POLITICAL ORDER
AND
POLITICAL DECAY

POLITICAL ORDER

AND

POLITICAL DECAY

From the

Industrial Revolution

to the

Globalization of Democracy

·

FRANCIS FUKUYAMA

FARRAR, STRAUS AND GIROUX

NEW YORK

Farrar, Straus and Giroux
18 West 18th Street, New York 10011

Printed in the United States of America
First edition, 2014

Library of Congress Cataloging-in-Publication Data
Fukuyama, Francis.
    Political order and political decay : from the industrial revolution to the globalization of
democracy / Francis Fukuyama.
    pages   cm
    ISBN 978-0-374-22735-7 (hardback) — ISBN 978-1-4299-4432-8 (e-book)
    1. State, The—History.   2. Order—History.   3. Comparative government—History.
4. Democracy—History.   5. Globalization—Political aspects.   I. Fukuyama, Francis.
Origins of political order. Continuation of: II. Title.

JC11 .F853 2014
320.1—dc23

                                                                              2014016973

Designed by Abby Kagan

Farrar, Straus and Giroux books may be purchased for educational, business, or
promotional use. For information on bulk purchases, please contact the Macmillan
Corporate and Premium Sales Department at 1-800-221-7945, extension 5442,
or write to specialmarkets@macmillan.com.

www.fsgbooks.com
www.twitter.com/fsgbooks • www.facebook.com/fsgbooks

1   3   5   7   9   10   8   6   4   2

Energy in the Executive is a leading character in the definition of good government. It is essential to the protection of the community against foreign attacks; it is not less essential to the steady administration of the laws ... A feeble execution is but another phrase for a bad execution; and a government ill executed, whatever it may be in theory, must be, in practice, a bad government. —ALEXANDER HAMILTON

The English race, consequently, has long and successfully studied the art of curbing executive powers to the constant neglect of the art of perfecting executive methods. It has exercised itself much more in controlling than energizing government. It has been more concerned to render government just and moderate than to make it facile, well-ordered and effective.

—WOODROW WILSON

When an American thinks about the problem of government-building, he directs himself not to the creation of authority and the accumulation of power but rather the limitation of authority and the division of power.

—SAMUEL P. HUNTINGTON

CONTENTS

POLITICAL ORDER
AND
POLITICAL DECAY

INTRODUCTION

Development of Political Institutions
to the French Revolution

Consider a number of very different scenarios that have been playing out at the beginning of the second decade of the twenty-first century.

In Libya in 2013, a militia armed with a panoply of heavy weapons briefly kidnapped the country's prime minister, Ali Zeidan, demanding that his government provide them with back pay. Another militia has shut down much of the country's oil production, which is virtually the only source of export earnings. Other militias were earlier responsible for the killing of U.S. ambassador Christopher Stevens in Benghazi, and for shooting dozens of demonstrators in the capital, Tripoli, who protested their continuing occupation of the city.

These militias were formed in various parts of the country in opposition to Libya's longtime dictator, Muammar Qaddafi, whom they ousted, with significant help from NATO, in the first year of the Arab Spring in 2011. The protests against authoritarian governments that broke out that year not just in Libya but also in Tunisia, Egypt, Yemen, Syria, and other Arab countries were often propelled by demands for greater democracy. But two years later, democracy as it is practiced in Europe and North America seems like a distant dream. Libya since then has taken some tentative steps toward establishing a constituent assembly that would write a new constitution. But at the moment, its most fundamental problem is that it lacks a state—that is, a central authority that can exercise a monopoly of legitimate force over its territory to keep the peace and enforce the law.

In other parts of Africa, states claiming a monopoly of force exist on paper and are less chaotic than Libya. But they remain very weak. Radical Islamist groups, having been pushed out of South Asia and the Middle East, have been setting up shop in countries with weak governments such as Mali, Niger, Nigeria, and Somalia. The reason that this part of the world is so much poorer in terms of income, health, education, and the like than booming regions like East Asia can be traced directly to its lack of strong government institutions.

Over the same time period, a very different scenario was playing out in the United States with regard to its financial sector. The United States is in many ways at the opposite end of the political spectrum from post-Qaddafi Libya: it has a very large and well-institutionalized state, one that dates back more than two hundred years and draws on a deep well of democratic legitimacy. But that state is not working well, and its problems may be related to the fact that it is too institutionalized.

Prior to the financial crisis of 2008, there were nearly a dozen federal agencies with regulatory authority over financial institutions, as well as banking and insurance regulators in each of the fifty states. For all of this regulation, however, the U.S. government was nonetheless unaware of the looming subprime mortgage crisis, allowing the banks to take on excessive leverage and permitting the emergence of a huge shadow banking system built around derivatives that were far too complex to properly value. Some commentators have tried to blame the crisis exclusively on government-guaranteed mortgages from agencies like Fannie Mae and Freddie Mac, which did in fact contribute to the meltdown.[1] But the private sector was a happy participant feeding the mortgage frenzy and could take undue risks because large banks knew that they would ultimately get bailed out by the government if they got into trouble. This is exactly the scenario that occurred in the wake of the Lehman Brothers bankruptcy in September 2008, leading to a near collapse of the global payment system and the deepest U.S. recession since the Great Depression.

What is perhaps more shocking, however, is what has happened since the crisis. Despite widespread recognition of the enormous risk posed by "too-big-to-fail" banks, the American banking sector became even more concentrated than it was in 2008. In the years following the crisis, Congress passed the Dodd-Frank Act that was supposed to solve this problem. But the legislation ignored simpler remedies, such as sharply raising bank capital requirements or putting hard caps on the size of financial institutions, in favor of a highly complex stew of new regulations. Three years after passage of the legislation, many of those detailed rules had not yet been written and would likely not solve the underlying too-big-to-fail problem even if they were.

There are two fundamental reasons for this failure. The first has to do with intellectual rigidity. The banks, in their own self-interest, have argued that strong new regulations of their activities would cut into their ability to lend, and therefore undermine economic growth, while producing harmful unintended consequences. Such arguments are often quite valid when applied to nonfinancial institutions like manufacturing industries, and appeal to many conservative voters who are distrustful of "big government." But, as the scholars Anat Admati and Martin Hellwig among others have shown, large banks are very different from nonfinancial firms, due to their ability to harm the rest of the economy in ways not possible for a manufacturing company.[2] The second reason for the failure is that the banks are very rich and powerful, and can hire a legion of high-priced lobbyists to work on their behalf. Despite enormous public anger against the banking sector and the taxpayer bailouts, these lobbyists have succeeded in blocking meaningful regulation that would have gone directly to the heart of the too-big-to-fail problem. Some legislators may have found the bankers' arguments against new regulation persuasive based on their ideological beliefs; for others, the arguments were a useful cover to protect the stream of campaign contributions flowing from the banking sector.[3]

A third scenario links the Arab Spring to the protests that broke out in Turkey and Brazil in 2013. These two countries were leading "emerging market" economies, which had seen rapid economic growth during the preceding decade. Unlike the Arab dictatorships, both were democracies with competitive elections. Turkey had been ruled by the Islamist Justice and Development Party (AKP in its Turkish initials), whose leader, Prime Minister Recep Tayyip Erdoğan, had initially made his mark as mayor of Istanbul. Brazil for its part had elected a president, Dilma Rousseff, who hailed from a Socialist party and had been jailed in her youth by the military dictatorship that ruled the country from 1964 to 1985.

Despite these impressive economic and political accomplishments, both countries were briefly convulsed with mass protests against their governments. In Turkey, the issue was a park in Istanbul that the government wanted to make over as a shopping mall. Many of the young protesters felt that Erdoğan, despite his democratic mandate, had authoritarian inclinations and was seriously out of touch with the younger generation of Turks. In Brazil, the issue was corruption and a failure of the government to provide reliable basic services, even while spending billions to host the football World Cup and summer Olympic Games.

What linked these protests to each other, and to the Arab Spring that occurred two years earlier, was the fact that they were driven primarily by the middle class. As a result of the economic development that had taken place over the preceding generation, a new middle class had emerged in both countries, whose expectations were much higher than those of their parents' generation. Tunisia and Egypt had experienced lower rates of growth than Turkey or Brazil; nonetheless, both produced large numbers of university graduates whose hopes for work and career were stymied by the cronyism of those countries' autocratic regimes. The fact that Turkey and Brazil held democratic elections was not sufficient to satisfy the protesters. Government actually had to deliver better results if it was to be regarded as legitimate, and needed to be more flexible and responsive to changing public demands. China, another economic success story, has begun to face similar challenges from its rising middle class, which now numbers in the hundreds of millions. While they have been the beneficiaries of the country's breakneck economic growth over the past generation, they, like their counterparts elsewhere, have different and higher expectations of government. The survival of the political systems of all these countries will depend critically on the degree to which they can adapt to the new social landscape created by economic growth.

THE PROBLEM WITH GOVERNMENT

These three examples may seem like very different cases, where problems are driven by specific policies, personalities, and historical context. But they are in fact linked by a common thread that serves as a background condition for all political life: institutions. Institutions are "stable, valued, recurring patterns of behavior" that persist beyond the tenure of individual leaders.[4] They are, in essence, persistent rules that shape, limit, and channel human behavior. Post-Qaddafi Libya's problem is a lack of basic institutions, most notably a state. Until there is a single, central source of authority that exercises a legitimate monopoly of force in that country, there will be no citizen security or the conditions for individuals to flourish.

At the other end of the scale, the United States has long-standing and powerful institutions, but they have been subject to political decay. Government institutions that are supposed to serve public purposes have been captured by powerful private interests, such that democratic majorities have a difficult time asserting their control. The problem is not just one of money and power; it also has to do with rigidities of the rules themselves, and of the ideas supporting them.

Finally, in the case of emerging market countries like Turkey and Brazil, the problem is one of social change outstripping existing institutions. By definition, institutions are persistent patterns of behavior that are created in response to the needs of a particular historical moment. But societies, especially those experiencing rapid economic growth, do not stand still. They create new social classes, educate their citizens, and employ new technologies that shuffle the social deck. Existing institutions often fail to accommodate these new actors and, as a result, come under pressure to change.

The study of "development"—that is, change in human societies over time—is therefore not just an endless catalog of personalities, events, conflicts, and policies. It necessarily centers around the process by which political institutions emerge, evolve, and eventually decay. If we are to understand the fast-changing political and economic developments of our contemporary world, it is important to put them in the context of the long-term story of the underlying institutional structure of societies.

The present book is the companion volume to *The Origins of Political Order: From Prehuman Times to the French Revolution*. This project started out as an effort to rewrite and update Samuel P. Huntington's classic *Political Order in Changing Societies*, first published in 1968. The current volume takes its title from the first chapter of the latter book, which in turn was based on an article originally published in *World Politics*. Huntington's work was critical in making people understand that political development was a separate process from economic and social growth, and that before a polity could be democratic, it had to provide basic order. For all of the differences between Huntington's book and my own in form and substance, I come to the same basic conclusions that he did. The first volume gave an account of the origins of three critical sets of political institutions: the state, the rule of law, and procedures promoting democratic accountability. It explained how these institutions separately or in combination emerged, or failed to emerge, in China, India, the Middle East, and Europe. For those who have not read the first volume, the following sections recap the story presented there.

SOCIAL ANIMALS

The first volume began not with primitive human societies but with mankind's primate ancestors, because political order is rooted in human biology. Contrary to the theories of philosophers such as Jean-Jacques Rousseau or modern neoclassical economists, science now shows us that human beings did not start out as isolated individuals who gradually came to form societies over the course of historical time. The behaviorally modern human beings who emerged somewhere in Africa about fifty thousand years ago were socially organized from the start, just like their primate forebears.

Natural human sociability is built around two phenomena: kin selection and reciprocal altruism. The first is a recurring pattern by which sexually reproducing animals behave altruistically toward one another in proportion to the number of genes they share; that is, they practice nepotism and favor genetic relatives. Reciprocal altruism involves an exchange of favors or resources between unrelated individuals of the same species, or sometimes between members of different species. Both behaviors are not learned but genetically coded and emerge spontaneously as individuals interact.

Human beings, in other words, are social animals by nature. But their natural sociability takes the specific form of altruism toward family (genetic relatives) and friends (individuals with whom one has exchanged favors). This default form of human sociability is universal to all cultures and historical periods. Natural sociability can be overridden by the development of new institutions that provide incentives for other types of behavior (for example, favoring a qualified stranger over a genetic relative), but it constitutes a form of social relationship to which humans always revert when such alternative institutions break down.

Human beings by nature are also norm-creating and norm-following creatures. They create rules for themselves that regulate social interactions and make possible the collective action of groups. Although these rules can be rationally designed or negotiated, norm-following behavior is usually grounded not in reason but in emotions like pride, guilt, anger, and shame. Norms are often given an intrinsic value and even worshipped, as in the religious laws of many different societies. Since an institution is nothing more than a rule that persists over time, human beings therefore have a natural tendency to institutionalize their behavior. Due to the intrinsic value with which they are typically endowed, institutions tend to be highly conservative, that is, resistant to change.

For the first forty or so thousand years of the existence of the modern human species, individuals were organized into what anthropologists label band-level societies, consisting of small groups of individuals, almost all of them genetic relatives, who subsisted off of hunting and gathering. The first major institutional transition, which occurred perhaps ten thousand years ago, was the shift from band- to tribal-level societies, which are organized around a belief in the power of dead ancestors and unborn descendants. We typically call these tribes; anthropologists sometimes use the term "segmentary lineages" to describe individuals who trace ancestry to a common progenitor who might be several generations removed. Such tribal societies existed in ancient China, India, Greece, Rome, the Middle East, and pre-Columbian America, and among the Germanic forebears of modern Europeans.

Tribal societies have no central source of authority. As with band-level societies, they tend to be highly egalitarian and have no third-party enforcement of laws. They prevailed over band-level societies largely because they were capable of achieving enormous scale simply by pushing back the dating of common ancestry. Both band- and tribal-level societies are rooted in kinship and hence human biology. But the shift to tribal organization required the emergence of a religious idea, belief in the ability of dead ancestors and unborn descendants to affect health and happiness in one's current life. This is an early example of ideas playing a critical independent role in development.

EMERGENCE OF THE STATE

The next important political transition was from a tribal to a state-level society. A state, in contrast to a band or tribe, possesses a monopoly on legitimate coercion and exercises that power over a defined territory. Because they are centralized and hierarchical, states tend to produce higher degrees of social inequality than earlier kinship-based forms of organization.

There are in turn two broad types of state. In those described by the sociologist Max Weber as "patrimonial," the polity is considered a type of personal property of the ruler, and state administration is essentially an extension of the ruler's household. The natural forms of sociability, reliance on family and friends, are still at work in patrimonial states. A modern state, on the other hand, is impersonal: a citizen's relationship to the ruler does not depend on personal ties but simply on one's status as citizen. State administration does not consist of the ruler's family and friends; rather, recruitment to administrative positions is based on impersonal criteria such as merit, education, or technical knowledge.

There are numerous theories about what is called "pristine" state formation, the formation of the first states out of tribal societies. There were necessarily a number of interacting factors at work, such as the availability of agricultural surpluses and the technology to support them, and a certain level of population density. Physical circumscription—what is called "caging," the bounding of territories by impassable mountains, deserts, or waterways—allowed rulers to exercise coercive power over populations and prevented enslaved or subordinated individuals from running away. Patrimonial states began to form in many parts of the world around eight thousand years ago, primarily in fertile alluvial valleys in Egypt, Mesopotamia, China, and the Valley of Mexico.

Development of modern states, however, required specific strategies for shifting political organization away from family- and friends-based organizations to impersonal ones. China was the first world civilization to establish a nonpatrimonial, modern state, which it did some eighteen centuries before similar political units appeared in Europe. State building in China was driven by the same circumstances that necessitated centralized states in early modern Europe: prolonged and pervasive military competition. Military struggle created incentives to tax populations, to create administrative hierarchies to provision armies, and to establish merit and competence rather than personal ties as the basis for recruitment and promotion. In the words of sociologist Charles Tilly, "War made the state and the state made war."

Modern states have to move beyond friends and family in the way that they recruit officials. China did this by inventing the civil service examination as early as the third century B.C., though it was not routinely used until later dynasties. Both the Arabs and Ottomans came up with a novel approach to the same problem: the institution of slave-soldiers by which non-Muslim boys were captured, taken from their families, and raised to be soldiers and administrators loyal to the ruler and lacking ties to the surrounding society. In Europe, this problem was solved on a social rather than a political level: early in the Middle Ages, the Catholic church changed the rules of inheritance to make it much more difficult for kin groups to pass resources down to their extended families. As a result, extended kinship among the Germanic barbarian tribes dissolved within a generation or two of their conversion to Christianity. Kinship was ultimately replaced by a more modern form of social relationship based on legal contract, known as feudalism.

THE RULE OF LAW

The rule of law, understood as rules that are binding even on the most politically powerful actors in a given society, has its origins in religion. It is only religious authority that was capable of creating rules that warriors needed to respect. Religious institutions in many cultures were essentially legal bodies responsible for interpreting a set of sacred texts and giving them moral sanction over the rest of society. Thus in India, the Brahmin class of priests was understood to be higher in authority than the Kshatriyas, the warriors who held actual political power; a raja or king would have to seek legitimation from a Brahmin before he could rightly rule. In Islam as well, the law (sharia) was presided over by a separate hierarchy of scholars known as the ulama; a network of qadis or judges did the routine work of administering religious law. Though early caliphs united political and religious authority in the same person, in other periods of Islamic history the caliph and sultan were separate individuals, and the former could act as a constraint on the latter.

The rule of law was most deeply institutionalized in Western Europe, due to the role of the Roman Catholic church. Only in the Western tradition did the church emerge as a centralized, hierarchical, and resource-rich political actor whose behavior could dramatically affect the political fortunes of kings and emperors. The central event marking the autonomy of the church was the investiture conflict that began in the eleventh century. This clash pitted the church against the Holy Roman Emperor, over the question of the latter's interference in religious matters. In the end, the church won the right to appoint its own priests and bishops, and emerged as the guardian of a revived Roman law based on the sixth-century Corpus Juris Civilis or Justinian Code. England developed an equally strong but different legal tradition: the Common Law emerged after the Norman Conquest out of the law of the king's court. There it was promoted less by the church than by early monarchs who used their ability to dispense impersonal justice as a means of cementing their legitimacy.

Thus in Western Europe, law was the first of the three major institutions to emerge. China never developed a transcendental religion; perhaps for this reason, it never developed a true rule of law. There, the state emerged first, and up to the present day law has never existed as a fundamental constraint on political power. The sequence was reversed in Europe: law preceded the rise of the modern state. When European monarchs aspired to behave like Chinese emperors from the late sixteenth century on and create modern, centralized absolutist states, they had to do so against the backdrop of an existing legal order that limited their powers. The result was that few European monarchs ever acquired the concentrated powers of the Chinese state, despite aspirations to do so. Only in Russia, where the Eastern Church was always subordinated to the state, did such a regime emerge.

DEMOCRATIC ACCOUNTABILITY

The last of the three sets of institutions to emerge was democratic accountability. The central mechanism of accountability, the parliament, evolved out of the feudal institution of estates, variously known as Cortes, Diet, sovereign court, *zemskiy sobor*, or, in England, Parliament. These institutions represented the elites in society—the upper nobility, gentry, and in some cases the bourgeoisie in independent cities. Under feudal law, monarchs were required to go to these bodies to raise taxes, since they represented the asset-owning elites in the agrarian societies of the time.

Beginning in the late sixteenth century, ambitious monarchs deploying novel theories of absolute sovereignty undertook campaigns to undermine the powers of these estates and to acquire the right to tax their populations directly. In each European country, this struggle played out over the next two centuries. In France and Spain, the monarchy succeeded in reducing the power of the estates, though they remained enmeshed in an existing system of law that continued to limit their ability to simply expropriate the property of their elite subjects. In Poland and Hungary, the estates were victorious over the monarch, creating weak central authorities dominated by rapacious elites that were in time conquered by their neighbors. In Russia, the estates and the elites supporting them were less well established than their Western European counterparts, and law exerted a much weaker influence; as a result, a more robust form of absolutism emerged there.

Only in England was there a relatively even contest between the king and the estates. When the early Stuart kings sought to build absolutist powers, they found themselves blocked by a well-organized and armed Parliament. Many members of this body were, in contrast to the monarchy's high church Anglicanism, Puritan Protestants who believed in a more grassroots form of organization. The parliamentary forces fought a civil war, beheaded King Charles I, and briefly established a parliamentary dictatorship under Oliver Cromwell. This conflict continued through the Restoration and culminated in the Glorious Revolution of 1688–1689, wherein the Stuart dynasty was deposed and a new monarch, William of Orange, agreed to a constitutional settlement embodying the principle of "no taxation without representation."

Accompanying William and his wife, Mary, from the Netherlands to London was the philosopher John Locke, whose *Second Treatise on Government* enunciated the principle that obedience to rule should rest on the consent of the governed. Locke argued that rights were natural and inhered in human beings qua human beings; governments existed only to protect these rights and could be overturned if they violated them. These principles—no taxation without representation and consent of the governed—would become the rallying cry of the American colonists when they revolted against British authority less than a century later in 1776. Thomas Jefferson incorporated Locke's ideas of natural rights into the American Declaration of Independence, and the idea of popular sovereignty would become the basis of the Constitution that was ratified in 1789.

While these new political orders established the principle of accountability, neither England in 1689 nor the United States in 1789 could be considered a modern democracy. The franchise was restricted in both countries to white male property owners who represented a very small part of the entire population. Neither the Glorious Revolution nor the

American Revolution produced anything like a genuine social revolution. The American Revolution was led by a merchant-planter-gentry elite who were jealous of the rights that the British king had infringed. These same elites remained in charge once independence was achieved, and they were the ones who drafted and approved the new country's constitution.

To focus on these limitations, however, is to radically underestimate the political dynamic that the new American order set in train and the galvanizing power of ideas. The Declaration of Independence boldly declared that "All men are created equal, that they are endowed by their Creator with certain unalienable rights." The Constitution squarely vested sovereignty not in a king or an amorphous state but rather in "We the People." These documents did not seek to re-create Britain's hierarchical, class-defined society in North America. While there were many political and social barriers to de facto equality in the United States over the next two centuries, the burden was on anyone claiming special rights or privileges for a particular class to justify how they were compatible with the nation's founding creed. This was one reason why the franchise was expanded to all white males a little more than a generation after ratification of the Constitution, long before any country in Europe was to do so.

The contradictions between founding principles and social reality came to a head in the decades before the Civil War, as southern defenders of their "peculiar institution," slavery, started to make novel arguments for why exclusion and subjugation of blacks was morally and politically justified. Some used religious arguments, some talked about a "natural" hierarchy among the races, and others defended it on the grounds of democracy itself. Stephen Douglas in his debates with Abraham Lincoln said he cared not whether a people voted slavery up or down, but that their democratic will should prevail.

Lincoln, however, made a decisive counterargument that necessarily harked back to the founding. He said that a country based on the principle of political equality and natural rights could not survive if it tolerated so blatantly contradictory an institution as slavery. As we know, it shamefully took another century after the Civil War and the abolition of slavery before African Americans finally won the political and juridical rights they were promised by the Fourteenth Amendment. But the country eventually came to understand that the equality proclaimed in the Declaration of Independence could not be made compatible with laws making some people second-class citizens.[5]

Many other social movements emerged in later years that expanded the circle of people bearing natural and hence political rights—workers, women, indigenous peoples, and other formerly marginalized groups. But the basic political order established by the Glorious Revolution and the American Revolution—an executive accountable to a representative legislature and to the whole society more broadly—would prove remarkably durable. No one subsequently argued that the government should not be accountable to "the People"; later debates and conflicts revolved entirely around the question of who counted as a full human being whose dignity was marked by the ability to participate in the democratic political system.

THE FRENCH REVOLUTION

The other great revolution of the late eighteenth century took place in France. Gallons of ink have been spilled describing and interpreting this cataclysmic event, and the descendants of those on opposite sides still have not resolved some of the bitter controversies it aroused.

It may seem surprising, then, that quite a number of observers from Edmund Burke to Alexis de Tocqueville to the historian François Furet have questioned whether the revolution was as consequential as many believed.[6] The revolution was originally animated by the "Declaration of the Rights of Man and of the Citizen," which, like the American Declaration of Independence, set forth a view of the universality of human rights grounded in the laws of nature. But the First Republic was short-lived. Like the Bolshevik and Chinese revolutions that were to follow, it established its own revolutionary dynamic of radicalization in which today's left-wingers became tomorrow's counterrevolutionaries, a cycle that led to the Committee of Public Safety and Reign of Terror in which the revolution devoured its own children. This unstable process was brought to an end by external war, the Thermidorian reaction, and finally the coup of 18 Brumaire that brought Napoleon Bonaparte to power in 1799.[7]

The violence of the revolution and the violence of the counterrevolution engendered a deep polarization in French society that made incremental political reform of a British sort much harder to achieve. The French would experience the July Revolution of 1830, the Revolution of 1848, and then, in the 1870s, occupation by Prussia and the Paris Commune, before a more enduring limited-franchise democracy could be established. By this point, there had been democratic elections under varying restrictive rules in many other European countries, including the arch-conservative Prussia. France, which had led the way toward democracy in 1789, proved to be something of a laggard. Worse, one of the revolution's legacies was a French left that in the twentieth century was prone to glorify violence and attach itself to totalitarian causes from Stalin's to Mao's.

So the question is reasonably asked, What did the French Revolution achieve? If the answer was not establishment of democracy in France, it did have a great, immediate, and lasting impact in the other institutional domains. First, it led to the development and promulgation in 1804 of Europe's first modern law code, the Civil Code or Code Napoléon. And the second was the creation of a modern administrative state, through which the code was implemented and enforced. Even in the absence of democracy, these constituted major advances that made government less arbitrary, more transparent, and more uniform in its treatment of citizens. Napoleon, looking backward after his defeat at Waterloo, claimed that the Civil Code constituted a greater victory than any he had won on the battlefield, and he was right in many ways.[8]

French law up to that point was a pastiche of rules that varied from region to region, some inherited from the Roman law, some based on customary law, as well as the countless accretions that had been added over the centuries from ecclesiastical, feudal, commercial, and secular sources. The resulting tangle of laws was often self-contradictory or ambiguous. The Code Napoléon replaced all this with a single modern code that was clear, elegantly written, and extremely compact.

The Code Napoléon cemented many of the gains of the revolution by eliminating from law feudal distinctions of rank and privilege. All citizens henceforth were declared to have equal rights and duties that were clearly laid out *ex ante*. The new Civil Code enshrined modern concepts of property rights: "the right to enjoy and to dispose of one's property in the most absolute fashion, provided that it is not used in a manner prohibited by law." Land was freed of feudal and customary entails, opening the way for development of a market economy. Seigneurial courts—courts controlled by the local lord, over which peasant grievances had boiled forth during the revolution—were abolished altogether and replaced with a uniform system of civil magistrates. Births and marriages now had to be recorded with civil rather than religious authorities.[9]

The Code Napoléon was immediately exported to the countries France was then occupying: Belgium, Luxembourg, the German territories west of the Rhine, the Palatinate, Rhenish Prussia, Geneva, Savoy, and Parma. It was subsequently forcibly introduced into Italy, the Netherlands, and the Hanseatic territories. The Civil Code was voluntarily accepted by many of the smaller German states. As we will see in chapter 4, this body of law was to become the inspiration for the reform of the Prussian Code that took place after the defeat by the French at Jena. It was used as a model for countless other civil codes outside Europe, from Senegal to Argentina to Egypt to Japan. While legal codes forcibly imposed on other societies do not have a great record of success, the Code Napoléon did: countries like Italy and the Netherlands that resisted its adoption eventually ended up with laws that were very similar in substance if not in name.[10]

The second major accomplishment of the revolution was the creation of a modern bureaucratic state, something China had achieved a couple of millennia earlier. The French Old Regime was a curious hybrid. Beginning in the middle of the seventeenth century, centralizing monarchs like Louis XIII and Louis XIV had created a modern system of administrators based on officials known as intendents. Sent from Paris to the provinces, they had no kinship or other ties with the local population and therefore could govern more impersonally. As Alexis de Tocqueville noted, this was the beginning of the modern centralized state in France.[11]

But the intendents had to operate in parallel with another administrative group, that of venal officeholders. French kings were perpetually short of money to finance their wars and lifestyles. Starting with a major bankruptcy known as the Grand Parti in 1557, the government resorted to increasingly desperate measures to raise money, including the outright sale of public offices to wealthy individuals. Under a system known as the Paulette, introduced in 1604 by Henry IV's minister Sully, these offices could not only be bought but also handed down to children as part of their inheritance. These venal officeholders, of course, had no interest in impersonal public administration or good government; what they wanted was to milk their offices for all they were worth.

Although French governments of the late eighteenth century made two major efforts to eliminate the venal officeholders, both were defeated because this elite group held great power and had too much to lose as a result of reform. The rottenness and unreformability of this system was one of the factors leading to the revolution itself. During that event, all of the venal officeholders were dispossessed of their offices, and in many cases of their heads for good measure. It was only after the decks had been cleared in this purge that a new Conseil d'État could be created in 1799, an institution that would become the pinnacle of a truly modern bureaucratic system.

The new administrative hierarchy would not have worked but for the creation of a more modern educational system designed to support it. The Old Regime had established technical schools in the eighteenth century to train engineers and other specialists. But in 1794 the revolutionary government created a number of Grandes Écoles (schools) such as the École Normale Supérieure and the École Polytechnique for the specific purpose of training civil servants. Such schools, the forerunners of the post–World War II École Nationale d'Administration (ENA), were fed in turn by a system of lycées or elite secondary schools.

These two institutional innovations—introduction of a new legal code and creation of a modern administrative system—are not the same thing as democracy. But they nevertheless achieved certain egalitarian ends. The law no longer privileged certain classes who got to manipulate the system to their own advantage; it was now committed to the equal treatment of all individuals, in principle if not always in reality. Private property was no longer subject to feudal restrictions, and a new, much larger market economy could begin to flourish as a result. The law, moreover, could not be implemented without the newly reformed bureaucracy, which was freed of the corrupt baggage it had accumulated over the centuries. And both together—law and an administrative state—acted in many ways as a constraint on the arbitrariness of would-be absolutist rulers. The sovereign had theoretically unlimited powers, but he had to exercise them through a bureaucracy acting on the basis of law. This is something that the Germans would label the Rechtsstaat. It had a very different character from the totalitarian dictatorships that would arise in the twentieth century under Lenin, Stalin, and Mao, whose reality was a despotic state unconstrained by either law or democratic accountability.

LAYING THE FOUNDATIONS

The American Revolution institutionalized democracy and the principle of political equality. The French Revolution laid the basis for an impersonal modern state, much as the Qin unification had done in China.

Both fortified and expanded the rule of law in its two sister versions, the Common Law and the Civil Code.

The first volume of this book concluded just at the historical moment when the foundations for the three sets of institutions had been put in place, but before any of them was fully developed into its modern form. In Europe and other parts of the world, law was the most developed institution. But as in the case of the Code Napoléon, a great deal of work had to be done to formalize, codify, reconcile, and update laws to make them truly neutral with respect to persons. The idea of a modern state had been germinating in Europe since the end of the sixteenth century, but no administration, including the new bureaucracy in Paris, was fully merit based. The vast majority of state administrations across the Continent remained patrimonial. And even though the idea of democracy had been implanted in England and particularly in its North American colonies, there was no society on earth in which a majority of the adult population could vote or participate in the political system.

Two monumental developments were unfolding at this moment of political upheaval. The first was the Industrial Revolution, in which per-person output moved to a much higher sustained level than in any previous period of human history. This had enormous consequences because economic growth began to change the underlying nature of societies.

The second great development was a second wave of colonialism, which was setting Europe on a collision course with the rest of the world. The first wave had begun with the Spanish and Portuguese conquests of the New World, followed a century later by British and French settlement of North America. The first colonial surge had exhausted itself by the late eighteenth century, and the British and Spanish empires were forced to retreat as a result of independence movements on the part of their New World colonies. But beginning with the Anglo-Burmese War of 1824, a new phase began that was to see virtually the entire rest of the world swallowed up into the colonial empires of the Western powers by the end of the century.

The present volume thus picks up the story from where the first one left off, giving an account of how state, law, and democracy developed over the last two centuries; how they interacted with one another and with the other economic and social dimensions of development; and, finally, how they have shown signs of decay in the United States and in other developed democracies.

PART ONE

·

The State

1

WHAT IS POLITICAL DEVELOPMENT?

Political development and its three components: the state, rule of law, and accountability; why all societies are subject to political decay; the plan for the book; why it is good to have a balanced political system

Political development is change over time in political institutions. This is different from shifts in politics or policies: prime ministers, presidents, and legislators may come and go, laws may be modified, but it is the underlying rules by which societies organize themselves that define a political order.

In the first volume of this book, I argued that there were three basic categories of institutions that constituted a political order: the state, rule of law, and mechanisms of accountability. The state is a hierarchical, centralized organization that holds a monopoly on legitimate force over a defined territory. In addition to characteristics like complexity and adaptability, states can be more or less impersonal: early states were indistinguishable from the ruler's household and were described as "patrimonial" because they favored and worked through the ruler's family and friends. Modern, more highly developed states, by contrast, make a distinction between the private interest of the rulers and the public interest of the whole community. They strive to treat citizens on a more impersonal basis, applying laws, recruiting officials, and undertaking policies without favoritism.

The rule of law has many possible definitions, including simple law and order, property rights and contract enforcement, or the modern Western understanding of human rights, which includes equal rights for women and racial and ethnic minorities.[1] The definition of the rule of law I am using in this book is not tied to a specific substantive understanding of law. Rather, I define it as a set of rules of behavior, reflecting a broad consensus within the society, that is binding on even the most powerful political actors in the society, whether kings, presidents, or prime ministers. If rulers can change the law to suit themselves, the rule of law does not exist, even if those laws are applied uniformly to the rest of society. To be effective, a rule of law usually has to be embodied in a separate judicial institution that can act autonomously from the executive. Rule of law by this definition is not associated with any particular substantive body of law, like those prevailing in the contemporary United States or Europe. Rule of law as a constraint on political power existed in ancient Israel, in India, in the Muslim world, as well as in the Christian West.

Rule of law should be distinguished from what is sometimes referred to as "rule by law." In the latter case, law represents commands issued by the ruler but is not binding on the ruler himself. Rule by law as we will see sometimes becomes more institutionalized, regular, and transparent, under which conditions it begins to fulfill some of the functions of rule of law by reducing the ruler's discretionary authority.

Accountability means that the government is responsive to the interests of the whole society—what Aristotle called the common good—rather than to just its own narrow self-interest. Accountability today is understood most typically as procedural accountability, that is, periodic free and fair multiparty elections that allow citizens to choose and discipline their rulers. But accountability can also be substantive: rulers can respond to the interests of the broader society without necessarily being subject to procedural accountability. Unelected governments can differ greatly in their responsiveness to public needs, which is why Aristotle in the *Politics* distinguished between monarchy and tyranny. There is, however, typically a strong connection between procedural and substantive accountability because unconstrained rulers, even if responsive to the common good, usually cannot be trusted to remain that way forever. When we use the word "accountability," we are mostly speaking of modern democracy defined in terms of procedures that make the governments responsive to their citizens. We need to bear in mind, however, that good procedures do not inevitably produce proper substantive results.

The institutions of the state concentrate power and allow the community to deploy that power to enforce laws, keep the peace, defend itself against outside enemies, and provide necessary public goods. The rule of law and mechanisms of accountability, by contrast, pull in the opposite direction: they constrain the state's power and ensure that it is used only in a controlled and consensual manner. The miracle of modern politics is that we can have political orders that are simultaneously strong and capable and yet constrained to act only within the parameters established by law and democratic choice.

These three categories of institutions may exist in different polities independently of one another, and in various combinations. Hence the People's Republic of China has a strong and well-developed state but a weak rule of law and no democracy. Singapore has a rule of law in addition to a state but very limited democracy. Russia has democratic elections, a state that is good at suppressing dissidence but not so good at delivering services, and a weak rule of law. In many failed states, like Somalia, Haiti, and the Democratic Republic of the Congo in the early twenty-first century, the state and rule of law are weak or nonexistent, though the latter two have held democratic elections. By contrast, a politically developed liberal democracy includes all three sets of institutions—the state, rule of law, and procedural accountability—in some kind of balance. A state that is powerful without serious checks is a dictatorship; one that is weak and checked by a multitude of subordinate political forces is ineffective and often unstable.

GETTING TO DENMARK

In the first volume, I suggested that contemporary developing countries and the international community seeking to help them face the problem of "getting to Denmark." By this I mean less the actual country Denmark than an imagined society that is prosperous, democratic, secure, and well governed, and experiences low levels of corruption. "Denmark" would have all three sets of political institutions in perfect balance: a competent state, strong rule of law, and democratic accountability. The international community would like to turn Afghanistan, Somalia, Libya, and Haiti into idealized places like "Denmark," but it doesn't have the slightest idea of how to bring this about. As I argued earlier, part of the problem is that we don't understand how Denmark itself came to be Denmark and therefore don't comprehend the complexity and difficulty of political development.

Of Denmark's various positive qualities, the least studied and most poorly understood concerns how its political system made the transition from a patrimonial to a modern state. In the former, rulers are supported by networks of friends and family who receive material benefits in return for political loyalty; in the latter, government officials are supposed to be servants or custodians of a broader public interest and are legally prohibited from using their offices for private gain. How did Denmark come to be governed by bureaucracies that were characterized by strict subordination to public purposes, technical expertise, a functional division of labor, and recruitment on the basis of merit?

Today, not even the most corrupt dictators would argue, like some early kings or sultans, that they literally "owned" their countries and could do with them what they liked. Everyone pays lip service to the distinction between public and private interest. Hence patrimonialism has evolved into what is called "neopatrimonialism," in which political leaders adopt the outward forms of modern states—with bureaucracies, legal systems, elections, and the like—and yet in reality rule for private gain. Public good may be invoked during election campaigns, but the state is not impersonal: favors are doled out to networks of political supporters in exchange for votes or attendance at rallies. This pattern of behavior is visible in countries from Nigeria to Mexico to Indonesia.[2] Douglass North, John Wallis, and Barry Weingast have an alternative label for neopatrimonialism, what they call a "limited access order," in which a coalition of rent-seeking elites use their political power to prevent free competition in both the economy and the political system.[3] Daron Acemoglu and James Robinson use the term "extractive" to describe the same phenomenon.[4] At one stage in human history, all governments could be described as patrimonial, limited access, or extractive.

The question is, How did such political orders ever evolve into modern states? The authors cited above are better at describing the transition than providing a dynamic theory of change. As we will see, there are several forces promoting state modernization. An important one historically was military competition, which creates incentives much more powerful than economic self-interest in motivating political reform. A second driver of change was rooted in the social mobilization brought about by industrialization. Economic growth generates new social groups, which over time organize themselves for collective action and seek to participate in the political system. This process does not always lead to the creation of modern states, but under the right circumstances it can and has.

POLITICAL DECAY

Following Samuel Huntington's definition, political institutions develop by becoming more complex, adaptable, autonomous, and coherent.[5] But he argues that they can also decay. Institutions are created to meet certain needs of societies, such as making war, dealing with economic conflicts, and regulating social behavior. But as recurring patterns of behavior, they can also grow rigid and fail to adapt when the circumstances that brought them into being in the first place themselves change. There is an inherent conservatism to human behavior that tends to invest institutions with emotional significance once they are put in place. Anyone who suggests abolishing the British Monarchy, or the American Constitution, or the Japanese emperor and replacing it with something newer and better, faces a huge uphill struggle.

There is a second source of political decay in addition to the failure of institutions to adapt to new circumstances. Natural human sociability is based on kin selection and reciprocal altruism—that is, the preference for family and friends. While modern political orders seek to promote impersonal rule, elites in most societies tend to fall back on networks of family and friends, both as an instrument for protecting their positions and as the beneficiaries of their efforts. When they succeed, elites are said to "capture" the state, which reduces the latter's legitimacy and makes it less accountable to the population as a whole. Long periods of peace and prosperity often provide the conditions for spreading capture by elites, which can lead to political crisis if followed by an economic downturn or external political shock.

In Volume 1 we saw many examples of this phenomenon. China's great Han Dynasty broke down in the third century A.D. when the government was reappropriated by elite families, who continued to dominate Chinese politics throughout the subsequent Sui and Tang Dynasties. The Mamluk regime in Egypt, built around Turkish slave-soldiers, collapsed when the slave-rulers began having families and looking out for their own children, as did the Sephahis and Janissaries—cavalry and infantry—on which

Ottoman power was built. France under the Old Regime sought to build a modern centralized administration from the middle of the seventeenth century on. But the constant fiscal needs of the monarchy forced it to corrupt its administration through the outright sale of public offices to wealthy individuals, a practice known as venality. Through these two volumes, I use a very long word—"repatrimonialization"—to designate the capture of ostensibly impersonal state institutions by powerful elites.

Modern liberal democracies are no less subject to political decay than other types of regimes. No modern society is likely ever to fully revert to a tribal one, but we see examples of "tribalism" all around us, from street gangs to the patronage cliques and influence peddling at the highest levels of modern politics. While everyone in a modern democracy speaks the language of universal rights, many are happy to settle for privilege—special exemptions, subsidies, or benefits intended for themselves, their family, and their friends alone. Some scholars have argued that accountable political systems have self-correcting mechanisms to prevent decay: if governments perform poorly or corrupt elites capture the state, the nonelites can simply vote them out of office.[6] There are times in the history of the growth of modern democracy when this has happened. But there is no guarantee that this self-correction will occur, perhaps because the nonelites are poorly organized, or they fail to understand their own interests correctly. The conservatism of institutions often makes reform prohibitively difficult. This kind of political decay leads either to slowly increasing levels of corruption, with correspondingly lower levels of government effectiveness, or to violent populist reactions to perceived elite manipulation.

AFTER THE REVOLUTIONS: THE PLAN FOR THIS VOLUME

The first volume of this book traced the emergence of the state, rule of law, and democratic accountability up through the American and French Revolutions. These revolutions marked the point at which all three categories of institutions—what we call liberal democracy—had come into being somewhere in the world. The present volume will trace the dynamics of their interaction up until the early twenty-first century.

The juncture between the two volumes also marks the onset of a third revolution, which was even more consequential—the Industrial Revolution. The long continuities described in the first volume seem to suggest that societies are trapped by their historical pasts, limiting their choices for types of political order in the future. This was a misunderstanding of the evolutionary story told in that volume, but any implicit historical determinism becomes even less valid once industrialization takes off. The political aspects of development are intimately linked in complex ways with the economic, social, and ideological dimensions. These linkages will be the subject of the following chapter.

The Industrial Revolution vastly increased the rate of growth of per capita output in the societies experiencing it, a phenomenon that brings in its train enormous social consequences. Sustained economic growth increased the rate of change along all of the dimensions of development. Between the former Han Dynasty in the second century B.C. and the Qing Dynasty in the eighteenth century A.D., neither the basic character of Chinese agrarian life nor the nature of its political system evolved terribly much; far more change would occur in the succeeding two centuries than in the preceding two millennia. This rapid pace of change continues into the twenty-first century.

Part I of the present volume will focus on the parts of the world that first experienced this revolution, Europe and North America, where the first liberal democracies appeared. It will try to answer the question, Why, in the early twenty-first century, are some countries, like Germany, characterized by modern, relatively uncorrupt state administrations, while countries like Greece and Italy are still plagued by clientelistic politics and high levels of corruption? And why is it that Britain and the United States, which had patronage-riddled public sectors during the nineteenth century, were able to reform them into more modern merit-based bureaucracies?

The answer as we will see is in some respects discouraging from the standpoint of democracy. The most modern contemporary bureaucracies were those established by authoritarian states in their pursuit of national security. This was true, as we saw in Volume 1, of ancient China; it was also true of the preeminent example of the modern bureaucratic rule, Prussia (later to become the unifier of Germany), whose weak geopolitical position forced it to compensate by creating an efficient state administration. On the other hand, countries that democratized early, before they established modern administrations, found themselves developing clientelistic public sectors. The first country to suffer this fate was the United

States, which was also the first country to open the vote to all white males in the 1820s. It was also true of Greece and Italy, which for different reasons never established strong, modern states before they opened up the franchise.

Sequencing therefore matters enormously. Those countries in which democracy preceded modern state building have had much greater problems achieving high-quality governance than those that inherited modern states from absolutist times. State building after the advent of democracy is possible, but it often requires mobilization of new social actors and strong political leadership to bring about. This was the story of the United States, where clientelism was overcome by a coalition that included business interests hurt by poor public administration, western farmers opposed to corrupt railroad interests, and urban reformers who emerged out of the new middle and professional classes.

There is another potential point of tension between strong, capable states and democracy. State building ultimately has to rest on a foundation of nation building, that is, the creation of common national identities that serve as a locus of loyalty that trumps attachments to family, tribe, region, or ethnic group. Nation building sometimes bubbles up from the grass roots, but it can also be the product of power politics—indeed, of terrible violence, as different groups are annexed, expelled, merged, moved, or "ethnically cleansed." As in the case of modern public administration, strong national identity is often most effectively formed under authoritarian conditions. Democratic societies lacking strong national identity frequently have grave difficulties agreeing on an overarching national narrative. Many peaceful contemporary liberal democracies are in fact the beneficiaries of prolonged violence and authoritarian rule in generations past, which they have conveniently forgotten. Fortunately, violence is not the only route to national unity; identities can also be altered to fit the realities of power politics, or established around expansive ideas like that of democracy itself that minimize exclusion of minorities from the national community.

Part II of the book also deals with the emergence, or nonemergence, of modern states, but in the context of a non-Western world that had been largely colonized and overwhelmed by the European powers. While societies in Latin America, the Middle East, Asia, and Africa had evolved indigenous forms of social and political organization, they were all of a sudden confronted with a radically different system from the first moment of contact with the West. The colonial powers in many cases conquered, subdued, and enslaved these societies, killing off indigenous peoples through war and disease, and settling their lands with foreigners. But even when physical force was not the issue, the model of government presented by the Europeans undermined the legitimacy of traditional institutions and cast many societies into a netherworld where they were neither authentically traditional nor successfully Westernized. In the non-Western world, therefore, it is not possible to speak of institutional development without reference to foreign or imported institutions.

There have been a number of theories put forward over the years of why institutions developed differently in different parts of the world. Some have argued that they were determined by the material conditions of geography and climate. Economists have argued that extractive industries like mining, or tropical agriculture favoring large plantations due to economies of scale, promoted the exploitative use of servile labor. These economic modes of production were said to spawn authoritarian political systems. Areas conducive to family farming, by contrast, tended to support political democracy by distributing wealth more equally across the population. Once an institution was formed, it was "locked in" and persisted despite changes that made the original geographical and climatic conditions less relevant.

But geography remains just one of many factors determining political outcomes. The policies undertaken by the colonial powers, the length of time they remained in control, and the kinds of resources they invested in their colonies all had important consequences for postcolonial institutions. Every generalization about climate and geography finds important exceptions: the small Central American country of Costa Rica should have become a typical banana republic, but it is today a reasonably well-governed democracy with thriving export industries and a vital ecotourism sector. Argentina by contrast was blessed with land and climate similar to that of North America and yet has ended up an unstable developing country subject alternately to military dictatorship, wild swings in economic performance, and populist misrule.

Ultimately, geographical determinism obscures the many ways people in colonized countries exercised agency; they played crucial roles in shaping their own institutions despite outside domination. The most successful non-Western countries today are precisely those that had the most developed indigenous institutions prior to their contact with the West.

The complex reasons for different development paths can be seen most vividly in the contrast between sub-Saharan Africa and East Asia, the worst- and best-performing regions of the world with respect to economic development over the past half century. Sub-Saharan Africa never developed strong indigenous state-level institutions prior to its contact with the West. When the European colonial powers began the "scramble for Africa" in the late nineteenth century, they soon discovered that their new colonies were barely paying for the cost of their own administration. Britain in response adopted a policy of indirect rule, which justified minimal investment on its part in the creation of state institutions. The terrible colonial legacy was thus more an act of omission than of commission. In contrast to areas of heavier political investment like India and Singapore, the colonial powers did not pass on strong institutions, least of all "absolutist" ones capable of penetrating and controlling their populations. Rather, societies with weak state traditions saw their established institutions undermined and were left with little in the way of modern ones to take their place. The economic disaster that beset the region in the generation following independence was the result.

This contrasts sharply with East Asia. As we have seen, China invented the modern state and has the world's oldest tradition of centralized bureaucracy. It bequeathed this tradition to neighboring Japan, Korea, and Vietnam. This strong state tradition allowed Japan to escape Western colonization altogether. In China, the state collapsed and the tradition was severely disrupted during the revolutions, wars, and occupations of the twentieth century, but it has been rebuilt by the Communist Party in a more modern form since 1978. In East Asian societies, effective public institutions have been the basis of economic success. Asian states were built around well-trained technocratic bureaucracies, which have been given enough autonomy to guide economic development, while avoiding the forms of gross corruption and predatory behavior that have characterized governments in other parts of the world.

Latin America lies somewhere between these extremes. Despite the existence of large pre-Columbian empires, the region never developed powerful state-level institutions of the sort found in East Asia. Existing political structures were destroyed by conquest and disease, and replaced by settler communities that brought with them the authoritarian and mercantilist institutions then prevailing in Spain and Portugal. Climate and geography facilitated the growth of exploitative agriculture and extractive industries. While most of Europe was similarly authoritarian at this point, the hierarchies in Latin America were marked by race and ethnicity as well. These traditions proved highly persistent, even in a country like Argentina, whose climate, geography, and ethnic composition should have facilitated North American–style equality.

Hence the widely varying contemporary development outcomes among sub-Saharan Africa, Latin America, and East Asia were heavily influenced by the nature of indigenous state institutions prior to their contact with the West. Those that had strong institutions earlier were able to reestablish them after a period of disruption, while those that did not continued to struggle. The colonial powers had a huge impact in transplanting their own institutions, particularly where they could bring in large numbers of settlers. The least developed parts of the world today are those that lacked either strong indigenous state institutions or transplanted settler-based ones.

While Parts I and II deal with development of the state, Part III of this book will deal with an institution of constraint—democratic accountability. This part is considerably shorter than Parts I or II. This is not because I believe that democracy is less important than other aspects of political development. It reflects the fact that a great deal of attention has been paid over the past generation to democracy, democratic transitions, democratic breakdowns, and the quality of democracy. The Third Wave of democracy that began in the early 1970s saw the number of electoral democracies around the world go from 35 to 120 by 2013, and so it is very understandable that a huge amount of scholarly attention has been devoted to this phenomenon. Readers interested in learning about these more recent developments are referred to the many excellent books that have been written on the subject.[7]

Instead of focusing on the Third Wave, Part III will look more closely at the "First Wave," the period of democratic expansion that occurred primarily in Europe in the wake of the American and French Revolutions. No country in Europe qualified as even an electoral democracy at the time of the Congress of Vienna in 1815 that brought to an end the Napoleonic Wars. The year 1848 saw the outbreak of revolutions in virtually every continental European country and has been compared to the

2011 Arab Spring. The European experience illustrates how difficult the road to real democracy is. Within less than a year of the revolutionary upsurge, the old authoritarian order had been restored virtually everywhere. The franchise was opened only very slowly over the following decades; in Britain, home to the oldest parliamentary tradition, full adult suffrage was not put in place until 1929.

The spread of democracy depends on the legitimacy of the idea of democracy. For much of the nineteenth century, many educated and well-meaning people believed that the "masses" simply did not have the capacity to exercise the franchise responsibly. The rise of democracy thus had much to do with spreading views of human equality.

But ideas do not exist in a vacuum. We live today in a world of globalized and expanding democracy due to the profound changes set in train by the Industrial Revolution. It set off explosive economic growth that dramatically changed the nature of societies by mobilizing new classes of people—the bourgeoisie or middle class, and the new industrial working class. As they became self-conscious as groups with common interests, they started to organize themselves politically and demanded the right to participate in the political system. Expansion of the franchise was usually a matter of grassroots mobilization of these newly emerging classes, which often led to violence. But in other cases it was the older elite groups that promoted democratic rights as a means of improving their own relative political fortunes. The timing of the spread of democracy in different countries therefore depended on the changing relative positions of the middle class, the working class, landowning elites, and the peasantry. Where the old agrarian order was built around large landowners dependent on servile labor, a peaceful transition to democracy became particularly difficult. But in almost all cases the rise and growth of middle-class groups was critical to the spread of democracy. Democracy in the developed world became secure and stable as industrialization produced middle-class societies, that is, societies in which a significant majority of the population thought of themselves as middle class.

Apart from economic growth, democracy worldwide has been facilitated by globalization itself, the reduction of barriers to the movement of ideas, goods, investment, and people across international boundaries. Institutions that took centuries to evolve in one part of the world could be imported or adapted to local conditions in a completely different region. This suggests that the evolution of institutions has sped up over time, and is likely to continue to do so.

Part III concludes with a view toward the future. If a broad middle class is indeed important to the survival of democracy, what will be the implication of the disappearance of middle-class jobs as a result of advancing technology and globalization?

The fourth and final part of the book will deal with the issue of political decay. All political systems are prone to decay over time. The fact that modern liberal democratic institutions supported by a market economy have been "consolidated" is no guarantee that they will persist forever. Institutional rigidity and repatrimonialization, the two forces contributing to decay in the cases detailed in Volume 1, are present in contemporary democracies.

Indeed, both of these processes are evident in the United States today. Institutional rigidity takes the form of a series of rules that lead to outcomes that are commonly acknowledged to be bad and yet are regarded as essentially unreformable. These include the electoral college, the primary system, various Senate rules, the system of campaign finance, and the entire legacy of a century of congressional mandates that collectively produce a sprawling government that nonetheless fails to perform many basic functions, and does others poorly. Many of the sources of these dysfunctions, I will argue in Part IV, are by-products of the American system of checks and balances itself, which tends to produce poorly drafted legislation (beginning with budgets) and ill-designed handoffs of authority between Congress and the executive branch. The deep American tradition of law moreover enables the courts to insert themselves into either policy making or routine administration in a manner that has few parallels in other developed democracies. It would be possible in theory to fix many of these problems, but most available solutions are not even on the table because they lie too far outside of American experience.

The second mechanism of political decay—repatrimonialization—is evident in the capture of large parts of the U.S. government by well-organized interest groups. The old nineteenth-century problem of clientelism (what was known as the patronage system), in which individual voters received benefits in return for votes, was largely eliminated as a result of reforms undertaken during the Progressive Era. But it has been replaced today by a system of legalized gift exchange, in which politicians respond to organized interest groups that are collectively unrepresentative of the public as a whole. Over the past two generations, wealth has become highly concentrated in the United States, and economic power has been able to buy influence in politics. The American system of checks and balances creates numerous points of access for powerful interest groups that are much less prominent in a European-style parliamentary system. Although there is a widespread perception that the system as a whole is corrupt and increasingly illegitimate, there is no straightforward reform agenda for fixing it within the parameters of the existing system.

A question for the future is whether these problems are characteristic of liberal democracies as a whole, or are unique to the United States.

I should note at the outset several topics that the present volume will not seek to address. It is not intended to be anything like a comprehensive history of the past two centuries. Anyone seeking to learn about the origins of the world wars or the cold war, the Bolshevik or Chinese Revolutions, the Holocaust, the gold standard, or the founding of the United Nations should look elsewhere. I have chosen instead certain topics within the broad field of political development that I feel have been relatively underemphasized or misunderstood.

This book focuses on the evolution of political institutions within individual societies, and not on international ones. It is clear that the current degree of globalization and interdependence among states means that national states are to a much lesser degree the monopoly providers of public services (if they ever were). Today there are a huge number of international bodies, nongovernmental organizations, multinational corporations, and informal networks that supply services traditionally associated with governments. For many observers, the word "governance" refers to government-like services provided by virtually anything other than a traditional government.[8] It is also reasonably clear that the existing structure of international institutions is inadequate to provide sufficient levels of cooperation, on issues from the drug trade to financial regulation to climate change. All these are again very worthy topics, but ones that I do not discuss at any length in this book.[9]

This book is backward looking—it tries to explain how existing institutions arose and evolved over time. Although it points to any number of problems that beset modern political systems under the heading of political decay, I avoid overly specific recommendations for fixing them. While I have spent a lot of my life in a public policy world that seeks very specific solutions to policy problems, this book aims at a level of analysis pointing to their deeper systemic sources. Some of the issues we face today may not in fact have any particularly good policy solutions. In a similar vein, I do not spend any time speculating about the future of the different types of political institutions discussed here. My focus rather is on the question of how we got to the present.

THREE INSTITUTIONS

I believe that a political system resting on a balance among state, law, and accountability is both a practical and a moral necessity for all societies. All societies need states that can generate sufficient power to defend themselves externally and internally, and to enforce commonly agreed upon laws. All societies need to regularize the exercise of power through law, to make sure that the law applies impersonally to all citizens, and that there are no exemptions for a privileged few. And governments must be responsive not only to elites and to the needs of those running the government; the government should serve the interests of the broader community. There need to be peaceful mechanisms for resolving the inevitable conflicts that emerge in pluralistic societies.

I believe that development of these three sets of institutions becomes a universal requirement for all human societies over time. They do not simply represent the cultural preferences of Western societies or any particular cultural group. For better or worse, there is no alternative to a modern, impersonal state as guarantor of order and security, and as a source of necessary public goods. The rule of law is critical for economic development; without clear property rights and contract enforcement, it is difficult for businesses to break out of small circles of trust. Moreover, to the extent that the law enshrines the unalienable rights of individuals, it recognizes their dignity as human agents and thus has an intrinsic value. And finally, democratic participation is more than just a useful check on abusive, corrupt, or tyrannical government. Political agency is an end in itself, one of the basic dimensions of freedom that complete and enrich the life of an individual.

A liberal democracy combining these three institutions cannot be said to be humanly universal, since such regimes have existed for only the last two centuries in the history of a species that goes back tens of thousands of years. But development is a coherent process that produces general as well as specific evolution—that is, the convergence of institutions across culturally disparate societies over time.

If there is a single theme that underlies many of the chapters of this book, it is that there is a political deficit around the world, not of states but of *modern* states that are capable, impersonal, well organized, and autonomous. Many of the problems of developing countries are by-products of the fact that they have weak and ineffective states. Many appear to be strong in what the sociologist Michael Mann labels despotic power, the ability to suppress journalists, opposition politicians, or rival ethnic groups. But they are not strong in their ability to exercise what Mann calls infrastructural power, the ability to legitimately make and enforce rules, or to deliver necessary public goods like safety, health, and education.[10] Many of the failures attributed to democracy are in fact failures of state administrations that are unable to deliver on the promises made by newly elected democratic politicians to voters who want not just their political rights but good government as well.

But weak states are not merely the province of poor developing countries. Neither Greece nor Italy ever developed high-quality bureaucratic administrations; both remained mired in high degrees of clientelism and outright corruption. These problems have contributed directly to their woes in the current euro crisis. The United States, for its part, was one of the last developed countries to put in place a modern state administration, having been characterized as a nineteenth-century "state of courts and parties" in which bureaucracy played a very minor role. Despite the growth in the twentieth century of an enormous administrative state, this characterization still remains true in many ways: courts and political parties continue to play outsized roles in American politics, roles that are performed by professional bureaucracies in other countries. Many of the inefficiencies of American government stem from this source.

Particularly over the past generation, thinking about states and the effective use of state power has not been a popular preoccupation. The experience of the twentieth century, with its history of maniacal totalitarian regimes from Stalin's Russia to Hitler's Germany to Mao's China, has understandably focused the attention of much of the world on the misuse of overweening state power. This is nowhere more true than in the United States, with its long history of distrust of government. That distrust has deepened since the 1980s, which began with Ronald Reagan's assertion that "Government is not the solution to our problem, government *is* the problem."

The emphasis on effective states should in no way be construed as a preference on my part for authoritarian government, or particular sympathy with regimes like those of Singapore and China that have achieved seemingly miraculous economic results in the absence of democracy. I believe that a well-functioning and legitimate regime needs to achieve balance between government power and institutions that constrain the state. Things can become unbalanced in either direction, with insufficient checks on state power on the one hand, or excessive veto power by different social groups on the other that prevent any sort of collective action. Few countries can decide to turn themselves into Singapore, moreover; replacing a poorly administered democracy with an equally incompetent autocracy buys you nothing.

Nor should this book's emphasis on the need for effective states be construed as a preference for a larger welfare state, or "big government" as it is understood in American political discourse. I believe that virtually all developed democracies face huge long-term challenges from unsustainable spending commitments made in years past that will only increase as populations age and birth rates decline. Much more important than the size of government is its quality. There is no necessary relationship between big government and poor economic outcomes, as one can see prima facie by comparing the large welfare states of Scandinavia to the minimalist governments of sub-Saharan Africa. There is, however, a very powerful correlation between the quality of government and good economic and social outcomes. Moreover, an expansive state that is nonetheless perceived as effective and legitimate will have a much easier time downsizing and reducing its own scope than one that is excessively constrained, feckless, or unable to exercise real authority.

This volume will not provide any straightforward answers, and certainly not any easy ones, to the question of how to improve the quality of government. That is something I have written about in other contexts. But one cannot begin to understand how bad governments might become good ones unless one understands the historical origins of both.

2

THE DIMENSIONS OF DEVELOPMENT

How political development fits into the larger picture of development; the economic, social, and ideological dimensions of development; how the world changed after 1800; why Huntington's theory needs to be modified but is still relevant in understanding events like the Arab Spring

Political development—the evolution of the state, rule of law, and democratic accountability—is only one aspect of the broader phenomenon of human socioeconomic development. Changes in political institutions must be understood in the context of economic growth, social mobilization, and the power of ideas concerning justice and legitimacy. The interaction among these different dimensions of development changed dramatically in the period following the French and American Revolutions.

Economic development can be defined simply as sustained increases in output per person over time. There are many arguments among economists and others whether this is an adequate way of measuring human well-being, since per capita GDP looks only at money and not health, opportunity, fairness, distribution, and many other aspects of human flourishing. I want to put these arguments to the side for the time being; per capita GDP has the advantage of being straightforward and relatively well defined, and a lot of effort has been spent trying to measure it.

The second important component of development—social mobilization—concerns the rise of new social groups over time and changes in the nature of the relationships between and among these groups. Social mobilization entails different parts of society becoming conscious of themselves as people with shared interests or identities, and their organization for collective action. In the early nineteenth century, the most economically advanced parts of the world, Europe and China, were still largely agrarian societies in which the vast bulk of the population lived in small villages and raised food for a living. By the end of that century, Europe saw an enormous shift as peasants left the countryside, cities expanded, and an industrial working class was formed.[1] The German social theorist Ferdinand Tönnies described this as the shift from Gemeinschaft to Gesellschaft, or what is typically translated in English as "community" and "society."[2] Other nineteenth-century theorists invented new dichotomies to describe the transition from the one form of society to the other, including Max Weber's distinction between traditional and charismatic to legal/rational authority, Émile Durkheim's opposition of mechanical and organic solidarity, and Henry Maine's move from status to contract.[3]

Each of these schema sought to explicate the shift from Gemeinschaft—the close-knit village where everyone knows each other and identities are fixed—to Gesellschaft, the big city with its diversity and anonymity. This transition has taken place in the late-developing countries of East Asia in the second half of the twentieth century and is in the process of occurring in South Asia, the Middle East, and sub-Saharan Africa today.

The industrialization process and economic growth constantly create new social groups, such as workers, students, professionals, managers, and the like. In the anonymous city, people become more mobile, live in more diverse and pluralistic societies, and have fluid identities that are no longer determined by the customs of the village, tribe, or family. These novel social relationships give rise, as we will see, to new forms of identity like nationalism, or to new forms of universalistic religious affiliation. It is social mobilization that lays the ground for changes in political institutions.

In addition to economic growth and social mobilization, there is an evolution in ideas concerning legitimacy. Legitimacy represents a broadly shared perception that certain social arrangements are just. Ideas regarding legitimacy evolve over time. This evolution is sometimes a by-product of changes in the economy or society, but there are numerous junctures at which they act as independent drivers of the other dimensions of development.

Thus, when the French regent Marie de Medicis called the Estates-General in 1614 to demand new taxes, it proved a weak and compliant body unable to block the rise of absolutist monarchy. When it was next called in 1789, however, the intellectual conditions in France were hugely different, with the blossoming of the Enlightenment and the spread of the ideas of the Rights of Man. This shift, needless to say, was one reason why the second Estates-General paved the way for the French Revolution. Similarly, there was a critical change in the thinking of English political actors during the seventeenth century: at the start, they spoke about defending the rights of Englishmen, that is, feudal rights inherited from time immemorial; a hundred years later, under the influence of writers like Hobbes and Locke, they demanded their natural rights as human beings. This made a huge difference in the kind of regime that would be created there, and in North America.

A historian of a Marxist bent might say that the adoption of these new ideas about universal rights reflected the rise of the bourgeoisie in both France and England, and that they constituted a superstructure masking economic interest. Karl Marx himself famously said that religion was the "opiate of the people." But the bourgeoisie could have made a case for itself on the basis of the special privileges of the old feudal order, rather than a doctrine that opened the door to universal human equality. The fact that it chose to justify itself in these terms hearkened back to yet other ideas of, alternatively, Christian universalism and the evolving doctrines of modern natural science. One wonders, moreover, what the history of the twentieth century would have looked like without Marx. There were of course many Socialist thinkers before and after him, reflecting the interests of the emerging working class. But none were able to analyze the conditions of early industrialization so brilliantly, link them to a larger Hegelian theory of history, and explain in self-professed "scientific" terms the necessity of the ultimate victory of the proletariat. From the pen of Marx emerged a new secular ideology that became, in the hands of leaders like Lenin and Mao, a substitute for religion that succeeded in mobilizing millions of people and materially changing the course of history.

We can bring the three components of political development together with economic growth, social mobilization, and ideas/legitimacy in Figure 1.

While each of the six dimensions of development can change independently, they are also all linked to one another in a multitude of ways. A model of political development would consist of a theory that explained these causal linkages. We can trace some of the more important linkages by outlining the sequence of events that took place in the wake of the industrialization of England, the United States, and other early modernizers.

FIGURE 1

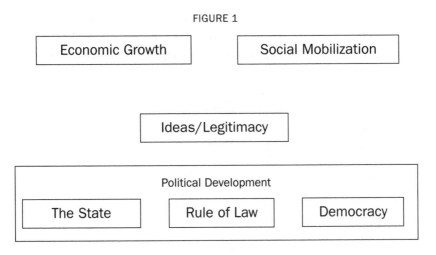

HOW THE WORLD CHANGED AFTER 1800

The rate of economic growth accelerated dramatically around the year 1800 with the takeoff of the Industrial Revolution. Prior to that moment, which corresponds to the historical period covered in the first volume of this book, much of the world lived under the conditions described by the English writer Thomas Malthus, whose 1798 *Essay on the Principle of Population* painted a gloomy picture in which population growth would outstrip economic resources in the long run. Figure 2 shows an estimate of per capita income over an eight-hundred-year period in England, where the Industrial Revolution started. The hockey-stick shape of the curve, and the sudden transition to a much higher rate of growth, reflects the fact that the later period saw continual year-on-year increases in productivity that vastly outstripped the rate of population growth. While we might speculate that this blessed interval of rapid growth may someday still be overwhelmed by population increase and by absolute limits to available resources, we are nonetheless fortunately still living in a post-Malthusian world.

What caused this sudden burst of economic growth? The Industrial Revolution had been preceded by a commercial revolution starting in the sixteenth century that vastly expanded the volume of trade both within Europe and across the Atlantic. This expansion, in turn, was driven by a host of political and institutional factors: the establishment of secure property rights, the rise of modern states, the invention of double-entry bookkeeping and the modern corporation, and new technologies of communications and transportation. The Industrial Revolution in turn rested on the systematic application of the scientific method and its incorporation into an institutional structure of universities and research organizations, which could then be translated into technological innovations.[4]

FIGURE 2. Real Income per Person in England, 1200–2000

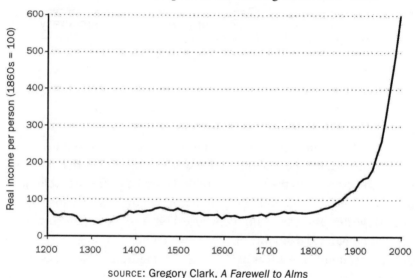

SOURCE: Gregory Clark, *A Farewell to Alms*

The sudden shift to a higher level of growth had a huge effect on societies via an expanding division of labor. The third chapter of Adam Smith's *Wealth of Nations* is titled "The Division of Labor is Limited by the Extent of the Market." Smith began the book with his famous description of a pin factory. Instead of a single craftsman pulling, cutting, and sharpening individual pins, each task is given to a specialized worker, which vastly increases the factory's productivity. But there would be no incentive to increase productivity in this fashion, Smith asserts, if a sufficiently large market did not exist. Smith thus argues that the expanding division of labor is stimulated in turn by improvements in transportation and communication that increase the size of markets. The commercial revolution of Smith's day seeded the Industrial Revolution that would soon unfold.

The expanding division of labor then becomes a central focus for subsequent thinkers, beginning with Karl Marx and Friedrich Engels, who in *The Communist Manifesto* talk about formerly proud craftsmen being reduced to robotic cogs in a huge industrial machine. Unlike Smith, they see specialization and the division of labor as an evil that alienates workers from their true beings. One gets a sense of how different this modern world was from the agrarian one that preceded it from the following passage written in 1848 just as the Industrial Revolution was shifting into high gear in England:

> The bourgeoisie cannot exist without constantly revolutionizing the instruments of production, and thereby the relations of production, and with them the whole relations of society. Conservation of the old modes of production in unaltered form, was, on the contrary, the first condition of existence for all earlier industrial classes. Constant revolutionizing of production, uninterrupted disturbance of all social conditions, everlasting uncertainty and agitation distinguish the bourgeois epoch from all earlier ones. All fixed, fast-frozen relations, with their train of ancient and venerable prejudices and opinions, are swept away, all newly-formed ones become antiquated before they can ossify. All that is solid melts into air, all that is holy is profaned, and man is at last compelled to face with sober senses, his real conditions of life, and his relations with his kind.

Silicon Valley thinks that it invented "disruptive innovation," but in fact the rate of social change across Europe and America was if anything higher at the time that Marx wrote than it is in the early twenty-first century.

Social mobilization creates political change by creating new groups that demand participation in the political system. Throughout industrializing Europe and America in the late nineteenth century, workers began to join together in trade unions and pushed for higher wages, as well as better and safer working conditions. They agitated for the right to speak out publicly, to organize, and to vote. Workers also began to support new political parties, which in turn started to win elections under banners like the British Labour Party and the German Social Democratic Party. In places without elections, such as Russia, they began joining underground Communist parties.

Spreading communications and transportation technologies fostered another important change that occurred in this period: the appearance of an early form of globalization that allowed ideas to spread across political boundaries in ways they had not done previously. The development of political institutions before 1800 took place largely within the context of single societies, even though some of those societies were rather large. For example, the Chinese introduction of merit-based bureaucracy in the third century B.C. had virtually no impact on the contemporaneous Greek and Roman worlds. While early Arab state builders could look to neighboring Persian or Byzantine models, they did not seek to emulate the feudal institutions of contemporary Europe, much less those of the Indians or Chinese.

The beginnings of a world system were laid first by the Mongols, who carried both trade and diseases all the way from China to Europe and the Middle East, and then by the Arabs who extended their networks from Europe to Southeast Asia. It was subsequently the Europeans who opened up trade with both the Americas and South and East Asia. For those who think that globalization is a unique feature of the early twenty-first-century world, consider the following passage from *The Communist Manifesto*: "The need of a constantly expanding market for its products chases the bourgeoisie over the whole surface of the globe . . . The bourgeoisie has through its exploitation of the world-market given a cosmopolitan character to production and consumption in every country . . . All old-established national industries have been destroyed . . . by industries that no longer work up indigenous raw material, but raw material drawn from the remotest zones; industries whose products are consumed, not only at home, but in every quarter of the globe."

What was true of commodities was also true of ideas concerning political and economic institutions: if something seemed to work in one part of the world, it was rapidly copied in another. For example, Adam Smith's ideas about the power of markets circulated widely throughout Europe and traveled all the way to Latin America where Spanish Bourbon reformers relaxed earlier mercantilist restrictions on trade. At the other end of the ideological spectrum, Marxism was from the start a self-consciously cosmopolitan ideology that was adopted by non-European revolutionaries from China to Vietnam to Cuba.

The conditions in which political development occurred after 1800 were very different from those that prevailed in the preceding periods covered in the first volume of this book. Continuous economic growth was rapidly driving new forms of social mobilization, creating new actors who then demanded participation in the political system. At the same time, ideas could spread from one society to another at the speed of the printing press or, later, the telegraph, telephone, radio, and eventually, the Internet. Political order under these conditions became highly problematic, as institutions developed to manage agrarian societies now presided over industrialized ones. The linkages between technological and economic change and political institutions continue into the present, with social media fostering new forms of mobilization in the Arab world, China, and beyond.

ALL GOOD THINGS DON'T ALWAYS GO TOGETHER

Britain was the first country to industrialize, and for many social theorists from Karl Marx on it became the paradigm for modernization as such. In Britain a causal path led from economic growth to social mobilization to changes in values to demands for political participation and, ultimately, to liberal democracy. European social theory crossed the Atlantic in the early twentieth century and became entrenched in the American academy under the rubric of modernization theory. The latter argued, in effect, that all good things ultimately go together. Modernization was a single, interconnected phenomenon in which change occurred simultaneously in all six of the boxes in Figure 1.[5] Everyone, in other words, would get to Denmark in short order. Modernization theory appeared at the historical moment that Europe's colonies were receiving their independence, and the expectation was that they would replicate the European development sequence.

Samuel Huntington's 1968 book *Political Order in Changing Societies* threw a dash of cold water on this theory. Huntington sharply contested the view that all good things necessarily go together. He argued that economic development bred social mobilization, and when the rate of social

mobilization exceeded the capacity of existing institutions to accommodate new demands for participation, political order broke down. Huntington pointed to the "gap" that emerged between the expectations of
newly mobilized populations and their government's ability or willingness to accommodate their participation in politics. He argued that both
poor traditional societies and fully modernized societies were stable; instability was characteristic of modernizing societies in which the different components of modernization failed to advance in a coordinated
fashion.[6]

In the forty-plus years since Huntington wrote his book, there has
been a tremendous amount of research into conflict and violence in developing countries by scholars including James Fearon, David Laitin,
and Paul Collier.[7] In light of this recent work, Huntington's theory would
have to be revised in many ways. He was right that instability reflected a
lack of institutions. This is true almost by definition, since institutions
are rules that organize behavior. But the instability and violence he observed in the 1950s and '60s was not necessarily the result of modernization upsetting otherwise stable traditional societies. His view that such
societies were stable is misleading: most developing countries had been
parts of colonial empires before the period in which he wrote, where authority was imposed externally. We have little reliable data, quantitative or
otherwise, on general levels of conflict in, say, sub-Saharan Africa before
the colonialists' arrival. Many of the new countries in the developing
world that emerged in this period, like Nigeria and the Belgian Congo/
Zaire, had never existed as independent polities previously and therefore
had no traditional institutions to speak of at a national level. It is therefore not surprising that they fell into conflict shortly after independence.
Countries with weak or nonexistent institutions would have been unstable whether they modernized or not.

More recent analyses of the causes of conflict contradict Huntington's assertion that instability afflicted primarily modernizing countries
somewhere in the middle between poverty and development. In fact,
they show that conflict correlates very heavily with poverty, and that it
is often both a cause and a result of poverty.[8] Almost all the authors
systematically studying the phenomenon of conflict point to weak governments and poor institutions as a fundamental cause of both conflict
and poverty. Many failing or fragile states are thus caught in a low-level
trap whereby poor institutions fail to control violence, which produces

poverty, which further weakens the ability of the government to govern. While many people believe that ethnicity is a cause of conflict when observing the Balkans, South Asia, Africa, and other places in the aftermath of the cold war, William Easterly shows that when one controls for the strength of institutions, any link between ethnic diversity and conflict disappears. James Fearon and David Laitin similarly show that higher levels of ethnic or religious diversity were not more likely to cause conflict when controlling for level of per capita income. Switzerland, after all, is divided among three linguistic groups and yet has been stable since the middle of the nineteenth century because of its strong institutions.[9]

Modernization and economic growth did not necessarily lead to escalating levels of instability and violence; certain societies were in fact able to accommodate demands for greater participation by developing their political institutions. This is what happened in South Korea and Taiwan in the period after World War II. Rapid modernization in both cases was overseen by repressive authoritarian governments. But these governments were able to satisfy popular expectations for jobs and economic growth, and eventually accommodated demands for greater democracy. Like South Korea and Taiwan in an earlier phase, the People's Republic of China has been able to maintain a high level of overall political stability without opening up its system to formal political participation, largely through its ability to supply stability, growth, and jobs to its citizens.

The years since the publication of *Political Order in Changing Societies* saw both dramatic economic development and the emergence of what Huntington himself labeled the "Third Wave" of democratic transitions. Global economic output roughly quadrupled between 1970 and 2008, increasing from $16 to $61 trillion,[10] and at the same time the number of electoral democracies around the world increased from about 40 to nearly 120.[11] While some of these transitions, including those in Portugal, Romania, the Balkans, and Indonesia, involved violence, this huge transformation of global politics occurred on the whole remarkably peacefully.

There are areas of the world, however, where Huntington's gap between increasing social mobilization and institutional development has in fact been a major driver of instability. While the Middle East experienced a large number of coups, revolutions, and civil conflicts in the 1950s, '60s, and early '70s, the subsequent decades saw the emergence of highly stable authoritarian regimes throughout the Arab world. Tunisia, Egypt, Syria, and Libya were ruled by dictators who did not permit opposition political parties to operate and who tightly controlled civil society. The Arab Middle East was in fact the one part of the world that did not participate in the Third Wave of democratic transitions.[12]

This all changed dramatically in early 2011 with the collapse of the Ben Ali regime in Tunisia, the fall of Hosni Mubarak in Egypt, a civil war in Libya and the death of Muammar Qaddafi, as well as serious political instability in Bahrain, Yemen, and Syria. The so-called Arab Spring was driven by a number of factors, among them the emergence of larger middle classes in Egypt and Tunisia. The Human Development Indices compiled by the United Nations, which are composite measures of health, education, and income, show an increase of 28 percent in Egypt and 30 percent in Tunisia for the period between 1990 and 2010.[13] There was also a substantial increase in the numbers of college graduates, especially in Tunisia.[14] The new middle classes, mobilized by new technologies such as satellite TV stations (Al Jazeera) and social media (Facebook and Twitter), led the uprisings against the Ben Ali and Mubarak dictatorships, even if these social groups could not retain control over subsequent developments.[15]

What the Arab world experienced, in other words, was a Huntingtonian event: under the surface of seemingly impregnable authoritarian governments, social change was occurring, and newly mobilized actors vented their frustrations at regimes that made no provision for incorporating them through new institutions. The future stability of that region will depend entirely on whether political institutions emerge to channel participation in peaceful directions. This means the growth of political parties, the opening up of media to permit broad discussion of political topics, and the acceptance of constitutional rules for regulating political conflict.

Huntington's basic insight, that modernization is not a seamless and inevitable process, was nonetheless correct. The economic, social, and political dimensions of development proceed on different tracks and schedules, and there is no reason to think that they will necessarily work in tandem. Political development, in particular, follows its own logic independent of economic growth. Successful modernization depends, then, on the parallel development of political institutions alongside economic growth, social change, and ideas; it is not something that can be taken for granted as an inevitable concomitant of the other dimensions of development. Indeed, strong political institutions are often necessary to get economic growth going in the first place. It is precisely their absence that locks failed or fragile states into a cycle of conflict, violence, and poverty.

The first and most important institution that fragile or failing states lack is an administratively capable government. Before a state can be constrained by either law or democracy, it needs to exist. This means, in the first instance, the establishment of a centralized executive and a bureaucracy.

3

BUREAUCRACY

How study of the state is the study of bureaucracy; recent efforts to measure the quality of government; variance in the quality of government across countries and the need for a historical understanding of these outcomes

For many people around the world, the central problem of contemporary politics is how to constrain powerful, overweening or, indeed, tyrannical governments. The human rights community seeks to use law as a mechanism for protecting vulnerable individuals from abuse by states—not just authoritarian regimes but also liberal democracies that are sometimes motivated to bend the rules in pursuit of terrorists or other threats. Prodemocracy activists, such as those that led the Rose and Orange Revolutions in Georgia and Ukraine, and the Tunisian and Egyptian protesters at the start of the Arab Spring, hoped to use democratic elections to hold rulers accountable to their people. In the United States, citizens are constantly vigilant against real and perceived abuses of government power, from excessively onerous environmental requirements to restrictions on guns to domestic surveillance by the National Security Agency.

As a consequence, much of the discussion of political development has centered in recent years on the institutions of constraint—the rule of law and democratic accountability. But before governments can be constrained, they have to generate the power to actually do things. States, in other words, have to be able to govern.

The existence of states able to provide basic public services cannot be taken for granted. Indeed, part of the reason many countries are poor is precisely that they don't have effective states. This is obvious in failed or failing states including Afghanistan, Haiti, and Somalia, where life is chaotic and insecure. But it is also true in many better-off societies with reasonably good democratic institutions.

Take the case of India, which has been a remarkably successful democracy since its creation in 1947. In 1996, the activist and economist Jean Drèze produced a Public Report on Basic Education that surveyed the state of primary education in a number of Indian states. One of the most shocking findings was that in rural areas, fully 48 percent of teachers failed to show up for their jobs. This understandably caused a huge outcry, and the Indian government launched a major program in 2001 to improve the quality of basic education. Although this reform effort led to a great deal of apparent activity, a follow-up study in 2008 showed that teacher absence rates were exactly what they had been more than a decade earlier, 48 percent.[1]

India, of course, had been a star performer among emerging market countries, with growth rates in the range of 7–10 percent per year up until 2010.[2] But alongside the billionaire tycoons and high-tech industries, contemporary India is characterized by shocking levels of poverty and inequality, with certain parts of the country on a par with the worst places in sub-Saharan Africa. This inequality has bred, among other things, ongoing Maoist insurgencies in its poorest states. The fact that education is grossly inadequate for so many citizens will ultimately be a constraint on growth as the country industrializes and looks for better-educated workers. With respect to providing such basic services, the country has done less well than neighboring giant China, not to speak of Japan and Korea, which have broken into first world status.

India's problem is not an absence of rule of law—indeed, many Indians would argue that the country has too much law. Its courts are clogged and slow, and plaintiffs often die before their cases come to trial. The Indian Supreme Court has a backlog of more than sixty thousand cases. The government often fails to invest in infrastructure because it, like the United States, is hamstrung with lawsuits of various sorts.

Nor is India's problem inadequate democracy. There is a free media that is perfectly happy to criticize the government for shortcomings in education, health, and other areas of public policy, and plenty of political competition to hold incumbents accountable for failure. In an area like education, there is no political conflict over the ends of public policy— everyone agrees that children should be educated and that teachers should show up for their jobs if they are to get paid. And yet, providing this basic service seems to be beyond the capacity of the Indian government.

The failure here is a failure of the state—specifically, the bureaucracies at local, state, and national levels that are tasked with providing basic education to children in rural India. Political order is not just about constraining abusive governments. It is more often about getting governments to actually do the things expected of them, like providing citizen security, protecting property rights, making available education and public health services, and building the infrastructure that is necessary for private economic activity to occur. Indeed, in very many countries democracy itself is threatened because the state is too corrupt or too incompetent to do these things. People begin to wish for a powerful authority—a dictator or savior—that will cut through the blather of politicians and actually make things work.

WHY GOVERNMENTS ARE NECESSARY

Someone of a libertarian bent (more often than not an American) will interject that the problem here is one of government itself: all governments are hopelessly bureaucratic, incompetent, rigid, and counterproductive, and the solution is not to try to make government better but to get rid of it altogether in favor of private or market-based solutions.

There are indeed reasons why government agencies are intrinsically less efficient than their private-sector counterparts. It is also the case that governments have often taken on tasks better left to the private sector, such as operating factories and businesses, or else have interfered with private decision making in destructive ways. The boundary between public and private will always be a matter up for renegotiation in every society.

But in the end, there has to be a public sector, because there are certain services and functions—what economists label public goods—that only governments can provide. A public good is, technically, one where my enjoyment of it does not prevent you from enjoying it as well, and which cannot be privately appropriated and thereby depleted. Classic examples are clean air and national defense. They fit these categories because neither can be denied to specific individuals within a society, nor does their use by some diminish the total stock available to others. No private actors have an incentive to produce public goods because they cannot prevent everyone from using and benefiting from them, and therefore cannot appropriate any income arising from them. Hence even the most committed free-market economist would readily admit that governments have a role in providing pure public goods. Besides clean air and defense, public goods include public safety, a legal system, and the protection of public health.

In addition to pure public goods, many goods are produced for private consumption that entail what economists call externalities. An externality is a benefit or harm imposed on third parties, such as the benefit an employer gets when I have paid for my own education, or the pollution that fouls the drinking water of a community downstream from a factory. In other cases, economic transactions may involve information asymmetries; for example, the seller of a used car may know about defects not readily apparent to the buyer, while a drug maker may be aware of clinical studies that show its products are ineffective or even harmful, which are unavailable to potential patients. Governments have classically played a role in regulating externalities and information asymmetries. In the case of education and basic infrastructure such as roads, ports, and water, the positive externality associated with it is great enough that governments traditionally provide a basic level to citizens for free or else at highly subsidized prices. In such cases, however, the extent of necessary government subsidy or regulation is often debatable, since excessive state intervention can distort market signals or choke off private activity altogether.

In addition to providing public goods and regulating externalities, governments engage in greater or lesser degrees of social regulation. There are many forms that this can take. Governments want their citizens to be upstanding, law-abiding, educated, and patriotic. They may want to encourage home ownership, small businesses, gender equality, physical exercise, or discourage cigarette smoking, drug use, gangs, or abortion. Most governments, even ones committed ideologically to free markets, end up doing things they believe will encourage investment and economic growth beyond the bare provision of necessary public goods.

Finally, governments have a role to play in controlling elites and engaging in a certain amount of redistribution. Redistribution is a basic function of all social orders: as Karl Polanyi noted, most premodern social systems revolved around the ability of the leader or Big Man in a group to redistribute goods to his followers, a practice that was much more common historically than market exchange.[3] As we saw in Volume 1, many early governments, from the post–Norman Conquest kings of England to the Ottomans to any number of Chinese emperors, saw their function as the protection of ordinary citizens against the rapacity of oligarchic elites. They did this not, in all likelihood, out of a sense of fairness, and certainly not because they believed in democracy, but rather out of self-interest. If the state did not control the richest and most powerful elites in society, the latter would appropriate and misuse the political system at everyone else's expense.

The most basic form of redistribution that a state engages in is equal application of the law. The rich and powerful always have ways of looking after themselves, and if left to their own devices will always get their way over nonelites. It is only the state, with its judicial and enforcement power, that can make elites conform to the same rules that everyone else is required to follow. In this respect, the state and the rule of law work together to produce something like the equality of justice, whether in the form of an English king's court finding in favor of a vassal against his lord in a tenancy dispute, or the federal government intervening to protect black schoolchildren against a local mob, or the police protecting a community against a drug gang.

There are other more overtly economic forms of redistribution that modern governments practice, however. One of the most common is mandatory insurance pools, in which the government forces the community to contribute to insurance plans which, in the case of social security, redistribute income from young to old, and in the case of medical insurance, from the healthy to the sick. Many American conservatives denounced President Obama's 2010 Affordable Care Act as "socialism," but the fact was that at the time, the United States was alone among rich democratic countries in the world in not having some form of mandated universal health insurance.

Liberal theorists from John Locke to Friedrich Hayek have always been skeptical of government-mandated redistribution, since it threatens to reward the lazy and incompetent at the expense of the virtuous and hardworking. And indeed, all redistributive programs incur what economists call "moral hazard": by rewarding people based on their level of income rather than their individual effort, the government discourages work. This was of course the case in former Communist countries such as the Soviet Union, where "the government pretended to pay us and we pretended to work."

On the other hand, it is morally difficult to justify a minimalist state that provides no safety net whatsoever for its less fortunate citizens. This would work only in a society where the playing field was always perfectly level, and in which accidents of birth or simple luck had no role in determining the life chances, wealth, and opportunities faced by individuals. But such a society has never existed in the past, and does not exist today. The real question facing most governments, then, is less whether to redistribute than at what level to do so, and how to redistribute in ways that minimize moral hazard.

The problem of inherited advantages usually increases over time. Elites tend to get more entrenched because they can use their wealth, power, and social status to get access to the government, and to use the power of the state to protect themselves and their children. This process will continue until nonelites succeed in mobilizing politically to reverse it or otherwise protect themselves. In some cases a reaction takes the form of violent revolution, as in the French and Bolshevik Revolutions; in others it can take the form of populist policies of redistribution as in Argentina under Juan Perón, or Venezuela under Hugo Chávez. Ideally, constraints on the power of elites should be exercised through democratic control of the state, where the state's policies reflect a broad consensus on the part of the population as to what constitutes a fair distribution of the resources at the state's disposal. As in the case of redistribution, the trick is to prevent the overrepresentation of elites without punishing them for their ability to generate wealth.

There is today a wide range of views on the appropriate scope of the state, ranging from those who believe it should provide only the most basic of public goods, to those who think it should actively shape the nature of society and engage in substantial redistribution. As noted, all modern liberal democracies engage in some degree of redistribution, but the extent of state intervention varies significantly from the social democracies of Scandinavia to the more classically liberal United States. Figure 3 shows a spectrum of state functions from minimal to activist in which modern governments can engage.

But while many contemporary political arguments concern how far state intervention should go, there is an equally important question about state capacity. Any given function, from fighting fires to providing

FIGURE 3. The Scope of State Functions

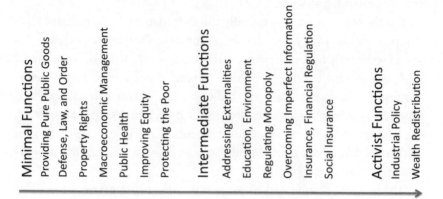

SOURCE: World Bank, *The State in a Changing World*

health services to undertaking industrial policy, can be done better or worse depending on the quality of the state bureaucracy charged with performing that function. Governments are collections of complex organizations; how well they perform depends on how they are organized and the resources, human and material, at their disposal. In evaluating states, then, there are two axes of importance, a horizontal axis defining the scope of state functions, and a vertical axis defining the capacity of the state to undertake a given function (see Figure 4 below).

FIGURE 4. State Scope and State Strength

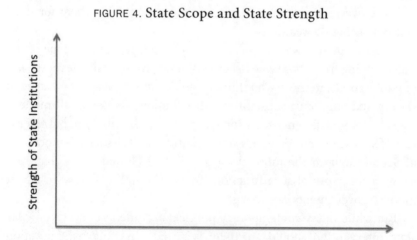

There are a number of rough measures for how far out on the horizontal axis a given state is. The one most typically used by economists is the proportion of total GDP taken in through taxes; alternatively, one could measure public spending as a proportion of GDP since that amount is often larger than taxes and covered by borrowing. These measures are not wholly adequate, however, since some activist functions, like regulation and industrial policy, have large impacts on society without necessarily affecting fiscal policy.

MEASURING THE QUALITY OF GOVERNMENT

Measuring the strength or quality of the state—that is, its position on the vertical axis—is far more complex. Max Weber famously identified a modern state with a set of procedures, the most important of which had to do with the strict functional organization of offices and the selection of bureaucrats based on merit and technical competence rather than patronage.[4] Some of Weber's criteria are not necessarily conditions that we would today accept as necessary for good bureaucratic functioning, such as the office constituting a lifetime career and the need for strict discipline and control through an administrative hierarchy. The idea, however, that bureaucrats should be chosen according to their technical qualifications and promoted on the basis of merit rather than through personal connections is both widely accepted and correlated with positive governance outcomes like low corruption and economic growth.[5] Whereas Weber highlighted bureaucratic form, political scientist Bo Rothstein has suggested the use of "impartiality" as a measure of government quality, a normative characteristic that he argues correlates strongly with efficient performance.[6] Conversely, one could also assess the quality of government through measures of dysfunction, such as perceived levels of government corruption like Transparency International's Corruption Perception Index.[7]

Measuring the strength of government through procedures alone is unlikely to capture its real quality, however. Weber's classic definition assumes that modern government is a rigid, rule-bound institution that is mechanically tasked with carrying out the functions set it by the principal. But in fact procedural rigidity, rather than being a virtue, is at the core of what people dislike about modern government. Weber himself spoke of bureaucratic administration as an "iron cage" in which people were trapped.[8]

An alternative method to a procedural approach is an assessment of the capacity of a government to formulate policies and carry them out, or what Joel Migdal calls the ability of a state to "penetrate" the society over which it presides.[9] Capacity, in turn, is defined by a number of factors, including the size of the bureaucracy, the resources at its disposal, and the levels of education and expertise of government officials. Some scholars use the rate at which a government can extract taxes from its population as a capacity measure, the same used to measure scope. The reason for this is that taxes, particularly direct ones like an income tax, are hard to collect and also represent resources at the government's disposal. However, the ability of an organization to perform its functions is never simply a matter of measurable resources. Organizational culture also matters—the degree to which the individuals who make up the organization can function cooperatively, engender trust, take risks, innovate, and the like. A Weberian bureaucracy defined only by formal procedures may or may not have the intangible qualities necessary to make it function effectively.

A different approach to measuring the quality of government would be to look not at what the government is, but rather at what it does. The purpose of government, after all, is not to follow procedures but to provide the population with basic services including education, defense, public safety, and legal access; an output measure like the degree to which children were being educated by the public school system would be more informative than data about teacher numbers, recruitment, or training. Lant Pritchett, Michael Woolcock, and Matt Andrews have argued that one of the big problems with developing countries' governments is that they engage in what they term "isomorphic mimicry," that is, copying the outward forms of developed countries' governments, while being unable to reproduce the kinds of outputs, like education and health, that the latter achieve.[10] Measuring what the government actually does rather than how it does it would avoid this problem.

Appealing as output measures are, however, they can be misleading. Good outcomes, like quality public education, are a complex mixture of inputs provided by governments (teachers, curriculum, classrooms, etc.) as well as characteristics of the population being served, including their income, social habits, and culture (that is, the degree to which learning is valued in the home). A classic study of educational outcomes in the United States was the 1966 Coleman Report, whose statistical analysis showed that quality education was much more a reflection of a student's friends and family than of the inputs being supplied by the government.[11] In any event, measuring outcomes is often difficult for the kinds of complex services offered by modern governments. For example, how does one measure the quality of a judicial system? Clearly a gross output measure of the number of cases closed or the number of convictions is meaningless in the absence of qualitative measures of whether the courts were adjudicating cases fairly, or using torture to extract confessions. Absent such judgments, police states will always seem to perform better than those that adhere to a strict rule of law.

In addition to considering procedural and output functions, there is a final dimension of government quality that is relevant when assessing the functioning of a state: the degree of autonomy that a government enjoys. All governments serve a political master, whether a democratic public or an authoritarian ruler, but they can be granted more or less autonomy in their ability to carry out their tasks. The most basic form of autonomy concerns the right to control the government's own staff and hire personnel based on professional rather than political grounds. But autonomy is important also for implementation, since highly complex or contradictory mandates seldom produce good results. Too much autonomy, on the other hand, can also lead to disaster, either in terms of corruption or bureaucracies that set their own agendas beyond any type of political control.

Good procedures, capacity, outputs, and bureaucratic autonomy are thus all possible ways of defining where a state lies on the vertical axis of Figure 4. It would be nice if there were scholarly agreement on a standardized way of measuring state quality, but no such measure exists. In recent years, a number of economists have tried to devise quantitative measures of the quality of government, with varying success. Comprehensive comparison is made more difficult by the fact that the quality of government within each country varies tremendously depending on region, function, and level (national, state, or local).

Despite these challenges, one commonly used cross-national measure of government performance is the World Bank Institute's Worldwide Governance Indicators (WGI), which has been produced annually since the early 2000s. These indicators measure six dimensions of governance

FIGURE 5. Government Effectiveness and Control of Corruption,
Selected Countries, 2011

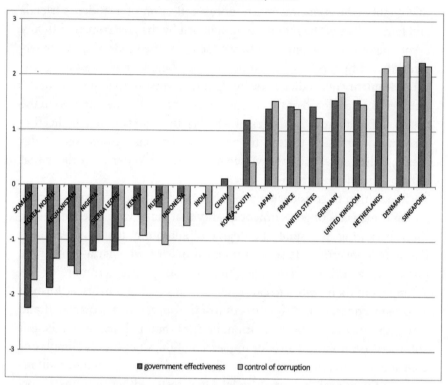

SOURCE: World Bank Institute, Worldwide Governance Indicators, 2011

for a wide range of countries (voice and accountability, political stability and absence of violence, government effectiveness, regulatory quality, rule of law, and control of corruption). Figure 5 extracts two of these dimensions, control of corruption and government effectiveness, for a selected group of developed and less developed countries, ranked in order of their scores on the effectiveness indicator.

It is hard to know what the WGI numbers actually represent, since they are a mixture of procedural, capacity, and output measures, often based on surveys of experts. The measures also fail to capture the variance in the quality of government that exists within each country; the U.S. Marine Corps is very different from a local police force in rural Louisiana, just as the quality of education differs greatly between Shanghai and a poor county in the interior of China. Nonetheless, these indicators broadly suggest the tremendous degree of variance in the quality of government that exists across the world, and the fact that government effectiveness and level of corruption are correlated. As any number of studies have indicated, the quality of government correlates very strongly with a country's degree of economic development.

We can fill in the two-dimensional matrix of state scope versus state strength from Figure 4 with some real data, using tax revenues as a percentage of GDP as a proxy for scope and the World Bank government effectiveness indicator as a proxy for strength (see Figure 6). Developed countries vary considerably in the size of their governments, but we see that they all lie in the upper portion of the matrix. That is, you can become a high-income country with a large state—Denmark, the Netherlands—or with a relatively small one—Singapore, the United States. But no country can get rich without an effective government. There are a number of emerging market countries, such as China, India, and Russia, that are at approximately the midpoint of the vertical axis;[12] the poor countries in the sample are all nearer the bottom, and the weakest states are closer to zero.

FIGURE 6. State Scope vs. State Strength

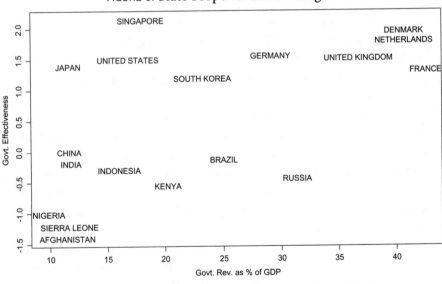

SOURCE: World Bank, Worldwide Governance Indicators, OECD

Taxes are for central governments only, excluding fines, penalties, and social security contributions.

Americans love to argue endlessly about the size of government. But what the cross-national data suggest is that the quality of government matters much more than its size for good outcomes.

What accounts for this variance in the performance of governments around the world? Why do some, like those in Northern Europe, provide a wide range of services with reasonably high effectiveness, engendering a high degree of social trust on the part of citizens, while others seem permanently mired in corruption and inefficiency, and as a consequence are regarded as parasites rather than facilitators by the population? And what is the relationship between good government and the other dimensions of development: the rule of law, accountability, economic growth, and social mobilization?

The following chapters will try to explain why some countries developed strong and capable states and why others did not. I will compare five cases: Prussia/Germany, Greece, Italy, Britain, and the United States. Prussia/Germany and Greece and Italy stand as bookends within the contemporary European Union. Germany has always had a reputation for strong and effective bureaucracy, and, after its disastrous performance in the first half of the twentieth century, has maintained sound macroeconomic policies throughout the postwar period. Greece and Italy, by contrast, have been known for high levels of clientelistic and corrupt government, and both have had problematic public finances that erupted during the 2010 euro crisis. Where this divergence came from and how it persisted into the present will be the topic of the comparison.

Britain and the United States constitute intermediate cases. Britain began the nineteenth century with an unreformed and patronage-ridden civil service. It cleaned up its bureaucracy beginning in the middle decades of the century, however, laying the foundations for a modern civil service that remains in place to this day. The United States similarly developed a party-led patronage system beginning in the 1820s, in which political appointees dominated the government at federal, state, and local levels. The American phenomenon is more accurately labeled clientelism rather than patronage, since it involved the mass distribution of individual benefits by politicians to supporters in a way that the less open British system did not. Yet the United States also by the second and third decades of the twentieth century succeeded in reforming this system, creating the core of a modern civil service. Britain and the United

States were able to eliminate one form of corruption in public administration in a way that Greece and Italy were not.

Key to these different outcomes was the sequence by which different countries reformed their bureaucracies relative to the moment they opened up their political systems to wider democratic contestation. Those countries that created strong bureaucracies while they were still authoritarian, like Prussia, created enduring autonomous institutions that survived subsequent changes of regime into the present. On the other hand, countries that democratized before a strong state was in place, such as the United States, Greece, and Italy, created clientelistic systems that then had to be reformed. The United States succeeded in this; Greece did not; and Italy was only partly successful.

One of the first European countries to acquire a modern state was Prussia, unifier of modern Germany. Prussia began to put together an effective bureaucracy before it industrialized and well before democratic accountability was introduced. I will therefore begin an account of the rise of the modern state with this story.

4

PRUSSIA BUILDS A STATE

How the Prussian-German bureaucracy became the model for modern bureaucracy; war and military competition as a source of state modernity; the meaning of the Rechtsstaat; why bureaucratic autonomy survived into the present; how war is not the only path to modern bureaucracy

When Max Weber wrote his famous description of modern bureaucracy early in the twentieth century, he was not thinking of the American bureaucracy, which he dismissed as hopelessly corrupt. In terms of the quality of its private sector, America was then the very model of a modern, industrialized nation, but its government was rightly viewed by Europeans as extremely backward. Weber was thinking, rather, of the bureaucracy of his native Germany, which by that time had grown into a disciplined, technically skilled, and autonomous organization that was easily the rival of the famous bureaucracy in neighboring France.

Germany at that moment was only incipiently a democracy; the Bismarck constitution under which the newly unified German state was operating since the 1870s provided for an elected Reichstag, or parliament, but gave extensive powers to an unelected emperor who had control over the military and exclusive right to appoint the chancellor. The main constraint on the executive's power was not democracy, which would not emerge until the formation of the Weimar Republic in the aftermath of World War I. Rather, it was the fact that the emperor had to rule through a highly institutionalized bureaucracy that incorporated a well-developed legal system. The resulting Rechtsstaat has been described as a liberal autocracy. It provided strong protections of the rights of its citizens in an impersonal manner, even though these citizens did not have the political right to hold their rulers accountable through elections.

The Rechtsstaat proved to be an excellent platform for economic development because it encompassed strong protection of private property rights and provided for the enforcement of contracts. The German kaiser was spoken of as an "absolute" ruler, but he could not arbitrarily confiscate the holdings of his citizens or personally intervene in their legal proceedings. As a consequence, Germany industrialized with great rapidity in the period from 1871 to 1914 and in many respects overtook Britain as the leading industrial power in Europe.

It took two devastating world wars and the division of the country for the western part of Germany to finally emerge as a consolidated liberal democracy in 1949. But throughout this time and into the period after 1989 when it was reunified, it could depend on a highly competent state administration, reflected in its high rankings in contemporary governance measures. Germany, in other words, developed both a strong state and rule of law early on, well before it developed accountable government. The reason it was able to do so was that the Prussian state that was the precursor of modern Germany engaged in a series of life-and-death military struggles with its neighbors over an extended period of time, just like the Qin state that unified China in 221 B.C. War, as we saw in Volume 1, creates incentives for efficient, meritocratic government that ordinary economic activity does not and therefore is one important path to state modernity.

Warlordism is probably an appropriate term to describe the state of much of Germany at the time of the Peace of Westphalia in 1648 that brought to an end the Thirty Years' War. At that time, the area constituted by modern Germany was fragmented into dozens of small sovereign entities, nominally unified under a transnational structure known as the Holy Roman Empire. What gave this region its warlord character was the fact that very few of these entities were strong enough to tax their own territories through a regular bureaucracy, raise a professional army, or create a monopoly of force that could reliably enforce their laws. Instead, the dynastic rulers of these polities tended to hire armed mercenaries and pay them with borrowed money; when resources ran out, these armed groups simply lived off the land by looting and pillaging. When these armies were not requisitioning food from hapless peasants, they were destroying crops and infrastructure to prevent their use by rivals. The ensuing famine and disease reduced the urban population of Germany by one-third and the rural population by two-fifths in the course of the Thirty Years' War.[1]

AN ARMY WITH A COUNTRY

When the young Frederick William of the house of Hohenzollern be- came the Elector of Brandenberg in December 1640, it was not at all ob- vious that his patrimony would serve as the core of a great nation, as opposed to larger rival states such as Saxony or Bavaria. Like many dy- nastic polities in this period, his domains were not contiguous, extending from east Prussia (now parts of Poland and Russia) all the way to Mark and Cleves in western Germany. The bureaucracy he inherited remained thoroughly patrimonial.[2] In each of his territories he had to share power with the estates, the feudal institution representing the landed nobility who were effectively sovereign on their own lands and needed to be con- sulted in matters of war and taxation. It had only been in the fifteenth and sixteenth centuries that the progenitors of this aristocracy had shifted from what economist Mancur Olson labeled "roving bandits" who gained resources largely through pillaging and feuding to "stationary bandits" who earned their keep by taxing a servile agrarian population for whom they provided a minimum of public goods like physical security and jus- tice in return.[3] These stationary bandits would come to be known as the Junkers.

As chronicled in Volume 1, accountable government first emerged in England at the end of the seventeenth century because the English es- tates, organized as a cohesive parliament, had the power to block the king's initiatives and indeed were able to depose two kings in the course of the century. In Brandenberg-Prussia, the opposite happened: the es- tates were weak and divided, and a series of resourceful and strong- minded rulers—the Great Elector Frederick William (1640–1688), King Frederick William I of Prussia (1713–1740), and Frederick II (Frederick the Great, 1740–1786)—succeeded in progressively stripping them of political power and concentrating it in the hands of a centralized royal administration.

The instrument by which this centralization occurred was the army. Very few rulers in this period maintained standing armies in periods of peace. The Great Elector established one by refusing to disband his army after the Peace of Oliva that ended the Swedish-Polish War in 1660 in which Prussia had participated. Having come of age at the conclusion of the Thirty Years' War, Frederick William recognized that Prussia's sur- vival as a largely landlocked state surrounded by powerful rivals could be guaranteed only through military power.[4] Through a variety of strata-gems, he took over the fiscal powers of the estates, disbanded independent militias, and centralized financial and military authority under a bureau-cracy he controlled. This process continued under the Great Elector's grandson Frederick William I of Prussia, whom historian Hajo Holborn characterized as "a boorish man, lacking not only in cultural graces but also in sensitivity for the human feelings of his fellow men . . . a formi-dable tyrant over his family, entourage, and state."[5] Frederick William was, however, a skilled state builder, who replaced the pleasure garden in front of his palace with a military drill ground and turned its ground floor into government offices. He created, in the words of historian Hans Rosen-berg, "a first-rate army which had to be supported by a country which was third-rate in terms of manpower, natural wealth, capital supply, and eco-nomic skills."[6]

There was, in addition, a critical cultural dimension to Prussian state building. The Hohenzollern family had become Calvinist in the mid-sixteenth century, which put them at odds with the largely Lutheran nobil-ity. Their Calvinism had at least three important consequences. First, the Great Elector and his successors staffed the new central bureaucracy with imported Dutch and Huguenot coreligionists, which increased the bu-reaucracy's autonomy from the surrounding society. Second, Puritan moralism infused the behavior of individual leaders, particularly Freder-ick William I, whose thrift, personal austerity, and intolerance of cor-ruption were legendary. And finally, the introduction of Calvinism in the Prussian lands created a whole series of new social institutions, from schools to parishes registering local populations to poor-relief houses, which were eventually taken over by and assimilated into a new, more modern state. This created competitive pressures for similar reforms among Lutherans and Catholics, not just in Prussia but also throughout Europe.[7]

Just as in Warring States China, creation of a substantial army was a matter not of princely caprice but of national survival, something the Ho-henzollern rulers recognized more clearly than their continental rivals.[8] Indeed, Prussia itself almost disappeared during the Seven Years' War, when Frederick the Great was almost captured and killed while fighting a much larger Russia and Austria simultaneously. It was only Frederick's enormous skill as a military commander and outright luck (the acces-sion of Peter III to the Russian throne) that saved the state and allowed it to remain a major European player. This is what led to the description of Prussia not as a country with an army but rather "an army with a country."[9]

The shift from a patrimonial to a modern bureaucracy in Prussia took place only in stages between 1640 and the conclusion of the Stein-Hardenberg reforms in the early nineteenth century. The Great Elector began the process in the second half of the seventeenth century with the separation of the civil and military bureaucracies, and the organization of the former into a series of technical *Regierungen* or councils. The need to raise resources made the war commissariat the primary instrument of centralization; its ability to administer an increasingly complex taxation system and its function as a military supply administration drove its evolution into the nation's chief economic policy body.[10]

By the late eighteenth century, the Prussian bureaucracy was a curious mixture of meritocratic and patrimonial recruitment and promotion: despite the fact that Frederick the Great promoted talented officers and bureaucrats, he often favored loyalty over competence. Once Frederick's wars came to an end, so did the pressure for advancement by merit. Prominent families developed near monopolies over certain service branches, and commissions and promotions could be had in return for loans and bribes. Prussia, in other words, underwent a process of repatrimonialization, just as China did at the end of the later Han Dynasty.[11]

HISTORY ENDS IN PRUSSIA

According to the philosopher Alexandre Kojève, history as such ended at the Battle of Jena-Auerstadt in 1806, when the half-patrimonial Prussian army was annihilated by Napoleon Bonaparte at the head of a much more modern military machine based on the *levée en masse* and organized according to modern bureaucratic principles. The young philosopher Georg Wilhelm Friedrich Hegel, who witnessed Napoleon riding through the university town of Jena, saw in that defeat the triumph of the modern state. He argued in *The Phenomenology of Spirit* that this type of state modernity represented the culmination of a long historical process of human reason making itself manifest. Kojève, interpreting Hegel in the 1930s, suggested that the idea of the modern state, once unleashed in the world, would eventually universalize itself because it was so powerful: those facing it would either conform to its dictates or be swallowed up.[12]

The groundwork for a modern state had already begun in the years before the Battle of Jena, with the 1770 civil service reform that introduced examinations as the basis for promotion. But the old system could not overcome its inertia without the disaster of military defeat. The post-Napoleonic reform was led by Baron Karl vom und zum Stein (1757–1831), an aristocrat descended from a family of Imperial Knights, who nonetheless studied at Göttingen and in England and was a follower of the liberal philosopher Montesquieu,[13] and Prince Karl August von Hardenberg (1750–1822), whose motto after Jena became "democratic principles in a monarchical government."[14]

The Stein-Hardenberg reforms finished the transformation of Frederick's personal dictatorship into a true liberal autocracy, or Rechtsstaat. The October Edict of 1807 abolished the legal privileges of the nobility, following the example of the French Revolution. Bureaucratic posts were opened up completely to commoners, and the French principle of the "*carrière ouverte aux talents*" (career open to talent) was enshrined. Patrimonial deadwood was purged from the bureaucracy, which remained an aristocracy, but one now based on education rather than birth. The employment regulations of 1817 required a classical secondary education as well as university study in law for recruitment into the higher civil service. There was at the same time a reform of the university system that had begun under Wilhelm von Humboldt prior to Jena, which would create an integrated system whereby the nation's best and brightest would be fed directly into the bureaucracy.[15] The Prussian system thus came to resemble that of France with its *grandes écoles*, or the system that the Japanese would create after the Meiji Restoration where a new academic elite would be sent directly from places like the University of Tokyo to work for the government.

The changing intellectual climate was reflected in the words of the philosopher Johann Fichte, who asserted that the nobles were "the first estate of the nation only in the sense that they were the first who ran away when there was danger."[16] The centrality of merit as an organizing principle was embodied in the German word *Bildung*, which can be translated as "education" but encompasses a broader sense of moral self-cultivation in addition to formal learning. The idea of *Bildung* had been promoted by a generation of Enlightenment thinkers at the end of the eighteenth century, including Lessing, Herder, Goethe, Fichte, Humboldt, and above all the great philosopher Immanuel Kant.[17]

THE RECHTSSTAAT

The Prussian state that had emerged by the nineteenth century and that would become the foundation for a unified Germany was the model of an absolutist dictatorship. But because the unaccountable sovereign ruled through an increasingly institutionalized bureaucracy, there was regularity and transparency in the government's behavior that over time evolved into a legal constraint on arbitrary despotism. In the end, however, the Rechtsstaat never amounted to the kind of constitutional constraint on executive power that the English achieved during their Glorious Revolution, or that the Americans were to enshrine in their Constitution. It was, however, good enough as a means of guaranteeing modern property rights and facilitated Germany's economic growth and rapid industrialization in the second half of the nineteenth century. As such, it became the model for liberal autocracy everywhere. Contemporary Singapore is sometimes compared to nineteenth-century Germany for just this reason.

The definition of the rule of law that I used in Volume 1 was law as a constraint on political power, including the most powerful political actors in the political system. I argued there that in many civilizations, the rule of law had its origins in religion, which provided both the substance of law as well as an institutionalized hierarchy of religious specialists who could interpret it. In Christian Europe, following the Catholic church's revival of Roman law in the eleventh century, a wide range of legal institutions were created centuries before the first absolutist monarch began accumulating power in the late sixteenth century. Indeed, that absolutist project was delayed and ultimately limited in scope by the strong legal traditions that prevailed across Europe.

This was nowhere more true than in Germany, which was virtually defined by legal institutions like the Diet of the Empire and the host of feudal rights and duties laid out in countless charters and contracts. The German states often seemed to spend as much time litigating against one another as fighting.

It was against this background that the new rising absolutist monarchs began trying to erode the earlier concept of law, which vested sovereignty in God (in practice, via God's agent, the church), and started to claim sovereignty for themselves. This argument was sometimes based on a divine right of kings—God's direct delegation of sovereign authority to a particular ruling house. But beginning in the mid-seventeenth century, a number of thinkers, including Hugo Grotius, Jean Bodin, Thomas Hobbes, and Samuel Pufendorf, began formulating novel theories that vested sovereignty in monarchs without appeal to religious authority. Pufendorf was particularly influential in Prussia, where he became a servant and eventually biographer of the Great Elector.

But the new secular grounding of absolutism in the state was not necessarily a boon to princely power. While sovereigns could claim absolute authority free of earlier religiously based legal constraints, the justification for this, according to these new theorists, lay in the fact that they in some sense "represented" the broader interests of the whole community. In Hobbes's *Leviathan*, for example, the monarch rules legitimately only because his authority rests on an implicit social contract by which he agrees to protect the citizens' fundamental right to life. Though the ruler is not elected, he in some sense embodies the public interest in peace and not the private interest of his family. As political theorist Harvey Mansfield points out, the state becomes an abstraction impersonally representing the whole community, and not the instrument of rule of one particular group within the society. The theoretical ground was thus laid for the distinction between public and private, which is critical to any modern understanding of the role of government.[18]

All of these ideas played themselves out in the evolution of Prussian law. As the Prussian state was being built, the personal authority of the sovereign prince was seen as the source of all law. But the prince ruled through a bureaucracy, which in turn used a new body of public administrative law to express its will. Indeed, much of what constituted the civil bureaucracy in Prussia was judicial, and the most common educational background for civil servants was legal training.[19] This did not constitute rule of law in the sense above of constraint on the executive; rather, it was what is sometimes referred to as rule "by law." In this sense it was very similar to the kind of law championed by the Chinese Legalists and embodied in various Chinese codes like those published in the Qin and Han Dynasties.[20]

Strong-minded leaders like Frederick William I and Frederick II could act in defiance of law (indeed, the former, who was the father of the latter, had his son thrown into prison for a period) and faced no powerful independent judicial institution that could stand in their way. And yet ordinary citizens in their dealings with one another and with the state could expect increasingly uniform and impersonal treatment. These newly emerging

civil codes incorporated a system of administrative courts that permitted citizens to sue the state when they believed they were being treated
illegally by the government. In France, lower court decisions could be
appealed all the way to the Conseil d'État, which could then force executive branch agencies to abide by its interpretation of the law.[21] (Administrative courts also exist in contemporary China and other parts of Asia
that have adopted the civil law; see chapter 25 below.) So although the
Rechtsstaat could not tell the king that he was behaving unconstitution-
ally, it could act as a constraint on arbitrary behavior on the part of lower
levels of the government.

The Prussian state sought to create a unified system of law first through
the efforts of Samuel von Cocceji, in the middle of the eighteenth century,
and then by way of the great Prussian law code, the Allgemeines Landrecht
of 1794. The latter, created by J. H. von Carmer and Karl Gottlieb Suarez,
was perhaps the most important innovation in the civil law tradition
prior to Napoleon's promulgation of the Civil Code in 1804, and sought
to define the law in a way that would make the state's purposes clear to
every citizen.

The Prussian Code remained a feudal document insofar as it divided
citizens into three classes—noblemen, burghers, and peasants—with different rights. While peasants had the right to remain on their land, noble
properties could be bought and sold only by other nobles. Carmer and
Suarez wanted to turn the code into a constitutional document protecting the people from arbitrary decisions by the Crown, but they were forced
to drop that paragraph by the king before its publication. While the code
recognized general rights to freedom of religion and conscience in private affairs, it gave the state considerable authority to control political
discussion and censor the media.[22]

It took the defeat at Jena and the Stein-Hardenberg reforms to sweep
away the unequal legal treatment of social classes. A particularly important reform triggered by Napoleon's victory was the opening of ownership of landed estates to all comers, which freed up land for the market
economy. There was no formal expansion of representation, but the bureaucracy saw itself performing a representative function: in the words
of historian Edward Gans, "The strength of the state lies in the constitutional order of administration . . . civil freedom lies in its legal order." In
Prussia's provinces, the office of Oberpräsident coordinated administrative agencies, chaired provincial assemblies, and served as a channel to

the central government, which was now ruled more by Hardenberg's Staatsrat (state council) than by the king.[23]

BUREAUCRATIC AUTONOMY AND THE PARADOX OF DEMOCRATIC ACCOUNTABILITY

One of the four criteria used by Samuel Huntington to define institutionalization is the degree to which the institution in question is "autonomous." Institutions are autonomous if "they have their own interests and values distinguishable from those of other institutions and social forces."[24] An autonomous judiciary thus adheres strictly to judicial norms in making decisions, rather than being under the thumb of political bosses or accepting bribes from wealthy defendants. An autonomous army can promote its officers based on military rather than political criteria. The opposite of autonomy is subordination, where an organization is effectively controlled by outside forces. The account given in Volume 1 of the Catholic church's struggle during the eleventh and twelfth centuries to be able to appoint its own priests and bishops during the investiture conflict was in effect a struggle to become autonomous from the court politics of the time.[25]

There has never been a formal rule of law in China, but since the Qin Dynasty there has always been a bureaucracy. That bureaucracy operated according to written rules and created stable expectations with regard to government behavior. Millennia earlier than in Europe, China's autonomous bureaucracy was putting the brakes on certain forms of arbitrary autocratic behavior on the part of the emperors. Indeed, one Chinese emperor during the Ming Dynasty thought he should be able to raise his own army and conduct a war; the bureaucracy politely but firmly disarmed him.[26]

The phenomenon of bureaucracies escaping the control of their masters is well understood by all executive agents, whether corporate CEOs, presidents of countries, or university chancellors. It is impossible to run a large organization, public or private, without a bureaucracy, but once authority has been delegated to the administrative hierarchy, the chief executive loses a great deal of control and often becomes a prisoner of that very bureaucracy. (This was the central premise of the BBC comedy series *Yes, Minister*, where the permanent secretary, Humphrey, a career bureaucrat, is able to completely stymie the initiatives of the political minister who is nominally his boss.) The more autonomous and capable the bureaucracy, the greater the potential loss of control.

So too under the Hohenzollerns. A vigorous king like Frederick the Great could intimidate the bureaucracy and make it subservient to his wishes. His famous political testament echoed the patrimonial view of France's Louis XIV, "*L'État, c'est moi.*"[27] But under his less forceful successors Frederick William II (1786–1797) and Frederick William III (1797–1840), the balance of influence shifted decisively in favor of the bureaucracy. Earlier kings had turned the bureaucracy into a powerful and cohesive status group; it was this internal solidarity that gave it a high degree of institutional autonomy. These officials increasingly saw themselves not as servants of the Hohenzollern dynasty but rather as servants of the Prussian state, a state whose interests transcended the fate of any particular occupant of the throne. This esprit de corps increased when the bureaucracy was opened after 1806 to ambitious, talented, and well-educated men from the bourgeoisie. Thus it was that one observer could say in 1799 that "far from being an unlimited monarchy," the Prussian state was an aristocracy that "rules the country in an undisguised form as a bureaucracy."[28] For this reason, Hegel in *The Philosophy of Right* saw the bureaucracy as the embodiment of a "universal class" that represented the whole community, as opposed to civil society, whose interests were necessarily partial and self-directed.

All effective institutions need to have a high degree of autonomy. But it is also possible to have too much of a good thing. If an army, for example, fails to give critical information to its political masters because it thinks they will misuse it, and goes on to set war aims independently, then it is improperly usurping a political prerogative. Economists understand this problem in principal-agent terms. Bureaucracies are supposed to be agents that do not have their own goals; those goals are set by the principal for whom they work. In a monarchical state, that principal is the king or ruling dynasty; in a democracy, it is the sovereign people who rule through their elected representatives. In a well-functioning political system, the agent should have enough autonomy to do its job well, but should also remain ultimately accountable to the principal. The bureaucratic autonomy that was a check on absolutist power in the monarchical period over time escaped the control not just of the emperor but also of elected legislatures as Germany democratized in the late nineteenth and early twentieth centuries.

In the years after Prussia led Germany to unification in 1871 under the leadership of Chancellor Otto von Bismarck, the bureaucracy protected its autonomy from both the emperor and the incipient forces of democracy. The franchise was opened up to popular vote in gradual stages after the 1870s, and new parties like the Social Democrats came to be represented in the Reichstag (see chapter 28). But the Constitution of the Empire protected the bureaucracy from interference from parliament; while bureaucrats could sit in parliament, parliament had no power over bureaucratic appointments. There emerged by this point what political scientist Martin Shefter has labeled an "absolutist coalition" of conservative and upper-middle-class parties that supported the autonomy of the bureaucracy and protected it from attempts by new political parties to place their own followers in positions of influence.[29]

This absolutist coalition retained its influence well into the twentieth century, after Germany's defeat in World War I and the emergence of the first true democracy under the Weimar Republic. After the emperor was forced to abdicate in 1918, the bureaucratic apparatus that ran the country remained largely intact. The new democratic parties—the Socialists, Democrats, and Centrists—that emerged in this period were reluctant to try to place too many of their own people in the bureaucracy, for fear of provoking a reaction that would turn it against the new republic. Even in the wake of the 1920 Kapp Putsch they hesitated to purge the civil service of entrenched right-wing elements. After ultranationalists assassinated Prime Minister Walther Rathenau in 1922, political appointments increased, but these new appointees were quickly eliminated when the Nazis came to power in 1933 and promulgated a Law for the Reestablishment of a Career Civil Service, which targeted Jews, Communists, and "party-made officials."[30]

The problem of excessive autonomy was greatest in the Prussian and later German military. The army was much slower than the civilian bureaucracy to open up to middle-class recruitment after the Stein-Hardenberg reforms and remained a bastion of privilege and a caste separate from civilian society well into the twentieth century.[31] The Prussian army's victories over Denmark, Austria, and France gave it the political capital to press for independence from control by the elected Reichstag, and under the Bismarck constitution the military was accountable to the emperor alone. This high degree of autonomy made the military an increasing driver of German foreign policy, or, as historian Gordon Craig puts it, a "state within the state." The General Staff's General Alfred von Waldersee began arguing at the time of the Bulgarian Crisis of 1887–1888 that war with Russia in support of Austria's interests in the Balkans was inevitable, and he pressed for preventive war. Bismarck, who wisely understood that the object of Germany's foreign policy should be to prevent emergence of a hostile anti-German coalition, was able to contain this threat, saying memorably that preventive war was like committing suicide out of fear of death. But his weaker successors failed to control the military's political influence. The General Staff under Generals Alfred von Schlieffen and Helmuth von Moltke (the Younger) drew up plans for a two-front war against France and Russia, urged an aggressive stance during the Moroccan crisis of 1905 (which drove Britain and France closer together), and pressed to support their Austrian ally in the lead-up to the assassination of Archduke Franz Ferdinand in Sarajevo in July 1914. The military's belief that a two-front war was inevitable became a self-fulfilling prophecy as the emperor was told he had no choice but to attack France on the army's timetable in response to events in the Balkans. World War I was the consequence.[32]

The tradition of autonomous bureaucracy that was established in the eighteenth century continues into the contemporary Federal Republic of Germany. The National Socialist regime on coming to power after 1933 had succeeded in subordinating the military to its will, but it left much of the civilian bureaucracy intact. In contrast to the Bolsheviks and the Chinese Communists, the Nazis neither created a parallel hierarchy of commissars nor sought to dismantle the bureaucracy wholesale. They added loyal personnel in some ministries (particularly the Ministry of Interior) and purged Communist and Jewish officials, but in the end found they needed to rely on the capacity of the civil service.[33]

As a result, when the Nazi regime was destroyed by the Allies in May 1945, that bureaucracy remained in place and in fact proved extraordinarily resilient despite the efforts of the Allied occupation authorities to purge it of people with Nazi backgrounds or sympathies. Some 81 percent of all Prussian civil servants had been party members, half having joined before 1933.[34] The American, British, and French occupation authorities sought to de-Nazify the German government by holding war crimes tri-

als for senior leaders at Nuremburg, and then by purging individuals
from the civil service. But as the new Federal Republic was formed in
1949 and pressure mounted to put in place a competent government that
could anchor the new NATO alliance against the Soviet Union, large
numbers of purged officials were reinstated. A federal law passed in 1951
granted all regular civil servants, including those with Nazi backgrounds
and those expelled by East Germany, a right to reinstatement.[35] Of the
fifty-three thousand civil servants initially purged, only about one thousand remained permanently excluded from service.

German society had changed enormously by the time of the formation of the Federal Republic in the middle of the twentieth century, with
the destruction of the aristocracy and old Junker class, the discrediting
of the Nazi regime, the disbanding of the state of Prussia, and the spread
of genuine democratic values throughout the larger society. The political
attitudes of German bureaucrats changed with the times as well. But the
traditions of high-quality, autonomous German bureaucracy remained
largely intact.

ONE PATH TO THE MODERN STATE

I've spent this much time on the history of the Prussian-German bureaucracy because it constitutes a widely recognized model for modern
bureaucracy. But it is also representative of a path taken by a select group
of countries that developed modern, nonpatrimonial states as a result of
military competition and saw those states survive into the modern era. In
this group I would include China at the time of the Qin and Han Dynasties some two millennia prior to Prussia, Sweden, Denmark, France, and
Japan. There is no broad correlation between war and high-quality modern government; many societies that have fought wars over prolonged periods remain corrupt or patrimonial. War has merely been an enabling
condition for a certain subset of countries.

Given the fragility of institutions in many developing states today,
what is impressive about the Prussian-German bureaucracy is its durability and resilience. The bureaucratic tradition established in eighteenth-
century Prussia survived Jena and Napoleon, transition to the German
Empire, Weimar democracy and the Nazi regime, and then the return
to democracy under the postwar Federal Republic. While the social

composition of the bureaucracy changed enormously from an aristocratic preserve to an elite, meritocratic body reflecting the German people more broadly, it retained an esprit de corps and, most important, political support for its autonomy.

There is no question that today the German bureaucracy is under full control of the German political system, and that it is ultimately accountable to democratically elected parties represented in the Bundestag. But this control exists largely through the political minister placed by each administration at the top of the bureaucratic hierarchy. What has never happened in German history is the wholesale distribution of government offices to party workers as a matter of political patronage, as occurred in the United States, Italy, and Greece. In German history, the autonomy of the bureaucracy was often a force for enormous conservatism, if not outright militarism and foreign aggression. However, the fact that this autonomy had been secured prior to the opening up of Germany's political system to democratic politics meant, as Martin Shefter points out, that patronage politics never got a start in Germany. In countries where democracy emerged prior to the consolidation of a strong state, the results as we will see below were less positive from the standpoint of government quality.

Germany, Japan, and a small number of other countries get high rankings for the quality of their governments and low levels of corruption in the present due to an inheritance from an authoritarian phase in their political development. We cannot call them lucky, since this bureaucratic autonomy was bought at the expense of military competition, war, occupation, and authoritarian rule that undermined and delayed the advent of democratic accountability. As Huntington made clear, in political development, not all good things go together.

5

CORRUPTION

Some definitions of corruption; how corruption affects politics and economic growth; patronage and clientelism as early forms of democratic participation; why patronage is bad from the standpoint of democracy, but not as bad as certain other forms of corruption; why clientelism may diminish as countries get richer

In 1996, James Wolfenson, the newly appointed head of the World Bank, gave a speech in which he pointed to the "cancer of corruption" as a major impediment to the economic development of poor countries. Officials at the World Bank of course knew from the organization's beginning that corruption was a big problem in many developing countries, and that foreign aid and loans had often gone straight into the pockets of officials in countries supposedly being helped.[1] Prior to Wolfenson's speech, however, there was also a widely held view among development practitioners that little could be done about this problem, and that some degree of corruption was either inevitable or not so serious as to impede economic growth. During the cold war, many corrupt governments were clients of the United States (Zaire under Mobutu Sese Seko being a prime example), and Washington was not eager to point fingers at close friends.

Since the end of the cold war, there has been a major push by international development organizations to combat corruption as part of a broader effort to build states and strengthen institutions. As we saw in the data from the Worldwide Governance Indicators in chapter 3, there is a strong correlation between government effectiveness and control of corruption. Having a strong and effective state involves more than just controlling corruption, but highly corrupt governments usually have big problems in delivering services, enforcing laws, and representing the public interest.

There are many reasons why corruption impedes economic development. In the first place, it distorts economic incentives by channeling resources not into their most productive uses but rather into the pockets of officials with the political power to extract bribes. Second, corruption acts as a highly regressive tax: while petty corruption on the part of minor, poorly paid officials exists in many countries, the vast bulk of misappropriated funds goes to elites who can use their positions of power to extract wealth from the population. Further, seeking such payoffs is often a time-consuming occupation that diverts the energies of the smartest and most ambitious people who could be creating wealth-generating private firms. Gaming the political system for private gain is what economists label "rent seeking."[2]

It has been argued that bribery might increase efficiency by lubricating the process of getting business registrations, export licenses, or appointments with high officials. But this represents a very poor way of doing business: it would be much better if registration processes were quick, if export licenses didn't exist at all, or if all individuals had easy and equal access to the government. A clear rule of law is in the end far more efficient.

Apart from its distorting economic impacts, corruption can be very damaging to political order. Perceptions that officials and politicians are corrupt reduces the legitimacy of the government in the eyes of ordinary people and undermines the sense of trust that is critical to the smooth operations of the state. Charges of corruption are frequently made not in the interest of improved government but as political weapons. In societies where most politicians are corrupt, singling one out for punishment is often not a sign of reform but of a power grab. The reality and appearance of corruption are among the greatest vulnerabilities of new democracies seeking to consolidate their institutions.

If we are to understand how states make the transition from patrimonial to modern ones, we need to understand more clearly the nature of corruption and its sources. Corruption takes many forms, some of them much more damaging to economic growth and political legitimacy than others, so it is necessary to have some clarity with regard to basic definitions.

PUBLIC AND PRIVATE

There is today a huge literature on corruption and its sources, and many suggestions for potential remedies. Yet despite the scholarly work on this subject, a commonly accepted taxonomy for understanding the different behaviors that are typically lumped under the heading of corruption does not exist.[3]

Most definitions of corruption center around the appropriation of public resources for private gain.[4] This definition is a useful starting point; under it, corruption is a characteristic primarily of governments and not, for example, of businesses or private organizations.

This definition implies that corruption is in some sense a phenomenon that can arise only in modern, or at least modernizing, societies, since it is dependent on a distinction between public and private. As we saw in the previous chapter, the distinction between the public sphere and private interest developed in Prussia only during the seventeenth and eighteenth centuries. Prior to that point, the Prussian government (as well as virtually all European states) was patrimonial. That is to say, the prince considered himself the owner of the territories he governed, as if they were parts of his household or patrimony. He could give away lands (and the people living on them) to relatives, supporters, or rivals because they were a form of private property. It made no sense to talk about corruption in this context, since there was no concept of a public sphere whose resources could be misappropriated.

It was only with the growth of centralized states in the seventeenth and eighteenth centuries that the ruler's domain came to be seen less as personal property and more as a kind of public trust that the ruler managed on behalf of the larger society. Early modern doctrines of state sovereignty put forward by Grotius, Hobbes, Bodin, and Pufendorf all emphasized the fact that the legitimacy of the sovereign rested not on ancient or inherited ownership rights but rather on the fact that the sovereign is in some sense the guardian of a larger public interest. He could legitimately extract taxes only in return for providing necessary public services, first and foremost public order to avoid the war of every man against every man described by Hobbes.

Moreover, the behavior of public officials, reaching up to the ruler himself, increasingly came to be defined by formal rules. Among the laws that made up the Prussian Rechtsstaat were rules that clearly established the boundary between public and private resources. Chinese Confucianism had developed a parallel doctrine many centuries earlier: emperors were not simply owners of the lands and people they ruled but rather moral guardians of the whole community, who had duties to communal well-being. Although Chinese emperors could and did appropriate public funds for their own uses (like the Wanli emperor toward the end of the Ming Dynasty), the distinction between these accounts was always well established.[5]

NOT SIMPLY CORRUPT

There are two phenomena that are closely related to corruption as defined above but that are not identical to it. The first is the creation and extraction of rents, and the second is what is referred to as patronage or clientelism.

In economics, a rent is technically defined as the difference between the cost of keeping a good or service in production and its price. One of the most important sources of rents is scarcity: a barrel of oil today sells well above its marginal cost of production because it is in high demand; the difference between the two is thus referred to as a resource rent. The owner of a condominium on Park Avenue in New York can charge a much higher rent than for an equal amount of square footage in the middle of Iowa because land is much scarcer in Manhattan.

While rents are created by natural scarcities of land or commodities, they can also be artificially generated by governments. A typical example is licensing. In New York City, the total number of legal taxicabs is set by the Taxi and Limousine Commission. Because this number has been capped for many years, the number of taxis has not kept up with demand for them, and the medallions awarded by the city that grant the right to operate a taxi sell for as much as a million dollars. The cost of a medallion is a rent generated by political authorities, one that would disappear immediately if the city allowed any individual to hang a sign on his or her car and take passengers for hire.

Governments have any number of ways of creating artificial scarcities, and thus the most basic forms of corruption involve abuse of this kind of power. For example, placing tariffs on imports restricts imports and generates rents for the government; one of the most widespread forms of corruption around the world lies in customs agencies, where the customs agent will take a bribe in order to either reduce the duties charged or expedite the clearance process so that the importer will have his goods on time. In Indonesia during the 1950s and '60s, corruption in the customs agency was so widespread that the government eventually decided to outsource the function to a Swiss company that would inspect all incoming containers.[6]

The ease with which governments can create rents through taxation or regulatory power has led many economists to denounce rents in general as distortions of efficient resource allocation by markets, and to see rent creation and distribution as virtually synonymous with corruption. The ability of governments to generate rents encourages many ambitious people to choose politics rather than entrepreneurship or the private sector as a route to wealth. Douglass North, John Wallis, and Barry Weingast make a fundamental distinction between what they label limited and open access orders: in the former, elites deliberately limit access to economic activity so as to create rents and increase their own income, preventing the emergence of a dynamic, competitive modern economy.[7]

But while rents can be and are abused in these ways, they also have perfectly legitimate uses that complicate any blanket denunciation of them. The most obvious type of a "good" rent is a patent or copyright, by which the government gives the creator of an idea or creative work the exclusive right to any resulting revenues for some defined period of time. The difference between the cost of production of the book you are holding in your hand and the price you paid for it (assuming you didn't steal or illegally download it) is a rent, but one that society legitimates as a means of spurring innovation and creativity. Economist Mushtaq Khan points out that many Asian governments have promoted industrialization by allowing favored firms to generate excess profits, provided they are plowed back into new investment. While this opened the door to considerable corruption and abuse, it also stimulated rapid growth at a rate possibly higher than market forces on their own would have produced.[8]

All government regulatory functions, from protecting wetlands, to requiring disclosure in initial public offerings of stocks, to certifying drugs as safe and effective, create artificial scarcities. Any ability to grant or withhold regulatory power generates a rent. But while we can argue about the appropriate extent of regulation, few people would like to see these functions abandoned simply because they create rents. Indeed, even the much criticized New York taxi medallion had its origin in the need to maintain a certain minimum level of service and ensure equality of access in public carriage. Without this type of regulation, many taxis would simply refuse short fares or rides to poor neighborhoods.

Thus the creation and distribution of rents by governments have a high degree of overlap with corruption, but they are not the same phenomenon. One must look at the purpose of the rent and judge whether it is generating a purely private good that is being appropriated by the government official, or whether it is actually serving a broader public purpose.

PATRONAGE AND CLIENTELISM

A second phenomenon that is often identified with corruption is that of patronage or clientelism. A patronage relationship is a reciprocal exchange of favors between two individuals of different status and power, usually involving favors given by the patron to the client in exchange for the client's loyalty and political support. The favor given to the client must be a good that can be individually appropriated, like a job in the post office, or a Christmas turkey, or a get-out-of-jail card for a relative, rather than a public good or policy that applies to a broad class of people.[9] The following is an example: "In Sicily, a student, interested in getting an introduction to a professor from whom he needs a favour, approaches a local small-town politician who owes him a favour. The politician puts him in contact with a cousin at the regional urban centre and the latter contacts an assistant to the professor who then arranges the appointment. The favour sought is granted and in return the student promises to campaign for the politician at election times."[10]

Patronage is sometimes distinguished from clientelism by scale; patronage relationships are typically face-to-face ones between patrons and clients and exist in all regimes whether authoritarian or democratic, whereas clientelism involves larger-scale exchanges of favors between patrons and clients, often requiring a hierarchy of intermediaries.[11] Clientelism thus exists primarily in democratic countries where large numbers of voters need to be mobilized.[12] What is traditionally referred to as the patronage system in American politics was by this definition actually a clientelistic system since it involved mass party organizations distributing widespread favors through complex hierarchical political machines.[13]

Clientelism is considered a bad thing and a deviation from good democratic practice in several respects. In a modern democracy, we expect citizens to vote for politicians based on their promises of broad public policies, or what political scientists label a "programmatic" agenda. People on the left may support government programs to provide health care and social services, while conservatives may prefer that the government allocate resources to national defense. In either case, voter preferences are supposed to reflect general views of what is good for the political community as a whole, not just what is good for one individual voter. Of course, voters in advanced democracies cast their ballots according to their self-interest, whether that lies in lower taxes for the well-to-do, or subsidies for a particular type of business, or programs targeted at the poor. Nonetheless, such targeted programs are justified in terms of broad concepts of justice or the general good, and even when targeted must apply impartially not to individuals but to broad classes of people. The government is in particular not supposed to give a benefit to specific individuals based on whether or not they supported it.

In a clientelistic system, politicians provide individualized benefits only to political supporters in exchange for their votes. These benefits can include jobs in the public sector, cash payments, political favors, or even public goods like schools and clinics that are selectively given only to political supporters. This has negative effects on both the economy and the political system for a number of reasons.[14]

First and perhaps most important is the impact of patronage and clientelism on the quality of government. Modern bureaucracies are built on a foundation of merit, technical competence, and impersonality. When they are staffed by a politician's political supporters or cronies, they almost inevitably perform much more poorly. Stuffing a bureaucracy with political appointees also inflates the wage bill and is a major source of fiscal deficits. Unlike the private sector, the public sector does not face the threat of bankruptcy or have easy metrics for performance, which means that governments staffed with patronage appointments become very hard to reform.[15]

The second way clientelism undermines good democratic practice has to do with the fact that it strengthens existing elites and blocks democratic accountability. A clientelistic relationship is by definition between unequals, in which powerful and/or wealthy politicians in effect buy the support of ordinary citizens. These politicians are typically interested in promoting their own narrow interests. They may be interested in promoting the welfare of the clients who provide their base of support but not the public at large. In Europe, inequality was reduced in the course of the twentieth century due to the rise of programmatic parties such as the British Labour Party or the German Social Democratic Party (see Part III below). These parties pushed for broad social programs that had the effect of redistributing resources from rich to poor on a relatively impartial basis. Many Latin American countries, by contrast, continue to experience high levels of inequality because the poor have tended to vote for clientelistic parties—the Peronist party in Argentina is a classic example—rather than programmatic ones. Instead of procuring broad benefits for the poor, clientelistic parties dissipate resources on what are in effect individual bribes for voters.

NATURAL MODES OF SOCIABILITY

Patronage and clientelism are sometimes treated as if they were highly deviant forms of political behavior that exist only in developing countries due to peculiarities of those societies. In fact, the political patronage relationship, whether involving family or friends, is one of the most basic forms of human social organization in existence. It is universal because it is natural to human beings. The big historical mystery that has to be solved is thus not why patronage exists but rather why in modern political systems it came to be outlawed and replaced by impersonal organization.

In Volume 1, I argued that human beings are social creatures by nature and that their social organization is rooted in biology. There are two basic biological principles that are shared not only by virtually all human societies but also by many other sexually reproducing species: kin selection or inclusive fitness, and reciprocal altruism.[16] In kin selection, individuals favor genetic relatives, in proportion to the number of genes they share; it is the basis of nepotism. Reciprocal altruism involves the exchange of favors between unrelated individuals on a face-to-face basis.

Neither kin selection nor reciprocal altruism is a learned behavior; every human child regardless of culture instinctively tends to favor relatives and exchanges favors with those around him or her. Nor are these behaviors rooted solely in rational calculation; human beings are born with a suite of emotions that fortify the development of social relationships based on cooperation with friends and family. To behave differently—to choose, for example, a highly qualified employee over a friend or relative, or to work in an impersonal bureaucracy—is a socially constructed behavior that runs counter to our natural inclinations. It is only with the development of political institutions like the modern state that humans begin to organize themselves and learn to cooperate in a manner that transcends friends and family. When such institutions break down, we revert to patronage and nepotism as a default form of sociability.

The earliest forms of human social organization are the band and the tribe. Both constitute what we would today call patronage organizations, and they were the only form of organization that existed for the first forty thousand or so years of human history. The band consists of small groups of a few dozen related individuals; the tribe is based on a principle of descent from a common ancestor, which allows the scale of the society to vastly increase. Both kin selection and reciprocal altruism are necessary to hold these two types of groups together: solidarity is based on genetic relatedness, and in both there is a reciprocal exchange of favors between the chief or Big Man who leads the group and his followers. Leaders in tribal organizations do not have the kind of absolute authority that they would acquire under state-level societies. If they fail to keep up the flow of resources to their followers, or make mistakes that hurt the group's interests, they can be replaced. There is consequently a real degree of reciprocity between leaders and followers in such organizations.

The patronage-dispensing Big Man and his followers has never been fully displaced as a form of political organization up through the present. This is not just because it comes naturally to people, but also because it is often the most efficient route to political power. Today, authority is mostly exercised through control of formal organizations such as states, corporations, and nongovernmental organizations. In their modern forms, they are structured to operate by impersonal and transparent rules. But these organizations are often rigid and hard to direct; leaders typically rely on smaller networks of supporters they have cultivated on their rise to the top. Joseph Stalin and Saddam Hussein based their power not just on their control of a state apparatus of army and police. They also commanded the loyalty of a much smaller group of followers—in Stalin's case, a group of fellow Georgians led by Lavrenty Beria, head of the secret police; in Saddam Hussein's, a network of kinsmen from Tikrit in central Iraq. These patronage networks were in turn used to control the state itself. Similarly, both Japan's Liberal Democratic Party and the Chinese Communist Party are riven with leadership factions based on patronage networks.

Many weaker and less politically developed societies are more overtly dominated by patronage organizations, such as the militias that have terrorized Libya, the Democratic Republic of Congo, Somalia, Sierra Leone, and Liberia.

Clientelism is a form of reciprocal altruism that is typically found in democratic political systems where leaders must contest elections to come to power. Compared to an elite patronage network, clientelistic networks need to be much larger because they are frequently used to get hundreds of thousands of voters to the polls. As a result, these networks dispense favors not based on a direct face-to-face relationship between the patron and his or her clients but rather through a series of intermediaries who are enlisted to recruit followers. It is these campaign workers—the ward heelers and precinct captains in traditional American municipal politics—who develop personal relationships with individual clients on behalf of the political boss.

Today, virtually every democracy makes overt vote buying illegal and discourages it through mechanisms like the secret ballot.[17] The problem, then, for the politicians is how to monitor the behavior of the clients to ensure that they are delivering their end of the bargain. The patrons must, furthermore, persuasively signal that they will deliver on their promises of individualized benefits. One of the reasons that ethnic voting is so common in democracies from urban America in the nineteenth century to India or Kenya today is that ethnicity serves as a credible indication that a particular political boss will deliver the goods to a targeted audience.[18]

Patronage and clientelism constitute substantial normative deviations from good democratic practice for all of the reasons outlined above, and are therefore illegal and frowned upon in virtually all contemporary democracies. As such, they are often considered another form of political corruption. There are a number of reasons, however, why clientelism should be considered an early form of democratic accountability and be distinguished from other types of corruption—or, indeed, not considered a form of corruption at all. The first reason is that it is based on a relationship of reciprocity and creates a degree of democratic accountability between the politician and those who vote for him or her. Even though the benefit given is individual rather than programmatic, the politician still needs to deliver something in return for support, and the client is free to vote for someone else if the benefit is not forthcoming.

Moreover, clientelism is designed to generate mass political participation at election time, something we regard as desirable.[19]

In this respect clientelism is very different from a purer form of corruption where an official steals from the public treasury and sends the money to a Swiss bank account for the benefit of himself and his family alone. This type of corruption is sometimes labeled, following Weber, prebendalism, based on the feudal prebend where a lord simply granted a vassal a territory that he could exploit for his own benefit.[20] While there is plenty of clientelism in sub-Saharan Africa, political scientist Nicolas van de Walle argues that the region suffers from the much more serious disease of widespread prebendalism that has deprived citizens of control over their elected officials.[21] As the successive wars in Afghanistan with the Soviets and NATO progressed, the traditional tribal relationships based on patronage and clientelism began to break down and were replaced by far more predatory forms of prebendalism in which individual governors or ministers simply appropriated vast sums of money without returning much in the way of services. The fact that a lot of these resources came from foreign assistance facilitated this process and served to deeply delegitimate the central government. In such a situation, a return to traditional patronage would constitute a huge improvement in the functioning of the political system.

A second reason for thinking that clientelism should be viewed as an early form of democracy rather than a form of corruption is that we see it taking hold in very many young democracies where voting and the franchise are new and politicians face the problem of how to mobilize voters. In societies where incomes and educational levels are low, it is often far easier to get supporters to the polls based on a promise of an individual benefit rather than a broad programmatic agenda. This was nowhere more true than in the first country to establish the principle of universal male suffrage, the United States, which in a certain sense invented clientelism and practiced it in various forms for more than a century.[22]

Clientelism should be broadly related to the level of economic development. This is a simple matter of economics: poor voters can be more easily bought than rich ones, with relatively small individual benefits like a cash gift or a promise of a low-skill job. As countries become wealthier, the benefits politicians need to offer to bribe voters increase, and the cost of clientelism rises dramatically. In the 1993 election, Taiwan's ruling Guomindang (KMT) bought enough votes to steal the election from the opposition Democratic People's Party, at the cost of around $300 Taiwanese (US$10) per vote, compared to $3 per vote in a 1998 election in the neighboring but poorer Philippines. Due to the fact that 45 percent of the bribed voters nonetheless failed to vote for the KMT, and that the opposition party made vote buying itself a campaign issue, this practice has largely faded from Taiwanese elections.[23]

Clientelism tends to retreat at higher income levels for reasons having to do with development of a robust market economy. Most poor countries lack a strong private sector and opportunities for entrepreneurship: indeed, this is why they are poor in the first place. Under such circumstances, politics is a much surer route to wealth for both patrons and clients. India today has a small but rapidly growing private sector; for the vast majority of Indians, however, participation in politics, either as a patron or a client, remains the main ladder of upward social mobility.[24]

As a stronger market economy develops, the opportunities for privately generated wealth increase, both absolutely and relative to the level of rents than can be extracted by entering politics. Ambitious young people who want to make large fortunes in today's America don't go into government. They go to Wall Street or corporate America, or start their own companies in places like Silicon Valley. Indeed, persuading people who've made private fortunes to go into government is often difficult given the reduction in income this entails. Moreover, for many voters in rich countries, programmatic issues like regulation, the environment, immigration policy, and the ability of unions to organize become much more important to their lives and well-being than the small bribes that could be offered by a clientelistic politician.[25]

Martin Shefter, whose framework forms the basis for much of the contemporary understanding of patronage and bureaucratic quality, argues that the supply of patronage is much more important than the demand for it. That is, patronage can exist only when politicians have access to state resources that they can distribute. This explains why what he labels "externally organized" parties like revolutionary Communist parties in Russia and China initially displayed much lower levels of patronage and corruption; they needed to be tightly disciplined and had no benefits to distribute before they came to power.[26]

There is no automatic process by which the demand for clientelistic favors drops as countries become richer. There are wealthy countries that still practice clientelism, such as Italy, Greece, and Japan. Why this is so requires a more detailed account of their specific historical paths and other factors that explain why reform coalitions failed to materialize.

6

THE BIRTHPLACE OF DEMOCRACY

How Greece and Italy came to be at the center of the European financial crisis; Greece and southern Italy as low-trust societies; the consequences of early democratization in Greece; how clientelism deepened in Greece despite modernization

Beginning in late 2009 and steadily intensifying thereafter, the European Union was shaken by a financial crisis that has threatened the future of the euro as a currency and the EU as an institutional framework for promoting peace and economic growth. At the center of the crisis lay the inability of certain EU countries, in particular Greece and Italy, to repay the sizable sovereign debt they had accumulated in the previous decade. The sovereign debt crisis quickly evolved into a banking crisis for Europe as a whole, as the viability of the financial institutions holding this debt was called into question.

I will return to an analysis of the problems of democratic government in Europe in Part IV of this book, and the failures of institutions at both a national and an EU-wide level to deal with economic management. The EU financial crisis, like the crisis that hit the United States in 2008–2009, is a complex one that has many contributing causes. But clearly one of the precipitating factors was the accumulation of public debt in Greece and Italy. As many observers have pointed out, the Maastricht Treaty creating the euro provided for a common currency and monetary policy without a corresponding common fiscal policy. This permitted countries with poor public finances to borrow during the boom times of the 2000s at low interest rates that did not reflect their underlying risk.

This problem was nowhere more true than in Greece, where public debt as a proportion of GDP reached 140 percent by 2010. As Figure 7 indicates, debt levels for Italy as well had reached unsustainable levels;

both countries were well above the average for the eurozone as a whole. This led to the fall of incumbent governments in both countries, and to leadership by technocratic caretaker administrations that sought to impose dramatic austerity programs to get public spending more in line with revenues. Within the eurozone, Greece and Italy also have the largest estimated "shadow economies," economic activity that is not regularly reported to the tax authorities.[1]

FIGURE 7. Central Government Debt as a Percentage of GDP

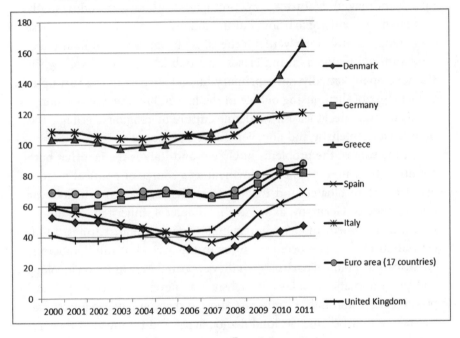

SOURCE: Eurostat

The ongoing euro crisis exposed a large rift between Northern and Southern Europe. There is no generic "crisis of the welfare state" in Europe: Germany, the Netherlands, and Scandinavia all have very large public sectors when compared to, say, the United States or Japan, yet these countries managed to weather the 2008–2009 Wall Street crisis better than the United States. Germany in particular put its public finances in order during the 2000s under Gerhard Schröder's Agenda 2010, trimming labor costs and controlling overall levels of debt. The countries that got into trouble—Greece, Italy, Portugal, Ireland, and Spain—also differed from one another. Ireland and Spain were relatively responsible fiscally in the run-up to the crisis; the problem started only when housing bubbles burst, leading to bank failures and the subsequent need for huge taxpayer bailouts, which in turn threw public finances into chaos. Unsustainably high levels of public debt based on excessive spending were problems primarily in Greece and Italy.

The differences between Northern and Southern Europe have led various observers to portray the problem as a cultural one, pitting a hardworking, Protestant, disciplined Northern Europe (Germany, Holland, and Scandinavia) against a lazy, profligate Catholic-Orthodox south. Although, as I will argue below, culture did play a role in the crisis, these large religious divisions were not the issue: Protestant Britain and Iceland suffered major banking crises and public deficits as well, while Catholic Spain actually ran a primary budget surplus in the run-up to the collapse of the housing bubble in the late 2000s. The real division is not a cultural one, at least if we define culture by religious heritage; it is between a clientelistic and nonclientelistic Europe.

At the root of the problems of Greece and Italy is the fact that both countries have used public employment as a source of political patronage, leading to bloated and inefficient public services and ballooning budget deficits. Germany, as we saw in chapter 4, inherited an autonomous, merit-based, modern bureaucracy from absolutist times. Modernization of the state occurred prior to the arrival of full democratic participation. Political parties when they appeared were based on ideology and programmatic agendas; clientelism was never a source of political power. Greece and Italy, by contrast, did not develop modern bureaucracies before they became electoral democracies, and for much of their recent history used public employment as a means of mobilizing voters. The result has been a chronic inability to control public-sector employment and hence the wage bill up until the present day. Greece and Italy followed a sequence closer to that of the United States in the nineteenth century than to their Northern European counterparts: democracy arrived before the modern state, making the latter subservient to the interests of party politicians.

As we will see in chapters 9–11, although the United States invented clientelism, it also uprooted this practice and laid the groundwork for a modern, merit-based state by the end of the Progressive Era. While patrimonialism has returned in the form of interest group politics, the particular clientelistic form that it took in the nineteenth century is no longer widespread. In Greece and Italy, by contrast, old-style clientelism continues, despite the fact that both are wealthy, industrialized societies. In the United States, economic development created new middle-class groups that were the basis for a progressive coalition. The Greek and Italian experiences, by contrast, suggest that economic growth by itself is not sufficient to explain the disappearance of clientelism. New social actors can be recruited into well-established clientelistic systems and be induced to play by their rules. This is further evidence that political development does not follow a single path, and that the different components of development can proceed along parallel but ultimately divergent trajectories.

LOW-TRUST SOCIETIES

I should note at the outset that when speaking of Italy, I am referring to a society that was politically unified only in the 1860s and that brought together a relatively prosperous and well-governed North with a poor and underdeveloped South. Many of the characteristics of clientelism and political corruption that foreigners associate with Italy as a whole were far more characteristic historically of the Mezzogiorno (the area south of Rome, including the island of Sicily) than of Lombardy, Piedmont, Veneto, and Tuscany. In Italian historiography this is known as Italy's "Southern Question"—the puzzle of why the historical differences between the two parts of the country exist in the first place, and why they seemingly have not narrowed over the course of the century and a half since unification. There is in fact a certain degree of political correctness among Italians about even raising the question of how the South is different, but these differences are too well established to be ignored.[2]

What is striking about sociological accounts of traditional life in southern Italy and in Greece is how similar they are with respect to the absence of social trust and of the importance of the family as the primary basis for social cooperation.[3] There is a long tradition of writing on southern Italy that notes the absence of civic structures—informal groups and associations—between the family and the state. Political scientist Edward Banfield, in his ethnographic account of a small, impoverished town in Basilicata, posits the concept of "amoral familism," whose code he describes as "Maximize the material, short-run advantage of the nuclear family; assume that all others will do likewise." Cooperation within the immediate family came at the expense of a broader capacity to trust strangers: "any advantage that may be given to another is necessarily at the expense of one's own family. Therefore, one cannot afford the luxury of charity, which is giving others more than their due, or even of justice, which is giving them their due . . . Toward those who are not of the family the reasonable attitude is suspicion."[4] According to political scientist Joseph LaPalombara, "Primary associations are still dominant; family, kinship, neighborhood, village are still the associational forms that have the greatest call on individual loyalties."[5] Another political scientist, Sidney Tarrow, in his study of peasant communism in southern Italy, writes of a culture built around "the prevalence of violence and the consciousness of death, the modest place of woman in society, and the almost occult role of corruption in economics and politics." Building on Banfield, he asserts that "in the Mezzogiorno, individuals participate in and directly perceive modern secondary organizations, but for some reason reject them as illegitimate or corrupt."[6] His insights were given broader empirical validation in Robert Putnam's classic study *Making Democracy Work*, in which he devises various empirical measures of civic engagement like newspaper readership or membership in sports clubs, and finds a striking divergence between the strong associational bonds in northern Italy and the weak or nonexistent ones in the South.[7]

Very similar observations have been made about the traditional Greek rural society that existed in the nineteenth century, in which, according to sociologist Apostolis Papakostas, "The only available way to organize people was through the family—a social organization which, in spite of local variations in its structure, has always played an important role in the social life of modern Greece."[8] As in southern Italy, loyalty to the family has a counterpart in distrust of strangers. According to political scientist Keith Legg,

> family members must join together to meet the threats from outsiders . . . To deceive the state, strangers, or even associates is accepted, and often applauded as evidence of cleverness. Villagers do not often attempt to establish new or direct relationships with strangers, since the Greek is in a relationship of tension even with associates and neighbors . . . Village houses are so placed that events in all but a few are shielded from the eyes of the rest of the community . . . When a rural

Greek is hospitalized, relatives are in constant attendance to keep a check on the doctor and the treatment he prescribes.[9]

Greece by this description resembles not just southern Italy but also other low-trust societies of the sort I described in *Trust*, like those of southern China and many parts of rural Spain and Latin America. In such societies, neighbors are not potential helpmates but dangerous rivals, which is why domestic architecture in all of these places tends to turn inward to hide the family's wealth from prying eyes. In such societies, businesses tend to remain small and family owned over the generations, rather than evolving into large-scale modern corporations run by hierarchies of professional managers. Businesses often keep two sets of books, an accurate one for the family and another for the tax collector; rampant tax evasion is socially approved because the state is regarded as just another dangerous stranger.[10]

The urbanization that occurred in Greece in the late nineteenth and early twentieth centuries did little to disrupt these social patterns. In Western European countries such as England, Belgium, and Germany, urbanization was the by-product of industrialization and the need of modern industries to locate in cities with communications links like ports and rivers. Under these circumstances, the discipline imposed by factory labor transformed Gemeinschaft into Gesellschaft, reorganizing traditional communities into a modern division of labor.

Greece, by contrast, fits a pattern more characteristic of many contemporary developing societies elsewhere in the Balkans, the Middle East, and Africa, where urbanization was driven not by industrialization but by the movement of entire villages to cities, preserving Gemeinschaft intact. In the words of Apostolis Papakostas, "Greek cities can be described as 'cities of peasants' and their inhabitants as 'urban villagers': a high level of social cohesion in the cities is based on interwoven networks and a high frequency of primary contacts with familiar faces."[11] The low-trust, family-oriented society of the Greek countryside thus became the urban society of the early twentieth century.

Events would conspire to make already low levels of trust even lower. Greece was occupied during World War II first by the Italians and then by the Germans. Greek society had split by this point along ideological lines, and a bitter civil war broke out just prior to the end of the German occupation between the Greek Communists and a government supported first by Britain and then by the United States. The war involved numerous atrocities on both sides and led to more than fifty thousand casualties, leaving a legacy of polarization that continues to this day.

There are of course important differences between southern Italy and Greece. The Mafia, which has been so prominent in the history of the Mezzogiorno, does not really have a counterpart in Greece. Nonetheless, both regions are notable for their familism, high levels of distrust, and lack of civic community. It is not at first glance obvious that social distrust should be related to the phenomena of clientelism and low-quality bureaucracy, but it is: strong, effective government produces social trust and is in turn facilitated by the existence of trust. Both trust and strong government were lacking in Greece and southern Italy.

What was the source of this distrust? To anticipate an argument I will make in the following chapter, it had less to do with culture than with the historical absence of a strong, impersonal state and a rule of law. Lacking a trusted public authority, families and individuals were thrown back on their own resources and engaged in a low-level war of "every man against every man."

GREECE'S EARLY DEMOCRACY

The Greek state never had a chance to consolidate into a strong, legitimate, autonomous body prior to the arrival of democracy in the nineteenth century. Indeed, as part of the Ottoman Empire, there was no sovereign Greek state at all, and the territory had a long tradition of resistance to tax collection by the Ottoman authorities,[12] who were known as *armatoloi kai kleftes* (guerrillas and thieves). The Greeks, inspired in part by the ideals of the French Revolution, declared independence in 1821 and began a revolt against Turkish rule. They did not succeed on their own, however; they achieved independence only after intervention by France, Britain, and Russia, which sent naval forces and an expeditionary army to drive the Turks out. The liberation of Greece was in a sense one of the first instances of what is now called "humanitarian intervention," in which strong moral concerns on the part of the international community were combined with strategic self-interest to promote military intervention. Greek independence had become a cause célèbre in liberal European circles, with the poet Lord Byron acting as the Bernard Henri-Lévy of his era.

Foreigners continued to dominate Greek politics long after it achieved formal independence in 1830, with the Great Powers placing Otto, prince of the Bavarian Wittelsbach family, on the Greek throne. The Bavarians brought in troops and skilled administrators in hopes of setting up a modern, centralized, impersonal administration. But like the outsiders in many contemporary efforts to build a modern state in a developing country, Otto's advisers were unable to control his Greek subjects. Facing increasing resistance to his rule, Otto conceded a constitution in 1844 and opened the country up to universal male suffrage by 1864. Greece thus became one of Europe's first electoral democracies, preceding Britain by a full generation. As in the United States, democracy was established before an indigenous modern state could be created.[13]

Britain, France, Germany, and Belgium began the process of industrialization well before the consolidation of democracy, which meant that there were already the beginnings of an organized industrial working class before the franchise was expanded. This permitted the emergence of programmatic Socialist or social democratic parties based on trade union movements. This sequence was reversed in Greece, as it has been in many contemporary developing countries. The Greeks were always superb traders and merchants, controlling a large proportion of commerce within the Ottoman Empire and serving as a bridge between the Middle East and Europe.[14] But Greece itself remained a predominantly agrarian society up through the 1870s, when foreign investment began to flow into the country. Large-scale urbanization occurred around the turn of the twentieth century, but this was based more on cities as administrative, cultural, and commercial centers than as sources of industrial employment—a process sometimes referred to as "modernization without development." A real industrial sector did not emerge until the late 1920s and early 1930s, and even then, it remained of a smaller scale than in Western Europe.[15]

This combination of a weak state dominated by foreigners, the absence of a strong entrepreneurial capitalist class, and the early opening of the franchise and democratic contestation laid the groundwork for Greece's pervasive clientelism. Politics in nineteenth-century Greece was not organized around broad social classes and their respective interests; rather, it was region and clan based. Constantine Tsoucalas argues that Greece had no bourgeois landowning class (as in England), no industrial proletariat, and none of the kinds of middle-class elites that organized politics as in Western Europe. People retreated into their families for security, and politics was organized around clientelistic chains of kin relations whose raison d'être was not ideology or programmatic policies but personal security.[16]

The absence of a strong capitalist market economy in Greece meant that the state became the de facto source of employment, and nineteenth-century Greek governments began packing the public sector with political supporters. By the 1870s, the Greek government had seven times the number of civil servants per capita as the British government of the same period, and a senior minister could earn half as much as the richest land-owner.[17] To use the terminology developed in chapter 3, the Greek state expanded dramatically in scope, taking on a range of activities, including the running of businesses that properly should have been left to the private sector, while remaining extremely weak in terms of administrative capacity.

Greek society in the middle of the nineteenth century was organized around rural patron-client relations, a system that morphed seamlessly into a democratic patronage system in which members of parliament controlled votes through the granting of jobs and favors. There was no attempt at public-sector reform until the modest ones undertaken by the governments of Trikoupis (1875–1895) and Venizelos (1910–1933), in which educational standards and life tenure were established for civil servants.[18] External events had the potential to pave the way for a deeper reform of the party system. In 1922, Greece was defeated by Turkey, a calamity that led to a transfer of populations that brought nearly a million and a half Greek refugees from Asia Minor back to the Greek mainland, one-fifth of the total population at the time. Many of these refugees were highly entrepreneurial and contributed to the takeoff of the industrial economy shortly thereafter. They were, moreover, unincorporated into the existing patronage networks. At the same time, the rise of the Soviet Union led to the formation of sympathetic Communist parties around the world based on an ideological form of mass mobilization. This included the Greek Communist Party, which joined the Moscow-led Third International in 1920. All of these developments promised the emergence of a new, non-clientelist form of politics.[19]

Unfortunately, while broader participation and new forms of political recruitment did emerge in the interwar years, Greek society was so intensely polarized that it could not achieve basic stability. It lurched through a series of coups and conflicts that led to the suppression of democracy by an oligarchic regime in the mid-1930s. This was succeeded by years of foreign occupation and civil war. Democracy was again interrupted by the brutal seven-year dictatorship of the colonels between 1967 and 1974, with stable liberal democracy emerging only after their departure from power. These social conflicts left deep divisions within Greek society and increased the overall level of distrust.[20]

What is notable about the evolution of Greek political institutions is that economic modernization did not, as in the case of Britain and the United States, lead to a middle-class coalition whose object was reform of the state itself and elimination of the pervasive system of clientelism. Rather, the emergence of a stable electoral democracy after 1974 led to the rollback of merit-based bureaucracy and the steady widening of a more sophisticated form of clientelism by the two dominant parties, the center-right New Democracy (ND) and the Pan-Hellenic Socialist Movement (PASOK). The restoration of formal democracy in Greece after the fall of the colonels has been rightly celebrated as an opening move in Huntington's Third Wave of democratizations. But insufficient attention has been paid to the quality of democratic government in Greece, the fact that Greece never created a truly modern, impersonal public sector. This seemed not to matter to anyone until the euro crisis in 2009.

COLONIZATION OF THE STATE

When we speak of clientelism in Greece after World War II, we are no longer talking about the system of local notables and their followings that dominated nineteenth-century Greek politics. The Greek parties, now dealing with mass electorates, evolved into much more sophisticated and well-organized vote-mobilizing organizations, similar to the machine politics of the United States in the late 1800s.[21]

This system has come to dominate Greek government, as George Mavrogordatos illustrates with examples from education and banking. Up until the 1980s there was automatic recruitment of university students into the secondary education system based on the order in which applications were submitted. There was limited meritocracy in this system, and it fueled an uncontrolled growth in the number of teachers, as candidates exceeded job openings. But it was at least not susceptible to political manipulation. All of this changed when PASOK came to power in 1993, and the party took control of temporary teacher postings and used them to reward its own party followers. In addition, the system of inspectors general was abolished and existing schools' principals effectively demoted, clearing the way for a system of automatic advancement that eliminated any trace of meritocratic evaluation of teacher performance. These were ideologically justified as anti-elitist or pro-Socialist measures. What they ensured was not popular participation (a questionable goal in any case in education) but party control over discretionary appointments.

Something similar happened to the state-owned National Bank of Greece. Up until the early 1980s, it had been a highly respected island of meritocracy within the Greek government, with some 90 percent of its personnel being recruited through examinations. This changed with PASOK's rise in 1981; the party expanded the bank's overall payroll by as much as 50 percent (to some sixteen thousand employees) and exempted the new hires from competitive examinations. The number of patronage appointees thus increased from 10 to 40 percent of the workforce, with promotions to higher grades being entirely controlled by the party. When Mavrogordatos asked the bank's personnel manager what total employment was, the latter said that only a court order could force him to divulge that figure.[22]

While it was PASOK that politicized the hiring of teachers and bank workers in the above cases, both parties participated in stuffing the public sector with their own followers. ND and PASOK traded places in power in 1981, 1989, 1993, 2004, and 2009. Following each election, they sought to purge their rival's political appointees and replace them with their own. However, the strong Greek public-sector unions have negotiated rules guaranteeing tenure for many public employees. So rather than turning over personnel with every change in party (as in the case of the American patronage system), the Greek state has simply expanded to make way for new recruits. Needless to say, neither of these practices was good for bureaucratic quality, and the ever-expanding public sector contributed mightily to Greece's budget deficits and debt woes. A report by the Organization for Economic Cooperation and Development on the Greek public sector after the onset of the euro crisis noted that Greece had more than seven hundred thousand public employees, a fivefold increase between 1970 and 2009. Only one public-sector worker has been laid off for every private-sector employee since the start of the crisis, and public-sector wages plus bonuses were one and a half times those in the private sector.[23]

The Greek state is large and expansive but, with a few exceptions, of very low quality. Its problems have become legendary across Europe since the start of the euro crisis: the frequent loss of land titles due to inadequate record-keeping systems, the backlog of court cases, long waiting times at hospitals and other government facilities.

The origins of clientelism in Greece are not hard to find; it is the result of the early arrival of electoral democracy, before a modern state had an opportunity to coalesce. In this respect the Greek experience is no different from that of America, and is similar to many other developing countries in Latin America and South Asia. What is noteworthy about Greece is the failure of a reform movement to arise as the country modernized and began to develop economically. Greece has never seen the emergence of a coalition of groups built around the middle class that has agitated for civil service reform. Instead, newly arrived social actors, such as urbanites and immigrants from Asia Minor, have gotten co-opted by the existing clientelistic system and been made to play by its rules.

Why have some countries been able to reform their clientelistic systems while Greece has not? I will return to this question more comprehensively in chapter 13, which summarizes the comparative experience of developed-country state building. But there are several factors that emerge from this case already that hint at parts of an answer.

The first has to do with the absence of a strong tradition of indigenous statehood. Although Greece was the "birthplace of democracy" in ancient times, it began the modern era as an Ottoman province in which domestic elites were recruited to work for an illegitimate foreign power. The Greeks fought bravely for their freedom but were unable to achieve it on their own; even after independence, foreign influence remained strong, as the linkages of the first Greek political parties to different Great Powers attest. These foreign influences were evident in the country's fluctuating borders over the centuries. This pattern of foreign influence continued up through World War II and the cold war, where Greece was a pawn in larger international struggles. As in other parts of the world including, as we will see below, Italy, Communist and other parties of the extreme left tended to reject clientelism in favor of mass mobilization based on ideology. The dynamics of the cold war, however, ensured that the United States would support a corrupt and clientelistic conservative party over a cleaner left-wing one.

And indeed today as it struggles with its financial crisis, the central issue in Greek politics remains resentment of the influence of Brussels, Germany, the International Monetary Fund, and other external actors, which are seen as pulling strings behind the back of a weak Greek government. Although there is considerable distrust of government in American political culture, by contrast, the basic legitimacy of democratic institutions runs very deep.

Distrust of government is related to the Greek inability to collect taxes. Americans loudly proclaim their dislike of taxes, but when Congress mandates a tax, the government is energetic in enforcement. Moreover, international surveys suggest that levels of tax compliance are reasonably high in the United States; higher, certainly, than most European countries on the Mediterranean. Tax evasion in Greece is widespread, with restaurants requiring cash payments, doctors declaring poverty-line salaries, and unreported swimming pools owned by asset-hiding citizens dotting the Athenian landscape. By one account, Greece's shadow economy—unreported income hidden from the tax authorities—constitutes 29.6 percent of total GDP.[24]

A second factor has to do with the late arrival of capitalism in Greece. The United States was an early industrializer; the private sector and entrepreneurship remained the main occupations of most Americans. Greece urbanized and took on other trappings of a modern society early on, but it failed to build a strong base of industrial employment. In the absence of entrepreneurial opportunities, Greeks sought jobs in the state sector, and politicians seeking to mobilize votes were happy to oblige. Moreover, the Greek pattern of urbanization in which whole villages moved from the countryside preserved intact rural patronage networks, networks that industry-based development tended to dissolve.

A final factor has to do with trust, or what has been described as social capital.[25] I began this chapter noting that Greece shared with southern Italy a reputation for being an extremely low-trust society. Some social scientists have argued that trust is the by-product of other forces in a society, like an effective government, or else strong economic growth that allows everyone to get richer together. Others have suggested that lack of trust is a cultural condition that exists independently (or exogenously, as economists would say) of the political or economic systems; it is a cause of systemic dysfunction rather than an effect.

In my view, Greek distrust is rooted in politics, particularly in the absence of a strong, impartial state, but over the years it has perpetuated itself as a cultural habit. Distrust has been pervasive in both traditional rural Greek society and in the bitter political struggles of the twentieth century. Greeks have been divided by family, kinship, region, class, and ideology, despite the fact that Greece is one of the world's most ethnically homogeneous societies. Feeding these social and political cleavages is the fact that the state has never been seen as the protector of an abstract public interest, in the manner of the German and French states. Rather, it is seen as an asset to be grabbed and exploited for narrow partisan benefit. Hence, no contemporary Greek political party has made reform of the state itself part of its agenda. When the European Union and the IMF demanded structural reforms in return for a restructuring of Greek debt, the Greek government was willing to consider virtually any form of austerity before agreeing to end party control over patronage.

The situation of Italy is in certain ways similar to Greece; deep distrust and cynicism play an important role in weakening public administration in that country as well. But the Italian situation is more complicated because Italy is a far richer and more diverse country. There has at least been an ongoing struggle against clientelism and the political corruption it engenders. But no more than in Greece has modernization by itself been sufficient to bring about the emergence of a fully modern state.

7

ITALY AND THE LOW-TRUST EQUILIBRIUM

How the quality of government varies across Italy; weaknesses of the Italian state in the South; where the Mafia came from; Italy's struggle with clientelism and corruption; the importance of trust for good government

One observer describes Sicily's leading city in the following terms:

Capital of the mafia, a national symbol of venality and corruption in local government, Palermo, Italy's sixth largest city, is balanced precariously between Europe and Africa. Behind the façade of a prosperous modern metropolis, the crumbling slums, narrow twisting alleyways, and dank courtyards of the old city harbor conditions of housing, health, and sanitation more reminiscent of a Cairo or a Calcutta than of a major European city. Life in Palermo is a perpetual drama, from the daily torment of the city's chaotic traffic to the routine collapse of yet another *palazzo* in the old city to the periodic breakdown of basic services like garbage collection or public transportation to not infrequent outbursts of mafia warfare, which leave the city's streets strewn with bullet-ridden corpses.[1]

One of the continuing failures of local government in southern Italy has been trash collection. In 1976, uncollected garbage piled up in the streets of Palermo for months at a time. In Naples during the late 2000s, a similar crisis reached up to the cabinet of Prime Minister Silvio Berlusconi.[2] Road building fared little better. *The New York Times* noted that between 2000 and 2011 Italy spent $10 billion, including $500 million in European Union subsidies, on the A3 highway from Salerno to Reggio

Calabria. Due to high levels of graft and corruption, the highway remains unfinished.[3]

In what has become a minor classic of contemporary political science, Robert Putnam demonstrated empirically the huge variance that exists in the quality of local governments across the different regions of Italy, and ascribed those differences not to structural economic or political factors but to different levels of civic engagement, or what has been labeled social capital. He argued further that one of the important sources of poor government performance was the region's long history of clientelism.

While much of the literature on Italy's "southern question" had previously been anecdotal, Putnam devised twelve quantitative measures of government performance, including cabinet stability, the promptness with which budgets were completed, legislative innovation, numbers of day care centers and family clinics, and bureaucratic responsiveness. He then collected data across all of Italy's regions over several decades and demonstrated that there is a consistent north-south axis in government quality, with Emilia-Romagna, Lombardy, and Umbria scoring consistently higher than Sicily, Basilicata, and Calabria. His measures correlate strongly with surveys of Italian citizens' satisfaction with their own local governments.[4]

At this point in his analysis, Putnam was providing only statistical confirmation of what Italians had long perceived. His argument became more controversial, however, when he posited the causes of these differences. An economic determinist might argue that the quality of government is the product either of a region's overall level of socioeconomic modernization or of resources. Since southern Italy is poorer than the North, it might simply not be able to afford good-quality government. Putnam pointed out that the gap between the regions has persisted over many generations and existed at a time when the North was poorer than today's South. Moreover, resources alone could not explain the difference, since postwar Italian governments had transferred enormous resources from north to south in the first couple of decades after World War II in a deliberate effort to help the region catch up. While the South did in fact develop substantially during this period, the North did so at a faster rate, such that the overall gap was maintained.

Nor is it possible to attribute the difference between regions to different institutions or policies. Italy's postwar political system was highly centralized; all the regions were ruled through French-style prefects in a uniform manner. This system was reformed in the 1970s when the central government devolved substantial local decision-making authority to the regions, within an overall structure that sought to equalize resources across the country.[5] Either way—as regions of a centralized state ruled from Rome, or as regions granted autonomy with more or less equal access to resources—it is hard to argue that the political order that has existed since 1861 is responsible for the developmental differences.

This is what led Putnam, following Edward Banfield and many other observers of the South, to argue that the region's dysfunctions lay in long-standing inherited cultural values, or social capital. Putnam argued that social capital was generated in self-governing city-states such as Genoa, Florence, and Venice, that flourished during the Middle Ages through the Renaissance. These republics cultivated virtues of loyalty and trust, and were organized around oligarchic institutions of self-rule. Southern Italy, by contrast, was shaped by the centralized and autocratic rule of the Norman kings of Naples and Sicily, whose predominant mode of social organization was the patron-client relationship. Thus the ultimate cause of the difference between the regions was political in nature, but this difference according to Putnam perpetuated itself across the centuries as social or cultural habits regarding trust and community.[6]

THE ORIGINS OF CLIENTELISM IN SOUTHERN ITALY

There are unfortunately several problems with a historical account that adduces strong authoritarian government as the cause of the South's lack of civic community. In the first place, the Norman kingdom of Sicily to which Putnam attributes the region's hierarchical politics formally ended in 1194, when it was succeeded by a Hohenstaufen dynasty whose base of power was in the North and whose members included a number of Holy Roman Emperors. (The story of how the southern Norman kingdom fought on the side of Pope Gregory VII against the Emperor Henry IV during the investiture conflict on behalf of an independent Catholic church is told in chapter 18 of the first volume of this book.) Even if one considers the Hohenstaufens a continuation of the earlier Norman tradition—Emperor Frederick II was indeed a great centralizer—this dynasty itself ended in 1268. At this point in European history there was also a powerful, centralized Norman kingdom ruling England, and a Viking kingdom in Denmark, yet neither England nor Denmark developed a pattern of clientelistic government. Needless to say, a lot happened in Italy between the thirteenth and nineteenth centuries that might better explain contemporary patterns of government.

There is a second problem in attributing clientelism to strong vertical political power in the South, in contrast to the republican traditions of the northern city-states. As I argued in Volume 1, the development of centralized state authority is a necessary condition for modern government, but it tells you little about the degree of political freedom that will exist in a given society. As Europe exited feudalism, the key to the eventual emergence of accountable institutions was the balance that existed between the monarch (or state) and the other elite power holders in the society. Where the monarch succeeded in co-opting the aristocracy and upper bourgeoisie, as in France and Spain, weak absolutism emerged; where the monarch and aristocracy joined hands against the peasantry, as in Prussia and Russia, there was strong absolutism; where the aristocracy was stronger than the monarchy, as in Hungary and Poland, there was local tyranny and national weakness. Only in England were the state and aristocratic elites relatively balanced; constitutional government arose out of the fact that neither one could prevail over the other. The English state often threw its weight into the balance in favor of nonelites against the aristocracy, not out of egalitarian ideology but because it wanted to clip the wings of a rival for power. While we are familiar with the story of King John's barons limiting his power through the Magna Carta, English kings were also instrumental in limiting the power of the barons and lords against their tenants and nonelite vassals.[7]

Putnam argues that the Normans established strong centralized government in southern Italy and that this vertical power undermined the ability of citizens to form horizontal linkages of trust or association. But at this point in the Middle Ages, no European government was able to set up a truly dictatorial centralized state capable of penetrating and controlling the whole of society in the manner of the Chinese or, later, the Russians. In the centuries following Frederick II, the reality of southern Italy was rather the opposite: a persisting weakness of centralized authority that was unable to prevent exploitation of the peasantry by the aristocracy. Southern Italy, in other words, resembled Hungary or Poland much more closely than it resembled Prussia or Russia.

As in the case of Greece, the weakness of indigenous central government in southern Italy had a lot to do with politics at an international level. The kingdoms of Sicily and Naples passed from the Hohenstaufens eventually to the House of Aragon, whose dynastic possessions were united under Spanish rule in the marriage of Ferdinand and Isabella. These possessions were consolidated in the empire of their grandson Charles V, who became the Habsburg heir and Holy Roman Emperor. Southern Italy remained a possession of first the Spanish Habsburgs and then, after the War of the Spanish Succession, the Spanish Bourbons, until it was invaded by Napoleon, who put his brother Joseph on the throne. Thus for nearly five centuries, the nominal sovereign over the Kingdom of the Two Sicilies was a distant foreigner, the legitimacy of whose rule was frequently contested in local uprisings. One school of Italian historiography maintains that the region's low trust emanates not from centralized dictatorship but from the policies of divide and rule practiced by the Spanish Habsburgs.[8]

In any event, the clientelism that persists in southern Italy is a modern phenomenon, and there are more proximate historical factors than the practices of an ancient Norman kingdom or even of the Spanish Habsburgs. We should look instead at the unified Italy that was created in 1861 under the aegis of the northern Piedmontese monarchy, after the Bourbons in the South were overthrown by Giuseppe Garibaldi. When the northerners first confronted the social reality of the South, they were shocked: the new governor of Naples after its liberation by Garibaldi reported to Italy's first prime minister, Camillo Benso, Count of Cavour, "This is not Italy! This is Africa: the bedouins are the flower of civic virtue besides these country bumpkins."[9]

Unlike Prussia, which was able to "nationalize" its bureaucracy and institutions when it unified Germany, Piedmont was too small a player to accomplish a similar feat. Faced with peasant revolts and chaos in the wake of the fall of the Bourbons, the northern bourgeoisie controlling the new national government made a pact with the local oligarchy in the South, what Antonio Gramsci labeled the "*blocco storico*," or historic alliance.[10] According to political scientist Judith Chubb, "In return for access to government patronage and for complete freedom of action in local administrations, [the southern elite] were prepared to provide unquestioning support in Parliament to any government majority, regardless of its program."[11]

Traditional patron-client relations have long existed in Italy. The very terms *patronus* and *cliens* were Roman and referred to a highly formalized legal relationship between a superior and an inferior that was the basis of power for Roman elites from the days of the late Republic onward.[12] The feudal relationship of lord and vassal can be seen as a contractual form of patronage in which respective duties and privileges of the two parties are clearly laid out. With the abolition of feudalism in the South, these formal relations shifted to informal ones, in which local landlords used their wealth and political connections to control the peasants living on their lands.

This traditional type of patronage (which existed in many rural communities around the world) evolved into a modern system of clientelism in stages, and as in the case of Greece had to do with the early introduction of democracy in a society that did not have a strong, autonomous state. According to Luigi Graziano, under the liberal republic that was in place between 1860 and 1922, "The organization of politics around personality and patronage rather than ideas and practical programs not only absorbed and neutralized the opposition but ultimately emptied the very concept of 'party' of any meaning beyond that of loose congeries of personal clienteles." As in America under the patronage system, this had a devastating effect on the quality of government: "The particularistic nature of the incentives which kept the system going required that the minister had to dispose of rewards and sanctions of an equally particularistic nature; that is, he had to be as free as possible from bureaucratic norms of conduct."[13] This system was by our earlier definitions not yet truly clientelistic because the country lacked mass politics. The franchise was expanded much more slowly in Italy than in Greece; in 1882, only 6.9 percent of the population had the right to vote, and universal male suffrage was not introduced until 1913.[14]

As in Greece, industrialization came relatively late to southern Italy. Under a unified national Italian government, tariffs were introduced to protect northern industry and the inefficient landowners of the South. It was now northern industries that increasingly supplied the South. This heightened the role of the local landowning classes at the expense of industry and encouraged the middle classes there not to go into entrepreneurship but to buy land for themselves and join the local oligarchy. Opportunities to do so expanded rapidly with the division of communal lands after the abolition of feudalism by Napoleon (which happened later in Sicily than in the continental Mezzogiorno), and the division of church lands after 1860. This led to a large number of social conflicts over land among different social classes. Thus the interests of the northern middle class were very much aligned with the project of creating a new and modern state, while the southern middle class was absorbed into the traditional oligarchy. The peasantry was deprived of a potential ally and relegated to an increasingly impoverished and marginalized state. According to Graziano, "The hate [the peasantry] harbored previously for a distant central authority, a hate somewhat mitigated by the paternalism of the Bourbon kings, was now concentrated against the new local ruling class."[15] There was no entrepreneurial middle class in the South that could lead a drive for state modernization.

THE WEAK STATE AND THE RISE OF THE MAFIA

The Mafia—the first and sometimes only thing that outsiders associate with Sicily—is not an ancient institution that somehow succeeded in surviving into the present era. It, as well as the Camorra in Campania and the 'Ndrangheta in Calabria, had very specific origins in the Mezzogiorno of the nineteenth century. One theory of the Mafia's origins is that the mafiosi were originally *gabelloti*, richer tenants who exploited their role between landlords and poor peasants to extort rents from both.[16] Diego Gambetta, however, presents an elegant economic theory of the Mafia's origins: mafiosi are private entrepreneurs whose function is to provide protection of individual property rights in a society in which the state fails to perform this basic service. That is, if one party to a private transaction is cheated by the other, he would normally take his partner to court in a well-ordered rule-of-law society. But where the state is corrupt, unreliable, or perhaps altogether absent, one must turn instead to a private provider of protection and task him to threaten to break the legs of the other party if he doesn't pay up. By this account, the Mafia is simply a private organization providing a needed service that is normally performed by the state—that is, use of the threat of violence (and sometimes actual violence) to enforce property rights. Gambetta shows that the Mafia arose precisely in those parts of southern Italy where there was economic conflict over land, mobile wealth and a high volume of transactions, and political discord in connection with the changes taking place in the nature of the Italian state after 1860.[17]

There are, of course, good reasons why the use of violence to protect property rights should be a monopoly of a legitimate state. Without a monopoly, protection markets themselves can become an object of violent competition. It is easy for a mafioso to move seamlessly from protection to extortion, protecting individuals from a threat that he himself creates. Private protection also easily evolves into other illegal rackets, such as prostitution and drug trafficking. The Mafia, as Gambetta argues, thrives in a low-trust society like that of Sicily because it can provide credible protection services in the short run. But it perpetuates a climate of violence and fear, which lowers levels of trust for the society as a whole.[18]

The inverse relationship between state strength and organized crime is illustrated by Italy's Fascist interlude. Fascism is generally understood to be a much stronger form of authoritarian government than the traditional absolutist governments of nineteenth-century Europe, involving as it does a mass party, guiding ideology, total monopoly over the state, charismatic leadership, and suppression of civil society.[19] Though Italy's Mussolini created fascism, his version never achieved quite the same degree of centralized power that Hitler's regime did, much less that of Stalin's Soviet Union. Mussolini's fascist party was never able to penetrate the South and reorganize politics on a mass basis. What the Fascists couldn't tolerate, however, were competitors in the violence game, and so they began a successful campaign to suppress the Mafia. But the latter's networks were not completely dismantled, and many of its leaders were co-opted into the system rather than killed or jailed. So the Mafia was poised to reemerge quickly after the foundation of a democratic regime in 1946.[20]

CLIENTELISM ARRIVES

Italy opened up the franchise shortly before World War I, but this democratic experiment was cut short a decade later by the rise of Mussolini. In this period, however, the first mass political parties emerged. On the left was the Socialist party, founded in 1894 by Filippo Turati, which then split in 1921 when the radical wing broke off to join the Third International as the Italian Communist Party (the Partito Comunista Italiano, or PCI).[21] On the right was the Partito Popolare, conceived by Don Luigi Sturzo, a Sicilian priest, as a mass-based Catholic party that sought to organize peasant cooperatives and pushed for land redistribution. All of these parties were banned under Mussolini, but they reemerged quickly after the fall of fascism in 1943.

The Italian Christian Democratic party—the Democrazia Cristiana or DC—was founded in 1943 as an heir to the Partito Popolare and originally conceived of itself as a progressive, mass-based party that would compete with the Italian Communists. Like the early American parties, however, the DC faced the problem of how to get masses of voters to go to the polls as the first democratic elections began under the new postwar republic. Even though it had strong connections with Catholic workers in the well-organized North, it faced a problem of penetrating the South where society remained organized around local elites and their patronage networks. In early elections after the war, a number of right-wing parties including the Monarchists and the populist Uomo Qualunque proved successful in gaining votes, and the DC shifted to a strategy of building on the region's existing traditions of patronage. However, the DC did this using modern organizational methods, building a centralized party hierarchy based in Rome, with networks of party bosses who could recruit voters on a clientelistic basis.

Under Amintore Fanfani (who would go on to be a long-serving prime minister in the 1950s), the party was transformed into a modern mass-based clientelistic party.[22] The shift was similar in many respects to the transformation of American political parties from ad hoc coalitions of patronage politicians to highly organized national political machines between the 1840s and 1880s. While ideology—and particularly the split between Italy's Catholic and Marxist subcultures—continued to play a critical role in post–World War II Italian politics, groups like the Socialist Party had increasingly to resort to clientelistic tactics themselves in order to remain competitive.[23]

Clientelism in the South was reinforced by the government's economic policies. Modern Italy established a highly centralized state modeled on that of France, in which Rome was able to reallocate resources among regions. In order to alleviate the region's poverty, liberal governments of the late nineteenth century began large investments in infrastructure, though this tended to facilitate the dominance of northern industries over southern ones.[24] In 1950, the government of the new republic set up a development arm, the Cassa per il Mezzogiorno, which was tasked with promoting economic growth in the South. It also made heavy use of the Institute for Industrial Reconstruction, a conglomerate of state-owned industries that could provide financing, jobs, and party patronage. The state spent considerable sums on infrastructure and made large investments in steel, petrochemicals, and other heavy industries.

The results of this industrial policy were highly mixed. There were large increases in per capita income and industrial output in the South, and a huge movement of peasants off of the land, with agricultural employment shrinking from 55 to 30 percent of the population between 1951 and 1971. Some went to cities in both the South and North, but many others left Italy altogether for the United States, Europe, and Latin America. There were, in addition, large improvements in social indicators such as literacy and infant mortality that made the South far less like "Africa" than in the nineteenth century. The years 1951–1981 in particular were ones of catch-up, in which the gap between North and South closed somewhat (see Table 1). What did not happen as a result of this investment was the creation of a large, self-sustaining industrial base in the South. Many of the successful companies in the South were offshoots of northern ones. Northern Italy grew even faster, and by the 1970s the development gap between the regions remained as wide as ever, despite the huge sums of money that had been transferred. Like Greece, southern Italy was a case of "modernization without development."[25]

TABLE 1. Per Capita Value Added in Italy's Regions, 1891–2001
(Italy = 1)

	1891	1911	1938	1951	1971	1981	2001
Northwest	1.16	1.22	1.43	1.52	1.28	1.22	1.24
Center/Northeast	1.01	1.00	0.99	1.04	1.04	1.11	1.13
South and Islands	0.88	0.84	0.70	0.61	0.73	0.70	0.68
Yearly Growth Rate (%)	–	2.29	0.85	0.96	6.33	2.79	2.08

SOURCE: Emanuele Felice, "Regional Inequalities in Italy in the Long Run (1891–2001)"

More important from a political standpoint, the growth of government-directed investments in the South proved to be a bonanza for political clientelism. In the words of one observer, "It is never the State or the national community that appropriates sums for this or that project, for the construction of houses or schools, for the realization of public works or industrial programs: it is always thanks to the interest of this or that local deputy or the local secretary of the DC."[26] As in Greece, political connections and the ability to manipulate the state became a much surer route to wealth and personal security than private entrepreneurship, thus reinforcing the existing north-south gap while creating a culture of political favoritism that would soon get out of hand. In addition, heavy public spending provided ample opportunities for more overt forms of corruption. The Mafia had played an important role in securing the electoral base for the DC in the South after the war; as in many other countries, they were rewarded through their control over public contracting. The rise of the 'Ndrangheta was tied to the completion of a highway from Salerno to Reggio Calabria in the 1960s, and that of the Camorra to the rebuilding of Naples in the 1980s.[27]

TANGENTOPOLI AND THE END OF THE COLD WAR

As in Greece, the Communists were the least clientelistic of Italian political parties because of their ideology-based organization. But the PCI was an ally of Moscow and widely suspected of wanting to use the democratic process only to seize power; it was therefore excluded from ruling coalitions despite the 25–30 percent and higher of the electorate that regularly voted for it. Also as in Greece, the government's American ally strongly preferred a democratic party tainted by corruption to a nonclientelistic Communist one and threw its weight into the balance. Except during the few interludes when the Italian Socialists and other minor parties were able to name a prime minister, the Christian Democrats dominated postwar politics. For all of its constantly changing cabinets, the Italian system was highly stable and oversaw the country's rise as a major industrial power.

This changed suddenly with the end of the cold war in 1989. The Italian Communists lost their link to Moscow with the collapse of the Soviet Union and the decline of Marxism as a legitimating ideology. The party was disbanded in 1991 and replaced by the Party of the Democratic Left (Partito Democratico della Sinistra). The end of the internal Communist threat in turn undermined the rationale for the continuing dominance of the DC, which by this point had dragged the country as a whole into a morass of corruption and criminality. New parties appeared, in particular the Lega Nord, or Northern League, a regional party based on small and medium-sized entrepreneurs who were sick of the Italian state's corruption and its constant subsidization of the South. The Lega Nord suggested at times that the North ought to secede entirely from the rest of Italy in order to make a break from southern corruption.

Many believed that the Mafia, clientelism, and corruption represented traditional social practices that would gradually erode as the country modernized economically. Instead, all three became stronger over time, breaking out of their southern redoubts to infect the whole of Italy. A culture of impunity had emerged by the 1980s surrounding the use of public resources for private gain, reflected in the words of a politician of an older generation:

> Maybe I'm ingenuous, but I would never have believed that there was such deep-rooted and diffuse corruption. I could certainly imagine that buying packs of membership inscriptions, financing conferences, offering dinners, publishing journals on glossy paper, all cost vast amounts of money. But—and I insist because it is the honest truth—I could never have supposed they were such blatant thieves. When I learned that the parties and factions were taking regular percentage cuts of public contracts, I was utterly appalled.[28]

All of this exploded in the 1992 "Tangentopoli" scandal. Surprisingly, this did not come out of the South but rather involved a Socialist politician from Milan, Mario Chiesa, who was arrested trying to flush a $6,000 bribe down the toilet and was soon found to be involved in a much larger series of scandals. The widening investigations netted Bettino Craxi, secretary of the Socialist Party, which had proved just as eager as the Christian Democrats to get in on the winnings.[29]

At the same time, the Mafia's influence spread beyond Sicily to infect the country as a whole. In the 1970s and '80s, the power of Italian organized crime grew dramatically due to the rise of the international drug trade, just as it did in Latin America. Conflicts over turf led to bloody battles between rival families in Palermo and other southern cities, and the rise of a particularly violent faction, the Corleonesi. While many individual southern politicians had Mafia ties, these became more systematic with the defection of Salvo Lima, the ex-mayor of Palermo, to longtime prime minister Giulio Andreotti's faction of the DC. Lima brought with him not just a formidable political machine but also all of his extensive ties with organized crime.[30]

There were, however, countervailing forces. The independence of the Italian judiciary had been reinforced by the recruitment of a generation of idealistic lawyers in the wake of the global uprisings of 1968. These left-leaning jurists rose steadily in the ranks and by the 1980s were in positions to take on the country's entrenched political elite. The targets of judicial investigations, from Andreotti to Craxi to Berlusconi, have charged the judiciary with political motives, and to some extent that is true. These judges tended to go after politicians on the right more often than those on the left. But many individual judges were willing to take highly courageous stands against corrupt politicians and Mafia bosses. In addition, there were a number of crusading judges such as Giovanni Falcone and Paolo Borsellino whose strong family traditions of civic responsibility ran against the general Sicilian tide. The investigations of the 1980s and '90s led to a virtual war between the Mafia and the uncorrupt parts of the Italian state, with a number of high-profile assassinations of judges and prosecutors by the Mafia. This culminated in the assassination in 1992 of Falcone, his wife, and his bodyguards, and of Borsellino shortly thereafter.[31] With the killing of police chief Alberto dalla Chiesa, prosecutor Gaetano Costa, and magistrate Rocco Chinnici, public opinion was gradually mobilized in support of anticorruption efforts. With the cold war no longer serving as a backstop to corrupt but conservative politicians, the revelations that came out of Tangentopoli and other investigations finally brought down Prime Minister Andreotti and the Christian Democratic Party as a whole. The DC did very poorly in the 1992 elections and ceased being a factor in Italian politics after 1994.[32]

THE FAILURE OF MODERNIZATION

Italy would have done well if the events that brought about the collapse of the post–World War II political system had paved the way for a strong reform coalition like the one that appeared in the United States at the turn of the twentieth century. Unfortunately, events did not play out in this manner. The right was reorganized under the leadership of media magnate Silvio Berlusconi, who used his corporate empire to build a new base of support. He came to power at the head of a coalition that included the Northern League of Umberto Bossi and the neo-Fascist Alleanza Nazionale of Gianfranco Fini. These parties, plus Berlusconi's Forza Italia, picked up the pieces of the old Christian Democratic Party; versions of this coalition ruled Italy in 1994, from 2001 to 2006, and again from 2008 to 2012.

Berlusconi's public face was one of a modern, free-market politician in the Reagan-Thatcher mold who wanted to reduce taxes, reform and reduce the size of the Italian state, and make it run more effectively, like one of his businesses. Unfortunately, Berlusconi was himself the product of the old system, a politician with a clientelistic mind-set who simply brought new media techniques to bear. If the essence of a modern state is the strict separation of public and private interest, Berlusconi moved in exactly the opposite direction, using his own business holdings in newspapers, television, and sports teams to build a mass political base. Not only did he fail to initiate, in any of his three terms, any serious reforms of the Italian public sector, he launched a broad attack on the independent judiciary and its corruption investigations against him. Operation Clean Hands, which had helped destroy the old party system, was itself undermined by his ministerial choices and decrees shielding various defendants.[33] Berlusconi used his parliamentary majority to vote himself immunity and failed egregiously to rein in either the appearance or substance of conflict of interest. And he did nothing to reform the clientelistic politics of the South, which has continued unabated: in the crisis over the euro in 2011–2012, the inability of Sicily to control its public finances led to people labeling it the "Greece of Italy," a crisis that has contributed overall to the country's weak fiscal condition.[34]

A reform coalition failed to materialize in Italy in part because of the Northern League and its leader, Umberto Bossi. The social base of the party was in the modern, northern parts of Italy and consisted heavily of small-business owners and middle-class professionals fed up with the corruption and inefficiency of the Italian state. Bossi, unfortunately, built his party not around state reform but around populist issues like opposition to immigration. He and his party were themselves not above using clientelistic methods to win voters, and they were willing to acquiesce in many of Berlusconi's antics in order to stay in power. A social group that should have been at the center of a reform coalition was thus neutralized.[35]

The left-wing governments that ruled between the Berlusconi prime ministerships did little better. Some modest reforms were launched in the 1990s focusing on universities, local governments, and bureaucratic red tape, with some effect. But there was never strong leadership or consensus about the need to change the nature of the Italian state itself, to free it completely of political patronage, to move more of the economy into the formal sector, and to control the state's overall size.

Outside forces could have supplied some of the missing political will to reform the system. Entry into the eurozone in 1999 put strong external pressure on Rome to meet budget targets. But once Italy was in, fiscal discipline relaxed as it did in Greece. A second opportunity came with the euro crisis in 2009–2011, which finally forced the replacement of Silvio Berlusconi with Mario Monti, an unelected technocrat. But Monti was forced to step down at the end of 2012, and new elections created, if anything, a consensus against more serious structural reforms. Whether Matteo Renzi, the new leader of the center-left, can change the system remains to be seen.

Both Greece and southern Italy have been home to clientelistic politics; both are notable because they are modern, industrialized societies that nonetheless have not succeeded in reforming their public sectors and eliminating political patronage as Germany, Britain, and the United States did. The similarities between Greece and southern Italy are striking. Both were impoverished and backward compared to other parts of Europe and saw late development of a capitalist economy. Both came to be heavily reliant on the state for employment and economic advancement; both experienced "modernization without development." And in both, governments were weak, in terms of legitimacy and capacity.

Greece and Italy differ importantly from one another insofar as Italy has had the makings of a reform coalition, while Greece has not. Although I have stressed regional differences between Italy's North and South, the conflict has not been strictly territorial. As many observers have pointed out, the South has produced civic-minded individuals like Giovanni Falcone, just as the North has experienced corruption and patronage. Judith Chubb has explained how Naples saw something of a civic renewal during the 1970s while Palermo did not, and Simona Piattoni has noted that there are varieties of clientelism practiced across the Mezzogiorno that are much less hostile to development than others.[36] In Greece, by contrast, it has been hard to locate an important constituency interested in reform of the public sector.

THE IMPORTANCE OF TRUST

I began the previous chapter by noting the degree to which Greek and southern Italian society were characterized by generalized social distrust, directed at both the government and fellow citizens. Is there a relationship between trust and good government, and if so, what is it?[37]

As a personal attribute, trust is not inherently good or bad. If I am living in a neighborhood full of thieves and swindlers, being a trusting person will get me into trouble. Trust becomes a valuable commodity only when it exists as the by-product of a society whose members practice social virtues like honesty, reliability, and openness. Trust makes no sense unless it reflects a general condition of trustworthy behavior; under these conditions, it becomes the marker and facilitator of cooperation. Of course, an opportunist could try to take advantage of other people's trust and try to cheat them. But if one wants to live in the community, this will quickly lead to ostracism and shunning.

Living in a high-trust society has many advantages. Cooperation is possible in low-trust societies, but only through formal mechanisms. Business transactions require thick contracts, litigation, police, and legal enforcement because not all people can be relied upon to meet their commitments. If I live in a neighborhood with high rates of crime, I may have to walk around armed, or not go out at night, or put expensive locks and alarms on my door to supplement the private security guards I have to hire. In many poor countries, as we will see in Part II, families have to leave a member at home all day to prevent their neighbors from stealing from their garden or dispossessing them of their house altogether. All of these constitute what economists call transaction costs, which can be saved if one lives in a high-trust society. Moreover, many low-trust societies never realize the benefits of cooperation at all: businesses don't form, neighbors don't help one another, and the like.

The same thing applies in citizens' relationship to their government.

People are much more likely to comply with a law if they see that other people around them are doing so as well. In the previous volume of this book, I presented evidence that faculties for norm following are genetically embedded as part of human nature. In most societies, law-abidingness is only in part the product of the degree to which governments can monitor compliance and enforce penalties for lawbreaking. The vast majority of law-abiding behavior is based rather on the fact that people see other people around them obeying the law and act in conformity to the perceived norm. Conversely, if a bureaucrat sees a fellow worker taking a bribe for allowing someone to jump the queue, or if a politician perceives that the rival party is benefiting from rake-offs from public contracts to his detriment, then he will be much more likely to behave in a similar fashion. If many citizens cheat on their taxes (as happens routinely in both Greece and Italy), then any given person is going to look stupid paying up in full.

The quality of government thus depends critically on trust or social capital. If the government fails to perform certain critical functions—if it cannot, for example, be trusted to protect my property rights, or if it fails to defend my person against criminals or public hazards like toxic wastes—then I will take it into my own hands to secure my own interests. As we saw in the case of Sicily, the Mafia had its origins in the failure of the Bourbon and later the Italian state to do precisely this, which is why individuals began hiring "men of honor" to provide them with private protection. But since the mafiosi were not themselves trustworthy individuals, distrust of government metastasized into distrust of everyone.

A low-trust society constitutes what economists call a collective action problem. Distrust is socially counterproductive, and everyone would be better off if they behaved in a trustworthy manner. But any given individual has no incentive to be the first person not to take a bribe or to pay her taxes. Since distrust feeds on itself, everyone is trapped in what is known as a low-level equilibrium, where everyone is worse off but no one can break out. By contrast, if the government were clean, honest, and competent, then people would be willing to trust it and follow its lead.

Both Greece and southern Italy had governments in the nineteenth and twentieth centuries that were, using the terminology developed in chapter 3, large in scope but weak in strength or capacity. Neither country on entering the modern democratic era inherited an autonomous, Prussian-style bureaucracy. The legitimacy of governments in both countries was tainted by connections to foreigners: both were ruled by external powers prior to the nineteenth century, and even after nominal independence Greece's institutions and political parties were strongly shaped by outside powers. In southern Italy it was a matter of internal colonization, with a northern-dominated central government shaping policy in the South. In both Greece and Italy, the government became an early source of patronage, and then overt clientelism as the systems democratized and shifted to mass political participation.

What was the relationship between these extensive but weak states, on the one hand, and low levels of generalized social trust on the other? The causality would seem to go in both directions. As we have seen, lack of trust in government leads individuals to seek private solutions to the provision of public goods like property rights. This can take a highly pathological form like the Mafia, or it can result simply in families leaning on their own resources as the only source of reliable behavior. The familism that is so pronounced in both societies is to some extent a defensive measure in societies with weak institutional support for extrafamilial trust.

On the other hand, once social distrust becomes culturally embedded, it takes on a life of its own. Cynicism about the government, or expectations that other people are out to take advantage of you, leads to behavior that reinforces these outcomes: you try to avoid paying taxes to a government that you think is corrupt and illegitimate; even if you are not inclined to actively take advantage of strangers, you have little expectation that working with them will lead to any good.

Of course, not all countries are trapped in this fashion. I have spanned the gamut of government quality in Europe, from a Weberian Germany to clientelistic Greece and Italy. I now turn to two intermediate cases, Britain and the United States, where government quality improved. Britain began the nineteenth century with a patronage-based civil service, and succeeded in reforming it by the 1870s. The United States had a patronage system in the early decades after ratification of the Constitution, but transformed it into a full-blown clientelistic system by the 1830s. Like Britain, the United States also reformed its system and laid the foundations for a modern Weberian state. But the peculiarities of the American form of government—its system of checks and balances—meant that this happened later than in Britain and took many more years to accomplish.

8

PATRONAGE AND REFORM

How Britain and America both started the nineteenth century with patronage-based bureaucracies; genesis of the Northcote-Trevelyan reforms in the Indian Civil Service; the middle-class coalition; why Britain never developed clientelistic political parties

Britain and the United States started the nineteenth century with patronage-laden governments that were not too different from those of Greece and Italy. Unlike the latter two countries, however, both reformed their public sectors and laid the groundwork for a much more modern bureaucracy. In Britain, an aristocrat-dominated, patronage-laden civil service was reformed over a brief fifteen-year period and replaced by highly educated professional civil servants. In the United States, patronage was deeply entrenched and took much longer to eradicate: the two political parties, Republican and Democratic, had evolved around the distribution of jobs in the civil service and resisted tenaciously the effort to replace political appointees with merit-based civil servants. It took two generations of continuing political struggle stretching into the early twentieth century to fix this system.

As we have already seen, democracy can make political reform difficult. The United States, by opening up the franchise to all white males a good sixty to seventy years earlier than Britain, not only pioneered the development of mass political parties but also invented the practice of clientelism. Britain by contrast remained a restrictive oligarchy throughout much of the nineteenth century and could thus reform its civil service before mass political parties were ever tempted to use public office as a currency for buying votes.

England's position as an island gave it considerable protection, and it never faced the existential threats that landlocked Prussia did. Thus while its Admiralty gained substantially in professionalism during the numerous wars it fought during the eighteenth and early nineteenth centuries, the rest of the civil service remained heavily patronage based. While the establishment of parliamentary accountability created pressures to rein in some of the worst abuses of public office, the elites were quite happy to use government service as a means of advancing their own interests and the interests of their relatives and supporters.[1] Personal connections rather than merit were the means by which individuals were placed in positions of responsibility. Consider the following letter from Mrs. Cecilia Blackwood to Lord John Russell in 1849: "A drowning man catches at a straw but I look upon it as a very substantial straw, you being not only the greatest man in England but the most powerful man in the world . . . When I reflect that your mother and my father were first cousins, I hope to come within the warmth of your rays. We now propose sending my son to Cambridge . . . I shall live in the hope that he may at some time, if not immediately, be placed by you in some suitable situation."[2] People in all societies trade upon their connections, but in early-nineteenth-century Britain, connections within a very small elite were all that existed for appointment to government office. As a result, there was no regular civil service as there was in Prussia, with its highly autonomous and elite bureaucracy. Rather, there was a collection of well-connected officeholders of questionable competence and often nonexistent training.

One of the early efforts to curb Crown patronage was inaugurated by the great statesman and philosopher Edmund Burke in 1780 with an attack on placemen (patronage appointees) and sinecures.[3] Another early target for reform was the Indian Civil Service (ICS). Britain did not rule India directly until the Rebellion of 1858; instead, it chartered a commercial corporation, the East India Company, which exercised quasi-governmental authority on the subcontinent. The very term "civil service" originated in India as a means of distinguishing the East India Company's civilian employees from its military ones.[4] The men who volunteered for the ICS were not the cream of British society; working conditions and long years away from home made it a haven for dropouts, adventurers, and men who had failed in occupations at home. In the words of Adam Smith, a thousand pounds of company stock gave a "share . . . not in the plunder, yet in the appointment of the plunderers of India." A directorship of the company paid a very small salary but entailed enormous benefits in a director's ability to dispense jobs and moneymaking opportunities to friends, relatives, and clients.[5]

The work of the ICS was, nonetheless, varied and demanding, and required a broad range of administrative skills. Recognizing the need to improve the quality of civil servants there, the company's directors established a college at Haileybury to train young recruits in oriental languages, mathematics, literature, law, and history. The government, recognizing the need for a better class of civil servants, pressed the directors to establish competitive selection in place of the nominations that were up to then used to fill vacancies. In the debate over the Government of India Act of 1833 that would renew the company's charter, Thomas Babington Macaulay (later Lord Macaulay) made an impassioned argument for open competition and educational qualifications as the basis for service in India. Macaulay would go on to serve on the Supreme Council of India between 1834 and 1838, where he introduced reforms of the educational system, making English a major language of instruction, and of the Indian penal code.[6]

The directors of the East India Company initially rejected these demands for open recruitment because it was not in their interest to do so: they were in effect a rent-seeking coalition that used their control over appointments to enrich themselves. Moreover, there was a strong class interest in keeping the recruitment pool very narrow; of the civilians sent to India between 1860 and 1874, almost three-quarters were sons of the aristocracy, gentry, army, navy, the ICS itself, or one of the learned professions. Reform of the ICS did not occur until the rise of an energetic young official in its ranks, Sir Charles Trevelyan.[7]

Trevelyan came from a baronet's family, attended Haileybury, and worked at a number of jobs for the East India Company including deputy secretary in Calcutta. His experience with the unreformed company made him a bitter enemy of patronage and a believer in a meritocratic society open to all. He was disgusted with India as the "sink to which the scum and refuse of the English professions habitually gravitates."[8] Trevelyan met Macaulay in India and later married Macaulay's sister, and the two collaborated closely on reform of the ICS. Trevelyan then moved on to the Treasury where in 1840 he became assistant secretary, in effect the head of the agency. While proving himself an able administrator, Trevelyan noted that the bureau was badly organized and suffered from many of the same dysfunctions as the ICS.[9]

Together with Sir Stafford Northcote, who had been William Gladstone's private secretary at the Board of Trade, Trevelyan drafted the Northcote-Trevelyan Report in 1854, a document of just over twenty pages that was actually not so much a break with the past as the culmination of a series of reports on public-sector reform, including the ICS, that had been produced in the previous decade.[10] It called for an end to patronage appointments and for civil service examinations as a gateway into government service. It also proposed splitting routine clerical duties from higher administrative functions, and setting high educational requirements for the latter. The kind of humanistic education that the report identified as necessary, while theoretically open to all social classes, in fact restricted the candidate pool to the aristocracy and upper middle class who had the money and connections to send their sons to Oxford and Cambridge. Nonetheless, these strict educational requirements shifted the British government much closer to the Prussian and French models, and meant that administrators would actually develop into a service with its own solidarity and autonomy.

While individuals like Trevelyan were motivated by their hatred of a government dominated by incompetent aristocrats, this kind of reform could not have been possible except under the exclusive conditions of British upper-class life. Trevelyan was, as noted earlier, related to Macaulay, who was in turn a confidant of Gladstone, chancellor of the exchequer at the time of the Northcote-Trevelyan Report, who would go on to be prime minister for the first of his four terms in office in 1868. Northcote was Gladstone's personal secretary, and all were friends of Benjamin Jowett, master of Balliol College, Oxford, and a leader in the movement to reform the university system.[11] These elite personal connections were sufficient to create a coalition in Parliament to push through the writing of the Trevelyan-Northcote Report and, eventually, the reform itself. This manner of operating stood in sharp contrast to the United States, where there was no cohesive elite, and where reform ideas had to be argued out and fought on a state-by-state basis in a much larger and more diverse society.

A second group of elites in England, led by John Stuart Mill, Edwin Chadwick, and an organization of businessmen called the Administrative Reform Association, also promoted meritocratic civil service recruitment and an examination system. The intellectual genesis of this group lay in the utilitarian ideas of Jeremy Bentham and John Stuart

Mill's father, James Mill, who emphasized rationality and efficiency in administration. They were popularized through groups like the Political Economy Club and the Society for the Diffusion of Useful Knowledge. John Stuart Mill himself had worked for the East India Company (of which he seems to have had a more positive impression than Trevelyan) and contributed an important memo on reform while the Northcote-Trevelyan Report was being drafted.[12] Unlike the Trevelyan-Northcote group, however, they favored not a humanistic or liberal education but a technical one focusing on the sciences, economics, and engineering, the type of training one would get at the London School of Economics rather than Oxford and Cambridge. They argued that these practical skills would be better suited to government service than knowledge of Greek and Latin, and would along the way decrease the advantages of the upper classes that dominated the Oxbridge system.[13]

These reformist ideas were circulated through a new popular media read by the middle class, and by the countless new clubs and societies that sprang up in the first half of the nineteenth century to promote industry, science, technology, and reform like the Society for the Diffusion of Useful Knowledge. They were also supported by a broad revolution in values that had been taking shape during the preceding century, a shift from what economist Albert Hirschman has called the passions to the interests. The older aristocracy was descended from a warrior caste that prized glory, honor, and bravery; it disdained commercial activity and moneymaking as unworthy of gentlemen. Work was not valued for its own sake, which is why children of the aristocracy were content to coast through Oxford and Cambridge based on their connections, riding, hunting, and drinking rather than studying. The new middle classes, by contrast, had only their hard work and talents to offer, and through their entrepreneurial energy were creating vast amounts of new wealth.[14]

The university system would not have been able to play the key role assigned to it had it not itself undergone considerable reform. At the beginning of the nineteenth century, British universities were characterized, in the words of Richard Chapman, by "lethargy, corruption, and sinecurism," with Oxford professors virtually having ceased to lecture. He reports how Lord Eldon graduated in 1770: "By way of examination he was asked only two questions to test him in Hebrew and History: 'What is the Hebrew for the place of a skull?' and 'Who founded University College?' By replying 'Golgotha' and 'King Alfred' he tells us that he satisfied the examiners who asked him nothing else."[15] In a process that intensified by the middle of the century, however, the universities were subject to successive waves of reform to improve their standards and increase their openness, including the Oxford Act of 1854, the Cambridge Act of 1856, and the Universities Tests Act of 1871 that eliminated religious tests as conditions for admission. In addition, the University of London was founded in 1836; it as well as other schools increased competition for Oxford and Cambridge and contributed to the debate on educational reform. Benjamin Jowett was a key figure in upgrading the examination system, which made him a natural coconspirator in the civil service reform efforts.

Behind all of this reform activity across a wide variety of institutions was one outstanding social fact: the Industrial Revolution was kicking into high gear in Britain and bringing with it a massive change in the country's social structure. The older agrarian society with its great landowners radiating power and authority was rapidly being displaced by an urban one led by industrialists and entrepreneurs. In the words of Richard Chapman,

> Middle-class radicals—whose significance had grown as a result of the industrial revolution and puritan attitudes associated with 'the onward march of the nonconformist conscience' . . . —felt that much that they believed to be wrong in government was primarily the result of patronage. This middle-class attack was based on the assumption that it was the landed aristocracy who exercised patronage, in their own interests; and it was, in fact, part of the aristocratic system of government (as with the Army and Navy) and it was both inefficient and indefensible.[16]

These middle-class groups had a direct interest in getting access for their children to Oxford and Cambridge, and to find employment for them in the civil service.[17]

The British middle classes chose to advocate universalistic, merit-based standards of advancement in all institutions. They did this out of self-interest, but as a general social class rather than as individuals. This stood in sharp contrast to the less entrepreneurial middle classes in southern Italy, who were co-opted by the local oligarchy and incorporated into its patronage networks.

Publication of the Northcote-Trevelyan Report in 1854 did not lead to the immediate adoption of its recommendations. Changing the conditions for entry into the civil service threatened the interests of the incumbent officeholders and the upper classes from which they came. In 1855, an Order of Council established a Civil Service Commission that authorized competition for a small number of jobs.[18] Enactment of the proposals in the full report by Parliament was delayed until 1870, when Gladstone had become prime minister. As the report had proposed, the new law divided the civil service into halves, an administrative one that would require a liberal humanistic education for entry, and a lower executive class whose qualification was a less exalted "English education" in English language and modern subjects. This two-tier system opened up employment for the offspring of both the upper and middle bourgeoisie while also preserving places for the old aristocracy that could use their Oxbridge educations to pass the new examination.

Contributing to the momentum for an overhaul of the civil service was the Crimean War (1853–1856). Operations of the British army were badly mismanaged, and in 1855 a Select Committee of Inquiry reported on the poor organization of the army in intelligence, strategy, and logistics. This caused a furor in the press, with demands for an overhaul of both the military and the civil service. Thus, even in a country that was nowhere as militaristically inclined as either Prussia or Japan, war and the risk of life to soldiers and civilians created pressures for reform that could not be generated in peacetime.[19]

It is critical that this reform of the British public sector took place before expansion of the franchise. There were three great reform bills passed during the nineteenth century that transformed Britain from an oligarchy to a genuine democracy (although full franchise expansion to women and minorities did not occur until the twentieth century). The 1832 reform eliminated certain gross abuses in the electoral system, such as rotten boroughs (electoral districts with few or no voters that became sinecures for elite politicians). Up through the 1860s, only one out of eight British citizens could vote.[20] Expansion of the franchise to include most householders had to await the 1867 and 1884 reforms, after which some 40 percent of British adult males, including lodgers, tenants, domestic servants, soldiers, and sailors, were still not permitted to vote. The comparable number of disenfranchised in the United States at the time was 14 percent.[21] (I will return to the question of why those bills passed in Part III below.) Thus the mobilization of voters that had occurred already in the United States by the 1830s, and the development of mass political parties, did not get under way in Britain until the 1870s, by which time the groundwork for an autonomous civil service had already been laid. At the point when British parties might have been tempted to use the mass distribution of government jobs as vote-getting opportunities, this avenue had already been closed off.

Even after the franchise was expanded, British parties were slow to marshal large numbers of voters. The most clientelistic party in this period was the Conservative or Tory party, many of whose leaders were influential landowners who could draw on support from their nonelite rural constituents. Indeed, one of the reasons why the Conservative prime minister Benjamin Disraeli, himself an inveterate user of patronage appointments, supported the 1867 Reform Bill was that he believed his party could keep control over an expanded voter base. The party was split over the next decades, however, between the older landed elite and a new elite of middle-class supporters, many of whom were incorporated into the party through the award of honorific titles rather than government jobs.[22] The opposition Whig or Liberal party was the party of the middle class, and again not inclined to broaden itself into a mass party.

It was the British Labour Party that would mobilize the working class and eventually replace the Liberals as the second party in British politics. The Labour Party was the political arm of the Trades Union Congress, which was organized in the late 1800s, and was founded in 1900. Growing out of various left-wing movements, and with a strong Socialist ideology, the Labour Party was an externally organized party that had to rally its supporters around programmatic issues like working conditions, wages, and state control of industry rather than through doling out government resources. When it first joined the government during World War I and finally came to power on its own in 1924, it had no access to the bureaucracy and was in any event already institutionalized as a modern party.[23]

While the Northcote-Trevelyan reforms constituted the most dramatic break with the traditional patronage system, it is fair to say that the British public sector has been undergoing a continuous series of incremental reforms from at least 1780 up to the present. There were many subsequent reform commissions, including the Playfair Commission of 1874–1875, the Ridley Commission of 1886–1890, the MacDonnell Commission of 1912–1915, the Reorganization Committee of 1919–1920, the Tomlin Commission of 1929–1931, and the Priestly Commission of 1953–1954.[24]

The last major public-sector reform effort was undertaken during the 1990s by Tony Blair under the heading of New Public Management.[25]

While reform of the British public sector was a prolonged and, in some sense, uncompleted process, elimination of the patronage system was relatively straightforward. Intellectuals and social critics made the case for reform, a case that was propagated and argued in the media in response to events like the Crimean War. An expert commission then studied the question in depth and came up with a series of recommendations, which were enacted into law by Parliament. The most important actors in the process were all part of a small elite based for the most part in London (though with common roots in British India). All had similar educations and knew one another personally; indeed, some were related. The British Westminster system is heavily biased toward rapid decision making because it has very few checks and balances: in the 1850s there was no federalism or decentralization, no supreme court to invalidate legislation, no separation of powers between executive and legislature, and strong party discipline (control of rank-and-file MPs by the party leadership). When the composition of the British elite began to change and middle-class actors began to displace the older oligarchy, their wishes could be reflected in legislation relatively quickly.

The same was not true in the United States, whose constitutional system of checks and balances makes large changes in public policy very difficult and time-consuming. But more important were social differences: there was no single cohesive elite in the United States, and indeed the democratic basis of its founding guaranteed that existing elites would be constantly challenged by new social actors. For this reason the United States did not go straight from an elite patronage system to a modern civil service; rather, it took a century-long detour through party-dominated clientelism. The American experience in contrast to the British suggests two things: first, that patronage and clientelism are not culturally specific phenomena, nor do they represent premodern practices that somehow survived as societies modernized. Rather, they are the natural outgrowth of political mobilization in early-stage democracies. Second, the experience of a more democratic America suggests that there is an inherent tension between democracy and what we now call "good governance."

9

THE UNITED STATES INVENTS CLIENTELISM

How America is different from other modern countries; the nature of early American government and the rise of political parties; the Jacksonian revolution and American populism; the patronage system and how it spread; clientelism and American municipal government

Since the era of Ronald Reagan and Margaret Thatcher in the 1980s, it has been common to contrast "Anglo-Saxon" capitalism to its continental variety. The former celebrates free markets, deregulation, privatization, and a minimal state, while the continental version, exemplified above all by France, is dirigiste and regulatory, and supports a large welfare state. But while the United States does indeed share many political characteristics and policy preferences with its English progenitor, this view lacks historical perspective and hides some important differences between British and American political development. In many ways Britain's political system is closer to its continental neighbors than it is to the American one.

In the second chapter of *Political Order in Changing Societies*, titled "Political Modernization: America vs. Europe," Samuel Huntington identified the "Tudor" character of American politics.[1] According to Huntington, the Englishmen who settled North America in the seventeenth century brought with them many of the political practices of Tudor, or late medieval, England. On American soil these old institutions became entrenched and were eventually written into the American Constitution, a fragment of the old society frozen in time.[2] Those Tudor characteristics included the Common Law as a source of authority, one higher than that of the executive, with a correspondingly strong role for courts in governance; a tradition of local self-rule; sovereignty divided among a host of bodies, rather than being concentrated in a centralized state; government with divided powers instead of divided functions, such that, for example, the judiciary exercised not just judicial but also quasi-legislative functions; and reliance on a popular militia rather than a standing army.

Huntington argued that after the Tudor period, England went on to develop the concept of a unified sovereignty and a centralized state in the eighteenth and nineteenth centuries. As we saw in the preceding chapter, England was slower to develop a rational, modern bureaucracy than either Prussia or France, but by the late 1800s this had occurred. The local governing bodies of medieval England evolved into parliamentary districts, with authority increasingly centralized in London; in the years following the Glorious Revolution, Parliament came to be understood as the sole source of sovereignty. While the Common Law remained sacrosanct, England never developed a theory or practice of judicial review by which the courts could invalidate an act of Parliament. Americans, by contrast, clung to Tudor institutions: "Political modernization in America has thus been strangely attenuated and incomplete. In institutional terms, the American polity has never been underdeveloped, but it has also never been wholly modern . . . In today's world, American political institutions are unique, if only because they are so antique."[3]

Huntington's observations echo those of a long tradition of writers on American exceptionalism who have described the ways the United States differs systematically from other developed democracies. This begins with writers such as Louis Hartz and H. G. Wells, who raised the question "Why no socialism in America?"[4] through Seymour Martin Lipset, who wrote extensively on American exceptionalism throughout a long scholarly career.[5] The United States was different, according to Hartz, because it lacked the inherited feudal class structure of Europe. As an area of new settlement (at least for Europeans), North America appeared as a land of equal opportunity where one's station in life reflected one's own work and talents. With few inherited inequalities, there was no demand for a strong state that would redistribute wealth, but rather widespread belief in a Lockean liberalism where individuals were free to help themselves. The one group that did face castelike restrictions to its mobility, African Americans, were therefore the most likely to favor a strong state to advance their interests, much like the white working class in Europe.[6]

There was another factor as well. Lipset noted that the United States was born in a revolution against the concentrated power represented by the British monarchy. Hence liberty, understood as antistatism and animated by strong distrust of government, was one of what he identified as five key components of American political culture.[7] America inherited from Tudor England traditions of the Common Law and, following the Glorious Revolution, accountable government based on the principle of no taxation without representation. What it did not inherit was the strong central state, which in England had always incipiently existed since the Norman Conquest and that had evolved into a powerful unified sovereignty by the beginning of the eighteenth century. The very struggle for independence from Britain amplified the American antistatist tendency and ensured that a host of constraints on government power would be enshrined in the new nation's Constitution in the form of multiple checks and balances. Nor did the physical conditions of the early United States encourage state building: America faced no powerful neighbors that could threaten it, and its physical size and dispersed rural population meant it would almost inevitably have to be governed on a decentralized basis.

FRIENDS OF GEORGE WASHINGTON

While Hartz was correct that the white population in America was not divided into sharply demarcated social classes as in Europe, there were in fact class distinctions in early America based on education and occupation, such as the merchant-banker elite in New York and Boston and the planter aristocracy in Virginia. The elite at this time was a small and homogeneous group, "descended from the same ancestors, speaking the same language, professing the same religion, attached to the same principles of government, very similar in their manners and customs," in the words of John Jay in Federalist No. 2. In the period immediately following ratification of the Constitution in 1789, the national public service at its upper levels has been described as a "Government by Gentlemen" and it did not look too different in certain respects from the one that existed in early-nineteenth-century Britain.[8] One might also label it government by the friends of George Washington, since the republic's first president chose men like himself who he felt had good qualifications and a dedication to public service.[9] Under John Adams, 70 percent, and under Jefferson, 60 percent of high-ranking officials had fathers who came from the landed gentry, merchant, or professional classes.[10] Many people today marvel at the quality of political leadership at the time of America's founding, the sophistication of the discourse revealed in the Federalist Papers, and the ability to think about institutions in a long-term perspective. At least part of the reason for this strong leadership was that America at the time was not a full democracy but rather a highly elitist society, many of whose leaders were graduates of Harvard and Yale. Like the British elite, many of them knew each other personally from school and from their common participation in the revolution and drafting of the Constitution.

History textbooks traditionally date the rise of the patronage system from the election of Andrew Jackson in 1828. By our earlier terminology, however, the U.S. government in the period from 1789 to 1828 was more properly a patronage system, while the one that arose thereafter was a clientelistic one. From the election of Thomas Jefferson in 1800 and the replacement of the Federalists by the Republicans, presidents began using their power of appointment to place their own political allies in positions of power, as British prime ministers did before 1870. Jefferson made seventy-three of ninety-two possible appointments since "continuation of everything in federalist hands was not to be expected"; his successors James Madison and James Monroe did much the same.[11] Both the Federalists and Jeffersonians made these appointments out of a fairly narrow range of local notables, with high social status, loyalty, and good breeding as the primary qualifications for office.[12]

The only Founding Father who showed an interest in strong and capable government was Alexander Hamilton, who laid out the case for "energy in the executive" in Federalist Nos. 70–77. As the first secretary of the treasury, he built up a large bureaucracy within what was at the time the U.S. government's chief administrative arm. But he was strongly opposed by Thomas Jefferson, who articulated America's enduring distrust of bureaucracy and large government in his first Inaugural Address: "We may well doubt whether our organization is too complicated, too expensive; whether offices and officers have not been multiplied unnecessarily and sometimes injuriously to the service they were meant to promote." And this was spoken at a time when the whole U.S. government encompassed only about three thousand individuals!

That government was destined to grow quite rapidly to twenty thousand employees by 1831. It still did not, however, constitute a large bureaucracy by European standards, given the size of the country.[13] Up until the Civil War, Washington, D.C., remained a small town by the standards of New York and Philadelphia, not to mention London and

Paris, with a population of only about sixty-one thousand.[14] The federal government was divided into two categories: high-ranking officials including cabinet members and their assistants, overseas ministers, territorial governors, bureau chiefs, and the like; and lower-level clerks, customs officials, postal employees, surveyors, etc.[15] While there was an incipient navy, the United States had no need to maintain a large standing army and relied entirely on local militias for security. The government that most Americans dealt with day to day was at a state or local level.

POLITICAL MOBILIZATION AND THE RISE OF PARTIES

It is impossible to understand the rise of clientelism except in the context of the emergence of modern democracy and the appearance of the first mass political parties. The United States was a pioneer in these respects.

Political parties did not exist prior to electoral democracy, unless one counts the mobs of clienteles that Roman politicians could mobilize to rally and intimidate opponents. What preceded them were elite factions of patrons and clients of the sort we saw operating in the British Parliament in the eighteenth and nineteenth centuries. Personalistic factions and patronage exist within all authoritarian systems, from the courts of monarchical Europe to the contemporary Chinese Communist Party. It was only the advent of electoral democracy that created incentives to form what we today recognize as modern political parties.[16]

It is well known that the American Constitution makes no provision for political parties, and that many of the Founding Fathers were hostile to the idea that parties should come to govern the country. James Madison in Federalist No. 10 famously warned about the danger of what he called "faction." By this he meant precisely the kinds of elite patronage networks that characterized court politics in Europe, which he saw as having led to the downfall of the classical republics in Greece and Rome. George Washington in his Farewell Address warned against "the baneful effects of the Spirit of Party; a conflict that would divide and potentially destroy the new nation," as did his successor, John Adams, who argued that "a division of the republic into two great parties . . . is to be dreaded as the greatest political evil under our Constitution." This hostility sprang from the very idea of parties as partial representations of the community whose competition would lead to division and disunity.

They hoped instead that the country would be led by public-spirited individuals who would seek only the good of the country as a whole. The Federalist Party of John Adams and Alexander Hamilton had many of the characteristics of an elite faction rather than a modern party; many historians credit the Jeffersonian Republicans who mobilized a coalition of opposing interests and succeeded in electing Jefferson president as founders of the first real political party in America.[17]

While the Founding Fathers were remarkably prescient in their design of institutions needed to govern the new democracy, they failed to see the need for a mechanism to mobilize voters and manage mass political participation. Political parties perform a number of critical functions and are now recognized as indispensable to well-functioning democracies: they provide for collective action on the part of like-minded people, they aggregate disparate social interests around a common platform, they provide valuable information to voters by articulating positions and policies of common concern, and they create a stability of expectations in a way that contests between individual politicians cannot.[18] Most important is the fact that they are the primary mechanisms by which ordinary citizens are mobilized to participate in competitive democratic politics.[19] Political parties thus emerged, unplanned, as a response to the requirements of a democratic political system with a rapidly expanding franchise.

Despite the exclusion of African Americans, women, Native Americans, and propertyless men from voting, America had from the beginning a much wider franchise than any country in Europe. Property qualifications for voting arose out of the old English Whig view that only those who paid taxes (and therefore had some level of property and income) should have a share in government. As Alexis de Tocqueville noted, however, America was founded on a deeper principle of equality and self-rule by the common man. In this spirit, many states began to lift property requirements for voting by the 1820s. Elections, which up to that point had been elite-driven affairs, were all of a sudden opened up to a whole new class of voters.

THE JACKSONIAN REVOLUTION

Andrew Jackson came from what was then frontier Tennessee and won military fame by defeating the British at the Battle of New Orleans during the War of 1812. He first ran for president in 1824 and won a plurality of both the popular and electoral college votes. But he was denied the presidency, which was decided in the House of Representatives as a result of a deal between the other candidates, John Quincy Adams and Henry Clay. The electoral college that made this possible had been designed by the Founding Fathers precisely to permit greater elite control over the selection of presidents; Jackson denounced the outcome as a "corrupt bargain" hatched by the eastern aristocracy. Riding a wave of populist anger, and empowered by newly enfranchised voters, he was able to defeat Adams soundly in 1828.

The contrast between Jackson, the plainspoken frontiersman, and the elitist John Quincy Adams was to become an enduring one in American political culture. Adams was a quintessential member of the northeastern elite, a Boston Brahmin who had traveled widely in Europe with his father, John Adams, spoke several languages, and graduated Phi Beta Kappa from Harvard College. Jackson, by contrast, came from a relatively undistinguished backwoods family, had a spotty formal education, and made his reputation largely as a fighter and brawler.[20] It was precisely Jackson's nonelite background that made him familiar to and popular with the country's newly expanded electorate. The Adams-Jackson contrast has strong echoes today when comparing the Yale-educated Boston Brahmin John Kerry with the anti-elitist conservative hero Sarah Palin.

Jackson's presidency was the foundation of what Walter Russell Mead has labeled the Jacksonian tradition of populism in American politics that continues up to the present day and finds echoes in groups like the Tea Party that emerged after the 2008 election of Barack Obama.[21] This tradition has its roots in the so-called Scotch-Irish settlers who began arriving in North America in the middle decades of the eighteenth century.[22] They hailed from northern Ireland, the Scottish lowlands, and the parts of northern England bordering on Scotland. These regions were the least economically developed in Britain, and it was indeed their high levels of poverty that drove hundreds of thousands of Scotch-Irish to emigrate. The Scotch-Irish were poor but intensely proud both in Britain and in the United States. The more elite English found this pride irritating since, in the words of historian David Hackett Fischer, they "could not understand what they had to feel proud about."[23]

These emigrants from Britain came from what had been an extraordinarily violent region, racked by centuries of fighting between local warlords, and between these warlords and the English. Out of this environment came an intense individualism, as well as a love of guns, which would become the origins of the American gun culture. The Scotch-Irish became pugnacious Indian fighters; Jackson led his Tennessee volunteers in campaigns to drive the Creeks from Georgia and northern Alabama and the Seminoles from Florida.[24] They settled in what at the time was the frontier, the mountains of Appalachia extending from western Virginia through the Carolinas into Tennessee and Georgia. They would lead the push westward; Davy Crockett and Sam Houston, heroes of the Alamo, had served under Jackson in the Creek War. The descendants of these Scotch-Irish settlers would go on to populate a band that stretched from the Appalachians through Texas and Oklahoma and on, particularly after the Dust Bowl of the 1930s, into Southern California.

Inevitably, the Scotch-Irish, driven by a strong frontier spirit, would come into conflict with existing American elites, dominated by the New England Puritans and the Quakers who had settled the Delaware Valley. The Adams-Jackson contests of 1824 and 1828 were about breaking the hold of these older elites on American politics and the assertion of a new populist brand of politics.

When Jackson came into office in 1829, he said that since he had won the election, he should decide who was appointed to federal offices, since the earlier patronage distribution of offices had turned officeholding into "a species of property" for the elite.[25] In addition, he enunciated a "doctrine of the simplicity of work," stating that "the duties of all public offices are, or at least admit of being made, so plain and simple that men of intelligence may readily qualify themselves for their performance."[26] This anti-elitist argument was articulated at a time when the average level of education in the United States did not go much beyond elementary school.[27] Jackson's system was one of frequent rotation of officials in office since "no one man has any more intrinsic right to official station than another," a practice that created enormous opportunities for placing party loyalists in bureaucratic positions.[28] These offices could then be used as a basis for mobilizing political followers in campaigns: Jackson had converted an existing elite patronage system into the beginnings of a mass clientelistic one. (In American history books, it is of course traditional to call this the "patronage" or "spoils" system.)[29]

The party system that evolved in the United States in the succeeding decades, both at the federal and municipal levels, emerged spontaneously from the political needs of a new democracy. With an expanded franchise, politicians needed a way to get supporters to the polls and to persuade them to demonstrate on their behalf at parades, marches, and rallies. Although programmatic issues such as tariffs or land rights were important to some voters, the promise of a job or a personal favor was a much more effective means of activating a new class of poor and relatively uneducated voters. The fact that this happened in the United States, the first country to experiment with an expanded democratic franchise, suggests that the ensuing clientelism should not be regarded as an aberration or deviation from "normal" democratic practice, but rather as a natural outgrowth of newly implanted democracy in a relatively underdeveloped country. No country, the United States included, ever leaps to a modern political system in a single bound.

A STATE OF COURTS AND PARTIES

The political system that emerged after the Jacksonian revolution became what political scientist Stephen Skowronek has labeled a "state of courts and parties."[30] That is, the two institutions of constraint, the rule of law and accountability, were the most highly developed. What did not exist in nineteenth-century America was a centralized, bureaucratic, and autonomous state of the sort that had been created in Prussia, France, and Britain.

The emerging political parties substituted for the state by exercising a high degree of control over the operations of the government. This can be seen in drawing up budgets, which in European parliamentary systems is most often done in the executive branch but which in nineteenth-century America was exclusively the domain of the parties in Congress. Party control brought "a measure of cohesion to national politics and a measure of standardization to governmental forms and processes . . . Parties organized governmental institutions internally . . . routinized administrative procedures with patronage recruitment, spoils rotation, and external controls over the widely scattered post offices, land offices, and customs houses."[31] The parties could play this integrative role only at the expense of developing clear programmatic goals, since the vast coalitions they represented had few common purposes. The courts did not restrict themselves to judicial functions but increasingly defined the boundaries between the responsibilities of the different parts of government, regulated relations between government and citizen, and involved themselves in substantive policy decisions.[32] Thus Huntington could argue that the United States divided powers rather than functions. The legislative and judicial branches began to take on functions normally performed by the executive in European political systems.

This does not mean that the United States was badly governed; for the first two-thirds of the nineteenth century, there was little that the national government needed to do beyond running customshouses and post offices, and distributing land. The American economy was agrarian and spread out over a vast territory, localized around isolated farms and villages; there were no significant foreign threats and therefore no need for mass military mobilization. Ideologically as well, nothing in the Lockean inheritance justified looking to the state as the protector of the common good, in the manner of Hegel's bureaucratic universal class.[33]

Without pressure to reform, party-managed clientelism developed over time, and reached a peak of sorts in the period just prior to the Civil War. In 1849, President Zachary Taylor replaced 30 percent of all federal officials during his first year in office; Democrat James Buchanan replaced a similar number of officials in 1857 despite the fact that he was succeeding another Democrat, Franklin Pierce.[34] Abraham Lincoln was overwhelmed by patronage requests after his election in 1860; when reelected four years later, he hoped to keep as many officeholders as possible in place because "the bare thought of going through again what I did the first year here, would crush me."[35] The military itself was open to political appointments, such as that of Dan Sickles, a New York politician who was made brigadier general in 1861, where his poor judgment caused major problems for the Union side at Chancellorsville and Gettysburg.[36] The satirist Artemus Ward suggested that the Union Army's retreat at the Battle of Bull Run was caused by a rumor of three vacancies at the New York Custom House.[37] Lincoln complained about the endless stream of office seekers he had to deal with, but he was trapped in a system in which doling out bureaucratic offices was an integral part of building political coalitions.

As in ancient China and early modern Europe, war proved to be a spur for American state building. During the Civil War, the size of the Union Army went from fifteen thousand to well over a million and involved the creation of a gigantic bureaucratic system to supply and move such large numbers of men. The U.S. Capitol building was renovated and its huge dome completed in this period. The Civil War also precipitated a shift in the way Americans thought of themselves: before the war, they would say, "The United States are," reflecting the country's federal origins, while after it, it became more common to say, "The United States is," signifying the union that Lincoln had gone to war to save.[38]

This moment of state centralization was, however, fleeting. The country quickly returned to its deeply embedded Tudor traditions. The Union Army was demobilized quickly after the war and returned to being a small frontier force dispatched to distant western forts. The executive branch structure responsible for war mobilization was dismantled and the control of government resources returned to the political parties. With Reconstruction and the return of the southern states to the Union, the period of Republican hegemony ended and a two-party system came to dominate politics until the end of the century. All that remained of the wartime state, according to historian Morton Keller, was a series of military metaphors applied to party politics: political campaigns, party standard bearers, rank and file, precinct captains, and the like.[39]

The political system that emerged in the 1870s and '80s was in fact a far more highly organized form of clientelism than the antebellum one. Because of the country's rapidly expanding size and growing social complexity, the older forms of face-to-face relationships gave way, at a national level, to a much more highly organized and hierarchical structure by which the parties distributed favors and offices.[40] Lord Bryce, a British observer, noted that "what characterizes [American politicians] as compared with the corresponding class in Europe is that their whole time is more frequently given to political work, that most of them draw an income from politics and the rest hope to do so, that they come largely from the poorer and less cultivated than from the higher ranks of society, and that . . . many are proficients in the arts of popular oratory, of electioneering, and of party management."[41] The very term "political machine" suggests the degree of organization that was required to make late nineteenth-century clientelism work.

BOSSES AND CITY POLITICS

American clientelism was most highly developed on a municipal level and survived there for the longest time. Political machines were erected in virtually all the major eastern, midwestern, and southern cities, where they served as mechanisms for mobilizing large numbers of nonelite voters.[42] They were particularly important in New York, Chicago, Boston, Philadelphia, and other cities that saw, toward the end of the century, a huge influx of emigrants from Eastern and Southern Europe who had never before voted. The spontaneous emergence of these machines in response to an expanding base of relatively poor voters again suggests that clientelism is an efficient way of energizing this type of population and therefore should be seen as an early form of democratic participation. It differed very much from the type of patron-client relationships that existed in southern Italy in the nineteenth century, where existing elites could use their wealth and social status to organize and dominate large numbers of poor voters. In America, by contrast, clientelism was a way for ambitious but nonelite politicians to become wealthy and increase their social status, while delivering concrete benefits to their supporters. Some early writers on machine politics suggested that there was a cultural or ethnic dimension to American clientelism, since many of the machines recruited voters who were Irish or Italian Catholics, while the reformers tended to be relatively high-status Anglo-Saxon Protestants.[43] But machines also were set up in Lexington, Kentucky, and Kansas City, Missouri, which didn't have significant numbers of recent immigrants or Catholic voters. The real issue was class, since clientelism has a more direct appeal to poorer and less-educated citizens.

Municipal-level political machines were simply modernized and highly organized versions of the Melanesian Big Man and tribal *wantok*, in which an elected leader develops a base of political support by giving out individualized benefits to his supporters.[44] In nineteenth-century America, the scale of organization required even in a relatively small city like Lexington was substantial: successful bosses tried to maintain personal relationships with as many supporters as possible, but they needed to recruit precinct captains and ward heelers as intermediaries to manage recruitment of voters, distribution of resources, and monitoring of voter behavior. It was these individuals who had to have detailed knowledge of their constituents and be able to cater to their needs. The individualized benefits given out could vary from jobs in the post office or city hall to Thanksgiving turkeys to hods of coal. Billy Klair, the boss of Lexington, used his control over the city's police force to selectively enforce anti-alcohol laws during Prohibition.[45]

There is no end of colorful characters and stories that can be told about American municipal machine politics.[46] Perhaps the most famous was New York's Tammany Hall, established in 1789 as a charitable organization formally known as the Society of Saint Tammany. In the mid-nineteenth century it was dominated by William Marcy Tweed. Boss Tweed, as he was known, and his Tweed Ring managed to enrich themselves substantially due to their control over public contracting. For example, the New York State legislature authorized a new courthouse in 1858 that was budgeted to cost no more than $250,000. By 1862, the building had not been completed and Tweed authorized an additional $1 million toward its construction. By 1871, the courthouse was still not finished, and total outlays now amounted to $13 million. A special commission was appointed to investigate the project, which was itself controlled by Tweed, and which managed to funnel $14,000 in printing costs for its report to a company owned by Tweed.[47] Similar stories could be told about contemporary India, Brazil, and Nigeria; anyone who thinks this sort of corruption was an invention of contemporary poor countries is unaware of history.

Despite these outrageous instances of corruption, municipal machines like Tammany Hall did play an important positive role in mobilizing otherwise marginalized citizens and allowing them to participate in the political system. This was particularly true of recent immigrants, who were often disdained by existing elites for their religion, habits, or sheer foreignness. Municipal machines took advantage of this fact and in return provided certain key social services—for instance, a ward boss who could interpret for the newcomer at City Hall—that few other institutions in nineteenth-century American society were able to perform.

While the poor gained advantages from the party machine, their long-term interests suffered. Because they were being organized on the basis of the distribution of individual benefits rather than broad programmatic agendas, it was much harder to recruit them into working-class or Socialist parties of the sort that emerged in Britain and Germany, where working-class parties demanded more formal types of redistribution such as universal health care or occupational safety programs. One of the reasons socialism never took hold in the United States is that the

Republican and Democratic Parties captured the votes of working-class Americans by offering short-term rewards instead of long-term programmatic policy changes.[48]

In chapter 5 I made a distinction between clientelism, which involves a reciprocal exchange of benefits, and more predatory forms of corruption in which public officials simply steal. This is an important difference, but clientelism often evolves into pure corruption because politicians have the power to distribute public resources as they wish; money that could go to clients often ends up in their own pockets. This became a widespread problem in the so-called Gilded Age that began with the presidency of Ulysses S. Grant in 1869, a period characterized by a number of scandals—the Crédit Mobilier affair, the Whiskey Ring, War Secretary Belknap's selling of Indian post traderships, the "Salary Grab" in which Congress voted itself a retroactive pay raise at the end of the session from $5,000 to $7,000 per year.[49] With the growth of industrialization and the vast new concentrations of money that came with it, lobbyists emerged to mediate between private interests and Congress. The railroads in particular paid legislators on both federal and state levels to do their bidding. Several western states were commonly believed to be wholly owned by railroad interests.[50]

America in the 1880s had many similarities to contemporary developing countries. It had democratic institutions and competitive elections, but votes were bought with the currency of public office. The quality of government was generally poor, a problem mitigated only by the fact that it wasn't expected to do much in terms of fighting wars or regulating the economy. These conditions changed dramatically as the country began to industrialize in the last decades of the nineteenth century; the United States needed a European-style state, and it slowly began to build one.

10

THE END OF THE SPOILS SYSTEM

Why the United States needed a modern state in the late nineteenth century; the Garfield assassination and the genesis of the Pendleton Act; reforming machine politics in American cities; what new social groups made up a reform coalition, and their motives; why strong presidential leadership was important in bringing about change

In the period between the early 1880s and America's entry into World War I, the clientelistic system on which federal employment was based was gradually dismantled, and in New York, Chicago, Boston, and other American cities a new generation of city managers replaced the old party bosses. The foundations were thus laid for a modern state along Weberian lines at both a national and local level. The United States, having invented clientelism, successfully modernized its administrative system.

It took the United States almost two generations to accomplish what the British were able to do in the period from the issuance of the Northcote-Trevelyan reforms in 1854 to the establishment of a modern civil service in the 1870s. This reflects the different social structure and political values of the two countries, and the fact that the United States was simultaneously more democratic and more suspicious of state power than Britain. It also reflects the greater capacity of the British Westminster system for decisive action than America's system of checks and balances. The United States to the present day has never succeeded in establishing the kind of high-quality state that exists in certain other rich democracies, particularly those coming out of absolutist traditions such as Germany and Sweden. Indeed, as we will see in Part IV of this book, the quality of the American state has decayed substantially since the 1970s, undoing much of this progress.

A LIBERTARIAN PARADISE

In the early 1880s, the United States constituted the kind of small-government society that Ron Paul and other contemporary libertarians hope it will someday become again. The federal government took in less than 2 percent of GDP in taxes, mostly in the form of customs revenues and excise taxes; the work of actual governing was largely done at state and local levels; the United States was on the gold standard, with no Federal Reserve able to create discretionary money; the military was small and involved in frontier security, with no entangling foreign commitments. Presidents were weak and real power lay with Congress and the courts. Although there were no formal term limits, intense competition between the two parties led to high turnover in Congress, ensuring that most members remained amateurs. Private interests were vigorous and expanding, and indeed succeeded in capturing a great deal of Congress through payoffs and patronage.[1]

This type of government was appropriate to the agrarian society the United States had been in the first half of the century. But by the final two decades of the nineteenth century, the nature of the American economy had changed enormously. Most important was a revolution in transportation and communications technology; railroads and the telegraph now united the country on a continental scale and vastly increased the size of markets. As Adam Smith explained, the division of labor is limited by the size of the market. Americans began leaving their farms and rural communities in increasing numbers, moving to cities and settling the country's new western territories. Economic growth was increasingly linked to the institutional application of science and technology to industrial processes. The expanding division of labor, in other words, was producing massive changes in the social dimension of development: trade unions, professional societies, and urban middle classes began to appear; educational institutions such as the land-grant colleges initially established under the Morrill Act during the Civil War were producing a new generation of university-educated elites; railroads and other new industries were escaping the confines of local-level regulation.

Change in the economic and social dimensions of development thus created a demand for change in the political dimensions, particularly with respect to the state. The United States needed something that looked like a European, Weberian state in place of the party-dominated clientelistic system that had run the country up to that point. This shift began to accelerate in the early 1880s.

BIRTH OF BUREAUCRACY

Prior to the landmark 1883 Pendleton Act, there were a number of efforts at public-sector reform. A career service track requiring examinations was created in technical agencies including the Naval Observatory and the Navy Medical Corps before the Civil War, with the development of more secure tenure for some job categories. However, this was meant less to protect excellence than to prevent the removal of political appointees. President Grant signed a law authorizing an Advisory Board for the Civil Service and the beginnings of a formal merit system in 1871, but Congress defunded this body two years later because of the threat it posed to patronage.[2]

As is often the case with reform movements, it took an external event to knock the system off of its equilibrium and move it toward a different institutional order. On July 2, 1881, the newly elected president James A. Garfield was shot by a mentally unbalanced individual named Charles Guiteau, an office seeker who thought he should have been appointed U.S. consul to France. It took more than two painful months for Garfield to die,[3] and the furor over the assassination created a public movement in favor of eliminating the spoils system. Although the new president, Chester A. Arthur, and the Republican-dominated Congress resisted reform, the Democrats and a faction of the Republican Party known as the Mugwumps began agitating for change. Soon after Garfield's death, the National Civil Service Reform League was founded and a bill was introduced by Senator George H. Pendleton proposing a makeover of the public sector. The 1882 midterm elections brought the Democrats to power, with many incumbents being defeated on the basis of their continuing support for the patronage system. Reading the handwriting on the wall, the old Congress passed the Pendleton Act by overwhelming majorities in January 1883, even before the new members could take their seats.[4]

The Pendleton Act's intellectual roots lay in Europe, and in particular the Northcote-Trevelyan reforms that had been enacted in Britain a decade previously. In 1879, Dorman Eaton, a well-known New York lawyer and founder of the National Civil Service Reform League, published a study of the British civil service at the request of President Rutherford Hayes.[5] The most famous advocate of European-style bureaucracy was, however, future president Woodrow Wilson, who in the 1880s had just completed a doctorate at Johns Hopkins University in political science, and published an article in 1887 titled "The Study of Administration."[6]

The science of administration, Wilson argued, had grown up in Europe and did not exist in America, where "not much impartial scientific method is to be discerned in our administrative practices. The poisonous atmosphere of city government, the crooked secrets of state administration, the confusion, sinecurism, and corruption ever and again discovered in the bureaux at Washington forbid us to believe that any clear conceptions of what constitutes good administration are as yet very widely current in the United States."

The kind of administrative system Wilson argued for was basically the one that Max Weber would later describe; anticipating the principal-agent framework, he argued in favor of a strict separation between politics and administration.[7] Administrators were simply agents whose only job would be effective implementation, like the bureaucracy in one of the modern corporations that were just beginning to appear. Wilson, who had learned German, referred to Hegel and the bureaucratic models of Prussia and France, whose governments "made themselves too efficient to be dispensed with." These were also too autocratic to fit America's democratic condition, but they nonetheless served as goalposts for reform. Most important, he followed in the tradition of Alexander Hamilton by arguing that strong centralized government was necessary for a whole host of purposes, from regulation of railroads and telegraph to control of large corporations that in many cases were seeking to monopolize the markets in which they operated. In a statement that perfectly summarizes the dilemma of American government, he said, "The English race, consequently, has long and successfully studied the art of curbing executive power to the constant neglect of the art of perfecting executive methods. It has exercised itself much more in controlling than in energizing government. It has been more concerned to render government just and moderate than to make it facile, well-ordered and effective."[8] As we will see, the father of American public administration found it very difficult to put his theories into effect when he became president.

The Pendleton Act was drafted by the reformer Dorman Eaton and incorporated the major features of the British reform.[9] The act revived the Civil Service Commission (whose second chairman Eaton would be) and created a classified (merit-based) service whose posts would no longer be the prerogative of the parties and Congress. It ended the practice of federal appointees being required to hand back a portion of their salary to the party that had appointed them. It did not create a higher civil service in the manner of the Northcote-Trevelyan reforms, given the egalitarian proclivities of American politics. It did, however, establish a requirement for civil service examinations and the principle of merit, though with less rigorous standards than those adopted in Britain. The British reform was deliberately aimed at pulling elite graduates of Oxford and Cambridge into the civil service. There was no parallel intention of restaffing the U.S. government with Harvard and Yale alumni, but rather with qualified people of more modest educational backgrounds.[10]

The American reforms were put into place very slowly. In 1882, only 11 percent of the civil service was classified; the number grew to 46 percent by 1900. (This figure was to reach 80 percent under Franklin D. Roosevelt and 85 percent in the immediate post–World War II period, declining thereafter.)[11] Congress continued to hold on to its patronage powers and agreed to an expansion of classification only when a change of administration allowed the outgoing party to use the system to protect its own political appointees. The unclassified service remained the domain of patronage. As administrations changed hands between Presidents Hayes, Garfield, Arthur, and Cleveland, anywhere from 68 to 87 percent of fourth-class postmasters across the country turned over.[12] The power of the Civil Service Commission varied with the energy of its chairman and the backing it received from the White House. Dorman Eaton was cautious in the use of the commission's powers, and his successors tended to be even more timid.

This changed only with President Harrison's appointment in 1889 of an up-and-coming young politician from New York named Theodore Roosevelt to the commission's leadership, who made civil service reform a centerpiece of his political ambitions. But when Roosevelt left this position in 1895, the number of patronage appointments once again increased. The Civil Service Commission's own bureaucracy was often not responsive; orders it issued to follow uniform rules for promotion were not actually enforced by many federal departments.[13]

A parallel reform process unfolded in each American city dominated by a boss and a political machine. For example, the Republican machine in Chicago at the end of the nineteenth century was run by William Lorimer, a congressman and later senator who handed out food, coal, pensions, scholarships, licenses, and jobs to political supporters. When testifying before a senate committee investigating his behavior, he said, "I got that patronage from the sheriff, the county clerk, the county treasurer, all the clerks of the different courts, the State administration . . . It rarely happened . . . that any appointments of any kind, big or little, were made in the section of the city in which I lived without my recommendation." Lorimer also owned a number of businesses that did contracting for the city, and through a process of what he suggested was "honest graft" managed to accumulate considerable wealth. His machine, like those in other cities, catered to the interests of the huge number of immigrants and working-class voters who were flocking into the city to work in its new industries.[14]

Lorimer and his machine were opposed by a coalition of businessmen, professionals, and social reformers who banded together in organizations like the Municipal Voters' League and the Legislative Voters League. They tended to be highly educated middle- and upper-middle-class individuals who lived in the new suburbs surrounding downtown Chicago. Out of a sample of fifty members of the Municipal Voters' League, thirty were professionals, with lawyers constituting the great majority. These groups began agitating against corruption through reports and publicity about the backgrounds of candidates published in sympathetic newspapers; they sought to professionalize government by making it nonpartisan. Ironically, while this group spoke in the name of democracy, it actually represented the upper crust of Chicago society, an overwhelmingly Protestant group that looked down on the way that Lorimer was empowering the city's new Catholic and Jewish immigrants. Lorimer for his part was contemptuous of the municipal reformers, calling them hypocrites who were using the reform cause as a means of increasing their own power and influence. Lorimer's political career ended when an investigation uncovered fraud in his election to the Senate; he was censured and his election invalidated. Lorimer's demise was not the end of machine politics in Chicago, of course. Richard J. Daley would go on to dominate the city's politics up through the 1960s, when the mayor could still "deliver" the city for candidate John F. Kennedy.

The Chicago case demonstrates that clientelism in American municipal politics often served a fundamentally democratizing function. The Lorimer machine was not under the control of local elites; they were indeed its opponents and forced its ultimate demise. The machine's ability to distribute resources performed an integrating and stabilizing function in a rapidly growing and ethnically diverse city, just as clientelism serves to integrate and balance ethnic and religious groups in contemporary India.

The situation was different in state-level politics in neighboring Wisconsin, where powerful railroad interests and lumber corporations dominated the state legislature. Robert La Follette was elected governor in 1900 based on a coalition that included farmers, university alumni, public officials, and ethnic Scandinavian voters. He then proceeded to build his own political machine to increase taxation of the railroads, a system of primaries to replace the boss-dominated convention system to nominate candidates, and a range of social legislation backed by the labor unions that supported him. He used his connections to the University of Wisconsin as a source of staffing and ideas, and even used the school's alumni to act as "intimidators" to counteract party stalwarts at the Republican convention. The fact that La Follette had to use machine tactics to beat the machine suggests that machines themselves are in some way intrinsic to politics—that is, all political leaders must assemble coalitions whose members do not always share the same goals, and must often be brought along with bribery, inducements, threats, and argument. Woodrow Wilson would learn this lesson when he became president.[15]

ECONOMIC GROWTH AND POLITICAL CHANGE

The political system of the United States in the 1880s appeared to constitute a stable equilibrium, in which all the major political actors benefited from their ability to distribute patronage. Why, then, did the system change?

The first explanation lies in the changes that were taking place in the underlying society as a result of economic development. We saw how the Northcote-Trevelyan reforms were driven by the demands of the British middle class for access to a civil service dominated by aristocratic patronage. The middle classes in the United States played a similar role in pushing for change; the difference was that their opponent was not an aristocracy but an entrenched party system. The new actors created by industrialization had little stake in the old clientelistic system. They were mobilized into interest groups that could challenge the status quo from within the old party system.

A second explanation is a change in ideas that occurred at the same time, which challenged the legitimacy of the old system, denounced it as corrupt, and posited a vision of a modernized American state that would be much closer to contemporaneous European models. Change on the level of ideas was related to change in society: reformers of the Progressive Era tended to come from precisely the strata of educated, professional, and middle-class people the modernization process was creating. But ideas are never simply "superstructure" or justifications for class interests; they have an internal logic of their own that makes them independent causes of political change.

The first group seeking reform was the business community, which wanted more efficient government. American capitalism was changing dramatically in this period, with the growth of large interstate corporations like the railroads, manufacturing that was dependent on foreign trade, and an agricultural sector that was shifting from subsistence farming to commercial cash cropping. Within this group of players were a number of diverse interests. Some, like the railroads, found it perfectly easy to make use of the patronage system to buy off state legislatures and protect their interests. By contrast, supporters of reform tended to be urban merchants and manufacturers whose interests were hurt more by the poor quality of government services that the old system produced. "Reformers harped on reports of post offices where bags of undelivered mail lay forgotten in locked rooms, and they lectured local chambers of commerce about customhouses in Prussia and Britain that were four and five times more cost efficient per volume of work done."[16] City merchants wanted clean streets, public transportation, and police and fire protection, all of which were jeopardized by party control of municipal government. One of the big controversies leading up to the Pendleton Act was an investigation of the New York Custom House through which a large volume of trade passed and from which the U.S. government derived nearly 50 percent of all its revenues. The Custom House was under the control of Republican boss Roscoe Conkling and a prime source of patronage. Conkling's ultimate defeat reflected a power struggle between the Stalwart and Half-Breed factions of the Republican Party, and the final outcome—merit-based recruitment into the Custom House—suited the interests of New York's business community.[17]

A second group in favor of reform was the stratum of middle-class professionals that emerged by the late nineteenth century. Demand for educated professionals was created by the growing private sector and its need for technical expertise, while supply was expanding through the efforts of federal and state governments as well as private funders to build a network of new colleges and universities across the country. This professional class had an elevated view of its own status and importance, and tended to resent the fact that the bosses controlling municipal politics were cruder and less educated than they were. They were also taxpayers who didn't like the fact that their hard-earned dollars were going into the pockets of machine politicians.[18]

A final group that formed part of the Progressive coalition were urban social reformers who dealt directly with the conditions of the contemporary city—people like Jane Addams, founder of Hull House in Chicago, who exposed the conditions of the urban poor, and William Allen, leader of the Association for Improving the Condition of the Poor, who attacked the Tammany machine's mismanagement of public resources.[19]

Social mobilization will not take place in the absence of ideas. New social classes may exist de facto—that is, groups of people with similar backgrounds, needs, and status—but they will not act collectively if they are not conscious of themselves as a group. In this respect, intellectuals play a critical role in interpreting the world, explaining to the public the nature of its own self-interest, and positing a different world that alternative public policies might make possible. Individuals like Dorman Eaton, Woodrow Wilson, and Frank Goodnow, author of a series of influential books on public administration, cast existing American institutions in a very negative light and suggested European models as alternatives.[20]

These intellectuals then organized or legitimated a series of new civil society organizations, such as the New York Municipal Research Bureau, which generated policy proposals for reform, the American Social Science Association, which made civil service reform on a "scientific" basis a top priority, and the Bar Association of the City of New York, formed in 1870 to defend the professional integrity of its members.[21] They would come to invoke the principles of Frederick Winslow Taylor's "scientific management," an approach that was seen as the cutting edge of modern business organization, as guidelines for a revamped American public sector.[22]

Much as the self-interest of the reformers was a basis of their activism, there was an important ethical dimension to this struggle as well. The attack on patronage and bossism took on a highly moralistic tone, with individuals across the country arguing passionately against the evils of the existing system. As described by Edmund Morris, Theodore Roosevelt's biographer,

> It is difficult for Americans living in the last quarter of the twentieth century to understand the emotions which Civil Service Reform aroused in the last quarter of the nineteenth. The movement's literature has about it all the faded ludicrousness of Moral Rearmament. How could intellectuals, politicians, socialites, churchmen, and editors campaign so fervently on behalf of customs clerks, Indian school superintendents, and Fourth-Class postmasters? . . . The fact remains that thousands, even millions, lined up behind the banner, and they were as evangelical (and as strenuously resisted) as any crusaders in history.[23]

Part of the answer to Morris's question as to why people became so impassioned on the question of civil service reform has to do with recognition, that is, the desire of people to have their status and dignity publicly acknowledged by other human beings. The civil service reform movement was led by professionals of various sorts—lawyers, academics, journalists, and the like. In Stephen Skowronek's words, they represented the "key link between America's old patrician elite and its new professional sector. Their roots lay in established American families and high New England culture."[24] This new middle-class elite sought reforms against the interests of a political class that had succeeded in mobilizing the vast mass of nonelite voters into the patronage system. The reformers tended to be upper-crust Protestants resentful of the barely literate Catholics and Jews who were flooding into the country, unfamiliar with American values and practices. They were trying, in a certain sense, to recoup the social status their predecessors had held in the period before the onset of Jacksonian populism. They saw themselves differently, of course, as leaders of modernization in a backward society.[25] They bitterly resented the fact that less-educated politicians held real political power and that they did not; their education and technical knowledge got little respect from the existing political class. So while many of them sought advancement of their material interests, the passionate moralism of the movement was generated by the demand for recognition of the values of education, merit, organization, and honesty that this class of individuals believed they themselves embodied.[26]

LEADERSHIP

The effort to eliminate clientelism from the federal civil service progressed slowly in the two decades after the passage of the Pendleton Act, since enforcement of the Civil Service Commission's edicts was dependent on the often nonexistent willingness of presidents to exert authority over their own cabinet departments. All of this changed, and a much stronger merit-based service emerged, only after two events that occurred shortly after the turn of the twentieth century.

The first was the election of 1896 that brought William McKinley to the presidency and gave the Republican Party a dominating majority in Congress. The previous two decades saw the two parties evenly matched, with power in Congress shifting from one to the other or being split between them every two years from 1875 to 1896.[27] The 1896 defeat of Democrat/Populist William Jennings Bryan was a so-called realigning election that shifted the balance of electoral power for the next generation to a Republican majority based on business interests in the Northeast, and the splitting off of a solidly Democratic South from the rest of the populist movement.[28]

The second development was the presidency of Theodore Roosevelt and the subsequent redefinition of executive leadership in the United States. The forgettable presidents of the late nineteenth century often acted as no more than clerks for decisions being made by the two parties in Congress. Teddy Roosevelt was an extraordinarily energetic individual who took the Hamiltonian view that the executive branch needed to exert independent authority, stretching existing views of the constitutional prerogatives of the presidency to a breaking point. Roosevelt had been a member of the Civil Service Commission for six years, and he used his presidential powers to greatly expand and strengthen the merit-based part of the federal government—something that was easier to do because his predecessor had been a Republican and had already filled the government with patronage appointments. Roosevelt came into office initially in 1901 on McKinley's assassination, but he and his party won a decisive majority in the 1904 election, a mandate that he used to great effect. He worked closely with the Civil Service Commission to strengthen its supervisory authority over federal agencies and to sever the ties between the protected service and the political parties. The commission was given more resources and, critically, control over recruitment and promotions all the way down to the local level.[29]

The reform effort flagged after Roosevelt's departure from office in 1909. His successor, William Howard Taft, was not nearly as energetic as a reformer and had to make peace with the Old Guard of the Republican Party that his predecessor had alienated. He appointed a Commission on Economy and Efficiency that recommended centralization of control over the budget through creation of a Bureau of Efficiency, plans he could not realize while still in office. Though Woodrow Wilson had been vice president of the National Civil Service Reform League and was regarded as the father of American public administration, he too had great difficulty pushing through a reform program when elected in 1912 as the first Democratic president since Grover Cleveland. Congress was in the process of reclaiming the powers that Roosevelt had usurped, and Wilson had to bargain hard with his own party, now anchored in a southern bloc that had little interest in reform. While Wilson was given special executive powers related to the mobilization effort for World War I, he did not oversee a lasting expansion of bureaucratic capacity. The Republican presidents who followed Wilson were in a sense throwbacks to the nineteenth-century system who showed very little interest in strengthening the bureaucracy.[30]

The end of the patronage system at a federal level did not arrive until the middle of the twentieth century. Despite the fact that Franklin Roosevelt and the New Deal oversaw an enormous expansion of the scope and functions of the federal government, the president himself used patronage appointments early on in his first term to ensure that the government was staffed by loyalists. The percentage of classified positions in the federal bureaucracy, which had risen to 80 percent by the late 1920s, fell back to about 60 percent by the mid-1930s. This trend was corrected by the end of the decade after the work of the Brownlow Commission, which regularized the process of personnel management throughout the federal government and comprehensively rewrote civil service rules.[31]

Between the 1880s and the 1920s, the United States gradually dismantled the clientelistic system of party government and laid the foundations of a professional bureaucracy comparable to the ones that had been operating in Europe for several generations. The fact that the United States had a clientelistic system in the first place had to do with the fact that it was democratic earlier than most European countries, and that it had not already created a strong, autonomous state at the point when the franchise was first opened up. A coalition in support of an autonomous bureaucracy eventually emerged, but it had to be put together under strong leadership over an extended period of time, both at a national level and in each city and state that was subject to machine politics.

The process of public-sector reform took far longer in America than in Britain because of differences at the level of institutions and in the broader society. Britain's Westminster system allows for rapid decision making by whatever party holds a majority in Parliament. In the United States, by contrast, power is divided between the president and Congress; Congress itself has a powerful upper house, and its two chambers can be held by different political parties. The federal system that distributes power to states and local governments means that reforms taken at a national level do not necessarily spread across the country. Some states began reform of their patronage systems before the federal government; others lagged well behind. Finally, the two nations were very different socially. In Britain, a rising middle class got early access to elite educational institutions like Oxford and Cambridge and negotiated reform in the clubs and back rooms of London. There was a comparable American elite in the graduates of Harvard and Yale who led the civil service reform movement, but they were dominant only in the Northeast and had to seek allies outside their social class over a geographically vast and diverse country.

The American experience contains some important lessons for contemporary developing countries that want to reform clientelistic political systems and create modern, merit-based, technically competent governments. The first is that reform is a profoundly political process, not a technical one. There are of course technical characteristics of a modern bureaucratic system such as job classifications, examination requirements, promotion ladders, and the like. But clientelistic systems do not exist because the officials staffing them, or the politicians who stand behind them, somehow don't understand how to organize an efficient agency. Clientelism exists because incumbents benefit from the system, either as political bosses who get access to power and resources, or as their clients who get jobs and perks. Dislodging them requires more than the formal reorganization of the government. The experience of public-sector reform mandated by international aid agencies for developing countries at the turn of the twenty-first century demonstrates the futility of a purely technical approach.[32]

A second lesson is that the political coalition favoring reform has to be based on groups that do not have a strong stake in the existing system. Such groups occur naturally as the by-product of economic growth and social change. New business interests that are excluded from the existing patronage system, middle-class professionals lacking access to politics, and civil society groups catering to the needs of underserved populations are all candidates. The problem in assembling a reform coalition is that the existing clientelistic politicians will also try to recruit these groups to their cause. In the United States, many of the railroads—exemplars of industrial modernity—learned to play the corrupt patronage game. This meant that the reform coalition had to include older, economically less modern groups like small farmers, and shippers whose interests were hurt by the railroads. Similarly, in older eastern cities, the masses of immigrants were often successfully mobilized by the existing urban machine, instead of being available for recruitment by the progressive coalition.

A third lesson is that while government reform reflects the material interests of the parties involved, whether entrenched patronage politicians or rising middle-class voters, ideas are critical in shaping how individuals see their interests. A middle-class voter could equally well take a proffered government job, or be persuaded that his or her family's long-term interests are better served by a system that recruits the best possible people on an impersonal basis. The choice actually made often depends on how these ideas are publically articulated. There is, moreover, a flipping point in such systems: if everyone around you is taking the patronage job, you will be more inclined to do so even if you think it is a bad idea. If few people do, it will seem like deviant behavior. Public discussion of the moral basis of public employment is critical in shaping these preferences.

A fourth lesson is that reform takes a great deal of time. The Pendleton

Act was passed in 1883, but it was not until the 1920s that a large majority of public servants were put under the merit classification system. Even then this pattern was reversed briefly early in the New Deal. The American system of checks and balances, as noted, puts up more roadblocks in the path of decisive political change than do other democratic systems. Since reform needs to go up against powerful entrenched interests, it should not be surprising that it does not happen overnight. Oftentimes reform is spurred by accidental events, like the assassination of James Garfield, or the exigencies of wartime mobilization. And at all times it benefits from strong leadership, as in the role that Theodore Roosevelt played both before and after he became president.

Even as the United States was laying the foundations of a modern public sector, the seeds for later problems in the growth of bureaucratic government were being planted. No sooner had a merit system been created than the new classified employees of the U.S. government banded together to form their own unions and lobby Congress to protect their status and jobs. In 1901, the newly created union of postal employees began to press for reclassification of positions and salaries, in response to which Congress sought to limit the ability of public employees to lobby on their own behalf. President Roosevelt supported the right of public-sector employees to unionize but wanted to limit their political activities so as to retain ultimate control over executive branch agencies. Public-sector employees were increasingly organized under the American Federation of Labor, which pressed for the passage of the Lloyd–La Follette Act of 1912, explicitly recognizing the right of public workers to organize and petition Congress on their own behalf (though not the right to strike).[33]

The organization of public-sector unions and the emergence of merit employees as a powerful interest group underscores one of the great inherent dilemmas of bureaucratic autonomy. On the one hand, the merit system was created to protect public employees from patronage and the excessive politicization of the bureaucracy. On the other hand, those same protective rules could be used to shield bureaucrats from accountability, making them hard to fire when they failed to perform. Bureaucratic autonomy could lead to high-quality government with public officials looking to the public good. It could also protect bureaucratic self-interest in job security and pay.

Today, these same public-sector unions have themselves become part of an elite that uses the political system to protect its own self-interests.

As we will see in Part IV, the quality of American public administration has declined markedly since the 1970s, in no small measure because of these unions' ability to limit merit as a basis for hiring and promotion. They are an integral part of the contemporary Democratic Party's political base, making most Democratic politicians loath to challenge them. The result is political decay.

The development of a modern, impersonal government is not just a matter of ending clientelism and overtly corrupt officeholding. One could have a clean and honest bureaucracy that nonetheless does not have the capacity or the authority to do its job properly. So a full account of the process of American state building should include not just the elimination of corruption but also the development of governments that are capable and autonomous enough to perform their functions at a high level, while remaining fundamentally accountable to a democratic citizenry. How this happened in certain key sectors in the United States is the subject of the following chapter.

11

RAILROADS, FORESTS, AND AMERICAN STATE BUILDING

Continuities in American political culture that have made state building a slow and laborious process; why it took so long to regulate the railroads; how Gifford Pinchot made the U.S. Forest Service into an autonomous bureaucracy; the ICC and Forest Service as contrasts in autonomy

Having a high-quality, modern government is not just a matter of eliminating patronage and corruption. Officials can be morally upright and well-intentioned but lack the necessary skills to do their jobs; their numbers could be insufficient to deliver adequate services; or they can lack necessary fiscal resources. A government, just like any private-sector firm, is an organization (or a collection of organizations), that can be well or badly managed. State building, therefore, requires more than just shifting from a patrimonial, patronage-based public sector to an impersonal bureaucracy; it also depends on the creation of organizational capacity.

In the United States, the creation of a modern state occurred considerably later than in Europe and a couple of millennia after its inception in ancient China. Moreover, the state-building project, once begun, was a slow and laborious process, subject to many setbacks and reversals. The reasons for this have to do with American political culture, which from the start has been highly resistant to government authority, and to the design of American political institutions, which throws up many roadblocks to decisive political reform. Americans are, in many ways, still living with this legacy: distrust of government remains high compared to other developed countries; strong institutional barriers to reform of government still exist; and the quality of the services that the U.S. government provides is oftentimes poorer than in other developed countries.

Why all this is so can be illustrated by the story of the nation's first national regulator, the Interstate Commerce Commission (ICC), whose job it was to oversee the railroads. It took almost two generations to create a modern regulator with adequate power to set rates and enforce rules. Yet the ICC remained hostage to political forces that ultimately made it an obstacle to the modernization of the American transportation system.

By contrast, the possibilities that exist for high-quality government and genuinely autonomous bureaucracy (as well as the reasons why such organizations are rare in the American experience) are embodied in the case of Gifford Pinchot and the U.S. Forest Service. I will tell each of these stories in turn.

RAILROADS AND THE LONG ROAD TO STATE POWER

The most transformative technology of the middle third of the nineteenth century, in both the United States and Europe, was the railroads. Particularly for regions of the United States west of the Mississippi River, railroads were critical in linking farmers to distant markets. With the creation of a single national market over a continental landmass, expansion of the division of labor, as Adam Smith had anticipated, could proceed apace. The impact of the railroads, in the words of historian Richard Stone, "was often the power of life and death over a particular location. In undeveloped areas railroads were the determining factor in exactly where settlement would occur . . . Stories are rife concerning towns which no longer exist because they could not attract a railroad, without which products could not get to market."[1] As a result, railroads were built at a furious pace; the ton-miles carried by the thirteen largest lines rose 600 percent between 1865 and 1880, and mileage doubled just between the years 1870 and 1876.[2]

Unlike in Europe, where the railroads were either developed by governments or were placed early on under strict government supervision, the railroads in the United States were almost entirely products of the free market. Competition in this particular service, however, led to huge conflicts among different economic interests, including among the railroads themselves. Competition was fiercest among the large trunk lines; these companies often overbuilt rail mileage and engaged in ruinous rate wars. There were, for example, twenty competitive routes between St. Louis and Atlanta in the 1880s.[3] Companies that went bankrupt could often undermine healthy ones (as in today's airline industry) by continuing to operate in receivership while lowering their costs. In response to steadily falling revenues, the railroads tried to create "pools" or cartels that would limit price competition, but these were often broken by opportunistic players operating in cooperation with shippers. On smaller feeder lines, by contrast, a single railroad often held a monopoly and could raise rates on hapless farmers and shippers at will. The lines were tempted to give volume discounts to large shippers sending goods over long distances, due to economies of scale; this angered smaller local producers and shippers, who were at a competitive disadvantage. There were moreover serious and often violent conflicts between railway owners and their workers.[4] In all of these cases, the different economic players turned to their elected representatives to defend their interests politically. They employed a mishmash of state and federal measures, like the prohibitions of rate discounting or of the pooling of rail service.

Railroads resemble other public utilities such as telephones, electricity, and broadband Internet in the need to reconcile conflicting interests: while the private parties investing in them want to maximize their returns on capital, which dictates selective provision of services to certain buyers—large shippers and producers in large cities—there is a countervailing political interest in subsidizing universal service to smaller players and rural communities. Although the economic conflicts of the late nineteenth century were often portrayed as pitting small farmers against oligarchic rail interests, owners of the railroads found themselves faced with volatile and often unprofitable markets. Certain individuals made enormous fortunes out of this system, while others went bankrupt or found their economic fate in the hands of others. The inconsistent profitability of this sector was reflected in generally falling prices of railroad stocks toward the end of the nineteenth century.[5]

In many ways, the railroads in the late nineteenth century resembled the American health-care system in the early twenty-first century. Both constituted large and critical parts of the total economy. In the 1880s, the railroads were the largest sector of the economy in terms of invested capital, just as the health-care sector in 2010 consumed almost 18 percent of American GDP. Both the railroads and the health-care system had evolved out of the private sector with increasingly heavy political inputs in response to perceived abuses. Politicians in the nineteenth century limited the ability of railroads to recover costs through differential pricing, just as politicians today try to limit price discrimination by insurance companies. Both railroads and health care pitted diverse interests against one another: shippers and farmers against the railroads, doctors and drug companies against insurers. Both sectors generated economic inefficiencies due to the inconsistencies with which policies were applied across the country. And finally, both were economic activities whose implications transcended the jurisdiction of individual states and called out for uniform federal regulation, something that was not forthcoming given America's traditions of federalism and antistatist political culture.[6]

In response to the conflicting interests driving expansion of the railroads, there was considerable political pressure to make the system fairer and more reliable for both providers and users of rail services. However, at this point in American history, there was no precedent for economic regulation on a national level; the Constitution's Commerce Clause reserved regulatory powers to the federal government only in cases of foreign and interstate commerce. In the period following the Civil War, a variety of states had passed Granger laws that sought to prohibit price discrimination, and some, including Massachusetts, established relatively effective commissions to stabilize the market. The right of individual states to set prices and regulate economic activity was upheld by the Supreme Court in 1877 in *Munn v. Illinois.*[7] But railroads could not be adequately regulated at a state level. They were the prime examples of interstate commerce that crossed numerous jurisdictional boundaries, a fact recognized in 1886 in *Wabash v. Illinois*, where the Supreme Court held that only the federal government could regulate railroads.

The failure of a purely free-market system to provide adequate service and reconcile competing interests was gradually recognized on a conceptual level. In 1885, a group of economists established the American Economic Association, which broke away from the American Social Science Association and began formulating a theoretical case for national railroad regulation. This group, led by Henry Carter Adams (who would go on to be the first chief economist of the Interstate Commerce Commission), argued that the government needed to step in to settle disputes over rates and prices because of market failures in the existing system. At this point in the nineteenth century, many of the economic concepts that are routinely taught today in introductory microeconomics courses—public goods, externalities, theories of monopoly and oligopoly, marginalism—were still in early stages of development.[8] As in the case of civil service reform, the academics looking at regulation pointed to the practical experience of countries such as Britain, which, having bequeathed a tradition of laissez-faire economics to the United States, nonetheless regulated railroads far more closely.[9]

The creation of the first federal-level American regulatory agency, the Interstate Commerce Commission, is a revealing case of late American state building. What is remarkable about this story is that it took more than forty years—from the mid-1880s until the period immediately following World War I—for the United States to put in place a "modern" regulator on a par with those that had been created in Europe by the mid-nineteenth century. While the economic logic of regulating railroads on a national level was impeccable, both American political culture and institutions conspired to delay the creation of an ICC with adequate powers for almost two generations.

During the 1880s, Congress tried on several occasions to create national rules for the railroads, not on the basis of a coherent theory of transportation economics but rather on the basis of the political coalitions of different regional interests that could be assembled around the bill. Western agrarian interests pushed strongly for a prohibition of pooling, a provision that might have made sense in other industries with low barriers to entry and small economies of scale, but not for railroads, which in many circumstances were natural monopolies. The obvious solution, not undertaken for several decades, was to permit pooling, but to strictly regulate rates in a way that would balance the interests of both the railroad operators and users. Similarly, the prohibition of rate discrimination between long- and short-haul shippers did not allow railroad pricing to reflect actual operating costs. Such discrimination was often efficient and allowed the railroads to make use of excess capacity in rural areas by taking more circuitous routes.

Both the antipooling provisions and the prohibition of rate discrimination were questionable policies in themselves and acted at cross-purposes. This tension was embodied in the Interstate Commerce Act of 1887, in which Congress finally authorized the creation of the ICC as a permanent regulatory body. Rather than create an authoritative executive agency, the new ICC was set up as an independent commission governed by a balanced board of party appointees serving staggered terms. Typically for a society governed by "courts and parties," the new agency was not given executive powers to set rates or broad policies; it could seek to adjudicate complaints only on a case-by-case basis and left enforcement of judgments up to the courts. Rather than trying to reconcile the conflicting interests pushing for legislation, Congress provided the commission with vague powers, the limits of whose authority would come to be defined by the other branches of government.[10]

The United States was facing, for the first time outside the realm of foreign policy, the issue of state autonomy: To what extent could an executive agency use its powers, delegated in an ambiguous and poorly thought-out piece of legislation, to set policy in what the government regarded as a rational manner? We saw in chapter 4 how Prussia moved to one extreme of the autonomy scale, creating a high-quality bureaucracy that could make decisions with virtually no accountability to democratic politicians. The inclination of the late-nineteenth-century Supreme Court was to move the United States in precisely the opposite direction from Prussia, toward a minimal delegation of authority, not in the interests of democratic accountability but to protect private property rights. The Court in the period after the *Munn* and *Wabash* decisions was becoming steadily more conservative, taking the view that corporations were legal "persons" whose rights deserved equal protection under the Fourteenth Amendment. The amendment, enshrining the right of all American citizens to the "due process of law," was enacted in the immediate aftermath of the Civil War to protect the rights of newly freed African American slaves, but the Court used it subsequently to protect private property rights. Between 1887 and 1910, the Court handed down 558 Fourteenth Amendment decisions, the most notable of which was the 1905 *Lochner v. New York* case in which a New York State law limiting working hours was held to violate "liberty of contract" that the Court argued was implicitly protected by the Fourteenth Amendment.[11]

The Supreme Court naturally took a dim view of the federal government's regulatory powers with regard to interstate commerce: in the words of Stephen Skowronek, "The Supreme Court, now firmly dedicated to saving the private economy from the impulsiveness of American democracy . . . rejected virtually every aspect of the commission's broad construction of the law [i.e., the Interstate Commerce Act] and reduced the ICC to a mere statistics-gathering agency."[12] Thus the parties and the courts reinforced one another in limiting executive autonomy: the first through the cumbersome commission structure, by which party appointees kept control over the ICC, and the latter by restricting the commission's powers to regulate.

It took a series of legislative acts in the first decade of the twentieth century to give the ICC the executive powers it should have had from the start. The Elkins Act of 1903 permitted the commission to set minimum rates; the 1906 Hepburn Act gave it powers to enforce those rates; and the 1910 Mann-Elkins Act shifted the burden of proof to the railroads to justify rate increases.[13] It was only at this point that the regulatory regime took a more modern form, with the government treating the railroads as a utility whose rates would be set administratively rather than by market forces alone.

The historian Gabriel Kolko has argued that these Progressive Era reforms were driven by railroad interests and big capital generally, which used their influence over Congress to limit competition by means of the ICC.[14] In this he is only partly correct. Railroad earnings stabilized and began to rise in the decade or so after the passage of the Interstate Commerce Act, but the political balance thereafter shifted toward the populist interests of small farmers and shippers who favored the prohibition of rate discrimination. The negative consequences of this shift for the railroads became evident only by World War I, when the needs of wartime mobilization dramatically increased demand for rail services. The capacity of the American railway system was severely inadequate, reflecting the underinvestment that had occurred by railroads increasingly unable to recover costs due to regulatory limitations on rates. As German submarines intercepted American shipping to Europe, goods piled up in American ports and the ICC proved unable to unsnarl the traffic. As a result, President Wilson nationalized the entire railroad system in December 1917, adjusted rates and wages, and had the government run the railroads directly until they were returned to private control in the Esch-Cummins Act of 1920.[15]

Stephen Skowronek celebrates the 1920 Transportation Act as a milestone in which "national administrative authority superseded the limits of courts and parties and in the process transformed the organizational, procedural, and intellectual landscape of American government."[16] He is certainly correct that the nation's first national regulator set a precedent for the growth of the powers of the federal government in the twentieth century. But the ICC's economic legacy was far more mixed. The commission structure that balanced party appointees prevented it from developing sufficient bureaucratic autonomy, and it remained hostage to underlying political interests. Over the following decades, the ICC shifted from having too little power to imposing an excessive regulatory burden. This impeded innovation and new investment in the national rail system. For example, the ICC did not permit the Southern Railway to realize the efficiency gains from its introduction of Big John aluminum hopper cars during the 1960s, making it uncompetitive with barges.[17] Railways faced increasing competition from trucking and ships, which were actually subsidized by other government programs, such as the building of the interstate highway system. By the 1970s, American railroads were in the midst of a full-blown crisis, with most railroads in major financial trouble and the Penn Central only the last of thirty-seven eastern carriers forced into bankruptcy.[18] In response, the intellectual climate shifted notably by the late 1970s toward a consensus on the need for deregulation of the entire American transportation system. The Carter administration began a series of reforms designed to unwind some of the regulatory burdens that had accumulated over the previous decades, relaxing common carriage rules and allowing railroads more flexibility in pricing.

The purpose of this discussion of the ICC is not to stake out a position on the appropriate level of regulation or deregulation. The point is that state power over the economy is potentially dangerous because it risks being captured by one interest group or another at the expense of the general public. Moreover, all bureaucracies tend to become increasingly rule bound over time, particularly when they are driven by the political demands of legislators. It is very difficult to create a government agency subservient to democratic will but at the same time sufficiently autonomous and free from capture by powerful interest groups.

Many people would say that the problem is one of government itself, and the solution is to severely cut back or abolish the regulatory state. But a national transportation system cannot be left up to market forces alone; the free market was what created the chaotic situation of the late nineteenth century in the first place. Bureaucrats are often blamed for being obtuse and inflexible, but missing from this perspective is an understanding that more often than not the original legislative mandate is the source of dysfunctional bureaucratic behavior. The ICC was caught between demands of consumers for low prices and of railroads for cartel-like agreements that would support their return on capital. The shifting policies of the ICC, sometimes favoring consumers and sometimes favoring railroads, were a response to the shifting political currents in Congress and the White House. Amtrak, the government-operated passenger rail service that was created in 1971 as part of the reorganization of the railroads, is today no one's model of a high-quality, innovative rail service. But the reason for this is not the mere fact that it is run by the government; government-operated railroads in Europe and Asia have often been leaders in service efficiency. Rather, the problem is that Amtrak operates under a contradictory political mandate: it is supposed to recover costs and invest in new capacity while at the same time providing service to a host of small towns and rural areas represented by the legislators who determine the company's budget. Were Amtrak freed of the latter mandate and allowed to focus on the dense Washington–New York–Boston corridor, it could become a highly profitable institution and provide much better service.

Had the ICC been created as an autonomous, high-quality executive agency rather than a commission, it might have played a much more effective role over the past century. A more autonomous bureaucracy would have had more flexibility to set rates and adjudicate between different interest groups, as the government actually did in the brief period from 1917 to 1920 when the railroads were fully nationalized. It might have been able to anticipate the fact that railroads no longer constituted a natural monopoly given the rise of road and air transportation, and permitted rates to reflect actual costs more realistically. The design of the American state, with its complex system of checks and balances, makes this kind of outcome difficult to achieve: the history of the ICC shows the continuing dominance of the courts and Congress over executive decision making. This particular limitation in the quality of government is rooted precisely in the strength of the rule of law and of democratic accountability in the American political system.

Does this mean that the United States is incapable of producing high-quality, autonomous bureaucracy? Yes and no. Even though the American system is biased against this type of strong government, individual cases of bureaucratic autonomy have arisen in the course of the country's history. One such case is the U.S. Department of Agriculture at the turn of the twentieth century, and in particular the role of Gifford Pinchot and the U.S. Forest Service.

GIFFORD PINCHOT AND AMERICAN FORESTS

The U.S. Department of Agriculture (USDA) was founded by President Lincoln in 1862 as part of a development strategy to upgrade the productivity of American farms, of a piece with the Morrill Act of the same year that created the system of land-grant colleges (Penn State, Michigan State, Cornell University, Kansas State, Iowa State, and others) that would train a new generation of agronomists. The Agriculture Department was originally intended to be staffed by scientists, but by the 1880s it acquired a different purpose: the free distribution of seeds. Supported by representatives from farm states, the Congressional free seed program came to dominate the agency's budget toward the end of the century. The USDA became, in other words, a variant of the patronage system that characterized the federal government as a whole at the time, disbursing not jobs but seeds to political clients.

The department under these circumstances found it very hard to retain trained scientific personnel. All of this began to change, however, after the passage of the Pendleton Act in 1883 and the establishment of the merit system. The USDA was one of the first federal agencies to protect its personnel from political patronage and began hiring large numbers of recent graduates of the new land-grant colleges who had up-to-date training in scientific agriculture. As political scientist Daniel Carpenter explains, many of the department's division and bureau chiefs enjoyed relatively long tenure and could shepherd along an entire generation of new recruits who had no roots in either the patronage or seed-distribution systems.[19]

In contemporary parlance, this shift in USDA personnel policy constituted "capacity building." The quality of the bureaucracy was dependent not just on the higher educational achievements of the new entrants but also on the fact that these individuals constituted a network of trust and possessed what has been labeled "social capital." Much like their German or Japanese counterparts, these new officials had similar backgrounds (indeed, often graduating together from the same schools) and embodied a common belief in modern science and the need to apply rational methods to the development of rural communities around the United States. This mind-set over time became the basis for the organizational ethos of the Agriculture Department and in particular of one of its key divisions, the U.S. Forest Service.

Today, the Forest Service manages over 150 national forests and more than 200 million acres of land. Prior to the formation of the Forest Bureau in the Department of Agriculture in 1876, forests were regarded largely as an impediment to the westward flow of settlers; land was cleared and abandoned over large stretches of the country. In the first decade of the twentieth century, older parts of the country, like New England, had been largely denuded of trees; there were concerns that most of the nation's forests would disappear altogether within another generation. The recovery of these lands and their return to productive use was one of the great achievements of government intervention. The U.S. Forest Service has long been regarded as one of the most successful American bureaucracies, whose quality and esprit de corps became legendary. This achievement was all the more remarkable given the fact that individual forest rangers live in highly dispersed locations, whose isolation prevents the kind of bonding usually seen in urban organizational settings.[20]

This state-building legacy was largely the work of one individual, Gifford Pinchot, who came to head the department's Forestry Division in 1898. To the extent that there is (or was) an American aristocracy, Gifford Pinchot was a member of it. He was born in his grandfather's summerhouse of wealthy parents from Pennsylvania who sent him to the Phillips Exeter Academy and then to Yale.[21] While at Yale he joined Skull and Bones, the secret society that would one day admit the forty-first president, George H. W. Bush. Like John Quincy Adams, Theodore Roosevelt, William and Henry James, and other elite nineteenth-century Americans, Pinchot traveled extensively in Europe as a young man, where he came into contact with, among other things, European theories of scientific forestry. He was, for all his privilege, incredibly motivated to make something more of his life. When Pinchot went traveling with Sierra Club founder John Muir through the Crater Lake country of Oregon in 1896, Muir wrote in his journal, "Heavy rain during the night. All slept in the tent except Pinchot."[22] Religion played an important role in shaping his character; while traveling in England, he and his mother were caught up in the revival led by Reverend James Aitken that taught a social gospel of responsibility. Pinchot in many ways embodied Max Weber's Protestant work ethic, observing that "my own money came from unearned increment on land in New York held by my grandfather, who willed the money, not to the land, but to me. Having got my wages in advance in that way, I am now trying to work them out."[23]

Perhaps because his own family were large landowners, Pinchot early on developed an interest in forestry and nature. At that time, however, Yale offered no courses in forest management. After graduating, he was advised to go to Europe, where he met an eminent German forester, Sir Dietrich Brandis, who had worked extensively managing forests on behalf of the British government in India and Burma. Brandis felt that Pinchot should spend several years studying scientific forest management, but the young American was too eager to bring the scientific forestry gospel back home. On returning to the United States in 1890, he began writing about forest management and was soon acknowledged as an expert on the subject. Pinchot was hired as a consultant by Phelps Dodge and later by George Vanderbilt, grandson of railroad magnate Cornelius, to manage the Vanderbilt family's forests in North Carolina.

The groundwork for a national forest service was laid not by Pinchot but by Bernhard Fernow, a Prussian who had trained at the Forest Academy at Münden and the Prussian Forestry Department, which had pioneered in developing techniques for the centralized planning of forest management. Fernow, on moving to America, became active in a number of scientific societies, serving as a secretary in the American Association for the Advancement of Science, and in the American Forest Congress. When Fernow was appointed to head the Agriculture Department's Forestry Division in 1886, it was run by two patronage appointees; he used his networks to begin staffing the organization with professionally trained agronomists. He also cultivated an extensive external constituency of local forestry associations, universities, private foresters, and other parties with an interest in forest management, through an aggressive campaign of scientific papers and bulletins. Fernow had tried unsuccessfully to recruit Pinchot to government work straight out of Yale; the latter took over as chief forester only in 1898. What Pinchot lacked in academic knowledge of forests, he made up for through his political connections and media savvy.[24]

Over the next three years, Pinchot turned the Division of Forestry into a Bureau of Forestry with a much larger budget and staff. Many of his closest associates in government had been fellow students at Yale—indeed, fellow members of Skull and Bones. He created a centralized system of training and socialization for national foresters built around the principles of expert, nonpartisan, and professional forest management for the benefit of multiple users. The purpose of the bureau was not, strictly speaking, conservation; Pinchot differed from early environmentalists like John Muir in believing that forests existed to be exploited. But economic benefit had to be extracted on a sustainable basis. Accordingly, he initiated a raft of new programs designed to help private owners of forests manage their properties better.

Pinchot's greatest triumph came in 1905 when he engineered the transfer of control over federally owned forests from the Department of the Interior to the Agriculture Department, lodging them under his own bureau's jurisdiction. The ethos of the Interior Department's General Land Office (GLO) was completely different from that of the Forest Service. The GLO was staffed by lawyers and accountants, with no expertise in forest management. They regarded their mission primarily as servicing the interests of private developers who wanted access to or ownership of public lands. The GLO was, however, politically very popular with western politicians and businessmen, who scoffed at the Forest Service as a bunch of "goggle-eyed, bandy-legged dudes from the East and sad-eyed, absentminded professors and bugologists" and bureaucrats "who were too indolent to go over the country and examine its geography, who simply sat in their offices and made the laws, doing the utmost injustice to the people." The GLO was an important source of Republican patronage. One of the biggest supporters of Interior Department control of forests was House Speaker Joe Cannon, Republican from Illinois (for whom the current building housing the U.S. House of Representatives is named), whose anti-conservationist inclinations were summed up in the words "not one cent for scenery." Cannon attacked Pinchot as having been "born with a gold spoon in his mouth," and criticized government scientists for being "industrious to fasten upon the public teat." Against this background, Pinchot began assembling a coalition of supporters in favor of a bill to shift authority over forests from Interior to Agriculture.[25]

The battle over control of public lands took place in the context of the big changes occurring elsewhere on the political scene. In contrast to the post–Civil War decades of shifting control of Congress between the two parties, the Republicans controlled both houses and the presidency after the realigning election of 1896. This had led to the appointment of James S. Wilson as secretary of agriculture, a post in which he would remain for a record sixteen years under three presidents. Wilson was critical in shifting the department from a seed-distribution agency to a forward-looking, science-based organization, not just with respect to the Forest

Service but also in areas like agricultural extension services, the regulation of pure foods and drugs, and the like.[26] Theodore Roosevelt had become president in 1901 on McKinley's assassination, and Roosevelt was of course a great outdoorsman who was converted to the cause of conservation by C. Hart Merriam of the Agriculture Department's Biological Survey and John Muir. Roosevelt, a friend of Pinchot's since his days as governor of New York, shared the chief forester's agenda and became a powerful patron of his initiatives.[27]

The mere fact that Pinchot had the support of the president and that his party was in charge of Congress did not, in America's system of separated powers, mean that the transfer of the land office was in any way a done deal. Joe Cannon was one of the most powerful House Speakers in American history, representative of the Republican Party's Old Guard and ally of a strong assemblage of western congressmen bitterly opposed to the transfer. This included Frank Mondell, representative from Wyoming and member of the Public Lands Committee, who led the opposition to the transfer bill. At Cannon's urging, the House in 1902 voted down the measure 100–73.

At this point, an ordinary bureaucrat in an ordinary bureau would have accepted his fate and backed down. But Pinchot was not just a bureaucrat; he also was a skillful political operator who had spent years cultivating a wide range of interest groups, newspaper editors, and scientific societies, including the Audubon Society, the Sierra Club, the General Federation of Women's Clubs, western ranchers' associations, the National Board of Trade, the National Live Stock Association, and many others. To build support, he reassured the Homestake Mining Company, a constituent of transfer opponent Senator Alfred Kittridge, that timber on federal lands would not be transferred out of state. He succeeded in provoking a huge outcry in the press, among academics, and among respected scientific authorities in support of the shift. His most daring move was to outflank Cannon by personally cultivating a friendship with Representative Mondell, traveling with him to the Yellowstone region and lobbying him ceaselessly to support the Department of Agriculture. Speaker Cannon found himself outfoxed by a midlevel bureaucrat, and the transfer of land management to Pinchot's bureau was passed by both houses of Congress in 1905.[28]

As Daniel Carpenter has argued, Pinchot's victory over Cannon represents a remarkable case of bureaucratic autonomy in a country not famous, as are Germany and France, for its powerful bureaucrats.[29] Pinchot achieved this degree of autonomy not because of any statutory authority he was given. Broad delegations of authority to the executive branch are rare in U.S. practice outside the realm of national security and foreign policy, and did not occur in this instance. What Pinchot did was to operate not bureaucratically but politically, building an informal network of allies both inside and outside government. In democratic America, this is how authority is exercised. His opponents, of course, accused him of bureaucratic imperialism and complained bitterly that "an individual executive officer of the Government [had no right] to legislate as to how lands shall be preserved." Another congressman criticized Pinchot's "publicity machine" that had mailed out more than nine million circulars annually with taxpayer dollars and accused the Forest Service of being "a new institution, made without Congress."[30]

Pinchot's downfall came three years later in the so-called Ballinger affair, and was the result of another power play on his part. Theodore Roosevelt had at this point been succeeded as president by William Howard Taft, whose commitment to conservation issues was questioned by those in the former president's inner circle. Of Taft, Pinchot said, "Weak rather than wicked, he was one of those genial men who are everything that fancy paints until a showdown comes along that demands real toughness of moral fiber."[31] The new secretary of the interior, James Garfield (son of the assassinated president), appointed former Seattle mayor Richard Ballinger to head the part of the General Land Office that had remained with the Interior Department, where he had authority over the opening up of land in Alaska to private development. A young GLO agent named Louis Glavis began noting questionable dealings between Ballinger and various Seattle land investors, including payments made to Ballinger after he was named to his office. When Glavis tried to report his findings to the president with the help of two of Pinchot's Forest Service agents, Taft issued a gag order and allowed Ballinger to fire the whistle-blower. Taft implored Pinchot to drop the issue, but the latter defied the president by defending the actions of his staff in a letter to Jonathan Dolliver, chairman of the Agriculture Committee, which was to be read on the Senate floor. For this, Taft fired Pinchot and ended his career as the nation's chief forester.[32]

Pinchot's decision to end-run President Taft might be regarded as an act of bureaucratic hubris by an official who had gotten too used to reading his own publicity notices. In the end, however, his last stand as chief forester had a positive effect for the cause of sustainable forestry. Taft was severely embarrassed by the incident, and the Old Guard of the party was put on the defensive. Speaker Cannon was to lose his powers of appointment in a revolt by the Progressive wing of the party two years later. Roosevelt's wing kept up pressure to maintain his legacy on conservation issues. The Forest Service's authority to purchase additional lands was approved by Congress in 1911 in the Weeks Act, which constituted the final consolidation of the bureau's powers.[33] Pinchot, for all of his political maneuvering, had created an institution, an organization that could survive the departure of its charismatic early leader.

Pinchot's career, moreover, was far from finished. He would go on to help Roosevelt in his 1912 Progressive Party bid for another term as president. He himself ran, unsuccessfully, for the Senate and was eventually twice elected governor of Pennsylvania.

CAPTURE AND AUTONOMY

The Interstate Commerce Commission and the U.S. Forest Service are only two examples of American state building and political development. There are others that occurred in the Progressive Era, though the next big wave of state building would have to await the New Deal in the 1930s. They would be followed by the plethora of agencies that constitute the American government today: the Federal Trade Commission, the Securities and Exchange Commission, the Food and Drug Administration, the Federal Aviation Agency, the National Labor Relations Board, the Environmental Protection Agency, and many, many others.

The ICC and the Forest Service were both necessary interventions on the part of the state. The railroads constituted potentially monopolistic enterprises whose scale and capital requirements generated huge social conflicts. Forests were not being well managed by their private owners, and distribution of the nation's public lands had become a huge source of patronage and corruption. In both cases the country needed an impartial regulator that was not under the thumb of the powerful interests involved. The U.S. state-building response to these problems occurred much later than it did in other industrializing countries, such as Germany and Britain, which were not constrained by America's institutional checks and balances or by its antistatist political culture.

These two government agencies differed greatly with regard to quality and the effectiveness with which they performed their mandates. The difference, I would argue, has to do with the degree of autonomy with which they operated. The ICC in some sense could never become autonomous due to its contradictory mandate and governance structure. Rather than being run as a hierarchical executive branch agency with a single head, it was structured as a commission with balanced representation of the two political parties. This ensured that it could never stray very far from its legislative overseers and that it would never have a visionary leader like Gifford Pinchot. When it tried to strike out on its own in its early years, it was immediately cut back by the courts, and then pulled in different directions by the political winds in Congress. As a result, the ICC, while eventually acquiring adequate enforcement powers to do its job, remained captive of the political forces that created it. Subject to rules not of its own making, the ICC over time appeared hidebound and nonadaptive. It was one of the first objects of the deregulatory trend that began in the 1970s, even before Ronald Reagan became president.

The Forest Service was very different. It was organized with a distinct ethos of scientific forestry by Bernhard Fernow and was lodged within a modernizing Agriculture Department that had strong and stable leadership under Secretary James S. Wilson for an extraordinary length of time. Its second leader, Gifford Pinchot, was one of the most energetic and remarkable men of the Progressive Era, working hand in glove with a president who shared his values, outlook, and exuberance. He and his political superiors did not simply fulfill a political mandate set by Congress; he created his own mandate. No elected official instructed him to publish reports on modern forestry techniques, or to cultivate newspaper editors, or to reach out to scientific societies and trade groups around the country. Needless to say, no one told him to conspire with sympathetic congressmen to move control over forests from the Interior Department; indeed, most legislators paying attention to this issue were strongly opposed in principle to a bureaucrat meddling in politics in this manner. Midlevel public officials, after all, are supposed to be mere agents, and

Congress the principal; here was a case of an agent run amok. Pinchot had an agenda for the country that he believed was in the long-term public interest, and that agenda was not necessarily coincident with that of the leaders of Congress. This is the meaning of state autonomy: a government that is responsive to interest groups but not owned by them, that is not too easily swayed by the short-term vagaries of democratic public opinion but rather looks to long-term public interest. The Forest Service became the nation's premier bureaucracy precisely because it was not hampered by mandated rules excessively limiting its discretion.

The fact that Gifford Pinchot as an agent was not under the strict control of his congressional principals suggests that the principal-agent framework by which contemporary economists understand the problems of organizational dysfunction is perhaps not adequate to really understand how good bureaucracies work.

It is impossible to talk about the Forest Service without reference to Gifford Pinchot's background and character. Like his friend Teddy Roosevelt, he represented a type of elite American that would fade away by the end of the twentieth century: of Anglo-Saxon stock, strongly Puritan in his religious beliefs, hailing from the old Northeast, familiar with European practices, and educated at Phillips Exeter and Yale (Roosevelt attended Harvard). The agency he created was staffed by some of his old Yale classmates; many young recruits would come out of the new Yale School of Forestry that his family endowed. In the tradition of John Quincy Adams, he was precisely the kind of northeastern elitist that western and southern populists in the Jacksonian tradition had learned to despise. But the more deeply democratic Jacksonians were the ones who had created the patronage system in America; their hostility to big government and rigid defense of property rights was what had turned the nineteenth-century American state into a machine for dispensing jobs, seeds, and land to private interests and political backers, often represented by one and the same individual. By contrast, it was the older northeastern elites, familiar with European traditions, that reversed course during the Progressive Era and created a modern state based on merit and the impersonal treatment of citizens.

The United States was the first democracy to open up the franchise to all white male voters, and it did so at a time before a modern state had been established. As a result, it invented the practice of clientelism and had a weak and ineffective national government for much of the nineteenth century. The United States followed Britain in reforming its public sector, but this process took far longer due to the country's institutional barriers to reform.

Reform of the American public sector at the beginning of the twentieth century did not end the problem of the political capture of the public sector by narrow private interests, or of political corruption. While American politicians no longer dole out public-sector jobs and Christmas turkeys to individual voters to the extent they did in the 1880s, they indulge in the wholesale granting of favors to political clients in the form of subsidies, tax breaks, and other legislative perks. As we will see in chapter 31, interest-group politics infected not just the ICC and railroad regulation but also the Forest Service itself, which by the 1980s had become an increasingly dysfunctional agency captured by its different constituencies.

Other countries around the world—indeed, probably a majority of those in the developing world—are where the United States was in the early nineteenth century. They have adopted democratic elections and opened up the franchise under conditions of great state weakness. They, like the United States from the 1830s on, have clientelist political systems in which votes are traded for individual favors.

Clientelist politics was ended in the United States as the result of a long-term political struggle between new middle-class actors who had a strong interest in creating a more modern form of government and the older entrenched patronage politicians. Underlying this shift was a social revolution brought about by industrialization, which mobilized a host of new political actors with no interest in the old clientelist system. However, as the Greek and Italian cases indicated, impersonal government is not the inevitable by-product of economic modernization.

In building a modern state and overcoming clientelism, the United States had one big advantage over many contemporary developing countries: from the first days of the republic, it had a strong national identity that was rooted less in ethnicity or religion than in a set of political values centering around loyalty to its own democratic institutions. Americans in some sense worshipped their Constitution, which embodied universalistic values making the assimilation of new, culturally different immigrants relatively easy. As Seymour Martin Lipset used to point out, in the United States one could be accused of being "un-American" in a way that one could not be "un-German" or "un-Greek," since Americanism constituted a set of values that could be adopted voluntarily rather than an inherited ethnic characteristic. Successful state building is dependent, therefore, on the prior existence of a sense of national identity that serves as a locus of loyalty to the state itself, rather than to the social groups underlying it.

12

NATION BUILDING

How national identities are critical to state building; how nationalism is properly seen as a type of identity politics; why identity is a modern phenomenon linked to technology and economic change; four routes to national identity

Critical to the success of state building is a parallel process of nation building, an often violent and coercive process that took place in all the countries under discussion in Part I.

State building refers to the creation of tangible institutions—armies, police, bureaucracies, ministries, and the like. It is accomplished by hiring staff, training officials, giving them offices, providing them with budgets, and passing laws and directives. Nation building, by contrast, is the creation of a sense of national identity to which individuals will be loyal, an identity that will supersede their loyalty to tribes, villages, regions, or ethnic groups. Nation building in contrast to state building requires the creation of intangible things like national traditions, symbols, shared historical memories, and common cultural points of reference. National identities can be created by states through their policies on language, religion, and education. But they are just as often established from the bottom up by poets, philosophers, religious leaders, novelists, musicians, and other individuals with no direct access to political power.

Nation building is critical to the success of state building. This reaches to the core meaning of the state: as the organizer of legitimate violence, the state periodically calls upon its citizens to risk their lives on its behalf. They will never be willing to do so if they feel that the state as such is unworthy of ultimate sacrifice. But the impact of national identity on state strength is not limited to its coercive power. Much of what passes for corruption is not simply a matter of greed but rather the by-product of legislators or public officials who feel more obligated to family, tribe, region, or ethnic group than to the national community and therefore divert money in that direction. They are not necessarily immoral people, but their circle of moral obligation is smaller than that of the polity for which they work. Citizens, for their part, may rationally calculate how loyal to be based on whether the state has upheld its end of the social contract. Political stability is bolstered enormously, however, if they feel that the state is legitimate and experience the emotions associated with patriotism. The contemporary Chinese Communist Party earns legitimacy today due to its economic performance. But it also has an important extra margin of support as an embodiment of Chinese nationalism.

If a strong sense of national identity is a necessary component of state building, it is also for that reason dangerous. National identity is often built around principles of ethnicity, race, religion, or language, principles that necessarily include certain people and exclude others. National identity is frequently formed in deliberate opposition to other groups and therefore serves to perpetuate conflict even as it strengthens internal social cohesion. National cohesion may express itself as external aggression. Human beings cooperate in order to compete, and compete to cooperate.[1]

NATIONAL IDENTITY AND MODERNIZATION

Nationalism is one specific form of identity politics that found its first major expression in the French Revolution. It is based on the view that the political boundaries of the state ought to correspond to a cultural boundary, one defined primarily by shared language and culture.[2]

Key to the idea of identity is the notion that there can be a disjunction between one's inner, authentic self and the social norms or practices that are sanctioned by the surrounding society. That inner self can be based on nation, ethnicity, race, culture, religion, gender, sexual orientation, or any characteristic that binds human communities together. The philosopher Charles Taylor, following Hegel, points out that struggles over identity are inherently political because they involve demands for recognition. Human beings are not satisfied, pace the economists, by material resources alone. They demand as well that their authentic selves be publicly recognized—granted dignity and equal status—by other people. This is why for nationalists the symbols of recognition—a flag, a seat in the United Nations, or legal status as a member of the community of nations—are of critical importance. Social mobilization, one of the six dimensions of development, is a by-product of the emergence of new identities as people become aware of shared experiences and values.[3]

Two major theorists of nationalism, Benedict Anderson and Ernest Gellner, link the emergence of nationalism to modernization, though their emphasis differs in certain key respects. Identity does not really exist as a problem in premodern societies. In either a hunter-gatherer or an agrarian economy, there is a differentiation of social identities—between hunters and gatherers, men and women, peasants, priests, warriors, and bureaucrats—but there is so little social mobility and such a restricted division of labor that one does not face much choice in one's associations. Indeed, in premodern India the entire division of labor was sacralized in the jati or caste system, which took a society with already limited mobility and froze it further through religious sanction. In agrarian societies, a person's important life choices—where to live, what to do for a living, what religion to practice, whom to marry—were mostly determined by the surrounding tribe, village, or caste. Individuals consequently did not spend a lot of time sitting around asking themselves, "Who am I, really?"

According to Anderson, all this begins to change with the emergence of commercial capitalism in sixteenth-century Europe, powered by the invention of the printing press and the growth of a market for books. The printing press sharply reduced the price of written communication and thus made possible publication of books in vernacular languages. Martin Luther, writing in German rather than Latin, became a bestselling author early in the sixteenth century and as a result played a key role in creating a sense of common German culture. Luther told his readers, moreover, that their salvation did not rest on conformity with rituals defined by the Roman Catholic church. It rested, instead, on an inner act of faith. By personal choice, individuals could be linked to a new community.

The emergence of a vernacular print language made possible for the first time what Anderson calls an "imagined community" of German speakers and readers. In a similar manner, the Filipino novelist José Rizal was able to create a common awareness of Philippine identity in the nineteenth century for a people spread out over seven thousand islands. The advance of newspapers, consumed by emerging educated middle-class readers, had an even more dramatic effect in building national consciousness in the nineteenth century. By reading, people who had never left the confines of their little village could all of a sudden perceive a connection to other people in other isolated villages. Well before the Internet and modern transportation, print media allowed people to travel virtually.[4]

Ernest Gellner also argues that nationalism emerged during a moment of profound social change, but he dates this shift to the transition from agrarian to industrial societies in the nineteenth century. In agrarian societies, there is no uniformity of culture: vast differences in language and ritual separate the different classes. Thus the Russian nobility spoke French, the Estonian and Latvian courts spoke German; the court language in the Austro-Hungarian Empire was Latin up until 1842. It was primarily peasants who spoke Russian, Estonian, or Latvian. These linguistic barriers, initially the result of conquest and dynastic politics, were deliberately kept in place because such stratified societies were set up to block mobility between social classes.

As Gellner explains, the requirements for an industrial society are very different:

> A society that lives by growth must needs pay a certain price. The price of growth is eternal innovation. Innovation in turn presupposes unceasing occupational mobility, certainly as between generations, and often within single life-spans. The capacity to move between diverse jobs, and incidentally to communicate and cooperate with numerous individuals in other social positions, requires that members of such a society be able to communicate in speech and writing, in a formal, precise, context-free manner . . .
>
> This is the general profile of a modern society: literate, mobile, formally equal with a merely fluid, continuous, so to speak atomised inequality, and with a shared, homogeneous, literacy-carried, and school-inculcated culture. It could hardly be more sharply contrasted with a traditional society, within which literacy was a minority and specialised accomplishment, where stable hierarchy rather than social mobility was the norm, and culture was diversifed and discontinuous.[5]

The expanding division of labor brought on by the process of industrialization thus prepares the ground for modern nationalism, where language-based culture becomes the central unifying source of social cohesion.[6]

The incentives for linguistic unification created by economic modernization are illustrated by the case of France. In the 1860s, a quarter of France's population could not speak French, and another quarter spoke it only as a second language. French was the language of Paris and the educated elite; in rural France, peasants spoke Breton, Picard, Flemish, Provençal, or any number of other local dialects. As in the highlands of Papua New Guinea, neighboring valleys could speak mutually incomprehensible dialects. With the expansion of the capitalist market economy during the nineteenth century, however, the use of French increased dramatically. In the words of Eugen Weber, "One has only to . . . browse through the Breton newspapers . . . to realize that more and more parents and children were becoming committed to integration, to Frenchification, which stood for mobility, advancement, economic and social promotion . . . Industrial development worked for the linguistic unification of the polyglot labor force that migrated to the cities." The final linguistic unification of France was not completed until World War I, when common service in the trenches completed a process begun by economic necessity.[7]

Social mobility fostered by an expanding division of labor immediately opens up the question of identity in an acute fashion. At one moment I am a peasant in a small village in Saxony; the next moment I'm working in a large Siemens factory in Berlin. In the early twenty-first century, similar migrations are occurring throughout China as peasants leave their villages in the interior for job opportunities in the industrial sector of Shenzhen and Guangzhou. The fixed, intimate, and limited social world that was defined by the peasant village is replaced by the large, anonymous, and diverse world of the modern city. This shift—the classic transition from Gemeinshaft to Gesellschaft first elaborated by Ferdinand Tönnies—not only involves a change in identities from one social occupation to another; it also opens up the question of identity itself. Now that I'm no longer living under the thumb of my family and friends back in the village, I have a much greater degree of choice over my own life course. "Who am I?" has all of a sudden become a real and pressing question. This shift is experienced as a crisis or trauma and produces a condition that Émile Durkheim labeled anomie, or normlessness. Durkheim saw anomie manifest in higher suicide rates in modernizing societies, but it also finds expression in higher rates of crime and family breakdown that are often associated with rapid social change.[8]

One problem with Gellner's theory linking nationalism to industrialization and to a linguistically grounded culture is that it fails to explain the emergence of nationalism in nonindustrial societies. In many countries in Western Europe and North America, economic growth drove social change in the following sequence: expanding commerce → industrialization → urbanization → new forms of social mobilization. This is not an inevitable sequence, however. In Greece and southern Italy, as we have seen, the industrialization stage was either skipped or sharply curtailed in its impact. Both societies urbanized without creating large industrial sectors—a phenomenon that I labeled "modernization without development." This pattern has prevailed in many non-Western societies as well, where colonialism fostered urbanization and the creation of a modernized elite, without engendering the wholesale transformation of society through large-scale industrial employment.

Nationalism had other, different sources in the former colonial world than it did in Western Europe. If these countries did not industrialize on a Western European pattern, they nonetheless acquired a new stratum of elites who confronted the totally different cultures of their colonizers. These elites felt enormous pressures to conform to the culture and mores of the colonial power, and many indeed got sucked into the dominant power structure. But this created a crisis of identity, as they were separated from their families and compatriots by language and Westernization. This was the crisis that struck the young British-trained lawyer Mohandas Karamachand Gandhi while practicing in South Africa and led him eventually into the struggle for Indian independence. It was this crisis that compelled three black writers from different French colonies, Aimé Césaire, Léon Damas, and Léopold Senghor, to develop the concept of "Négritude." They sought the transvaluation of the meaning of the word *nègre*, which for white Frenchmen at the time had an entirely pejorative and racist connotation, into something that was a source of pride.

The ideas of collective national identity and demands for recognition of the dignity of indigenous identities were among the many things exported from Europe to the colonial world. As Liah Greenfeld explains, "As the sphere of influence of the core Western societies (which defined themselves as nations) expanded, societies belonging or seeking entry to the supra-societal system of which the West was the center had in fact no choice but to become nations."[9] This meant, however, that nationalism took on a very different form in the former colonial world. In Western Europe, the preeminent nationalist movement was that of the Germans, which sought to unite all German speakers under a single sovereignty. In India, Kenya, and Burma, nationalism could not be built around language, since these were ethnolinguistically fragmented societies with no dominant group that could unite the whole country around its culture. Thus the Mau Mau rebellion in Kenya, led by Jomo Kenyatta, was dominated by Kikuyus, who comprised a bit more than 20 percent of the population. They could not hope to permanently dominate the country or impose their language or customs on the whole of the society. Indeed, in many countries the language of the colonizer remained the lingua franca because, first, it was regarded as a more neutral choice than any of the languages of the ethnic subgroups, and second, it connected the former colony to the wider global economy better than any indigenous language.

FOUR ROUTES TO NATIONAL IDENTITY

Most scholars studying the phenomenon of national identity assert that it is "socially constructed." They contest the view of many nationalists that nations are primordial, biologically based groupings that have existed since time immemorial. Ernest Gellner argues that nationalism is a modern phenomenon, which responds to the needs of an industrial, urbanized society. Others go further, unmooring national identity from its connection to large social forces like industrialization and making it a product of the creativity of artists and poets. Another school influenced by economics argues that identities are essentially coordinating mechanisms used by political entrepreneurs to promote underlying economic interests.[10]

It is certainly correct that nationalism was a by-product of modernization, and that specific national identities were socially constructed. But the social constructivist view begs a number of important questions. Who is it that constructs new national identities? Is it a top-down or bottom-up process? Some national identities, once created, become incredibly durable, while others fail to stick. The Soviet Union, for example, spent seventy years trying to create a "new Soviet man" who would be cosmopolitan and transcend categories like ethnicity and religion. And yet, when the USSR broke up into its constituent union republics in 1991, older national identities thought to be long dead reasserted themselves. Today there are no Soviets in a place like the Crimea, only Russians, Ukrainians,

Tatars. Similarly, the European Union has been trying to construct a postnational sense of European citizenship since the 1950s, a project that has run up against clear limits in the wake of the euro crisis that began in 2009. What are the limits and possibilities of nation building?

Far from being an open-ended process of social construction, national identity is formed through four basic processes, which can occur separately or in combination. Some are overtly top-down and political, requiring the power of states to enforce. Others are more bottom-up, the result of spontaneous actions by populations. There must be some complementarity between the top-down and the bottom-up processes, otherwise identities won't take root.

First, there is the defining of political borders to fit populations; second, the moving or physical elimination of populations to fit existing borders; third, the cultural assimilation of subpopulations into the dominant culture; and fourth, modification of the concept of national identity to fit what is politically feasible, given the social and physical endowments of the society. Most successful national identity projects resulted from the interaction of all four approaches. Note, however, that the first three of these processes often involve violence and coercion.

1. Moving borders to fit posited national identities. Dynastic polities around the world from the Roman and Mauryan to the Ottoman and Austro-Hungarian Empires were constructed without regard to cultural identity. As the nationalist principle took hold from the French Revolution onward, the large extant political units began to break apart into more ethnolinguistically homogeneous ones. Thus Turkey was reduced to its Turkish-speaking core in Anatolia, and Austria-Hungary fragmented into the myriad small nations of the Balkans. The most recent of these imperial dissolutions was that of the former Soviet Union, a country built on ostensibly universalistic ideological principles which collapsed after 1991 into smaller states based on ethnolinguistic solidarity. In other cases, borders were expanded to include conationals, as in German and Italian unification.

2. Moving or eliminating populations to create more homogeneous political units. During the Balkan wars following the breakup of the former Yugoslavia, this is what came to be known as "ethnic cleansing." Ethnic cleansing was in a sense the natural concomi-

tant to the shift in legitimating principle from dynastic rule to national solidarity.

The great agrarian polyglot empires were compatible with both impersonal administration and rule of law. Indeed, they depended on such universalistic institutions in order to function, since they thrived on the interactions of ethnically and linguistically diverse people. At the height of the Roman Empire in the second century A.D., travelers moving from Britain to North Africa, Syria, or Asia Minor could expect to find similar administrative structures, laws, and roads. Fin de siècle Vienna was one of the most liberal and cosmopolitan cities in the world, reflecting the diversity of the empire of which it was the capital.

When multiethnic empires broke apart into states organized on a nationalist principle, various minority populations were left stranded in them. They could have been accommodated had the new national states adopted a liberal rule of law, but the power of ethnonationalist self-assertion guaranteed that this seldom happened. The result was huge movements of populations as various minority groups were forced out of the new would-be nation-states or traded for minorities in neighboring countries. Thus the mixed Greek and Turkish populations in Asia Minor and the eastern Aegean who had lived side by side since the time of the Byzantine Empire sorted themselves out during the Greek-Turkish War of 1919–1922. World War II was triggered, in some sense, by stranded populations such as the Sudeten Germans in Czechoslovakia and the Baltic Germans in Poland. The end of the war in 1945 saw massive transfers of populations (as well as substantial redrawing of borders) among Germany, Poland, Ukraine, Czechoslovakia, and other countries. Ethnic cleansing in the Balkans was thus not an invention of the post–cold war period. As some observers pointed out at the time, the stability of modern Western Europe was built on ethnic cleansings that had taken place in earlier historical periods, which modern Europeans had conveniently forgotten.

3. Cultural assimilation. Subordinate populations can adopt the language and customs of the dominant group, or in some cases intermarry to the point of eventually disappearing as a distinct minority. Assimilation can happen voluntarily, as minorities decide that it is in their self-interest to conform to the dominant culture. The

reduction in the number of regional languages in France and the adoption of Parisian French as a national standard is an example. Similarly, most immigrant groups arriving in the United States learned English and took on American customs because that was a route to upward social mobility.

Perhaps one of the greatest assimilation stories is China. Remarkably for so large a country, ethnic Han Chinese today constitute over 90 percent of the population. China was not always so homogeneous; its current ethnic makeup is the result of more than two millennia of relentless assimilation. The seat of ethnic Han civilization lay in the northerly Yellow River valley four millennia ago. The first Han state was established by the conquests of the state of Qin (in what is now north-central China) in the third century B.C. This state then expanded to the southeast, southwest, west, and northeast over the centuries. In doing so, the Han people ran into ethnically diverse indigenous populations, particularly among the Turkic-Mongolian nomads to the north and west. This original cultural diversity is preserved in the different forms of spoken Chinese that exist today. But the literary language was unified from the time of the original Qin Dynasty and served as the basis of a common elite culture for the entire empire. China was heavily influenced by non-Han ethnicities, but almost all of the foreign populations ultimately adopted Chinese cultural norms and intermarried so extensively with Han Chinese that those remaining in China were no longer distinguishable as ethnic minorities. The major exceptions are the Muslim Uighurs in the western province of Xinjiang, the Mongols in Inner Mongolia, and the Tibetans. Assimilation continues relentlessly as a matter of government policy, with the settling of ethnic Han Chinese in each of these areas.

We should not underestimate the degree of power and often coercion that is required to bring about cultural assimilation. Choice of a national language is a political act on the part of those who speak it. Few minorities voluntarily give up their mother tongues, particularly if they themselves are concentrated in a particular region where they have lived for generations. The primary instrument of cultural assimilation is the public education system and secondarily the choice of language in public administration.

Control over the school system is thus a hugely contested issue and the central objective of would-be nation builders.

4. Adjusting posited national identities to fit political realities. All nation-building projects eventually run into practical obstacles to achieving correspondence between idea and reality, and it is often the idea that gives way first in the face of simple power politics. The identity question cannot be separated from the territorial question. Ideas can be adjusted in a variety of ways: territorial claims can be scaled back, identity can be shifted from ethnicity or religion to ideology or a more flexible concept of shared culture, or entirely new concepts of identity can be introduced to supersede existent ones. Changing the definition of national identity to fit reality is the least coercive and most promising path to national unity.

HISTORICAL AMNESIA

Identity-building projects are extremely contentious because the world never consisted of compact, homogeneous "nations" ready to be turned into political units. As a result of conquest, migration, and trade, all societies were and still are complex mixtures of tribes, ethnicities, classes, religions, and regional identities. Any idea of a nation inevitably implies the conversion or exclusion of individuals deemed to be outside its boundaries, and if they don't want to do this peacefully, they have to be coerced. This coercion can be accomplished from the top down by states, but it can also take the form of communal violence, as one community kills or drives off its neighbors. The twenty-five or so nations that made up Europe at the middle of the twentieth century were the survivors of the five hundred or more political units that had existed there at the end of the Middle Ages.

In all of the cases discussed up to now—Germany, Greece, Italy, Britain, and the United States—contemporary outcomes, including high levels of economic development and liberal democracy, were dependent on earlier histories of violence and coercion. I have already touched on this with regard to Germany and Greece, both of which had large diaspora populations interspersed with other ethnicities to their east. The formation of the contemporary German and Greek states began with an act of violence—Bismarck's wars against Denmark, Austria, and France on the one hand, and the Greek revolution against the Ottomans on the other. That violence continued over the next century as populations were physically moved and borders continually redrawn.

Ernest Renan, one of the first writers to describe the phenomenon of modern nationalism, speaks of a historical amnesia that accompanied the process of nation building. According to him, "Forgetting, I would even say historical error, is essential to the creation of a nation, which is why the advance of historical study often poses a threat to nationality. Historical inquiry, in effect, brings to light the violent events that are at the source of all political formations, even those whose consequences have been beneficial." He argues that this amnesia extended all the way back to the barbarian conquests of Europe, in which wifeless warriors, having subdued the decadent remnants of the Roman Empire, married the local women and adopted their customs. Historical amnesia continued through the centuries, as we have forgotten once proud and independent entities like Burgundy, the Grand Duchy of Parma, or Schleswig, all of which now exist only as regions subordinate to larger territorial states.[11]

Britain and the United States are sometimes seen as exemplars of peaceful political development, which managed to avoid the violent upheavals of other societies in establishing their national identities through a process of gradual, piecemeal reform. But this is true only to a certain extent; Renan's historical amnesia applies in both cases. Britain's original Celtic Gaelic-speaking inhabitants were repeatedly invaded from across the channel, first by the Romans, then by succeeding waves of Angles, Saxons, and Danes, and finally a French-speaking Norman dynasty. The transformation of England into Britain involved the often violent efforts to incorporate Wales, Scotland, and Ireland, the limits of which were reached during Ireland's Easter Rebellion in 1916 and the formation of an independent Irish Republic. Needless to say, Northern Ireland has not been an entirely happy member of the British family since then, and at this writing Scotland has scheduled a referendum on independence.

Renan's observation about historical amnesia echoes a similar thought of Niccolò Machiavelli. Writing about the beginnings of Rome in *Discourses on the First Ten Books of Livy*, Machiavelli noted that the great city's founding was based on a fratricide, the killing of Remus by Romulus. He makes a broader observation that all just enterprises originate in a crime.[12] So too with the founding of democracy in the United States. North America was not a land of "new settlement" as is sometimes asserted. It was a territory thinly occupied by indigenous tribal groups who had to be exterminated, moved, or driven off their lands into reservations to make way for the democratic institutions of the settlers. American national identity is based on principles of equality, individual rights, and democracy, but that identity could not take hold except at the expense of the country's indigenous inhabitants. This didn't make the outcome less democratic or just, but it also does not mean that the original crime was not a crime. Moreover, the question of whether America's identity should give priority to political union based on the assertion of equality in the Declaration of Independence, or to the Constitution's protection of the rights of states, could not be peacefully resolved through democratic processes. So while Germans and Greeks may have more vivid memories of the violence in their recent histories, Britons and Americans should not forget that their contemporary national identities are also the beneficiaries of bloody struggles in the distant past.

13

GOOD GOVERNMENT, BAD GOVERNMENT

Why some developed-country governments are more effective than others; how political reform happens; why modernization is neither a sufficient nor a necessary condition for reform, yet helps; the role of outsiders in promoting reform

It is time to draw some general conclusions about the process of state building and modernization of the public sector. The purpose of this part of the book has been to explain why some developed countries managed to enter the twenty-first century with reasonably effective and uncorrupt governments, while others continue to be plagued by clientelism, corruption, poor performance, and low levels of trust both in government and in society more broadly. Providing an explanation may give us some insight regarding strategies that contemporary developing countries might use to deal with problems of corruption and patronage today.

All modern societies began with what Weber called patrimonial states, governments that were staffed with the friends and family of the ruler, or those of the elites who dominated the society. These states limited access to both political power and economic opportunity to individuals favored by the ruler; there was little effort to treat citizens impersonally, on the basis of universally applied rules.[1] Modern government—that is, a state bureaucracy that is impersonal and universal—develops only over time, and in many cases fails to develop at all.

I've selected cases that vary in terms of the success or failure of this modernization process. Germany developed the core of a modern state by the early decades of the nineteenth century. Japan, as we will see in chapter 23, created a modern bureaucracy almost from scratch shortly after the country was opened up during the Meiji Restoration. Italy and Greece, by contrast, never developed strong modern states and continue clientelist practices today. Britain and the United States are intermediate cases: both had patronage-ridden bureaucracies in the first half of the nineteenth century, or in the case of the United States, full-blown clientelism. Britain reformed its system fairly decisively following the Northcote-Trevelyan Report in the 1850s, while the United States reformed its public sector incrementally from the early 1880s through the 1930s.

Patrimonial states can be highly stable. They are constructed using the basic building blocks of human sociability, that is, the biological inclination of people to favor family and friends with whom they have exchanged reciprocal favors. Elites build power through the management of patronage chains by which clients follow patrons in pursuit of individual rewards. All of this is reinforced by ritual, religion, and ideas legitimating a particular form of elite rule. These elite groups are much better organized than others in the society—particularly dispersed and poverty-stricken peasants in agrarian societies—and have better access to weapons and training in the use of violence. As the scale of the society increases, informal patronage networks are converted into more formally organized clientelistic hierarchies. But the basic organizing principle of politics—reciprocal altruism—remains the same. Once they achieve political power, the elites running this type of system can be displaced by other, better-organized elite groups but seldom by the nonelites below them. These types of premodern states have succeeded in enduring for centuries and continue to exist around the world at the present moment.

ROUTES TO MODERN GOVERNMENT

How, then, did any society succeed in making the transition from a patrimonial to a modern state? The admittedly limited number of cases selected here suggests that there are at least two important routes.

The first comes by way of military competition. Ancient China, Prussia, and Japan all felt themselves engaged in prolonged struggles with their neighbors in which efficient government organization was critical to national survival. Military competition creates imperatives far more powerful than any economic incentive: nothing is worth very much, after all, if I and my entire family are likely to be slaughtered at the end of a war. The need to create an army puts a premium on meritocratic recruitment; it necessitates new taxes and revenue-raising capacity; it requires bureaucratic organization both to tax and to manage the fiscal and logistics chain that supplies the troops in the field; and it upsets interelite relationships by forcing the recruitment of nonelites to serve in and often lead the army.

To the extent that nation building has been critical to successful state building, war has also played a critical role. Once nationalism as a principle took hold at the time of the French Revolution, national identities were forged by adjusting political boundaries to correspond to existing cultural, ethnic, or linguistic communities. As we saw in the last chapter, this usually required the violent redrawing of borders, or the killing, moving, or forcible assimilation of populations living within them.

In Volume 1 we saw a number of examples of state modernization via war, particularly in the case of China, which I argued was the first society to set up a coherent, universal, and impersonal state. It was the Chinese who invented meritocracy and the civil examination in the third century B.C., a practice that did not get widely implemented in Europe until the nineteenth century. Both the Mamluks and the Ottomans arrived at a reasonably modern form of public administration through what seems today like the bizarre institution of military slavery: young men were captured in foreign lands and taken from their families, to be raised to be soldiers and administrators.

Prussia, too, felt the pressure of military competition and gradually put into place the elements of modern autonomous bureaucracy that has survived into the present. This began with the Great Elector's decision in 1660 not to disband the army after the Peace of Oliva but rather to maintain a standing military whose revenue needs necessitated reorganization of the country's entire administrative structure. Prussia's defeat by Napoleon in 1806 forced the opening of the bureaucracy to the middle classes under the Stein-Hardenberg reforms. Establishment of an elite, merit-based bureaucracy created an absolutist political coalition in support of the continuing autonomy of the bureaucracy. Thereafter, any time a politician or political party tried to place political appointees in the bureaucracy, the latter's supporters would express great opposition, and the politician would be forced to back down. In Prussia this autonomy was carried too far, such that democratically elected leaders found it impossible to bring the military part of the bureaucracy to heel. Bismarck forged a modern German nation through war, and unleashed an aggressive nationalism that culminated in the two world wars. State modernity and national identity were therefore purchased at a terribly high price.

The second route to state modernization was via a process of peaceful political reform, based on the formation of a coalition of social groups interested in having an efficient, uncorrupt government. Underlying the formation of such a coalition is the process of socioeconomic modernization. As noted in the general framework of development presented in chapter 2, economic growth often drives social mobilization through an expanding division of labor. Industrialization leads to urbanization, requirements for higher levels of education, occupational specialization, and a host of other changes that produce new social actors not present in an agrarian society. These actors have no strong stake in the existing patrimonial system; they can either be co-opted by the system, or they can organize an external coalition to change the rules by which the system operates.

The latter scenario unfolded in Britain and the United States. Both countries were early industrializers, and the new middle-class groups formed thereby led a drive for civil service reform whose legislative expressions were the Northcote-Trevelyan reform and the Pendleton Act. The British reform process unfolded much more quickly than the American one for several reasons: first, the British elite was more compact and had considerable control over the reform process; second, the Westminster system posed many fewer obstacles to decisive political action than America's complex system of checks and balances. The courts, opposition on a state level, and the difficulty of achieving a clear legislative majority all slowed the American reform process but were unimportant in the British case. The most important difference, however, was the fact that clientelism had become deeply rooted in American politics prior to the onset of reform and hence was much harder to eradicate.

This brings us to the question of clientelism, and why it is so much more powerful and pervasive in some countries than others. Here the answer suggested by these cases is basically that of Martin Shefter: it is a question of the sequence by which modern institutions are introduced and, in particular, the stage at which the democratic franchise is first opened.[2] I defined clientelism as the trading of votes and political support for individual benefits rather than programmatic policies, and distinguished it from elite patronage systems in which the scope of clientelist recruitment is far more limited and less well organized. Clientelism appears when democracy arrives before a modern state has had time to consolidate into an autonomous institution with its own supporting political coalition. Clientelism is an efficient form of political mobilization in societies with low levels of income and education, and is therefore best understood as an early form of democracy. In the United States, Greece, and Italy, the franchise was expanded prior to the creation of a modern state: in the 1830s in the United States, from 1844 to 1864 in Greece, and in the period after 1946 in Italy. Political parties in all three countries used their public bureaucracies as sources of benefits to political clients, with predictably disastrous consequences for state capacity. The principle of effective government is meritocracy; the principle of democracy is popular participation. These two principles can be made to work together, but there is always an underlying tension between them.

The interactions between the different dimensions of development are of course considerably more complicated than this and can be illustrated in the figures below.

FIGURE 8. The Prussian/German Development Path

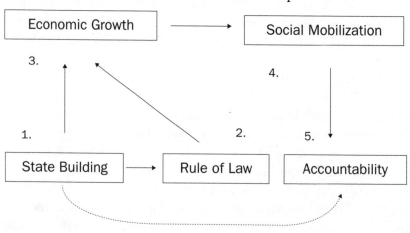

Figure 8 illustrates the Prussian/German development path. Prussia began building a strong state for reasons that had nothing to do with economic development; rather, it was needed for national survival. (The dotted line linking state building and accountability indicates that the impact of the former on the latter was negative.) While state building occurred under absolutist governments, it did, as we have seen, have a positive impact on development of the rule of law. The bureaucracy ruled through law; while the state did not accept the principle of democratic accountability, its sovereignty was increasingly based on the notion that the bureaucracy was the guardian of the public interest.

The combination of a modern state and rule of law then set the stage for the takeoff in economic growth that began around the middle of the nineteenth century. Economic historian Alexander Gerschenkron noted that in late-developing Germany the state played a much larger role in promoting economic growth than it did in England, a state that had a high-capacity at the beginning of the industrialization process.[3] Economic growth then led to the emergence of a working class and its mobilization under the banner of German Social Democracy. The German road to liberal democracy went through war, revolution, and repression in the early twentieth century. The early development of a strong and autonomous state had a very negative impact on democratic accountability, helping to drive the country into World War I and then undermining Weimar democracy. A fully institutionalized liberal democracy emerged only with the birth of the Federal Republic of Germany in 1949.

The United States took a very different path toward political modernization (see Figure 9). The United States inherited from Britain a strong rule of law in the form of the Common Law, an institution that was in place throughout the colonies well before the advent of democracy. The rule of law, with its strong protection of private property rights, laid the basis for rapid economic development in the nineteenth century. The early introduction of universal white male suffrage, however, had a decidedly negative impact on American state building by making clientelism pervasive throughout virtually all levels of government (the dotted line in Figure 9). Growth, however, created new social groups, mobilized through civil society and as new factions within the existing political parties. A reform coalition then led the drive to modernize the American state.

Finally, Figure 10 illustrates the Greek/southern Italian path. The entry point for development was neither state building nor economic growth;

FIGURE 9. The American Path

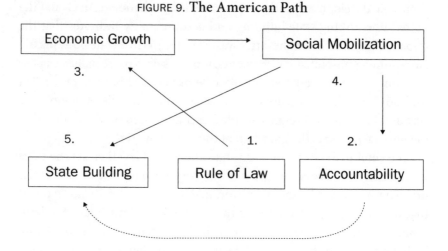

rather, it was social mobilization (what was earlier described as modernization without development) and early democratization. The weakness and lack of opportunity in the capitalist economy made the state an early object of capture, first by elite social groups and then by mass political parties as democracy deepened. Extensive clientelism weakened state capacity, which then further constrained prospects for economic growth (the dotted lines).

FIGURE 10. The Greek/Southern Italian Path

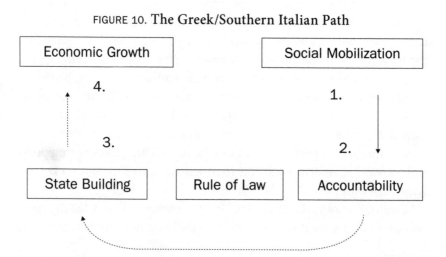

CORRUPTION AND THE MIDDLE CLASS

In Britain and America, economic modernization drove social mobilization, which in turn created the conditions for the elimination of patronage and clientelism. In both countries, it was new middle-class groups that sought an end to the patronage system. This might lead some to believe that socioeconomic modernization and the creation of a middle class will by themselves create modern government. But this view is belied by the Greek and Italian cases, societies that are wealthy and modern and yet continue to practice clientelism. There is no automatic mechanism that produces clean, modern government, because a host of other factors is necessary to explain outcomes.

One factor is the quality of economic growth. We saw that industrialization came late to both Greece and southern Italy, and that the process of urbanization had a very different character from what went on in Britain and the United States. In the latter countries, new occupational groups and social relationships were created by industrialization; in Greece and southern Italy, the population of the countryside simply moved into the cities, bringing with them rural habits and ways of life. In a thriving capitalist economy, one's self-interest is often best advanced through broad public policies, like lower tax rates, different forms of regulation, and consistent standards for internal and external trade. When Gemeinschaft is preserved intact by the ruralization of cities, by contrast, it is much easier to preserve clientelistic forms of social organization. The individual payoffs that are the essence of clientelism matter more than policies.[4]

Second, there is no guarantee that a member of the middle class will support an anticlientelistic reform coalition. Even within the United States, not all of the new social actors produced by industrialization signed up with the Progressive movement. As we saw, the railroads figured out how to make use of the existing patronage system to their own benefit; in many cases it was rather the customers of the railroads—the merchants, shippers, and farmers—who led the charge against what they perceived as a cozy relationship between the railroads and politicians. There was in a sense a race between the newly organizing middle-class interests opposed to patronage and the existing urban machines to sign up new social groups like recent immigrants.

In Greece and Southern Italy, the race to recruit the middle classes to a reform coalition was lost almost before it began. In Italy, there was a strong reformist middle class in the North that could have led a coalition to try to change the nature of politics in the South. But these groups found the job far too ambitious, given the weakness of the existing state; it was easier to guarantee peace and stability by making use of local elites and their chains of clients. In both places, the least clientelistic groups were those on the extreme left, the Greek and Italian Communists. But both parties had an agenda of overturning the democratic political system as a whole and were therefore strongly opposed by external powers including Britain and the United States. (In Italy, the Communists succeeded in coming to power locally in Turin and Bologna, and were generally credited with running relatively clean and effective municipal governments.) While the Progressives in the United States tended to be on the left as well, they had a strong stake in preserving the existing American system and therefore had a much better chance of taking power at a national level.

Third, there may be cultural factors that explain the difference in outcomes between Germany, Britain, and America on the one hand and Greece and Italy on the other. Self-interest explains only part of the reason that different social groups push for change, and it does not capture the high degree of moralism that often accompanies such movements. In each of these countries, individual leaders of reform movements were motivated by personal religiosity. They included the Great Elector and Frederick William I of Prussia, whose Calvinism induced them to import coreligionists from abroad and gave them a disciplinary vision of an austere and moral society led by an upright state. Calvinism also infused the Dutch state, which had accumulated extraordinary wealth and power in the seventeenth century after winning its independence from Catholic Spain.[5] From well before the English Civil War, Puritanism was an important driver of reform in England, and it continued to shape the behavior of the new middle classes in the nineteenth century. This was true as well of the upper-crust Progressive Era reformers in late-nineteenth-century America, who did not think merely that political bosses and patronage politics got in the way of making money. They were morally outraged that public offices were being perverted for private ends. While Americans may distrust state authority, they also believe that their democratic government is deeply legitimate, and that manipulation of the democratic process by monied interests and corrupt politicians is a strike against the democratic principle itself. Individual leaders like Gifford Pinchot were driven by a kind of Protestant religiosity that has largely disappeared from contemporary American public life.

Putting loyalty to the state ahead of loyalty to family, region, or tribe requires a broad radius of trust and social capital. Britain and the United States are traditionally societies with good endowments of both, at least in comparison to Greece and southern Italy. It is impossible to create social movements if people cannot be motivated to join civil society organizations, and they will not be inspired unless there is some ideal of civic responsibility to a larger community present among their fellow citizens.

The sources of social capital in Britain and the United States were varied. One had to do with the sectarian form of Protestantism, noted above, that took root in both countries and encouraged the grassroots organization of religious life that did not depend on centralized, hierarchical institutions. But the second source had to do with strong national identity organized around institutions—in Britain's case, the Common Law, Parliament, and the monarchy, and in America's, a similar Common Law tradition and the democratic institutions emanating from the Constitution. By the nineteenth century, government in both countries came to be seen as a legitimate expression of national sovereignty and an object of considerable loyalty.

Greeks and Italians always had a more troubled sense of national identity. Greek society was very homogeneous on ethnic, cultural, and religious levels, but the Greek state was frequently seen as a tool of foreign powers and therefore illegitimate. Loyalty was therefore limited to a narrow circle of trust around the immediate family; the state was an object of suspicion. Italy, particularly in the South, had also been the playground of various foreigners who set Italians against one another. The unified country that emerged after 1861 yoked together regions of very different cultures and levels of development, and never generated the kind of centralized political power that could assimilate the South to the North. To this day, regional loyalties often trump national identity, as the very existence of the Northern League suggests. There have been heroic individuals inspired by a strong sense of civic duty, like Alberto dalla Chiesa and Giovanni Falcone. There is also the residue of a strong civic republican tradition in the cities of the North. But especially in the South, the lack of legitimate state institutions narrowed the radius of trust to friends and family, a tendency that then became institutionalized through organizations like the Mafia.

REPATRIMONIALIZATION

Before Americans, Britons, or Germans get too self-satisfied about their own political systems, however, it is important to note that the problem of patrimonialism is never finally solved in any political system. I argued in Volume 1 of this book that reliance on friends and family is a default mode of human sociability and will always return in different forms in the absence of powerful incentives to behave otherwise. The modern, impersonal state forces us to act in ways that are deeply in conflict with our own natures and is therefore constantly at risk of erosion and back-sliding. Elites in any society will seek to use their superior access to the political system to further entrench themselves, their families, and their friends unless explicitly prevented from doing so by other organized forces in the political system. This is no less true in a developed liberal democracy than in other political orders, and one can make the argument that the process of repatrimonialization continues into the present.

The Progressive Era reforms in the United States eliminated one particular form of clientelism, the ability of the political parties to secure support through the distribution of jobs in the bureaucracy at federal, state, and local levels. It did not, however, end the practice of distributing other kinds of favors, such as subsidies, tax breaks, and other benefits, to political supporters. One of the big issues afflicting American politics in recent years has been the impact of interest groups that are able to effectively buy politicians with campaign contributions and lobbying. Most of this activity is perfectly legal, so in a sense the United States has created a new form of clientelism, only practiced at a much larger scale and with huge sums of money at stake. This is an issue to which I will return in the last part of this volume.

This is not only an American problem. Japan, as noted, has a tradition of strong, autonomous bureaucracy, and jobs in the bureaucracy were never the currency of corruption there. On the other hand, budgetary perks have for many decades been the currency of so-called money politics in Japan, with the Liberal Democratic Party maintaining its hegemony over several decades by skillfully handing out political pork. The ability of Japanese interest groups like the electric power industry to capture regulators was evident in the crisis that enveloped the country in 2011 after the Tohoku earthquake and the Fukushima nuclear disaster.

GIVE WAR A CHANCE?

Military competition was an important driver of state modernization in the cases selected here, but it is in itself neither a sufficient nor a necessary condition to achieve this end. Our sample was deliberately biased toward successful cases, but a number of observers have pointed out that prolonged military competition in other parts of the world has not produced modern states. This is true among the tribes of Papua New Guinea and other parts of Melanesia, which have been fighting one another for some forty thousand years now and were nonetheless unable to achieve even state-level forms of organization prior to the arrival of European colonizers. This has also been largely true in Latin America, whose wars have ended with patrimonial elites still in power (see chapter 17 below). There are clearly other conditions, such as physical geography, class structure of societies, and ideology, that combined with war to produce modern states in Asia and Europe but not elsewhere.

Conversely, other countries have created modern, nonclientelistic governments without military competition. While Sweden and Denmark fought large numbers of wars in the early modern period, their neighbors Norway, Finland, and Iceland did not, and yet all have very similar clean governments today. Korea was the victim of outside aggression, occupation, and violence beginning in the late nineteenth century up through the end of the Korean War, and yet it has a bureaucratic system equal in quality to that of Japan, as does the former British colony of Singapore. Canada, Australia, and New Zealand have modern, nonclientelistic states and yet were never militaristic.

In many of these cases, high-quality government was the result of a direct colonial inheritance (Norway became independent of Denmark in 1813, Iceland in 1874, and Canada separated from Britain in 1867). In others, it was due to a deliberate copying of other models. Singapore and Malaysia created effective modern governments virtually from scratch out of materials that seemed initially very unpromising, in response to perceived challenges from leftist forces that were mobilizing across Southeast Asia.[6]

These observations have important implications for the present. In a half-serious vein, the military analyst Edward Luttwak once suggested that the international community needed to "give war a chance" in weak-state zones like sub-Saharan Africa.[7] Modern states, he argued, had been forged over the centuries in Europe through relentless military struggle; Africa, with its irrational colonial era state boundaries, had not been allowed to sort itself out in a similar manner. The states there created neither strong bureaucracies nor overarching national identities.

Apart from the fact that no one should wish Europe's violent experience on anyone else, it is not clear that even a couple of centuries of conflict would actually produce strong states in other parts of the world. Why this is so, and what alternative approaches might be taken to state building in Africa, will be addressed in the following part of this book on legacies of colonialism. On the other hand, the fact that other states achieved modern governments without war suggests that developing states today might choose similar peaceful paths.

The fact that the early introduction of democracy encouraged clientelism, and that today's strong states were often forged prior to the onset of democracy, might further suggest that contemporary developing countries should try to follow the same sequence. This was in fact a conclusion drawn by Samuel Huntington in *Political Order in Changing Societies*— that societies needed order before they needed democracy, and that they were better off making an authoritarian transition to a fully modernized political and economic system rather than trying to jump directly to democracy. His book praised not just existing Communist regimes for their ability to expand political participation and force the pace of economic growth; he also wrote approvingly of systems like the one created by Mexico's Institutional Revolutionary Party (Partido Revolucionario Institucional, or PRI), which ruled the country from the 1940s up until 2000, and returned to power in 2013. The PRI created a tremendously stable political order that replaced the coups, military caudillos, and violent social conflicts that characterized Mexico's first century of national existence, but at the expense of democracy and economic vitality.[8] Huntington's student Fareed Zakaria has made a similar argument about the importance of sequencing, emphasizing less political order in itself than a liberal rule of law as a necessary first step prior to the onset of democracy.[9]

While this type of argument would seem to flow logically from the cases presented here, it is not in fact such a good guide to policy in the present.[10] It is fine to say that societies should create a strong, autonomous Weberian bureaucracy first, or else put into place a liberal rule of law with its independent courts and well-trained judges. The problem is that, as a matter of institutional construction, it is not very easy to do either. Institutions were often predetermined by historical legacies, or shaped by external powers. Many poor societies in the developing world have been able to create authoritarian states that stay in power through some combination of repression and co-optation. But for the reasons that we saw, hardly any has been able to create a Chinese mandarinate or Rechtsstaat, in which authoritarian power is embodied in a highly institutionalized bureaucracy and operates through clearly articulated rules. Many contemporary authoritarian states are riddled with patronage and high levels of corruption. The only countries in the contemporary world that come close are some Persian Gulf monarchies, as well as Singapore, whose peculiar circumstances make them difficult models for anyone to emulate. Under these circumstances, what is the point of putting off democratization, in favor of a ruthless and/or corrupt and incompetent dictatorship?

The final reason why a deliberate effort to sequence the introduction of political institutions is problematic is a moral or normative one. Accountability through periodic free and fair elections is a good thing in itself, apart from any effects it may have on the quality of government or economic growth. The right to participate politically grants recognition to the moral personhood of the citizen, and exercise of that right gives that person some degree of agency over the common life of the community. The citizen may make poorly informed or bad decisions, but the exercise of political choice in and of itself is an important part of human flourishing. This is not simply my private opinion; around the world, large masses of people are now mobilized to defend this right of political participation. The Arab Spring of 2011 is just the latest demonstration of the power of the idea of democracy, in a part of the world where many assumed there was a cultural acceptance of dictatorship.

In countries like Prussia and Britain that did experience a sequenced introduction of modern political institutions, the older nondemocratic regimes were traditional monarchies that had their own sources of legitimacy. This is not true for the vast majority of authoritarian countries that emerged in the wake of colonialism in the mid-twentieth century, which were founded in military coups or elite power grabs. The most stable among them—Singapore and China—maintained their legitimacy through good economic performance but do not have clear wellsprings of support like the Hohenzollern dynasty.

For better or worse, then, most contemporary developing countries do not have a realistic option of sequencing, and, like the United States, have to build strong states in the context of democratic political systems. That is why the American experience during the Progressive Era is singularly important. No country today can realistically try to imitate Prussia, building a strong state through a century and a half of military struggle. On the other hand, it is possible to imagine civil society groups and political leaders in democratic countries organizing reformist coalitions that press for public-sector reform and an end to gross corruption. The single most important lesson to be drawn from the American experience is that state building is above all a political act. The structure of a modern state may be specified by certain formal rules (for example, selection of officials based on merit rather than connections), but implementation of these rules inevitably hurts the interests of some entrenched political actors who benefit from the status quo. Reform therefore requires dislodging these actors, working around them, and organizing new social forces that will benefit from a cleaner and more capable form of government.

State building is hard work, and it takes a long time to accomplish. Elimination of patronage at a federal level took over forty years, from the Pendleton Act to the New Deal. In New York, Chicago, and other cities, political machines and patronage survived until the 1960s. I noted that the American political system puts up high barriers to reform, and not every country is like this. Oftentimes countries can make use of external crises like financial meltdowns, disasters, or military threats to accelerate the process. But there are very few historical precedents for this type of political modernization happening overnight.

We saw that state building in Greece was particularly difficult because of the role of outside powers. Greece was ruled for centuries by the Turks; foreigners helped the country win its independence; they imposed Otto of Bavaria as the first king of the newly independent country; they attempted a crash modernization of its political system and continued to intervene to either support or oppose domestic groups like the Greek Communists. All of this weakened the legitimacy of Greek governments, increased levels of distrust in the state, and ultimately failed to produce a fully modernized political system. In a way, the struggle among the European Union, the IMF, and the Greek government over the financial crisis early in the twenty-first century is only the latest version of this ongoing story.

Greece therefore prefigures the topic of the next part of the book, which is the effort to transplant modern political institutions from one part of the world to another. The process of globalization began in earnest with the European voyages of discovery in the fifteenth century and the onset of colonialism, which suddenly brought entire regions of the world in contact with one another. The confrontation of indigenous societies all over the world with Western culture and institutions had profound and often deadly consequences. It also meant that political development would forever cease to be something that happened largely within the confines of a single region or society. Foreign models would be forcibly imposed or voluntarily adapted by locals, with very different conditions for institutional development. Why this process worked better in some parts of the world than in others will be the topic of the following section of this book.

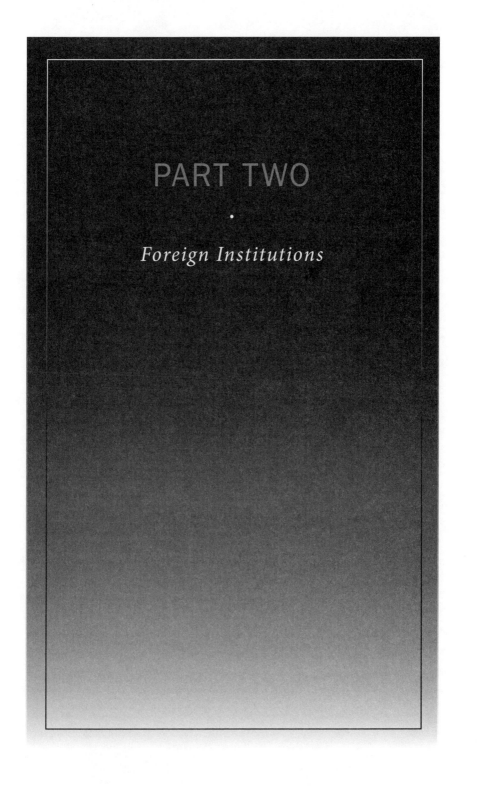

PART TWO

·

Foreign Institutions

14

NIGERIA

Political corruption in Nigeria; how Nigeria, despite possessing abundant natural resources, has failed to develop; why this failure is squarely rooted in weak institutions and bad politics; how Nigeria's experience differs from that of other developing countries

While the governments of Greece and Italy differ from their Northern European neighbors with regard to clientelism and corruption, they still possess modern cores and have been able to provide basic public goods at a level sufficient to turn their societies into wealthy developed countries. When we turn to the African country of Nigeria, however, we observe clientelism and corruption of an entirely different order of magnitude and, correspondingly, one of the most tragic development failures in the contemporary world.

Consider the following story related by Peter Cunliffe-Jones, a British journalist who lived in Nigeria for several years, and whose distant relative was a participant in the region's original colonization. A German businessman named Robert married a Nigerian woman and set up a plant to process soybeans in his wife's home state, a crop that was grown locally and for which there was a good market. The business was hard to set up, given the need for machinery that couldn't be purchased locally and a very unreliable electricity supply. With some perseverance, however, Robert and his wife were able to get the plant running. Cunliffe-Jones relates:

> Then, three months later, the problems started. After they sold the first cartons of soybean oil, a local government official appeared at the factory gate and said that regulations had been broken in setting up the plant . . . The council chairman wanted 10 percent of their revenue, paid to a special

account, to make the problem go away. Robert refused to pay. He went to the police. The council chairman sent round thugs to smash up his car. The police chief got involved. Not to help, but to demand a cut for himself.

Robert and his wife realized they had to play the game, and paid up. They were left alone for a while, and their business succeeded in making a profit. Then the state governor heard about his operation and demanded a cut for himself:

> When Robert again refused to pay, he was arrested for breaking employ-
> ment laws and bribing officials . . . To get himself out of jail, Robert had to
> pay off the governor, the police chief, the council chairman, and the judge
> now handling the case. He closed the business and sold the equipment to
> recoup some of his costs. He and his wife then left for Germany . . . The
> 200 jobs they had created disappeared with the business. All that re-
> mained was an empty warehouse, some unemployed workers, a large
> pile of soybeans, and a lot of angry farmers.[1]

Although this might seem like a typical story about developing world corruption, it raises some troubling questions. The willingness of Robert and his wife to establish a business should have led to a win-win situation for everyone: for the soybean farmers, for the consumers of their products, for the two hundred employees of Robert's company, and indeed for the public officials who would have seen long-term tax revenues rise and who might have been rewarded at the next election for having encouraged the creation of so many jobs. It is not sufficient to say that the officials were personally greedy and chose private gain over public benefit. Even by this selfish calculus, they shortsightedly killed the goose that was laying the golden egg. Once Robert left the country, there was no one from whom they could extract a bribe, no one further to tax. The potential win-win became a lose-lose.

POOR PERFORMANCE

Nigeria is sub-Saharan Africa's largest nation by population, at around 160 million. Nigeria got substantially richer during the great commodity boom of the early 2000s, and the Nigerian government "rebased" its estimate of the size of its 2013 economy to make it suddenly 60 percent larger than prior estimates by organizations like the World Bank. But very little of that money flowed down to its population as a whole.

Figure 11 shows that Nigerian per capita income in the fifty years from 1960 to 2010 grew by some 90 percent, which amounts to a miserable compound annual rate of just over 1 percent per year. In the three decades from the start of the country's oil boom in the 1970s, per capita income actually declined and did not return to its 1979 level until 2005. This performance is poor by the standards of "emerging" Africa, and particularly poor when compared to countries in East Asia. It is perhaps unfair to compare Nigeria to highfliers like South Korea and Taiwan, but as political scientist Peter Lewis has shown, Indonesia provides a highly revealing counterpoint.[2] Like Nigeria, Indonesia is a large (2010 population 233 million), ethnically diverse, oil-rich country. In 1960, Indonesia's per capita income was only 60 percent of Nigeria's. By 2010, it was 118 percent higher.

FIGURE 11. **Per Capita GDP, Constant 2000 US$**

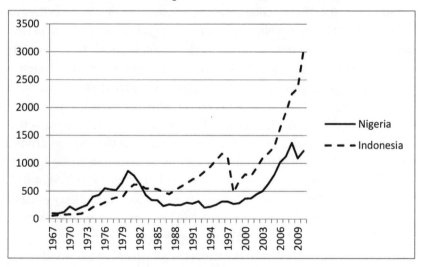

SOURCE: World Bank

What growth there's been in Nigeria over this period was related almost entirely to oil exports. Oil production began in the Niger River Delta in 1958, and the country experienced an economic boom as prices rose during the energy crises of the 1970s. However, oil turned out to be much more of a curse than a blessing in virtually every respect. Nigeria suffered from "Dutch disease," a phenomenon experienced by Holland during a natural gas boom in the 1950s during which a commodity-led currency appreciation undermined the competitiveness of sectors other than energy. Whereas Nigeria used to export substantial amounts of cocoa, groundnuts, palm oil, and rubber in pre-oil days, it came to be almost completely dependent on oil exports for both export earnings and government revenues.[3] As a major energy producer, Indonesia faced similar challenges but was much better able to promote the growth of nonoil exports and manufacturing. While Indonesia reduced energy as a proportion of exports from 75 to 22 percent between 1975 and 2003, Nigeria's dependence increased. The paltry 4 percent of Nigerian exports not related to energy is testimony to the complete failure to create either a modern commercial agriculture industry or manufacturing sector, which would have been sustainable routes to economic development.[4]

It is estimated that from the 1970s to the early 2000s Nigeria took in about $400 billion in oil revenues.[5] Unlike the East Asian export-led economies, this money was not plowed back into investments in either physical or human capital (that is, education). Nor did it have much of an effect on the incomes of ordinary Nigerians: indeed, poverty rates increased dramatically, and other indicators of development, such as child mortality rates, barely budged. Table 2 shows that, in comparison to Indonesia's relative success at poverty reduction, Nigeria entered the twenty-first century with more than two-thirds of its population living in poverty.

So where did all this money go? The answer, not surprisingly, is that it went into the hands of Nigeria's political elite. That elite centers around a series of ogas, or Big Men, and their patronage networks. Some ogas are descendants of the traditional elite that ruled prior to the arrival of British colonialism, but others are self-made men—former military officers, businessmen, or politicians who succeeded in using the political system to enrich themselves. And some are very rich indeed, like Aliko Dangote, a northern patriarch said to be the richest black person in the world with a 2014 net worth estimated at $25 billion.[6] Many of the worst offenders are state governors, like Diepreye Alamieyeseigha, elected to run one of the poorest states in the Niger delta, who owned properties in London and Cape Town and was found by the British police with £914,000 in cash lying around his flat in 2002.[7]

TABLE 2. Percentage of Population Below the Poverty Line

Year	Indonesia	Nigeria
1976	40.1	–
1980	28.6	28.1
1984	21.6	–
1985	–	46.3
1990	15.1	–
1992	–	42.7
1996	17.5	65.6
1999	23.4	70.6
2003	17.4	70.2

SOURCE: Peter Lewis, *Growing Apart: Oil, Politics, and Economic Change in Indonesia and Nigeria*

Politics is the general route to riches in Nigeria; very little income has been earned through entrepreneurship and genuine value creation. Transparency International ranked it 143 out of 183 countries in terms of perceived corruption.[8] The stories of corruption-driven incompetence are legendary. In the mid-1970s, for example, the military regime of Yakubu Gowon announced the purchase of sixteen million metric tons of concrete to build a series of military facilities and other ambitious infrastructure projects, quadrupling imports from the previous year. Ships full of concrete poured into Lagos harbor but could not unload for as long as a year because they were not actually needed; much of the concrete was ordered so that government officials could collect demurrage fees. The concrete hardened in the ships' holds, and many of them had to be scuttled in place, clogging the harbor for years to come.[9]

Corruption at a high level filters down and affects all segments of Nigerian society. The only thing many Westerners know about Nigeria is that it is the source of e-mail scams offering bogus windfalls. This is a variety of what in Nigeria are known as 419 frauds, named after a section of the Nigerian penal code. Reflecting Nigeria's weak protection of property rights, middle-class Nigerians often paint large signs on their houses stating that they are not for sale. The reason for this is that they could go away on a vacation and return to find their house occupied by a stranger who had stolen the legal title from them.[10]

In a country with so much poverty and corruption, it is not surprising that there is also a lot of violence. This is particularly true in the Niger River Delta, where Western oil companies have been operating since the 1950s. The failure of resources to flow down to the region's mostly Ijaw and Ogoni population is especially notable here; the delta is one of the poorest parts of Nigeria. Nearly 1.5 million tons of oil have been spilled into the delta over the past fifty years, polluting the waterways and killing off the fisheries by which the population traditionally lived. This has spawned an insurgency that regularly targets the oil industry as well as numerous gangs sponsored by local ogas who live off of robbery and extortion. The federal government in Abuja has tried to appease this anger by sending substantial resources to the South. Much of this money, however, ends up in the pockets of local politicians.[11]

More recently, there has been a string of deadly attacks in the North by Boko Haram, a radical Islamist group linked to al-Qaeda, that have targeted government facilities, Christian churches, and the UN compound in the capital, and in 2014 captured more than two hundred schoolgirls. Boko Haram's violent tactics can in no way be justified by northern Nigeria's poverty, but it and other dissident groups find the country's corrupt government an easy target for their activities due to its extraordinarily weak legitimacy. That government's response to these attacks has been, in turn, slow and feckless.

DICTATORSHIP AND DEMOCRACY

Many outside observers of Nigeria's political institutions focus on the presence or absence of democracy there, and the way that democratic institutions interact with the country's complex ethnic and religious makeup. When Nigeria was granted independence from Britain in 1960, it was bequeathed a democratic constitution that provided for regular elections. There was also continuity in the legal institutions that had been set up under the colonial government, down to the wig-wearing judges in Nigeria's British-style courts. But democracy did not last long: after a violent and contested election in 1964 that led to a breakdown of order throughout the country, the civilian government was overthrown by the military in 1966. The military was itself split between Igbos from the East and northern Muslims; after a countercoup, the Igbos declared an independent state of Biafra and a civil war ensued, resulting in between one and three million deaths. It was finally resolved through the military defeat of the breakaway state amid widespread starvation there.[12]

The military remained in power in Nigeria during the oil boom years and gave way to an elected government in 1979 under the title of the Second Republic. Another chaotic and contested election in 1983 led the military to take over again. The country was led by a series of generals until new democratic elections were held in 1999, when a former strongman, Olusegun Obasanjo, became president. While Nigeria has been an electoral democracy since then, the quality of its democratic institutions is not strong: the 2007 election that brought Umaru Musa Yar'Adua into office was marked by substantial fraud and violence, and was described by former U.S. ambassador John Campbell as an "election-like event."[13]

The presence or absence of formal democracy has made very little difference either to Nigeria's rate of economic growth or to the quality of government. The performance of the economy is linked almost exclusively to global commodity prices, given the country's heavy energy-export dependence. Thus the country's economy grew under military rulers in the 1970s, shrank under both civilian and military rulers during the oil price collapse of the 1980s and early 1990s, and then rose again in the 2000s under civilian governments as prices increased. Neither poverty rates, health outcomes, levels of corruption, nor income distribution have shown much correlation to the type of regime.

This then poses the interesting question: Why hasn't democracy made a significant difference? Shouldn't opening up a political system to the free flow of information and democratic contestation lead ordinary people to vote for candidates who are more honest or who provide public goods for everyone rather than just their supporters? If democracy means rule by the people, the question that contemporary Nigeria forces on us is, Why don't people get angrier and try to take charge of the situation, as they did in the United States or Britain during the nineteenth century?[14]

The answer that scholars such as Richard Joseph have given is that politics in Nigeria is what he labels "prebendal," involving a fatal mixture of rent seeking, clientelism, and ethnicity. Because of oil, the state has ready access to a steady flow of resource rents, which the elites have shared among themselves. While all poor people—the 70 percent of the population below the poverty line—in theory have a common interest in ending corruption and redistributing those resources more fairly, they are divided into more than 250 ethnic and religious communities that do not want to work with one another. Their ties are instead vertical, to clientelistic networks controlled by the elites, who dole out just enough patronage and subsidies to mobilize support at the next election. The system is stable because members of the elite rent-seeking coalition realize that using violence to grab a larger share of the total pie will hurt everyone's interests, including their own. The typical response to violence like the armed attacks in the delta is a combination of repression and increased subsidies to buy off discontent.[15]

This is why the impact of democracy on corruption and government performance in Nigeria has been so limited and disappointing. There is no question that democracy is an improvement over military governments: there is a free and lively press that often exposes corruption scandals and criticizes poor performance on the part of politicians and bureaucrats. In the 2000s, the government of President Obasanjo set up an Economic and Financial Crimes Commission (EFCC), whose first chairman, Nuhu Ribadu, succeeded in prosecuting some officials. But the simple availability of information about corruption tends not to produce genuine accountability because the politically active part of the population are members of clientelistic networks. Elections are hotly, violently, and often fraudulently contested because there is so much at stake in terms of access to state resources. The leaders who organize these networks have no interest in seeing anticorruption measures go too far; Ribadu was dismissed and the EFCC neutralized as soon as it looked like it was becoming independent of its political masters. In 2014, Lamido Sanusi, Nigeria's central bank governor, was dismissed after noting that as much as $20 billion had gone missing from the national oil company. Ethnically and religiously based clientelism displaces any broader political mobilization around issues of ideology or public policy.

In a clientelistic political system, it is rational for voters to respond to individual rewards offered by politicians in return for their votes. As a large literature on African clientelism has shown, ethnicity becomes a convenient signaling device and commitment mechanism between patrons and clients that guarantees that voters will support a candidate and that candidates will deliver on targeted goods and services after the election.[16]

INSTITUTIONAL ROOTS OF POVERTY

Nigeria is in no way typical of Africa. Its economic and social performance over the decades has lagged behind the continent as a whole, and only during the resource boom of the 2000s has it begun to catch up. It is, nonetheless, the continent's largest country by population, and, by recently revised estimates, the region's largest economy. Its problems are only a more extreme form of a phenomenon common not just in other parts of sub-Saharan Africa but in underdeveloped countries around the world.

The roots of Nigeria's development problem are institutional; indeed, it is hard to find a better example of weak institutions and bad government trapping a nation in poverty. Of the three categories of basic political institutions—state, rule of law, and accountability—lack of democracy is not the core of the country's problems. However poor the quality of Nigeria's democratic institutions, substantial political competition, debate, and opportunities for the exercise of accountability have existed since the end of military rule in 1999.

Nigeria's real institutional deficits lie in the first two categories: lack of a strong, modern, and capable state; and absence of a rule of law that provides property rights, citizen security, and transparency in transactions. These two deficits are related. Rather than having a modern state that can provide necessary public goods like roads, ports, schools, and public health on an impersonal basis, the Nigerian government's main activity is predatory or, in Joseph's term, prebendal: it is engaged in the extraction of rents and their distribution to other members of the political elite. This leads to the routine violation of the rule of law, as in the story of Robert, where public officials force a job-creating businessman out of the country in their pursuit of bribes.

The Nigerian state is weak not only in technical capacity and its ability to enforce laws impersonally and transparently. It is also weak in a moral sense: it has a deficit of legitimacy. There is little loyalty to a nation called Nigeria that supersedes ties to one's region, ethnic group, or religious community. The country's complex electoral laws require that a president be elected not just by a plurality of votes in a national election, but that he or she receive a certain number of votes in different regions of the country. This clever rule effectively makes it difficult for a candidate representing one region or ethnic group to dominate the system as a whole.

But it does not guarantee that Nigerians will feel a common sense of national identity, or that they will trust the president and other national leaders to treat their group fairly. Stability in recent years has been maintained by an informal elite pact that provides for, among other things, alternating rule between a northern Muslim and a southern Christian.

Why is it that the Nigerian state and rule of law ended up being so extraordinarily weak? And if strong political institutions are critical for economic development, where do they come from? One answer that has been put forward by a variety of observers is the physical conditions of climate and geography.

15

GEOGRAPHY

Montesquieu's theories about the origins of institutions, and the effects of climate and geography thereupon, and their modern counterparts; how economists have revived these debates in recent years; where geography has had a clear effect on the nature of institutions; a framework for understanding the three regions to be discussed

Since the beginning of the Industrial Revolution, there has been a huge divergence between levels of wealth in the developing and developed worlds. In the year 1500, differences in levels of per capita wealth among Europe, pre-Columbian America, China, and the Middle East would not have been all that great, but in the past two hundred years a certain part of the world has pulled ahead economically in a dramatic way. This "great divergence" is illustrated in Figure 12.

Since at least the time of Adam Smith, one of the chief preoccupations of economists has been to explain why Europe and the West more broadly succeeded in pulling ahead of other parts of the world. Not only was the West the first region to industrialize; it has succeeded in maintaining its lead over most other parts of the world for the last two hundred years. Only in the second half of the twentieth century did parts of East Asia—Japan, Korea, Taiwan, Singapore—begin to catch up and close the gap. In the twenty-first century, there was another set of so-called emerging market countries labeled the BRICS—Brazil, Russia, India, China, and South Africa—that seemed poised to join the rich countries' club. Even if this eventually happens, however, it is a puzzle as to why it took so long.

The difference in economic outcomes corresponds to a difference in political institutions. There is a strong correlation between the richest countries, in per capita terms, and those that have the strongest institutions: countries with effective, relatively uncorrupt states; enforceable,

FIGURE 12. Per Capita Incomes, Industrialized Countries vs. Nonindustrialized

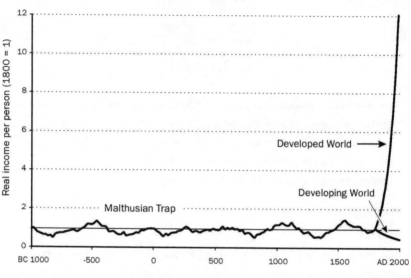

SOURCE: Gregory Clark, *A Farewell to Alms*

transparent legal rules; and open access to legal and political institutions. As the case of Nigeria suggests, there is a linkage between economic and political outcomes. If a country is ruled by an elite whose primary objective is to appropriate public resources, if property rights aren't respected, if the country can't set coherent policies or educate its own people, then even the possession of valuable natural resources like oil is not going to lead to sustained economic growth. The existence of formal democratic institutions is not sufficient to guarantee good outcomes; state and rule of law are important parts of the mix.

What, then, accounts for the difference in institutions in different parts of the world, and why did the West have a large initial advantage? If institutions are so critical to wealth and growth, why doesn't everyone simply adopt the best ones and get on with it?

THE SPIRIT OF THE LAWS

Charles Secondat, Baron de Montesquieu (1689–1755) is perhaps best known for his arguments in favor of separated powers as a check on tyranny and his observations concerning the softening effects of commerce on morals and politics. Montesquieu was in some sense the first modern comparative political scientist. His observations on politics are drawn not just from the experience of different European countries including England and his native France, but also from non-Western societies such as China and Turkey. Books XIV–XIX of his great work *The Spirit of the Laws* contain an extensive discussion of the impact of climate and geography on political institutions.

There are several avenues by which Montesquieu sees geography having an effect on the nature of institutions. The first is through the way it shapes what later would come to be called national character. Climate had a direct effect on personality, as he argues in Book XIV:

> Put a man into a close, warm place, and . . . he will feel a great faintness. If under this circumstance you propose a bold enterprise to him, I believe you will find him very little disposed towards it; his present weakness will throw him into despondency; he will be afraid of everything, being in a state of total incapacity. The inhabitants of warm countries are, like old men, timorous . . . the people in cold countries are, like young men, brave. Northern people, transported to southern regions, did not perform such exploits as their countrymen, who, fighting in their own climate, possessed their full vigor and courage.

Montesquieu goes on to note that "in cold countries they have very little sensibility for pleasure; in temperate countries, they have more; in warm countries, their sensibility is exquisite." He makes an observation many people today would likely affirm: "I have been at the opera in England and in Italy, where I have seen the same pieces and the same performers; and yet the same music produces such different effects on the two nations: one is so cold and phlegmatic, and the other so lively and enraptured, that it seems almost inconceivable."

The second mechanism through which geography influences institutions is its effects on power. In Book XV, he discusses the institution of slavery. He notes Aristotle's theory of natural slavery but doubts that natural slaves exist; he also rejects the view that African slavery is based on some inherent biological inferiority of blacks. Slavery, he argues, is the product of human convention and coercion. But who coerces whom into slavery is very much the product not of biology but of physical geography.

In Book XVII, Montesquieu comes to the following conclusion, which deserves to be quoted at length:

> In Asia they have always had great empires; in Europe these could never subsist. Asia has larger plains; it is cut out into much more extensive divisions by mountains and seas; and as it lies more to the south, its springs are more easily dried up; the mountains are less covered with snow; and the rivers being not so large form more contracted barriers.
>
> Power in Asia ought, then, to be always despotic; for if their slavery was not severe they would make a division inconsistent with the nature of the country.
>
> In Europe the natural division forms many nations of a moderate extent, in which the ruling by laws is not incompatible with the maintenance of the state: on the contrary, it is so favorable to it, that without this the state would fall into decay, and become a prey to its neighbors.
>
> It is this which has formed a genius for liberty that renders every part extremely difficult to be subdued and subjected to a foreign power, otherwise than by laws and the advantage of commerce.
>
> On the contrary, there reigns in Asia a servile spirit, which they have never been able to shake off, and it is impossible to find in all the histories of that country a single passage which discovers a freedom of spirit; we shall never see anything there but by the excess of slavery.

Other political theorists, from Aristotle to Rousseau, have argued that climate and geography had an effect in shaping the nature of political institutions. By the second half of the twentieth century, however, when the European colonial empires were being disbanded and countries of the developing world were emerging as independent states, this line of reasoning began to fall out of favor. This was particularly true of arguments having to do with the effects of climate on national character and consequently development. Many of Montesquieu's views on the differences between courageous inhabitants of northern climates and pleasure-seeking but indolent southerners were dismissed as crude stereotyping or racist prejudice. These and related arguments about the cultural determinants of development were attacked for "blaming the victim."

The idea that there were intrinsic differences between Europeans and southern people of color had been biologized during the late nineteenth century when the great colonial empires were being carved out of Asia,

Africa, and the Middle East. Europeans justified their conquests of much of the rest of the world on the basis of a social Darwinist doctrine regarding their own inherent racial superiority. The peoples being colonized were regarded as unfit for democracy or self-rule because they were lower down on an evolutionary scale and would require centuries of tutelage before they were ready to operate modern institutions on their own. The Nazis with their doctrine of Aryan racial superiority produced the most extreme and grotesque variant of this theme, which Germany used to justify conquest of Poland, Russia, and other neighbors. There was an understandable reaction against this type of biological determinism in the period after World War II, and the rise of a countervailing belief in the inherent equality of both individuals and of human societies.[1]

Montesquieu never attributed differences in behavior between North and South to human biology. Rather, he seemed to believe that human beings around the world were fundamentally similar to one another. What differed were conditions of climate and geography that, operating on the biology of otherwise indistinguishable individuals, produced systematic differences in political behavior. Slavery for him was not natural and needed to be explained in terms of the ability of certain societies to better organize themselves for war and conquest. The political freedom that Northern Europeans enjoyed was not the product of any inherent natural or even cultural characteristic. They were as likely as anyone else to want to conquer one another and indeed were rather good at it. European freedom was for Montesquieu instead the result of the fact that physical geography kept European states divided into a relatively balanced number of competing polities, none of which was able to conquer all the others. The great Asiatic empires of China, Persia, and Turkey, by contrast, were facilitated by the flatness and extent of open terrain on which they operated, which made the military centralization of power much easier to achieve.

ENTER THE ECONOMISTS

In recent years there has been a revival of arguments that climate and geography are the chief determinants of both modern institutions and economic growth.[2] Perhaps not surprisingly, this case has been made chiefly by economists, for whom materialistic explanations of behavior are second nature. Jeffrey Sachs, for example, points out that there is a strong correlation between contemporary levels of development and geography: industrialized countries are largely located in temperate zones, while the bulk of poor countries are in the tropics. Geography, according to him, operates in two important ways to facilitate or impede economic growth. First, access to waterways and other means of transport is critical in allowing a country to benefit from commerce, just as Adam Smith noted it had been in the early development of trade and commerce in Europe. Landlocked countries in the interior of Africa and Central Asia face huge disadvantages in exporting products compared to those with harbors or navigable rivers. Second, people in the tropics are subject to a much wider variety of diseases than those in temperate climates. Sachs estimated that the incidence of intensive malaria alone shaves 1.3 percentage points off of the potential per capita growth rates of countries in the tropics.[3] Sachs's argument reproduces, in a sense, the first of Montesquieu's causal channels in a more modern form: hot southern climates directly affect economic performance not by making people lazy and pleasure loving but by debilitating them with chronic diseases that hinder their ability to work and flourish.

Jared Diamond's metahistorical work *Guns, Germs, and Steel* similarly points to material obstacles to development that were primarily the products of geography and climate. Europe's ability to dominate other parts of the world has to do with a number of geographical factors like the east-west lines of communication that link the Eurasian continent compared to the north-south axes of South America across different climatic zones that pose big obstacles to movement. This allowed appropriate technologies to diffuse laterally across similar climatic zones, while differences in climate prevented similar diffusion in the western hemisphere. Europeans furthermore succeeded in cultivating wheat and rye, which became major cash crops, and domesticated the horse, which was critical to mobility. Greater mobility in turn facilitated the development of immunities to a variety of diseases by creating greater genetic diversity through the intermarriage of peoples. The relative homogeneity of genotypes in the New World, by contrast, left populations there particularly vulnerable to diseases introduced from outside. All of these factors came together to explain, according to Diamond, the almost effortless conquests of the Spanish in the New World.[4]

Neither Sachs nor Diamond pays much attention to the question of institutions in their initial accounts of development outcomes. By contrast, the economic historian Douglass North attributes Latin America's poor performance relative to North America to institutional differences regarding property rights and rule of law, which in turn was a function of the identity of the colonizer. It was England that seeded North America and gave it the institutions of Common Law and parliamentary government, while South America was colonized by a mercantilist and absolutist Spain or Portugal.[5]

The economic historians Stanley Engerman and Kenneth Sokoloff argue in a similar vein that institutions were critical, but that they were themselves the product of the geographical and climatic conditions that the colonizers found in the New World. They note the persistence of hierarchical, authoritarian governments in Latin America, coupled with exploitative economic institutions, and contrast that with the democratic governments and open markets of North America. Engerman and Sokoloff trace these institutional differences not to the identity of the colonizer but to what economists call factor endowments, that is, the types of crops and minerals that can be grown or extracted based on the climate and geography of different parts of the Americas. They point out that at the time of the American Revolution, Cuba and Barbados were wealthy colonies due to the relative efficiency of large-scale plantation agriculture employing slaves. Barbados was no less a British colony than Massachusetts or New York and yet saw the emergence of a highly exploitative society involving the rule of a small planter elite over a large slave population.

Similarly, the Spanish colonies of New Spain (Mexico) and Peru were built around the extraction of gold and silver. These colonies did not have to import slaves from Africa but could make extensive use of the large indigenous populations as a source of involuntary labor. The concentration of economic power in mining spilled over into land ownership and led to the growth of large estates that persisted over the next several centuries, in sharp contrast to the family farming that was more characteristic of North America. Engerman and Sokoloff trace the origin of different political institutions—authoritarian and oligarchic on the one hand, and democratic and egalitarian on the other—to these original conditions of climate and geography.[6]

These institutions persisted over time even when the conditions that gave rise to them changed. The elites empowered by these institutions used their political clout to preserve their initial advantage. Thus the

Creole elites in Latin America were able in later years to block immigration into their societies, so as to prevent competition in labor markets. They also restricted the franchise much later into the nineteenth century than did the United States. As a result, Latin America remains overall the most unequal region of the world, despite the fact that its political institutions are today largely democratic.

The economists Daron Acemoglu, James Robinson, and Simon Johnson modify this argument in an often-cited paper, arguing that the variation in early institutions was due not to factor endowments so much as early settler mortality, which was driven in turn by the diseases to which they were subject. Where Europeans found it safe to settle, they demanded rights for themselves and institutions that would limit the ability of the state to take away their property arbitrarily. Where disease made it too costly to settle, the colonial powers set up what they labeled "extractive" economic institutions enforced by "absolutist" political structures. These early institutional structures proved very durable because existing power holders were able to continue to restrict access to both the economic and political systems over subsequent centuries.[7]

Any simple geographical determinism of the Sachs or Diamond variety that links wealth to temperate northern climates and poverty to southern tropical ones is belied by the "reversal of fortune" that occurred between 1500 and the present, as a number of economic historians have pointed out. For much of human history, the wealthiest and most productive regions tended to be southern. This was true first and foremost in Europe: the Roman Empire was centered around the Mediterranean, with North Africa being a major grain-producing region, while Britain and Scandinavia were impoverished peripheries inhabited by tribal barbarians. The Chinese Empire started in the northerly Yellow River valley and then expanded south and southwest rather than north; colder areas—Manchuria, Korea, and Japan—were significantly less developed. And in the Americas, the Aztecs and Incas, the richest civilizations, developed in tropical/subtropical Mexico and Peru. The temperate zones of both North and South America were sparsely inhabited by relatively impoverished hunter-gatherer or pastoral societies. This pattern continued after the European conquest of the western hemisphere. The Spanish located their empire in the seats of the former indigenous civilizations, while a rich slave-based planter economy grew up in the Caribbean and northeastern (that is, subtropical) Brazil. At the beginning of the seventeenth century, it is estimated that the sugar island of Barbados was two-thirds richer than the thirteen North American colonies in per capita terms; Cuba was far richer than Massachusetts at the time of the American Revolution.[8]

The pattern noted by Sachs and other writers wherein the richest parts of the world were temperate northern climates is thus a modern pattern that came about only after the Industrial Revolution. Normally, economic theory would predict that those tropical and subtropical regions that hosted wealthy agrarian communities should have an advantage with regard to industrialization, since they had the largest stocks of labor and capital. Acemoglu, Robinson, and Johnson argue that the reason this did not happen was due again to institutions: older wealthy regions with dense populations attracted European colonists, who enslaved those populations and created extractive institutions. Those institutions then served to block the development of more open, competitive market economies that were necessary for industrial development. By contrast, poor, sparsely settled regions were not burdened with the legacy of bad institutions and permitted more inclusive ones to appear.

What all of these arguments have in common is that they trace the origins of political institutions to factors that are broadly economic, which include but are not limited to climate and physical geography. While Acemoglu and Robinson criticize what they characterize as the geographical determinism of writers like Sachs and Diamond, and point to good institutions as the cause of development, they nonetheless trace the origin of institutions in turn to conditions of climate and geography. Geography and factor endowments remain determinative insofar as they shape political institutions, which then persist. The impact of climate and geography can obviously change over time as a result of technology; thus the Caribbean sugar trade could not have happened absent transatlantic shipping, and it became far less competitive with the development of alternatives to sugarcane like beet sugar. Nonetheless, all the writers in this tradition agree that economic factors such as geography, climate, diseases, the availability of resources like labor, precious metals, rainfall levels, and the feasibility of plantation agriculture are the final determinants of the nature of institutions. They explicitly argue that nonmaterial factors—ideas or ideology, culture, or the particular traditions of individual colonizing societies—were much less important in explaining contemporary political and economic development outcomes.

ONE, TWO, THREE, MANY DETERMINISMS

This broad line of argument by economists met with substantial criticism, precisely because of its apparent determinism. Writers such as Jeffrey Sachs seemed to be saying that unalterable factors like location in the tropics or the absence of access to waterways condemned certain countries to poverty and backwardness. Critics pointed to economically successful Singapore and Malaysia, both located in the tropics with a history of extractive colonial institutions, to show that the past didn't necessarily predict the future. In general, people don't like these types of arguments because they seem to deny the possibility of human agency and the ability of human beings to take control of the conditions of their existence.

But before we dismiss the importance of climate and geography to the shaping of institutions, we should consider a number of broad historical facts that suggest they are indeed very important. Geography and climate were critical to early state formation. As noted in Volume 1 of this book, the first states to appear anywhere in the world arose under very specific geographical conditions. Most appeared in alluvial valleys including those of the Nile, the Tigris and Euphrates, the Yellow River in China, and the Valley of Mexico, where high soil fertility allowed productive agriculture and high population densities. Further, these valleys needed to be neither too small nor too large. If they were too small, like many of those in Papua New Guinea and the highlands of Southeast Asia, they could not support sufficiently large populations that were capable of dominating their regions and taking advantage of economies of scale in creating state-level institutions. On the other hand, if they were too large and open, they could not prevent slaves and other subservient people from running away from state authority. Tribal societies are egalitarian and can subsist over very large ranges of territory. States by contrast are coercive and typically need to compel the obedience of their citizens. Anthropologist Robert Carneiro argues that some degree of geographical circumscription was necessary to permit the creation of the earliest states. Archaeologist Ian Morris has noted the rise of civilizations in widely separated places sharing common environmental conditions (what he labels the "lucky latitudes"), such as those prevailing in Europe and China.[9]

These geographical conditions go quite far to explain the distribution of levels of political organization around the world. There are today a number of surviving tribal and/or band-level societies that have resisted incorporation into states. But they exist only under very specific environmental conditions: either mountains (Afghanistan or highland Southeast Asia), deserts (the Bedouin in the Arabian peninsula, the nomads of the Sahara, the !Kung San in the Kalahari), jungles (tribal groups in India and parts of Africa), or extreme Arctic conditions (Eskimos, Inuits in the far north of Canada). They have survived simply because it is difficult for states to project military force into such regions. The failure of an indigenous state to emerge in Papua New Guinea despite the fact that it has been inhabited by modern humans for some forty thousand years would seem to be related to the fact that there is no large open alluvial valley there that would support a correspondingly large civilization, only a seemingly endless series of small mountain valleys. Afghanistan has been a settled crossroads for thousands of years but to this day has never consolidated into a strong centralized state, despite the efforts of a long series of invaders from the Greeks to the Persians to the British, Soviets, and NATO. Mountainous terrain and Afghanistan's being landlocked and surrounded by powerful Iran, Russia, India, and Pakistan would seem to explain this outcome.[10]

Physical geography also played a role in the presence or absence of absolutism and democracy. The mechanism through which this operated, however, was not any of those discussed by the economists. Rather, it was the factor pointed to by Montesquieu, which had to do with the suitability of certain terrains for military conquest or defense. Economists tend to believe that political power derives from economic power and serves economic interests. But political power often rests on superior military organization which, in turn, is the product of leadership, morale, motivation, strategy, logistics and, of course, technology. Resources are naturally an important component of military power, but there is no simple translation of economic power into military power. For nearly two thousand years, tribally organized horsemen riding out of Central Asia were able to conquer settled agrarian civilizations that were far wealthier and more complex in their organization. The most famous of these groups were the Mongols who, breaking out of their home territories in inner Asia early in the thirteenth century, conquered present-day Russia and Ukraine, Hungary, Persia, the whole of Song China, the Levant, and parts of northern India.

These conquests were made possible by two material factors: first, the domestication of the horse which, as Jared Diamond notes, was unknown in the New World until its introduction by the Spanish; and second, the fact that much of Eurasia is relatively flat and open plain. The Mongols' extraordinary mobility was due to the fact that they were unencumbered by heavy logistics trains, living largely as predators off the richer civilizations they attacked. The ability of nomadic invaders to overwhelm agrarian cultures led to the repeated cycle, noted by the great Arab historian Ibn Khaldun, of civilizational flowering and decay that characterized the Middle East, China, and other regions bordering on Central Asia.

The limits of the power of these and other horse-mounted tribal groups were also set by physical conditions. In Europe, the Mongols eventually ran into a series of mountain ranges and, more important, thick forests that prevented the rapid movement of their horses. In India, their bows started to delaminate in the heat and humidity of the Gangetic plain. The limits of conquest by horse- and camel-mounted Arabs in West Africa were set by the tsetse fly, which in forest zones killed their horses. This explains the line that divides the Muslim north of the West African countries Nigeria, Benin, Togo, Ghana, and Cote d'Ivoire from the Christian/ animist South.[11] The entire period of barbarian conquests out of Central Asia came to an end only with the European adoption of gunpowder and artillery, which allowed soldiers in defensive positions to decimate cavalry at a distance.

The political impact of these geographical and technological conditions can be seen in the differing political paths taken by Russia and the Baltic and Eastern European polities just to its west. Russia itself was conquered by Mongol commanders Batu Khan and Subutai in the 1230s, and the so-called Mongol yoke continued for the next 250 years. The Mongols had no particular interest in the well-being of their Russian subjects and set up a predatory state that extracted tribute through a series of local Russian agents. The Mongols destroyed the nascent state formed around the Kievan Rus', cut Russia off from trade and intellectual exchange with Byzantium, the Middle East, and Europe, and undermined Russia's Byzantine-Roman legal traditions. The clock of Russian political development was set back during the so-called appanage period that followed on the Mongol invasion, when power was decentralized into hundreds of tiny principalities. There was, consequently, no development of a deeply rooted feudalism that provided strong local government as in Western Europe; indeed, no time to build the fortified castles that were critical to the protection of feudal power.

Geography continued to play a critical role in the consolidation of a strong absolutist Russian state, one whose authority and power over society came to be far greater than anything experienced under the absolutisms of Western Europe. Power was centralized under the Rurik dynasty in Moscow under Ivan III (1440–1505), which under subsequent tsars underwent a huge territorial expansion. The openness of the Russian steppe, combined with the relative weakness of the aristocratic boyar class, gave the Muscovites a huge first-mover advantage. Organizing a middle service class as a Mongol-style light cavalry, the Muscovite tsars ran into few natural defensive obstacles until they encountered the better-organized communities in Poland and Lithuania, and the Turks to the south. Independent commercial cities like Novgorod, that were so important to the development of political freedom in Western Europe, were militarily overwhelmed and subordinated to Moscow's centralized control.

Montesquieu was thus deeply insightful about the impact of geography in the development of political freedom in Europe when he said that "the natural division forms many nations of a moderate extent." Europe's geography, unlike that of Africa, promoted the formation of strong states. Political competition among its nations required the construction of strong states with good laws; without this, "the state would fall into decay, and become a prey to its neighbors." On the other hand, Europe's great rivers, mountain ranges, and forests made it very difficult for any one state to achieve predominance. As a result, no one conqueror has ever been able to subdue the whole of Europe and subject it to a single political authority, in the manner of Chinese emperors or Russian tsars. Another fortuitous feature of European geography that contributed to its freedom was the existence of a large, hard to conquer island just off the continent, which was able to accumulate substantial wealth and maritime power and act as a balancer against those that sought to dominate the rest of the region. This happened when England resisted the Spanish armada at the end of the fifteenth century, the expansionist plans of Louis XIV in the seventeenth century, Napoleon in the early nineteenth century, and Hitler in the twentieth.

THREE REGIONS

In the following chapters, I will trace the development of political institutions in three regions of the developing world: Latin America, sub-Saharan Africa, and East Asia.

East Asia is of course today the great star, with Japan, Korea, Taiwan, Hong Kong, and Singapore having successfully joined the club of developed countries, and China on its way to overtaking the United States as the world's largest economy. Sub-Saharan Africa, by contrast, is the poorest region, despite the relatively good performance of a number of countries there in the early 2000s. Latin America lies somewhere in the middle: it is full of what the World Bank labels "middle-income countries," such as Mexico, Brazil, and Argentina, but with the possible exception of Chile, none seems poised to reach the high income levels of Europe, North America, or northeast Asia anytime soon.

These economic growth outcomes are indeed related to the institutional legacies of colonialism, as the economists argue. Geography and climate had a large impact on the kinds of institutions that the colonial powers were initially able to establish. But geography is not destiny: in each region, there are many significant cases of countries that escaped the fates of their neighbors and performed either better or worse because other factors, like ideology, policies, and the choices made by individual leaders, shifted the societies onto new development paths.

Moreover, the literature on colonialism gives too much weight to colonial legacies in general. Contemporary institutional outcomes, and thus contemporary growth outcomes, were influenced not just by the policies of the colonial powers but also by the nature of preexisting indigenous institutions. In particular, the superior performance of East Asia in modern times is directly related to the fact that many East Asian countries developed strong, modern states prior to their contact with the West. In China and Japan, this prevented their total conquest and subordination by foreign powers. In sub-Saharan Africa, by contrast, half the continent was still tribally organized at the time of its conquest by the Europeans. The "states" that existed were very primitive and weak. The colonial powers therefore had no strong indigenous state traditions to build on. Latin America was again an intermediate case: while the Spanish encountered large empires and concentrated populations in Mexico and Peru, these polities were much less formidable than they seemed, and not at all modern in the Chinese sense. They collapsed almost immediately, even before disease took its toll, and left almost nothing by way of institutional residue. This left the new colonial powers free to construct their own feudal institutions on New World soil.

16

SILVER, GOLD, AND SUGAR

How resources and population affected institutions in the New World; the nature of Spanish institutions, and how Madrid sought to transfer them; how inherited class structure and ethnicity weakened rule of law and accountability

Latin America was the first part of the non-Western world to be colonized by Europeans. It is also the part of the world for which contemporary economic theories of the origin of political institutions were originally developed. The establishment of authoritarian, highly unequal political institutions in much of the region was attributed to the "extractive" nature of economic production there, based in turn on geography, climate, resources, and other material conditions that the colonialists encountered. By this view, institutional characteristics persisted over the centuries, even after the original economic and technological conditions that created them began to change. The different kinds of political institutions that emerged in North America—more democratic, egalitarian, and economically liberal—reflected the rather different conditions of agricultural production found there.

This basic story is correct. Latin America has been characterized by a "birth defect" of inequality from which it has not yet recovered. But the economic interpretation of the origin of institutions is far from a complete one. Latin American institutions are overdetermined: that is, their authoritarian and illiberal character has multiple sources and does not simply lie in the material conditions found by the colonialists. It is not as if the Spanish and Portuguese had created liberal, egalitarian institutions back in Europe and would have implanted them in the New World if only conditions were right. In fact, they sought to re-create a version of their own political system in their colonies. Conditions at home began to change with a modest series of liberal reforms that took place under the Bourbon monarchy in the eighteenth century, and as Spain itself liberalized, the types of institutions exported to the Americas liberalized as well.

The real differences between North and Latin America lie less in these initial institutional conditions than in what happened later. Virtually all of Europe, including England, was authoritarian, hierarchical, and unequal at the beginning of the sixteenth century. But the countries there went through a series of violent wars and revolutions over the next two centuries that, first, produced a series of strong, consolidated modern states, and second, produced changes in political institutions that ultimately created modern democracy. Sometimes things that don't happen are as important in explaining subsequent events as those that do, as Sherlock Holmes said of the dog that failed to bark. In Latin America, there also was a dog that didn't bark: the large-scale and continuous political violence that was so critical in shaping Western European states and national identity simply didn't convulse the New World. On the one hand, this was a good thing: Latin America has been a much more peaceful continent than either Europe or Asia. On the other hand, its political institutions developed more slowly as a result, and the older forms of authoritarian government as well as the social inequalities on which they were based persisted for much longer.

EXPLOITATION

The Spaniards did not conquer the New World for strategic reasons, as the European powers were to do in Africa during the late nineteenth century, nor did they necessarily want to impose their way of life there. They established colonies because they wanted to get rich, and for this purpose they were attracted to the regions that were already wealthy and populous, such as the seats of the Aztec and Inca Empires in Mexico and Peru. The Valley of Mexico where the Aztec capital of Tenochtitlán (now Mexico City) was located had perhaps a million inhabitants at the time of Hernando Cortés's expedition, with several million more in the surrounding countryside. The Inca Empire stretched from Ecuador to northern Chile and encompassed as many as ten million inhabitants. The Spanish located their two viceroyalties in Mexico and Peru precisely because they found precious gold and silver there and because they could draw on dense populations as sources of servile labor.

The Spaniards enriched themselves at first by simply plundering the wealth of their conquered kingdoms. (The Inca ruler Atahualpa was told to fill a large room with gold and silver to ransom his life, which he did, whereupon the Spanish killed him anyway.) When these sources were exhausted, they discovered new ones, the silver mines in Zacatecas, Mexico, the mercury mines in Huancavelica, and the silver mountain of Potosí high in the Andes (then part of Upper Peru, now in Bolivia).

Legally, indigenous people were considered to be full subjects of the Crown, with their property protected by the same legal rights as that of Europeans. The *encomienda*, an institution by which the Spanish Crown granted the conquistadores rights over people but not land, was considered to be an alternative to slavery. Under it, the indigenous could be made to work in return for paternalistic protection. In some cases, the church joined hands with the local representatives of the Spanish Crown in trying to protect native populations from abuse by settlers. In practice, these legal protections were not observed, and de facto slavery became a common practice, led by the Spanish settler community. Under the viceroy Francisco de Toledo late in the sixteenth century, the Inca institution of the *mita* (corvée labor) was reconfigured into a much harsher form of coercive labor that required long absences from the workers' local communities and the endurance of extremely dangerous conditions in the mines. The colonial authorities resorted to forced relocations of their steadily declining populations, called *reducciones*, in order to be better able to control and draft laborers.[1]

The elites in Latin America were both the Spanish colonial authorities—the *peninsulares*—and the white settler population, known as Creoles. Early Spanish policy tried to prevent the establishment of a landed aristocracy through institutions like the *encomienda*, which did not give the settlers rights to land. But the Creoles' presence on the ground allowed them to become major landowners nonetheless, a process that was accelerated by the *mayorazgo*, a form of primogeniture imported from Spain that permitted landowning families to concentrate and enlarge their holdings. Carried over from Spain as well was the tendency for landowners to live in cities rather than on their estates; peasant labor was controlled by managers for the benefit of wealthy absentee landowners.

Also part of the elite were merchants who benefited from the trade monopolies granted by the Crown under mercantilist rules. These two groups lived symbiotically, the merchants exporting the primary products produced by the landowners to protected markets that guaranteed them a steady income. This urban-merchant elite, over time, bought titles and offices from a weakening Habsburg colonial regime and cemented their power in a manner very similar to elites in old regime France and Spain.[2]

The ethnic and racial divides that existed in the Americas strongly entrenched class differences. In the words of historian David Fieldhouse, "Because the peoples of Mexico and Peru filled the role of a European working class, there was no place in Spanish America for a white proletariat; and this distinguished Spanish colonies from others in North America which became 'pure' European settlements."[3] Class differences overlapped with racial and ethnic ones, marking off the poor visibly from the rich—or rather, given the degree of intermarriage, creating a continuum from white to black whose different shades marked rungs on a social ladder. It is this social stratification that has shaped the region's politics over the centuries, and in many ways it persists to the present moment.

THE SLAVERY-PLANTATION COMPLEX

If there was a single area where climate and geography could be said to have direct political implications, it was the emergence of a plantation complex involving the export of tropical agricultural products to Europe, in particular sugar. Sugar differs from staple crops like wheat or corn because it is not suitable for family farming. Families cannot live on sugar; it is purely an export crop. It needs to be processed near where it is grown, requiring substantial capital investment and benefiting from economies of scale. And it grows best in wet, hot climates like those found in tropical or subtropical regions. Sugar was cultivated in Portugal and other parts of southern Europe beginning in the fifteenth century but soon moved to Portugal's West African colonies such as São Tomé. And there it began its fateful association with African slavery, since the kingdoms of Kongo and Benin provided nearby sources of labor to work the sugar plantations.[4]

Slavery had existed in West Africa for several centuries prior to the arrival of the Europeans late in the fifteenth century, largely as a result of the trans-Saharan trade from North Africa and the Middle East. The Portuguese found ready sources of slaves there, whom they put to work in the sugar plantations of São Tomé. When the Treaty of Tordesillas in 1494 gave Portugal possession of what would become Brazil, this system of labor would prove to be exportable. Unlike Peru and Mexico, the Portuguese found little gold or silver in their New World lands, nor large concentrations of people. But northeastern Brazil had a perfect climate for growing sugar, which the Portuguese quickly brought over from Africa. And from West Africa, it was relatively easy to transport slaves to the new colony being established in Brazil, where prevailing winds made for a much easier east-to-west journey than farther north in the Atlantic where prevailing winds blew in the opposite direction. Under the harsh work conditions of sugar production in the tropics, slave populations did not reproduce themselves sufficiently, so a triangular trade developed: slaves were exported to Brazil, sugar and sugar products like rum were exported back to Europe, and European manufactured goods were sent to Africa in return for more slaves.

Thus Brazil, now a charter member of the emerging market BRICS club and Latin America's industrial powerhouse, got its start as a plantation colony based on slave labor. Portugal did not have the power or resources to rule Brazil the way the Spanish ruled Mexico and Peru. Instead, it gave authority and grants of land to a group of "captains donatory" who acted as virtual sovereigns in the territory they controlled. These land grants were huge, extending 130 miles along the coast and going inland as far as 500 miles. De facto authority came to lie in the hands of a powerful yet provincial slave-owning planter class, which by the end of the sixteenth century had accumulated substantial political power in a relatively decentralized political system.[5]

The second phase of the sugar revolution occurred farther north, in the Caribbean, where conditions and trade winds were favorable to exports to Britain and other parts of Northern Europe. The Carib and Arawak indigenous populations encountered by Christopher Columbus had long since been wiped out by disease and their few descendants assimilated into the settler populations, both white and slave. Beginning in the mid-sixteenth century, Barbados and the Windward and Leeward Islands became the center of a huge export industry, a center that later shifted westward to the French colony of Saint-Domingue (today Haiti),

Jamaica, Puerto Rico, and eventually Cuba. England, France, Spain, Holland, and even Denmark participated in both the process of colonization and the creation of a plantation industry there. In the early days, the commercial companies investing in plantations were as willing to use white indentured laborers as readily as African slaves, but they found that the latter had greater immunity to local diseases than the Europeans and could be made to work under harsher conditions. This is not to say that Africans flourished in the New World; as in Brazil, the slave population could not replenish itself and so was dependent on a continuing flow of new bodies from Africa. As a result, the number of Africans transported to the Americas outnumbered white Europeans by a factor of five in the years between 1600 and 1820.[6] Slavery was thus integral to a burgeoning transatlantic commercial economy. Exports from Britain's slave colonies exceeded the value of exports from free ones by almost a factor of ten.[7]

Climate and geography thus had a clear effect on the rise of what Philip Curtin calls the "plantation complex" and the institution of slavery that it spawned. The identity of the colonial power made no initial difference to where slavery arose; the more liberal British and Dutch were just as eager participants in this trade as the authoritarian Spaniards.

If there is a single historical case that proves the importance of physical conditions to institutions, it is the rise of slavery and cotton in the southern United States. Slavery of course existed throughout the United States at the time of the War of Independence, including the northern colonies. But many people at the time believed that it was a dying institution. While George Washington and Thomas Jefferson owned slaves, the economics of growing crops like tobacco and wheat with servile labor was not especially favorable.

All of this changed dramatically with the spread of cotton in the American South, facilitated by the invention of the cotton gin and the enormous increases in demand for raw cotton coming from Britain's emerging textile industry at the beginning of the nineteenth century. Cotton, like sugar, benefited from economies of scale on large plantations, and strongly revived demand for servile labor. Unlike in the Caribbean and Brazil, slave populations reproduced well in the continental United States, so even after the end of the slave trade in 1807 there was a growing population of servile labor that increasingly constituted a major source of the region's capital.

There has been a prolonged and often bitter debate among historians over the economics of North American slavery. Some have argued, along with a number of slavery critics prior to the Civil War, that the practice was an economically inefficient one that could not compete on equal terms with free labor, and would have died out on its own under free-market conditions. A number of Marxist historians have argued that the Civil War itself was driven not by moral considerations concerning slavery but rather by a competition between free and servile forms of labor. On balance, however, it would seem that right up to the time of the Civil War, slavery-based plantation production was a fully competitive form of economic enterprise and that per capita incomes in the South began to decline relative to those in the North only after the war and the abolition of slavery.[8]

The emergence of a powerful economic interest in slavery in North America soon overwhelmed whatever democratic and egalitarian political proclivities the English settlers brought with them. Prior to the Civil War, southern defenders of the "peculiar institution" began raising a host of novel arguments to defend slavery, drawing from the Bible, from arguments regarding the natural order of races, and from simple manufactured traditions of hierarchy and racial domination. Abraham Lincoln was to underline the contradictions between these theories and the country's founding assertion that "all men are created equal," something that nonetheless did not prevent economic self-interest from trumping principle.

INDIGENOUS STATES

One of the great puzzles of institutional development in Latin America is why the indigenous political institutions of pre-Columbian America did not play a greater role in shaping later developments. Latin America's institutions were largely created by European settlers, either ones they imported from Europe or ones they created in response to the conditions they found on the ground. In tropical Africa and large parts of Southeast Asia, European settlement was limited by disease, as it was in the Caribbean. In other parts of the world—South Asia, the Middle East, and East Asia—large-scale European settlement was blocked or slowed by the existence of big and often well-organized indigenous populations that could be displaced only with great difficulty. In the core areas of the Spanish New World empire—Mexico and Peru—diseases affecting settlers were not a limiting factor, but well-organized local populations should have been. In contrast to the nomadic tribal societies that existed in North America, or groups like the Mapuches who resisted white settlers in Argentina and Chile, the Aztecs and Incas were organized into complex, state-level societies and projected centralized authority over tremendous distances. And yet the speed and completeness with which their power collapsed—as told by authors from William Prescott to Jared Diamond—is astonishing.[9] Francisco Pizarro defeated the Inca king Atahualpa, who commanded an army of perhaps 80,000 soldiers, with 168 Spanish troops of his own, and did not suffer a single casualty.

Diamond attributes this success to a number of technological factors, such as the Spanish use of horses, muskets, and steel swords, none of which were possessed by the Incas, as well as a healthy dose of tactical surprise. The Spanish brought with them Old World diseases, as is well known, which devastated native populations and eventually killed as many as 90 percent of the local inhabitants.[10]

This account of the Aztec-Inca collapse is not, however, entirely convincing. As political scientist James Mahoney points out, the Europeans held similar technological advantages over more primitive groups in other parts of the Americas, and yet it took decades to defeat them. Disease was certainly a factor in the ultimate demise of the indigenous civilizations over the long run, but the disastrous declines in population did not start until the second half of the sixteenth century, well after the political collapse of the Aztecs and Incas. The real explanation, it seems, would have to be more political and institutional in nature. Although this risks amounting to an ex post "just so" story, the fact of their collapse suggests that neither civilization was nearly as institutionalized as it appeared.

This is most evident if we compare the Aztec or Inca state to the one that developed in China. Chinese states gradually evolved out of tribal groups during the Eastern Zhou Dynasty, particularly in the violent five hundred years comprising the Spring and Autumn and Warring States periods (770–221 B.C.). At the end of this period the total number of political units in northern China had been reduced from perhaps a thousand to seven, each of which had developed centralized bureaucratic institutions. The country was unified under the Qin and Earlier Han Dynasties, the first taking power in 221 B.C., the latter in 202 B.C. At the time of the Qin-Han unification, China consisted not just of the remnants of the seven early warring states but also of pockets of tribal and aristocratic influence spread throughout the country. It took the Han bureaucracy, modeled on that of the western state of Qin, nearly two hundred years to fully suppress these pockets of resistance and create a uniform, modern administrative system that ruled over a population as large as the contemporaneous Roman Empire.

The level of political development of the New World indigenous empires seems to have resembled that of China at a point sometime in the middle of the Eastern Zhou period, rather than of the mature Han state. Both the Aztec and Inca Empires remained organized around segmentary lineages at a local level (such as the *ayllu* in Inca lands, a social unit that survives to the present day in Bolivia and the highlands of Peru) and confederations of tribes. These empires were highly mixed ethnically, speaking related but often mutually unintelligible languages. The Aztec Empire had been created through conquest a couple of centuries before the confrontation with Cortés; the Inca Empire only in the decades preceding the Spanish arrival. Both empires were maintained through repression—notably, with the Aztecs, involving the widespread use of human sacrifice of subject peoples. This made it easy for the conquering Spaniards to find local allies who would fight for liberation from their indigenous rulers. Cortés established alliances with the Tlaxcala and the Totonacs and was able to attack Tenochtitlán with tens of thousands of indigenous soldiers. The same was true of Pizarro in Peru, who arrived on the heels of a bloody conflict between two princes, Atahualpa and Huáscar, over succession to the throne of the Sapa Inca, or supreme chief. As in Mexico, the Spaniards were able to play on Inca divisions. Local allies proved critical in the final defeat of Túpac Amaru, the Inca prince who tried to rally the last organized resistance in the eighteenth century, and who is still a symbol of indigenous pride in contemporary Peru.

While both the Aztec and Inca Empires are sometimes described as "bureaucratic," the level of administrative development was nothing close to what China achieved by the middle of the Earlier Han Dynasty. Perhaps the clearest indication of this was in the use of language. Chinese administrators were already communicating with one another with written memoranda during the second millennium B.C. Shang Dynasty that preceded the Zhou. By contrast, the Aztecs had a hieroglyphic form of writing that is sometimes described as a form of protowriting, useful for ritual purposes but not something that could be used for routine communications throughout a bureaucratic hierarchy. The Incas had no written language at all, although they had a system of colored strings known as the quipu by which they could record statistical information. Otherwise, they had to rely on runners using spoken Quechua to communicate with distant parts of their empire. This meant that neither indigenous civilization could create a literary corpus similar to the Chinese classics that became not just the common curriculum of bureaucratic education but also the basis for a shared cultural identity. Needless to say, neither New World civilization could penetrate its respective societies in the manner of China, promulgating written legal codes enforced by a complex bureaucratic hierarchy.[11]

The kind of civilization that existed in Mexico and Peru would thus seem to be closer to that of India under the Mauryas in the third century B.C. than to the Qin-Han civilization of the same period. The Mauryas succeeded in violently unifying the northern two-thirds of the subcontinent under Ashoka, but their empire went into decline within three generations because they were never able to create a powerful administrative system. Like the Incas, they had no written administrative language.[12]

While both New World empires covered vast territories, they nevertheless were very weak. When the Spanish defeated and killed Montezuma and Atahualpa, symbols of military centralization, the empires shattered into their constituent ethnic and tribal groups, never to be reconstituted. Many of these subordinate groups simply transferred loyalty from their indigenous leaders to the Spaniards. All of this happened *before* the indigenous populations suffered their disastrous demographic decline due to imported Eurasian diseases. That decline sealed the fate of any surviving institutions. Mexico's population fell from ten million at the time of Cortés's arrival to two million in 1585, and then to one million by the beginning of the sixteenth century. Peru's preconquest population shrank from nine million to somewhat over one million by 1580, and then down to six hundred thousand by 1620.[13]

The indigenous cultures of the New World have shaped contemporary Latin America in myriad ways, from the Day of the Dead ceremonies in Mexico to *ayllu* clan organizations that characterize social life in the Andes. But the higher-level political legacy of the pre-Columbian

civilizations played a much smaller role than state-level indigenous organizations in other parts of the world, particularly those in East Asia.

WEAK ABSOLUTISM

Geography and climate were not the only factors determining the nature
of political institutions in Latin America. The Spanish and Portuguese
also sought to export their own institutions to their colonies.

The Habsburg Spain that first colonized the New World was characterized by what I labeled weak absolutism in the earlier volume. The Spanish monarch, beginning with the defeat of the Comunero revolt in 1520,
emasculated the Spanish estates (the Cortes) and centralized power in the
court. But he was still strongly limited by the existing system of law,
whose Roman roots ran deeper in Spain than in other parts of Western
Europe. Charles V, who acquired a huge empire both in the Old World
and the New, had legal taxing authority only in Castile, which bore the
burden of his expensive wars in Italy and the Low Countries. In the
course of the sixteenth century, this led to heavy borrowing from foreign
bankers, the repeated bankruptcy of the Crown, and attempts to meet
revenue needs by debasing the currency. Eventually, the Spanish state,
like its French counterpart, turned to the selling of public offices to
wealthy elites, legalizing corruption and weakening the capacity of the
state to administer its realm uniformly and impersonally. Unlike a
strong absolutist state that has the power and autonomy to master its
own elites, the Spanish government was over time captured by them.[14]

Under these circumstances, revenue from the New World in the form
of exports of gold and silver was critical. The Spanish government, however, imposed strict rules limiting economic exchange—a system known
as mercantilism—under the mistaken belief that this would maximize
its income from the colonies. Exports from the New World could go only
to Spain, indeed, to a single port in Spain; they were required to travel
in Spanish ships; and the colonies were not permitted to compete with
Spanish producers of manufactured goods. Mercantilism, as Adam
Smith was to demonstrate in *The Wealth of Nations*, created huge inefficiencies and was highly detrimental to economic growth. It also had
very significant political consequences: access to markets and the right
to make productive economic investments were limited to individuals or

corporations favored by the state. This meant that the route to personal wealth lay through the state and through gaining political influence. This then led to a rentier rather than an entrepreneurial mentality, in which energy was spent seeking political favor rather than initiating new enterprises that would create wealth. The landowning and merchant classes that emerged under this system grew rich because of the political protection they received from the state.

The formal structure of Spanish rule in the New World was an authoritarian system built around the Council of the Indies (Real y Supremo Consejo de las Indias). The council, along with the Casa de Contratación overseeing economic matters, wrote laws and issued autocratic decrees—some four hundred thousand by the year 1600. These executive agencies were balanced by a parallel system of *audiencias* or administrative courts run by lawyers or judges who were not allowed to marry local women or otherwise get involved in the politics of the regions over which they presided.[15] This structure broke down as the sixteenth and seventeenth centuries progressed under the pressures of fiscal constraint and resistance from the Creoles who increasingly sought a voice in government.

However much the Spanish state may have wanted to deliberately shape New World institutions, it did not have either the power or the authority to impose its will on its colonies. This problem was crystallized in the saying "Obedézcase, pero no se cumpla" (Obey, but do not comply). The reconquest of the Iberian peninsula from the Moors had been accomplished not by a modernized state but rather by "freelances" operating under royal contract, and many of these individuals, like Cortés and Pizarro, were quasi-independent agents. It took the Spanish Crown the better part of the sixteenth century to bring these individuals under control, by use of institutions like the *encomienda* that gave the settlers control over people rather than territory. But by that point the peninsular government back in Europe was itself weakening, with mounting debts from its European and Mediterranean wars. The same practices of venal officeholding resorted to in Spain itself were gradually exported to the New World colonies, shifting the balance of power there to local elites. The *regimientos* and *cabildos*—institutions of local government that had earlier been elected—were by 1600 sold by the Crown as heritable property. State institutionalization thus went into reverse, from a modern, bureaucratic system to a patrimonial one.

Ideas mattered a great deal as well in the evolution of institutions. In the first centuries of colonial rule, there was no Spanish Hobbes or Locke to tell the settlers that they possessed natural and universal rights as human beings. What they had instead were particularistic feudal privileges that they had inherited or bought. In contrast to the British settlers of North America, the Creole populations of Latin America were thus much more likely to demand protection of their privileges than of their rights.[16]

The ideas exported from Spain began to change again, as James Mahoney points out, during the liberal Bourbon phase of empire that began around 1600. In line with reforms taking place on the peninsula itself, the Crown prohibited the sale of *audiencia* seats—the bulk of which had gone to Creoles—beginning in the 1650s, and began staffing administrative courts with more professional officials brought from Europe whose offices were appointive rather than purchased. The intendant system borrowed from France was extended to the colonies, where professional appointed delegates replaced the corrupt local *corregidores* and *alcaldes mayores*. Trade was liberalized through Charles III's Decree of Free Trade: the old restrictions limiting exports to certain ports and ships were abolished, and direct trade with North America became legal. An effort was made to erode the power of merchant monopolies in Peru and Mexico, and to increase the ability of new actors to compete within the economic system.[17]

The impact of these new institutions was dramatic. The center of gravity within the empire began to shift from its old centers in Peru and Mexico to temperate, more lightly settled areas farther south in Argentina and Chile. Argentina, which had been part of the Viceroyalty of Peru, became the seat of its own viceroyalty in 1676. The population of the port of Buenos Aires grew to fifty thousand by the year 1800. Trade expanded significantly with the shift away from mercantilism; between 1682 and 1696, the value of goods exported to Spain increased tenfold. In response to this rising prosperity, emigrants from Europe began shifting their destinations to these new areas and constituted social groups distinct from the entrenched Creole landowners and merchants who made up the old elite. These immigrants themselves also had more liberal ideas and set the stage for the vicious conservative-liberal political conflicts that would dominate the politics of postindependence Latin America.[18]

Ideas mattered once again in the wake of the American and French

Revolutions, which spread notions of equality and made slavery progressively more unacceptable in moral terms as time went on. The American Revolution did not of course have any direct effect on the institution of slavery in the American colonies. It did, however, give all New World settler populations the idea that they too might become free of European tutelage, and it helped bankrupt France and prepared the ground for the events of 1789. The French Revolution had an immediate and direct impact on the large slave colony of Saint-Domingue, where a slave rebellion broke out in 1791 under the leadership of Toussaint Louverture and continued in several phases until the colony won complete independence under slave leadership in 1804 as the new country of Haiti. The British Parliament ended the slave trade in 1807, and the British navy was deployed over the succeeding decades to enforce the ban on slave trading off the African coast. Religious ideas were critical, such as those of William Wilberforce whose conversion to a form of evangelical Protestantism led him to found the Society for Effecting the Abolition of the Slave Trade. Slavery itself was not ended in the British colonies until the Slavery Abolition Act of 1833. The practice hung on in the United States until passage of the Thirteenth Amendment in 1865, and continued in Cuba until 1886 and Brazil until 1888.

LATIN AMERICA'S BIRTH DEFECT

Latin America was born with a birth defect. The Spanish and Portuguese implanted their own authoritarian and mercantilist institutions in the New World, responding to the economic opportunities they saw there. In so doing, they reproduced the class structure that existed back on the Iberian peninsula, as well as a political system in which an authoritarian state was nonetheless partially captured by local elites and consequently never able to dominate them. This class structure differed in an important way from the one that existed in Europe, however, because economic class came to correspond in many Latin American countries to racial and ethnic divisions, which were far more difficult to overcome.

When the countries of Latin America began to win their independence from their colonial masters early in the nineteenth century, they inherited this legacy. The constitutions of most of these newly independent states were nominally representative; many, indeed, were modeled on the presidential system that had been established in the United States in 1787. But all the countries in this region with a very few exceptions had big problems thereafter both in sustaining stable democracy and in maintaining consistent levels of economic growth.

The two phenomena of unstable politics and poor long-term economic performance are closely related to the underlying problem of inequality. The class structure and unequal distribution of resources created sharp political polarizations, in the nineteenth century between liberals and conservatives, and in the twentieth between conservative governments and a variety of Marxist or populist opponents. Economic growth occurred in Latin America in different periods, particularly in the late nineteenth century and in the middle of the twentieth, when a number of countries there were able to close the gap with the developed world to some degree. But the gap reopened as a result of political instability that interrupted normal economic life and reversed the gains from earlier periods. Economic elites were able to dominate nominally democratic political systems to maintain their social status, thereby blocking more democratic access to economic opportunities.[19]

The impact of this historical legacy can be best seen in Mexico, one of the two seats of the Spanish Habsburg Empire in the New World. Efforts to liberalize the economy under the eighteenth-century Bourbons had limited effect as the economic elites in Mexico City fought to protect their positions against new entrants. In the countryside as well a system of mobile wage labor did not take hold as it did in the newly opened lands of Argentina. Rather, large landowners were able to control masses of peasants through debt peonage and other semicoercive means.[20]

The eighteenth-century mining boom was already slowing when the Mexican War of Independence began in 1810; as will be detailed in the following chapter, it began as a social revolution led by two priests and their armies of impoverished followers, and was extraordinarily prolonged and turbulent. The war continued into the mid-1820s and destroyed Mexico's mining industry, its major source of exports.[21] In the wake of this upheaval, Mexico remained unusually unstable politically, with six coups bringing to power a series of caudillos over the next forty years.

In contrast to the United States, where the revolution only briefly disrupted economic growth, Mexico's economy did not recover until the rise of Porfirio Díaz. He ruled the country for a total of thirty-five years

(1876–1911), in a dictatorship known as the Porfiriato. Inheriting a country that was essentially bankrupt from decades of conflict and low growth, he needed economic allies. He got them by creating a banking sector in which a small number of government-connected banks could make large amounts of money. This gave the government access to resources that it could use to suppress lawlessness and provide essential political stability. This led to an extraordinary period of economic growth in which Mexico succeeded in partially catching up to both North America and more liberal emerging powers such as Argentina. Díaz did not, however, create an open or liberal economic order but rather a system we would today label crony capitalism. It was similar in certain ways to the old mercantilist system, only run by local elites rather than the Spanish Crown.[22] It did nothing to empower the mass of the Mexican population either economically or politically. The resulting social tensions exploded in the Mexican Revolution, another convulsive affair that led to Díaz's overthrow in 1911 and lasted until 1916. Indeed, the country was not really stabilized until the rise of the Partido Revolucionario Institucional in the 1940s, meaning that economic growth stagnated or indeed went into reverse for a generation.

The PRI would remain the dominant party controlling Mexican politics until 2000, when it lost the presidency to Vicente Fox, a candidate of the rival Partido Acción Nacional. The 1950s and '60s, in particular, were years of strong economic growth that saw Mexico once again begin to close the gap between itself and the United States. But the fundamental problem of inequality and class had not been solved. The PRI did have some significant accomplishments to its credit: it undertook a major land reform in the 1930s that broke up Mexico's large haciendas, and just as important, it created a strong sense of national identity by continuing the revolution's revival of pre-Columbian symbols. But it achieved stability through the clientelistic distribution of state resources to favored political groups, which limited competition and prevented Mexico from developing a strongly competitive private sector. While the Mexican economy has liberalized substantially (particularly after negotiation of the North American Free Trade Agreement in 1994), it is still dominated by large oligopolies and neomercantilist restrictions on trade. The PRI returned to Los Pinos (the president's residence) in 2012 after a twelve-year absence, this time hopefully more committed to a program of serious structural reform including liberalization of the critical energy sector.

Climate and geography were among the original sources of the Latin American birth defect. The extractive slave economies established by the Spanish in Mexico, Peru, and elsewhere left a legacy of inequality that persisted long after the last silver mine closed and slowed the creation of a North American–style open economy.

But although these material conditions influenced the nature of political institutions in Latin America, they did not altogether determine them. Formal institutions evolved over time in a democratic direction, just as in Europe. What remained much more constant was the region's class structure—its division into whiter, wealthier elites, and poorer, darker masses—which then shaped the way that formal institutions operated. This meant that the emergence of formal democracy in the nineteenth and twentieth centuries did not necessarily lead to empowerment of ordinary people but rather to the continued indirect elite domination of democratic political systems that maintained the social status quo.

17

DOGS THAT DIDN'T BARK

How war, which was critical to the formation of modern states in China and Europe, was much less prevalent in Latin America; why this was so, and how the incentives for state modernization were much weaker; whether we should regret the fact that Latin America experienced lower levels of violence

To say that Latin America was born with a birth defect of social inequality does not, in a way, say anything particularly interesting. In the year 1808, when the Latin American wars of independence began, few societies in any part of the world were characterized by high degrees of economic or social equality. With the exception of more liberal England and Holland, most of Europe consisted of agrarian orders ruled by feudal elites with deeply entrenched privileges. China didn't have feudalism, but it did have a powerful authoritarian state, a class of landlords, and a vast mass of dependent and impoverished peasants. The same could be said of all the other great agrarian empires in India, Turkey, Persia, and in the kingdoms of Southeast Asia. North America was one of the few parts of the world not encumbered by such deeply rooted social inequality, at least for its white population. And apart from France, hardly any countries had modern states.

In the succeeding two centuries, however, some countries evolved in a very different direction. Prussia, Denmark, the Netherlands, Britain, and other European countries followed France in the development of centralized bureaucracies organized along Weberian lines. The French Revolution had, moreover, unleashed not just demands for popular political participation but also a new form of identity by which a shared language and culture would be the central source of unity for the new democratic public. This phenomenon, known as nationalism, then prompted the redrawing of the political map of Europe as dynastic states linked by marriage and feudal obligations were replaced by ones based on a principle of ethnolinguistic solidarity. The levée en masse of the French Revolution represented the first coming together of all these trends: the revolutionary government in Paris was able to mobilize a significant part of the available able-bodied male population to defend France. Under Napoleon, this mobilized expression of state power went on to conquer much of the rest of Europe.

What is interesting about Latin America in the nineteenth and twentieth centuries, then, is the dogs that didn't bark. Strong states like France and Prussia never appeared anywhere in the region, with the possible exception of Chile. Nationalism and patriotic fervor did not emerge in anything like the form they took in Europe, where entire populations could be aroused in anger and competition against their neighbors. With one or two exceptions, states never achieved the capacity to dominate and mobilize their populations. In many respects, the independent governments that appeared after liberation from Spain and Portugal continued to resemble their colonial predecessors. Old regime Spain was characterized by weak absolutism: the state was centralized and autocratic but relatively weak in capacity and unable to dominate its own elites. Although many of the new postindependence Latin American governments were nominally democratic, they were never able to generate more than a moderate amount of state capacity. The failure to create modern states was marked first and foremost by the inability of Latin American states to extract significant levels of taxation from their own populations. As a result, governments met fiscal deficits as old regime Spain did, by inflating the money supply. Inflation is a backdoor form of taxation that has many distorting and unfair consequences for the populations that have to endure it. More than in any other region, inflation became the hallmark of nineteenth- and twentieth-century Latin America.

So why did strong, modern states not emerge in Latin America as they did in Europe? If there is a single factor that explains this outcome, it is the relative absence of interstate war in the New World. We have seen how central war and preparation for war were in the creation of modern states in China, Prussia, and France. Even in the United States, state building has been driven by national security concerns throughout the twentieth century. Though Europe has been remarkably peaceful since 1945, the prior centuries were characterized by high and endemic levels of interstate violence. Over the past two centuries, the major political acts that reconfigured the map of Europe—the French Revolution and Napoleonic Wars, and the wars of unification of Italy and Germany—all involved high levels of violence, culminating in the two world wars of the twentieth century.

There has been plenty of violence in Latin America, of course: today the region is infested with drug cartels, street gangs, and a few remaining guerrilla groups, all of which inflict enormous sufferings on local populations. But in comparison with Europe, Latin America has been a peaceful place in terms of interstate war. This has been a blessing for the region, but it has also left a problematic institutional legacy.

A PEACEFUL CONTINENT

The sociologist Miguel Centeno has documented the fact that Latin America over the past two centuries has been much more peaceful than Europe, North America, and Asia. This is true whether measured by cumulative battle deaths (see Figure 13), mortality rates, percent of the population mobilized for war, or intensity of war, that is, the rate at which people were killed in a given year (see Figure 14). He points out two further facts: first, that levels of violence decreased steadily over time, making twentieth-century Latin America one of the most peaceful regions in the world; and second, that Latin American violence has tended to occur in civil rather than interstate wars. Centeno argues further that when Latin American wars occurred, they tended to be limited in nature, seldom involving the kinds of mass mobilizations of entire populations that occurred following the French Revolution or during the two world wars.[1]

The wars that Latin America did fight came in a couple of waves. The first was the wars of independence from Spain, which were triggered not by the ideas of the American or French Revolutions but by the French occupation of the Iberian peninsula and Napoleon's placing his brother Joseph on the Spanish throne in place of the Bourbon royal family in the years 1808–1810. In Portugal, the monarch moved the seat of government from Lisbon to Rio de Janeiro, though the royal family was to return to the peninsula after Napoleon's defeat. The collapse of legitimate authority in the home countries led to Creole uprisings in Buenos Aires,

FIGURE 13. Cumulative Battle Deaths

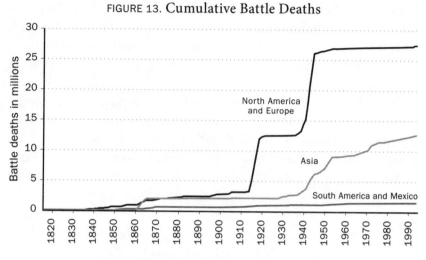

SOURCE: Miguel Angel Centeno, *Blood and Debt*

FIGURE 14. Total Wars by Region

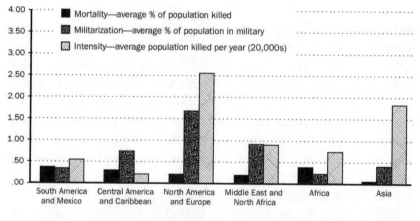

SOURCE: Miguel Angel Centeno, *Blood and Debt*

Caracas, and northern Mexico, which royalist forces were able initially to suppress. But after the restoration of the Bourbon Ferdinand VII to the Spanish throne in 1815, a second wave of revolts broke out and led to independence for virtually the whole of South America by the mid-1820s.

The Latin American wars of independence went on for much longer than the American Revolution, and did far more damage to the infrastructure of the region, setting it back economically for much of the first half of the nineteenth century. The most notable feature of these wars, however, is how little they affected the class structure of the underlying societies and their extremely limited impact on state building.

The missing social revolution was reflected in the dominance of conservative groups in virtually every newly independent country. It is ironic that Hugo Chávez, the populist Venezuelan president, virtually beatified the region's liberator, Simón Bolívar, as a hero of the Left. Bolívar came from a wealthy Creole family. Although he performed truly heroic military feats in defeating Spanish forces, he had inconsistent political commitments, sometimes expressing liberal views and at other times more authoritarian ones. The last thing he wanted to be was a social revolutionary. The same was true of José de San Martín, the other military genius who liberated the southern half of the continent, who proposed establishment of a monarchical government in Peru once Spanish rule ended. The only genuine social revolutionaries were two priests, Miguel Hidalgo and José María Morelos, who mobilized an army of poor indigenous and mixed-blood people that threatened the Creole elite in Mexico City. Morelos's program promised "a new government, by which all inhabitants, except *peninsulares*, would no longer be designated as Indians, mulattoes, or mestizos, but all would be known as Americans."

Both Hidalgo and Morelos were captured and executed, and their movements suppressed. The local Creole elites came to support independence in Mexico and Peru only because Ferdinand VII back in Spain agreed to accept the liberal constitution of 1812; independence for them was thus meant to prevent liberal reform from spreading to the New World.[2] The makers of the American Revolution, by contrast, were liberal and democratic to the core. Independence from Britain served to embed democratic principles in the institutions of the new nation, even if it did not bring about a social revolution. The leaders of the independence movements in Latin America were far more conservative, despite the fact that they felt compelled to adopt formally democratic institutions. Even less did they envision upsetting the region's class structure.

Independence did, however, create a large state-building task as the different components of the Spanish empire sought to create freestanding political orders, which as in Europe involved a splitting apart of certain political units and the merging of others into more centralized polities. Simón Bolívar created an entity known as Gran Colombia in

1819, which incorporated much of present-day Venezuela, Colombia, Panama, northern Peru, Ecuador, and parts of Brazil. This huge region, spread over mountainous and jungle terrain, resisted centralization and split apart into separate countries by 1830 (Panama was detached from Colombia with help from the United States in 1903). Similarly, Agustín de Iturbide, leading an independent Mexico, made himself emperor over territory that included Central America. That area broke free in 1823 as a unified Federal Republic of Central America, but it soon broke apart into the separate nations of El Salvador, Guatemala, Nicaragua, Honduras, and Costa Rica, which resisted several subsequent efforts to reunify them. These new polities often corresponded to Spanish administrative districts, but they did not have their own strong cultural identities the way that France and Germany did. On the other hand, Argentina and Mexico, which had broken down into regional fiefdoms, were unified under authoritarian rulers such as Juan Manuel de Rosas in Buenos Aires, who gradually suppressed regional revolts and accumulated power around centralized governments.[3]

The second big wave of interstate wars took place in the middle of the nineteenth century and can be seen as the finale to this period of postindependence territorial reshuffling. Argentina and Brazil had fought a series of conflicts over control of the mouth of the Río de la Plata, which eventually led to the creation of the independent buffer state of Uruguay in 1828. The two countries continued to contest for influence over Uruguay; this eventually triggered intervention by Britain and France, which sought to protect their commercial interests in the region. Brazil and Argentina were also involved in the War of the Triple Alliance, a bizarre conflict that pitted these two large countries against impoverished Paraguay. This was an utter disaster for Paraguay, which was thereafter "removed . . . from the geopolitical map."[4]

The two other major conflicts of the time were the Mexican-American War, by which Mexico lost the entire area from Texas to California to a rapidly expanding United States, and the War of the Pacific, fought among Chile, Peru, and Bolivia, which led to Chilean acquisition of the rich resources of the Atacama and turned Bolivia into a landlocked country. After the War of the Pacific concluded in 1883, Latin America's borders were largely fixed, and no major interstate conflicts broke out thereafter (with the exception of the Chaco War between Bolivia and Paraguay in the 1930s, a conflict little remembered even in Latin America).[5]

Interstate wars in Latin America have been so infrequent and politically unimportant that many major surveys of Latin American history barely cover them. Compared to Europe and ancient China, or indeed North America, war had a marginal effect on state building. Charles Tilly's aphorism "war made the state, and the state made war" remains true, but begs the question of why wars are more prevalent in some regions than in others.

The region's lagging state building is evident from a number of measures of state capacity, but above all in taxation. In China and early modern Europe, the resource requirements of long-term warfare led states to tax their citizens, create finance ministries and bureaucracies to administer the tax extraction, build administrative hierarchies to manage extensive logistical systems, and the like. All of this led to a dramatic expansion of the revenue needs of early modern European states in the seventeenth and eighteenth centuries, and the growth of civilian bureaucracies. Organized violence also promoted political development through the wholesale elimination of certain social classes that were bulwarks of the old patrimonial state, like the venal officeholders of Old Regime France or the Junker class in Prussia.[6]

Similar developments never materialized in Latin America. Centeno notes that in Brazil and Mexico, two countries for which nineteenth-century data is available, governments extracted no more than a quarter to a half of the taxes per capita that Britain did in the same period. Moreover, they were much more heavily reliant on indirect taxes like customs and excise duties. These are much easier to collect than direct taxes on businesses and individuals, and are always the first kinds of taxes that developing countries with weak administrative capacity tend to use. Even when it was fighting wars, the Brazilian government did not collect more than 4 percent of total revenues from taxes on wealth and production. Chile—sometimes called the "Prussia of Latin America" for its military prowess against its neighbors—collected an even lower percentage. In this regard, they were simply following the pattern set by Latin America's colonial master, Spain, which was itself perpetually unable to raise sufficient tax revenues from its own people, and was forced to declare bankruptcy ten times between 1557 and 1662.[7]

The relative absence of interstate war may explain why Latin America has fewer strong states than Europe, but it does not explain why some countries in the region have more effective governments than others. Political scientist Marcus Kurtz points out that there has been a relatively constant rank ordering of effective states since the nineteenth century, with Chile and Uruguay consistently topping the tables, and Bolivia, Paraguay, and Haiti typically coming out close to the bottom.[8] He argues that Chile, Uruguay, and Argentina were able to build strong states initially due to a combination of free agricultural labor and relatively strong elite consensus, but that Argentina's state subsequently deteriorated as a result of the class conflict after the 1930s. The historical contingency of these outcomes suggests the difficulty of providing a parsimonious theoretical model of state building.[9]

Nonetheless, the lower intensity of interstate war in Latin America did lead to some familiar outcomes. There was much less competitive pressure to consolidate strong national bureaucracies along French-Prussian lines prior to the arrival of mass political participation in the late nineteenth and early twentieth centuries. This meant that when the franchise was opened up in the early twentieth century, there was no "absolutist coalition" in place to protect the autonomy of national bureaucracies. The spread of democratic political competition created huge incentives in Argentina, Brazil, Mexico, Colombia, and other countries for democratic politicians to use clientelistic methods to recruit voters, and consequently to turn public administration into a piggy bank for political appointments. With the partial exceptions of Chile and Uruguay, countries in Latin America followed the paths of Greece and southern Italy and transformed nineteenth-century patronage politics into full-blown twentieth-century clientelism.

Having created patronage-ridden states, the countries of Latin America have faced what political scientist Barbara Geddes has called the "politician's dilemma." As in nineteenth-century America, there was a clear public interest in reforming the state and putting it on a more meritocratic foundation. But doing so would cut into the politicians' fund of political capital, so few had incentives to proceed. Geddes argues that reform took place only under special conditions, such as when the political parties were balanced and none would get a special advantage by pushing for reform.[10]

External shocks, not in the form of military threat but of financial crisis, were sometimes also effective in forcing change. Thus, following the Latin American debt crisis of the early 1980s, there was a major effort to professionalize central banks and finance ministries, which has led to much better state performance in managing macroeconomic policy. And there are at least the beginnings of a middle-class coalition against clientelism and corruption in Brazil and elsewhere, where prosecutions of the notoriously corrupt political class have increased in the 2000s. Brazil today offers a mixed picture, with some excellent ministries and agencies coexisting with highly corrupt and underperforming ones.[11]

NO MORE WAR

Why was it that interstate war was rare in Latin America compared to Europe and East Asia, and that the wars that occurred did not motivate governments to engage in serious and prolonged state building of the sort that happened in Asia and Europe? There are a number of possible reasons.

The first has to do with the class stratifications already noted, which in Latin America had significant ethnic and racial dimensions. War and violence, as noted earlier, were endemic to Latin America; the difference with Europe lay in the fact that in the nineteenth and twentieth centuries war was all internal rather than between states. Mexico, Argentina, Uruguay, Colombia, Nicaragua, and a host of other countries experienced prolonged internal conflicts that disrupted economies and impoverished their societies. These internal conflicts reflected the bitter social and class divisions that existed. They limited the degree to which elites in any given country were willing to push for total mobilization of the population, since this would entail putting guns into the hands of restive nonelites. The elites themselves were often internally divided into factions based on region, ideology, or economic interest. Social mistrust also limited the degree of loyalty that marginalized populations felt toward the state. In Europe, demands for expanded popular participation came on the heels of war; the rise of the British Labour Party in the 1920s, for example, was in some ways a consequence of the sufferings of the working class in the trenches of World War I. In Latin America, by contrast, elites usually pulled back from interstate conflicts precisely to avoid having to turn to the masses for help.

A second factor has to do with geography. Europe is cut up into geographically defined regions that make it difficult for a single power to dominate the continent as a whole. But within each region, there is open territory that permits the accumulation of substantial economic and military power. There are also large, navigable rivers that enable commerce and communication with inland areas. Latin America by contrast is divided by the spine of the Andes and the dense forests of the tropics, which have physically separated its different parts. Though Venezuela, Colombia, Peru, and Bolivia border on Brazil, none has strong communications links with the largest economy in the region simply because of the difficulty of penetrating the Amazonian jungle. Colombia, Latin America's third-largest country, is so internally divided by Andean cordilleras that its government to this day has trouble projecting power across the whole of its territory, creating havens for guerrillas and drug traffickers. At the beginning of the twenty-first century, not a single road connects Panama to Colombia despite the fact that they used to be part of the same country. Obviously, projecting military power under such circumstances is very difficult.

A third factor has to do with national identity, or rather, the weakness of national identity in many of the region's societies. This too was deeply affected by ethnic and racial diversity. The strong European states that emerged in the nineteenth century were built around a national principle that made language and ethnicity the core of national identity. Part of the reason that Europe in the twentieth century was so violent is that ethnic identities did not correspond to existing political borders and had to be rearranged through war. European war was tightly connected to the nation-building process.

The same could never be true in Peru, Bolivia, Guatemala, and Mexico, where large numbers of Indian and mixed-blood people lived their lives in rural communities largely untouched by the state or its services, and as a consequence felt almost no sense of obligation to it. They in turn were regarded by the European elites at best with indifference and at worst with distrust and hostility. Language, moreover, could not serve as a source of identity that both unified nations and distinguished them from one another, since all of the elites spoke either Spanish or Portuguese, while the nonelites continued to speak Quechua, Aymara, Nahuatl, Mayan, or some other indigenous language. To the present day, the business elites in Guatemala City have virtually nothing in common with the indigenous groups living in the highlands. And indeed, these two sets of actors faced off in a brutal civil war during the 1980s.

A final factor inhibiting Latin American state building was powerful external actors—the United States, Britain, France, and other European powers—who sought to influence developments there. The United States in particular upheld a conservative political and social order in the region, intervening to help topple left-wing leaders such as Jacobo Árbenz in Guatemala and Salvador Allende in Chile. The United States under the Monroe Doctrine also sought to prevent outside powers like Britain and France in the nineteenth century and the Soviet Union in the twentieth from forming alliances with Latin American countries that might have helped both in institution building. As a result of their own experience in a country with historical social mobility, American policy makers are often blind to deeply embedded social stratifications that characterize other societies. The only successful political revolution in the western hemisphere that also resulted in a social revolution was that of Fidel Castro's Cuba in 1959, a revolution that the United States spent the next fifty-plus years trying to contain or reverse.

Should we then regret the fact that Latin America has not seen more violence over the past two centuries, either in the form of massive interstate wars or social revolutions? It goes without saying that the social revolutions that occurred in Europe and Asia were purchased at enormous cost: tens of millions of people killed in purges, executions, and military conflict, and hundreds of millions more displaced, incarcerated, starved to death, or tortured. Political violence, moreover, oftentimes begets only more political violence rather than progressive social change. We would not want to "give war a chance" in Latin America any more than in other parts of the world. These observations should not blind us, however, to the fact that just outcomes in the present are often the result, as Machiavelli noted, of crimes committed in the past.

18

THE CLEAN SLATE

Exceptions to the materialist account of institutions in Latin America; why Costa Rica didn't become a "banana republic"; why Argentina should have looked like Canada or Australia but regressed instead

The Spanish and Portuguese went to the New World to exploit its resources and brought with them authoritarian political institutions that left a legacy of inequality and poor government up to the present. But while it is possible to spin a larger story of the relationship among geography, climate, and resources to political outcomes at the level of the region as a whole, there were important exceptions and qualifications to this pattern. Certain countries did better than their material endowments would suggest, and others did much worse. All of this points to the fact that material conditions are not the only factors explaining outcomes in the twenty-first century. Human beings make political choices at critical junctures in their history that force their societies onto very different trajectories for better and worse. Human beings, in other words, are agents who have control over their destinies, even as material conditions shape the choices they face.

LA COSTA POBRE

A good example of a country escaping the Latin American birth defect is Costa Rica. It is a small country in Central America of fewer than five million people that is today substantially wealthier than most of its neighbors. Its per capita income in 2011 was over $12,000, compared to its neighbors in Guatemala (less than $5,000), Honduras ($4,000), and

Nicaragua ($3,000).[1] Many foreigners know it as an ecotourism destination, with its lush tropical rain forests; they may be less aware that it has also been host to multinationals like Intel and Boston Scientific that have set up assembly plants there. Perhaps more significant is what hasn't happened in Costa Rica. Unlike El Salvador, Nicaragua, and Guatemala, there were no military coups, dictatorships, bloody civil wars, death squads, or foreign intervention on the part of the United States, Cuba, or other outside parties for the last sixty years. Rather, it has been a stable democracy since 1948 with competitive elections and regular turnovers of power between political parties. This has been the case despite the fact that Costa Rica's development has been based primarily on tropical agricultural products—coffee and bananas—and that its climate and resource endowments are virtually indistinguishable from those of its neighbors.[2]

The fact that Costa Rica turned out so differently from the rest of Central America has generated theories and myths as to why this was so. The Costa Ricans themselves argue that they have always had an egalitarian and democratic culture, based on the absence of a landed oligarchy that characterized much of the rest of Spanish America, and that their racial and ethnic homogeneity has contributed to their political stability. There are even cultural hypotheses that trace the country's success to the fact that its early settlers were alleged to be Spanish Marranos (Jews converted to Catholicism).[3]

There is some truth to at least the first of these explanations. Compared to Guatemala, which was the seat of an important imperial *audiencia* from early in the sixteenth century, Costa Rica was a relative backwater, isolated and unattractive because of its lack of precious metals or exploitable indigenous population. Although Christopher Columbus managed to stop in Costa Rica in 1502, the territory was largely avoided by later Europeans as being too remote—hence the national joke that the country should have been named "Costa Pobre" (poor coast) rather than Costa Rica (rich coast). As the coffee industry grew in the nineteenth century, there tended to be far fewer large estates than in Guatemala and El Salvador, and thus less concentrated political power in the hands of a conservative agrarian oligarchy.[4] While African slaves constituted one-sixth of the population in 1800, both they and the indigenous inhabitants soon died out or were assimilated into the broader mestizo population. In this respect it differs sharply from Guatemala, with its large Indian population and high levels of inequality.[5]

But like all national stories, this historical legacy does not begin to explain the country's success in the second half of the twentieth century. Up until 1948, Costa Rica experienced many of the same political dysfunctions as its neighbors. While family farming was more extensive than elsewhere, growth of the coffee and banana export industries nonetheless created an oligarchy of rich growers who proved perfectly willing to use violence to protect their economic interests. Despite adoption of a democratic constitution when Costa Rica became independent in 1821, the country was ruled by a series of dictators in the nineteenth century and plagued by constant battles between liberals and conservatives who were happy to use electoral fraud and force to seize and keep power. While Costa Ricans date their democracy to the election of 1889, there was a subsequent military coup in 1914 and increasing political polarization as the country began to industrialize. As elsewhere, conservative elites looked on with fear as labor unions formed and new Socialist and Communist parties emerged. All of this resulted in a civil war in 1948 between a left-wing administration under Rafael Ángel Calderón that sought to hold on to power after losing an election, and a coalition of opposition forces led by Social Democrat José Figueres and the candidate who had won the election, the strongly anticommunist Otilio Ulate Blanco.[6]

El Salvador, Nicaragua, and Guatemala were at this point also dominated by conservative landowning oligarchies that were increasingly challenged by newly mobilized actors like trade unions, Christian social activists, and emerging Socialist and Communist parties. In these three countries, the old elites turned to the military to suppress the Left and protect their interests, while the Left responded by becoming more radical, seeking help from the international Communist movement, and undertaking armed struggle. In El Salvador, a peasant rebellion led by Farabundo Martí was violently suppressed in the 1930s, inspiring a Marxist revolutionary group, the Farabundo Martí National Liberation Front, to challenge the government in the 1970s. In Nicaragua, the Sandinista movement fought the dictatorship of Anastasio Somoza and came to power in 1979 with help from Cuba and the Soviet Union, which then led the Reagan administration to fund the contra movement seeking to overthrow it. In Guatemala, a U.S.-aided coup toppled the left-wing Jacobo Árbenz in 1954 and provoked a long and bloody civil war during the 1970s and '80s. These conflicts were not resolved until the early 1990s and to this day have left a legacy of polarization and distrust.

Why did Costa Rica's civil war not lead to a similar spiral of mistrust and violence? It is hard to explain this except by reference to the choices made by individual leaders at the time. Although Calderón's left-leaning coalition included some Communists, it did not pursue a particularly radical agenda, and indeed in response to charges that it had stolen an election established a new electoral tribunal to more fairly administer future electoral contests. When the conservative rebels led by Figueres overturned the Calderón government by force, they went on to implement a social democratic agenda close to that of Calderón and then restored power to the legitimate winner of the 1948 election, the conservative Ulate. This government accepted in turn a new constituent assembly that strengthened the nonpartisan electoral tribunal and extended the vote to women.[7]

Most important—and uniquely, for Latin America—the 1949 constitution abolished the standing army. Thus a broadly conservative coalition agreed to deprive itself of the one coercive instrument that was to become the basis for oligarchic power elsewhere throughout the region. This choice influenced the subsequent development of the Left in Costa Rica, which abjured armed struggle and Marxism for a more reformist social democratic path.

The decision of a major political player to use constitutional rules to bind not just its opponents but also itself was very rare in Latin America. It was similar to the settlement coming out of England's Glorious Revolution, which established the very principle of constitutional government. That is, the English revolutionaries did not seize power and exploit the state in their own narrow interests; they accepted binding rules on the grounds of their general validity.

Like Botswana, an African country that has defied the odds to become far more economically and politically successful than its neighbors, it is very difficult to fit Costa Rica into any of the existing theoretical structures that purport to explain economic or political development. The bare facts of its climate, geography, population, and indeed its political history up through the middle of the twentieth century would never have led one to predict that it would perform so differently from the rest of Central America. Contemporary outcomes appear to be the product of a series of happy historical accidents, including the fact that one of its early dictators, Tomás Guardia, was far more enlightened than his contemporaries and did much to promote education as well as to curtail the power of the coffee elite. The good choices made by political leaders like Figueres during the crisis of 1948 were shaped by earlier choices, such as the relative moderation of the anticommunist right, and the corresponding lack of radicalism on the part of the Communists themselves.[8] Costa Rica's experience thus underlines the fact that the material conditions of geography and climate, and the social structure they produce, can be offset by good leadership and the choices made by individuals.

THE CLEAN SLATE

If anyone needs further convincing that geography, climate, and population influence but do not finally determine contemporary development outcomes, consider Argentina. It is in some sense the polar opposite of Costa Rica. Whereas Costa Rica succeeded in breaking free of the broader pattern of plantation agriculture and its resultant class and ethnic divisions, Argentina did the opposite. Blessed with geographical circumstances that should have facilitated North American–type democratic and capitalist development, it succumbed to the same kind of class polarization and inconsistent long-term economic performance that characterized old centers of the Spanish empire like Peru and Mexico. The fact that Argentina never became the Canada of the South suggests the limits of all general theories of development that are purely economic in nature.

In contrast to Mexico and Peru, which in pre-Columbian times hosted large indigenous populations, Argentina was founded in a region that used to be referred to as a "land of new settlement," much like the United States, Canada, Australia, and New Zealand. Of course, these were not actually lands of new settlement. They were in fact lightly settled by hunter-gatherer and in some cases agrarian communities including the Pehuenches, Tehuelches, and Puelches, whose relatives also inhabited southern Chile. These groups put up often tenacious resistance against the settler communities, but eventually they were physically marginalized like those in North America. At this point the settlers could believe they were occupying a *terra nullis*, an empty land where they were free to set up their own institutions.

The Argentine population was thus among the most European of any in Latin America. Unlike Mexico and Peru, it was not divided between a white settler class and a vast mass of Indians and mestizos. Slavery did exist in the late colonial period, and at one time blacks constituted as much as a quarter of the population of Buenos Aires. But slavery was abolished early on and the black population gradually was absorbed into the larger European one.[9] There was in fact a massive "whitening" of Argentina's population as a result of the huge migrations from Europe that took place toward the end of the nineteenth century, which increased the country's population from 1.7 million in 1869 to 7.9 million in 1914. Of these new immigrants, 46 percent came from Italy and 32 percent from Spain. While Argentina was divided by region and by the large cleavage between the metropolis of Buenos Aires and the rural hinterlands, ethnicity and race were not big political issues.[10]

Argentina was the classic example of the "reversal of fortune" that took place in the eighteenth and nineteenth centuries: tropical and semitropical regions that had been rich in the sixteenth century became poor and were displaced by more temperate regions of the former periphery (see chapter 16 above). Argentina during the Habsburg period had been a provincial backwater within the Spanish New World empire, but beginning in the late eighteenth century it began to rapidly overtake the older colonial centers. Indeed, Argentina in the late nineteenth century came to be regarded much as China and Singapore are today, an economic miracle that incited envy, wonder, and a significant level of European investment. Between 1870 and 1913, Argentine exports were the fastest growing in the world, increasing at a rate of 6 percent per annum; at the end of the nineteenth century, per capita GDP was about the same as that of Germany, Holland, and Belgium, and higher than that of Austria, Spain, Italy, and Sweden.[11] While much attention has been paid to the country's growth in the late nineteenth century, James Mahoney points out that the acceleration of output dated from a much earlier point, with Argentine per capita GDP reaching a level slightly higher than that of the United States in the year 1800. The country's early growth performance was therefore not a flash in the pan but lasted more than a hundred years from independence up until the Great Depression in the 1930s.[12]

Argentina in this period was fully incorporated into the global economy. Built around the port of Buenos Aires, it produced not gold and silver but beef, wool, wheat, and other commodities for the European market. Its temperate climate and extensive pampas provided ideal conditions for growing a wide range of foodstuffs, which improved transport technology like refrigerated ships could make available to distant markets. In return, it received high levels of investment from more developed countries, particularly Britain, which equipped the country with railroads, communications, and other infrastructure that vastly stimulated productivity.

The reasons for Argentina's success in the nineteenth century are fairly straightforward. The country was settled after the onset of the more liberal Bourbon period of Spanish colonialism and was therefore never saddled with the kinds of restrictive trade practices, monopolies, and regulations that characterized Habsburg mercantilism. It also didn't have the social legacy of a merchant and landowner elite like those in Mexico and Peru that continued to dominate the economy even after the more liberal reforms were put in place. Argentina was, in the words of historian Tulio Halperín Donghi, a country that was "born liberal."[13]

Then, beginning in the 1930s, the reversal of fortune was itself reversed, and Argentina began a long period of economic stagnation and decline. Instead of moving from middle- to high-income status like Canada, Australia, and New Zealand, Argentina fell behind. From a position where it was as rich as or richer than Switzerland, Italy, and Canada, it was reduced by 1978 to one-sixth of the per capita GDP of Switzerland, half of Italy's, and one-fifth of Canada's.[14] Argentina went on to become one of the charter members of the club of Latin American countries that experienced the debt crisis of the early 1980s, defaulting on its sovereign debt. Hyperinflation followed, with rates reaching as high as 5,000 percent per year in 1989. The 1990s saw a brief return to monetary stability and growth, as the country pegged the peso to the U.S. dollar via a currency board. But then Argentina succumbed to a major economic crisis in 2000–2001 as the dollar peg was abandoned, and the country fell into a huge depression. Growth returned in the first decade of the twenty-first century on the back of a global commodity boom, but it did so under the leadership of yet another populist government that encouraged short-term expansion at the expense of long-term sustainability. Argentina, for all of its advantages, had regressed to an earlier Latin American mean.

Argentina's poor performance has generated a small industry devoted to the question of what sociologist Carlos Waisman labels the "Argentine riddle" of reversed development.[15] A proximate answer to this question is simply bad economic policies implemented by generations of officials and political leaders. Any textbook on international monetary policy or financial crises will feature Argentina, since it has repeatedly brought upon itself cycles of rapid growth, inflation, devaluation, and economic collapse. It is also a textbook case of the evils of economic nationalism: efforts in the 1950s to encourage domestic manufacturing through import substitution—that is, the protection of uncompetitive domestic industries—led to huge inefficiencies, including efforts to develop a car, the Di Tella, that never found a market outside Argentina. These bad policies continue: the populist spending policies of the 2000s have produced the second highest level of inflation in Latin America, something the government has tried to cover up by corrupting the national statistical agency.

But to say simply that the country's poor growth record is the result of bad policy begs the question of why bad policies were adopted in the first place and why the national elites seem to have such a hard time learning from earlier mistakes and putting the country on a sounder footing. The answer lies, of course, in politics. Despite the fact that Argentina in the first decades of the twentieth century appeared to be on its way to developing a liberal and inclusive political order based on a broad middle class, a series of bad political choices in the 1930s and '40s shifted the country into a type of polarized politics much more typical of older states like Peru and Mexico. A society that did not inherit deep class divisions nonetheless developed them, along with a uniquely Argentine brand of personalistic politics and clientelistic mobilization that continues to distort policy choices down to the present day.

If one wants to look for deeper historical causes of the twentieth century reversal, there are two that stand out. The first is the concentration of land ownership, particularly in the agricultural regions radiating out from the port of Buenos Aires. Beginning in the 1820s, the Argentine state leased out huge tracts of land that were eventually purchased by a small number of families for very low prices. As late as the third decade of the twentieth century, a group of fifty families owned eleven million acres of property, or 13 percent of the land in Buenos Aires province. The six largest landowners at the time of World War I had incomes larger than the national budget of Argentina's main ministries. This consolidation took place in a temperate agricultural zone with moderate amounts of rainfall, conditions perfectly suitable for family farming.

Democracy does not automatically spring up under favorable climatic conditions. It is the result of deliberate political choices about the way that resources are distributed, which in turn are driven by ideas and ideology. In American history, there was always a strong tension between demands for the egalitarian distribution of federal lands in the West to individual families, and those of large land speculators and corporations that wanted to consolidate landholdings. These battles were fought in Congress, and to the extent that family farming prevailed, it was due to passage of measures like the 1787 Northwest Ordinance and the 1862 Homestead Act, which deliberately encouraged smallholding.[16] Unlike the United States, early postindependence Argentine governments decided on very different policies that concentrated land ownership and created a landed oligarchy that then dominated the country's politics up through the 1930s. The United States made one choice and Argentina another; climate and geography had little to do with these outcomes.[17]

The second long-term historical factor is leadership style and Argentina's ambivalent embrace of institutions. One of the country's founding leaders was the dictator Juan Manuel de Rosas, a caudillo who was governor of Buenos Aires province from 1835 to 1852. Rosas was himself a wealthy landowner who built a political base by conquering Indian lands and giving them away to his followers as estancias, or large estates. In doing so he established the hegemony of his class over Argentine politics. He was also good at rallying supporters around opposition to a variety of enemies, such as neighbors Brazil and Paraguay, the European powers, and the opposition Unitarios who supported a strong, centralized government. Among other acts, he decreed that all official documents be prefaced with the slogan "Death to the Vile, Filthy, Savage Unitarios." These were not simply words; in the course of his dictatorship, Rosas had thousands of opponents put to death, including 3,765 individuals who had their throats cut. A George Washington he was not.[18]

Rosas was not an institution builder. His dictatorship produced few laws, least of all a constitution on which a new national government could be based. In a precedent that would be followed by later Argentine leaders, he built a following based on loyalty to his person rather than to any coherent set of ideas or institutions. Argentina did not get a constitution until 1853, and it was not until 1880 that the final regional rebellions and Indian uprisings had been suppressed, and Buenos Aires made the national capital.[19]

Argentina thus was saddled with two bad historical legacies: a powerful landed oligarchy and a tradition of personalistic authoritarian leadership. The decades following this consolidation of national power demonstrated, nonetheless, that these historical legacies did not necessarily condemn the new republic to economic decline or political decay; it was just the opposite. Economic growth took off in the last decades of the nineteenth century, and at the beginning of the twentieth, the political system began to open up as well.

Samuel Huntington argues that for political order to be achieved during the process of modernization, institutions must accommodate increasing demands for political participation. This is in fact exactly what happened in Argentina between 1880 and 1930. The political system of the late nineteenth century, like that of Italy, Germany, and any number of other European countries, was based on a limited male franchise with strict property qualifications that allowed the system to be dominated by the landed elite. This oligarchic republic soon came under challenge. Economic growth and incipient industrialization, as well as the huge number of foreigners flooding into the country, created new social groups that sought representation in the political system. The first was the middle class—professionals like lawyers and doctors, civil servants, and other more educated people who made their livelihoods outside of the agrarian economy. This group formed a base of support for the Unión Civica Radical, or Radical Civic Union, in the 1890s. The Radicals were initially excluded from political participation by widespread fraud and vote manipulation on the part of the landed oligarchy, and in response staged several violent revolts to gain power. A more enlightened wing of the ruling conservative party came to power in 1911 under President Roque Sáenz Peña, which expanded suffrage to all adult males. This vastly expanded the voter rolls (though immigrants remained excluded) and resulted in the election in 1916 of Hipólito Yrigoyen, whose Radical Party remained in power for the next fourteen years.

The Radical Party was not, in fact, very radical; its leadership included members of the rural oligarchy, and it had no intention of trying to up-end the existing social order or commodity-based export economy. Instead it behaved much like early democratic political parties in the United States, Greece, and Italy, building a large political base through the clientelistic distribution of public offices to supporters and creating a modern machine run by professional political functionaries. Using these techniques, the Radical Party became the first truly national party in Argentina. In addition, Yrigoyen himself perfected the personalistic political style of Rosas, building a cult of personality around himself rather than around the ideas represented by his party. The Radical Party thus engineered the transition from traditional oligarchic patronage to modern clientelism, much as the Italian Christian Democrats were to do after World War II.[20]

Up to this point, there was really no reason why Argentina could not have developed politically in the manner of the United States or Britain. Industrialization was leading to the mobilization of new social groups—first the middle classes and then a growing working class. The political system was adjusting to the demands for participation posed by these groups, in the shape of an expanded franchise and new political parties representing their interests. There was violence as each of these rising groups sought representation, but there was plenty of violence as well in the United States and Britain at comparable periods of their industrial development. The old landowning oligarchy could feel its influence slipping away, but no one in the new political constellation that emerged by the 1920s was fundamentally challenging its position. Indeed, one social fact that distinguished Argentina from Peru and Mexico was that it had no impoverished peasantry that could organize to demand radical land reform.

Whereas the Costa Rican elite made good political choices in 1948, the Argentine elite made some very bad ones, beginning with the military coup that took place in September 1930 that brought down Yrigoyen's radical party government. The coup was the result of collaboration between the old landowning oligarchy and the military. The 1929 stock market crash in New York and the beginning of the Great Depression had reduced demand for Argentina's exports and brought on an economic crisis. While the setback was not nearly as great as in other countries of the western hemisphere, it nonetheless triggered great fears among the old elite that their economic and social position was under threat.

The military, ironically, was the one part of the Argentine state that had undergone considerable modernization. The government had sought the advice of—who else?—the German military in seeking to professionalize its own armed services, and in the early decades of the twentieth century saw the emergence of a much more autonomous army that could control its own promotions and protect its interests from politicians. Many in the military were unhappy with Yrigoyen's interference in their chain of command. They had also by that time developed their own ideas about the need for a quasi-Fascist corporatist organization of a new Argentine state, along lines that Hitler was to implement in Germany during the 1930s. The military was thus prepared to join forces with the old oligarchy to close off the system to the new social actors.[21]

Argentina's landed oligarchy could easily have continued to enjoy their lifestyles and wealth even as they lost political power, just as the landowning aristocracy in England did. The coup could not prevent the larger process of social change from occurring as Argentina industrialized; this group would lose power in any event over the next generation. Had the global economic crisis occurred a decade later, things might have turned out differently. But the elite's commitment to democratic norms at this point was still fragile, and they judged their own self-interest poorly.

The period following the 1930 coup is known in Argentina as the "infamous decade," in which a series of military men turned politicians tried to rule the country through electoral fraud, repression, and outright illegality. The conservative oligarchy did not achieve any of the goals the authors of the coup intended, and a decade of jockeying for power prepared the ground for a second military coup in 1943. This event in turn paved the way for the rise of Juan Perón, a military officer who used his position as labor minister in the military government to build a party and a power base for himself.[22]

It is not my intention to provide a detailed account of the subsequent history of Perón and Peronism, and the complex sequence of military coups and democratic restorations that occurred in the period from 1943 until 1983 when democracy was more stably restored in Argentina and the military exited from politics. What makes these struggles hard for outsiders to understand is that they do not fit neatly into the ideological categories used to describe twentieth-century European politics. Perón and his first wife, Eva, could be seen as left-wing figures insofar as they built a power base among the working class and labor movement, and followed redistributive social policies that were highly beneficial to the industrial proletariat. On the other hand, Perón was a military officer whose mobilizational techniques borrowed much from fascism, with its effort to organize the state in a corporatist fashion. He had little use for Marxism, emphasizing nation and Argentine patriotism instead. Rather than building a disciplined Leninist party with its ideologically motivated cadres, he built a populist mass party based on his ability to shower clientelistic favors on supporters. In addition, he and particularly his wife Evita followed in the tradition of Rosas and Yrigoyen in building a highly personalistic following in which loyalty was owed less to a party with a clear program than to a particular charismatic leader. This ideological incoherence continued long after Perón departed the scene: the Peronist party followed a conservative neoliberal policy under Carlos Menem in the 1990s, and then a leftist-populist program under Néstor and Cristina Kirchner in the 2000s.

Perón invented a populist tradition that continues to the present day, engaging in social policies that won him votes in the short run but that were economically disastrous and unsustainable over time. He tried to maintain full employment through customs tariffs and quantitative restrictions on imports, overvalued the peso to make imports cheaper, and taxed agricultural exports to pay for his generous social policies. These measures introduced a host of distortions into the economy, required an ever-more-complex set of exchange controls to administer, and in the end led to long-term declines in productivity and deficits that could be covered only through the printing of money. Under Perón, the Argentine working class became the hyperpoliticized political base of a single, controversial individual.[23]

But in another respect, the real damage was done by the first coup in 1930, which brought the military into politics and signaled that Argentine elites were not willing to play by liberal democratic rules of the game. The coup undermined the rule of law: the Argentine Supreme Court retroactively approved what should have been clearly denounced as an unconstitutional seizure of power, as a result of the new government's ability to pack the court with its own members. This practice of court packing—something the U.S. public rejected soundly when Franklin Roosevelt tried to do it in 1937—has been practiced by virtually every subsequent Argentine president, with terrible consequences for the rule of law.[24]

Argentina was born with a clean slate. Unlike Mexico and Peru, it did not inherit a society that was highly stratified by class or ethnicity. It did well in its early days precisely because it could adopt, like Britain's settler colonies, a set of liberal economic policies that encouraged entrepreneurship and growth. What Argentina's political elites did was to turn the country into a polarized, class-ridden society whose divisions made it incapable of achieving consensus around sensible pro-growth economic policies. These elites included the old oligarchy that feared losing power and social status, the military, which sought to protect its own autonomy at the country's expense, the leadership of a working class that soon had benefits to protect, and a broader political class that traded on personality rather than policy.

Costa Rica and Argentina have something in common: they both failed to follow the predictions of materialist theories of how early colonial institutions or natural resource endowments determine contemporary success, in either economic development or political institution building. This doesn't mean that the theories are necessarily wrong. It does mean that they are insufficient to fully explain the process of political development in many specific cases. This process is highly complex, involving multiple factors including leadership, international influences, and ideology in addition to climate and geography.

What these deviant cases demonstrate is that human agency matters a great deal in institutional development. Costa Rica could have ended up like El Salvador or Nicaragua but for certain good political choices made by leaders in the late 1940s. Argentina, by contrast, squandered many natural advantages because its elites had exaggerated fears of social change, and because of the behavior of its early leaders. Counterfactual histories are very easy to imagine in all of these cases.

Latin America and the Caribbean were the oldest non-Western societies colonized by European powers. We will now turn to sub-Saharan Africa, the region where colonialism began centuries later and failed to leave nearly as deep an institutional imprint. If Latin America's problem was that early Spanish and Portuguese institutions left a legacy of authoritarian government, inequality, and class polarization, Africa's problem was that the colonial authorities wanted to exercise dominion on the cheap and failed to leave behind much of an institutional legacy at all. If states in Latin America were weak and failed to evolve into modern Weberian bureaucracies, in sub-Saharan Africa states were often missing altogether.

19

STORMS IN AFRICA

Why sub-Saharan Africa's situation is today not as bad as commonly perceived; how certain nations there nonetheless are near the bottom of global development rankings; how the central obstacle to development is lack of an effective state; how and why the Europeans colonized Africa

During the 1990s and early 2000s, Western audiences were bombarded with pictures of starving African children and appeals from figures in the entertainment world like Bono and Angelina Jolie to support debt relief and foreign assistance to impoverished countries there. It is ironic that this campaign was reaching a crescendo just as Africa was effecting a major turnaround in its fortunes. Following a long period of decline, the countries of sub-Saharan Africa as a whole achieved economic growth rates of more than 4.6 percent per year in the period from 2000 to 2011, according to the World Bank.[1] Some are resource-rich states including Angola and Nigeria that rode a commodity boom in the 2000s driven by demand from China and other emerging market countries. Economist Steven Radelet points out, however, that even if one excludes these highly corrupt countries, there is still a core of about seventeen states that have not only grown economically but have also been governed democratically, holding reasonably free and fair multiparty elections. There are obviously countries with very bad records either with regard to economic growth or democratic government, such as Somalia, Zimbabwe, and the Democratic Republic of Congo. But just as Asia encompasses countries performing at widely varying levels, from Singapore and South Korea on the one hand to Burma and North Korea on the other, so too the African story is a complex one that does not fit current stereotypes of a continent of starving children.[2]

Sub-Saharan Africa's recent turnaround should not, however, obscure its disastrous overall performance in the generation that stretched from independence in the 1960s to the mid-1990s. The story told about Nigeria in chapter 14 is not typical of Africa; Nigeria had a particularly bad case of a disease afflicting many countries in the region. Figure 15 traces per capita GDP for sub-Saharan Africa compared to the developing countries of East Asia. It shows, first, that incomes in the latter region went from being a fraction of Africa's to a level nearly four times as great, and that from the early 1970s to the mid-1990s African per capita incomes actually dropped.

FIGURE 15. Sub-Saharan Africa and East Asia, Per Capita GDP, 1960–2011

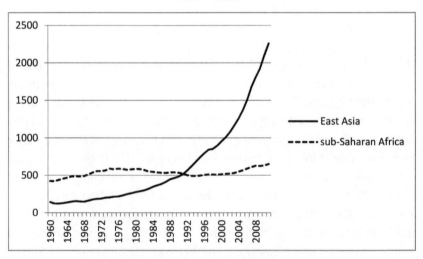

SOURCE: World Bank

These aggregate statistics mask, moreover, the misery of life for many Africans in this period. Somalia, Liberia, and Sierra Leone fell apart entirely and were taken over by warlord gangs that drugged child soldiers and turned them into pathological killers. Independence from Portugal triggered long civil wars in Angola and Mozambique fueled by outside powers. Sudan fought a long war with its own south, which finally became an independent country in 2011, while committing atrocities against the population of Darfur. South Sudan itself collapsed into civil war soon after independence. Uganda, Equatorial Guinea, and the Central African Republic suffered under grotesque dictators, while the Democratic Republic of Congo went from kleptocratic bankruptcy under Mobutu Sese Seko to breakdown and a prolonged internal conflict that has killed as many as five million people. Many of these conflicts were driven by global demand for African commodities such as diamonds, copper, cobalt, cotton, and oil, and were facilitated by weapons and mercenaries provided by developed countries.[3]

Africa's poor economic performance in this period and its troubled political institutions are clearly linked. Countries will obviously not grow if they are racked by bloody conflicts. For this reason, economist Paul Collier and a number of other Africanists have spent their academic careers studying conflict and ways to mitigate it. But as Collier himself would be the first to admit, conflict is itself driven by weak institutions. If a country has legitimate, strong, and effective political institutions, the discovery of diamonds or oil on its territory will not tempt rebel groups to grab them or foreign powers to meddle in their exploitation. Norway did not fall apart when it discovered offshore oil. In a similar vein, many people blame ethnic divisions for creating conflict. But Collier and others have found that ethnicity is often a tool that political leaders use to mobilize followers, rather than a fundamental source of conflict in itself. Switzerland with its strong institutions has grown rich despite its internal ethnic differences.[4]

AFRICA'S WEAK STATES

Even though Africa encompasses a wide variety of political regimes from stable democracies to authoritarian kleptocracies to failed states, there are certain generalizations that can be made about many of them. There is an African mode of governance that characterizes many states on the continent, and it is distinctly different from those found in Latin America or East Asia.

Political scientists have labeled this type of governance "neopatrimonialism." Throughout this book I have used Max Weber's term "patrimonial" to refer to governments staffed by the family and friends of the ruler, and run for their benefit. Modern governments, by contrast, are supposed to be staffed by officials chosen on the basis of merit and expertise, and run for the sake of a broad public interest. A neopatrimonial government has the outward form of a modern state, with a constitution, presidents and prime ministers, a legal system, and pretensions of impersonality, but the actual operation of the government remains at core a matter of sharing state resources with friends and family.[5]

The first characteristic of African neopatrimonial rule is its personalism. In the wake of independence, politics centered around the figure of the president or Big Man (virtually all African postcolonial political systems were presidential rather than parliamentary, and all presidents were male), to whom individuals owed loyalty. While leaders set up political parties, these were far less well organized and important than in Asia and Europe, where ideology was an organizing principle. African leaders cultivated images that were part father figure and part Mafia boss: Mobutu of Zaire wore a leopard-skin hat and sunglasses, and carried a ceremonial stick; Julius Nyerere of Tanzania had himself referred to as "the teacher"; President Gnassingbé Eyadéma of Togo was said to have occult powers. The authority of presidents was enormous and not shared with legislatures, courts, or ministers, regardless of what the constitution said.[6] Moreover, very few African presidents until recent times observed term limits or were willing to peacefully turn over power to successors, as George Washington did after serving two terms. Kenneth Kaunda of Zambia served for twenty-seven years, Mobutu for thirty-two, Jomo Kenyatta for fourteen, Sékou Touré of Guinea for twenty-six, Kwame Nkrumah of Ghana for fifteen, Meles Zenawi of Ethiopia for seventeen, Paul Biya of Cameroon for thirty-two, Teodoro Obiang of Equatorial Guinea for thirty-five, Yoweri Museveni of Uganda for twenty-seven, and Eduardo dos Santos of Angola for thirty-five (Biya, Obiang, Museveni, and dos Santos are still in power, as of this writing). Among the reasons that Nelson Mandela, the first black president of South Africa, stood out among revolutionary African political leaders was the fact that he voluntarily relinquished the presidency after a single five-year term.

A second characteristic of African neopatrimonialism was massive use of state resources to cultivate political support, which resulted in pervasive clientelism. To an even greater degree than in nineteenth-century America, presidents distributed offices and favors to their supporters in a particularly blatant way, which resulted in the immense expansion of executive branches. Mobutu's Zaire, for example, had six hundred thousand names on the civil service payroll, when the World Bank estimated it needed no more than fifty thousand. The central bank alone employed half again as many people as the entire private banking sector. Mobutu initially used nationalized Belgian properties to build his political base, according to journalist Michela Wrong:

> Mobutu, of course, did best out of the share-out, seizing fourteen plantations which were merged into a conglomerate that employed 25,000 people, making it the third largest employer in the country, responsible for one fourth of Zairean cocoa and rubber production. Members of his Ngbandi tribe were the next to benefit, their plum positions in the newly nationalised companies and prime enterprises making up for all those jibes about rural backwardness. But Mobutu was careful to ensure all the major ethnic groups whose support he needed profited. The social class known as the "Grosses Legumes" (Big Vegetables)—a term used by ordinary Zaireans with a mixture of resentment and awe—was born.[7]

Zambia had by one estimate 165,000 people in public administration in the 1990s, while state employees in Kenya grew from 18,213 in 1971 to 43,230 in 1990. During the boom years of the 1960s and '70s when commodity prices were rising, these rapidly expanding state sectors could be supported, but Africa as a whole was thrown into a severe debt crisis as commodity prices collapsed in the 1980s, and bloated public payrolls became unsustainable.[8]

For all of the size and symbolic authority of neopatrimonial governments of postcolonial Africa, however, the single most important characteristic, as Jeffrey Herbst has argued, is their underlying weakness.[9] Using again the Weberian definition, the strength of a state is measured by its ability to make and enforce rules over a defined territory, something that is a matter not just of physical coercion but also of legitimate authority. While African leaders could jail and intimidate political opponents, the basic capacity of their states to deliver basic public services like health and education outside of cities, to maintain law and order and adjudicate disputes, or to manage macroeconomic policy was often nonexistent.

State capacity, if measured by the ability to extract taxes, was lower in sub-Saharan Africa than in Latin America, and a fraction of what it is in the developed world. Many of the region's poorest countries extract no more than 7–15 percent of GDP in taxes, and many of those taxing at higher levels do so only because of natural resource wealth.[10] The types of taxes collected also reflect weak state capacity: they are overwhelmingly customs duties and indirect taxes of various sorts (now often value-added taxes, following recommendations of foreign donors) rather than more difficult to collect personal income taxes. State budgets therefore have had to be financed from other sources. For some countries, like Angola, Nigeria, and Sudan, those were resource rents; for many of the others, foreign aid has become a major source of budget support. At the nadir of Africa's decline in the 1990s, funding from foreign donors amounted to anywhere from 8 to 12 percent of GDP, and in many cases represented a majority share of total government budgets.[11]

As we have seen, state capacity can also be understood in terms of whether the government exercises a monopoly of force over its own territory. Sub-Saharan Africa after independence has been subject to a host of civil wars, separatist movements, rebellions, coups, and other internal conflicts, many of which are ongoing. Sierra Leone, Liberia, and Somalia all experienced total state failure and collapsed into warlordism during the 1990s. Zaire had a large army that looked impressive on paper, but when the country was invaded from the east by troops of the Alliance of Democratic Forces for the Liberation of Congo-Zaire in 1996, its military collapsed overnight. The army did more damage to the Congolese population than the invading forces as it fled and stripped whatever assets it could steal. The new government of Laurent Kabila proved no better and was unable to defend the country from a range of predatory militias and soldiers from neighboring countries. This failure to control violence is endemic to Africa's weak states.

A final measure of state weakness concerns the human capital of postcolonial African governments, something that translates directly into poor public policies. Unlike East Asia, Africa had no long-standing tradition of bureaucratic government, and no trained cadre of state officials who were capable of taking over the administrative systems left behind by the departing colonial governments. For example, the Congo had fewer than a dozen university-educated administrators at the moment that the Belgians departed in 1960.

Newly independent governments, operating without administrative expertise, made a series of huge policy errors. One of the most significant was the use of agricultural marketing boards that artificially depressed prices paid to farmers under a mistaken view that this would promote capital for industrialization. At a moment when export agriculture represented the most promising path for economic growth, it went into a sudden decline throughout the region.[12] Cocoa production in Ghana, for example, fell from 560,000 tons in 1965 to 249,000 tons by 1979 as a result of these perverse incentives. The Zaireans who took over operation of the Gécamines mine—at the time constituting 70 percent of export earnings—diverted its earnings into a special presidential account, failing to invest not just in new capacity but also in maintenance of existing operations, and thus oversaw a collapse of the mine's output from 470,000 tons per year at its peak to just 30,600 tons by 1994.[13]

The great institutional deficit that distinguishes sub-Saharan Africa from East Asia is not democracy. Even though democracy had a rocky history in Africa, the region overall was more democratic than East Asia in the period between 1960 and 2000. Nor was the deficit so much in the rule of law, either. Many of Asia's star performers in the early postcolonial period, like South Korea, Taiwan, Singapore, Malaysia, China, and Indonesia, were authoritarian states with relatively weak judicial systems whose rulers could skirt the law whenever they chose. What East Asia had that Latin America needed more of and that Africa lacked almost entirely were strong, coherent states that could control violence and carry out good, economically rational public policies.

THE ORIGINS OF STATE WEAKNESS

The African deficit in state capacity must of course be traced back to the legacy of colonialism, as well as to the nature of African societies prior to the onset of European colonial rule. In this respect, Africa's inheritance was totally different from that of Latin America. In the latter region, Spain and Portugal succeeded in wiping out the indigenous regimes and reproducing their own authoritarian, mercantilist political systems on the soil of the New World. Old World class hierarchies were amplified by the racial and ethnic differences that appeared as the Europeans extracted resources from their colonies. Latin America was bequeathed what I characterized as "weak authoritarian" states, which then failed to develop into either strong authoritarian or strong democratic states in the nineteenth century.

Africa had another legacy. Due to the late start of colonialism and its short duration, the colonial rulers succeeded in undermining existing traditional sources of authority while failing to implant anything like a modern state that could survive the transition to independence. Europeans discovered that they could extract very little from sub-Saharan Africa (with the exception of South Africa) and found the climate of the tropics highly inhospitable. As a consequence they invested minimally in terms of settlers or resources in their colonies. Colonialism on the cheap left Africa with very little by way of modern political institutions when the Europeans decided to leave in the decades after World War II.

Africa was intensively colonized only in the period after 1882, in what David Abernethy labeled the third phase of European colonialism. Phase one had begun with the Spanish and Portuguese conquests in the New World, and phase two was a period of contraction from the revolt of the North American colonies to the aftermath of the Napoleonic Wars. Phase three began with the Anglo-Burmese War of 1824 and culminated in the "scramble for Africa" that began in the last decades of the century.[14]

There were a number of important differences between the earlier and later phases of expansion. By the nineteenth century, the technological lead of Europe over the non-Western world was even greater than it had been when the Spanish encountered the New World. Europe was industrializing; inventions like the steamboat and the Maxim gun gave small groups of European conquerors huge advantages over their adversaries. The factor of disease, which had severely limited European expansion and settlement in earlier years, was itself reduced in importance by European medicine and the introduction of drugs like quinine. Abernethy points out that while thirty-nine of forty-eight Europeans died in Macgregor Laird's expedition up the Niger in 1832, not a single one did during an expedition on the same river in 1854.[15]

These differences had profound consequences. The first wave of colonization in the New World produced economic surpluses for the metropolitan powers in the form of gold, silver, sugar, cotton, and other commodities that could be expropriated to the benefit of the colonizers. Many Europeans during the nineteenth-century expansion hoped to duplicate the Spanish achievement in Mexico and Peru, and some did so on a small scale. The Congo was colonized as a personal project of King Leopold II of Belgium, who succeeded in personally enriching himself by establishing a brutal regime that plundered the region's resources. But the new colonies, and particularly those in tropical Africa, did not yield, overall, a new El Dorado. Theorists of imperialism like Vladimir Lenin and J. A. Hobson argued that Europe's surplus capital needed an outlet and new markets outside Europe. But Africa's output of groundnuts, cocoa, ivory, and palm oil hardly constituted a bonanza that would save global capitalism, or even pay for the costs of its own administration. Indeed, Europe largely lost interest in what Africa could produce after the abolition of slavery and the end of the triangular trade in slaves, sugar, rum, and manufactured goods that had been so critical in the seventeenth and eighteenth centuries.

It wasn't so much resource extraction as the intensifying European Great Power rivalry that drove the second wave of colonialism. There were a number of new actors on the scene, particularly a newly unified Germany after 1871, and an expansionist Russia, which the older Great Powers sought to balance and contain, even as they played out their own rivalries. Italy, Belgium, Japan, and the United States entered the game, pushing the competition into previously unoccupied parts of the world. David Fieldhouse argues that the scramble for Africa was triggered by the announcement by Germany under Chancellor Otto von Bismarck of its long-term goal of establishing an overseas empire. Germany's ambitions led directly to the Berlin Conference of 1884–1885, at which the European powers agreed on general rules for carving up the hinterlands of their coastal beachheads. Between 1878 and 1914, Europe added 8,653,000 square miles to its colonial possessions, claiming a staggering 84.4 percent of the land surface of the earth as under its control.[16]

This latest wave of European conquest was legitimated by novel theories of race. When the Spanish colonized the New World, they debated whether the indigenous people they found had souls; the Catholic church, at least, concluded that they did and tried—ineffectively—to prevent the worst depredations of the local settlers. In the nineteenth century, the situation was different. The scramble for Africa occurred after the publication of Charles Darwin's *Origin of Species* and the rise of a doctrine of "scientific racism" asserting that the existing hierarchy among the world's races was the result of the inherent biological superiority of white Europeans over everyone else. These views emerged despite the steady spread of democracy and representative government in Europe and North America, and they legitimated the use of force against nonwhite people. As a result, settler populations were granted an expanding set of political rights completely denied to Africans, setting up a sharp dichotomy between citizens on the one hand and subjects on the other.[17]

Once the scramble for Africa got under way, it unfolded with extraordinary rapidity. There were several specific characteristics of Africa that made this possible. Foremost was the fact that indigenous African societies themselves did not possess strong state-level institutions, in sharp contrast to East Asia. Prior to the scramble, state-level societies existed in only about half of the continent; the rest was populated by acephalous tribal societies based on kin ties.

Jeffrey Herbst has provided a penetrating analysis of why so few strong state-level societies existed, despite the fact that the human species originated in Africa and inhabited the region for some fifty thousand years (see Volume 1, chapters 3–5). In the first place, population densities were low. Although Africa today has some of the highest birth rates in the world, the continent was one of the least populated in the late nineteenth century. It was only in 1975 that Africa's population density reached the level that Europe enjoyed in the year 1500. While Japan had a population density of 118.2 persons per square kilometer and China 45.6 in 1900, sub-Saharan Africa's was only 4.4.[18] As noted in the first volume, while technological innovations like higher-productivity agriculture allowed populations to expand, the economist Ester Boserup and others have argued that the reverse was also true, with larger populations spurring the need for technological change by increasing demand and permitting a greater specialization. Whichever direction causality ran, the level of technological backwardness of precolonial Africa was striking: the plow had not been adopted in agriculture, which everywhere remained rain fed rather than irrigation based, and sophisticated metalworking was not developed. The latter had huge political consequences: in contrast to the Japanese, who had a long-standing metalworking tradition and could manufacture their own guns shortly after coming into contact with Europeans, the Africans remained dependent on imported firearms until well into the nineteenth century.[19]

A second factor limiting state formation in Africa was physical geography. As noted above, political consolidation depends on the ability to project military power and exert a monopoly of force. Large, powerful states were formed in Europe and China because relatively flat land bounded by rivers and mountain ranges could be easily traversed by horses. Projecting military power in this fashion was of course critical to the establishment of centralized states. In Africa, the only flat, open land lies in the empty Sahara desert and in the savanna belt running just below it. It is therefore not surprising that those parts of the continent possessing state-level structures tended to cluster in these regions where horses and camels could be used.

The tropical forests south of the savanna belt proved to be an enormous obstacle to state formation, unless one went all the way down to South Africa where larger political units like the Zulu kingdom existed in precolonial times. Although Africa has large rivers, few of them are navigable for long stretches. (The Nile is of course an exception, and it did facilitate the growth of a large state-level civilization.) It was for this reason that early European settlements on the coasts, created for the slave trade or as trading entrepôts, remained cut off from their hinterlands. Maps of the interior were not available until the explorations of Richard Burton, David Livingstone, Henry Morton Stanley, and John Hanning Speke in the later part of the nineteenth century. Road construction, which was critical in knitting together empires as diverse as those of the Romans and Incas, is enormously more difficult to accomplish in the forested tropics.

In the first volume I noted the theory of Robert Carneiro that circumscription was an important condition for the transition from tribal- to state-level societies.[20] In open, unconstrained geographies, tribal units coming under pressure from a centralized political authority have the option of simply moving away. This in fact was the situation throughout much of tropical Africa, where land was always abundant and the bush close by. This was why, according to Herbst, political authority was not seen in territorial terms in much of Africa. Since it was so hard to project physical control over long distances, authority was exercised more over persons. Rulers did not have precise maps of their domains, as feudal lords in densely populated Europe did; rather, they saw webs of authority radiating out through networks of tribute-paying clients.[21]

What Herbst is describing is less, it seems to me, an alternative concept of stateness than societies that were at the boundary of the tribal- to-state-level transition and that remained more at the tribal end. In this respect they resembled Chinese society during the Western Zhou Dynasty in the first half of the first millennium B.C., or Europe in the time of Clovis in the fifth century. In such societies, social organization remains based on segmentary lineages, which can aggregate upward into very large units when they come under attack as a group. But lineages can fracture very easily back into much smaller ones as circumstances dictate (see Volume 1, chapter 3). Power can occasionally be concentrated into chiefdoms, which have statelike characteristics but which, unlike states, cannot prevent the departure of subunits and do not exercise territorial control.

It is important to note that when I speak of political organization in precolonial Africa being "tribal," this has a very specific meaning that is different from the way the word is used (or misused) in contemporary politics. Kenya today, particularly since the contested presidential election of 2007, is fractured along ethnic lines that have pitted groups like the Kikuyu, Luo, Kalenjin, and Maasai against one another. The politics of countless other African countries is built around similar ethnicities, like the Tutsis slaughtered by the Hutus in the Rwandan genocide of 1994. An ethnic group like the Kikuyu is sometimes loosely spoken of as a "tribe" and ethnic politics as a form of tribalism. There is a tendency to believe that modern African politics is simply an extension of ancient cultural patterns.

But African ethnic groups are largely a modern phenomenon, created either in the colonial period or consolidated in postcolonial times. A classic segmentary lineage—a tribe, speaking anthropologically—is a group that traces common ancestry to a progenitor who may be two, three, or more generations distant. The system is held together by a very specific set of beliefs about the power of dead ancestors and unborn descendants to affect the fortunes of the living. As described in E. E. Evans-Pritchard's classic study of the Nuer in South Sudan, these lineages are scalable depending on how many generations back one chooses an ancestor. For most day-to-day purposes, the relevant ancestor is very proximate and the kin group correspondingly very small.

Modern ethnic groups, by contrast, encompass hundreds of thousands if not millions of people. They may claim descent from a common ancestor, as the Roman tribes claimed descent from Romulus, but that ancestor is so distant as to be more a matter of myth and fabulism than a real person. The contemporary African sense of ethnic identity was, as we will see in the following chapter, often cultivated by the colonial authorities, who believed that certain groups were more "martial" and therefore suitable as recruits for the military, or else who wanted to play one group against another in order to make them more tractable. Today, one of the main functions of ethnic identity is to act as a signaling device in the clientelistic division of state resources: if you are a Kikuyu and can elect a Kikuyu president, you are much more likely to be favored with government jobs, public works projects, and the like.

PUSHING ON AN OPEN DOOR

There were few strong centralized states in Africa prior to the scramble, and the Europeans did not create any once the continent had been carved up among them by the time of World War I. The reasons for this derive from the characteristics of the second wave of colonialism described above. The interests of European governments were much more strategic than economic; they wanted to make sure that they could protect existing dependencies and prevent new powers from outflanking them. They were much more interested in creating zones of influence or protectorates than ruling indigenous Africans directly, and they did not want to spend a lot of state resources in the process. If these territories yielded economic benefits, so much the better.

The actual extension of colonial authority was thus often driven by actors other than national governments. Among them were local agents who, without the knowledge or approval of their home ministries, expanded their country's claims; settlers in existing colonies who demanded protection and new opportunities to acquire land; the commercial interests of various local traders and chartered companies which, if not of vital economic interest to their home governments, nonetheless constituted powerful lobbies; and missionaries, who saw Africa as ripe for conversion and cultural conquest.

It is said that the British Empire was created in a fit of absentmindedness; this was in fact true not just of that empire but also of those of many other Europeans. Thus, for example, Afrique Occidentale Française, one of the two large divisions of the French Empire in Africa, was created by a group of French officers who trekked into the upper Niger valley and ultimately into Chad in disregard of orders from Paris. French traders lobbied for the appointment of General Louis Faidherbe to be governor of Senegal and to push up the Senegal River valley to reduce tribute they owed to African chiefs there. The Congo Free State was the creation not of the Belgian government but of King Leopold II, who made this huge territory his personal property and whose debts Belgium was later forced to assume. British expansion in West Africa actually came about as an accidental by-product of their efforts to suppress the slave trade. Freetown in Sierra Leone had been a naval base and haven for freed slaves; areas surrounding it were progressively annexed to prevent traders from evading customs at the port. Bismarck found few German companies willing to invest in Africa; nonetheless, fear that the German foothold in Tanganyika would threaten lines of communication to India led the British to cement their hold over Uganda, Zanzibar, and other parts of East Africa.[22]

This mixture of motives for the colonization of Africa resulted in a constant tug-of-war between European groups on the ground that wanted to extend imperial control and deepen investments there, and governments (and the taxpayers standing behind them) who were skeptical of the value of these new African possessions. The colonial powers experienced what today is labeled "mission creep," which has been the bane of American post–cold war foreign policy: a small intervention, designed to be of limited purpose and duration, creates on-the-ground interests and commitments that then require further interventions to make the whole effort sustainable. For example, the need to suppress terrorists in Afghanistan spills over into Pakistan, generating new requirements to stabilize Pakistan through military and economic aid, and requires logistics bases in Central Asia, which then become bargaining chips in a larger U.S.-Russian relationship. This dynamic leads to ever-expanding involvement without necessarily creating a consensus at home as to the wisdom of undertaking the project in the first place.

In Africa, this logic led to colonialism on the cheap, an effort to maintain influence while failing to invest sufficiently in sustainable political institutions. In Singapore, the British created not just a port where none had existed before but also a crown colony and administrative structure designed to support their interests throughout Southeast Asia. In India, they created a British Indian army and a higher civil service, institutions that were bequeathed to an independent Indian republic in 1947 and still exist. In Africa, by contrast, they created a system of minimal administration that went under the title of "indirect rule." In so doing they failed to provide postindependence African states with durable political institutions and laid the ground for subsequent state weakness and failure. It is this system to which we turn next.

20

INDIRECT RULE

Sierra Leone and the crisis of state breakdown; how states can be brutal and weak at the same time; what "indirect rule" was and why it developed; how French direct rule differed and why in the end it proved to be no more successful in implanting modern institutions

During Sierra Leone's horrific descent into civil war during the 1990s, the Revolutionary United Front (RUF), led by warlord Foday Sankoh, began the practice of recruiting child soldiers—young boys of twelve or thirteen, or even younger—who would be given marijuana, amphetamines, and cocaine, and forced to kill their parents in front of their friends. These traumatized children, then implicated in the most horrible of crimes, would go on to commit further atrocities, like slicing open the bellies of pregnant women to determine the sex of their children, or amputating the hands of captured soldiers or ordinary civilians so that they would never use them against the RUF in the future. Women would be routinely raped and forced to serve as wives of the child soldiers. In 1999, the RUF launched an assault on Sierra Leone's capital, Freetown, known as "Operation No Living Thing," in which entire neighborhoods were looted and their inhabitants indiscriminately raped and killed.[1]

How does one explain this level of human degradation? One answer, usually not articulated too openly but often tacitly assumed, is that things were somehow always like this in Africa. The Sierra Leone conflict, portrayed in the popular film *Blood Diamond*, as well as others like the insurgency of the Lord's Resistance Army in northern Uganda, or the Tutsi genocide in Rwanda, have reinforced Western notions that Africa is a place of brutality and barbarism. Robert D. Kaplan and others have suggested that in West Africa the veneer of civilization had broken down, and these societies were returning to an older, primordial form of tribalism, only fought with modern weapons.[2]

This answer reflects a great deal of ignorance about historical Africa, and about tribalism more broadly. Tribally organized societies are orderly: segmentary lineages are a form of political order that both keep the peace and limit power. Very few tribal chiefs or Big Men have the power or authority to tyrannize their fellows; most tribal societies are indeed egalitarian when compared to their state-level counterparts. They have clear rules regulating personal behavior and strict (if informal) methods for enforcing them. Tribal segments often skirmish with one another, but they do not exist in some sort of Hobbesean state of anomic violence of the sort represented by Sierra Leone and Somalia in the 1990s. Nor do they constantly innovate in coming up with new forms of grotesque cruelty.

An alternative explanation of why a country like Sierra Leone came to be racked by horrific violence is colonialism. The history of European colonialism includes systematic and intensive brutality against indigenous populations.[3] The practice of hacking off hands and arms as warnings in Sierra Leone that so outraged Western opinion was originally practiced by the Force Publique in Leopold's Belgian Congo: according to one account, "Soldiers in the Congo were told to account for every cartridge fired, so they hacked off and smoked the hands, feet and private parts of their victims. Body parts were presented to commanders in baskets as proof that soldiers had done their work well."[4] While the slave trade had been suppressed, the economies of colonial Africa were highly dependent on different types of coerced labor and economic extraction. Involuntary impressment was also a widespread European practice; all colonies required corvée labor of most men, including work in unbearable and unhealthy conditions that led to the deaths of thousands. Many thousands more were drafted into European armies for service and often died on battlefields very far from home. The British, in prosecuting the Hut tax war in Sierra Leone, hanged ninety-six tribal chiefs whom they blamed for the insurrection.[5] European colonial officials often behaved like petty tyrants, dispensing justice (or injustice) arbitrarily with few checks on their power. Consider the following vignette from German-controlled Cameroon, where the "imperial chancellor of the protectorate, Leist, had the wives of Dahomey soldiers whipped in the presence of their husbands, which resulted in December 1893 in a revolt of the sol-diers. He had female convicts brought to him from the prison at night for his sexual gratification. He was brought before a disciplinary council and condemned to be transferred to an equivalent post, with a loss of seniority, for 'an error in the cause of duty.'"[6] Indeed, an entire academic discipline devoted to exposing the horrors of European colonialism emerged in the late twentieth century, which sought to explain how con-temporary Africa's many problems are rooted in the colonial experience. Many of the newer economic theories tracing poor governance to ex-tractive colonial institutions have joined hands with this earlier school of thought.

There is something wrong, however, with any theory directly con-necting a particular colonial practice with a contemporary outcome. In the first place, Sierra Leone is no more typical of contemporary Africa than the Belgian Congo was typical of colonial Africa. Sierra Leone was one of a handful of failed states in a continent of more than fifty sovereign entities, the vast majority of which were far more peacefully governed and stable. Similarly, the Belgian Congo stood out among colonial administra-tions as particularly brutal and exploitative. The practices of the Force Publique and Belgian companies were exposed by Protestant missionaries and activists like E. D. Morel seeking to protect ordinary Congolese from their depredations. Public opinion back in Europe eventually forced the Belgian government to clamp down on Leopold's private enterprise. The vast majority of colonial governments, especially as they began to ap-proach independence, used significantly lower levels of coercion.

There were in fact large continuities between the colonial state and the states that emerged after Africa's independence, but that continuity was different from inheritance of one particular abhorrent practice. Bru-tality was part of the picture, but the primary colonial legacy was hand-ing down weak states that did not have the power or authority to compel obedience on the part of their populations. While the outward show of postindependence African presidencies was enormous, it masked an un-derlying inability of the state to penetrate and shape society. The horrors of Sierra Leone—and of Liberia, Somalia, and the Congo—represented an extreme version of state weakness, where the postindependence state collapsed completely. The vacuum was filled not by traditional African society but by a half-modernized hybrid of deracinated young men who organized themselves to take advantage of the global economy and exploit natural resource rents from diamonds and other commodities.

It might seem contradictory to say that a state can be brutal and weak at the same time. Don't strong states kill, jail, and torture their opponents? But the two in fact go together. All states concentrate and use power—that is, the ability to violently coerce people—but successful states rely more heavily on authority, that is, voluntary compliance with the state's wishes based on a broad belief in the government's legitimacy. In peaceful liberal democracies, the fist is usually hidden behind layered gloves of law, custom, and norms. States that make heavy use of overt coercion and brutality often do so because they cannot exercise proper authority. They have what Michael Mann labels "despotic power" but not "infrastructural power" to penetrate and shape society.[7] This was true of both the colonial African state and the independent countries that emerged after the end of colonial rule.[8]

The reality of the colonial state was not a transplanted absolutist regime imposed by the Europeans but rather "indirect rule," a policy that had been practiced since the Indian Rebellion of 1858 but was systematically articulated for the first time by Lord Frederick Lugard, the British governor of, among other places, Northern Nigeria (from 1900 to 1906) and Hong Kong (from 1907 to 1912). Lugard's experience in Africa taught him that Britain did not remotely have either the resources or the personnel to govern its huge African domains directly, in the manner in which it governed the small city-state of Hong Kong. In writings like *The Dual Mandate in British Tropical Africa*, he asserted that efforts to impose European law and institutions on unwilling African subjects were counterproductive, and that indigenous peoples were better and more justly governed using their own customary practices. This led to a regime, first put into place among the Muslim emirates in Northern Nigeria, whereby administration was put into the hands of local chiefs carefully selected by the British and presided over by a skeletal hierarchy of white officials led by a district officer or commissioner.[9]

The thinness of the European presence in Africa during the height of colonialism is truly astonishing. Table 3 gives the number of administrators for select regions, showing that the ratio of administrators to population ranged from a high of 1 for every 18,900 in Kenya (where a large white settler population required greater attention), to a low of 1 for every 54,000 in Nigeria and Cameroon.

TABLE 3. Density of European Administrators in Africa

	Population	Year	Administrators	Ratio
Nigeria and Cameroon	20,000,000	late 1930s	386	1 : 52,000
Kenya	3,100,000	late 1930s	164	1 : 18,900
French West Africa	14,500,000	1921	526	1 : 27,500
Belgian Congo	11,000,000	1936	316	1 : 34,800
Ghana	3,700,000	1935	77	1 : 48,000

SOURCE: Michael Crowder, "The White Chiefs of Tropical Africa," in Gann and
Duignan,eds., *Colonialism in Africa 1870–1960*, and Karen Fields, *Revival and Rebellion in Colonial Africa*

The extreme thinness of the European presence virtually guaranteed that the colonial administration would have to rely on a hierarchy of chiefs, village elders, headmen, clerks, translators, and other black officials to do the actual work of government. Treasuries in the metropolitan capitals were not interested in subsidizing their impoverished territories; in the words of Earl Grey, "The surest test for the soundness of measures for the improvement of an uncivilised people is that they should be self-sufficient." As many observers have pointed out, indirect rule was less a novel policy than simply a recognition of the reality of British administration on the ground. These facts alone suggest that the institutional legacy of colonialism would not be strong, centralized states, since Britain was setting something of the opposite—the preservation of customary law—as its explicit policy goal. It was, as historian Sara Berry describes it, "hegemony on a shoestring."[10]

THE SEARCH FOR "NATIVE LAW AND CUSTOM"

There was something superficially appealing about indirect rule in the British colonies. In contrast to the French, whose objective was assimilation of their colonies into a single homogeneous French empire, Lugard's theory had a moral component. He argued that rather than trying to turn Africans into second-rate Europeans, they ought to be ruled under their own laws and customs through traditional sources of authority. This was in line with the practice of many earlier empires, which realized that they could not export their own institutions to people of very different cultural backgrounds. The aspiration to recover local tradition led to a scramble to uncover what was termed "native law and custom." Whatever else one might say about the search for tradition, it gave a tremendous boost to the new field of anthropology, where colonial governments promoted the work of researchers such as Charles Meek and E. E. Evans-Pritchard who sought to identify "authentic" legal traditions.[11]

This was far easier said than done. European colonial officials assumed, according to Berry, "that African communities consisted of mutually exclusive sociocultural units—tribes, villages, kin groups—whose customs and structures had not changed very much over time."[12] This was appropriate for certain parts of Africa like Northern Nigeria (where Lugard had direct experience), whose Muslim emirates actually had written laws and established administrative systems. But it didn't work for much of the rest of Africa, where tribal identities were overlapping and in constant flux. In many regions, colonial officials were hard-pressed to find a tribal "chief" to whom they could delegate authority, and in such situations they created one, sometimes by simply elevating the houseboy or aide of the district officer. Indeed, following the belief that "every African belonged to a tribe," the colonial authorities created tribes where none existed, "working through a mishmash of ethnic affiliations to create 'purer' and clearer tribal identities as the basis for tribal authorities."[13]

This "invention of tradition," in Terence Ranger's words, was based on a profound misunderstanding of African society:

> In comparing European neo-traditions with the customary in Africa the whites were certainly comparing unlike with unlike. European invented traditions were marked by their inflexibility. They involved sets of recorded rules and procedures—like the modern coronation rites. They gave reassurance because they represented what was unchanging in a period of flux . . .
>
> Almost all recent studies of nineteenth-century pre-colonial Africa have emphasized that far from there being a single "tribal" identity, most Africans moved in and out of multiple identities, defining themselves at one moment as subject to this chief, at another moment as a member of that cult, at another moment as part of this clan, and at yet another moment as an initiate in that professional guild.[14]

The effect of indirect rule, then, was not to achieve a modernizing objective in terms of the development of indigenous institutions but to freeze in place an imagined set of power relationships.

Mahmood Mamdani has gone further, to charge that the tyrannical postindependence Big Man was largely the product of the "decentralized despotism" created by indirect rule. The British had two long-term economic policy objectives that indirect rule was meant to serve. First, they sought to convert customary land tenure into modern property rights, at the behest of both commercial agricultural interests and white settlers. Modern property rights are formal, freely alienable, and held by individuals or by legal entities operating as individuals. As elaborated in Volume 1, customary land tenure is a complex informal system of private property rights, sometimes mistakenly said to be communal in the sense of a Communist collective farm. Traditional customary property is intimately connected with the kinship system and heavily entailed by kin obligations; individuals usually are not free to alienate their holdings.[15] The chief in particular does not have any right to alienate land. While customary property in this sense once existed in barbarian Europe, the feudal property rights that prevailed in the European Middle Ages were more modern in the sense of being formal, contractual, and individual. Moving from a customary to a modern land tenure system was therefore much more revolutionary than the shift from feudal to modern land tenure in Europe; it involved huge changes within the authority structure of the kin groups involved. When colonial authorities sought to buy land from customary owners, they found no one actually in charge who had the authority to alienate property. One reason to create a subordinate tribal chief under indirect rule was to empower an African equivalent of a European feudal lord who had the authority to alienate communal property into a modern property rights system.[16]

A second reason for empowering indigenous chiefs was to serve as tax collectors. All colonial governments established poll or capitation taxes on each male in the colony to raise revenues so that the colony could pay for its own administration. But they served another purpose as well: by making subjects pay a tax in cash, they were encouraged to move out of the bush and into the cash economy where they could serve as a labor force for European commercial agriculture. The chief function of the new native authorities thus came to be tax collection, which they could enforce much more effectively when given modern weapons and backed by threats of coercion from colonial armies. The Europeans were thus imposing their own models of political authority on societies organized very differently.

Mamdani argues that the new chiefs were as a consequence far more despotic than true traditional authorities. Tribal societies tend to be consensual and egalitarian, with plenty of checks on the power of the Big Man. He quotes an exchange in 1881 between the Cape Commission on Native Laws and Customs in South Africa and the former Zulu king Cetshwayo, leader of a society long held to be the most absolutist in Africa:

> *As the king of the Zulus, was all power invested in you, as king, over your subjects?*
> —In conjunction with the chiefs of the land.
> *How did the chiefs derive their power from you as king?*
> —The king calls together the chiefs of the land when he wants to elect a new chief, and asks their advice as to whether it is fit to make such a man a large chief, and if they say "yes" the chief is made . . .
> *Is a man killed for trying to kill a king?*
> —He is simply fined cattle, and is talked to very severely . . .
> *What is the punishment for a man deserting from his tribe?*
> —If the chief of his district had given him any property he would be asked by the chief to return that property, and then he would be at liberty to go.[17]

According to Mamdani, the new chiefs established under British indirect rule were far more authoritarian than the Zulu king, having the powers associated with a modern European state: the power to unilaterally take title to land, the power to extract taxes, and the power to make formal law and to punish crimes. Thus while central colonial governments may have seemed extremely weak, they set up a far more dictatorial system on a local level, one that was freed of the checks and balances that existed in truly traditional African societies. They also established a bright line between citizens and subjects: the first were white settlers (and occasionally mixed-race or Asian populations) who were given access to modern legal systems, with their attendant rights and privileges, while the latter were subject to invented customary law. Legal pluralism masked the fact that the rights of white settlers would be protected much more carefully than those of black Africans. And Africans were never given leave to truly apply their own law as they wished. Customary law had to be in accord with European morals, which barred certain practices as repugnant (suttee, the burning of widows in India, was perhaps the most famous case of this). The ultimate expression of this double standard would be the apartheid regime in South Africa.[18]

The views of Ranger, Mamdani, and others on the malign effects of indirect rule and invented tradition have been sharply debated. Thomas Spear argues that the ability of European officials to manipulate African society—in effect, creating dictators, tribes, ethnic identities, and the like where none existed before—has been greatly exaggerated. New traditions, in order to be accepted, had to be based on something actually already existing in the culture. Nor did they simply freeze things in time; there was a constant process of adaptation between rulers and ruled that generated "unresolvable debates over the interpretation of tradition and its meaning for colonial governance and economic activity." While some new tribal chiefs acted like dictators, others tried to soften European demands, faking tax rolls or shielding individuals from colonial justice. In order to exercise authority, local agents had to seek legitimacy, which generally means trying to incorporate the interests and wishes of the ruled. It was not just chiefs but also interpreters and personal aides who mediated between the white district officer and local populations. Social-engineering efforts that sought to combine, move, or separate different tribes often failed. Far from manipulating African societies, it was the Europeans who were often manipulated by Africans. Administrators seeking to understand "customary" rules were told stories that benefited particular African power holders or interests, and they were too naïve or ignorant to know better. In the words of Karen Fields, "Indirect rule was a way of making the colonial state a consumer of power generated within the customary order. It did not transfer real power from the Crown to African rulers. Just the inverse: Real power issued from the ruled."[19]

The truth in this debate probably lies somewhere in between: the colonial authorities were able to impose their wishes in certain cases, while Africans were able to exert agency in resisting it in others. Compared to the Europeans who conquered the New World, however, the overall institutional imprint of colonialism was much shallower.

This complex process is evident in Kenya, a country that has been racked in recent years by bloody ethnic conflict. Today's ethnic groups—Kikuyus, Kalenjin, Luo, etc.—did not really exist as such before the territory was taken over as a British protectorate. The colonial authorities clearly came to use ethnicity as a means of controlling Kenya's population, but they did not "create" ethnic identities out of whole cloth. What they did was set in motion a process of slow economic modernization that created identity on a broader basis, and then formalized ethnic identification as an instrument of rule. The gradual absorption of rural Kenyans into a market economy demanded social relatedness at higher levels of aggregation. Thus two Kikuyus from different segments meeting in rural Kenya might regard each other as strangers, but would see themselves as co-ethnics when meeting in Nairobi and rubbing up against a Kalenjin or Luo.

In the end, then, the legacy of indirect rule was mixed. It did produce local despotisms, misrule, and injustice, but on a local level as well as on a central one the power of the colonial state was not strong enough to achieve routine compliance with the state's wishes. By trying to adapt to local conditions, the colonial authorities got more buy-in from local populations. But they also frequently misunderstood what those local conditions were, and failed to understand that many Africans wanted to acquire modern property and participate in the broader market economy.[20] Indirect rule had no application in the growing urban areas of Africa, where new sources of identity like ethnicity and class were taking shape. As a result, the Europeans were taken by surprise by the new nationalist movements that suddenly appeared in the 1940s and '50s, which did not want a return to tradition but sought to move forward to independence and national sovereignty. Today, Northern Nigeria, the region where indirect rule was invented, is significantly poorer than the southern half of the country, which was more exposed to modernizing forces.

The impact of indirect rule was thus profoundly conservative. And the one thing it never did, either in aspiration or in practice, was lay the basis for a strong, modern state.

COLONIALISM THE FRENCH WAY

While the Belgians, like the British, practiced a decentralized form of rule in the Congo, the French and Portuguese ran much more centralized administrations in their African colonies. For the French, this was second nature, since the French state itself was highly centralized administratively. The French believed that Roman law had universal validity and were unwilling to bend to customary practices.

Since indirect rule did not seem to leave much in the way of strong political institutions to postindependence Africa, did direct rule make a difference? The answer, in short, is no: whatever the theoretical differences between the British and French approaches, limitations of resources and knowledge prevented French authorities from shaping their colonies any more than the British. Indeed, the French developed a high degree of cynicism in dealing with Africans the way they were rather than the way they were supposed to be, a cynicism that has infected their policy toward Francophone Africa for decades after independence.[21]

The French governed through chiefs, as did the British, but regarded them not as representatives of local communities with their own traditional legitimacy but as simple agents of the French state. The relationship was "that of an officer to an NCO."[22] The rules that applied up until the 1940s were first set down in 1854 under the authoritarian Second Empire, and were implemented in the early years by military officers like Louis Faidherbe, governor of Senegal. Following a model developed in French Algeria, independent polities in sub-Saharan Africa were progressively attacked and subdued. Large areas, including French West Africa and French Equatorial Africa, were broken down into smaller "cercles," which were in turn divided into cantons and villages. The shift from the Second Empire to the Third Republic in 1870 did not change things all that much. If anything, the French republican tradition was stricter in its desire to impose uniform rules. The stated goal was "assimilation" of the colonies into the French system. But while French language and education were imposed, there was no long-term path for most African subjects to eventually become French citizens.[23]

Many of the important differences between the French and British were rooted in the way their colonial services were internally administered, as well as their training and recruitment practices. All bureaucracies operating over large geographical areas have to choose between favoring generalists who are good leaders and administrators, and specialists who have developed intimate knowledge of particular places. The latter are advantaged by their local knowledge (what James Scott calls mētis, Greek for "wisdom") but tend to get captured by local interests and often develop parochial views.[24] The generalists are more reliable and often more effective but tend to apply general theories to situations where they don't apply. British administration tended to reward the specialists, while the French model encouraged generalists. Thus French colonial officers were moved around every few years, not just within Africa but to completely different parts of the empire. As a result, very few of them learned to speak indigenous languages or acquired local knowledge.[25]

The French and British also differed in the types of people recruited into their colonial service. In Britain they tended to come from upper-middle-class or gentry families; there was a very high proportion that attended public school (private school in American terminology) and good universities like Oxford or Cambridge. (We have already seen in chapter 8 above how reform of the British civil service began with re-form of the Indian colonial service.) In France, recruits came from the bourgeoisie, which in contrast to their British peers had disdain for local chiefs as feudal or monarchical survivals. As a consequence, the colonial service found itself unable to attract sufficient numbers of quality candidates. There are numerous anecdotes about the character of those who went to the colonies. According to one doctor, "Power-crazy psychopaths are particularly numerous in the colonies—far more so, proportionately, than in France. They belong to a large class of unbalanced individuals who seek out colonial life; their psychic make-up is particularly attracted by the exotic." As the director of the École Coloniale said in 1929, "When a young man left for the colonies, his friends asked themselves, 'What crime must he have committed? From what corpse is he fleeing?'" The pathological Mr. Kurtz in Joseph Conrad's *Heart of Darkness* was based in the end on some reality. All of this began to change in the 1930s as the French improved the education and professionalism of their officials, while better health conditions encouraged them to serve tours accompanied by their families. But this led to a new problem familiar to contemporary development agencies: they would then spend all their time in expatriate communities with their wives and children, rather than with the locals.[26]

In the end, the French found that their policy of assimilation was unworkable. Officials with field experience coming out of the École Coloniale began to argue for a more flexible policy of association, in which their societies would be helped to "evolve within their own structures."

By the middle of the twentieth century, norms all across Europe were changing: there was much greater appreciation for the integrity of traditional cultures and a realization that the effort to impose foreign institutions by brute force was having a damaging impact on native societies. The discipline of anthropology, having started out as a tool of European colonialism, became a powerful voice arguing for the equal dignity of indigenous cultures.[27] In the words of one French Jesuit, "Custom belongs to the community itself, but to remove from the community the right of interpretation and of transformation is an act of violence more serious, though less visible, than the confiscation of arable land or of forest."[28] The French presence on the ground, just as thin as that of the other colonial powers, had in any event failed to implant powerful French-style institutions in any of the colonies. So in the end, direct rule was as much of a failure as indirect rule.

Ironically, the failure of French policy to turn Africans into Frenchmen had the reverse effect of turning Frenchmen into Africans. The French in their postindependence dealings with Africa were more willing to play the local power games according to local rules, in comparison to the Americans and British who at least paid lip service to universal principles like democracy and human rights. Thus the French were happy to work with authoritarian rulers like Mobutu or Félix Houphouët-Boigny in the Ivory Coast, or to use their paratroopers to prop up often unsavory regimes that served French foreign policy interests. This also led to corruption at home like the Elf affair of the early 1990s in which senior business and government officials were implicated in taking kickbacks for lucrative contracts.[29]

Africa did not possess states that were strong or modern prior to European colonialism. This was one reason why the continent could be conquered so easily. The legacy of late colonial rule in Africa was to undercut existing social structures—even when the explicit objective of policy was to preserve them—while failing to implant much by way of modern state institutions. The weak postindependence African state was the heir to the weak colonial state.

The breakdown of Sierra Leone was one long-term consequence of this legacy. As one of Britain's oldest colonies in Africa, Sierra Leone was ruled indirectly, through a network of chiefs who were alternately bribed and intimidated by the white administration in Freetown. When the country received its independence in 1961, there was no modern state to

speak of. What was left of the colonial administrative structure deteriorated, particularly after the rise of Siaka Stevens, a former police constable who took power in 1968 and was known for both his demagogy and
shameless corruption.

The deterioration accelerated when the market for alluvial diamonds
(i.e., those found in rivers) gave all of Sierra Leone's political actors something to fight over. Paul Collier has argued that it was greed rather than
social grievance that drove this and other African conflicts.[30] But rivalry
over natural resource wealth does not inevitably produce conflict;
Botswana used its diamonds to benefit its population. Sierra Leone's
problem was its total lack of a state that could keep order and fairly and
peacefully exploit its resources. The country's civil war and drug-crazed
child soldiers did not constitute a return to traditional Africa, nor did they
reflect any deep social or cultural traditions in the country other than
poverty. They were a modern innovation in response to the economic
incentives posed by a global diamond industry, and utter state failure.[31] As
one observer of the war, Lansana Gberie, notes, "The lesson . . . is that there
is no alternative to the building of strong bureaucratic states that function
at the social level, effectively providing services like education and thereby
employment, and avoiding the kind of corrosive corruption and misuse
of public funds that are such a mark of the continent's misgovernment."[32]

There are many similarities between the British and French experiences in sub-Saharan Africa, and contemporary nation-building exercises
in, for instance, Iraq, Afghanistan, and Haiti. In the following chapter,
I will ask the question, Did anyone do any better in giving their colonies
strong institutions?

21

INSTITUTIONS, DOMESTIC OR IMPORTED

Indirect rule as a precedent for contemporary state-building interventions; "good enough" governance as an alternative to Denmark; the United States and Japan as nation builders

One might think that colonial history is irrelevant to the world that has emerged early in the twenty-first century. Most of the colonial empires were dismantled in the three decades following World War II; one of the last large ones, that of the former Soviet Union, fell apart in 1991. Why, then, be concerned with the success or failure of foreign powers to implant institutions?

The question remains relevant because both individual powers like the United States and the international community more broadly have been heavily engaged, since the end of the cold war, in trying to build states in poor developing countries. This is most evident in the U.S. occupations of Afghanistan and Iraq in the 2000s, where creating viable states has been central first to America's "war on terrorism," and then to its ability to exit these countries with a modicum of credibility. But there have been numerous other peacekeeping and state-building interventions around the world: in Cambodia, Bosnia and Kosovo, Sierra Leone and Liberia, Haiti, Somalia, Timor Leste, the Democratic Republic of Congo, Papua New Guinea, the Solomon Islands, and others.

The moral framework of these interventions is obviously different from colonialism. Colonial powers made no pretense that they were occupying foreign countries in the interests of the indigenous inhabitants, though they tried to justify their behavior to themselves in terms of their civilizing mission. Until the last decade or so before their departure, colonial governments did not pursue overtly developmental aims—indeed, they were wary of industrialization in their colonies because their domestic manufacturers did not want competition. They were also not especially worried about democracy, since they justified their own rule on a nondemocratic basis.

This framework changed in the course of the twentieth century. Following World War I, the League of Nations (predecessor to the United Nations) granted mandates to colonial powers like Britain and France but now said that these territories had to be governed in the interest of their inhabitants. The international legal framework changed once more after World War II, with the issuance of the Universal Declaration of Human Rights and the growing weight of newly independent former colonies in international forums like the UN General Assembly. The cold war and the Soviet veto blocked the Security Council from authorizing too many peacekeeping missions, but with its end the floodgates opened and the peacekeeping directorate of the UN Secretariat became a very busy place. By the late 1990s, in the wake of atrocities committed in places like Bosnia and Rwanda, a new doctrine called the "responsibility to protect" had emerged, which enjoined the international community to take positive action to safeguard the human rights of peoples threatened by conflict and repression.[1]

The goal of these new postconflict interventions quickly evolved. They began with efforts to promote cease-fires and keep the peace in conflict zones. But it soon became evident that there would be no lasting peace without institutions, and that the international community's ability to exit these troubled places in fact depended on the societies acquiring stable governments that could provide security without outside help. Thus the mandate for intervention expanded from peacekeeping to state building.

East Timor had been a province of Indonesia when it voted for independence and became a sovereign state in 1999. What little administrative apparatus it possessed was wrecked by the departing Indonesians, and the United Nations was called upon to set up a mission, UNTAET, to in effect create a new state. The United States found itself in a similar position in Afghanistan and Iraq. Afghanistan had become a haven for terrorists since the collapse of the state in the 1980s. Preventing al-Qaeda from reestablishing itself involved the uphill struggle to set up a national government in Kabul. Similarly, Iraq had a functioning state under Saddam Hussein, which collapsed following the American invasion in March 2003 and the early decision to disband the Iraqi army. As the country moved to full-scale civil war in 2005–2006, state building became a central objective of the American occupation.[2]

The record of the international community's success in stabilizing conflict or postconflict zones is mixed. In some cases, like Bosnia, Kosovo, East Timor, the Solomon Islands, and El Salvador, the peacekeeping mission largely prevented the reemergence of conflict. In Afghanistan and the Democratic Republic of Congo, they did not. Indeed, there is some argument that well-meaning humanitarian interventions in Somalia and the eastern Congo actually prolonged the crisis by inadvertently aiding one of the parties to the conflict.[3]

Results of state building are very disappointing. The United States is scheduled to withdraw its forces from Afghanistan in 2016 without having created a functional, legitimate centralized state. Iraq seemed to have more of a state, but the latter's authority in the areas north of Baghdad collapsed in 2014. Repeated interventions and billions of dollars in foreign assistance have yet to create functional governments in either Haiti or Somalia. In other cases, like the Balkans and the Solomon Islands, basic stability has been maintained only through heavy continuing outside involvement.

These failures have engendered a prolonged discussion of the conditions under which institutions are created and strengthened, and the role that outsiders can potentially play in promoting them. And this brings us back to the study of colonialism, since colonialism provides a rich source of experience of outsiders seeking to implant institutions in culturally different societies.

Many of the precedents and examples set by European colonialism are irrelevant to present-day interventions. Colonial powers were most successful in implanting modern institutions in places where the indigenous peoples were so weak, small in numbers, and primitively organized that they could be effectively killed off by war or disease, herded into reservations, or otherwise eliminated from the picture. This was the story of the United States, Canada, Australia, and New Zealand—British colonies that are today models of liberal democracy. This pattern will not be repeated. Even if we could find parts of the world so lightly inhabited, contemporary views on the rights of indigenous peoples would correctly present insuperable obstacles to this form of colonization.

The British and French colonial administrations in sub-Saharan

Africa are actually far better precedents for contemporary state-building interventions because they were lightly resourced, didn't involve large-scale European settlement, and in their later years began to actually take on developmental goals. Indirect rule by Britain is of particular interest because it sought to deal with what I have labeled the "getting to Denmark" problem by declaring that producing "Denmark" was not the goal of foreign rule in the first place.[4]

The problem is that Denmark did not get to be Denmark in a matter of months or years. Contemporary Denmark—and all other developed countries—gradually evolved modern institutions over the course of centuries. If outside powers try to impose their own models of good institutions on a country, they are likely to produce what Lant Pritchett, Michael Woolcock, and Matt Andrews call "isomorphic mimicry": a copying of the outward forms of Western institutions but without their substance. To succeed, institutions need to accord with local customs and traditions: for example, law codes imported from abroad wholesale often don't win acceptance because they don't reflect local values. Institutions are often complementary: you can't build a steel plant in a country in which there is no market for steel, no supply of competent managers or workers, no infrastructure to move product to market, and no legal system to protect the rights of the plant's investors. Strategies seeking to prioritize some goals over others require intimate understanding of the nature of local institutions. Moreover, institutions evolve based on the interests and ideas of local elites and power holders. Outsiders often don't understand who these elites are, how they interpret their interests, and therefore what resistance they will pose to well-meaning plans for reform or change.[5]

In light of these considerations, a number of observers have suggested that the international community ought to dramatically scale back its ambitions and go for "good enough" governance, seeking to get not to Denmark but to some more realistic objective, like Indonesia or Botswana.[6] Rather than importing entire modern legal codes from the United States or Europe, why not try in some circumstances to rely on customary law? Instead of insisting that the entire civil service be squeaky-clean with regard to corruption, why not wink at petty corruption by low-level officials and deal with only the most egregious cases? Rather than requiring people to vote for nonexistent programmatic parties, why not accept the reality of clientelism and aim instead for rent-seeking coalitions that nonetheless promote stability and some degree of economic growth?

One could have imagined, for example, a very different American policy in Afghanistan following the initial rout of the Taliban in the fall of 2001. Rather than seeking to reestablish a centralized, unitary democratic state, the United States could have tried to create a coalition of tribal leaders, warlords, and other power brokers who would among them have agreed to keep the peace and suppress al-Qaeda and other terrorist groups. Instead of attempting to build a democracy in Iraq, the United States could have kept Saddam Hussein's army intact and put it under the charge of a general with no ties to the old regime.

British indirect rule in Africa was in fact an early version of this "good enough" governance strategy. Lugard and other administrators made a virtue of necessity and recognized that they had neither the resources nor the manpower to rule their African colonies the way they ruled Hong Kong and Singapore, and therefore sought to make use of as many local traditions and existing facts on the ground as possible. As we saw, the French, though espousing a very different policy of direct rule and assimilation, ended up in much the same place as the British.

As we have seen, indirect rule had many pitfalls and often led to unanticipated and undesirable consequences. In the first place, the local knowledge requirements were huge and often overwhelmed the capabilities of the foreign administration. The search for "native law and custom" was easily manipulated by locals and led to misunderstandings of local practices. The formalization of informal law then froze in place certain customs that had previously been much more fluid. In other cases, colonial authorities were not actually willing to permit local chiefs to make decisions, either when they went against the interests of European settlers, or when they were judged to be contrary to "civilized morals." In still other cases, an otherwise admirable respect shown for local traditions failed to recognize that the objectives that Africans themselves sought were changing. The latter didn't want to preserve their traditional cultures, they wanted to modernize. To underline an uncomfortable fact, Northern Nigeria, where indirect rule was born and most consistently practiced, has for decades been the poorest and least educated part of the country, precisely because locals were left to their own traditions.

These same contradictions are evident in the contemporary indigenous rights movement. Public opinion in Western countries has shifted 180 degrees from colonial days, when indigenous peoples were regarded as savages needing to be forcibly "civilized," to what has now become a scrupulous regard for the right of the world's surviving indigenous communities to continue their traditional ways of life. This has led to violent conflicts in countries like Peru and Bolivia between mining or energy companies and indigenous communities supported by a worldwide network of international NGOs.

In principle, it is hard to argue that traditional communities should not be allowed to govern themselves under their own traditions. The alternative for most is not life in Denmark, but rather a marginal existence in a squalid urban settlement. The problem with outside promotion of indigenous rights, however, is that it is very difficult for outsiders to accurately judge the real interests of local communities, just as it was for the practitioners of indirect rule. Many of these communities are already half modernized, just as many Africans were in the early twentieth century, and many would actually have jumped at the chance to join the modern world. Continuing to live in a traditional village and speaking a local language may represent a dramatic closing of opportunities, something often overlooked by the well-meaning outsiders claiming to speak on their behalf.

Many of the problems created by indirect rule reappear in the practices of present-day development programs in Africa and other poor regions. For example, the World Bank, the U.S. Agency for International Development, and other donor agencies have been sponsoring so-called community-driven development (CDD) projects since the first one was launched in Indonesia in the 1990s.[7] The theory behind CDD is very plausible and appealing: local people know better than people in Washington or London what they need and should be the drivers of development projects intended to help them. Like colonial officials trying to implement indirect rule, CDD projects solicit community views on what sorts of local investments to make with donor funds, whether irrigation, roads, latrines, and the like. The outside donors hire local facilitators who presumably have sufficient local knowledge to be able to organize village communities and get fair representations of their views. The very act of organizing as a community will build, it is hoped, social capital that will last beyond the termination of the project.

CDD projects run into two distinct problems, however. The first is knowing what the real views of the community are. Like communities everywhere, villages are dominated by local elites, often older men who claim to speak on behalf of the group as a whole. It is very hard to know whether a particular community spokesperson is really reflecting general interests or is a locally powerful person who simply wants the latrine built near his house. In order to get around problems like this, the outside donors force the community to include women, minorities (if there are any), or other marginalized people, in accord not with local but with Western standards of fairness. This leads to a situation where the outsider either is forced to leave things up to local elites, or else tries to engage in a very intrusive form of social engineering. Few donors have enough local knowledge to understand what they are actually accomplishing. This dilemma would have been very familiar to district officers in colonial times trying to implement indirect rule, with the difference that most of them had much longer tenures and thus better local knowledge than the aid officials administering CDD programs today. Although such projects have proliferated around the world, their total impact on development is at this point quite uncertain.[8]

Reo Matsuzaki has suggested that to the extent state building has been successful, it has depended on the autonomy of agents on the ground who could make use of local knowledge to achieve developmental objectives. He points to the relative success of Japanese administration in building institutions in Taiwan in the years that it was ruled as a colonial dependency (from the Sino-Japanese War of 1895 to Japan's defeat in 1945). Japan's aims in Taiwan were not benevolent. As in Korea, Tokyo sought to Japanize the island, including making Taiwanese speak Japanese and using it as a platform for commodity exports to Japan. But they also pursued developmental objectives, building substantial infrastructure, schools, and a local state administration, all of which survived after the Japanese departed.

Matsuzaki argues that this came about because the governors-general like Kodama Gentarō appointed to run the island were powerful military bureaucrats whose stature allowed them to make decisions without heavy oversight from Tokyo. Kodama in turn appointed and protected his man on the spot, Goto Shimpei, who could implement policies based on his intimate knowledge of actual conditions in Taiwan. In dealing with land issues and education, they shifted policies frequently in response to local developments; moreover, they served in Taiwan long enough to develop sufficient local knowledge to recognize when things weren't working.

This contrasts with American overlordship of the Philippines, where local administrators (like future president William Howard Taft, civil governor there from 1901 to 1903) were constantly being overruled by politicians in Washington. Congressional leaders controlling the purse strings were eager to impose American models of government on a society they only dimly understood. Thus the American administration missed a big opportunity to redistribute Catholic church lands to poor peasants due to a Catholic lobby back home. American administrators left land distribution up to the Philippine court system rather than to an executive agency, since that was the way it was done in the United States. They failed to recognize that in the Philippines, in contrast to America, widespread illiteracy meant that legal proceedings would be dominated by educated elites, who then succeeded in grabbing large estates despite the Americans' explicit desire to promote land reform. By exporting the nineteenth-century U.S. model of a government of "courts and parties" to the Philippines, the United States permitted the growth of a landed oligarchy that continues to dominate that country.[9]

We should thus be wary of foreigners bearing gifts of institutions. Foreigners seldom have enough local knowledge to understand how to construct durable states. When their efforts at institution building are halfhearted and underresourced, they often do more damage than good. This is not to say that Western models of development don't work, or don't have some degree of universal validity. But each society must adapt them to its own conditions and build on indigenous traditions.

Institutions are best created by indigenous social actors who can borrow from foreign practices but also are well aware of the constraints and opportunities presented by their own history and traditions. Some of the most remarkable cases of institutional development were those in East Asia, where local elites could draw on a long experience of state- and nationhood. In many other places, however, such traditions did not exist and had to be created.

As I noted earlier, it is not enough to create formal state institutions, whether based on borrowed or indigenous models. State building needs to be accompanied by a parallel process of nation building to be effective. Nation building adds a moral component of shared norms and culture and underpins the state's legitimacy. It is also potentially a source of intolerance and aggression, and so often must be accomplished using authoritarian methods. Two paired comparisons, between Nigeria and Indonesia on the one hand, and Kenya and Tanzania on the other, illustrate this point.

22

LINGUA FRANCAS

How national identity is important and problematic in developing countries; how Indonesia and Tanzania succeeded in creating national identities while Nigeria and Kenya did not; whether national identity is better established under democratic or authoritarian conditions

We saw in previous chapters that existence of a strong national identity was critical to the success of state building in Europe. In the contemporary developing world, weak states are frequently the by-product of weak or nonexistent national identities. This was a particular problem in sub-Saharan Africa, whose independent states were colonial creations with arbitrary borders that did not correspond to a single ethnic, linguistic, or cultural community. As administrative units within larger empires, their peoples had grown used to living with one another, but they had no sense of shared culture or common identity. In the vacuum left by colonialism, some newly independent countries like Nigeria and Kenya made little effort to create a new national identity, and they have been plagued in later years by high levels of ethnic conflict. Indonesia and Tanzania, by contrast, had founding leaders who articulated ideas around which national unity could be created. Indonesia, of course, is not an African country, but as noted in chapter 14, there are many points of similarity between it and Nigeria, while Kenya and Tanzania share many characteristics. Both Indonesia and Tanzania face great political challenges, of course, including corruption and ethnic conflict. But relative levels matter; their governments are much more coherent and stable because of their early investment in nation building, and as a result they have achieved better social and economic results in recent years.

OIL AND ETHNICITY

Like many developing countries, Nigeria was never a historical nation. But it was also never the object of a serious nation-building project, either on the part of the colonial authorities, or by the new national leadership after independence. When the British took over Nigeria, they did not conquer a large, well-established centralized state, as when they subdued the Mughal Empire in India. The indigenous people were loyal primarily to very small tribal-level units.[1] The territory now called Nigeria was first consolidated into a single political unit on January 1, 1914, by Frederick Lugard, codifier of indirect rule, who was serving as governor. It was based on a merger of the Protectorate of Northern Nigeria and the Colony and Protectorate of Southern Nigeria, the latter itself the product of a merger that had taken place between Lagos Colony and the Niger Delta Protectorate in 1906. These territories had little in common since they were divided by religion, ethnicity, and wealth, especially between the Muslim North and the South that was being steadily converted to Christianity through the work of European missionaries. The merger had been undertaken for reasons of administrative convenience—the poorer North kept running a fiscal deficit, which would be easier to subsidize in a united colony. The colonial authorities of course never thought to consult the locals themselves about the wisdom of this plan.[2]

What the British didn't find in Nigeria, they didn't create, either. In India, where the British had a presence since the seventeenth century, they established an army, a national bureaucracy, an educated middle class, and a lingua franca (English) that could unite the subcontinent's diverse ethnicities, religions, and castes. Sunil Khilnani argues that, in a certain sense, the very "idea of India" as a political unit was created in colonial times around these institutions and the democratic ideals that were slowly being transmitted. India was, moreover, central to British strategic purposes as the anchor of their empire.[3]

By the time they got to Nigeria, however, the British were in a sense exhausted by the burdens of a global empire. Indirect rule was the policy that remained once they had decided that they could not invest in Africa the way they invested in India. So they deliberately decided not to try to implant a strong state structure, or do much to develop the economy. The British had very little interest in creating a class of educated Nigerians.

On the eve of independence, the literacy rate in English was only 2 percent in the North, and there were only one thousand university-educated Nigerians in the whole country. Nigerians were barred from the senior civil service; only seventy-five Africans served at other levels at the end of World War II.[4]

As noted earlier, one of the ways that strong state structures and uncorrupt administrations are formed is when people have to organize to fight for their freedom. What is notable about Nigeria is that it never had a strong nationalist party that contested British rule or sought to pursue a nation-building strategy once in power. Rather, sovereignty was handed to the Nigerians on a platter by the British. They wrote the new country's constitution and announced some years in advance that they would be leaving, which they eventually did in 1960. The political parties that came to power in independent Nigeria were heavily regional and ethnic from the start, more suspicious of each other than of their former colonial master, and lacking in any concept of a Nigerian nation or how to define the new country's identity. The lack of a national identity soon led to the breakdown of the country and its descent into civil war.[5]

The discovery of large new reserves of oil in the Gulf of Biafra gave Nigeria's competing ethnic groups a valuable prize to fight over, but it also produced a mechanism that ensured future political stability. The government controls economic resources, which are distributed to elites, who in turn distribute those resources to networks of followers (while taking hefty cuts for themselves). Whenever some disgruntled group threatens the rent-seeking coalition with violence, they are bought off by greater subsidies and payments. Political corruption and clientelism are the price that Nigerians have had to pay for stability and for their lack of an overarching national identity.

Indonesia started out much like Nigeria but developed very differently in subsequent years. Prior to the twentieth century, the country of Indonesia did not exist. Stretching over an archipelago containing more than eleven thousand islands, the area known variously as the Indian Archipelago, the Indies, the Tropical Netherlands, or the Dutch East Indies consisted of a wide variety of sultanates, tribes, trading posts, and ethnic groups speaking hundreds of different languages. Few of the indigenous inhabitants were aware of a world much beyond their village or, at most, island.[6]

This all began to change at the end of the nineteenth century and the beginning of the twentieth, as the Dutch extended their political control and trading networks beyond Batavia (the location of present-day Jakarta), headquarters of the Dutch East India Company. Regular steamship travel gave people a sense of the archipelago as a whole, as did the possibility of making the hajj to Mecca, which connected Indonesian Muslims to the broader Muslim community. A very small indigenous elite with access to European education emerged and began to adopt concepts like nationalism and Marxism from the West.[7]

By the third decade of the twentieth century, there were quite a lot of ways this colony's identity could have been defined. Since a large majority of the inhabitants were Muslim, they could have seen themselves as a Muslim state as Pakistan was to do. The Communist Party of Indonesia (PKI) wanted a class revolution that would link them to the global Communist International, as the Chinese and Vietnamese parties had done. And there were many regional and local identities that could have supported their own regional political units, especially on the larger islands of Java and Sumatra.

Instead, a completely new idea for a country to be called Indonesia emerged during the late 1920s with the creation of the Indonesian National Association, the Congress of Indonesian National Political Associations, and a nationalist youth group Young Indonesia.[8] The second Indonesia Youth Congress meeting in Batavia in October 1928 adopted a national anthem, "Indonesia Raya" (one of the first public uses of the word "Indonesia"), and declared Bahasa Indonesia the national language.

The adoption of Indonesian as a national language was a critical element of identity formation for the nascent country. Indonesian is a standardized version of classical Malay, one that had been in use for many centuries as a lingua franca of traders and travelers operating within the archipelago. It was the first language of only a relatively small number of the region's inhabitants, the vast majority of whom continued to speak Javanese, Sundanese or, for the educated elite, Dutch. It is more egalitarian than Javanese, the language of the colony's politically dominant ethnic group, lacking an elaborate system of registers reflecting the relative status of the speakers and those spoken to. Many of the early young nationalists could not speak Indonesian, or speak it well.

Adoption of Indonesian and the promulgation of a broad, multiethnic idea of Indonesia succeeded in trumping other concepts of identity in circulation in the early twentieth century. There had been a number of regional movements on Java, Sumatra, and the Celebes at the time, which dissolved themselves with the formation of the broader Indonesian groups. The Dutch had played the game of divide and rule, and many in the new nationalist elite recognized that formation of the broadest possible coalition was critical to winning independence.

One of the most important forces behind the idea of Indonesia was the country's first postindependence president, Sukarno, who published a short pamphlet in 1927 titled *Nationalism, Islam, and Marxism*. In it he took on the three major intellectual currents at the time and argued that there was no fundamental inconsistency among them that would prevent creation of a broad political front against Dutch rule. Sukarno claimed that the messages of Islam and Marxism were similar insofar as they both opposed usury. He criticized "fanatical" Muslims who sought a theocratic state on the grounds that this would breed conflict with Indonesia's other religious communities. Similarly, he argued against doctrinaire Marxism for its hostility to religion. The one political principle Sukarno was not interested in including in his synthesis was Western liberalism, precisely because this doctrine did not provide a justification for a strong state that would play an integrative role in forging a national identity, or engage in the redistributionist policies he felt necessary for "social justice."

These ideas were later articulated by Sukarno as the "Five Pillars" (Pancasila) in a speech in 1945, and were to become the basis of the Pancasila doctrine that underlay the independent Indonesian state.[9] Sukarno was an extremely woolly theorist, seeking to synthesize ideas that were in fact sharply contradictory. His purpose, however, was not philosophical but practical: he wanted to create an integrative national identity that would allow him to both coalesce and at the same time keep at bay the alternative political currents running through Indonesia. He defined the Indonesian nation in the broadest possible terms, without reference to any of the country's ethnic groups, while he accepted religion but neutered it by reference not to Islam but to generic monotheism.[10]

Sukarno's national synthesis could be implemented only in the context of an increasingly authoritarian state. Indonesia's original constitution upon independence in 1950 provided for multiparty democracy and sidelined President Sukarno as a weak figurehead. After the first general elections in 1955, Sukarno began an attack on parliamentary democracy as such, and with the outbreak of ethnic rebellions on the outer islands, martial law was declared in March 1957. Backed by the army and the PKI, Sukarno crushed the liberal opposition and created a National Front based on Nasakom. That acronym represented the three forces of his article—the nationalists, Muslims, and Communists. Increasingly dependent on support from the Communists and externally from China and the Soviet Union, Sukarno used the state to mobilize mass support on the basis of his Pancasila ideology.[11]

Sukarno ultimately failed because he could not in fact synthesize his three pillars, particularly the nationalist one represented by the army and the Marxist one represented by the PKI. These two sources of support became increasingly suspicious of one another. An attempted coup by Sukarno's presidential guard and the murder of a number of generals led the army, headed by General Suharto, to strike back, forcing Sukarno out of power and leading to the bloody purge in which the PKI was decimated and anywhere from five to eight hundred thousand people were killed.[12]

The resulting New Order of General Suharto dropped the Marxist part of Sukarno's program but retained his reliance on a strong, centralized state as a guarantor of national unity, and Pancasila ideology as the source of national identity. Indonesia's small Chinese minority, from which the PKI recruited heavily, were forced to take Indonesian names and assimilate into the broader population. The crisis had revealed a bitter antagonism between the country's Muslim majority and its Chinese minority, and the PKI's defeat strengthened the hand of various Muslim organizations. But the New Order regime continued to use Pancasila ideology as a means of keeping at bay demands for greater Islamicization of the Indonesian state. Suharto, indeed, was to come to rely on the Chinese business community as a support for his regime.[13]

The mechanism for cultural assimilation was education. Bahasa Indonesia was the language of instruction in public schools from the beginning, and the state introduced programs to train teachers and have them work (and often marry) outside of their home provinces. The Indonesians thus replicated an administrative system similar to the one employed by Chinese emperors to rule their provinces, or by the Ottomans to govern their *sanjaks*. One of the more important achievements of Suharto's New Order period was the expansion of primary education, where coverage rose from 55.6 to 87.6 percent of the population between 1971 and 1985. After Bahan had been taught in the school system for more than two generations, the number of its speakers has risen steadily and today approaches 100 percent of the population.[14]

Indonesian national identity was entrenched in a way that Nigerian national identity would never be—through articulation of a clear integrative ideology, establishment of a national language, and the backing of both by authoritarian power based on a national army. The limits of this integrative process were made clear, however, in places like Timor Leste (formerly East Timor), West Papua (the former West New Guinea), Ambon, and Aceh, which never accepted the national narrative coming out of Jakarta.[15] West Papua and Timor Leste are both substantially Melanesian by ethnicity, largely non-Muslim, and were formally annexed by Indonesia only in 1963 and 1976, respectively. Sukarno in his 1927 essay referred to Ernest Renan's definition of a nation as a group that shares a common history and acts as a common community; by this standard, neither place ever thought of itself as part of the Indonesian nation. Neither belonged to the ancient Majapahit Hindu kingdom that preceded the Islamicization of Indonesia, a historical period that was sometimes evoked by modern nationalists as an imagined source of Indonesian identity. Both had other more proximate sources of identity connected to their Melanesian roots and, in the case of Timor, Portuguese overlordship. When early Indonesian nationalists visited the eastern parts of the archipelago, they found it to be an utterly foreign place, inhabited by tribal peoples and, as one put it, "cannibals."[16] The Indonesian government moved transmigrants from Java and other parts of Indonesia into both places in an effort to change the ethnic balance, taught Indonesian, promoted Pancasila ideology through the school system, and relied on outright force to retain sovereignty in the face of armed local insurgencies. Timor Leste nonetheless voted for independence in a 1999 referendum, and became, despite terrible violence by pro-Indonesian militias, an independent country in 2002. West Papua has remained within Indonesia, but there is a continuing low-level insurgency and independence movement there.

Notwithstanding the clear limits to the radius of the national identity that the Indonesian state has been able to impose, the government has achieved a remarkable degree of national integration for a region that was not remotely a single nation one hundred years earlier. Indeed, Indonesian identity by the 1990s had become sufficiently secure that when the country as a whole transitioned to democracy after the Asian financial crisis in the late 1990s, it was able to permit a substantial devolution of power to its provinces and localities without fear of further fragmentation. Indonesia remains a highly fractured country, as communal violence against the Chinese and Christian communities and other minorities continues. Levels of corruption remain high as well. But all success is relative: given the kind of ethnic, religious, and regional fractionalization with which the country started, its nation-building success is quite remarkable. Indonesia could have looked much more like Nigeria.[17]

Tanzania's record in nation building has been very similar to that of Indonesia, despite obvious differences in region, religion, and race. Tanzania is highly diverse ethnically, being divided into some 120 different ethnic groups; like Indonesia, it was ruled for many years by a strong one-party state that made nation building an explicit goal and, to a large extent, succeeded at that. Like Indonesia, it used top-down, authoritarian power to achieve this goal.

The country to which Tanzania can best be compared is the state to its immediate north, Kenya. Both were British colonies or mandates, and both are very similar with regard to climate and culture. Indeed, the border between the two countries is an unnaturally straight line drawn by colonial authorities running from Lake Victoria in the west eventually to the Indian Ocean, which artificially separates the peoples who straddled it.

During the cold war, the two countries were frequently compared because Kenya had adopted what Joel Barkan labeled "patron-client capitalism," while Tanzania adopted "one-party socialism."[18] For the first two decades after gaining independence in 1963, Kenya grew substantially faster than Tanzania, arguably demonstrating the superiority of market-based economics (see Table 4).

TABLE 4. GDP Growth Rates, 1965–1990

	1965–1980	1981–1985	1986–1990
Kenya	6.8	3.2	4.9
Tanzania	3.9	0.4	3.6

SOURCE: World Bank

But then, beginning in the late 1980s, the countries reversed positions, with Kenya suffering a precipitous economic decline relative to Tanzania (see Figure 16). More recently, Tanzania has shared in sub-Saharan Africa's overall strong growth with rates of around 6 percent in the period 1999– 2011. Kenya by contrast has been racked, particularly since the presiden‧ tial election of 2007, by violence among its ethnic groups. GDP growth has been lower and much more volatile during the 2000s, reflecting ongo- ing political conflict. Tanzania has remained much more stable. The rea- sons for this can be traced ultimately back to the fact that Tanzania's one-party dictatorship engaged in a policy of nation building, while Kenya's more liberal state did not.

FIGURE 16. GDP Growth Rates, 1989–2011

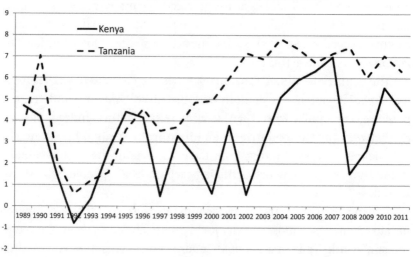

SOURCE: World Bank

Tanzania had certain preexisting advantages over Kenya in formu- lating a national identity. None of its 120 ethnic groups is large enough to potentially dominate the country, whereas Kenya has five major ones, constituting some 70 percent of the population.[19] An alliance of any two of these larger groups—Kikuyu, Kalenjin, Luo, Kamba, Luhya—is often sufficient to gain control of the government. Equally important was the role of Swahili as a national language in Tanzania. Swahili, a Bantu lan- guage borrowing heavily from the Arabic of the traders in Zanzibar and other coastal areas, is spoken throughout many countries in East Africa.

It played a role similar to Bahasa Indonesia as a colonial-era lingua franca and language of merchants and traders. When Tanganyika was controlled by the Germans during the late nineteenth century, the colonial authorities made a much more concerted effort to turn it into a national language than did the British in their Kenyan colony. It was therefore more heavily used in Tanzania than in Kenya at independence.[20]

Tanzania's founding president, Julius Nyerere, played a role similar to that of Sukarno in Indonesia. He explicitly built national identity around socialist ideology rather than ethnicity with his doctrine of *ujamaa* or African socialism, articulated clearly and at great length in his writings and in documents like the 1967 Arusha Declaration.[21] He argued that ethnic fractionalization was a grave threat to the socialist project and therefore made efforts to suppress what he labeled "tribalism." Like Sukarno, he had little patience with Western liberal notions of pluralism and wanted one-party rule in order to restructure society. To accomplish this, he created a political instrument, the Tanganyika African National Union (TANU, which evolved into the Chama Cha Mapinduzi), that would maintain Leninist discipline and centralized control over its cadres throughout the country. Unlike many other new African rulers, Nyerere focused not only on the cities but also sought to have TANU penetrate the countryside in what was still a heavily rural society.[22] In the process, Nyerere's government made a much stronger effort than did Jomo Kenyatta's to turn Swahili into a national language, making it compulsory in all secondary schools in 1965. In the words of Henry Bienen, "Swahili was an essential component of Tanganyika's national identity; it was equated with 'Tanganyikaness.'"[23]

Things were very different in Kenya. One large ethnic group, the Kikuyu, made themselves dominant after independence by virtue of their leadership role in both politics and the economy. The Mau Mau rebellion against British colonial authority was largely led by Kikuyus, who also contributed the country's founding president, Jomo Kenyatta. Although Kenyatta established his own nationalist party, the Kenya African National Union, this was conceived not as an ideologically based Leninist organization but as a patronage-distribution system. The state was not seen as a neutral arbiter standing above different ethnic groups; it was a prize to be captured. Thus when Kenyatta was succeeded by Daniel arap Moi in 1978, patronage shifted abruptly from the Kikuyu to the Kalenjin and other ethnic groups supporting Moi. While TANU sought to redistribute resources from rich to poor, the Kenyan government re-distributed from one ethnicity to another. The open exploitation of pa-tronage by ethnic groups arriving at political power was captured by Michela Wrong in the phrase "It's our turn to eat."[24]

Kenya's economic decline can be directly traced to Moi's ascendancy and increasing levels of patronage and corruption that followed. Since that time, much of Kenyan politics has revolved around a zero-sum game between the country's ethnic groups to grab the presidency and state resources. This culminated in mass killings in the wake of the 2007 presidential election between Mwai Kibaki, a Kikuyu, and Raila Odinga, a Luo.[25] Uhuru Kenyatta, son of the country's founder, was elected presi-dent in 2013 but is under indictment by the International Criminal Court for his role in the 2007 communal violence.

The Tanzanian push for a national language, in addition to TANU's efforts to stamp out all manifestations of regionalism and ethnic iden-tity, has meant that ethnicity over time has come to matter considerably less in Tanzania than in Kenya and other countries that did not make nation building an explicit goal. Economist Edward Miguel finds that despite similar levels of ethnic diversity in Tanzania and Kenya, the for-mer provides higher levels of public goods, suggesting the lower salience of ethnicity there.[26]

Strong national identity does not by itself create good outcomes; it must be linked to sensible policies as well. In the period from independence through the early 1990s, Julius Nyerere's effort to build African social-ism in Tanzania was an utter disaster in every respect other than nation building. In economic policy, Tanzania destroyed incentives by seizing the commanding heights of the economy and redistributing wealth away from producers. It undermined the country's agricultural sector, which was the chief source of export earnings, in favor of import-substituting industries that were not sustainable over the long term. And it discour-aged foreign private investment in favor of "self-sufficiency." In the politi-cal realm as well, Tanzania made many serious early mistakes. It declared itself officially to be a one-party state, with TANU cadres seeking to oversee all aspects of political and social life. Not just other political par-ties, but civil society organizations also were banned or strictly con-trolled, and press freedom limited. Perhaps the worst policy to come out of the socialist period occurred between 1973 and 1976, when 80 percent of the rural population was forced into communal *ujamaa* villages. This effort at massive social engineering, like its counterparts in the Soviet Union and China, had predictably negative consequences for the economy as well as individual freedom.[27]

These poor economic policies ended after Tanzania's debt crisis in the late 1980s and since then have been replaced by more sensible market-oriented ones. This shift, combined with the fact that it has avoided Nigerian- or Kenyan-style ethnic conflict, has given it an impressive rate of economic growth in the late 1990s and 2000s. No more than in Indonesia does this mean that ethnicity (or religion) has disappeared as a potential source of conflict and instability. The Muslims in Zanzibar have been increasingly mobilized in favor of a separate state. But both Indonesia and Tanzania have succeeded in creating more effective political orders as a result.

I suggested earlier that successful democracies have benefited from historical nation-building projects that were achieved by violent and nondemocratic means. What was true for Europe is also the case in developing countries like Indonesia and Tanzania. Both are reasonably successful democracies today: Indonesia in 2013 received an overall freedom rating of 2.5 from Freedom House (on a scale that goes from 1, the best, to 7, the worst), and Tanzania's was 3.0. Yet both countries were far more authoritarian in the periods in which their national identities were being built. Conversely, it is hard to see how either Nigeria or Kenya could embark on a nation-building project today, given their existing divisions and constraints on national power. No one would have the authority to write a national narrative or declare a new national language. Sequencing and history therefore matter with regard to common identity, as they did to the creation of a modern state.

When we turn to the countries of East Asia, we find a very different situation with regard to national identity and state traditions. China, Japan, and Korea, at least, are among the most ethnically homogeneous societies in the world and have long had strong national identities based on shared language and culture. Things were not always like this—Chinese civilization expanded over the centuries out of the Yellow River valley with conquests to the south, southeast, and west; it assimilated countless nonethnic Han populations and was itself colonized by a variety of Turkic barbarians from the north and northwest. China, as chronicled in Volume 1, invented not just one of the first states, but the first modern state, which was built around a common literary corpus of classical writings that served as the basis for the education of generations of bureaucrats. National identity and state building were connected from the start in Chinese history. The same was true of the other societies on China's borders touched by Confucian culture—Korea, Japan, and Vietnam. All of this happened well before any of them had significant contact with European colonialism or Western ideas. This fact has had a very powerful impact on contemporary development outcomes: unlike Nigeria or Indonesia, none of these Asian countries had to undertake a nation-building project in parallel with its efforts to create a modern state in the nineteenth and twentieth centuries. Like their European contemporaries, those nations had already been formed.

23

THE STRONG ASIAN STATE

How China, Japan, and other East Asian societies could presuppose strong, modern states before their contact with the West, and how East Asia's problem is not state weakness but the inability to constrain the state; how Japan introduced law under foreign pressure and how bureaucratic autonomy got completely out of control

East Asia is the only part of the non-Western world that boasts of industrialized, high-income societies that are also liberal democracies—Japan, South Korea, and Taiwan. It is also home to China, Singapore, Vietnam, Malaysia, and other fast-developing countries that lack democratic political institutions but nonetheless have very effective states. East Asia stands at the opposite end of the spectrum from sub-Saharan Africa with its weak states and poor economic performance.

There is a huge literature on the "East Asian miracle" and why countries there have grown so rapidly. Interpretations of growth there are polarized between those who see the region's success resting on its market-friendly policies and others who stress the importance of industrial policy and other forms of state intervention to promote economic growth. There are also cultural theories that attribute the region's success to the Asian values of thrift and a work ethic. Since a great deal of variation exists across the region, one can make a plausible case for either a market-oriented or a state-driven interpretation of the sources of growth: Hong Kong has always been more open and less statist than mainland China and South Korea, but all three have grown rapidly. Regardless of the degree of government intervention, the fast-growing economies of East Asia share a common feature: they all possess competent, high-capacity states.[1]

A capable state is particularly important for activist governments pursuing industrial policy, essentially trying to "pick winners" in the economy and promote them through subsidized credits, special licensing arrangements, or infrastructural support. Contrary to free-market fundamentalists who say that industrial policy never works, it has proved highly successful in certain places.[2] But the conditions for success are very specific. Any effort to override the price signals given by the market can be dangerous if politicians get their hands on the process: investment decisions will be made on political rather than economic grounds. The history of developing countries in Latin America, Africa, and the Middle East is littered with cases of industrial policy gone bad and collapsing in a flurry of corruption and rent seeking, like the Argentine effort to create a domestic car industry noted in chapter 18. For government intervention to work, the state must have what Peter Evans labels "embedded autonomy": bureaucracies have to respond to social needs, but also must be free of pressures to satisfy rent-seeking political constituencies, allowing them to promote longer-term goals that serve a broad public interest. This kind of policy worked in Japan, South Korea, Taiwan, and China but failed elsewhere. The difference in outcomes lies in the quality of government.[3]

Where does this strong Asian state come from? While Singapore and Malaysia were colonial creations, China, Japan, and Korea all had strong traditions of state- and nationhood centuries prior to significant contact with the West. These traditional states were severely disrupted in the nineteenth and twentieth centuries by confrontation with Western colonial powers, and state institutions needed to be dramatically restructured and reformed. But governments did not have to be built from scratch as in many parts of Africa. Moreover, China, Japan, and Korea already had strong national identities and shared cultures; indeed, they constituted some of the most ethnically homogeneous societies in the world. These long state traditions and national identities were the basis of the region's remarkable success in economic development.

Much of East Asia therefore resembled Europe insofar as it could take a strong state for granted as industrialization began. However, the region's path of political development took quite a different course from that of Europe. Europe established legal institutions in the late Middle Ages, prior to the burst of state building that occurred from the late sixteenth through the eighteenth century. This meant that modern European states always had more limited powers than their counterparts in East Asia, despite the absolutist pretensions of European monarchs. Having been limited by law, state power in Europe was further constrained by the rise of new social actors such as the middle classes and industrial working class, who organized themselves into political parties and demanded rights against the state. Law and accountability worked hand in hand to restrict the power of the state. Law established the rights of feudal estates like the English Parliament to require the king to seek its permission for new taxes. Originally established on a narrow oligarchic basis, parliaments could become the vehicles for the assertion of power by rising new social forces that organized political parties and sought broadened representation.

By contrast, East Asian political development began not with rule of law but with the state. Because of its lack of a transcendental religion, China never developed a body of law that stood outside the positive enactments of the emperor and had no legal hierarchy independent of executive power. The emperor ruled by law, using law as an instrument of bureaucratic governance. Chinese rulers had at their disposal a precociously modern state that could prevent the subsequent emergence of social actors that might want to oppose their purposes, like religious organizations, an entrenched blood nobility living (as they did in Europe) in impregnable castles, or a commercial bourgeoisie ruling themselves in free cities. As a result, traditional Asian governments could be far more absolutist than those in Europe.

East Asia's political challenge then was very different from that of much of the rest of the colonial world. State authority could be taken for granted. The problem was rather the opposite: how to limit the power of the state through law and representative government. The state-society balance, skewed heavily in favor of society in other parts of the world, strongly favored the state in East Asia. Social organizations that could serve as a counterbalance to state power existed, but they were tightly controlled and seldom allowed to flourish on their own. This pattern continues up to the present day.

JAPANESE BUREAUCRACY

Japan, the first non-Western country to modernize and join the developed world, is in some sense paradigmatic of this larger pattern. Its inherited traditions of stateness were strong enough that it succeeded in resisting colonization altogether, even as its traditional institutions were restructured through borrowings from imported European models. Key to this process was the creation of a centralized national bureaucracy, which from the late nineteenth century on was the primary source of government authority. This eventually resulted in an out-of-control military so autonomous that it was able to drag the entire country into a disastrous war. Law and democratic accountability were put in place in the end not through popular mobilization of democratic forces but through outside intervention by the United States and other foreign powers.

During the Tokugawa Shogunate (1608–1868), the shogun, while nominally a vassal of the emperor, in fact exercised real authority in the latter's name. The country was not ruled as a centralized bureaucratic state; authority rather was split between the *bakufu*—the shogun's administration in the capital of Edo (Tokyo)—and a few hundred domains (*han*) ruled over by a daimyo or military lord. The resulting "bakuhan" system has often been characterized as being similar to European feudalism, since power was decentralized at the domain level. Each daimyo had his own castle and following of samurai warriors.

Calling this system feudal, however, masks considerable uniformity in administration and the extraordinary ability of the premodern Japanese state to penetrate society. In its premodern period, Japan inherited a tradition of bureaucratic government that was heavily shaped by Chinese norms and practices. In the words of Peter Duus, "Despite its outwardly feudal structure Japan was in many respects a model bureaucratic state . . . Government offices were stacked high with records and documents of every conceivable kind, from land surveys to population registers, which recorded the existence of most of the population in some way or another. (In the domain of Nambu, a horse breeding area, even the pregnancies and deaths of horses were recorded.)"[4] As in the case of China, Japanese government was modern in many ways, well before it began its post-1868 economic modernization.

The latter began after the arrival of U.S. Commodore Matthew Perry's "black ships" in 1853 and presents a paradigmatic case of what Samuel Huntington labeled "defensive modernization." Demands by Perry and other Western powers to open Japan to outsiders led to the concession of various unequal treaties granting foreigners market access. This capitulation delegitimized the Tokugawa government and sparked an armed rebellion, which set in motion the restoration of a centralized state in 1868 in the name of the Emperor Meiji. The urgency of the restoration was animated by the desire to avoid the fate of China, which had lost pieces of coastal territory to foreign powers. Abrogation of the unequal treaties, and the colonial powers' recognition of Japan as an equal, remained central to Japan's drive to modernize through the first decades of the twentieth century. As in Prussia, perception of military threat drove state building.[5]

Japan's political development occurred with astonishing rapidity during the decade of the 1870s. All of the domains were abolished in a single stroke in 1871 and ordered to incorporate their military forces into a national army. The samurai elite, who under the Tokugawa system were the only individuals permitted to bear arms, were stripped of their stipends by 1876 and forbidden to wear their two symbolic katana, or swords. A new conscript army was set up on modern organizational principles, and its ranks were filled with formerly despised peasants. These changes led to a samurai revolt known as the Satsuma Rebellion in 1877, which was militarily suppressed in short order by the new conscript army.[6]

We tend to accept these historical facts as the natural consequence of Japan's decision to modernize. But compared to other parts of the world, these developments are extraordinary. In Europe, the abolition of feudal privileges and the creation of a modern, centralized state was a process that extended, depending on the country, from the late sixteenth to the late nineteenth century and involved enormous levels of often violent social conflict. In the contemporary developing world, such consolidation has not yet occurred despite years of effort. Pakistan, for example, continues to be dominated by an entrenched quasi-feudal landed elite that has no intention of giving up its privileges. Somalia and Libya have been unable to force their militias into a new national army. In Japan, by contrast, consolidation of a modern state was accomplished in just over a decade.

Of the various reasons that have been given for this difference, one that stands out is Tokugawa Japan's extraordinarily strong sense of national identity. As an island nation ruled from the start by a single, unbroken dynasty, Japan enjoyed an unusually high degree of ethnic and cultural uniformity. The Meiji oligarchs were careful to cultivate this identity through such policies as the elevation of Shinto and emperor-worship as a state religion. Shinto had direct political implications, providing a source of legitimacy for the new emperor-centered state.[7] These traditions had existed for centuries but were simply given greater emphasis after 1868. In contrast to most developing country elites, the leaders of the Meiji Restoration only had to build a state, and not a nation.

Under the new system, the Japanese emperor did not actually rule; real power was held by a small circle of oligarchs including Itō Hirobumi, Yamagata Aritomo, and Inoue Kaoru, as well as various anonymous officials in the Imperial Household, who operated behind the scenes to make policy in the emperor's name. One of their first acts was to create a modern Weberian bureaucracy, whose departments they themselves often supervised. Over time, it was difficult to distinguish between this more political group and the upper levels of the bureaucracy itself. Personnel from the old *han* or domain governments became the core of a new national bureaucracy. These local governments lost their independence in the period 1868–1878 and were turned into prefectural administrative units subordinate to the central government in Tokyo.

As in Europe, education became the gateway into higher bureaucratic service. The Law Faculty of Tokyo Imperial University (now Tokyo University) became the preferred entryway into elite ministries like Finance and Commerce and Industry. By 1937, over 73 percent of higher bureaucrats were Tokyo University graduates.[8] The growth in capacity of the Japanese bureaucracy was remarkable for both its speed and quality. Of those appointed prefectural governor before 1900, more than 97 percent had no formal university education; in the period from 1899 to 1945, fully 96 percent of such officials had not only a university education but a Western-style education from one of the many new universities that had been established in the last decades of the nineteenth century.[9] It is hard to think of many contemporary developing countries outside of East Asia that have succeeded in building human capital within their state administrations so rapidly.

As in the Prussian bureaucracy, Japanese officials were screened in competitive examinations and entered as a class. It was difficult to make patronage appointments because there was almost no opportunity for lateral or midcareer entry. A civil service career track was created in 1884 with a pension system that rewarded long service. The examination system was established in 1887 and strengthened in 1893 to put strong emphasis on jurisprudence and law. By 1899, the Chokunin Civil Service Appointment Ordnance restricted recruitment into the highest levels of the civil service to those who had passed through the upper civil service.[10] This, plus the fact that many bureaucrats came from the former domains of Satsuma and Chōshū that had led the Meiji Restoration, resulted in a high degree of internal cohesion among a very small group of senior public officials.[11]

Like the German state, the Japanese state was forged in war. Japan fought China in 1894–1895, after which it annexed Taiwan, defeated Russia in the 1905 Russo-Japanese War, gained a foothold in China, and colonized Korea in 1910. As in Prussia, modernization of the administrative structure of the military was seen as key to national survival. The army and navy received huge increases in their budgets, and new academies were set up to train officers in European military techniques. The state paid special attention to those who had fallen in the country's wars, opening the Yasukuni Shrine in Tokyo in 1869 as a place to inter the souls of the war dead. The Tokugawa regime had always been a military oligarchy infused with the warrior ethic of bushido. This ethic was merged with modern organizational techniques in an increasingly autonomous military bureaucracy. Japanese nationalism had a military flavor from the beginning. This tradition continues up to the present day, as conservative politicians seek to visit Yasukuni much to the consternation of Japan's Chinese and Korean neighbors.[12]

THE SPREAD OF LAW IN JAPAN

By the time of the Russo-Japanese War, Japan could take for granted the existence of a modern Weberian state. Its problem, then, was completely different from that of the vast majority of contemporary developing countries: rather than build state power, it needed to create institutions that would limit the power of the state. This was necessary to protect property rights, and hence the prospects of economic growth, from an overweening state, as well as protection of individual citizens from abuse. This meant the establishment of a rule of law.

Like China, premodern Japan had a long history of rule by law, as opposed to rule of law. That is, law was seen as the regularized administrative commands of the sovereign, binding on subjects but not on the sovereign himself. Japan's first written law was borrowed from the Chinese Tang Code of the seventh and eighth centuries, the Taiho Ritsuryō

and Yoro Ritsuryō in A.D. 702 and 718, respectively. Like its Chinese counterpart, early Japanese law was largely a schedule of criminal penalties;
there was no concept of private law, including contracts, property, or torts.
As in China, but differently from Europe, India, and the Middle East, law
did not grow out of an independent religious authority with its own hierarchy of judges and interpreters. Law was simply the administrative arm
of the government, whether national or domain based. By the time of the
Meiji Restoration, traditional Japanese criminal and administrative law
was written, formal, and relatively uniform across the whole of the country. Administrative regulation penetrated deeply into rural Japanese society, as evidenced by the personal registration system that identified
every individual citizen within the country's borders.[13]

As part of their modernization effort, the Japanese invited Western
legal scholars to come to Japan to advise them, and sent out students and
officials to study Western law. The fact that traditional Japanese codes
did not cover entire large domains of law, especially in areas related to
the economy, meant that this had to be imported from the outside. Indeed, there were much deeper problems: the Japanese language had no
word equivalent to the French *droit*, German *Recht*, or English *right*.
There was no concept, so basic to European and American law, that
rights inhered in individuals prior to their coming together in society,
and that part of the role of government was to protect those individual
rights. The idea of natural rights embodied in the U.S. Declaration of
Independence was considered but explicitly rejected in the formulation
of the Meiji constitution.[14]

Given this tradition, then, it was probably inevitable that after studying English Common Law, Japan passed it up in favor of a civil law system
based on those of France and Germany. The English version, with its
sprawling decentralized system of judge-made law, was less suited to
Japanese traditions than the more compact civil system that could be
grafted onto existing Japanese bureaucratic traditions. Many parts of the
civil code were imported wholesale, culminating in an expanded Civil
Code in 1907; traditional Japanese law was retained in family matters,
where rules regarding the *ie* or household were extended from the samurai class to the whole of society.[15]

By adopting the Civil Code, Japan had implemented a modern rule
by law. Rule of law, however, implies further the notion that rules will be
binding not just on ordinary citizens but also on the sovereign himself,

which meant in this case the emperor. In modern political systems, this is typically done through adoption of a formal, written constitution that spells out the source of sovereign authority and clearly defines (and thereby limits) the powers of government. The Japanese government did this in 1889 by promulgating the Meiji Constitution, which remained in effect until adoption of the American-written post–World War II constitution in 1947.

The Meiji Constitution was drafted in secrecy by five men, one of whom was a German constitutional expert, Carl Friedrich Hermann Rösler. It followed on a thirteen-month trip to Europe undertaken by the most powerful Meiji oligarch, Itō Hirobumi, to study European constitutionalism. The fact that he chose to spend this much time abroad studying the issue, and the fact that his colleagues allowed him to do so, is indicative of the importance the leadership accorded the law for Japan's future. (Itō would later serve as resident-general of Korea, and was assassinated in 1909 by a Korean nationalist.)

The Meiji Constitution rejected the English model of parliamentary sovereignty in favor of a more conservative one closer to the Bismarck constitution of the German Empire.[16] It vested sovereignty not in the people of Japan, but in the emperor. All of the powers of subordinate bodies were therefore derived from the emperor's authority. He had the right to appoint ministers, make war and peace, and thereby had exclusive control over the military. The constitution provided for a hereditary House of Peers and a Diet that was elected under an extremely limited property franchise that included no more than 1 percent of the population. The Diet had budgetary authority, but it lacked the power to lower the budget; in the event it failed to support the government's proposed budget, the previous year's one would take effect. The constitution enumerated a long list of citizen rights but immediately qualified them by saying that they were subject to law and the requirements of peace and order. These rights were regarded, in any event, not as natural or God-given but as the result of the generosity of the emperor who bestowed them.[17]

Evaluations of the Meiji Constitution vary substantially depending on whether the observer sees the glass as half empty or half full. George Akita points out that Japan's turn to militarism during the 1930s has led many contemporary Japanese scholars to emphasize the Meiji Constitution's deviations from good democratic practice, and to see those as inevitably preparing the ground for later unbridled authoritarianism. He argues, however, that it makes more sense to see the glass as half full. Japan went from a situation in which there were no formal limitations whatsoever on imperial power to one in which power was regularized and limited in a variety of ways. Although the emperor appointed ministers, all of his decrees had to be countersigned by one of them. Executive powers were shared with the privy council (modeled on the British precedent), a council of elder statesmen known as the genro, and, during the 1910s and '20s, with the prime minister and his cabinet. And the elected Diet's ability to in effect veto budget increases gave it substantial leverage over the government in an era of steadily rising fiscal expenditures, a power that became evident the moment the first Diet was seated. As in the German Rechtsstaat, the formal vesting of sovereignty in the emperor did not lead to the capricious and arbitrary exercise of authority, since the sovereign was committed to governing through a rule-bound bureaucracy.[18]

It is of course much better to have a fully democratic constitution protecting individual rights than the kind of semi-authoritarian one represented by the Meiji Constitution, or for that matter the Bismarck constitution. Political orders that concentrate too much power in a small set of hands invite abuse in both economic and political affairs. A true rule of law has to be binding on the state itself and the major elites that stand behind the state. Since there is no third party to enforce the constitution, its durability depends much more on the degree to which major interest groups see it in their self-interest to abide by its terms. So the question that needs to be asked about Japan's constitution is, Who were the social and political actors that were pushing for limitations on the sovereign powers of the emperor? Why did the Japanese oligarchs accept legal limitations on their power, when they could have ruled in a much more arbitrary fashion?

In this respect, the Japanese settlement of 1889 was very different from the English one of 1689 because the Japanese state faced very few organized opposition groups, of either an elite or a grassroots variety. The most powerful and dangerous class were former samurai, who had suffered the greatest loss of status and income as a result of the Meiji Restoration. Not allowed to carry their swords and made to cut off their traditional topknots in favor of shorter Western hairstyles, many of them were forced into ignoble occupations like business or farming, or else sank into poverty. Former samurai staged half a dozen armed uprisings after the restoration, but with the military defeat of the Satsuma Rebellion in 1877 they disappeared from politics. Another disgruntled group were peasants, many of whom were hit hard by the Meiji reforms of the land tax and military conscription. They staged a number of protests during the 1870s, but in the end discontent remained local and the group was never organized into a national movement or party. Finally, there were middle-class liberals who adopted Western ideas of freedom and democracy. This group formed the Popular Rights Movement and established a Jiyūtō (Liberal Party). They circulated petitions and organized protests, and faced repression by the Meiji regime, which led some members to turn to assassinations and armed resistance. But the wind was taken out of the sails of the Popular Rights Movement when the government announced in 1871 the emperor's intention to grant a constitution by the end of the decade.[19]

Thus the Japanese constitution, in contrast to the English one, was not the result of a prolonged conflict between two well-established social groups who agreed, in effect, to share power. Nor was the Meiji Constitution the product of grassroots mobilization on the part of middle- and lower-class social groups who sought to force a constitution on a reluctant monarch, as happened during the French Revolution. Virtually all observers agree that both the writing and the granting of the new constitution were heavily top-down processes, pushed by actors at the pinnacle of power like Itō Hirobumi. The oligarch's hand may have been forced by the Popular Rights Movement, but he remained in control of the political process at all times. There was no equivalent of the Arab Spring in Japan.[20]

The force ultimately driving Japan to establish a constitution was not a domestic social group but the example of foreigners. No Western power was, at this point, overtly trying to coerce Japan to grant a constitution. Rather, the Japanese themselves saw adoption of a constitution as a necessary condition for their recognition as a great power with rights equal to those of the West. They were following a syllogism that said, "All modern states have constitutions; Japan aspires to be a modern state; therefore Japan must have a constitution." The immediate political pretext for making these changes was the desire to abolish the unequal treaties, something that was in fact accomplished by 1899. But this objective was driven less by economic interest than by the desire for the recognition of Japan's status as a modern society in the eyes of Western powers.[21]

BUREAUCRATIC AUTONOMY GOES BERSERK

As in Germany, the modern Weberian bureaucracies created by Japan after the Meiji Restoration became so autonomous that they led the country to disaster. I would argue that the origin of Japan's turn to the right in the 1930s was rooted in this development rather than in any deeper social causes.

One of the most famous efforts to explain Japan's "fascist" turn in social terms is that of Barrington Moore. He argues that there were three distinct paths to modernity, and that peasants played a critical part in each. The first was the democratic one exemplified by England and the northern American states, in which peasant agriculture and feudal political arrangements were forcibly converted into commercial agriculture (England), or didn't exist in the first place because of the predominance of family farming (the American North). The second route was modernization via peasant revolution, which was the path taken by Communist Russia and China. And the third path was the fascist one, in which a repressive system of agriculture bred an authoritarian state that then escaped the control of its creators.[22]

Moore's arguments for why there was never a Chinese- or Russian-style peasant revolution in Japan are fairly convincing. The Tokugawa system of taxation encouraged increases in agricultural productivity in the century preceding the Meiji Restoration. Peasants were actually growing richer over time. Moreover, the collective manner in which taxes were assessed, and the relative impersonality of the government as tax collector, led to a high degree of communal solidarity or social capital at a village level. This stands in sharp contrast to China, where tax farming—that is, the outsourcing of tax collection to often predatory private agents—as well as family-centered individualism bred distrust on the part of the peasantry.[23] There was a much higher degree of peasant discontent and anger in Qing China than in Meiji Japan, an anger that would be ultimately mobilized by the Chinese Communist Party. While there were peasant revolts accompanying the increasing commercialization of agriculture in Japan both before and after the Meiji Restoration, they did not reach a level that was sufficient to breed a nationwide uprising.[24]

Less convincing is Moore's effort to relate rural land tenure to the rise of the militarist governments of the 1930s. He wants to draw parallels between Japan and Prussia, a country whose military was indeed implicated in the increasingly repressive system of agrarian land tenure from the sixteenth century on. The Prussian officer corps was recruited directly from the class of Junker landlords who in civilian life were busy repressing their own peasants. But in Japan, feudal land tenure was already being replaced by freer forms of tenancy and commercial agriculture by the late nineteenth century. There were large landlords who survived until the American-imposed land reform of the late 1940s, forming part of the conservative parties' political base. But they were politically a much less important part of the conservative coalition in Japan than were the Junkers in Germany before World War I, or the large estancia owners of Argentina at the time of the 1930 coup, and they were actually opposed by bureaucratic activists within the emerging militarist state.[25]

Indeed, absent an autonomous military, it would be perfectly possible to posit a counterfactual history where Japan evolved in a more English-style democratic direction. Having sat out World War I, the country experienced a vigorous period of economic expansion, which led to the rapid growth of an urban middle class and the spread of higher levels of education. The boom suddenly came to an end in 1920 with the return of the European powers to Asian markets. The prolonged recession that followed saw the growth of trade unions and labor unrest, the rise of various Marxist and left-wing groups, and the consolidation of industrial capitalism on the part of the country's huge industrial groups, or *zaibatsu*. None of these developments should have been necessarily fatal to democracy, since they were also occurring in Britain, France, and the United States at the time. Had participation by these new groups been accommodated by parties that were increasingly able to contest for power in the Japanese Diet, democracy would have been consolidated by the 1930s.[26]

What blocked this path were decisions taken by Japan's military, which was deployed not in Japan but in Japan's overseas empire. In a sense, Japanese authoritarianism was born in Manchuria, rather than in Tokyo or in the Japanese countryside. The navy was smarting from concessions made to Britain and the United States at the Washington Naval Conference of 1930. The army, for its part, hoped to establish a state-within-a-state in Manchuria. Lower-ranking officers of the Kwantung Army there assassinated the warlord Chang Tso-lin, and after the September 1931 Manchurian Incident seized most of southern Manchuria. The civilian government back in Tokyo was divided and failed to respond adequately. The Meiji Constitution gave the elected civilian government no direct authority over the military in any case. To an even greater extent than in pre–World War I Germany, the emperor became captive of the armed forces rather than being their commander. Thus began a period of mounting political violence in which military or right-wing political zealots, acting in the name of the emperor, began assassinating civilian politicians, including Prime Ministers Hamaguchi and Inukai in 1930 and 1932. Radical officers attempted a coup in 1936; although they were stopped, the civilian government was so intimidated that it was unable to prevent the Kwantung Army from provoking the Marco Polo Bridge incident in 1937 and plunging into a full-scale invasion of China.[27]

Unlike German and Italian fascism, Japanese militarism was not connected to a mass political party. While the military had civilian allies in various right-wing groups, it did not rest on a strong social base within Japan as the German military did. It was a creature of the younger officers in Japan's field armies, like Ishiwara Kanji, architect of the Manchurian Incident, who in his travels and studies developed a concept of the coming "total war" between the great powers. The Japanese military developed its own anticapitalist national ideology, deploring the materialism and selfishness of industrial society, and looked back nostalgically to an imagined agrarian past. But what it celebrated was less peasant life than the honor-bound ethos of the old military aristocracy. Bureaucratic autonomy within the military was especially strong due to "the time-honored right of local commanders to undertake operations in emergency situations without waiting for direct orders from central military headquarters."[28] In the course of the 1930s, the agents succeeded in turning themselves into principals.

LAW AND DEMOCRACY

A genuine rule of law finally arrived in Japan with its defeat in the Pacific War and adoption of an American-drafted constitution in 1947 that has remained in force without amendment until the present day. There were a number of important legal steps leading up to this result, including the August 16, 1945, announcement by the emperor that Japan had accepted the Potsdam Declaration and unconditional surrender, and the Imperial Rescript of January 1, 1946, in which the emperor renounced the doctrine of imperial divinity.[29] The government of the defeated and occupied Japan had drafted a set of minor revisions to the Meiji Constitution which, when leaked to the press, induced General Douglas MacArthur, the Supreme Commander for the Allied Powers, to order the drafting of a very different document, which was delivered to a shocked Japanese government in February 1946.

The American draft contained a number of key changes. Sovereignty was no longer vested in the emperor, but in the Japanese people; the peerage system was abolished; a list of basic rights was enumerated and not qualified in the manner of the Meiji Constitution; and the famous Article 9 renounced Japan's right of warmaking and maintenance of a military. The constitution was debated before a newly elected Diet and came into effect on May 3, 1947.[30]

Contemporary Japanese nationalists like Ishihara Shintaro, former governor of Tokyo, have criticized Article 9 and the postwar constitution as a whole as having been imposed on Japan, and argue for amending it to restore the right to military power and self-defense. Before we accept this narrative, however, we should note that the Americans tried to impose a lot of different policies on Japan after 1945, some of which became very durable and some of which failed. Besides the democratic system embodied in the constitution itself, the durable policies included land reform that ended the system of tenancy and distributed agricultural land to individual farmers, and the strengthening of women's legal and political rights. The vast majority of Japanese were subsequently quite grateful that these changes had been forced on them, particularly women, whose rights were secured due to the tenacity of a young woman named Beate Sirota who served on the constitutional drafting committee.[31] The Japanese system had been stuck, in effect, in an equilibrium where the existing actors would never have agreed to certain changes—popular rather than imperial sovereignty, land reform, and women's rights—on their own. The Americans did not force Japan to accept a distasteful outcome as much as help the Japanese to reach a more positive equilibrium.

On the other hand, the Americans failed to bring about certain other changes they desired. One was a dismantling of the *zaibatsu*, the huge industrial conglomerates that were held to be responsible for funding and pushing for war. The *zaibatsu* formally disbanded but quickly reconstituted themselves on an informal basis as *keiretsu* (built around famous brands like Sumitomo, Mitsui, and Mitsubishi), where they went on to be the basis for the country's subsequent economic miracle.[32]

Moreover, both the borrowed and imposed legal codes that make up contemporary Japanese law are implemented quite differently in Japan than they are in Europe and North America. Japan as well as other Asian countries has always been less litigious than the United States, and the number of lawyers and lawsuits per capita actually declined during the three decades following the end of the Pacific War. The Japanese make much heavier use of arbitration and informal dispute resolution processes than do Westerners.[33]

A final area of the failure of imposed institutions was the effort to bring Japan's bureaucratic apparatus under greater democratic control, or in other words, to reduce its autonomy. As in Germany, the Allied occupation authorities sought to purge the bureaucracy of what they regarded as war criminals and ultranationalists. But the need to keep Japan stable and well governed, especially under the pressures of an emerging cold war, cut short this effort. In many cases, only the wartime ministers and vice ministers were removed from their positions; younger bureaucrats simply moved up the promotion ladder while keeping their bureaucratic traditions alive. So even under its new democratic constitution, the bureaucracy remained the center of Japanese political decision making. While the long-dominant Liberal Democratic Party (LDP) controlled spending decisions and doled out pork-barrel subsidies to favored interests, it never succeeded in penetrating the bureaucracy and placing its own people there. Rather the reverse: the bureaucracy produced countless officials who, after retirement (called *amakudari*, or "descent from heaven"), went on to important political leadership positions and facilitated the hand-in-glove cooperation between the LDP and the government. This bureaucracy became one leg of the "iron triangle" that included the business sector and Liberal Democratic Party that dominated Japanese politics for two generations.

Indeed, it has become clear in retrospect that much of the bureaucratic system centering around the Ministry of International Trade and Industry (MITI, now the Ministry of Economy, Trade and Industry) that guided Japan's postwar economic miracle was the descendant of the wartime planning bureaucracy. This agency had its distant origins in a group of officers connected with the Kwantung Army in Manchuria, which instituted a centrally planned economic system for that territory. This system was brought back in 1941 to Japan itself and became the core of the wartime resource allocation system.[34] Thus the American trade negotiators of the 1970s and '80s were contending over economic issues with descendants of the bureaucrats their fathers had fought during the Pacific War.

While the Japanese bureaucracy was powerful relative to other parts of the political system, in its postwar incarnation it was never as centralized and decisive as its Chinese counterpart. Power tended to be diffused among a variety of agencies, each of which was pervaded by cliques and factions that had to seek consensus before being able to make a decision. In recent years, this has reinforced a tendency to put off making difficult choices, whether concerning nuclear power or agricultural subsidies. Moreover, there is strong evidence that the bureaucratic system itself has decayed, with the end of the *amakudari* system in 2007, which reduced incentives for elite recruitment, and the efforts of political parties to place their supporters in key bureaucratic roles.

JAPAN'S MISSING SOVEREIGNTY

Japan's political development since the mid-nineteenth century set a pattern that would be followed, with variations, by a number of other East Asian societies.

Prior to its encounter with the West, Japan was already endowed with a strong state that had many characteristics of Weberian bureaucracy, with a state-society "balance" heavily weighted in favor of the state. There were different social groups—farmers, merchants, and warriors—but they were not organized for collective action in a manner comparable to Europe's independent cities, churches, guilds, and the like. Thus civil society had a much harder time constraining the state through demands for a rule of law and accountable government.

Japanese civil society grew enormously after the country democratized, with the emergence of environmental, feminist, media, nationalist, and religious groups of various sorts. But the ability of Japanese civil society to mobilize for political ends remains weak relative to other industrialized democracies. The rise of the Democratic Party of Japan and its capture of the prime ministership in 2009 represents, in some sense, the emergence of a stronger oppositional culture. But its poor subsequent performance in response to events like the 2011 Tohoku earthquake and Fukushima nuclear crisis casts doubts on the durability of this shift.

What compensated for a missing indigenous civil society were foreign pressures. The Meiji oligarchs accepted constraints on their powers not because there was a powerful domestic mobilization of citizens demanding their rights, but rather because they wanted the Western powers to accord them equal status. The 1947 constitution was even more directly imposed on the country. The only reason that it has remained legitimate and stable for almost seventy years is Japan's position in the international system. Through Article 9 and the 1951 U.S.-Japan Security Treaty, Japan has in effect outsourced an important element of its security, the capacity for self-defense, to the United States. Only as long as the U.S. commitment to defend Japan remains credible in the face of threats from countries like North Korea and China will the 1947 constitution remain viable. (Germany, the other defeated power from World War II, did much the same thing, outsourcing its sovereignty to NATO and the European Union.) The strongly nationalist prime minister Shinzō Abe who returned to power in 2012 has stated his intention to seek revision of Article 9, and return Japan to the status of a more normal sovereign country. If this happens, many of the features of the postwar settlement may change as well.

Japan set a further precedent to be followed by other Asian countries, which lay in the moral qualities of its authoritarian rulers. These qualities were rooted, in turn, in Japan's Confucian heritage. In the words of George Akita, the Meiji leaders

> believed first of all in a benevolent elitism which stemmed from the acceptance of a natural hierarchy based on ability . . . Like good Confucians, the Meiji leaders were fully aware that only a thin line divided enlightened from despotic elites . . . If the sovereign and the governed were expected to exert efforts for the common good, the implication is that the masses could be educated and trained to rise up to the point where they could meaningfully participate in the government.[35]

The Meiji oligarchs, as well as the senior bureaucrats like Kishi Nobusuke who led Japan in the 1950s, or Sahashi Shigeru who directed MITI during its postwar heyday, were arrogant, disdained the rights of ordinary citizens, and hungered for power. But compared to authoritarian leaders in other parts of the world, they had a keen sense of themselves as servants of a higher public interest. The Meiji oligarchs were so self-effacing that hardly anyone today who is not a careful student of Japanese history even knows their names. They were also extremely competent in building on tradition while simultaneously moving the country forward toward development goals for which there was no historical precedent.

This Confucian tradition originates of course in China, to which we turn next.

24

THE STRUGGLE FOR LAW IN CHINA

How the state preceded law in China; rule by law in dynastic China; the beginnings of constitutionalism in modern China; Mao and the absence of law; rebuilding rule-based behavior in contemporary China

Japanese institutions ultimately came from China. In China, a centralized state with many of the characteristics that Weber identified as modern existed already at the time of the Qin Dynasty in 221 B.C. and was consolidated during the Former Han Dynasty (206 B.C.–A.D. 9). China built a centralized, merit-based bureaucracy that was able to register its population, levy uniform taxes, control the military, and regulate society some eighteen hundred years before a similar state was to emerge in Europe.[1]

This precociously modern state was then able to forestall the emergence of powerful social actors that could challenge its predominance. In Europe, an entrenched blood nobility, independent commercial cities, and religious organizations from the Catholic church to various Protestant sects all had independent bases of power and could limit the power of states. In China, these groups had their counterparts, but they were initially weaker, and the strong state acted to keep them that way. Thus there was a Chinese aristocracy, but it did not exercise territorial sovereignty to the extent of its European counterpart; religions like Buddhism and Daoism were kept under strict control; and cities resembled the administrative centers of Europe east of the Elbe rather than the self-governing independent metropolises of Western Europe. Critically, power was dispersed in Europe at an international level to a far greater degree than in China, due as noted earlier to the region's different geography. This meant that any European state that tried to concentrate power and build an empire would face immediate resistance from its neighbors. These neighbors could fight aggression militarily at a state level and were more than happy to support internal opponents of the imperial power. European state consolidation by the mid-twentieth century reached a level that China experienced midway through the Warring States period (475–221 B.C.), when the total number of large states was reduced to half a dozen or so. Perhaps the European Union will one day complete the process of unification that China achieved at the beginning of the Qin Dynasty, but the fact that it has not happened yet suggests how different the state-society balance has been in Europe than in China.

The China that the European colonial powers encountered was ruled by the Qing (1644–1911), a foreign dynasty from Manchuria, late in its dynastic cycle. The first Qing emperor, Shunzhi, had simply taken over Ming institutions and used Ming personnel to run the existing administrative apparatus.[2] In those years, the agrarian economy of China was not terribly different from what it was during the Han Dynasty some sixteen hundred years earlier. But all of this changed dramatically beginning in the seventeenth century, as a much more extensive commercial economy started to take off. Like Europe and the Ottoman Empire, China experienced both price inflation and a rapidly growing population from the seventeenth century on.[3] British, Portuguese, and Dutch traders began showing up in southern Chinese ports, tying China to a broader system of global trade. A much larger and more independent commercial class emerged. Rather than being completely dependent on the government for their well-being, China's merchants became a source of capital and were thus modestly able to increase their autonomy vis-à-vis the government. Toward the end of the nineteenth century, a small middle class began to appear in Chinese cities, from which many of the leaders of the 1912 Chinese revolution that ended dynastic China would be drawn.

Historian Kenneth Pomeranz argues that Europe had no significant technological or institutional advantages over China in the middle of the eighteenth century. In his view, Britain's subsequent takeoff during the Industrial Revolution was largely the accidental by-product of its access to abundant coal and foreign supplies of raw materials like cotton.[4] The Industrial Revolution, however, was the result not only of the availability of certain resource inputs but also of the integration of several critical subsystems: a scientific system that could induce general theories from observed facts; a technological system that allowed this knowledge to be applied to the solution of practical tasks; a property rights system that created incentives for technological innovation; a certain degree of cultural curiosity about the outside world; an educational system that increasingly focused on training students in scientific and technical fields; and finally, a political system that allowed and indeed encouraged all of these things to happen at the same time. China may have had several of these pieces in place; what it lacked might be called the "systems integration" capacity that could pull all of them together at the same time. This systems integration function ultimately needs to be provided by the political regime. As Japan would shortly demonstrate, and as contemporary China now proves, there are no deep cultural reasons why Asian societies are incapable of such integration. But this did not happen in the rigid and conservative China of the nineteenth century.[5]

The late Qing Dynasty could draw on a two-millennium-long tradition of stateness that allowed it to avoid total colonization in the manner of Africa. But by the nineteenth century it was deeply mired in ritual practices and rigidities that prevented it from adapting to the competitive pressures brought to bear by the European powers. China's "century of humiliation" began in 1839 when the Qing government tried to ban imports of opium and were forced by the British to open their ports during the First Opium War. The Treaty of Nanking in 1843 ceded Hong Kong to Britain, gave extraterritorial rights to foreign nationals, and paved the way for further concessions to France, the United States, and other Western powers. A protonationalist Boxer Rebellion at the turn of the twentieth century sought to expel foreign influence, but it was defeated by the Western powers and led to the imposition of a huge indemnity on China. Japan defeated China in the 1895 Sino-Japanese War, which led to the loss of Taiwan, and of Korea as a vassal state. China itself was progressively occupied by Japan during the 1930s.[6]

The experience of chaos and backwardness in early twentieth-century China convinced many Westerners that Chinese society had always been shambolic and impoverished. But they were encountering a foreign and declining political order that did not reflect the strength of past regimes. The rise of China in the second half of the twentieth century better demonstrates what a young and vigorous dynasty is capable of. Throughout this entire turbulent period, neither the Chinese government nor the Chinese tradition of centralized rule had disappeared. Despite the huge disruptions of the early twentieth century, there are large continuities between dynastic China and the polity presided over by today's Chinese Communist Party.

Then, as now, the central problem of Chinese politics has not been how to concentrate and deploy state power but rather how to constrain it through law and democratic accountability. The task of balancing state, law, and accountability that was completed in Japan by the late 1940s has been only partially accomplished in China. Under Mao Zedong, law virtually disappeared and the country became an arbitrary despotism. Since the reforms that began under Deng Xiaoping in 1978, China has been moving slowly toward a political system that is more rule based. But the rule of law is still far from secured, and the regime's sustainability will depend heavily on whether this becomes the main line of political development in the twenty-first century.

THE NATURE OF CHINESE LAW

China represents the one world civilization that never developed a true rule of law. In ancient Israel, the Christian West, the Muslim world, and India, law originated in a transcendental religion and was interpreted and implemented by a hierarchy of religious scholars and jurists. The keepers of the law in each case were a social group separate from the political authorities—Jewish judges, Hindu Brahmins, Catholic priests and bishops, the Muslim ulama. The degree to which law limited the arbitrary power of rulers depended on the institutional separation of the legal-religious hierarchy from the political one, as well as the degree to which one or the other group was united or divided. This separation was the most dramatic in Western Europe, where the investiture conflict of the late eleventh century resulted in the Catholic church's ability to appoint its own priests and bishops. In stark contrast to China, the rule of law was established well before the creation of modern states, and law put limits on state building that did not exist in China.

In China, by contrast, there was never a transcendental religion, and there was never a pretense that law had a divine origin. Law was seen as a rational human instrument by which the state exercised its authority and maintained public order. This meant that, as in Japan, China had rule by law rather than rule of law. The law did not limit or bind the sovereign himself, who was the ultimate source of law. While the law could be administered impartially, this was not due to any inherent rights possessed by citizens. Rights were rather the gift of a benevolent ruler. Impartiality was simply a condition for good public order. It was for this reason that property rights and private law—contracts, torts, and other issues arising between individuals and not involving the state—were given very little emphasis. This stood in sharp contrast to both the Common Law and the Roman Civil Law traditions in the West.[7]

There was in fact an active hostility to the very idea of law embedded in traditional Chinese culture. The Confucians believed that human life should be regulated not by formal, written laws, but by morality. This revolved around the cultivation of *li*, or correct moral conduct, through education and correct upbringing. The Confucians argued that reliance on written law, or *fa*, was detrimental because formal rules were too broad and general to produce good outcomes in specific cases. Confucian ethics is highly situational or context dependent: the right outcome depends heavily on the relationship and status of the parties involved, the specific facts of the case, and conditions that cannot be known or specified in advance. Good outcomes are produced not by the impersonal application of rules but by a sage or superior man who can weigh local context. Having a good emperor at the top of the system is a condition for its proper functioning.[8]

In contrast to the Confucian viewpoint, the Legalist school in ancient China argued in favor of written law. Unlike the Confucians, who saw human nature as essentially good and educable, the Legalists believed that human beings were selfish and prone to disorder. Behavior needed to be regulated not through morality but through strict incentives—above all, extremely harsh punishments for transgressions. The Legalists argued, in the words of one historian, that a government must "publicize its laws to all and to apply them impartially to high and low alike, irrespective of relationship or rank," and that "Law is the basis of stable government because, being fixed and known to all, it provides an exact instrument with which to measure individual conduct." By contrast, "A government based on *li* cannot do this, since the *li* are unwritten, particularistic and subject to arbitrary interpretation."[9] In many ways, the Legalist tradition comes much closer to the contemporary Western understanding of law as general, clearly stated, and impartial rules, and of human behavior being determined primarily by incentives rather than moral norms. If the Western tradition seeks to limit the autonomy of governments through law, the Chinese tradition seeks to maximize it through a more flexible system of morality.[10]

Although the Legalist school disappeared after the beginning of the Han Dynasty in the second century B.C., subsequent Chinese government was always something of an amalgamation of the Confucian and Legalist positions. Major legal codes were promulgated during the Han, Tang, Ming, and Qing Dynasties, which were mostly lists of punishments for criminal offenses in the Legalist tradition. However, the law specified many different outcomes dependent on circumstance, along Confucian lines.[11] Formal law always played a much smaller role in regulating Chinese social behavior than it did in the West. Many disputes were adjudicated under customary (that is, unwritten) rules of the lineage, clan, or village rather than being settled through the court system. Formal litigation was denigrated. Judges were not a separate, high-status group as in Israel, the Middle East, India, and Europe, but were just another species of bureaucrat without their own separate training institutions and guildlike traditions. In Europe, the first bureaucrats in the Middle Ages were recruited out of the ranks of lawyers, and lawyers played central political roles in later events like the French Revolution. Nothing like this was ever remotely the case in China.[12]

CHINA GETS A CONSTITUTION

The Manchu regime ruling Qing China was much slower to react to the Western challenge than were the rulers of Meiji Japan. Responding to Western criticisms of traditional Chinese law, particularly with respect to the cruelty of punishments, a commission led by Shen Jiaben was established in 1902 to recommend revisions to the Qing Code.

The Chinese reformers were motivated, as were the Japanese, by fear that their military and political weakness stemmed from defects in their traditional institutions. Much like contemporary developing countries facing the International Monetary Fund, they understood that they had to align their own practices with Western standards as a condition for being treated as sovereign equals. Members of the commission traveled to Japan, Europe, and the United States to study alternative constitutional models, and by 1911 they had drafted an extensively revised code that contained new provisions related to commercial law, procedure, and judicial organization. Like the Japanese, the Chinese reformers considered and then rejected Common Law in favor of Civil Law; in their revisions of criminal law they borrowed a great deal of the German code virtually intact. They copied much of the Japanese approach since Japan had so successfully used it to overturn the unequal treaties in the previous decade. Two Japanese scholars, Okada Asataro and Matsuoka Yoshitada, established the first modern law school in Beijing in 1906. These reforms met substantial resistance from conservatives in the court, who were particularly upset with changes affecting the traditional family.[13]

The old regime proposed a nine-year plan to replace the old empire with a constitutional monarchy, based on wholesale importation of the Meiji Constitution (minus its modest restrictions on imperial powers). Neither the revised code nor the proposed constitution could be implemented, however, before the regime faced an armed uprising in 1911. A last-minute promulgation of a constitution known as the Nineteen Articles was too little and too late to save the regime, which was replaced by a Chinese republic the following year.[14] In the ensuing period of warlordism and civil war, constitutions were enacted by various political actors to burnish their legitimacy, but few had any real effect in limiting power.[15]

The leading exponent of Chinese revival following the 1911 Revolution was Sun Yat-sen, leader of the Nationalist movement. While he appealed to Abraham Lincoln and the French Revolution as sources of inspiration, the Guomindang party (KMT) he created was both Leninist and authoritarian. After KMT's break with the Communists in 1927, the party, under the leadership of Chiang Kai-shek, promulgated an organic law that was to serve as a provisional constitution for the Republic of China. This law entrenched single-party rule by the KMT for a period of tutelage, which was formally ended only in 1946 by adoption of a constitution of the Republic of China (ROC). Once it had retreated to Taiwan after the Communist victory in 1949, the KMT government remained a dictatorship through emergency powers granted on the basis of the existence of a "Period of Communist Rebellion." True constitutional government came to the Republic of China on Taiwan only in 1991, with the formal ending of the "rebellion" and the lifting of military rule.[16]

While the constitutions of the early twentieth century were largely meaningless, the same cannot be said of the revisions to the civil code that were published by the KMT in 1929–1930, some of which have been preserved in contemporary laws of the People's Republic of China. There were three major areas of reform, some carried forward from the proposed revisions to the Qing Code of 1911. The first was the shift from the old Qing Code's schedules of proscriptions and punishments to a system recognizing the rights and responsibilities of citizens. For the first time, Chinese citizens were seen not simply as the subjects of state power but as individuals with positive legal entitlements. The second shift was economic. The old Qing Code had embedded property rights in the lineage or patrilineal kin group, and the right to alienate property was severely entailed by the obligations of one family member to another. The KMT code, by contrast, recognized property rights that were individual and freely alienable. It put into effect a whole domain of private law involving contract and torts, which had been regarded as "minor matters" in Qing law. And finally, it attacked the legal basis of the patrilineal family by giving women full rights to inherit property and the ability to contest those rights before the courts. This was one area in which Chinese legal reform outpaced reform that had taken place in Japan up to that date.[17]

MAO'S ASSAULT ON LAW

When the Chinese Communists came to power in 1949, they liberated the mainland from foreign occupation and restored the sovereignty of a centralized state. Mao Zedong had by this point acquired such stature as "the Great Helmsman" that he was able to embark on a personal dictatorship so extreme that it completely dismantled all semblance of law. Even though emperors in dynastic China were in theory absolute sovereigns, their power was in fact limited by the bureaucracy and the myriad rules, procedures, and rituals by which the court operated. One would have to go back to Qin Shi Huangdi, unifier of China in the third century B.C., Wu Zhao, the "evil empress Wu" of the Tang Dynasty in the seventh century, or the first Ming emperor, Zhu Yuangzhang, in the fourteenth, to find precedents for Mao's personal exercise of power. It is no accident that Mao celebrated Shang Yang, the Legalist mastermind of the dictatorial state of Qin that unified China, as a protototalitarian predecessor.[18]

One of Mao's first acts on coming to power was to abolish at one stroke all of the codes developed by the KMT government. Where law was used, it was an arbitrary terroristic weapon to fight the Chinese Communist Party's (CCP) "class enemies." In 1952–1953, law itself became a target as judges and clerks with legal training under the former nationalist government were purged and replaced with party cadres. The criminal law was used to go after perceived enemies, and the police began to operate independently of the judicial system, creating a vast network of detention camps and attacking groups like "landlords," "counter-revolutionaries," and "rich peasants." In a country where private property was being eliminated, civil law essentially did not exist. As Premier Zhou Enlai was to explain in 1958, "Why should we proletarians be restrained by laws?! . . . Our law should be developed in pace with the changes of the economic base. Institutions, rules and regulations should not be fixed. We should not be afraid of changes. We have advocated uninterrupted revolutions and the law should be in the service of the continuing revolution . . . It does not matter if we make a law today and change it tomorrow."[19] Mao himself asserted that "[we must] depend on rule of man, not rule of law."

No society, of course, can live entirely without rules, and as the Communist Party sought to stabilize and expand the economy in the 1950s, it began rebuilding law by importing statutes from the Soviet Union. But this process was cut short by the Anti-Rightist Movement in 1957 and the Great Leap Forward of 1958. The latter was an ideologically driven campaign whose goal was to mobilize mass support for industrialization but instead brought about a famine estimated to have killed thirty-six million people.[20] After this disaster, there was another brief effort to rebuild a legal system during the early 1960s, which was in turn brought to an end by Mao's Cultural Revolution of 1966–1976. Mao's revolution ended any semblance of rule-based administration, undermined the operations of government, and terrorized the party itself, much like Stalin's purges of the Soviet Communist Party during the 1930s.[21]

REBUILDING RULE BY LAW AFTER 1978

It is impossible to understand the China that emerged after the death of Mao and the reforms that began in 1978 except in relation to the trauma experienced by those who lived through the Cultural Revolution. The Communist elite that survived this period, led by one of the greatest statesmen of the twentieth century, Deng Xiaoping, was determined that Mao's form of personal dictatorship must never be allowed to occur again. The political reform process that unfolded subsequently centered around the slow construction of a series of rules that would limit the ability of any future charismatic leader to emerge and wreak havoc on the whole of Chinese society in the manner of Mao. In addition, law was seen as a mechanism by which the party could channel and monitor popular grievances against the government. As a result, nearly forty years after Mao's death, China has become a far more law-governed and traditionally bureaucratic society.

It has not, however, become a society governed by a rule *of* law. Even though leaders at the top levels of the Chinese Communist Party have agreed on rules to manage their relationships with one another, they have nonetheless never acknowledged the supremacy of law itself over the party. The evolution of constitutions since the founding of the People's Republic of China (PRC) tells a story about the failure of the Communist Party to create a true rule of law.

Virtually all Communist countries followed the lead of the former Soviet Union in adopting formal constitutions that were essentially worthless pieces of paper in terms of any real constraints on political power. The PRC's first constitution, which was adopted in 1954, enshrined the Socialist principles from the CCP's 1949 Common Program and imported many provisions from the Soviet constitution wholesale. The gradual implementation of "social transformation" noted in this document was then rejected in favor of a more leftist constitution drafted during the Cultural Revolution in 1975 that openly called for the dictatorship of the party over the state.

Since Mao's death in 1976 and the fall of the so-called Gang of Four, there have been new constitutions or major constitutional revisions promulgated in 1978, 1982, 1988, 1993, 1999, and 2004. These revisions largely reflected the shift to the right and the opening toward a market economy that was taking place in the political realm. Article 18 of the 1982 constitution, for example, provided a basis for foreign investment and its protection, while the 1988 revision provided for the commercial transfer of land use rights. The 1992 revision substituted "socialist market economy" for "planned economy," and "state-run enterprises" with "state-owned enterprises." The newer versions also returned some powers from the party to the state, reflecting the latter's larger role in economic management.

These constitutional provisions, however, were more declarations of new policy initiatives decided on by the party than serious legal instruments that would govern the party's own behavior. The contemporary Chinese constitution is built around two potentially contradictory principles. On the one hand, Deng Xiaoping asserted in 1978 that "democracy has to be institutionalized and written into law, so as to make sure that institutions and laws do not change whenever the leadership changes, or whenever the leaders change their views."[22] The Chinese constitution provides for an elected National People's Congress (NPC), which is held to be the "supreme organ of state power," along with people's congresses at lower levels of government. The constitution further states that the Communist Party must operate under its provisions and the law. China scholar Kenneth Lieberthal notes that in the decades after 1978, the NPC has played a greater role in policy deliberation and has passed "a remarkable corpus of formal law" in areas not regarded as inherently political by the party. This contrasts with the virtually lawless state of affairs under Mao.[23]

On the other hand, the Four Fundamental Principles with which the constitution begins enshrine the domination of the political system by the Communist Party, which in practice exercises strict control over the government and legislature. No one has authority to modify the constitution other than the party, and all existing constitutional documents were rubber-stamped by NPCs with little discussion. Prior to the 2004 constitutional revisions, it appeared that the party was permitting some open discussion of them by academics and other commentators, but these were quickly shut down and the final changes were essentially dictated to the NPC for ratification. The party clearly operates above and not under the law. As in dynastic China, law remains an instrument of rule, and not an intrinsic source of legitimacy.[24]

THE SPREAD OF RULES

China since the beginning of the reforms in 1978 has seen a large and gradual increase both in formal laws and informal rules that define and therefore constrain the behavior of lower levels of the government. It is not just the number of formal laws passed but the degree to which decision making is actually rule based that is the measure of an emerging rule by law there. The spread of rule-based decision making, as well as its limitations, can be seen in two areas: property rights and the regulations governing promotion and succession at the top levels of the Communist Party.

When the Deng-era reforms began, China faced a huge legal vacuum, especially in the area of private or civil law. The desire to encourage economic growth and a market economy has led to a rapid proliferation of new laws regarding contracts, joint ventures, land use, insurance, arbitration, and the like. The sources of law in the contemporary PRC are very eclectic, however, and were adopted piecemeal according to discrete requirements rather than implemented as a system, as in the Japanese adoption of the German code in the 1890s. Criminal law, for example, is still largely based on imported Soviet law from the early days of the PRC. In 1986, the NPC adopted the General Principles of Civil Law (GPCL) that was explicitly said to be derived from German civil law. In fact, the derivation came via the Japanese adaptation of the German code and the latter's adoption by the KMT government in the 1930s. Despite the formal cancellation of the KMT codes in 1949, Jianfu Chen notes that "the KMT Civil Code . . . [has] been the very basis upon which civil law and civil law science have been developed in the PRC."[25]

Among the things inherited from the continental civil law tradition by the Chinese is the right of private citizens to sue the government in administrative courts for illegal behavior. The NPC passed an Administrative Litigation Law in 1989 setting forth rules under which government decisions could be appealed or challenged. The party saw this as a useful way of disciplining lower levels of the government, and the number of such suits has risen steadily in the decades since adoption of the GPCL. There are, however, strict limits to the usefulness of such litigation. One study from the 1990s showed that the likelihood of a plaintiff winning a judgment against the government is only about 16 percent in the most progressive provinces. Moreover, it is only the government and not the party that can be sued in this fashion.[26]

The adoption of a civil code ultimately derived from Western sources under the GPCL laid the foundations for the equivalent of Western private law. It recognized a sphere of independent legal actors who could acquire property, enter into contracts, alienate property, and defend their rights before a court system. The reformers faced principled opposition from ideologues within the party who were opposed to ownership of property by anyone other than "the whole people" (that is, the state). They squared this circle by creating a set of usufructuary (usage) rights that could be bought, sold, mortgaged, or transferred, in which the state nonetheless retained formal ownership. Thus, in China's booming real estate market, no one technically "owns" an apartment or house. One owns the equivalent of a lease whose term extends up to seventy years, which is acquired in exchange for land-use fees.[27] Laws regulating contracts similarly try to square individual rights with ultimate state power. They fall short of full freedom of contract because they retain provisions that allow the state to "manage" contracts or void them entirely under poorly defined force majeure conditions.[28]

The 1986 GPCL was never intended to be a comprehensive civil code but rather a statement of general principles that left it up to subsequent ad hoc legislation to fill in the gaps. In addition, the code was modified in certain ways to meet ideological or political criteria. For example, the German and KMT codes in defining legal personhood differentiated between "natural" and "juristic" persons; the GPCL in effect abolished natural personhood by replacing it with the concept of citizenship. This seemingly minor point is in fact important in distinguishing Chinese and Western legal concepts: the latter see natural persons as bearers of rights and duties independently of any action of the state, whereas in China citizenship is something conferred on individuals by the state.[29] Contemporary Chinese law thus continues the traditional Qing practice of not recognizing a separate sphere of individual rights bearers, and of seeing property rights as something benevolently granted to individuals by the state.[30] In practice, the state could at any moment legally take that property for its own purposes. The state has at times tried to promote a rule of law as a means of dampening discontent. This has led to the development of a greater consciousness about legal rights on the part of ordinary Chinese citizens, but also to dashed expectations and increased cynicism about the law given the highly inconsistent enforcement of rules.[31]

Thus while contemporary China is increasingly rule governed, it does not possess Western-style property rights and contract enforcement. Theoretically, the government has not conceded the principle of private ownership, nor has it created a legal system that takes on the fundamental duty to protect private property. Chinese law, courts, litigation, arbitration, and a host of legal or quasi-legal undertakings have mushroomed in the three decades since the beginning of the reform period. But the judiciary still does not have anything like the stature and independence that courts do in Europe, North America, and Japan. Western businesses operating in China face a complicated terrain. While there have been increasingly clear rules promulgated regarding foreign investment, for example, many foreigners find that their Chinese partners treat the contract less as an enforceable legal document than as a symbol of a personal relationship between them. Particularly when dealing with powerful and politically well-connected entities like state-owned enterprises, they have found that their rights are often not protected.[32]

The degree of protection of property rights or contract enforcement remains, in other words, a fundamentally political rather than a legal issue. The Chinese Communist Party has seen fit to protect most property rights because it recognizes that it has a self-interest in doing so. But the party faces no legal constraints other than its own internal political controls if it decides to violate property rights. Many peasants find their land coveted by municipal authorities and developers who want to turn it into commercial real estate, high-density housing, shopping centers, and the like, or else into public infrastructure like roads, dams, or government offices. There are large incentives for developers to work together with corrupt local officials to illegally take land away from peasants or urban homeowners, and such takings have been perhaps the largest single source of social discontent in contemporary China.[33]

Apart from property rights and contracts, a critical area in which rules have spread concerns term limits, retirement, and procedures for leadership recruitment and promotion. One of the biggest liabilities of authoritarian governments in other parts of the world is the unwillingness of leaders to step down after a decent interval, and the lack of an institutionalized system for deciding on succession.[34] I have already noted the length of tenure of many presidents in sub-Saharan Africa, both authoritarian and democratic. One of the drivers of the Arab Spring was the fact that Tunisia's Zine al-Abidine Ben Ali, Egypt's Hosni Mubarak, and Libya's Muammar Qaddafi had clung to power for twenty-three, thirty, and forty-one years respectively. Had any of these leaders set up a regularized system for succession and then stepped down after a term of eight or ten years, he would have left a far more positive legacy for his country and might not have been swept away in a revolutionary upsurge.

One of the factors contributing to the stability and legitimacy of authoritarian rule in China is the fact that the CCP has put such rules in place. The Chinese constitution specifies that senior leaders will serve maximum terms of ten years, and since Deng Xiaoping's retirement there have already been two ten-year cycles of leadership replacement at the 16th and 18th Party Congresses in 2002 and 2012. There are other less formal rules as well, such as one specifying that no one can be a candidate for the Standing Committee of the Politburo of the Communist Party past the age of sixty-seven. Mandatory retirement rules have also been set more broadly for lower levels of the party. While the actual politics of leadership succession at the highest levels remain completely obscure, there is at least an institutionalized process for leadership turnover.[35]

These rules are the direct result of the experience of Mao's Great Leap Forward and Cultural Revolution. As in the Soviet Union under Stalin, it was the senior ranks of the party itself that suffered directly from the unchecked personal dictatorship of a charismatic leader. Many of the rules they subsequently put in place were therefore designed to prevent another such leader from emerging. One of the speculations concerning the sacking of Chongqing party leader Bo Xilai in 2012 was that he was building precisely such a charismatic political base, making use of both populist appeals and Maoist-era nostalgia in a bid to become a member of the Politburo's Standing Committee.

The Bo Xilai affair illustrates both the strengths and weaknesses of rule-based decision making in the contemporary Chinese system. On the one hand, there are both formal and informal rules regarding succession, promotion, and acceptable political behavior on the part of aspiring political leaders. On the other, these rules fall short of genuine constitutional limitations on political power. They reflect a consensus in favor of collective leadership that exists among the current elite of the Communist Party, and particularly those who were old enough to have experienced the Cultural Revolution. But the rules themselves can be modified by that same leadership at a moment's notice.

Among the liberal democracies of Latin America, there has been a flurry of attempts by democratically elected presidents to hang on beyond the term limits specified in their constitutions. Some, like Carlos Menem in Argentina and Rafael Correa in Ecuador, succeeded in amending their countries' constitutions. But because the rules are embedded in stronger rule of law systems, such efforts are both politically costly and not always certain of success. Menem, for example, tried but ultimately failed to add not just a second but a third term to his presidency. Álvaro Uribe in Colombia, having secured an amendment to grant a second term, was stopped from getting a third term by an independent Constitutional Court. For all of the new rules affecting leadership change in China, these sorts of formal checks on power have yet to be created.

Creation of a rule of law that would limit political authority in China is thus still very much a work in progress. The precedent for an expanding rule of law has been set, however, and greater adherence to China's own constitution is an obvious path for future reform.[36] It is for this reason that attacks by China's current leader, Xi Jinping, on the principle of constitutionalism itself are highly regressive.

25

THE REINVENTION OF THE CHINESE STATE

How China's chief historical legacy has been high-quality bureaucracy; the organization of the Chinese party-state; bureaucratic autonomy in China and how it is achieved; the "bad emperor" problem and why China ultimately needs democratic accountability

During the Former Han Dynasty a couple of centuries before the birth of Jesus Christ, a centralized government existed in China that had many of the characteristics that Max Weber associated with modern bureaucracy. The government had the capacity to perform cadastral surveys and register the country's large population. It created a centralized bureaucracy that was literate, well educated, and organized into a functional hierarchy. The beginnings of a civil service examination system were already in place that included a channel of upward social mobility for bright but poor young men. This bureaucracy could impose land taxes on its large peasant population and conscript them into military service. The Chinese state mandated uniform weights and measures to promote commerce. The bureaucracy also sought to be impersonal: for example, the central government rotated officials in and out of provinces to make sure they did not develop close family ties with the local population. The civilian government exerted careful control over the military, which was moved to the frontiers and played little role in court politics. The Chinese state had the resources and technical ability to engage in huge public works projects, like the building of the Great Wall and a canal system to promote commerce and divert water to arid regions. The state was strong enough to be highly tyrannical when it wanted, moving entire large populations and confiscating the property of its own elites.[1]

There are many things that government during the Han Dynasty didn't do that are expected of modern states. It did not provide universal education, health care, or pensions. The provision of public goods and services was still rudimentary and often did not penetrate very far into the rural hinterland. Many of its famous projects, like the Grand Canal and the Great Wall, took centuries to complete. The civil service examination system was on again, off again, and did not fully emerge until the beginning of the Ming Dynasty in the fourteenth century. Moreover, China's precociously modern system didn't last. The centralized state broke down in the third century A.D. and wasn't reconstituted for another three hundred years. When it was restored in the Sui and Tang Dynasties, it was dominated not by a meritocratic elite but by aristocratic families that succeeded in capturing state power. Then as now, corruption on the part of government officials was a huge problem. The cycle of political development and political decay was to repeat itself several times in subsequent years, up through the early twentieth century.

I would argue that the state that has emerged in China since the beginning of reforms in 1978 bears more resemblance to this classical Chinese state than it does to the Maoist state that preceded it, or even to the Soviet state that the Chinese tried to copy. Contemporary China has been engaged in the recovery of a long-standing historical tradition, whether or not participants in that process were aware of what they were doing.

At one level this argument seems absurd. Chinese civil servants today don't engage in the elaborate rituals of the Qing court or wear pigtails. They no longer study Confucian classics but a combination of Marxist-Leninist tracts, engineering textbooks, and Western management literature. The mentality of a Mao-era party cadre or Soviet-style bureaucrat is still evident in the behavior of party and state officials. Many of the actual institutional structures created in that period, such as the work group (*danwei*) and population registration system (*hukou*), still exist. Yet if one looks not at the surface style but at the essence of Chinese government, the continuities with the past are striking.

The changes in the nature of Chinese government after 1978 were at least as great as those that took place in economic policy. Indeed, one could argue that the massive shift from a centrally planned economy to a more open and marketized one could not have occurred without corresponding changes in the nature of government. Most observers of modern China have focused on the economic policy shifts, without paying attention to the political infrastructure that made those shifts possible.

RETREAT OF THE MAOIST STATE

Under Chairman Mao, the Chinese state was first completely politicized and subordinated to the Chinese Communist Party. It then disintegrated almost entirely during the Cultural Revolution, as did the hierarchy of the party itself.

In previous cases covered in this book, politicization of a bureaucracy has usually meant capture of a state by politicians who want to use bureaucratic positions for patronage purposes. This is what happened to the American state after the Jacksonian revolution, and to the Greek and Italian states as they democratized and opened themselves up to political competition.

In China, the state was colonized not by patronage politicians but by a disciplined Leninist party that sought to subordinate it to its own ideological purposes. Following the Bolshevik model, a Leninist party is built around an elite core whose members are recruited into a strict hierarchy on the basis of ideological loyalty, and a mass base that is used to penetrate the rest of the society. Before the Cultural Revolution, party members constituted 2.5 percent of China's total population; today they number some 86 million members, or 6 percent of the total.

The party's hierarchy replicates the hierarchy of the state itself, from local party committees to municipal- and provincial-level bodies up through the national-level Central Committee, Politburo, Politburo Standing Committee, and finally the party chairman. Control over the state is exercised through a variety of mechanisms: at the top level, the state apparatus including all of the functional ministries is headed by a party member who wears two hats; at a local level, in each urban neighborhood and rural village, the work group is overseen by a party cadre. At the height of China's "Soviet" period in the 1950s, the state had greatest autonomy from the party at the level of the higher centralized ministries. Political control increased as one went down the hierarchy to the local level.[2]

One area where Chinese practice departed from the Soviet precedent was in civil-military relations. While the Soviet Red Army played an important role during the civil war that followed the Bolshevik Revolution, the military was always strictly subordinated to the Communist Party of the Soviet Union. This control was cemented in the bloody purges of the 1930s, when a quarter to a half of the officer corps were purged by Stalin.

In China, by contrast, the party was able to come to power largely through the prolonged struggle of the People's Liberation Army (PLA) against both the Japanese and the Nationalists. Many party leaders, like Deng Xiaoping and Mao himself, were also famous and successful generals during the Chinese civil war, and thus the PLA always enjoyed a somewhat greater degree of autonomy than its Soviet counterpart.[3]

This familiar party-state structure was then completely upended during the Great Leap Forward and the Cultural Revolution. The Great Leap Forward made use of the party apparatus to organize a military-style mass campaign of workers and peasants to meet Mao's totally unrealistic production goals for industrialization. This disrupted the routine operations of the economic ministries and replaced them with a chaotic, bottom-up process of mass mobilization. The results were famine and economic disaster, but the hierarchy of the party survived. The same cannot be said of the Cultural Revolution, which undermined not just the government but the party as well. Mao launched the Cultural Revolution partly out of fear of the erosion of his personal authority and partly due to opposition to the very principle of bureaucratic government. In an effort to restore the zeal of the original revolution, Mao bypassed all intermediate levels and connected his personal authority directly to the "masses" through organization of local Revolutionary Committees. Heads of different ministries would show up for work and find out that their organizations had been taken over by their underlings. While Stalin made use of the secret police under his personal control to purge the Soviet Communist Party during the 1930s, Mao made use of the Revolutionary Committees and youthful Red Guards to purge, execute, or send to the countryside party members. The PLA was used arbitrarily in this period, sometimes to restore "discipline" and sometimes on behalf of Revolutionary Committees. The party, normally the agent of politicization, was itself controlled and purged from without, and as a result ceased any kind of normal functioning along with the government.[4]

Deng Xiaoping, who was twice purged during the Cultural Revolution, saw both restoration of party discipline and reconstruction of government authority as critical parts of his reforms. Deng never contested the need for dominance of the party over the government, but he believed that both had to operate by rules, the antithesis of Mao's anarchistic approach to governance. The constitutional revision efforts described in the previous chapter were reflections of his view that the party needed to restore its own authority, and that the government's political overseer needed to retreat so that the ministries could properly manage the large changes he foresaw in the economy. It was also important for the party to reassert control over the PLA, which had emerged as something of an arbiter between competing political factions in the delicate period following Mao's death. Whether he was conscious of it or not, Deng was restoring much of the institutional legacy of traditional Chinese government. Only this time, it was the Communist Party that played the role of the emperor with his eunuch cadres supervising a vast bureaucracy.

The kind of government that emerged bears little resemblance to its Maoist predecessor. It is far more professionalized. China reintroduced a merit-based civil service examination system after the 1978 reforms. The political scientist Dali Yang has pointed to a series of reforms taking place in the late 1990s and early 2000s that increased competition for merit-based civil service positions and disciplined large numbers of officials who failed to make the grade.[5] In 2012, 1.12 million people across China competed for twenty-one thousand positions in the civil service.[6] China also restored its university system and instituted competitive entrance requirements for admission (something that many continental European countries have failed to do).[7] The reformers were deliberately seeking to establish a Western-style Weberian bureaucracy, but in doing so they inadvertently recovered some of their own traditions.

The contemporary Chinese government is centralized, massive, and extraordinarily complex. The party remains in control of the government, duplicating its bureaucratic structure from top to bottom and overseeing activities at every level. Nonetheless, party control began to retreat in the 1990s, and the nature of that control has itself changed substantially.

One of the first problems that any centralized bureaucracy faces is that of delegation. Dynastic China was nominally ruled by a bureaucracy in the capital, but the difficulties in managing so large and populous a country in an age of poor communications technology meant that authority had to be delegated to subordinate units at a province or county level. Oftentimes the central government in Chang'an, Luoyang, Kaifeng, or Beijing had no idea what was going on in other parts of the country and would issue orders only to find months or years later that they had not been implemented. The post-Mao leadership early on recognized the importance of delegation. While China remains a unitary rather than a federal state, provinces and cities have been delegated substantial powers to implement directives from the center in ways that they see fit. Thus there is considerable variation in policies across China's different regions. Southern provinces like Guangdong and cities like Shenzhen are far more market-friendly than is, say, Beijing. Shenzhen has, for example, privatized much of its municipal water supply to some twenty-six companies, while municipal water in Beijing is still controlled by a single state-owned company.[8]

In China, many individual provinces are larger than major European countries. Guangdong and Jiangsu both have nearly eighty million permanent residents, plus tens of millions more migrants. The city of Chongqing, which was split off from Sichuan Province as a separate administrative unit in 1997, by itself has a population of almost thirty million. As a result, the bureaucratic structure of the central government is replicated at the provincial and municipal levels, with each having the same functional division of offices and party oversight agencies.

The overall size of the Chinese bureaucracy is correspondingly huge, and it has been growing rapidly. Political scientist Minxin Pei puts the number at over forty million officials in the year 2000, though he notes that accurate statistics are hard to come by. Each of China's subordinate levels of government replicates the division of labor of the higher levels, which leads to a highly complex system in which lines of authority are often in conflict. For example, management of municipal water resources is the primary responsibility of the municipality, but a regional agency managing the watershed that supplies the city's water also has authority, as does the national water ministry.[9] In addition, the Communist Party maintains a smaller, parallel hierarchy that oversees the work of the government agencies.

THE AUTONOMY OF THE CHINESE STATE

If there is a single quality that would seem to distinguish the Chinese party-state from those of other developing countries, it is its degree of autonomy. The Chinese government has not acted as a simple transmission belt for powerful societal interest groups, but has been able to set an independent policy agenda by its own lights. This autonomy is evident at the level of the senior leadership of the Communist Party, which sets overall policy directions, and at the level of implementation, where lower-ranking cadres have considerable discretion in the way that they fulfill directives from above. I will consider each of these in turn.

A high degree of state autonomy free of any form of democratic accountability and unencumbered by a rule of law is a very dangerous thing. This was the story of China during the Maoist period, when a single leader with unlimited policy discretion could unleash untold suffering and cause the deaths of tens of millions of people through willful innovations like the Great Leap Forward and the Cultural Revolution. But that same degree of autonomy in the hands of a wiser and less crazed leader like Deng Xiaoping could bring about transformations for the better that would be scarcely conceivable in a liberal democracy. Chinese-style autonomy frees the state of many of the interest group pressures, lobbyists, and formal procedural constraints that prevent liberal democracies from acting quickly and weaken the quality of decisions ultimately made. In the hands of a competent leadership that wants to serve public purposes, such autonomy allows the government to move much more quickly and dramatically on policy issues than its democratic counterparts.

This is not to say that interest groups do not exist in China. While there were no K Street lobbyists in China representing powerful private interests, the party-state had powerful factions and entrenched interests that were committed to some version of the Maoist status quo. Deng's early reforms had spurred a rapid rise in expectations, especially among the urban intelligentsia and students. The contemporaneous Gorbachev reforms in the former Soviet Union inspired the Tiananmen protest movement and the government's bloody crackdown in June 1989. The killing of student protesters undermined hopes for an early democratic transition and was widely condemned around the world. It also gave comfort to leftists in the party who hoped for a return to greater Communist orthodoxy. Deng himself, however, realized that the party's survival would be undermined by such a conservative reaction. Following his famous "southern tour" in 1992, he returned to a reformist agenda that liberalized prices, privatized a number of state-owned enterprises, and openly promoted transition to a market economy. So even though Deng's ultimate victory was never assured, the fact that he was able to shift policy so massively remains a testament to the autonomy of the Chinese state in this period.

At a lower level, the CCP has granted subordinate levels of the government a high degree of autonomy to carry out its mandates. This is evident in the first instance in the large delegations of authority to China's provinces and municipalities to implement policies in a manner that suits local conditions. This authority often clashes with, and frequently trumps, the interests of the line ministries headquartered in Beijing.

Most Western observers focus on the reform's creation of market incentives through the household responsibility system, which decollectivized agriculture and allowed peasants to keep a much larger proportion of their output. They also point to the creation of four special economic zones open to foreign investment. These were indeed critical: agricultural output doubled in the first four years following the reform as private incentives kicked in, and export industries were seeded in southern cities like Shenzhen. But equally important were changes in the governance structure that created a fiscal responsibility system for local governments. As political scientist Jean Oi has documented, the early gains were accomplished not by the private sector but by so-called township and village enterprises (TVEs), in which local governments essentially turned themselves into profit-making businesses.[10]

One of the fundamental tenets of Western public administration is that public-sector agencies are not allowed to retain earnings and thus have no incentive to control costs or perform more efficiently. This explains why there is a big effort to push money out the door whenever an agency ends the fiscal year with a surplus.[11]

The Chinese party-state upended this verity by in effect permitting local governments to keep surplus revenues and use them for their own purposes. Localities were put under a hard budget constraint, given the authority to extract certain types of taxes, and allowed to start profit-making businesses to supplement their tax revenues. Seventy percent of such retained earnings had to be plowed back into new investment, but the remainder constituted a surplus that could be used at the discretion of the TVE. Some of this surplus was spent on public purposes, but a certain amount ended up in the pockets of local government officials. Many outside observers interpreted this phenomenon as outright corruption, but it was in fact a profit-sharing system designed to incentivize local governments to spur economic growth. And it succeeded spectacularly: much of China's industrial output in the early reform years came not from the new private sector but from TVE-sponsored businesses.[12] In a sense, the Chinese independently discovered the principles of what in the West has gone under the label of New Public Management, an approach that sought to extend marketlike incentives to the public sector.

The TVE was not an institution that any orthodox U.S.-based economist would ever have recommended. Operating behind a veil of ignorance in which outside observers knew the characteristics of the system but not the actual country in question, most would have predicted that it would become a sink of corruption and self-dealing. Had Nigeria or Pakistan tried to implement such a system, one can imagine all sorts of ways the TVEs would have been abused. The central governments would likely have failed to impose hard budget constraints or reinvestment targets, allowing local governments to impose more predatory levels of taxation and appropriate the entire surplus. Or more likely, the higher levels of government would have colluded with the lower ones to split the surplus, while using their rule-setting powers to favor the state-owned businesses.

But China is not Nigeria or Pakistan. The central government was able to impose strict discipline on the TVEs in a way that focused their attention on promoting long-term growth, in a manner similar to the industrial policies set by other states in East Asia. When conditions changed, the policy changed as well. The TVEs by the early 1990s had gotten rich, and the profit-sharing system was plagued by high levels of outright corruption. Many of the complaints of the student protesters in Tiananmen Square were against corruption on the part of government and party officials. The 1994 tax reform took away many of those revenues and forced local governments into a different type of fiscal discipline that encouraged them to promote a more market-friendly form of industrial development. The emerging Chinese middle class that had provided the social basis for the Tiananmen protests was thus increasingly co-opted into supporting the continuation of Communist Party rule.[13]

Dingxin Zhao and Hongxing Yang argue that the 1994 tax reform was a good illustration of the autonomy of the Chinese state. They claim that the specific content of the policies involved is less interesting than the fact that the Chinese government could shift gears so quickly when it became clear that an earlier initiative was producing unanticipated consequences, and then could successfully implement the new course in the face of large vested interests. Deng and the Communist Party recognized that their legitimacy rested on continuing strong performance, and they were not trapped by ideology or past practice in making dramatic and rapid course corrections.[14] These reforms were followed by others during the Jiang Zemin years which, as documented by Dali Yang, cracked down on smuggling perpetrated by government agencies, stripped the People's Liberation Army of many of its profit-making businesses, and imposed a more transparent set of rules with regard to government procurement.[15]

This system of incentivizing local governments represented an approach remarkably different from the old ideology-driven cadre system of the Maoist era, one that violated many basic principles that underlie any Marxist-Leninist regime. Just as striking was the state's focus on promoting long-term growth rather than on maximizing short-term rents. One could say that the senior leadership of the Communist Party was acting in its own self-interest by promoting growth and hence its own legitimacy and grip on power. But this long-term understanding of self-interest and focus on legitimacy does not come automatically to many governments. It has eluded a very large number of developing country governments outside of East Asia. (Recall the story of Robert in Nigeria at the beginning of chapter 14.) It is here that China's millennia-long Confucian tradition of government probably had an important impact.

One of the biggest questions hanging over the future of China is the degree to which the top levels of government can remain as autonomous as in the past. Minxin Pei argues that the quality of government services has declined over time, in large measure because subordinate units of the state have become too autonomous, or rather, autonomous in the wrong way. That is, they are able to protect their own political and economic positions regardless of performance, and resist discipline from higher levels of the state and party. These subunits include powerful state-owned enterprises like China Telecom and the China National Offshore Oil Corporation, which now rank among the world's largest corporations. These SOEs during the 2000s gained in relative power over their private-sector rivals and foreign investors, and have been able to use their political clout to avoid competitive threats to their positions.[16] In addition, bureaucracies like the Ministry of Railways have become fiefdoms that the Communist Party has had difficulty controlling. This ministry is a gigantic organization, presiding over some fifty-seven thousand miles of track and employing 2.5 million people across China.[17] The central government has been trying, without success, to get control of the money-losing ministry for many years. Following the highly publicized crash of a new high-speed rail train near Wenzhou in mid-2011, the ministry tried to hide evidence of malfeasance by burying the cars involved, until discussions on China's microblogs forced it to unbury them. The central government used this as an opportunity to sack railway minister Liu Zhijun on charges of corruption, and announced that it intended to break the agency apart into two separate organizations. Like many of the government reorganizations that the central government has announced, the breakup never came about, presumably because the powerful and secretive ministry had enough political clout to protect its position.[18]

Any administrative system that relies so heavily on monetary incentives will invite corruption. The Western economists predicting that it would lead to rent seeking and corruption were not entirely wrong; they simply would not be able to predict the degree of corruption, or the level of real services the government was able to provide in return. There continues to be a great deal of patronage, nepotism, factionalism, political influence, and outright corruption pervading the Chinese political system. Minxin Pei argues that China's gradual political transition has resulted in a system of "decentralized predation," in which locally empowered officials throughout an enormous government system take advantage of the opportunities provided by their political control to extract a host of rents and bribes. Higher levels of the party understand that pervasive corruption is strongly resented by ordinary people and that the legitimacy of the party's continued rule depends heavily on its ability to control itself. The party has made numerous public commitments to control and punish corruption. This happened most recently following the 18th Party Congress in 2012 in the early pronouncements of the new leadership of General Secretary Xi Jinping and Wang Qishan, head of the Central Discipline Inspection Commission responsible for rooting out corruption. But Pei argues that the monitoring capacity of the party has been declining over time, as the government becomes larger and more complex, and officials have more resources and more ways of hiding them.[19]

THE ACCOUNTABILITY OF THE CHINESE STATE

The People's Republic of China is an authoritarian state whose constitution grants a leading role to the Communist Party. The party has no intention of permitting free and fair multiparty elections, and is careful to suppress any open discussion of democracy.

All authoritarian regimes encounter resistance to their rule in one form or another, and all respond with a mixture of repression and co-optation. When compared to a totalitarian state like North Korea, or the Arab dictatorships of Hosni Mubarak in Egypt or Muammar Qaddafi in Libya, the Chinese balance has tended to lean much more in the direction of co-optation. Thus while there are no formal mechanisms of accountability, the party and the state can be said to be responsive to the demands of various actors in Chinese society.

There are several mechanisms by which this happens. The Chinese government has permitted village elections in rural areas since 1989 to elect village committees and village leaders with certain limited local powers. They are part of a larger electoral system stretching up to the National People's Congress, in which delegates have started to act with a certain degree of independence.[20] In addition to these formal mechanisms, as political scientist Lily Tsai describes, Chinese peasant communities provide informal feedback mechanisms for informing local officials of complaints and ideas for better delivery of government services. There are also formal complaint channels created by both government and party organizations through which citizens can register their views. The government of course is under no legal obligation to respond, but local officials are nonetheless frequently incentivized by higher-level authorities to head off social instability by preempting problems.[21]

The most important feedback mechanism, however, is public protest. When coupled with the government's almost paranoid concern for social stability and "harmony," protests lead not simply to repression but also to significant accommodation. In 2010 there were estimated to be some 180,000 officially reported acts of social protest—peasants angry at land requisitions, parents worried about pollutants from a nearby factory, migrant workers feeling mistreated by local officials.[22] Under Hu Jintao's leadership, the party changed the relative priority of economic growth versus promoting stability in its evaluations of official performance, elevating the latter to the point where a single incident of disorder could mean the end of an official's career. Many local officials find it easier to buy off protesters through various concessions, subsidies, or rule changes, and have come under severe pressure to meet these conflicting goals.[23]

There is a very strong popular belief in China that the higher levels of government are more responsive and less corrupt than lower levels.[24] Confidence in the good intentions of the higher levels is critical to the legitimacy of the government as a whole, which is why the government tries to be responsive. But it is not really clear whether the higher levels are in fact less corrupt than the lower ones. The revelations coming out of the 2012 Bo Xilai case suggest that senior leaders have reached rather shocking levels of malfeasance as well.

With regard to policy and politics, lower levels of the government are supposedly subject to strong discipline by higher levels. But in a centralized system they have to be granted considerable autonomy with regard to implementation. In dynastic China, emperors faced huge problems of information, trying to monitor the behavior of the bureaucracy they supposedly controlled. They attempted to solve this problem by piling more centralized monitoring institutions on top of one another. Household eunuchs, for example, were more trusted than the bureaucracy and were used to monitor the bureaucrats. But then the corps of eunuchs themselves became unreliable, so emperors in the Ming Dynasty had to create a "Eunuch Rectification Office" to monitor the behavior of the eunuchs. So too in contemporary China: higher levels watch over the behavior of lower levels; the party's Organization Bureau monitors the behavior of the government; and special offices within the party, like the Central Discipline Inspection Commission, watch over the rest of the party. In this sort of atmosphere, many of the actors have strong incentives to cover up bad behavior and prevent the upward flow of information. In the end, the only solution is a system of downward accountability, in which the state is monitored by a free press and a genuinely empowered citizenry.

The vast majority of the rules, laws, and procedures that have been put in place in post-Mao China are designed to regularize the behavior of lower levels of the government and make them more responsive to higher ones. The ultimate performance of a political system that has only upward but no downward accountability therefore depends heavily on the choices and intentions of the people at the top. In the last chapter I described the old argument between Legalists and Confucians, in which the former argued for clear procedures while the latter argued in favor of a more flexible and contextually based leadership morality. Premodern Chinese governments opted for moral rather than formal legal constraints on higher leaders; procedures were used only to regularize the manner in which the emperor transmitted commands to the rest of society. The contemporary Chinese government, despite its rhetorical commitment to

Marxism-Leninism, continues in this tradition. Citizens have to rely more on the good intentions of their leaders than on any formal procedural constraints on their power.

In the hands of good leaders, such a system can actually perform better than a democratic system that is subject to rule of law and formal democratic procedures like multiparty elections. It can make large, difficult decisions without being hampered by interest groups, lobbying, litigation, or the need to form cumbersome political coalitions or educate the public as to their own self-interest. The historical "embedded autonomy" of fast-growing states in Asia including Singapore, South Korea, Taiwan, and Japan has been widely admired. So too with China: compared to authoritarian regimes in other parts of the world, its post-1978 performance has focused on widely shared goals such as economic growth, stability, and the broad provision of public services. Deng Xiaoping and the leaders of the party who followed him understood that the party's survival would depend on legitimacy, which could no longer rest on ideology but would have to be based on their performance in governing the country.

The problem with such a system is what the Chinese have historically identified as the "bad emperor" problem. An authoritarian system can move much more quickly and decisively than a democratic one, but its success is ultimately dependent on having a continuing supply of good leaders—good not just in a technocratic sense but in their commitment to shared public goals rather than self-enrichment or personal power. Dynastic China addressed this problem through a sophisticated bureaucratic structure that limited the actual powers of the sovereign, as well as an elaborate system for educating rulers that encased them in oppressive ritual. Even so, this system was not sufficient to prevent the emergence of periodic bad emperors who were alternately despotic, lazy, incompetent, or corrupt.

Contemporary China faces precisely this kind of problem. Compared to most authoritarian and many democratic regimes, China has performed extremely well over the past several decades in terms of economic growth, reduction of poverty, and provision of basic social services. But does the current Chinese system guarantee a continuing supply of "good emperors"?

Chinese authoritarian government faces several kinds of threats to the sustainability of its system. First, it could produce a charismatic leader who exploited populist passions and built a personal following that upset all of the consensual understandings that have characterized the post-Mao leadership. There are plenty of unaddressed social discontents on which to build, beginning with the extremely high level of economic inequality in China and perceptions of rampant corruption.

A second threat is less dramatic but much more likely: the government will lose its autonomy over other social actors and will be captured by the powerful interest groups generated as a result of economic growth. Minxin Pei suggests that this has already happened: the government now faces powerful entrenched groups—state-owned enterprises, individual ministries, and even entire regions that resist its authority. While it tries to control corruption at lower levels, the government can itself fall prey to corruption at the top. The party's authority is substantially diminished in any event since the days of Mao and Deng, and as its performance weakens, as it inevitably must given China's difficult path from being a middle-income to a high-income country, authority will weaken further. Under Hu Jintao, political reform was largely suspended and economic policy turned in a less liberal direction. Following the 18th Party Congress and the rise of Xi Jinping, the party has promised new economic reforms but accompanied this agenda with a clampdown on dissent and a renewed emphasis on ideology and discipline. Whether Xi will be able to effect large policy changes remains to be seen.

A final threat has to do with the system's lack of an intrinsic source of legitimacy. The Chinese government often argues that it constitutes a different, non-Western political and moral system. It is true, as I have argued, that there are many continuities between dynastic China and the current government. But the Chinese Communist Party still officially bases its legitimacy on an imported Western ideology, Marxism-Leninism. This prevents it from fully and forthrightly basing its legitimacy on traditional Chinese values. On the other hand, it cannot simply discard Marxism-Leninism. As a result, it must seek legitimacy in continuing high levels of economic growth and in its ability to be the standard-bearer of Chinese nationalism. If that growth slows or goes into reverse, the CCP will not have a coherent story to tell about why it deserves a monopoly of power.

The only way to solve the bad emperor problem and the associated evils of corruption and arbitrary rule in the long run is to increase the formal procedural constraints on the state. This means in the first instance steadily expanding rule-based decision making and applying the law to higher levels of government and party. Formal constraints require in the second instance broadening political participation. The information problem that plagued Imperial China and that confronts the present-day government ultimately cannot be solved without formal safeguards concerning access to information. China's economic growth has created a large and growing middle class that is less accepting of paternalistic authoritarianism that seeks to hide its own corruption. The transition to more formal constraints on power can be gradual and should focus initially on law rather than accountability. The existing Chinese constitution is not a bad basis from which to build a growing foundation of law. But both are ultimately necessary if the Chinese political system is to be sustainable over the long run.[25]

What is the dynamic process by which either the rule of law or democratic accountability can be expected to spread? This will not happen as a result of top-down mandates by the current leadership, which is brimming with self-confidence and shows little inclination to move on the political front. Change is more likely to occur as new social actors appear on the scene who press for stronger institutions of constraint. In the past, the Chinese state was strong enough to prevent the emergence of powerful social groups that might challenge its power. But social mobilization is occurring in contemporary China at a pace without precedent in all of Chinese history. A huge middle class, currently numbering in the hundreds of millions, has appeared. In many other societies, the middle class has been the dynamic force responsible for political change and, ultimately, democracy. The future of rule of law and democracy in China will depend on whether these new social groups can shift the classic balance of power between state and society that persisted in China's past. This is the general phenomenon to be addressed in Part III of this book.

26

THREE REGIONS

Latin America, sub-Saharan Africa, and Asia compared; how the strength of states is critical in distinguishing them and explaining their economic performance; how colonial legacies explain only part of contemporary outcomes

The first part of this book asked why modern, Weberian states emerged in some parts of the developed world but not in others. Part II has continued this investigation for places that developed later and had to confront Western colonialism, focusing on Latin America, sub-Saharan Africa, and East Asia. While there are large variations within each region, there are also certain systematic differences among them that allow us to talk about separate regional development paths.

Of the three regions, East Asia has had the highest rates of growth from the second half of the twentieth century on, as indicated in Table 5. It may surprise some people that per capita income is higher overall in Latin America than in East Asia. That is due to the existence of a number of large, relatively poor countries in the latter region such as Indonesia and the Philippines, and the fact that China, while a star performer in many ways, still has a large, impoverished rural population.

Things are quite different with regard to political institutions, where Latin America does much better than East Asia, and significantly better than sub-Saharan Africa. The region as a whole is above the fiftieth percentile for all six of the World Bank's Worldwide Governance Indicators (see Figure 17), and ranks particularly high with regard to "voice and accountability," a measure of democracy and political participation. East Asia does significantly less well in this category, and sub-Saharan Africa lags behind substantially on all six indicators. This reflects the fact that although all regions saw increases in the number of democracies during the Third Wave of democratization that began in the early 1970s, this trend was most powerful in Latin America. Asia's largest and most economically dynamic country, China, remains a Communist dictatorship, as do Vietnam and North Korea. The only such country in the western hemisphere is Cuba, though there has been significant backsliding on democracy in the 2000s in Venezuela, Ecuador, Nicaragua, and other countries.

TABLE 5. Growth Rates and GDP Per Capita

	Growth Rate, 1961–2011 (%)	Per Capita GDP, 2011*
East Asia	7.3	$7,294
Latin America	3.8	11,595
Sub-Saharan Africa	3.5	2,233
OECD (Developed Countries)	3.2	38,944

SOURCE: World Bank

*GDP per capita is in parity purchasing power.

FIGURE 17. Regional Comparison, Worldwide Governance Indicators (percentile ranks)[1]

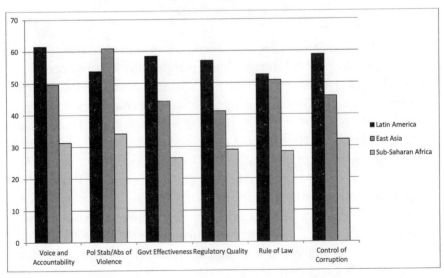

SOURCE: World Bank, Worldwide Governance Indicators

While Latin America outperforms East Asia in terms of democracy, it has a much smaller advantage with regard to state institutions. The scores for political stability and rule of law are roughly comparable between Latin America and East Asia, and sharply lower in sub-Saharan Africa.

FIGURE 18. Gini Coefficients, Selected Countries

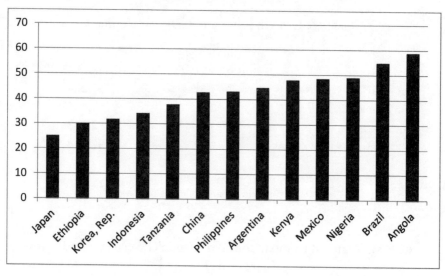

SOURCE: World Bank

The difference among regions can also be measured in terms of inequality, as indicated in Figure 18, which presents Gini index numbers for a selected group of countries (Gini indexes range from 0 to 100, with 0 representing perfect equality and 100 representing complete inequality). The countries of sub-Saharan Africa vary widely: Ethiopia is relatively equal, while oil-rich Nigeria and Angola have very high levels of inequality. In East Asia, Japan and South Korea have had low rates of inequality since the 1950s, as did China at the end of the Maoist period. But with its rapid economic growth during the 2000s, China's income distribution has skewed to almost Latin American levels. During this same decade, Latin America's rate of inequality began to decrease slightly. Nonetheless, the region is still subject to large gaps between rich and poor that have troubling political consequences.[2]

Statistical averages of economic growth and governance of course mask important differences within each region. Latin America includes extremely poor Haiti, Guatemala, and Paraguay, as well as Brazil, which exports high-tech products such as jet aircraft to the rest of the world. Nonetheless, each of these regions has certain characteristics that make countries within them similar to one another and different from those in other regions. Many Latin American countries have experienced a cycle of rapidly rising inflation, currency crisis, devaluation, and economic downturn, most recently during the debt crisis in the early 1980s (and, in Argentina, in the early 2000s). East Asia's fast-growing economies, by contrast, got through this period largely unscathed. Sub-Saharan Africa experienced a similar and even more severe debt crisis than Latin America a few years later, which led a number of countries to require debt relief from their creditors before they could start growing once again. While Latin America is largely democratic today, this was not always the case; during the 1960s and '70s, repressive military governments took power in Brazil, Argentina, Chile, Peru, Bolivia, and other places. Most of what are labeled "developmental states"—countries that have successfully used state power (often under authoritarian regimes) to promote rapid economic growth—have clustered in East Asia. It is hard to find comparable countries in Latin America or sub-Saharan Africa.[3]

PATHS OF DEVELOPMENT

Part II began with various theories put forward to explain contemporary development outcomes as the result of geography, climate, and colonial legacies. All of these have some merit. But the nature of human social behavior is so complex that few theories that trace outcomes to single factors hold up across the board.

Theories that link political (and consequently economic) development to geography and climate can explain certain important outcomes. Economists focus on endowments of natural resources: the requirements of gold and silver mining, or of plantation agriculture, led to the enslavement of indigenous peoples or the importation of slaves from Africa. The exploitative industries created an economic basis for authoritarian governments on New World soil.

But authoritarian institutions in Latin America were overdetermined. The political orders created in Peru and Mexico were settler colonies that succeeded in eradicating virtually any institutional trace of the dense pre-Columbian state structures that preceded them. As settlement colonies, they tended to replicate the class-based, mercantilist society found back on the Iberian peninsula, in which indigenous laborers and mestizos took the place of the white European peasantry. The Spanish Crown initially tried to create a strong form of absolutist direct rule in the Americas, but the realities of distance meant that it was able to exert substantially less authority over its colonies than it could at home. The Spanish form of absolutism was a weak one, unable to tax adequately or meet its own revenue needs in Europe, and even less able to do so with respect to its restive Creole colonists in the New World. The Creoles thus created for themselves oligarchic governments based on privileges rather than liberties, which survived the transition to independent states when the colonies broke away from Spain in the early nineteenth century. Latin America in the twenty-first century continues to live with this legacy as the most unequal region of the world.

Geography was important in other ways as well, as Montesquieu pointed out. Certain topographies were better suited to the raising and deployment of large armies. In Eurasia (China and Russia primarily), relatively open land encouraged consolidation of large centralized states, while in sub-Saharan Africa, the difficulties of projecting power across vast deserts and tropical forests inhibited state formation. Europe was somewhere in between: its geography encouraged the formation of medium-sized political units, but it prevented any one of them from growing to a size that allowed conquest of the entire region.

Latin America's geography put it closer to sub-Saharan Africa than to Europe. The continent as a whole was divided by mountains, jungles, and deserts, and by the prevailing north-south lines of communications, into mutually inaccessible regions that did not facilitate the creation of large territorial empires. Following the demographic collapse of the region's indigenous populations, there were few parts of the continent with population densities great enough to support powerful states. Moreover, once Spanish and Portuguese colonization began, surpluses were not locally reinvested but exported back to the home country under highly inefficient mercantilist rules.

In the second half of the eighteenth century, Latin America as a whole didn't look that different from Europe in political terms. Both were dominated by autocratic regimes and economic oligarchies that used political power to protect their privileges. Yet in the succeeding two centuries, Europe underwent a profound series of political changes that left it much more democratic and economically equal than Latin America. One of the principal reasons for this was the extraordinarily high level of violence experienced by Europe during this period, beginning with the French Revolution and Napoleonic Wars, continuing through the wars of Italian and German unification, and ending with the cataclysms of the two world wars. High levels of military competition led to the formation and consolidation of strong, modern states, as in the Stein-Hardenberg reforms in Prussia. At the same time, rapid industrialization was drawing millions of peasants off the countryside and into dense, diverse cities. This shift created the conditions for the emergence of modern ethnolinguistic concepts of national identity, which in turn provoked further military competition. Nationalism helped to facilitate the consolidation of modern states. And both internal revolution and external war succeeded in wiping out entire social classes, like France's venal officeholders and the Junker class in Germany, which had been pillars of the old oligarchic order.

Latin America's development path was very different. There was no equivalent of the French Revolution to unseat old oligarchies, nor was there prolonged international competition to stimulate the formation of modern states. National identities remained weak, due to ethnic diversity and slow or absent industrialization, which meant that conflict was more often an internal one between classes rather than an external one between nations. By 1945, Europe's exhausted elites were ready to concede both liberal democracy and redistributive welfare states to ensure social peace. While Latin America's elites faced the threat of social upheaval, especially after the Cuban Revolution, it was never severe enough to promote either state building or redistribution on a European scale. There was no European-style social consensus built around moderate center-left and center-right parties, but rather sharp polarizations between rich and poor. Only in the 2000s does a more European type of political order appear to be emerging in Chile and Brazil.

Geography, climate, and colonial legacies do not explain present-day outcomes across the board. Argentina, whose climate and colonial history freed it from the inequality and slow growth of the rest of the continent during the nineteenth century, should have continued to flourish. It did not do so because of the poor choices made by its elites in the early twentieth century. Despite its more favorable climate and geography, it inherited some of the political culture from the older parts of Latin America, such as caudillismo and personalistic leadership. Conversely, Costa Rica should have evolved into another Central American banana republic characterized by dictatorship and civil conflict, and yet it developed into a stable democracy because of good choices made by elites at a certain critical historical juncture.

The situation in sub-Saharan Africa was completely different. The deadly legacy of European colonialism was not an "extractive" authoritarian state but rather the profound absence of strong institutions altogether. The scramble to colonize Africa came very late, in the closing decades of the nineteenth century, when the Spanish and Portuguese territories in the New World were already four and a half centuries old. Unlike in Latin America, early European colonialists did not find either large populations or substantial mineral resources to exploit in Africa. Tropical diseases and climate, moreover, made the region inhospitable to extensive European settlement, except for more temperate regions in the south. There simply weren't the time or resources to build institutions before demands for independence arose in the middle decades of the twentieth century. The fact that the African colonies could barely be made to pay for the costs of their own administration led the Europeans to seek a cheap way out through "indirect rule," using local African agents to extract taxes or force young men into corvée labor. This ramshackle system, imposed over territories that reflected the outcomes of strategic competition rather than ethnic realities, was the political legacy bequeathed to much of sub-Saharan Africa on independence after World War II.

Also unlike in Latin America, postindependence Africa did not have deeply entrenched elites who could pull strings behind the scenes. Independence from colonial rule opened up opportunities for new elites to emerge, largely the urban educated class that had been close to the colonial administration. Not having a secure social base either as a landed aristocracy or in the small capitalist economy, many saw the state itself as their main route to economic advancement. Low-capacity states were thus stuffed with patronage employees, vastly increasing their size and further weakening their ability to deliver real services. Politics came to be a neopatrimonial contest over capture of the state and its resources, with different groups lining up for their "turn to eat." Under these conditions, there was no permanent bureaucracy that could represent a broader public interest or that could discipline elites and force them to play by economically rational rules.

It is commonly observed that many of sub-Saharan Africa's travails are due to the fact that the territorial boundaries bequeathed to newly independent states did not conform to the realities of existing ethnic and tribal identities. This bit of conventional wisdom is misleading insofar as it implies that a more intelligent form of boundary drawing would have led to more coherent postindependence states. This is true only to a limited extent: Sudan, for example, could have been spared two long and costly civil conflicts if South Sudan and Darfur had not been attached to the Arab core around Khartoum by the British. But for much of the rest of Africa, ethnic groups were far too small and intermingled to become the basis for a modern European-style nation-state. In contrast to East Asia and Europe, strong indigenous state-level units had not performed the hard and violent work of identity formation prior to European colonization. To the extent that the colonial powers shaped identity, it was replacing tribalism with ethnicity—that is, replacing small-scale kin groups with much larger ones, done for the sake of divide-and-rule. The colonial rulers of Africa had neither the time nor the incentive to create strong states that could help shape national identity, and most of the elites that emerged after independence did not make nation building a priority. Weakness of national identity in sub-Saharan Africa is thus far more a matter of omission rather than commission. Tanzania is the exception that proves the rule. Nyerere's creation of a Tanzanian identity demonstrates that where elites did embark on such a project, it could be a success despite considerable prior ethnic diversity.

Societies with strong state institutions and equally strong national identities existed, prior to their confrontation with Western colonial powers, in other parts of the world, primarily in East Asia. China indeed invented the modern state at the time of the Qin unification, some eighteen hundred years before its rise in early modern Europe. The Chinese created a state that was centralized, bureaucratic, and impersonal, ruling a vast territory with far greater uniformity than its Roman counterpart. The power of the Chinese state waxed and waned over the following millennia, as it was recaptured by internal kin groups or invaded by barbarians from without. Nonetheless, China and surrounding countries like Japan, Korea, and Vietnam developed governments based on the strong-state model and succeeded in reaching levels of political organization substantially higher than any of the indigenous societies of Latin America and sub-Saharan Africa. These state-building efforts were enhanced by great ethnic homogeneity, the result of many centuries of conquest and assimilation. These societies had a strong sense of shared culture based on a common written language and widespread elite literacy.

It should be noted that these generalizations do not apply to East Asia as a whole. Many of the countries of Southeast Asia have had very different political development trajectories. As noted in chapter 22, Indonesia did not even exist as a state in the nineteenth century and was nearly as fragmented ethnically as Nigeria. Singapore and Malaysia were direct creations of British colonialism, whose modern success did not depend on the existence of precolonial indigenous states. It is interesting to note, however, that even so, they were able to build relatively strong and coherent states. How this came about is a fascinating story that unfortunately remains outside the scope of this book.[4]

Early state institutionalization in East Asia made it easier to resist threats from the outside. Japan was the most successful in preventing Western colonization. And although China was attacked and partly occupied by the Western powers, and the Qing court in Beijing repeatedly humiliated during the nineteenth century, the Western powers never managed to fully dissolve the connective tissue of the Chinese state. While state authority did break down briefly in the 1920s, '30s, and '40s during the period of warlordism, civil war, and Japanese occupation, a strong centralized state was soon reestablished under the leadership of the Chinese Communist Party in 1949. Similarly, though Vietnam was occupied by France, it succeeded in eventually ousting the colonial regime and defeating its American-supported successor. It is no accident that East Asia was host to the two best-organized and most powerful nationalist revolutions in the world, those of China and Vietnam, whose leaders converted their military prowess into state power immediately upon victory in their civil wars/wars of national liberation.

China and the countries influenced by it were heirs to a Confucian moral and bureaucratic system that oriented rulers, through education and socialization, toward a broader concept of the common good. That, plus the Confucian emphasis on literacy and education, left a critical if unintended benefit for modern economic development. East Asia's rapid rise from the second half of the twentieth century on has been driven by strong technocratic states whose leadership, however authoritarian, remains oriented toward shared goals of economic and social development. It is very hard to prove in a social scientific manner a causal connection between these older historical and cultural traditions and the behavior of Itō Hirobumi, Yamagata Aritomo, Park Chung Hee, Lee Kwan Yew, and Deng Xiaoping, and the governments they led, but the connection is still there. While some were corrupt and most quite authoritarian, levels of malfeasance overall were kept in better check in Asia than in sub-Saharan Africa. Just as important, leaders in East Asia were much more competent in their economic management and understood better the importance of professional state administration. This is not to say there isn't a lot of corruption in the region. Compared to other parts of the world, however, bribe payers there got a lot more back for their money in terms of public goods and broad-based development.

China, Japan, Vietnam, and Korea could seek to modernize their economies while taking for granted the existence of a strong and coherent state as well as a well-established national identity. The newly independent countries in sub-Saharan Africa, by contrast, could not, and they needed to do everything at once—build modern states, establish national identities, create rule-of-law institutions, stage democratic elections, and promote economic development at the same time. While Europe and East Asia sequenced institutional development differently from one another, they had the luxury of doing this sequencing over long periods of time.

The strong states of East Asia developed bureaucratic institutions before they had a rule of law, while in Europe the sequence was reversed. The precociously strong East Asian state was for centuries able to head off the emergence of independent social actors that could challenge its power. While European liberal democracy grew out of a rough balance of power between state and society, the state-society balance in East Asia favored the state. This meant that, in contrast to most of the rest of the developing world where state weakness was the central issue, what is lacking in East Asia is the limitation of state power through law or political accountability.

In Part I, we saw that states that democratized before they had acquired modern state institutions were prone to large-scale clientelism. This has been much less of a problem in East Asia than in other parts of the world, because the region developed a smaller number of democracies than either Latin America or Africa, and the first ones to appear tended to be concentrated in industrialized countries already possessing strong states.

Although I have not discussed the Philippines at any length, it would seem to be an exception that proves the rule: like the United States in the nineteenth century, that country democratized before it had a modern state and has therefore experienced substantial amounts of patronage and clientelism.

The state-society balance in East Asia is changing rapidly under the impact of two forces that didn't exist or were much less powerful in the premodern world. The first is industrialization, which mobilizes powerful new social actors like a middle class and working class that didn't exist in agrarian times. The second is the much more intense interaction among societies internationally, what we now label globalization. Goods and services, people, and ideas travel across international boundaries much more readily than they once did, which makes foreign actors far more important to the process of domestic development. So if East Asian states were traditionally strong, they today face both resistance from new groups in their own societies and the influx of ideas from other parts of the world. The same kind of social mobilization that changed European societies and laid the basis for democracy there is taking place in contemporary East Asia.

We need, then, to look more closely at the dynamic process by which democracy spreads. Democracy has become the dominant form of political organization around the world not just because it is a good idea, but also because it serves the interests of and is promoted by certain social groups. These groups in turn are the by-products of broader economic and social developments. Ideas matter in this process, but they interact with and shape the material interests of different classes in society.

PART THREE

·

Democracy

27

WHY DID DEMOCRACY SPREAD?

The Third Wave of democratization; theories of why democratic waves occur; how democracy is rooted in the interests of specific social groups; social mobilization as the link between economic change and democracy; political parties as key agents in the struggle over democracy

Japan, China, and other societies in East Asia were heirs to a long tradition of government and could presuppose the existence of a strong state as they began to industrialize in the nineteenth and twentieth centuries. Prior to this point, they were highly unequal agrarian societies in which a small elite exercised a monopoly of power over a large mass of largely unorganized peasants. I suggested that the state-society balance began to change with the onset of rapid economic growth, and that the authoritarian system in contemporary China will face significant challenges as new social groups are mobilized and begin to demand a share of political power. Will this lead to the eventual appearance of formal democratic accountability in China? We have no way of predicting such an outcome. What we can do is to try to understand the process of democratization in other parts of the world and what implications it may hold for the future.

Between 1970 and 2010, the number of democracies around the world increased from about 35 to nearly 120, or some 60 percent of the world's countries, in what Samuel Huntington called the Third Wave of democratization. According to him, the first long wave began in the 1820s and continued through the end of the nineteenth century, while the second short wave happened in the immediate aftermath of World War II. The Third Wave began with the democratic transitions in Spain and Portugal in the early 1970s and continued through the end of military rule in Greece and Turkey, followed by a series of Latin American countries including Brazil, Argentina, Peru, Bolivia, and Chile; then it moved to Asia with the democratization of the Philippines, South Korea, and Taiwan; and culminated in the collapse of communism and the transition to democracy in Eastern Europe and some of the successor states of the former Soviet Union. Democracy expert Larry Diamond has argued that there has been a recession of the Third Wave in the 2000s. While the outbreak of the Arab Spring in early 2011 suggested to some observers the start of a Fourth Wave, setbacks in Egypt, Libya, and Syria have made this a less compelling argument.[1]

Why did these waves of democratization occur? Why did they occur in some regions and societies and not others? Why were some waves successful in establishing relatively stable democracies while others were rolled back? And why did democracy become a global phenomenon only during the twentieth century and not in the roughly four hundred prior centuries of human history?

One answer to the question of why democracy spread has been put forward in a number of different variants: democracy has taken hold as the result of the power of the underlying idea of democracy. This was stated forcefully by Alexis de Tocqueville in his introduction to *Democracy in America*. He noted that the idea of human equality that underlies modern democracy had been gaining ground for the preceding eight hundred years, and it had acquired an unstoppable momentum that aroused in him a "kind of religious dread." He regarded its progress as a providential fact.[2] Other authors have agreed that ideas were critical and have traced them to specific historical and cultural roots, either in ancient Athens or in Christianity. Both Hegel and Nietzsche understood modern political democracy to be a secularized version of the Christian doctrine of the universal equality of human dignity. Hegel in particular saw developments in the material world such as the French Revolution and the emergence of the principle of equal recognition as the working out of the inner logic of human rationality. During the Third Wave itself, as well as during the more recent Arab Spring, ideas clearly propagated rapidly across international borders via radio, television, the Internet, and flows of activists bringing news of political upheavals elsewhere. The wave of democratic transitions occurring in sub-Saharan Africa during the early 1990s was clearly inspired by the fall of the Berlin Wall and the dramatic developments taking place in Eastern Europe shortly before.

In terms of the framework built around the six dimensions of devel-

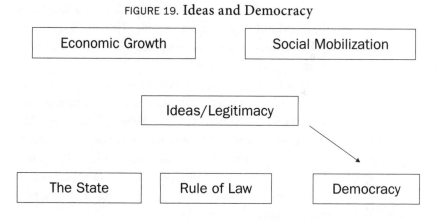

FIGURE 19. Ideas and Democracy

opment laid out in chapter 2, theories focusing on ideas or cultural values would posit a causal relationship looking something like Figure 19.

But while ideas are indeed powerful and can explain much about political institutions, this kind of explanation begs as many questions as it settles. Why, for instance, do the ideas of human equality or democracy take off in some periods and not in others? The idea of democracy has been around at least since ancient Athens, and yet it did not become institutionalized anywhere until the end of the eighteenth century. Tocqueville does not explain why the idea of human equality became progressively more powerful, except to suggest that it was an act of God. Democracy did not arise in all parts of the world, nor has it gained traction equally across the globe. This has led to the assertion, made by parties as diverse as Samuel Huntington, the contemporary Chinese government, and a variety of Islamists, that liberal democracy does not represent a universal trend but is something culturally specific to Western civilization. If this is true, it still begs the question of why this particular idea arose in the West and not elsewhere.

An alternative school of thought understands democracy not as the expression of an idea or a set of cultural values but as the by-product of deep structural forces within societies. Social scientists have long noted that there is a correlation between high levels of economic development and stable democracy: most of the world's rich industrialized countries today are democracies, whereas most remaining authoritarian states are much less developed. One well-known study shows that while countries may transition from authoritarian to democratic government at any level of development, they are much more likely to remain democracies if they rise above a certain threshold of per capita income. This suggests prima facie that there may be something in the process of economic development that makes democracy more likely.[3]

But what is the connection between economic development and democracy? Do people's values somehow magically flip over to favor democracy when they achieve a certain level of well-being? The statistical correlations linking development and democracy provide no insight as to specific causal mechanisms that connect the two. Within all of these correlations, moreover, there are many exceptions: for example, according to this view, impoverished India should not be a stable democracy yet wealthy Singapore should.

In chapter 2, I suggested an alternative causal path by which economic growth could affect democratic institutions, via social mobilization. The key concept here is the division of labor. Adam Smith asserted that the division of labor is limited by the size of the market, or, put differently, that as markets expanded through increased trade in a commercial and later an industrial economy, a new division of labor would arise and deepen. This division of labor entailed the creation of new social groups. Although Smith himself never made this argument explicitly, it follows logically that these new groups, excluded from participation in the political institutions of the old agrarian society, would demand a share of political power and therefore increase pressures for democracy.

FIGURE 20. Growth and Social Mobilization

"The Division of Labor is limited by the extent of the market"

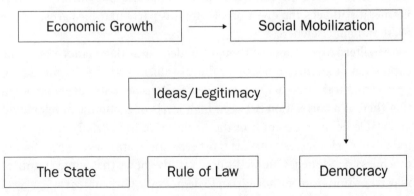

Economic growth, in other words, engendered social mobilization, which in turn led to increasing demands for political participation (along the lines of Figure 20).

Smith's description of the changing division of labor was one of the central concepts that preoccupied the major social theorists of the nineteenth century. First was Karl Marx, who made the division of labor integral to his own doctrine by transforming it into a theory of social classes.

MARX'S INSIGHT

Marx's framework can be summarized as follows. Out of the old feudal order, the first new social class to be mobilized is the bourgeoisie, townsmen who were regarded contemptuously by the old landowners but who accumulated capital and used new technologies to bring about the Industrial Revolution. This revolution in turn mobilized a second new class, the proletariat, whose surplus labor the bourgeoisie unjustly appropriated. Each of these three classes wanted a different political outcome: the traditional landowning class wanted to preserve the old authoritarian order; the bourgeoisie wanted a liberal (i.e., rule of law) regime protecting their property rights that might or might not include formal electoral democracy (they were always more interested in the rule of law than in democracy); and the proletariat, once it achieved consciousness of itself as a class, wanted a dictatorship of the proletariat, which would in turn socialize the means of production, abolish private property, and redistribute wealth. The working class might support electoral democracy in the form of universal suffrage, but this was a means to the end of control over the means of production, not an end in itself.

One of the most important scholars working in a post-Marxist tradition was Barrington Moore, whose 1966 book *Social Origins of Dictatorship and Democracy* has already been noted in connection with Japan (see chapter 23 above). This complex book presented a series of historical case studies, including Britain, Germany, Japan, China, Russia, and India, and tried to explain why democracy emerged in some countries and not in others. He is probably best remembered for his blunt observation: "No bourgeoisie, no democracy." By this he did not mean that the rise of the bourgeoisie inevitably produced democracy. In Germany, for example, the industrial bourgeoisie allied itself with the autocratic Junker land-owning aristocracy in the famous marriage of "iron and rye" that upheld Bismarckian authoritarianism, and later played some role in the rise of Hitler. Rather, Moore argued that democracy could emerge if a rapidly enlarging bourgeoisie succeeded in displacing the older order of land-owners and peasants. This happened in England, he noted, as an entre-preneurial bourgeoisie in the countryside succeeded in commercializing agriculture, driving peasants off the land, and using the proceeds to fund the Industrial Revolution. This cruel process had the effect of weak-ening the power of the old landed aristocracy while producing a modern working class.

Moore also paid particular attention to the form of agricultural pro-duction in a way that Marx did not. Marx largely ignored the peasantry, assuming that it would be eliminated by capitalist industrialization as it had been in England. However, revolutions broke out in Russia and China, where the vast majority of the population were peasants. Lenin and Mao came to power on the backs of peasants, despite the fact that Marx believed they were a class destined ultimately to disappear. Moore, taking these cases into account, argued that democratization faced spe-cial obstacles under conditions of what he called "labor-repressive" agri-culture, in which peasants were tied to the land in large, concentrated estates. The result was the survival of an authoritarian landowning class, which in turn spawned worker-peasant revolutionary movements. Be-tween these two extremes, the prospect of a middle-class democracy was poor. We have already seen this scenario play out in several Latin Amer-ican countries noted above.

Barrington Moore's book has spawned a vast literature that contests many of the points he made, but particularly his assertion that the bour-geoisie or middle classes were critical to the emergence of democracy.[4] Without going into the details of the scholarly controversy, it is clear that his hypothesis would have to be modified in certain important ways. For example, the bourgeoisie is far from being a unified group. It in-cludes large industrialists like the Thyssens and Rockefellers as well as small shopkeepers and urban professionals that the Marxists frequently referred to contemptuously as "petty bourgeois." The interests of these different segments varied according to circumstance; in many cases, im-portant middle-class groups did not invariably support democracy.[5] And though the working class could be recruited into radical antidemocratic Communist or agrarian movements, many working-class organizations in fact lined up solidly in support of democratic voting rights and rule of law.

It is important to note that the two components of liberal democracy—liberal rule of law and mass political participation—are separable political goals that initially tended to be favored by different social groups. Thus the middle-class authors of the French Revolution were not, as many historians have pointed out, committed democrats in the sense that they wanted immediate expansion of the franchise to peasants and workers. The Rights of Man were conceived as legal guarantees that would protect the property and personal freedoms of the bourgeoisie, limiting the power of the state but not necessarily empowering the mass of French citizens. Similarly, the Whigs, who forced the constitutional settlement on the English king during the Glorious Revolution in the previous century, were largely wealthy taxpayers that included part of the aristocracy, the gentry, and the upper middle classes. Their ranks were joined in the succeeding two centuries by the growing numbers of commercial and industrial bourgeoisie, as well as by middle-class lawyers, doctors, civil servants, teachers, and other professionals set off from the working classes by their education and property ownership. These groups constituted the base of support for the British Liberal Party during the nineteenth century. The main interest of the Liberals tended to be rule of law much more than democracy—that is, legal protection for private property and individual rights, as well as policies such as free trade, meritocratic civil service reform, and public education that would make possible upward mobility.

Over time, however, the liberal and the democratic agendas began to converge, and democracy became a middle-class goal. Rule of law and democratic accountability are, after all, alternative means of constraining power, and in practice are often mutually supportive. Protection of property rights against arbitrary state predation requires political power, which in turn can be achieved through expansion of the franchise. Similarly, citizens demanding the right to vote can be protected by a rule of law that restricts the government's ability to repress them. The right to vote came to be seen as just another protected legal right. Liberal democracy—a political system embodying both rule of law and universal suffrage—thus evolved into a single package desired by both middle-class groups and a significant part of the working class.

Barrington Moore was not himself a Marxist in the sense of wanting to see the victory of communism around the world. He saw liberal democracy as a desirable outcome while appreciating the powerful social forces that often made it unattainable. In this spirit, the Marxist analytical framework as modified by Moore remains extremely useful as a means of understanding how and why democracy spreads. The key insight is that democracy is desired most strongly by one specific social group in society: the middle class. If we are to understand the likelihood of democracy emerging, we need to evaluate the strength of the middle class relative to other social groups that prefer other forms of government, such as the old landed oligarchy who are inclined to support authoritarian systems, or radicalized groups of peasants or urban poor who are focused on economic redistribution. Modern democracy has a social basis, and if we don't pay attention to it, we will not be able to properly evaluate the prospects of democratic transitions.

We can summarize the major social actors whose relative strength and interactions determine the likelihood that democracy will emerge in a given society. These were the dominant groups that existed in Europe as the continent democratized during the nineteenth and early twentieth centuries; they are also groups that exist in many contemporary developing countries.

1. The middle classes, defined in occupational and educational terms rather than by level of income. They tended to support the liberal part of liberal democracy. That is, they wanted legal rules that protected their rights and particularly their property from predatory government. They may or may not have been supporters of democracy, understood as universal political participation, and they were even more ambivalent about if not overtly opposed to economic redistribution that might affect their own property and income. Middle-class groups were the primary leaders of the democratic transitions that took place in Denmark, Greece, France, Argentina, Portugal, and Spain in the nineteenth century, and were important parts of the coalitions that pressed for full democratization in Finland, Sweden, the Netherlands, Belgium, Germany, and Britain in the early twentieth.[6]

2. The working classes—Marx's famous industrial proletariat—were conversely more interested in the democratic part of liberal democracy, meaning their own right to participate politically. They

joined forces with middle-class groups to press for full expansion of the franchise in Denmark, Belgium, Finland, Sweden, the Netherlands, Germany, and Britain.[7] However, they were more interested in economic redistribution than the middle classes and often more focused on redistribution than liberal guarantees of property rights. For this reason significant parts of the working class around the world were willing to support nondemocratic anarchosyndicalist parties in the nineteenth century (as in Southern Europe or much of Latin America), or Communist or Fascist parties in the twentieth, parties that promised redistribution at the expense of liberal individual rights.

3. Large landowners, and particularly those making use of repressive labor (slavery, serfdom, or other nonmarket conditions of labor), have almost everywhere been authoritarian opponents of democracy. One of the most enduring of Barrington Moore's insights is the need to break the power of this particular social group by one means or another before full democracy can flourish.[8]

4. The peasantry had complicated and sometimes inconsistent political aspirations. In many societies they were an extremely conservative group, embracing traditional social values and willing to live in subordinate positions as clients of the landowning class. One of the earliest counterrevolutionary movements was the peasant uprising of the Vendée in 1793 that opposed the revolutionary government in Paris. As we saw in the Greek and Italian cases, they could be mobilized by conservative parties using clientelistic methods. Under the right circumstances, however, they could be radicalized to join forces with the working classes as supporters of revolution. They became the foot soldiers of the Bolshevik, Chinese, and Vietnamese revolutions.

These four groups constituted the major social actors whose interactions determined the course of political development and democratic transition in the nineteenth century. At the beginning of this period, virtually all of the world's most advanced countries were dominated by the last two of these groups, a landowning oligarchy and the peasantry. Increasing industrialization induced peasants to leave the countryside and enter the working class, and by the beginning of the twentieth century they were the largest social group. Under the impact of expanding trade, the number of middle-class individuals began to swell, first in Britain and the United States, then in France and Belgium, and by the late nineteenth century in Germany, Japan, and other "late developers." This then set the stage for the major social and political confrontations of the early twentieth century.

THE CENTRALITY OF POLITICAL PARTIES

Useful as it is, one of the weaknesses of Marx's analytical framework is his use of "class" as a key determining variable. Marx sometimes talks as if social classes—the bourgeoisie, the proletariat, feudalists—were clearly defined political actors capable of purposive rational decision making. In reality, social classes are intellectual abstractions, useful analytically but incapable of producing political action unless they are embodied in specific organizations. Newly mobilized social groups can participate politically in a wide variety of ways: through strikes and demonstrations, by use of the media, or today, through channels like Facebook and Twitter. Citizens can organize civil society groups to press for particular causes, or for mutual support. But if participation is to be enduring, it needs to be institutionalized, which for the past two centuries has meant the formation of political parties.

Thus the four groups listed above did not spring into the world as cohesive political actors like Athena from the head of Zeus. They had to be politically mobilized and represented by political parties. It is for this reason that political parties have been considered necessary to the success of any democracy, despite the fact that they were unanticipated by many early democratic theorists. Conservative parties like the Tory Party in Britain or the German Imperial Party started out as elite political factions that only later were forced to organize themselves as mass parties that could contest elections. The middle classes were represented by various liberal parties, like the Liberals in Britain or the Progress Party, the Left Liberals, or the National Liberals in Germany. The working class was mobilized under the banner of Socialist parties like the British Labour Party and the German Social Democratic Party, or, by the early twentieth century, the various Communist parties that had begun to appear on the fringes of the political landscape in virtually all industrializing societies. The peasants were the least well-organized social group. In Britain, the United States, Denmark, and Sweden, they had largely disappeared by the late nineteenth century because they had been converted into independent family farmers, or else simply driven off the land. In Greece and Italy, peasants were actually represented by conservative parties that used patronage to control them; in Bulgaria, they succeeded in forming their own party.

A central problem with any simple class-based analysis of democratization is that there were a number of cross-cutting issues that united people across class lines and blurred the class profiles of political parties. Among the most important were ethnicity, religion, and foreign policy. Thus the German Reichstag in the late nineteenth century contained parties representing the Polish and Danish minorities, as well as the Centre Party, which stood for Catholic interests and was itself divided into left and right wings. Issues like imperial policy and the building of a navy were conservative causes that drew working-class support. In Britain, there were sharp divisions over Irish Home Rule and empire that were often as important as class considerations in determining election outcomes. In the contemporary Middle East, Islamist parties tend to have a social base in the lower classes and in rural areas, but their overt message is based on religion rather than class.

Thus, while political parties may try to represent the interests of particular social classes, they are very often also autonomous political actors that can get power by mobilizing voters from different classes by shifting their agendas from economic ones to identity politics, religion, or foreign policy. They do not actually have to represent the true interests of the social classes that support them. At one extreme, the Communist Parties in Russia and China ended up being among the greatest oppressors of workers and peasants in human history. In the United States, the Republican Party, traditionally the bastion of business interests, gets substantial support from working-class voters who support it on cultural rather than economic grounds.

Like state bureaucracies, political parties are not simply robotic arms controlled by underlying social classes. Rather, they can exercise a great deal of choice in how they represent their constituents. Political parties are created by political entrepreneurs who organize followings around particular ideas and who then go on to organize real-world political machines. Successful Communist parties required the organizational genius of leaders like Vladimir Lenin to come to power. Conservative parties were animated by ideas about tradition, religion, monarchy, and stability.

As their underlying social bases went into decline and they were forced to compete for mass electorates, some, like the British Conservatives, were able to change their agendas to make themselves appealing to middle- and working-class electorates. Others, like the Italian Christian Democrats, survived and prospered through their ability to organize vast clientelistic networks. Those conservative parties that failed to adapt to these new conditions of electoral politics were tempted to resort to nondemocratic methods for preserving their power, like the Argentine coup of 1930 (see chapter 18 above). Clientelistic party organization often went hand in hand with a personalistic political style, in which supporters were rallied around particular charismatic individuals like Juan and Eva Perón rather than around a coherent program. Organizational capacity was thus not something that could be readily predicted simply by looking at the strength of different social classes. It depended on historically contingent factors like leadership, personality, and ideas.

ECONOMIC GROWTH, SOCIAL MOBILIZATION, AND DEMOCRACY

Why did democracy spread, and why might it spread farther in the future? Democratic institutions are driven by multiple causes, but one of the most important centers on economic change. Economic growth is linked to democracy in a multistage process, as illustrated in Figure 21. Economic growth engenders social mobilization via the spreading division of labor, and social mobilization in turn produces demands for both rule of law and greater democracy. The traditional elites that dominated the old agrarian order frequently try to block entry of the newer groups into the system. A stable democratic system will emerge only if these newly mobilized groups are successfully incorporated into the system and allowed to participate politically. Conversely, instability and disorder will occur if those groups do not have institutionalized channels of participation.

In this context, ideas can still be very important, but they are related to changes in the other dimensions of development. For example, the idea of the universal equality of human dignity has been around for centuries, but in static agrarian societies it never gained much traction because such societies had an extremely low degree of social mobility. Peasants periodically revolted and challenged the political status quo. This could be

FIGURE 21. Economic Development and Democracy

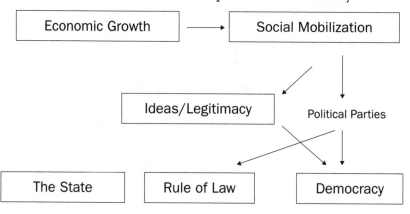

sparked by some outrageous violation of their rights, or out of sheer hunger and desperation. But while individual leaders of such revolts might aspire to join the oligarchy, it never occurred to them to displace the class-bound system as such. Hence they never became true revolutionaries. The idea of social equality acquired a broad galvanizing power only when in parts of Europe during the seventeenth and eighteenth centuries an expanding capitalist economic system started reordering the social system. Modern capitalism both required and produced social mobility, and as a consequence demands for equality of access and opportunity expanded. There are thus multiple lines of causality linking social mobilization to democracy and the rule of law. Ideas were important and had their own autonomy—neither Adam Smith nor Karl Marx could be understood as a mere spokesman for the social class out of which he sprang—but receptivity to ideas was shaped by social context and deep economic changes.

Democracy emerged in Europe in gradual stages over a 150-year period, as a result of struggles among the middle classes, working class, old oligarchy, and peasantry, all being shaped in turn by underlying changes in the economy and society. The Marx-Moore framework, with a few emendations, remains basically sound. It is this story that I will flesh out in the following chapter.

28

THE LONG ROAD TO DEMOCRACY

How European democracy advanced in the nineteenth century as societies changed; arguments against democracy before its triumph; how conservative parties often determined the nature of democratic advance

I told the story in Volume 1 of the rise of accountable government in England and the United States. Accountability was the result of what seems
in retrospect to be the almost accidental survival of a feudal institution,
the medieval estate or parliament, into the modern era. In the Middle
Ages, taxing authority was vested in these estates, which represented the
oligarchic layer of property owners in the society. In France, Spain, Sweden,
Prussia, and Russia, the monarchy succeeded from the late sixteenth century on in undermining the power of the estates and consolidating absolutist rule. In Poland and Hungary, by contrast, the estates were victorious
over the monarchy and created a weak decentralized political system that
was soon militarily overwhelmed by foreign conquerors. Only in England
was the power of the Parliament evenly matched against that of the monarchy. The former succeeded in fighting the latter to a standstill in the
course of the seventeenth century, an impasse that eventually resulted in
the constitutional settlement of 1688–1689, the Glorious Revolution.

Accountable government is not simply a matter of opposition groups
overwhelming a government and forcing it to do their bidding. Throughout human history, out-groups have fought in-groups, and once they
succeeded in displacing the power holder became the new oppressive in-
group. Accountable government, by contrast, means formal recognition
of the principle of accountability to a broader public and the legitimacy
of opposition. This is where ideas came to play a critical role. John Locke
explained that the authority of all governments lay not in divine right

but in their ability to protect the individual rights of their citizens. Governments are potentially the prime violators of those rights. He further argued that "no government can have a right to obedience from a people who have not freely consented to it"; what we today call legitimacy therefore flowed from the ability of a people to "choose their government and governors." "No taxation without representation" and "consent of the governed" were the animating principles of the Glorious Revolution and of the American Revolution that took place less than a century later. The shift in understanding from the "rights of Englishmen" (that is, traditional feudal rights) to "natural rights" (universal rights held by all human beings) meant that these new revolutions would never simply be about the displacement of one elite group by another.

But even though the Glorious Revolution established the principle of parliamentary accountability, England was still very far from anything like true democracy at the beginning of the eighteenth century. Those sitting in Parliament were elected by a small, well-to-do part of the country, no more than 3 percent of the whole population as late as 1830. So the story of the arrival of democracy, as opposed to accountability, takes place in the centuries following the settlement of 1689.

Since the rule of law and democratic accountability can be conceived of as alternative means of constraining the government, it is not surprising that the two have been closely associated with one another historically and promoted in common. During the English Civil War, one of the biggest grievances of the parliamentary side against the king was the fact that he was trampling on the Common Law. The early Stuarts had prosecuted opponents through bodies of questionable legality like the King's Court of the Star Chamber. The parliamentary demands were that the monarchy be accountable to them on matters of taxation and that it act under the law. It is adherence to the rule of law that guarantees that an out-group that succeeds in displacing an in-group will not use its newfound access to power as a means of prosecuting its opponents in revenge.

Though the two components of liberal democracy that constrain the state—the liberal rule of law part and the democratic accountability part—are often associated, they remain conceptually separable. As noted in the last chapter, they tend to be championed by different social groups. This means that liberal democracy seldom arrived in a neat package but was introduced sequentially over time. It also makes the dating of the onset of democracy very difficult. When, for example, did the United States become a liberal democracy? Rule of law arrived much earlier than democracy, with introduction of the Common Law into the colonies well before the revolution and the Constitutional Convention. But equal access to the law still took centuries to implement. Though most Americans assume democracy arrived with the adoption of the Constitution in the late eighteenth century, the franchise was severely limited in 1787 and was progressively opened up to white men without property, African Americans, and women in a slow process that wasn't completed until ratification of the Nineteenth Amendment in 1920. Indeed, various constraints on voting by blacks in the South meant that full legal enfranchisement had to wait until passage of the Voting Rights Act in 1965.

If we apply these different criteria of liberal democracy backward in time to the nineteenth century, we see that the democratization of Europe and other countries in the First Wave was an extremely protracted process. Table 6 presents the dates on which different countries achieved various milestones with regard to expansion of the franchise, and indicates both the length of time required to get to universal suffrage and the variance across different countries. Besides limiting the franchise, authoritarian governments in nineteenth-century Europe did many other things to check democracy. Prussia, for example, adopted universal male suffrage in 1849, but under a three-tier voting system and an open ballot that wasn't abolished until 1918. Some countries like Britain, Italy, and Denmark had unelected upper houses that could veto or otherwise alter legislation. Many countries imposed restrictions on political organization, particularly on the part of new working-class groups operating under socialist or communist banners. Democratization in this period was not, moreover, a one-way process; some countries like France granted rights to their citizens, only to take them away with the return to power of authoritarian regimes, in a recurring cycle.

THE FRANCHISE

The European route to democracy unfolded in stages, punctuated by long periods of stasis or active regression. The simplest reason for this circuitous route is that Europe was not socially ready for democracy until the final third of the nineteenth century.

TABLE 6. Expansion of the Franchise in Selected Countries[1]

Country		Year	
	% of Pop. Enfranchised	Manhood Suffrage	Universal Suffrage
Austria	6.0 (1873)	1907	1919
Belgium	1.0 (1831)	1919	1949
Britain	2.3 (1830)	1918	1929
Denmark	14–15 (1848)	1849	1915
Finland	–	1906	1906
France	0.25 (1815)	1875	1945
Greece	–	1864	1952
Iceland	9.8 (1903)	1920	1920
Ireland	0.2 (1830)	1918	1923
Italy	2.3 (1871)	1919	1945
Japan	1.0 (1899)	1899	1946
Luxembourg	2.0 (1848)	1892	1919
Netherlands	2.4 (1851)	1917	1917
Norway	–	1898	1915
Prussia/Germany	–	1849/1867	1919
South Korea	–	1948	1948
Sweden	4.8 (1865)	1920	1920
Switzerland	–	1848	1959–1990
United States	9.4 (1828)	1820s	1920

SOURCE: Rokkan and Eisenstadt, *Building States and Nations*; Tilly, *Democracy*

As noted in the preface, while the French Revolution brought the Code Napoléon to much of Europe and secured a modern administrative state in France itself, it did not establish democracy. Napoleon's defeat ushered in a prolonged period of authoritarian reversion under the aegis of the Austrian-Prussian-Russian Holy Alliance, in which conservative monarchical regimes tried to turn back the clock to the period before 1789. There was a gradient of absolutism stretching from west to east. Republican government existed only in some Swiss cantons and German city-states. France, the Netherlands, Belgium, Norway, and some of the other German states (as well as, of course, Britain) had constitutional monarchies in which the king's formal powers were limited by law. In the Austro-Hungarian Empire, Prussia, Italy, and Russia, monarchs faced far fewer checks on their power, though most ruled through bureaucracies that were grounded in some form of civil law.[2]

The second great surge toward democracy occurred with the Revolutions of 1848, raising hopes that were just as quickly dashed. In the words of historian Eric Hobsbawm, "1848 appears as the one revolution in the modern history of Europe which combines the greatest promise, the widest scope, and the most immediate initial success, with the most unqualified and rapid failure."[3] The "Springtime of Peoples," to which the Arab Spring has been compared, affected virtually every country in the core of Europe. It started in France with the downfall of the July Monarchy and proclamation of a Second Republic in February, and then spread to Bavaria, Prussia, Austria, Hungary, and Italy the following month. The only countries not destabilized were at the periphery of the continent: Sweden, Britain, Greece, Spain, and Russia. The revolutions were then rapidly suppressed, beginning with the Habsburg recovery in May and continuing through the rest of the continent by the end of the year. The brisk spread of revolutionary ideas demonstrates that the "contagion effect" of democratic awakenings was not the by-product of the Internet and social media but could occur in an age of newspapers as well.[4]

Both the outbreak of these revolutions as well as their ultimate failure reflected the incomplete nature of the social transformations that were occurring in Europe. At the beginning of the nineteenth century, the greater part of Europe was still agrarian, with landowners and peasants as the major actors. Only in Britain and the Netherlands were there middle-class groups of any significant size or political weight. But by the middle of the century, a small commercial and industrial bourgeoisie had emerged virtually everywhere, and with the spread of education and literacy, newspapers and public discussions became much more common. The decade of the 1840s saw the organization of what today we would call "civil society" throughout continental Europe: voluntary private associations, often organized around banqueting or public festivals, in which like-minded people could gather, exchange views, and express opinions critical of governments. (Such organizations had existed in Britain at a much earlier point.) Political parties, however, were in most places illegal. In the more repressive territories, activists had to organize secret societies, like the Young Italy of Giuseppe Mazzini. It was these middle-class groups, legal and illegal, that would spearhead the Revolutions of 1848.[5]

The social transformation was at this point very incomplete, however; even in the most economically advanced European societies, the middle class still constituted a minority of the population. These middle classes were themselves split between those who wanted strong legal protections for their persons and property rights, and those interested in broader democratic participation. The majority of European populations remained peasants, artisans and tradesmen, and an incipient working class that was at this point largely unorganized. The European situation was thus comparable to that of emerging market countries like Thailand and China today. The conservatives in 1848 were able to break the revolutionary momentum by splitting the ranks of the middle class through appeals to nationalism, and by playing on its fears of disorder.

The decades immediately following the restoration of the conservative order post-1848 would prove to be the most economically and socially transformative in European history, as they were in the history of the United States. The more advanced countries—Britain, France, Germany, Belgium, and the Netherlands—went from being majority agrarian societies to urban-industrial ones on the eve of World War I. This led to an enormous change in social classes and created the basis for a new mass democratic politics.

Hobsbawm's judgment about the completeness of the failure of the Revolutions of 1848 is therefore too severe. The outbreak of revolution and fear that it might recur lay in the back of the minds of all authoritarian leaders in the second half of the nineteenth century, and set an agenda for political changes that would unfold in the succeeding two generations. Prussia, for example, put in place a universal franchise between 1847 and 1867, albeit with an open ballot and tiered voting. The newly unified Germany after 1871 adopted a formal constitution that for the first time created a role for an elected Reichstag. The legalization of political parties provided an opening for the Social Democratic Party to organize; despite the arch-conservative Chancellor Bismarck's attempts to suppress it, the Social Democrats became the largest group within the Reichstag by the eve of World War I. Bismarck implemented Europe's first social security and health insurance systems in the 1880s in an effort to steal the thunder of the new working-class parties.

Similarly in France, Louis Napoleon, who came to power via a coup in 1851 and declared himself the Emperor Napoleon III, nonetheless felt he had to legitimate his rule by staging a plebiscite (having been once elected president of the republic that emerged in the wake of the 1848 revolution). The French had gotten used to the idea of voting, even if under highly managed conditions. The Second Empire was, moreover, a liberal one in which diverse political views could be openly expressed. The economic expansion that took place under it paved the way for the more genuinely democratic Third Republic that was declared after defeat in the Franco-Prussian War and the Paris Commune. Many of the moves toward more liberal societies and greater democracy were thus the work of conservative leaders who lived through 1848 and were conscious of the fact that they faced societies mobilized in ways they had not been earlier in the century.

The middle-class supporters of constitutional government at midcentury would turn out to be inconsistent democrats, however, because the democratic impulse was hijacked, in many countries, by nationalism. The German liberals sitting in the Frankfurt and Berlin parliaments were often more interested in the creation of a united Germany than they were in the democratization of the existing German states. As elites, they were willing to let themselves "represent" the nation without actually wanting to give their fellow citizens the right to vote. Many of them ended up supporting Bismarck and his authoritarian Reich when he proved to be the one individual capable of creating a united Germany. As leaders and beneficiaries of German capitalism, they did not hesitate to abandon economic liberalism when the state offered tariff protections to their industries. Similarly, many of the liberals in the component territories of the Austro-Hungarian Empire were more interested in securing their own privileges as national elites than in expansion of the franchise. In Britain, opposition to Irish Home Rule and support for the empire allowed the conservatives to attract support not just from the middle class but also from the working class in the late nineteenth century. This would not be the last time that nationalism would trump class interest in Europe.

ARGUMENTS AGAINST DEMOCRACY

Resistance to the spread of democracy lay in the realm of ideas as well as in the material interests of Europe's existing elites. In the nineteenth century, many serious intellectuals were willing to make thoughtful arguments against a universal franchise, or the principle of one man, one vote. It is worth reviewing some of those arguments, since a number of them remain salient even if few people are willing to articulate them openly today.

One of the most sustained critiques of democracy was provided by the philosopher John Stuart Mill, whose *On Liberty* has been a foundational text for liberals since its publication in 1859. In *Thoughts on Parliamentary Government*, published in 1861 before the Second Reform Act, Mill made several arguments against a universal and equal franchise. He began with the classic Whig argument that "the assembly which votes the taxes, either general or local, should be elected exclusively by those who pay something towards the taxes imposed."[6] The idea that only taxpayers should vote was the flip side of the principle "no taxation without representation" that was the motto of both the English and American Revolutions. Mill therefore believed it was better to impose direct rather than indirect taxes, since that would remind citizens of their obligations to be vigilant about how the government spent their money. This implied further that the "receipt of parish relief should be a peremptory disqualification for the franchise." In other words, people on welfare should not have the right to vote, since they were essentially freeloading off of taxpayers.

Mill's second argument against an equal franchise had to do with the qualifications and sense of responsibility of voters. He did not contest the principle of universal franchise, since "the possession and the exercise of political, and among others of electoral, rights, is one of the chief instruments both of moral and of intellectual training for the popular mind." He did, however, contest one man, one vote. In an argument that sounds particularly foreign to contemporary ears, he noted that "if it is asserted that all persons ought to be equal in every description of right recognised by society, I answer, not until all are equal in worth as human beings."[7] This led to a conclusion that different classes of people should have different numbers of votes based on their level of education: an unskilled laborer, one vote; a foreman, three; and a lawyer, physician, or clergyman, five or six. He noted that Louis Napoleon had just been elected president of France by millions of "peasants who could neither read nor write, and whose knowledge of public men, even by name, was limited to oral tradition."[8] Very similar arguments would be used by whites in the American South to restrict or take away voting rights from African

Americans in the decades following the Civil War as Jim Crow laws spread.

Other thinkers made the argument that only elites were capable of objective guardianship of the public interest and should therefore be trusted to represent those who did not have the right to vote. Back in the eighteenth century, for example, Edmund Burke suggested that members of the House of Commons elected from rotten boroughs or otherwise unequal franchises did not enjoy better roads, prisons, or police than those who were underrepresented, since that privileged class of people were able to "stand clearer of local interests, passions, prejudices and cabals, than the others" and therefore to produce "a more general view."[9] The working classes in themselves were not qualified to rule: "The occupation of a hairdresser, or of a working tallow-chandler cannot be a matter of honor to any person . . . The state suffers oppression if such as they . . . are permitted to rule."[10]

This perspective was taken up by Walter Bagehot's classic work *The English Constitution*, published in 1866 just before the introduction of the Second Reform Bill, in which he asserted: "I do not consider the exclusion of the working classes from effectual representation a defect in *this* aspect of our parliamentary representation. The working classes contribute almost nothing to our corporate public opinion, and therefore, the fact of their want of influence in Parliament does not impair the coincidence of Parliament with public opinion. They are left out in the representation, and also in the thing represented."[11] What Bagehot called the "dignified" parts of the government—the monarchy and the House of Lords—actually attracted considerable public support and therefore sufficed as a basis for legitimacy in the absence of the active participation of the working classes and poor in government.[12]

A different sort of argument was made against democracy by a series of conservative Italian thinkers, who asserted that it was pointless to open up the franchise since true democracy was impossible to achieve. This view was first articulated by Gaetano Mosca, who stated that the different regime types—monarchy, aristocracy, democracy—made little difference to actual life because all were in the end controlled by elites. The "political class" maintains itself in power under a wide variety of institutions and will simply use democratic ones to do the same. Even "Communist and collectivist societies would beyond any doubt be managed by officials." The economist Vilfredo Pareto (familiar to economics students as the inventor of the Pareto optimum) made a similar case for continuing elite domination regardless of the type of regime. Based on his statistical studies of income distribution, he formulated a "Pareto's law," which argued that 80 percent of wealth was held by 20 percent of the population across time and space. Since this was akin to a natural law, efforts to remedy it through political measures like expansion of the franchise or income redistribution were pointless.[13]

These conservative Italian thinkers were making a variant of the argument put forward by Marx himself, namely, that the advent of formal democracy and an expanded franchise would not improve the lives of the mass of the population but would simply preserve elite dominance in a different form. Mosca and Pareto believed that different institutions would not change this situation, and therefore they argued in favor of a continuation of the status quo. Marx believed, of course, that a solution existed in the form of a proletarian revolution. His followers would go on to try to engineer a truly egalitarian society following the Bolshevik and other Communist Revolutions of the twentieth century. In one sense, the Italians were proved right: communism did not eliminate the distinction between rulers and ruled, or end oppression by elites; it merely changed the identity of those in charge.

The fact that the Communist solution to the problem that Marx, Mosca, and Pareto identified—continued elite dominance despite the advent of formal democracy—ended in failure does not mean that the original critique was entirely wrong. Democratic procedures like regular elections and press freedoms do not guarantee that the people will be adequately represented. (I will return to this problem in chapter 31 and in Part IV below.)

The argument that uneducated people could not exercise the franchise responsibly was vulnerable to the spread of mass public education, which most European societies began to implement toward the end of the nineteenth century. The same was not true for novel antidemocratic arguments based on biology. After publication of Charles Darwin's *On the Origin of Species* in 1859, a school of "scientific" racism sprang up to explain and justify not just the ongoing colonial conquest of non-European peoples but also the failure to grant equal rights to blacks, immigrants, and ethnic minorities. Women as well were held to be insufficiently rational to be granted the vote, and in any event destined by their biology to be unqualified for male workplace occupations.[14]

It is important to note that all of these nineteenth-century antidemocratic arguments accepted many of the modern conceptual foundations
underpinning democracy. They granted the notion that governments
should be accountable to citizens, and that all citizens capable of exercising good political judgment ought to have the right to political participation. Where they differed from contemporary norms was in their
assessment of the ability of different classes of individuals—the poor or
propertyless, the uneducated, blacks and other racial and ethnic minorities, women—to responsibly exercise political power. This meant that they
were vulnerable to certain empirical facts: when society did not disinte-
grate as a result of extending the franchise to workers or to women, or
when poor people or blacks could be educated and rise socially, it became
much harder to maintain principled arguments in favor of their continuing political exclusion.

Very few contemporary politicians would dare to make overt arguments in favor of franchise restrictions, or for qualifying voters on the
basis of education or income. This is particularly true in a country like
the United States where franchise restrictions have corresponded to racial
hierarchy.

But echoes of virtually all of these nineteenth-century conservative
arguments remain in contemporary political discourse. It is common, for
example, for elites to complain about democratic voters choosing "populist" policies. From their perspective, democratic electorates do not always choose well: they may choose short-term demands over long-term
sustainability; they often vote on the basis of personality rather than policies; they sometimes vote for clientelistic reasons; they may want to redistribute income in ways that will kill incentives and growth. In the
end, these fears do not amount to a convincing argument for systematic
franchise restriction. As in the nineteenth century, elites are often good
at dressing up their own narrow self-interest as universal truths.

But voters in democracies don't get things right all the time either,
especially in the short term. Moreover, it is not clear that the solution to
contemporary governance problems lies in ever-higher levels of popular
participation. As political scientist Bruce Cain argues, most voters simply do not have the time, energy, or expertise to devote to the careful
study of complex public policy issues. When higher levels of democratic
participation are encouraged by putting more issues before voters through

mechanisms like public referenda, the result is often not the accurate representation of popular will but the domination of the public space by the best-organized and most richly resourced interest groups.[15] The creation of merit-based bureaucracies, ultimately accountable to the public but protected in many ways from the vagaries of democratic politics, is one expression of the concerns raised in these now-forgotten arguments against the spread of democracy.

CONSERVATIVES IN CHARGE

Both classical Marxists and contemporary economists have reduced the struggle for democracy to a fight between the rich and the poor, in which the poor organize and threaten the rich with the objective of redistributing wealth and income to themselves. Democracy emerges when the threat is severe enough that the rich make concessions with regard to political rights and outright redistribution.[16] The middle classes can make alliances in either direction, but more often than not they are bought off by the rich to support at most very limited democracy. Any arguments regarding justice or legitimacy are merely "superstructure" masking hard economic self-interests. In the Marxist version of this story, the rich never concede enough to bring about true democracy; this happens only after a violent seizure of power by the poor. A statistical study by Adam Przeworski shows that most franchise extensions were in fact undertaken in response to popular mobilizations, and that democracy was therefore conquered rather than granted.[17]

But conservative social groups can interpret their self-interest in a variety of different ways, some of which are much more conducive than others to nonviolent transitions to democracy. The reason why liberal democracy was peacefully consolidated in Britain by the third decade of the twentieth century when compared to places like Germany and Argentina (not to speak of Russia and China) had much to do with the tactical behavior of the British Conservative Party. The Conservatives at the beginning of the nineteenth century were the party of the old landed elite, comparable to the parties representing the Junkers in Prussia or the large estate owners in Argentina. But instead of trying to resist spreading social and political mobilization through violence or authoritarian rule, the British Conservatives reinterpreted their own self-interest in ways that permitted preservation of their political power while allowing expansion of the franchise.

Britain was one of the slower European countries to fully democratize. Franchise expansion stretched out over three major reform bills in 1832, 1867, and 1884. As noted in Table 6, universal adult male suffrage did not arrive until 1918 and female suffrage took until 1929.[18] The 1832 Reform Act could indeed be seen as a worried conservative response to threats and agitation coming from below as a result of economic change. But the 1867 and 1884 Acts, which genuinely democratized Britain, were the work of a Conservative prime minister, Benjamin Disraeli, and a Liberal one, William Gladstone, who were operating not under the threat of imminent revolution but under a rather different political calculus.

Virtually all contemporary observers were agreed that the "Great" Reform Act of 1867 was not driven by grassroots agitation. There was a sense on the part of the elites that "silent changes were taking place in the minds of members of the working classes, not unlike movements of the earth's crust," and there was a general expectation that the 1832 reform would be followed by subsequent political initiatives. It was not the Liberals led by Gladstone who brought about this shift, but his Conservative archrival Disraeli who introduced a radical reform bill that led to an immediate doubling of the franchise.[19]

Disraeli's motives have been debated ever since. Many of his fellow Conservatives denounced him as a traitor to their class interests, or at best an opportunist who in the heat of a political struggle broke with principle. Historian Gertrude Himmelfarb has argued, however, that Disraeli's actions sprang from a different kind of principle, a belief that the Tories were a national party representing a natural order in which the aristocracy and the working class were allies. The Tory creed had an impetus toward democracy because of "the belief that the lower classes were not only naturally conservative in temperament but also Conservative in politics."[20] In other words, the views expressed by Burke in the previous century that the conservative oligarchy could "represent" the interests of the whole nation were not just an ideological smokescreen hiding class interest; it was a view that people of Burke's social class genuinely believed.

And it was not just the wealthy Tories who believed it. After accepting a second expansion of the franchise in 1884, the Conservatives went on to dominate British electoral politics for much of the next generation.

Disraeli was right: many working-class and poor rural constituents voted for the Tories in subsequent elections, despite their class interests. (This is a phenomenon familiar to Americans in the early twenty-first century, where many working-class voters prefer Republican candidates despite the toll that Republican economic policies like free trade and de-unionization have taken on their incomes.) The Conservatives represented a set of values revolving around church, tradition, monarchy, and British national identity that had appeal for working-class voters, and were able later to shift the agenda to other issues like foreign policy. This allowed the Tories to change their social base: it was no longer the party of large landowners but of a rising urban middle class. On certain issues (for example, protection of property rights) these voters sided with the old oligarchy, but on others the new middle-class electorate accepted arguments being put forth for an expanded franchise. These trends combined with a great penchant for political organization to make the Conservatives a winning party.[21]

The British pattern of democratization being initiated by elite parties rather than pushed from below by grassroots mobilization was not unique. Political scientist Ruth Collier notes that the kind of top-down process she labels "electoral support mobilization" drove the "ins" to enfranchise the "outs" in Switzerland, Chile, Norway, Italy, and Uruguay, as well as in Britain. These cases illustrate the way institutional arrangements can become self-reinforcing: once the principle of electoral politics is established under a limited franchise, incumbent parties can attempt to stay in power by seeking new voters, shifting to new issues, and reaching out across class lines.[22]

Some elite groups, of course, chose not to play by democratic rules, but turned to the army or nondemocratic forms of mobilization to protect their interests. This is what happened in Italy and Germany in the 1920s and '30s, Argentina in 1930, and many other Latin American countries in the wake of the Cuban Revolution in 1959. Which path they chose to take depended on any number of factors: whether Conservatives believed they could retain control of a democratic opening; how united they were; how united and therefore threatening the democratic forces were; and what elites in other countries had done. The newer industrial middle class tended to be more open to change than the old landed oligarchy, not just because its capital was more mobile but also because it was more urbanized, better educated, and more likely to rub shoulders with other cultural and international elites bearing more progressive ideas.

Ideas and norms shaped material interests: the British landed upper classes were far more ready to let their daughters marry wealthy up-and-coming commoners than were their Prussian Junker counterparts, and much more willing to be persuaded by Whiggish notions that the spread of education and literacy would make it safe to permit their working-class countrymen the right to vote.[23]

Unfortunately, the story of democratization in most of Europe did not end with gradual and peaceful franchise extensions. For Europe as a whole, the national question took precedence over the class question as the continent was engulfed in two world wars. The solidarity of the Second Socialist International was undermined as the working classes in Germany, Austria, Britain, France, and Russia lined up behind their respective governments in August 1914. In many countries, including Britain, full adult male suffrage had to await the end of the Great War in 1918 when the sacrifices of the working classes in the trenches made it morally impossible to deny them the vote. The defeat of Germany and Austria in the war led to the abdication of the German emperor and the creation of the Weimar Republic, and the dissolution of the Austro-Hungarian Empire.

But while the political structures of the old authoritarian order were dismantled, the social bases of the political right in Central and Eastern Europe were not eliminated. The old landed oligarchies continued to exercise power behind the scenes through their influence over the civilian bureaucracy and the army. The middle classes, whose savings and security were destroyed in the postwar inflation and economic turmoil, were ripe for recruitment into the new Fascist parties that sprang up in the 1920s. The working classes, for their part, had been radicalized by the war and by the recent example of the Bolshevik Revolution, and were recruited into new Communist parties with little commitment to liberal democracy. The ensuing polarization hollowed out the political center in Germany, Austria, and Italy, facilitated the rise of Hitler and Mussolini, and paved the way for World War II. It was not until the second half of the twentieth century that stable liberal democracy finally spread throughout Western Europe, and not until the collapse of communism in 1989–1991 that it was extended into Eastern Europe as well. The European road to democracy was long indeed.

29

FROM 1848 TO THE ARAB SPRING

Origins of the Arab Spring; differences and similarities between the contemporary Middle East and nineteenth-century Europe; religion and nationalism as alternative routes to political mobilization

The Arab Spring began in January 2011 with the self-immolation of a Tunisian street vendor named Mohamed Bouazizi, which brought down the dictatorship of Zine al-Abidine Ben Ali and triggered a cascade of uprisings that spread to Egypt, Yemen, Libya, Bahrain, and Syria, and threatened the stability of every regime in the region. Bouazizi, according to press reports, had his produce cart confiscated on several occasions by the police; when he went to protest, he was slapped and insulted by police officials. Denied recognition of his basic dignity, he doused himself with gasoline and set himself on fire, eventually dying of his burns two weeks later. His story, broadcast around the Arab world, evoked sympathy and outrage, and proved to be the trigger for a major political revolution.

Some observers had believed that Muslim or Arab countries faced special obstacles to democratization absent in other regions of the world, since it was the one region largely unaffected by the Third Wave of democratization. Either Islam or Arab culture was held somehow responsible for resistance to liberal democracy. Any simple arguments that the Arabs were exceptional and would passively accept dictatorship ended with the events of early 2011.[1]

Predictions that Arab societies will not be able to sustain liberal democracy may prove correct in the longer run. Four years into the Arab Spring, it does not appear that this form of government is likely to emerge anytime soon in countries affected by it, with the possible exception of the country in which it began, Tunisia. In Egypt, the formerly banned Muslim Brotherhood was elected and dominated the new parliament and presidency for a year, until the military pushed its president, Mohamed Morsi, out of power in the summer of 2013. The Egyptian state then launched a bloody crackdown against not only Islamist groups but against liberal critics as well. The Tahrir Square uprising was not a revolution that displaced the military-led state; it only pushed it into a tactical retreat. Libya remains chaotic in the wake of the military struggle against Muammar Qaddafi, with the central government unable to disarm the country's many militias. Peaceful protests against Syria's Bashar al-Assad were ruthlessly crushed, and the country descended into a prolonged civil war that has pitted radical Islamist fighters against the Ba'athist dictatorship. In Bahrain and the other Arab Gulf states, protests were violently repressed and the traditional monarchies remain in power. Throughout the region, violence and instability have helped the fortunes of jihadist groups that are overtly antidemocratic.

These unfavorable outcomes have led many observers in the West to decry the phenomenon of the Arab Spring as a whole. Some are speaking from a perspective of simple national self-interest: the United States, Israel, and other countries had developed mutually beneficial relationships with the old dictatorships in the Arab world, and are now facing instability and uncertainty within the region. But others make a broader argument that the Arab Spring does not represent a democratic wave but rather the self-assertion of political Islam, and will result at best in illiberal democracy or at worst in the spread of radical Islam and continuing chaos.[2]

It is of course impossible to predict the long-term consequences of the Arab Spring. However, those observers who criticize the chaotic results of this upheaval and argue that they cannot lead to a good democratic outcome in the long run often fail to remember what a long, chaotic, and violent process the democratization of Europe was. A stable, well-functioning liberal democracy involves the interaction of a number of different institutions: not just elections for a president or legislature but also well-organized political parties, an independent court system, an effective state bureaucracy, and a free and vigilant media. In addition, there are a number of cultural conditions necessary: politicians and voters cannot have a winner-take-all attitude toward their opponents, they must respect rules more than individuals, and they must share a collective sense of identity and nationhood.

Bringing down dictators like Ben Ali or Mubarak eliminates only one source of authoritarian power. Putting the other institutions in place is not a process that happens overnight. The American architects of the 2003 Iraq invasion expected that democracy would appear spontaneously in the wake of their removal of Saddam Hussein. They discovered to their dismay that they had to preside over a chaotic and violent society from which institutions were largely absent.

What lessons do earlier democratic transitions hold for the future of the Arab Spring? There are many obvious differences between the Middle East and regions like Eastern Europe and Latin America, beginning with culture and the impact of Islam. Indeed, nineteenth-century Europe may constitute a better precedent for political change in the Arab world than the democratic transitions of the Third Wave that took place from the 1970s on. In the late-twentieth-century transitions in Latin America and Eastern Europe, we are dealing mostly with countries that already had had some experience with democracy. Those early democratic periods, some of which had lasted for decades, were interrupted by military takeovers in Latin America and by foreign occupation in Eastern Europe. Democratization was therefore in some sense the restoration of an older political order that had roots in the national experience of each country. In Latin America especially, there were already well-established democratic political parties that regenerated themselves rather quickly once an opening occurred. In Eastern Europe, the countries of Western Europe and the European Union constituted nearby and powerful examples of successful democracy that could offer substantial assistance and incentives to democratize.

By contrast, the Arab world today and Europe in the nineteenth century had no prior experience of democracy. While there is today a large international community providing both political models and concrete democracy assistance, it is largely based in the United States and other Western countries, and therefore suspect by many in the Arab world. This differs markedly from the open embrace of the European Union, NATO, and other Western institutions by Eastern European countries newly liberated from Soviet domination.

While both the contemporary Middle East and nineteenth-century Europe had no direct experience with democracy, there are also important differences between the regions, beginning with political Islam. Religion played a major role in nineteenth-century Europe as well: the

German Centre Party and the Christian Democratic parties in France and Italy were organized to defend religious as opposed to class interests. But still, class and nation tended to be more important sources of identity than religion in Europe, while the reverse is more often the case in the Middle East today. (This was not always so; from the 1950s to the 1970s Arab politics was dominated more by secular nationalists than by Islamists, with a sprinkling of left-wing Socialist and Communist parties.)

Conservative forces have a different character as well. Of today's Muslim countries, only Pakistan has a social structure of large landowners dominating masses of peasants, as most European countries did in the early nineteenth century. Conservatives in most Muslim and Arab countries are recruited from tribal elites, traditional monarchical families and their clients, military officers, crony capitalists surrounding the old authoritarian regimes, and Islamists. Europe's conservatives did not have external sources of support, except for the help they rendered each other. Middle Eastern conservatives, by contrast, have gotten substantial external assistance from the United States and other Western countries over the years, and from the bonanza represented by oil and gas in the Persian Gulf. The working classes throughout the region are much less powerful than they were in nineteenth-century Europe, since much of the region, similar to Greece and southern Italy, has experienced "modernization without development." Trade unions exist in Egypt and other parts of the Arab world, and although they played important roles in the initial fight against the authoritarian regime, they do not represent massive and growing segments of the population in the way they did in nineteenth-century Britain or Germany.

Nonetheless, there are a number of similarities between the Arab world and Europe a century ago. In the first place, the democratization process was rooted in social mobilization driven by underlying socioeconomic change. As industrialization progressed in nineteenth-century Europe, it created an expanding middle class and a proletariat. Masses of former peasants left the countryside for cities, where they were available to recruitment by new political parties and susceptible to appeals based on identity politics.

Something similar has been going on in the Middle East since the later decades of the twentieth century. The region is urbanizing rapidly, growing from 30 to over 50 percent of the population between 1970 and 2010.[3] The Human Development indices compiled by the United Nations (a composite of indicators of health, education, and income) increased by 28 percent in Egypt and 30 percent in Tunisia between 1990 and 2010. The numbers of college graduates increased at an even faster rate, and in both countries the latter complained about the lack of jobs commensurate with their levels of education. It was these groups that were the most savvy about using the Internet and social media to spread images of repression and organize demonstrations against the regime.

Samuel Huntington argued in *Political Order in Changing Societies* that the middle classes are critical to political change. Revolutions, he noted, are never organized by the poorest of the poor, because they have neither the resources nor the education to organize effectively. The middle classes, by contrast, are the group most likely to have experienced rapid increases in their social status and therefore face the sharpest disappointment if their subsequent mobility is blocked. It is the gap between their expectations and reality that creates political instability.

In both the Arab world and in the European Revolutions of 1848, the middle classes were the key actors in organizing the revolution and pressing for political change. The Tunisian uprisings against Ben Ali and the Tahrir Square demonstrations against Mubarak were led by urban, middle-class individuals who felt that their chances for social and economic advancement were being thwarted by the authoritarian regime. (The upheavals in Libya and Yemen were more complicated; the middle classes there were less numerous and complex tribal rivalries also were at work. There was a somewhat larger middle class in Syria, but sectarian identity quickly overwhelmed class or economic grievance.)

A new middle class was not the only product of urbanization, however. In many respects, the rise of political Islam in the Middle East can more appropriately be seen as a form of identity politics than as a matter of revived religiosity per se, and as such has displaced class as a rallying cry for the mobilization of political outsiders. That is, the Middle East experienced the same kind of shift from Gemeinschaft to Gesellschaft, from traditional villages to modern cities, that Europe experienced in the late nineteenth century, with all of the anomie and identity confusion that such a shift entails. For a generation after independence from colonialism, secular nationalism worked as a source of identity, but it was discredited by the late 1970s by its failure to produce consistent and shared economic growth, and by its political failure in dealing with issues like the Israeli-Palestinian conflict. The vacuum was filled by religion, which became a clear source of identity to recently urbanized rural folk who now had access to satellite television and the Internet. One of the reasons for the strength of political Islam today is that it can speak to issues of identity, religion, and social class simultaneously.

Social class remains important in the contemporary Middle East under the veneer of religious politics. The supporters of Western-style liberal democracy tend to be largely drawn from the educated, urban middle classes, while the Islamist parties like the Muslim Brotherhood in Egypt and Ennahda in Tunisia tend to recruit from rural areas or from poor and marginalized communities within urban areas. As banned parties under the old authoritarian regime, these organizations turned to the direct provision of social services to the poor and therefore were in a good position to mobilize these populations when a democratic political space opened up. The same is true of Islamic conservatives in Iran, who tend to recruit from the poor and less educated layers of society.

The European experience in 1848 indicates, however, that the initial toppling of an authoritarian regime and the organization of democratic elections is only the beginning of a much longer process of political development. Democracy is built around the institutionalization of mass participation in an agreed political process, which requires in the first instance well-organized political parties. The middle-class liberals who lead the revolution have to go on to organize themselves to be able to contest elections, and they have to be able to form coalitions with other groups. The liberal revolutionaries of 1848 failed to do either in the short period they had before they were overwhelmed by the military counter-moves of the authoritarian establishment. The middle-class groups that led the Arab revolutions had similar problems in organizing themselves on a long-term basis to contest elections in the first couple of years after the uprising, being internally divided and centered on individual leaders rather than mass political followings. Now they face a revitalized military government that will actively restrict their ability to organize.

In Europe, the middle-class groups that led the push for democracy were seldom able to bring it about on their own. All required cross-class coalitions of various sorts. In Denmark, the middle-class groups aligned with the peasantry (or, more properly, farmers, since the old peasantry had largely disappeared by this point) to demand an end to absolutism in 1848; in 1915, they aligned with the working class to demand universal suffrage. In Germany, the middle classes aligned with working-class parties in support of the Weimar Republic, as they did in Sweden, Belgium, and the Netherlands. And in Switzerland, Britain, and Italy, they aligned with conservative parties to expand the franchise.

As noted in chapter 28, however, middle-class groups do not inevitably end up supporting liberal democracy. They can align with conservative forces not to extend democracy but to restrict it from popular forces that threaten their interests. This was the strategy followed by many middle-class groups in Latin America during the dictatorships of the 1960s, '70s, and '80s, and in Turkey up through the end of the 1990s. This pattern repeated itself in Egypt in 2013, where many former liberals became so disgusted with Islamist President Morsi who had been elected the previous year that they supported the military coup removing him from power.

In nineteenth-century Europe, popular mobilization for democracy got hijacked by nationalism. This phenomenon first manifested itself during the French Revolution, when calls for the Rights of Man quickly evolved into the militant assertion of the rights of the French nation. It was evident in Germany in the 1870s, when many of the liberals of the 1840s and '50s became fervent supporters of Bismarck and his forceful unification of the German nation. And it appeared in August 1914, when rank-and-file members of working-class parties that had been charter members of the Second Socialist International lined up behind their national governments and plunged into war.

There is an obvious cultural factor that has gravely complicated the possibility of democracy in the Middle East—Islam. A large number of Muslim-majority societies have had to contend with militant and antidemocratic Islamist groups; there was no equivalent threat to the Third Wave democratic transitions in Eastern Europe or Latin America. A number of observers have suggested that Islam itself constitutes an insuperable obstacle to the emergence of democracy, since it has never accepted the principle of the separation of church and state, and harbors a long tradition of violent religious militancy. Islamist organizations like Ennahda in Tunisia and the Muslim Brotherhood in Egypt that have played by democratic rules are often accused of using democracy instrumentally to gain power; their real agenda remains creation of illiberal theocratic states. The rise of these groups has then provoked conservative authoritarian governments to crack down on them, leading to politics that is polarized between two nondemocratic alternatives.

Whether political Islam will remain a permanent obstacle preventing the emergence of liberal democracy in Muslim majority countries is not so obvious, any more than an assertion that nationalism makes democracy impossible in Europe. Political Islam has waxed and waned over the decades, and in the twentieth century it often took a backseat to other movements based on secular nationalism or liberal authoritarianism. All large, complex cultural systems can be and have been interpreted in a variety of ways over time. Although there is an egalitarian doctrine at the heart of Christianity (as there is in Islam), Christian churches aligned themselves with authoritarian rulers and justified illiberal orders over the centuries. Part of the story of the Third Wave of democratizations in Europe and Latin America has to do with the reinterpretation of Catholic doctrine after Vatican II in the 1960s to make it compatible with modern democracy.[4]

So too with radical Islam. It seems likely that its current expansion is due more to the social conditions of contemporary Middle Eastern societies than to the intrinsic nature of the religion. Indeed, the spread of political Islam can be seen as a form of identity politics very comparable to its nationalist variant in Europe. This was an argument first made by Ernest Gellner, whose theory of the origins of nationalism was noted back in chapter 12. Gellner, it will be recalled, argued that nationalism is a response to the identity dislocation that occurs as societies modernize and transition from Gesellschaft—the small village—to Gemeinschaft—the large city. It occurs primarily in modernizing countries, where the narrow old forms of identity based on kinship and locality disappear and are replaced by more universalist doctrines linking individuals to broader cultural movements. He argued that the rise of modern Islamism responded to very similar imperatives in the Middle East, where religion plays the role that nation played in Europe. To the confused former peasant now living in Cairo or Karachi, or to a second-generation Muslim immigrant in Europe, a figure like Osama bin Laden can provide a convincing answer to the question "Who am I?" The rise of political Islam in the last part of the twentieth century does not therefore reflect the return of an eternally unchanging Islam, as both the proponents of radical Islam and their critics maintain, but rather is a response precisely to the half-modernized state in which much of the Middle East finds itself.

So just as the nineteenth-century European impulse toward democracy got diverted into nationalism, so the Middle Eastern popular mobilization risks being hijacked by religion.[5]

The Third Wave transitions in Eastern Europe and Latin America are thus misleading precedents for the Arab Spring. It is really Europe's long and tortured journey from autocracy through nationalism to democracy that provides the better model. This line of analysis does not offer comfort to those hoping for the emergence of liberal democracy anytime soon in the Arab world. We can only hope that such a transition, if it eventually occurs, will not take anywhere as long as it did in Europe. Europe in the nineteenth century had no prior experience of democracy and therefore no clear institutional models to follow. The same is not the case in the contemporary Middle East. Regimes that balance strong states with legal and democratic constraints on power have become a normative standard around the world. Getting there, however, depends on the creation of a complex set of interlocking institutions, which in turn are facilitated by changes in the nature of underlying economic and social conditions. The social basis for stable democracy did not exist in the Europe of 1848, and it may not yet exist in many parts of the Middle East today.

30

THE MIDDLE CLASS AND
DEMOCRACY'S FUTURE

How the working class became the middle class in the developed world and upset Marx's predictions; technology, globalization, and the future of middle-class societies; some reflections on the role of violence in bringing about modern democracy

According to Karl Marx, modern capitalism was headed for an ultimate crisis of what he called "overproduction." Capitalist use of technology would extract surpluses from the labor of the proletariat, leading to greater concentrations of wealth and the progressive immiseration of workers. The bourgeoisie who ran this system could not, despite their wealth, consume everything that it produced, while the proletariat whose labor made it possible were too poor to buy its products. Ever-increasing levels of inequality would lead to a shortfall in demand, and the system would come crashing down upon itself. The only way out of this crisis, according to Marx, was a revolution that would give political power to the proletariat and redistribute the fruits of the capitalist system.[1]

Marx's scenario seemed quite plausible through the middle decades of the nineteenth century in all industrializing countries. Working conditions in new factory towns were appalling, and huge new agglomerations of impoverished workers appeared out of nowhere. Rules concerning working hours, safety, child labor, and the like were either nonexistent or poorly enforced. European conditions were, in other words, very similar to those found in the early twenty-first century in parts of China, Vietnam, Bangladesh, and other developing countries.

But a number of unexpected developments occurred on the way to the proletarian revolution. First was the fact that labor incomes began to rise. Early gains were the result of extensive economic growth as new workers were mobilized out of the agrarian population, but that process reached natural limits and the price of labor relative to capital began to increase. This dynamic is happening today in China, as the cost of labor has risen rapidly in the first decades of the twenty-first century.

Second, many countries, beginning with the United States, began to put into place universal public education systems as well as increasing investments in higher education. This was not simply a matter of public generosity: new industries required engineers, accountants, lawyers, clerical staff, and hourly workers with basic literacy and numeracy skills. Higher labor costs could easily be justified if they were matched by enhanced productivity, which was in turn the result of better technology and increasing human capital.

Third, the spread of the franchise described in the previous chapter led to expansion of the political power of the working classes. This happened through the struggles to legalize and expand trade unions, and in the rise of political parties associated with them like the British Labour Party and the German Social Democratic Party. The nature of conservative parties began to change as well: instead of representing wealthy landowners, they shifted their base of support to the new middle-class elites. The working classes' newfound political power was then used to implement social legislation regulating working conditions, which led to agitation for broader welfare state policies like pensions and publicly provided health care.

Fourth, by the middle decades of the twentieth century, the working class simply stopped growing, both in absolute numbers and as a share of the workforce. Indeed, the relative size of Marx's proletariat shrank as workers saw substantial increases in their standards of living that allowed them to move into the middle class. They now owned property and had better educations, and were therefore more likely to vote for political parties that could protect their privileges rather than ones pushing to overturn the status quo.

Fifth, a new class of poor and underprivileged people emerged below the industrial working class, often consisting of recent immigrants, racial and ethnic minorities, and other marginalized people. These groups worked in lower-paying service jobs or remained unemployed and dependent on government benefits. Workers in manufacturing industries who were represented by trade unions became a kind of aristocracy within the labor force. The vast majority of workers had no such representation; in countries where benefits like pensions were tied to regular jobs, they entered the informal sector. Such individuals had few legally defined rights and often did not possess legal title to the land or houses they occupied. Throughout Latin America and many other parts of the developing world, the informal sector constitutes perhaps 60 to 70 percent of the entire labor force. Unlike the industrial working class, this group of "new poor" has been notoriously hard to organize for political action. Rather than living in large barracks in factory towns, they live scattered across the country and are often self-employed entrepreneurs.

Finally, the political Left throughout the world lost its focus on economic and class issues, and became fragmented as the result of the spread of identity politics. I have noted already how working-class solidarity was undermined by nationalism at the time of World War I. But the rise of new forms of identity in the developed world by the middle of the twentieth century around black empowerment, feminism, environmentalism, immigrant and indigenous rights, and gay rights created a whole new set of causes that cut across class lines. The leadership of many of these movements came out of the economic elites, and their cultural preferences often stood at cross-purposes to those of the working-class electorate that had once been the bulwark of progressive politics.

The displacement of class politics by identity politics has been very confusing to older Marxists, who for many years clung to the old industrial working class as their preferred category of the underprivileged. They tried to explain this shift in terms of what Ernest Gellner labeled the "Wrong Address Theory": "Just as extreme Shi'ite Muslims hold that Archangel Gabriel made a mistake, delivering the Message to Mohamed when it was intended for Ali, so Marxists basically like to think that the spirit of history or human consciousness made a terrible boob. The awakening message was intended for *classes*, but by some terrible postal error was delivered to *nations*." Gellner went on to argue that in the contemporary Middle East, the same letter was now being delivered to religions rather than nations. But the underlying sociological dynamic was the same.[2]

The first four of these six developments unanticipated by Karl Marx all center around a single phenomenon, which was the conversion of the working class into a broad middle class. At the conclusion of the tumultuous first half of the twentieth century, the developed democracies of Europe and North America finally found themselves in a happy position. Their politics was no longer sharply polarized between a rich oligarchy and a large working class or peasant majority, who engaged in a zero-sum struggle over the distribution of resources. The old oligarchies in many developed countries had either evolved into more entrepreneurial capitalist elites or had been physically eliminated through revolution and war. The working classes through unionization and political struggle won greater privileges for themselves and became middle class in political outlook. Fascism discredited the extreme Right, and the emerging cold war and threat from Stalinist Russia discredited the Communist Left. This left politics to be played out among center-Right and center-Left parties that largely agreed on a liberal democratic framework. The median voter—a favorite concept of political scientists—was no longer a poor person demanding systemic changes to the social order but a middle-class individual with a stake in the existing system.

Other regions were not so lucky. Latin America had a legacy of high levels of inequality, and in many countries the old landowning oligarchies had not been eliminated through the political struggles that consumed Europe. The benefits of economic growth were shared by the organized working classes but not by the mass of workers in the informal sector, and as a result a highly polarized politics emerged reminiscent of nineteenth-century continental Europe. The persistence of radical, anti-systemic groups—the Communist parties led by Cuba, the Tupamaros in Uruguay, the Sandinistas in Nicaragua, the FMLN in El Salvador, and most recently the Bolivarian movement of Hugo Chávez in Venezuela—was a symptom of this fundamental class conflict.

From the days of Aristotle, thinkers have believed that stable democracy would have to rest on a broad middle class; societies with extremes of wealth and poverty are susceptible to oligarchic domination or to populist revolution. Karl Marx believed that the middle classes would always remain a small and privileged minority in modern societies. Yet by the second half of the twentieth century, the middle class constituted the vast majority of the population of most advanced societies, thereby undercutting the appeal of Marxism.

The emergence of middle-class societies also increased the legitimacy of liberal democracy as a political system. In chapter 28 I noted the critique of liberal democracy made by writers as varied as Mosca, Pareto, and Marx that its advent was in the end a fraud, masking the continued rule by elites. But the value of formal democracy and an expanded franchise became evident in the twentieth century. Democratic majorities in

Europe and North America used the ballot box to choose policies beneficial to themselves, regulating big business and putting into place redistributive welfare state provisions.

WHO IS MIDDLE CLASS?

Before proceeding to analyze further the political consequences of the
rise of the middle classes, it is necessary to step back and define what the
middle class is. There is a difference in the way that economists and sociologists think about it. The former tend to define middle class in income
terms. A typical way is simply to choose some band like the middle three
quintiles of the income distribution, or to count those individuals who
fall within 0.5 to 1.5 times the median income. This makes the definition
of middle class dependent on a society's average wealth and thus incom-
parable cross-nationally; being middle class in Brazil means a much lower
consumption level than in the United States. To avoid this problem, some
economists choose an absolute level of consumption, ranging from a low
of US$5 a day, or $1,800 in parity purchasing power per year, up to a range
of $6,000–$31,000 annual income in 2010 U.S. dollars. This fixes one
problem but creates another, since an individual's perception of class
status is often relative rather than absolute. As Adam Smith noted in *The
Wealth of Nations*, a pauper in eighteenth-century England might have
lived like a king in Africa.

Sociologists, in a tradition beginning with Karl Marx, tend not to
look at measures of income but instead at how one's income is earned—
occupational status, level of education, and assets. For the purpose of
understanding the political implications of a growing middle class, the
sociological approach is vastly preferable. Simple measures of income or
consumption, whether relative or absolute, may tell you something about
the consumption habits of the person in question but relatively little concerning his or her political inclinations. Huntington's theory of the de-
stabilizing impact of the gap between expectations and reality is much
more closely tied to social and occupational status than to any absolute
level of income. A poor person of low social status and education
who briefly rises out of poverty and then sinks back is likely to be
more preoccupied with day-to-day survival than with political activism.
A middle-class person, by contrast—someone, say, with a university

education who cannot find an appropriate job and "sinks" to a social level he or she regards as beneath his or her dignity—is far more challenging politically.

Thus, from a political standpoint, the important marker of middle-class status would be occupation, level of education, and ownership of assets (a house or an apartment, or consumer durables) that could be threatened by the government. Marx's original definition of "bourgeoisie" referred to ownership of the means of production. One of the characteristics of the modern world is that this form of property has become vastly democratized through stock ownership and pension plans. Even if one does not possess large amounts of capital, working in a managerial capacity or profession often grants one a very different kind of social status and outlook from a wage earner or low-skilled worker.

A strong middle class with some assets and education is more likely to believe in the need for both property rights and democratic accountability. One wants to protect the value of one's property from rapacious and/or incompetent governments, and is more likely to have time to participate in politics (or to demand the right to participate) because higher income provides a better margin for family survival. A number of cross-national studies have shown that middle-class people have different political values from the poor: they value democracy more, want more individual freedom, are more tolerant of alternative lifestyles, etc. Political scientist Ronald Inglehart, who has overseen the massive World Values Survey that seeks to measure value change around the world, has argued that economic modernization and middle-class status produce what he calls "post-material" values in which democracy, equality, and identity issues become much more prominent than older issues of economic distribution. William Easterly has linked what he labels a "middle class consensus" to higher economic growth, education, health, stability, and other positive outcomes. Economically, the middle class is theorized to have "bourgeois" values of self-discipline, hard work, and a longer-term perspective that encourages savings and investment.[3]

From the earlier discussion of Europe in the nineteenth century, however, it should be clear that the middle classes are not inevitably supporters of democracy. This tends to be particularly true when the middle classes still constitute a minority of the population. Under these circumstances, opening up a country to universal political participation may lead to large and potentially unsustainable demands for redistribution.

In this case, the middle classes may choose to align themselves with authoritarian rulers who promise stability and property rights protection.

Such is arguably the case in contemporary Thailand and China. The Thai political system went from an authoritarian military regime to a reasonably open democracy between 1992 and 1997, preparing the way for the rise of the populist politician Thaksin Shinawatra. Thaksin, one of the country's richest businessmen, organized a mass political party based on government programs to provide debt relief and health care to rural Thais. The middle classes, who had strongly supported the democratic opening in the early 1990s, turned against Thaksin and supported a military coup that forced him from power in 2006. He was charged with corruption and abuse of power, and has had to exercise power from exile since then. The country subsequently became sharply polarized between Thaksin's Red Shirt supporters and middle-class Yellow Shirt adherents, and saw an elected government pushed out of power by the military in 2014.[4]

A similar dynamic may exist in China. The size of the Chinese middle class in 2014 depends obviously on definition but is estimated to be perhaps 300–400 million people out of a population of 1.3 billion. These new middle classes are often the source of resistance to the authoritarian government; they are the ones who are on Sina Weibo (the Chinese Twitter equivalent) and who are likely to publicize or criticize government wrongdoing. Survey data from sources like AsiaBarometer suggest that there is widespread support for democracy in China, but when asked about the specific content of democracy, many respondents associate it either with greater personal freedom or with a government responsive to their needs. Many believe that the current Chinese government is already providing them with these things and do not oppose the system as a whole. Middle-class Chinese are less likely to express support for a short-term transition to multiparty democracy under universal suffrage, although it is very difficult to get accurate polling data on this subject.

The Thai and Chinese cases, as well as the nineteenth-century European ones, suggest that the size of the middle class relative to the rest of the society is one important variable in determining how it will behave politically. When the middle class constitutes only 20–30 percent of the population, it may side with antidemocratic forces because it fears the intentions of the large mass of poor people below it and the populist policies they may pursue. But when the middle class becomes the largest group in the society, the danger is reduced. Indeed, the middle class may at that point be able to vote itself various welfare-state benefits and profit from democracy. This may help to explain why democracy becomes more stable at higher levels of per capita income, since the size of the middle class relative to the poor usually increases with greater wealth. Middle-class societies, as opposed to societies with a middle class, are the bedrock of democracy.

Such societies appeared in Europe by the early decades after World War II, and they have been gradually spreading to other parts of the world ever since. The Third Wave of democratization was not "caused" by the rise of the middle class, since many democratic transitions occurred in countries—like those in sub-Saharan Africa—that did not have appreciable middle classes at the time. Contagion, imitation, and the failures of incumbent authoritarian regimes were all significant factors triggering democratic transitions. But the ability to consolidate a stable liberal democracy is greater in countries that have large and broad middle classes, in contrast to ones in which a relatively small middle class is sandwiched between a rich elite and a mass of poor people. Spain, the country that kicked off the Third Wave, had been transformed from a backward agrarian society at the time of the civil war in the 1930s to a much more modern one by the early 1970s. Surrounded by examples of successful democracies in the European Union, it was much easier to contemplate a democratic transition then than it had been a generation earlier.

This suggests that the prospects for democracy globally remain good, despite the setbacks that occurred during the early twenty-first century. A Goldman Sachs report projects that spending on the part of the world's middle three income quintiles will rise from the current 31 percent of total income to 57 percent in 2050.[5] A report by the European Union Institute for Security Studies projects that the numbers of middle class people will grow from 1.8 billion in 2009 to 3.2 billion in 2020, and 4.9 billion in 2030 (out of a projected global population of 8.3 billion).[6] The bulk of this growth is slated to occur in Asia, particularly China and India, but all regions of the world will participate in this trend.

Economic growth by itself is not sufficient to create democratic stability if it is not broadly shared. One of the greatest threats to China's social stability today is its rapid increase in income inequality since the mid-1990s, which by 2012 had reached Latin American levels.[7] Latin America itself had reached middle-income status well before East Asia but continued to be plagued by high levels of inequality and the populist policies that flowed from it. One of the most promising developments for the region, however, has been the notable fall in income inequality in the decade of the 2000s, as documented by economists Luis Felipe López-Calva and Nora Lustig.[8] There have been significant gains to the Latin American middle class. In 2002, 44 percent of the region's population was classified as poor; this had fallen to 32 percent by 2010 according to the UN Economic Commission for Latin America.[9] The cause of the decline in inequality is not entirely understood, but a certain portion of it is attributable to social policies like conditional cash transfer programs that have deliberately distributed benefits to the poor.

THE MIDDLE CLASS AND CLIENTELISM

The arrival of a large middle class may also have important effects on the practice of clientelism and the forms of political corruption associated with it. I argued earlier that clientelism is an early form of democracy: in societies with masses of poor and poorly educated voters, the easiest form of electoral mobilization is often the provision of individual benefits such as public-sector jobs, handouts, or political favors. This suggests that clientelism will start to decline as voters become wealthier. Not only does it cost more for politicians to bribe them, but the voters see their interests tied up with broader public policies rather than individual benefits.

Civil service reform, where it has taken place, has typically come on the back of a rising middle class. We saw in chapter 8 how the Northcote-Trevelyan reforms in Britain served the interests of the new British middle classes who found themselves excluded from the old aristocratic patronage networks. A middle class created by capitalist growth is almost by definition a supporter of meritocracy. Similarly, in the United States the civil service reform movement during the Progressive Era was driven by middle-class groups who stood outside the existing patronage system. These educated, often Protestant businessmen, lawyers, and academics looked down on the machine politicians who mobilized masses of immigrant voters in the country's growing cities. Merchants and industrialists, moreover, needed a competent civil service to provide the increasingly complex services expected from the government. Contemporary anticorruption movements in China, India, and Brazil all recruit heavily from the middle classes.

As in the case of democracy, however, the simple emergence of a middle class does not mean that this group will automatically support clean government and an end to clientelistic politics. New social actors are perfectly capable of being recruited into existing patronage networks and profiting from it. In the United States, the railroads—exemplars of technological modernity during the nineteenth century—quickly learned how to buy politicians and manipulate the patronage system to their own benefit. Many legislatures in western states were said to be owned lock, stock, and barrel by railroad interests. Indeed, the railroads' ability to play this political game is the reason that older agrarian groups like midwestern farmers were eager to join the Progressive coalition in support of civil service reform.

Thus as economic growth occurs, there is something of a race between different interests to recruit the new middle classes to their cause. The old patronage politicians are perfectly happy to extend their largesse to middle-class supporters. As in a democracy, their willingness to support the reformist side in this struggle will depend on their numbers, their sense of economic security, and their social status. If they feel excluded and unrecognized by those above them, as in Britain, or by those below them (who nonetheless held political power), as in America, they are much more likely to turn their indignation to reform or overthrow of the existing clientelistic system.

THE FUTURE OF DEMOCRACY

The existence of a broad middle class is neither a sufficient nor a necessary condition to bring about liberal democracy. But it is extremely helpful in sustaining it. Karl Marx's Communist utopia did not materialize in the developed world because his global proletariat turned into a global middle class. In the developing world, new middle classes have enhanced democracy in Indonesia, Turkey, and Brazil, and promise to upset the authoritarian order in China. But what happens to liberal democracy if the middle class reverses course and starts to shrink?

There is unfortunately a lot of evidence that this process may have begun to unfold in the developed world, where income inequality has increased massively since the 1980s. This is most notable in the United

States, where the top 1 percent of families took home 9 percent of GDP in 1970 and 23.5 percent in 2007. The fact that so much of the economic growth in this period went to a relatively small number of people at the top of the distribution is the flip side of the phenomenon of the stagnation of middle-class incomes since the 1970s.[10]

In the United States and other countries, this stagnation was hidden from view by other factors. The same period saw the entry of large numbers of women into the workforce, increasing household income at the same time that many middle-class men found their paychecks getting smaller in real terms. In addition, politicians across the world saw cheap, subsidized credit as an acceptable substitute for outright income redistribution, leading to government-backed housing booms. The financial crisis of 2008–2009 was one consequence of this trend.[11]

There are a number of sources of this growing inequality, only some of which are subject to control through public policies. One villain most commonly cited is globalization—the fact that lower transportation and communications costs have effectively added hundreds of millions of low-skill workers to the global labor market, driving down wages for comparable skills in developed countries.

With rising labor costs in China and other emerging-market countries, a certain amount of manufacturing has started to return to the United States and other developed countries. But this has happened in part only because labor costs as a proportion of total manufacturing costs have gotten much smaller due to increases in automation. This means that renewed onshore production will not be likely to replace the huge numbers of middle-class jobs that were lost in the initial process of deindustrialization.

This points to the much more important long-term factor of technological advance, which in a sense is the underlying facilitator of globalization. There has been a constant substitution of technology for human labor over the decades, which in the nineteenth and early twentieth centuries brought huge benefits not just to elites but also to the broad mass of people in industrializing countries. The major technological innovations of this period created large numbers of jobs for low-skill workers in a succession of industries—coal and steel, chemicals, manufacturing, and construction. The Luddites, who opposed technological change, proved very wrong, insofar as new, higher-paying opportunities for work opened up to replace the ones they lost. Henry Ford's invention of the assembly line for producing automobiles in his Highland Park, Michigan, facility actually lowered the average skill levels required to build an automobile, breaking apart the complex operations of the earlier carriage craft industry into simple, repeatable steps that a person with a fifth-grade education could accomplish. This was the economic order that supported the rise of a broad middle class and the democratic politics that rested on it.

The more recent advances in information and communications technology have had very different social effects, however. Automation has eliminated a large number of low-skill assembly-line jobs, and with each passing year smart machines move up the skill ladder to take away more occupations formerly performed by middle-class workers.[12] Indeed, it is impossible to separate technology from globalization: without high-speed broadband communications and falling transportation costs, it would not be possible to outsource customer support and back-office operations from the United States and Europe to India and the Philippines, or to produce iPhones in Shenzhen. The lower-skill jobs that are being destroyed in this process are being replaced, as in earlier periods, by newer, higher-paying ones. But the skill requirements, and the numbers of such jobs, are very different from Henry Ford's time.

There has always been inequality as a result of natural differences in talent and character. But today's technological world vastly magnifies those differences. In a nineteenth-century agrarian society, people with strong math skills didn't have many opportunities to capitalize on their talent. Today, they can become financial wizards, geneticists, or software engineers, and take home ever-larger proportions of national wealth.

In addition, modern technology has created what Robert Frank and Philip Cook call a "winner-take-all" society, in which a disproportionate and growing share of income is taken home by the very top members of any field, whether CEOs, doctors, academics, musicians, entertainers, or athletes. In the days when the markets for such skills and services were localized due to the high costs of communications and transportation, there were plenty of openings for people farther down the hierarchy because mass audiences did not have access to the best of the best. But today, anyone can attend a performance by the Metropolitan Opera or the Royal Ballet live on a high-definition screen, which many would watch in preference to a third- or fourth-tier local company.[13]

MALTHUS REVISITED

Thomas Malthus's *Essay on the Principle of Population* had the bad luck to be published in 1798, on the eve of the Industrial Revolution, just as a technological tsunami was gathering force. His prediction that human population growth would outstrip increases in productivity proved very wrong in the two centuries that followed, and human societies succeeded in enriching themselves on a per capita basis to a historically unprecedented degree. Malthusian economics has ever since been derided, along with the Luddites, as backward looking and ignorant of the nature of modern technology.[14]

However, Malthus did not specify the time period over which population growth would outstrip productivity. The developed world has been on a high-productivity trajectory for only a little over two hundred of the fifty thousand or so years that the human species has existed in its current form. We assume today that revolutionary new technologies equivalent to steam power and the internal combustion engine will continue to appear into the future. But the laws of physics do not guarantee such a result. It is entirely possible that the first 150 years of the Industrial Revolution captured what Tyler Cowen calls the "low-hanging fruit" of productivity advance, and that while future innovations will continue, the rate at which they improve human welfare will fall. Indeed, a number of laws of physics suggest that there might be hard limits on the carrying capacity of the planet to sustain growing populations at high standards of living.

Moreover, even if technological innovation continues to occur at a high rate, there is no guarantee that it will provide large numbers of jobs for middle-class people in the manner of the early-twentieth-century assembly line. The new employment and rewards go to the creators of the machines and those who figure out how to employ them, who are almost always better educated than those whose jobs are lost.

Indeed, many foreseeable future innovations will actually make the productivity situation worse because they are in the area of biomedicine. Many economists and politicians assume that any new technology that extends human life spans or cures disease is an unqualifiedly good thing. And it is true that the longer life spans that citizens of developed countries have come to enjoy have been of economic benefit. But many biomedical technologies have succeeded in extending life spans at the expense of quality of life and sharply increased dependency on caregivers. In all developed countries, the costs of end-of-life care have accelerated faster than the overall rate of economic growth, and they are on their way to becoming the single largest component of government spending. Death and generational turnover are classic cases of outcomes that are bad for individuals but good for society as a whole. There are many reasons to think that societies will be worse off in the aggregate if life spans are extended another ten or twenty years on average, beginning with the fact that generational turnover is critical to social change and adaptation, both of which will occur at a slower pace as average life expectancies increase.[15]

There is no way of predicting the nature of future technological change—either its overall rate, its effects on middle-class employment, or its other social consequences. However, if technological change fails to produce broadly shared economic benefits, or if its overall rate slows, modern societies risk being cast back into a Malthusian world that will have big implications for the viability of democracy. In a shared-growth world, the inevitable inequalities that accompany capitalism are politically tolerable because everyone is ultimately benefiting. In a Malthusian world, individuals are in a zero-sum relationship—one person's gain inevitably means another person's loss. Under these circumstances, predation becomes as viable a strategy for self-enrichment as investment in productive economic activities—the situation that human societies were in for most of their history prior to the Industrial Revolution.

ADJUSTMENT

In *The Great Transformation*, Karl Polanyi argued that there was a "double movement" in which capitalist economies continually produced disruptive change and societies struggled to adjust to that change. Governments frequently had to be involved in the adjustment process since private markets and individuals on their own could not always cope with the consequences of technological change.[16] Public policy must therefore be factored into the fate of middle-class societies.

Across the developed world, there has been a range of responses to the challenges of globalization and technological change. At one end of the spectrum are the United States and Britain, where governments provided minimal adjustment help to communities facing deindustrialization beyond short-term unemployment insurance. Indeed, both public authorities and pundits in academia and journalism have often embraced the shift to a postindustrial world. Public policy supported deregulation and privatization at home and pushed for free trade and open investment abroad. Particularly in the United States, politicians intervened to weaken the power of trade unions and to otherwise increase the flexibility of labor markets. Individuals were advised to embrace disruptive change and were told that they would find better opportunities as knowledge workers doing creative and interesting things in the new economy.

France and Italy stood at the other end of this spectrum, seeking to protect middle-class jobs by imposing onerous rules on companies attempting to lay off workers. By not recognizing the need for adjustment in work rules and labor conditions, they stopped job loss in the short run while losing competitiveness to other countries in the long run. Like the United States, they tend to have highly adversarial management-labor relations, but while the owners of capital usually come out on top in the Anglo-Saxon world, labor has done much better protecting its privileges in Latin Europe.

The countries that came through the 2008–2009 crisis the most successfully were those like Germany and the Scandinavian nations that steered a middle course between the laissez-faire approach of the United States and Britain, and the rigid regulatory systems of France and Italy. Their corporatist labor-management systems have created sufficient trust that unions were willing to grant companies more flexibility in layoffs, in return for higher benefits and job retraining.

The future of democracy in developed countries will depend on their ability to deal with the problem of a disappearing middle class. In the wake of the financial crisis there has been a rise of new populist groups from the Tea Party in the United States to various anti-EU, anti-immigrant parties in Europe. What unites all of them is the belief that elites in their countries have betrayed them. And in many ways they are correct: the elites who set the intellectual and cultural climate in the developed world have been largely buffered from the effects of middle-class decline. There has been a vacuum in new approaches to the problem, approaches that don't involve simply returning to the welfare state solutions of the past.

The proper approach to the problem of middle-class decline is not necessarily the present German system or any other specific set of measures. The only real long-term solution would be an educational system that succeeded in pushing the vast majority of citizens into higher levels of education and skills. The ability to help citizens flexibly adjust to the changing conditions of work requires state and private institutions that are similarly flexible. Yet one of the characteristics of modern developed democracies is that they have accumulated many rigidities over time that make institutional adaptation increasingly difficult. In fact, all political systems—past and present—are liable to decay. The fact that a system once was a successful and stable liberal democracy does not mean that it will remain one in perpetuity.

It is to the problem of political decay that we will turn in the final part of this book.

PART FOUR

·

Political Decay

31

POLITICAL DECAY

How the U.S. Forest Service's mission came to center on fighting wild-fires; the failure of scientific management; how the Forest Service lost autonomy due to conflicting mandates; what political decay is, and its two sources

The creation of the U.S. Forest Service (USFS) under Bernard Fernow and Gifford Pinchot was the premier example of American state building during the Progressive Era. Prior to passage of the 1883 Pendleton Act and the spread of merit-based bureaucracy, American government was a clientelistic system in which public offices were allocated by the political parties on the basis of patronage. The Forest Service, by contrast, was staffed with university-educated agronomists and foresters, chosen on the basis of merit and technical expertise. Its defining struggle, chronicled in chapter 11 above, was the successful effort by Pinchot to secure for the USFS authority over the General Land Office in the face of vehement opposition by Joe Cannon, the legendary Speaker of the House of Representatives. The central issue in this formative stage of American state building was bureaucratic autonomy: the idea that professionals in the USFS and not politicians in Congress should be the ones to make decisions on allocations of public lands, and that they should be in charge of recruiting and promoting their own staff. The U.S. Forest Service for many years afterward remained the shining example of a high-quality American bureaucracy.

SMOKEY THE BEAR; OR, HOW THE FOREST SERVICE
LOST ITS AUTONOMY

It may be surprising to learn, then, that the Forest Service is today regarded by many observers as a highly dysfunctional bureaucracy performing an outmoded mission with the wrong tools. Although it is still staffed
by professional foresters, many of whom are highly dedicated to the
agency's mission, it has lost a great deal of the autonomy it won under Pinchot. It operates under multiple and often contradictory mandates from
Congress and the courts that cannot be simultaneously fulfilled, and in
the process ends up costing taxpayers a huge amount of money. The service's internal decision-making system is often gridlocked, and the high
degree of staff morale and cohesion that Pinchot worked so hard to foster has been lost. The situation is sufficiently bad that entire books have
been written arguing that the Forest Service ought to be abolished altogether.[1] No political institution lasts forever, and the current condition
of the Forest Service tells us a great deal about the forces that work to undermine high-quality government.

Civil service reform in the late nineteenth century was promoted by
academics and activists like Francis Lieber, Woodrow Wilson, and Frank
Goodnow, who had a great deal of faith in the ability of modern natural
science to solve human problems. Wilson, like his contemporary Max
Weber, distinguished between politics and administration. Politics was a
domain of final ends subject to democratic contestation, whereas administration was a realm of implementation that could be studied empirically and subjected to scientific analysis. A similar intellectual revolution
had been going on in the business world, with the rise of Frederick Winslow Taylor's doctrine of "scientific management," which used among
other things time-and-motion studies to maximize the efficiency of factory operations. Many of the Progressive Era reformers sought to import
scientific management into government, arguing that public administration could be turned into a science and protected from the irrationalities
of politics. They hoped that the social sciences one day could be made as
rigorous as the natural sciences.[2]

After the experiences of the twentieth century, this early faith in science, and the belief that administration could be turned into a science,
seems naïve and misplaced. This period was one in which natural science created weapons of mass destruction, and bureaucratic manage-

ment ran death camps. But the context in which these early reformers operated was one where governments were run by political hacks or corrupt municipal bosses, much like many developing countries today. No public university today would want hiring and tenure decisions to be made by the state legislature, nor would anyone want Congress to choose the staff of the Centers for Disease Control. So it was perfectly reasonable to demand that public officials be selected on the basis of education and merit.

The problem with scientific management is that even the most qualified scientists occasionally get things wrong, and sometimes get them wrong in a big way. This was what happened to the Forest Service with regard to what became its central mission, fighting forest fires.

The evolution in the Forest Service's mission began with the Great Idaho Fire of 1910, which burned some three million acres in Idaho and Montana, and led to the death of eighty-five people. The political outcry over the damage caused by this conflagration led the USFS to increasingly focus on wildfire suppression. William Greeley, a Forest Service chief, asserted that "fire fighting is a matter of scientific management"—that is, readily accommodated under its existing mandate.[3] By the 1980s, this mission had ballooned in size in what one observer called a "war on fire." The Forest Service, whose permanent staff had grown to around thirty thousand, employed tens of thousands of firefighters in peak fire years, owned a large fleet of planes and helicopters, and spent as much as $1 billion a year on the firefighting mission.[4]

The problem with fighting wildfires is that the early proponents of "scientific forestry" didn't properly understand the role of fires in woodland ecology. Forest fires are a natural occurrence and play an important function in maintaining the health of western forests. Shade-intolerant trees like giant ponderosas, lodgepole pines, and sequoias require periodic fires to clear areas in which new trees can regenerate; the forests were invaded by species like Douglas firs once fires were suppressed. (Lodgepole pines in fact require fires to propagate their seeds.) Over the years, these forests developed high tree densities and huge buildups of dry understory, such that fires that did occur became much larger and more destructive. Instead of destroying the small invasive species, these fires now burned the larger old-growth trees. The public began to take notice after the huge Yellowstone fire in 1988, which ended up burning nearly eight hundred thousand acres and took several months to control.

Ecologists began criticizing the very objective of fire prevention, which led the Forest Service to reverse course by the mid-1990s and implement a "let burn" policy.

Years of misguided policies could not simply be reversed, however, since the western forests had become gigantic tinderboxes. Moreover, as a result of population growth in the West, more people were living in areas close to forests and therefore vulnerable to wildfires. By one estimate, the wildland-urban interface expanded more than 52 percent from 1970 to 2000 and would continue to expand well into the future. Like people choosing to live on floodplains and on barrier islands, these individuals were exposing themselves to undue risks that were mitigated by government-subsidized insurance. Through their elected representatives, they lobbied hard to make sure the Forest Service and the other federal agencies responsible for forest management were given the resources to continue fighting fires that could threaten their property. Ultimately, it proved very difficult to do any kind of rational cost-benefit analysis; the government could easily spend $1 million to protect a $100,000 home because it was politically impossible to justify a decision not to act.[5]

In the meantime, the original mission of the Forest Service around which Pinchot had created a high-quality agency had eroded. That mission, it will be recalled, was neither fire suppression nor conservation per se but rather the sustainable exploitation of forest resources—in other words, timber harvesting. This original mandate was greatly diminished in scope: in the last decade of the twentieth century, timber harvests in national forests plunged from twelve to four billion board-feet per year.[6] The reason for this had partly to do with the economics of timber, but it more importantly reflected a change in national values that had taken place over the previous century. With the rise of environmental consciousness, natural forests were increasingly seen not as resources to be exploited for economic purposes but as preserves to be protected for their own sake. This shift was of a piece with many other changes in social attitudes taking place at the time. Dams and other big hydroelectric projects, earlier seen as heroic efforts to master nature, were later understood to entail huge unintended environmental consequences. In North America, dams had virtually ceased being built by the 1970s. The change in the Forest Service's mission was written into law when President Lyndon Johnson signed the 1964 Wilderness Act, which enjoined the Forest Service along with the National Park Service and the Fish and Wildlife

Service to review and protect the more than nine million acres of land under their control.[7]

Even in its original core mission of sustainably harvesting timber, a number of critics noted that the Forest Service was not doing a good job. Timber was being marketed at well below the cost of operations, meaning that the government was failing to derive proper benefit from what should have been a productive asset. The reasons for this were multiple: timber pricing was inefficient, and many of the agency's fixed costs were not taken into account in setting prices. Like all government agencies, the Forest Service could not retain earnings and therefore had no incentive to contain costs. Quite the contrary, it had an incentive to increase its own budget and staffing year to year regardless of the revenues this would generate.[8]

Why did the performance of the Forest Service deteriorate over the decades? The story is suggestive in pointing to the broader forces underlying the phenomenon of political decay.

Gifford Pinchot's original USFS was regarded as the gold standard of American bureaucracies because he won a high degree of autonomy for an organization of well-trained professionals dedicated to a central mission, the sustainable exploitation of American forests. The old Forest Bureau, and the Department of Agriculture of which it was a branch, had been part of the clientelistic party-based nineteenth-century political system, whose main purpose was to deliver political benefits to members of Congress. The Forest Service's ability to appoint and promote its own staff, and its freedom from congressional interference in individual transactions, was critical to its mission.

The problem began when the Forest Service's clear, single mission was replaced by multiple and potentially conflicting mandates. In the middle decades of the twentieth century, the firefighting mission began to supersede the timber exploitation focus both in budgetary and personnel terms. But then, firefighting became controversial and was itself supplanted by a preservationist/environmentalist function. None of the old missions were discarded, however, and each one tended to link up to different external interest groups that supported different factions within the Forest Service: consumers of timber, environmentalists, homeowners, western developers, young people seeking temporary jobs as firefighters. Congress, which had been excluded from the micromanagement of land sales back in 1905, reinserted itself. This came about not through old-style corruption typified by the Ballinger affair in 1908 that led to

Pinchot's firing by President Taft; rather, it worked through the issuing of legislative mandates that forced the Forest Service to pursue differing and often contradictory goals. For example, the protection of the properties of the increasing number of homeowners living at the wildland-urban interface meant that the "let burn" policy desired by environmentalists could not be implemented in any straightforward way. What was good for the long-term health of forests was not good for individual homeowners, and each of the parties to this process used their access to Congress and the courts to try to force the agency to protect their favored interests.

The small, cohesive agency created by Pinchot and celebrated by Herbert Kaufman in *The Forest Ranger* slowly evolved into a large, balkanized one. It became subject to many of the maladies affecting government agencies more generally: bureaucrats came to be more interested in protecting their budgets and jobs than in the efficient performance of their mandates. And they clung to old mandates even when both science and the society around them were changing. Like Pinchot, many reached out to interest groups to protect their autonomy, but without a single, coherent mandate, they ultimately could not avoid recolonization by their clients.

ACROSS THE BOARD

It would be one thing if the U.S. Forest Service were an isolated case of political decay. Unfortunately, there is substantial evidence from public administration specialists that the overall quality of the American government has been deteriorating steadily for more than a generation. In the words of Paul Light, "The federal government has become a destination of last resort for [young people wanting to make] a difference"; according to Patricia Ingraham and David Rosenbloom, the federal service has been in the process of "decomposing" since the 1970s.[9] This conclusion is supported by the work of the two Volcker Commissions on public service in 1989 and 2003.[10]

Many Americans have the impression that the size of the U.S. government has been growing relentlessly over the decades. This is only partly true: the mandates placed on the government to do various things, from reducing child poverty to fighting terrorism, have indeed expanded dramatically. However, the actual size of the federal workforce has been capped at approximately 2.25 million since the end of World War II, and subject to repeated bouts of downsizing; in 2005 it numbered about 1.8 million. What has expanded are, first, a series of public authorities that perform public functions while remaining separate from government, and an army of unaccountable contractors who do everything from providing cafeteria services to protecting diplomats to managing the computer systems for the National Security Agency.[11]

There are numerous ways that the U.S. bureaucracy has moved away from the Weberian ideal of an energetic and efficient organization staffed by people chosen for their ability and technical knowledge. The system as a whole has changed from being merit based. Following two Middle Eastern wars, half of all new entrants to the federal workforce have been veterans, and of that group, a large portion is disabled. While the Congressional mandate leading to this outcome is perhaps understandable, this is not the way most corporations would voluntarily choose to staff themselves. Surveys of the federal workforce paint a depressing picture. According to Light, "Federal employees appear to be more motivated by compensation than mission, ensnared in careers that cannot compete with business and nonprofits, troubled by the lack of resources to do their jobs, dissatisfied with the rewards for a job well done and the lack of consequences for a job poorly done, and unwilling to trust their own organizations."[12]

According to the 2003 National Commission on the Public Service, "Those who enter the civil service often find themselves trapped in a maze of rules and regulations that thwart their personal development and stifle their creativity. The best are underpaid, the worst, overpaid."[13] Government work has always been driven, of course, more by a service ethic than by monetary rewards alone, but these same surveys indicate that young people hoping to serve the public interest are much more likely to go into a nonprofit than the government. When one survey asked how well their organizations were at disciplining poor performance, only 9 percent answered "very good," while 67 percent responded "not too good" or "not good at all." These trends have all accelerated in the early decades of the 2000s.[14]

HOW INSTITUTIONS DECAY

The travails of the Forest Service are but one small example of a broader phenomenon of political decay. Political institutions develop over time, but they are also universally subject to political decay. This problem is not solved once a society becomes rich and democratic. Indeed, democracy itself can be the source of decay.

Much of the best-known writing about decline, by Oswald Spengler, Arnold Toynbee, Paul Kennedy, and Jared Diamond, has focused on the systemic decline of entire societies or civilizations.[15] It is possible that there are general processes of civilizational decay at work, though I seriously doubt that one could extract anything close to a universal law of social behavior from the available cases. The kind of decay I am interested in here is related to the workings of specific institutions and may or may not be related to broader systemic or civilizational processes. A single institution may decay while others around it remain healthy.

Samuel Huntington used the term "political decay" to explain political instability in many newly independent countries after World War II. Traditional political orders undergoing rapid change had collapsed into disorder all around the globe. Huntington argued that socioeconomic modernization led to the mobilization of new social groups over time, whose participation could not be accommodated by existing political institutions. The source of political decay was thus the inability of institutions to adapt to changing circumstances—specifically, the rise of new social groups and their political demands.[16]

Political decay is therefore in many ways a condition of political development: the old has to break down in order to make way for the new. But the transitions can be extremely chaotic and violent; there is no guarantee that political institutions will continuously, peacefully, and adequately adapt to new conditions.

We can use this model as the starting point for a broader understanding of political decay. Institutions, according to Huntington, are "stable, valued, recurring patterns of behavior" whose most important function is to facilitate human collective action. Without clear and stable rules, human beings would have to renegotiate their interactions at every turn. The substantive content of these rules varies, both across different societies and over time. But the faculty for rule making as such is genetically hardwired into the human brain, having evolved over centuries of social life.

Individuals may come to accept the constraints of institutions out of a calculation of their own self-interest. But human nature has provided us with a suite of emotions that encourage rule or norm following that is independent of the norm's rationality. Sometimes rule following is reinforced by religious belief; in other cases we follow rules simply because they are old and traditional. We are instinctively conformist and look around at our fellows for guidelines to our own behavior. The tremendous stability of normative behavior is what creates enduring institutions and has allowed human societies to achieve levels of social cooperation unmatched by any other animal species.[17]

The very stability of institutions is also the source of political decay. Institutions are created to meet the demands of specific circumstances. However, the original environment in which institutions are created is subject to change. The kind of social mobilization described by Huntington is only one form of change in the conditions surrounding the institution that may lead to dysfunction. Environmental change is another: anthropologists have speculated that shifts in climate are what led to the decline of Maya civilization and the Indian cultures of the American Southwest.[18]

Institutions fail to adapt to changing circumstances for a number of reasons. The first is cognitive. Human beings follow institutional rules for reasons that are not entirely rational. Sociologists and anthropologists have speculated, for example, that various religious rules have rational roots in different functional needs—for example, the need to regulate sexuality and reproduction, the requirements for conveying property, organization for warfare, etc. But fervent religious believers will not abandon their beliefs simply in the face of evidence that they are wrong or lead to bad outcomes. This kind of cognitive rigidity extends well beyond religion, of course. Everyone creates and uses shared mental models of how the world works, and sticks to them in the face of contradictory evidence. This was just as true of Marxism—an avowedly secular and "scientific" doctrine—as of contemporary neoclassical economics. We saw a vivid case of this in the U.S. Forest Service's belief that it possessed "scientific" knowledge about forest management, which led it to persist in its fire suppression policy in the face of accumulating evidence that this was undermining its goal of forest sustainability.

The second important reason that institutions fail to adapt is the role of elites or incumbent political actors within a political system. Political institutions develop as new social groups emerge and challenge the existing equilibrium. If successful institutional development occurs, the rules of the system change and the former outsiders become insiders. But then the insiders acquire a stake in the new system and henceforth act to defend the new status quo. Because they are insiders, they can use their superior access to information and resources to manipulate the rules in their favor. We saw how the new classified (merit-based) civil servants created by the Pendleton Act immediately began to unionize in the first decade of the twentieth century in order to protect their own jobs and privileges. This became a bulwark of protection not just against corrupt politicians but also against superiors demanding better performance and accountability.

Modern state institutions, which are supposed to be impersonal even if not necessarily democratic, are particularly vulnerable to insider capture in a process that I labeled "repatrimonialization." As we have seen, natural human sociability is built around the twin principles of kin selection and reciprocal altruism—the favoring of family or of friends with whom one has exchanged favors. Modern institutions require people to work contrary to their natural instincts. In the absence of strong institutional incentives, the groups with access to a political system will use their positions to favor friends and family, and thereby erode the impersonality of the state. The more powerful the groups, the more opportunities they will have to do this. This process of elite or insider capture is a disease that afflicts all modern institutions. (Premodern or patrimonial institutions don't have this problem only because they are captured from the start as personal property of the insiders.)

In the first volume of this book I offered numerous examples of repatrimonialization. China, which created the first modern state in the third century B.C., saw the state recaptured by elite family networks at the end of the Later Han Dynasty, a domination that continued well after the reconstitution of a centralized state in the Sui and Tang Dynasties of the seventh and eighth centuries. The degree of impersonality that existed during the Han Dynasty wasn't restored until the time of the Northern Song in the eleventh century. Similarly, the Mamluk slave-soldiers who legitimated themselves by defending Egypt and Syria against the Mongols and Crusaders themselves became an entrenched elite. Indeed, by the end of the dynasty, the older Mamluks found themselves presiding over elite patronage networks designed to block the upward mobility of their younger peers. This, coupled with their disdain for new technologies like firearms, led to their conquest by the Ottomans and the collapse of the Mamluk state. And finally, the French state under the Old Regime progressively sold itself off to wealthy elites from the late sixteenth century on. The power of entrenched venal officeholders made it impossible to modernize the state; reform could occur only when the revolution violently dispossessed these individuals.

Democracy, and particularly the Madisonian version of democracy that was enshrined in the U.S. Constitution, should theoretically mitigate the problem of elite capture by preventing the emergence of a dominant faction that can use its political power to tyrannize the country. It does so by spreading power among a series of competing branches of government and allowing for competition among different interests across a large and diverse country. Rather than trying to regulate these factions (or, as we would say today, interest groups), Madison argued that their numbers and diversity would protect the liberty of individuals. If any one group obtained undue influence in a democracy and abused its position, the other groups threatened by it could organize to counterbalance it.

But while democracy does provide an important check on elite power, it frequently fails to perform as advertised. Elite insiders typically have superior access to resources and information, which they use to protect themselves. Ordinary voters will not get angry at them for stealing their money if they don't know that this is happening in the first place. Cognitive rigidities may also prevent social groups from mobilizing in their own self-interest. In the United States, many working-class voters support candidates promising to lower taxes on the wealthy, despite the fact that this hurts their own economic situations. They do so in the belief that such policies will spur economic growth that will eventually trickle down to them, or else make government deficits self-financing. The theory has proved remarkably tenacious in the face of considerable evidence that it is not true.

Furthermore, different groups have different abilities to organize to defend their interests. Sugar producers or corn growers are geographically concentrated and focused on the prices of their products, unlike ordinary consumers or taxpayers who are dispersed and for whom the prices of these commodities are only a small part of their budgets. This, combined with institutional rules that often favor such interests (like the fact that Florida and Iowa where sugar and corn are grown are electoral swing states in presidential elections), gives those groups an outsized influence over agricultural policy. To take another example, middle-class groups are usually much more willing and able to defend their interests, like preservation of the home mortgage deduction, than are the poor. This makes universal entitlements to social security or health insurance much easier to defend politically than programs targeting the poor only.

Finally, liberal democracy is almost universally associated with a market economy, which tends to produce winners and losers and amplifies what James Madison termed the "different and unequal faculties of acquiring property." This type of economic inequality is not in itself a bad thing, insofar as it stimulates innovation and growth, and when it occurs under conditions of equal access to the economic system. It becomes highly problematic politically, however, when economic winners seek to convert their wealth into unequal political influence. They can do this on a transactional basis by, for example, bribing a legislator or bureaucrat, or more damagingly by changing the institutional rules to favor themselves— by, say, closing off competition in markets they already dominate. Countries from Japan to Brazil to the United States have used environmental or safety concerns to in effect protect domestic producers. The level playing field becomes progressively tilted in their direction.

The decay of American political institutions is not the same thing as the phenomenon of societal or civilization decline, which has become a highly politicized topic in the discourse about America.[19] America's greatest strengths have never been the quality of its government; the private sector has from the start always been more innovative and vital. Even as government quality deteriorates, new opportunities open up in sectors like shale gas or biotechnology that lay the basis for future economic growth. Political decay in this instance simply means that many specific American political institutions have become dysfunctional, and that a combination of intellectual rigidity and the power of entrenched political actors, growing over time, is preventing the country from reforming them. Institutional reform is an extremely difficult thing to bring about, and there is no guarantee that it will be accomplished without a major disruption of the political order.

32

A STATE OF COURTS AND PARTIES

How the judiciary and legislature continue to play outsize roles in American government; how distrust of government leads to judicial solutions for administrative problems; how "adversarial legalism" reduces the efficiency of government

The three categories of political institutions—state, rule of law, and democracy—are embodied in the three branches of government of a modern liberal democracy—the executive, the judiciary, and the legislature. The United States, with its long-standing traditions of distrust of government power, has always emphasized the role of the institutions of constraint—the judiciary and legislature—over the executive in its institutional priorities. As we saw in chapters 9–11 above, American politics during the nineteenth century was characterized by Stephen Skowronek as a "state of courts and parties," where government functions that in Europe were performed by an executive branch bureaucracy were performed in the United States by judges and elected representatives. The creation of a modern, centralized, merit-based bureaucracy capable of exercising jurisdiction over the whole territory of the country began only in the late 1880s, and the number of classified civil servants did not reach 80 percent until the time of the New Deal more than fifty years later.[1]

This shift to a more modern administrative state paralleled an enormous growth in the size (or what I labeled in chapter 2 the "scope") of government as well. Table 7 displays total tax revenues as a percentage of GDP for a selected group of developed countries over time. Spending has grown even faster than tax revenues, as indicated in Table 8.

Much of the literature on American state building, or the "rise of the modern administrative state," tends to assume that history is a one-way

TABLE 7. Tax Revenue as a Percentage of GDP

Country	1965	1975	1985	1990	1995	2000	2005	2011
Australia	21.0	25.8	28.3	28.5	28.8	31.1	30.8	26.5
Austria	33.9	36.7	40.9	39.6	41.2	42.6	42.1	42.3
Belgium	33.1	39.5	44.4	42.0	43.6	44.9	44.8	44.1
Canada	25.7	32.0	32.5	35.9	35.6	35.6	33.4	30.4
Denmark	30.0	38.4	46.1	46.5	48.8	49.4	50.7	47.7
Finland	30.4	36.5	39.7	43.5	45.7	47.2	43.9	43.7
France	34.1	35.4	42.8	42.0	42.9	44.4	43.9	44.1
Germany	31.6	34.3	36.1	34.8	37.2	37.2	34.8	36.9
Greece	17.8	19.4	25.5	26.2	28.9	34.1	31.3	32.2
Iceland	26.2	30.0	28.2	30.9	31.2	37.2	40.7	36.0
Ireland	24.9	28.7	34.6	33.1	32.5	31.7	30.6	27.9
Italy	25.5	25.4	33.6	37.8	40.1	42.3	40.9	43.0
Japan	18.2	20.9	27.4	29.1	26.8	27.0	27.4	28.6
Luxembourg	27.7	32.8	39.5	35.7	37.1	39.1	37.8	37.0
Mexico	n/a	n/a	17.0	17.3	15.2	16.9	19.1	19.7
Netherlands	32.8	40.7	42.4	42.9	41.5	39.7	38.8	38.6
New Zealand	24.0	28.5	31.1	37.4	36.6	33.6	37.5	31.5
Norway	29.6	39.2	42.6	41.0	40.9	42.6	43.5	42.5
Portugal	15.9	19.7	25.2	27.7	31.7	34.1	34.7	33.0
South Korea	n/a	15.1	16.4	18.9	19.4	23.6	25.5	25.9
Spain	14.7	18.4	27.6	32.5	32.1	34.2	35.8	32.2
Sweden	35.0	41.2	47.3	52.2	47.5	51.8	49.5	44.2
Switzerland	17.5	23.9	25.5	25.8	27.7	30.0	29.2	28.6
Turkey	10.6	11.9	11.5	14.9	16.8	24.2	24.3	27.8
United Kingdom	30.4	35.2	37.6	36.1	34.0	36.4	35.8	35.7
United States	24.7	25.6	25.6	27.3	27.9	29.9	27.3	24.0
OECD Total	24.2	29.4	32.7	33.8	34.8	36.0	35.7	34.1

SOURCE: Vito Tanzi and OECD

ratchet that, once turned, cannot be reversed. This would seem to be
borne out in terms of government scope. Table 7 indicates that the overall levels of taxes have for the most part continued to grow since the 1970s
despite the Reagan and Thatcher revolutions in the United States and the
United Kingdom, despite efforts by those leaders to reverse growth of state
sectors. To the relief of progressives and the consternation of conservatives, "big government" seems to be very difficult to dismantle.

TABLE 8. Government Revenue, Spending, and Deficits as a
Percentage of GDP, 2011

Country	Government Revenue	Spending	Deficit
Australia	22.9	26.1	3.2
Austria	48.3	50.8	2.4
Belgium	49.7	53.6	3.9
Canada	38.5	44.1	5.6
Denmark	55.7	57.6	2.0
Finland	54.2	55.2	1.0
France	50.6	55.9	5.4
Germany	44.4	45.2	0.8
Greece	42.9	52.5	9.6
Iceland	41.8	47.4	5.6
Ireland	34.1	47.2	13.1
Italy	46.1	49.9	3.7
Korea	32.2	30.3	−2.0
Luxembourg	42.7	42.7	−0.1
Netherlands	45.7	49.9	4.3
New Zealand	34.9	41.7	6.8
Norway	57.3	43.9	−13.4
Portugal	45.2	49.5	4.3
Spain	36.4	46.0	9.6
Sweden	51.5	51.5	0.0
United Kingdom	40.5	48.2	7.7
United States	30.9	41.5	10.6
OECD Total	23.7	29.7	6.0

SOURCE: World Bank; OECD

(Figures for Australia, New Zealand, and OECD exclude subnational revenues)

Focusing only on the United States for the moment, the apparently irreversible increase in the scope of government in the twentieth century has masked a large decay in its quality (or what I labeled state "strength" in chapter 2). This deterioration in the quality of government has in turn made it much more difficult to get fiscal deficits under control. The quantity, or scope, problem will be very difficult to address until the quality, or strength, problem is fixed at the same time. To put it in less abstract language, the American system of checks and balances makes it harder, relative to other democracies with different institutional arrangements, to make decisions. In the past, this slowed the growth of the American welfare state. But the cumbersomeness of the process also makes it very hard to cut that state back. Performing the core function of any political order—responsible budgeting—will be difficult unless those processes are somehow streamlined and implementation of policies becomes more efficient.

The decay in the quality of American government is rooted in the fact that the United States has returned in certain ways to being a state of "courts and parties"—the courts and legislature have usurped many of the proper functions of the executive, making the operation of the government as a whole both incoherent and inefficient. The story of the courts is one of the steadily increasing judicialization of functions that in other developed democracies are handled by administrative bureaucracies, leading to an explosion of costly litigation, slowness of decision making, and highly inconsistent enforcement of laws. The courts, instead of being constraints on government, have become alternative instruments for the expansion of government.

There has been a parallel usurpation by Congress. Interest groups, having lost their ability to directly corrupt legislatures through bribery and the feeding of clientelistic machines, have found new, perfectly legal means of capturing and controlling legislators. Interest groups exercise influence way out of proportion to their place in society, distort both taxes and spending, and raise overall deficit levels through their ability to manipulate the budget in their favor. They also undermine the quality of public administration as a result of the multiple and often contradictory mandates they induce Congress to support. All of this has led to a crisis of representation, in which ordinary people feel their supposedly democratic government no longer truly reflects their interests but is under the control of a variety of shadowy elites. What is ironic and peculiar is that this crisis in representativeness has occurred in part because of reforms designed to make the system more democratic.

Both phenomena—the judicialization of administration and the spread of interest-group influence—tend to undermine people's trust in government. This distrust then perpetuates and feeds on itself. Distrust of executive agencies leads to demands for more legal checks on administration, which reduces the quality and effectiveness of government. That same distrust leads Congress to impose new and often contradictory mandates on the executive, which prove difficult if not impossible to fulfill. Both processes lead to a reduction of bureaucratic autonomy, which in turn leads to rigid, rule-bound, uninnovative, and incoherent government. Ordinary people then turn around and blame bureaucrats for these problems, as if bureaucrats enjoy working under a host of detailed rules, court orders, earmarks, and complex mandates coming from courts and legislators over which they have no control. The problem with American government lies rather in an overall system that allocates what should properly be administrative powers to courts and political parties.

The problems of American government arise, then, because there is an imbalance between the strength and competence of the state on the one hand, and the institutions that were originally designed to constrain the state on the other. There is, in short, too much law and too much "democracy" relative to American state capacity.

AN UNUSUAL WAY OF PROCEEDING

One of the great turning points in twentieth-century American history was the Supreme Court's 1954 *Brown v. Board of Education* decision, which overturned on constitutional grounds the nineteenth-century *Plessy v. Ferguson* case that had upheld legal segregation. This decision was the starting point for the civil rights movement that unfolded over the following decade, which succeeded in dismantling the formal barriers to racial equality and guaranteed the rights of African Americans and other minorities. Use of the courts to enforce new social rules was the model followed by many subsequent social movements in the late twentieth century, from environmental protection to women's rights to consumer safety to gay marriage.

So familiar is this heroic narrative to Americans that they are seldom aware of how peculiar their approach to social change is. The primary mover in *Brown* was the National Association for the Advancement of Colored People (NAACP), a private voluntary association that filed a class action suit against the Topeka, Kansas, Board of Education on behalf of a small group of black parents and their children. The initiative had to come from private groups, of course, because the state government was under the control of prosegregation forces. The NAACP continued to press the case on appeal all the way to the Supreme Court, and was represented by future Supreme Court justice Thurgood Marshall. What was arguably one of the most important changes in American public policy came about not because Congress as representative of the American people voted for it, but because private individuals litigated through the court system to change the rules. Later changes like the Civil Rights and Voting Rights Acts were the result of congressional action. But even in these cases, enforcement of national law was left up to the initiative of private parties who were given standing to sue the government, and was carried out by courts.

There is no other liberal democracy that proceeds in this fashion. All European countries went through similar changes in the legal status of racial and ethnic minorities, women, and gays in the second half of the twentieth century. But in Britain, France, or Germany, the same result would have been achieved not using the courts but through a national justice ministry acting on behalf of a parliamentary majority. The legislative rule change would have been driven by public pressure from social groups and the media but would have been carried out by the government itself and not by private parties acting through the justice system.

The origins of the American approach lie in the historical sequence by which its three sets of institutions evolved. In Britain, France, and Germany, law came first, followed by a modern state, and only later by democracy. The pattern of development in the United States, by contrast, was one in which a very deep tradition of English Common Law came first, followed by democracy, and only later by a modern state. While the last of these institutions was put into place during the Progressive Era and the New Deal, the American state always remained weaker and less capable than its European and Asian counterparts. More important, American political culture since the founding has been built around distrust of executive authority, so that functions routinely entrusted to administrative bureaucracies in other countries are parceled out in the United States to courts and legislators.

During the Progressive Era and New Deal, reformers tried to construct a European-style administrative state. This brought them directly into conflict with the conservative courts of the time, culminating in the Roosevelt administration's effort to pack the Supreme Court and the subsequent backlash that forced it to back down. More compliant courts in the middle of the twentieth century permitted the emergence of an ever-larger administrative state. But Americans remained highly suspicious of "big government" and new federal agencies. Distrust of the government is not a monopoly of conservatives; many on the left worry about the capture of national institutions by powerful corporate interests, or about an unconstrained national security state, and prefer grassroots activism via the courts to achieve their preferred policy outcomes.

ADVERSARIAL LEGALISM

This history has resulted in what the legal scholar Robert A. Kagan labels a system of "adversarial legalism." While lawyers have played an outsized role in American public life since the beginning of the republic, their role expanded dramatically during the turbulent years of social change in the 1960s and '70s. Congress passed more than two dozen major pieces of civil rights and environment legislation in this period, covering issues from product safety to toxic waste cleanup to private pension funds to occupational safety and health. This constituted a huge expansion of the regulatory state founded during the Progressive Era and New Deal, a shift that American businesses and conservatives are so fond of complaining about today.[2]

Yet what makes this system so unwieldy is not simply the level of regulation per se, but the highly legalistic way it is pursued. Congress mandated creation of an alphabet soup of new federal agencies—EEOC, EPA, OSHA, etc.—but it was not willing to cleanly delegate to these bodies the kind of rule-making authority and enforcement power that European and Japanese state institutions enjoyed. What it did instead was turn over to the courts responsibility for monitoring and enforcement of the law. Congress deliberately encouraged litigation by expanding standing (who has a right to sue) to wider circles of parties, many of whom were only distantly affected by a particular rule.[3]

As an example, political scientist R. Shep Melnick has described the way that the federal courts rewrote Title VII of the 1964 Civil Rights Act, "turning a weak law focusing primarily on intentional discrimination into a bold mandate to compensate for past discrimination." Instead of providing a federal bureaucracy with adequate enforcement power, "the key move of Republicans in the Senate . . . was to substantially privatize the prosecutorial function. They made private lawsuits the dominant mode of Title VII enforcement, creating an engine that would, in the years to come, produce levels of private enforcement litigation beyond their imagining." Across the board, private enforcement cases grew from fewer than 100 per year in the late 1960s to 10,000 in the 1980s, and more than 22,000 by the late 1990s.[4] Expenditures on lawyers increased sixfold during the same period. Not only did direct costs of litigation soar; costs were incurred due to the increasing slowness of the process and uncertainties as to outcomes.[5]

Thus conflicts that in Sweden and Japan would be solved by quiet consultations between interested parties through the bureaucracy are fought out through formal litigation in the American court system. This has a number of unfortunate consequences for public administration, leading to a process characterized, in the words of Sean Farhang, by "Uncertainty, procedural complexity, redundancy, lack of finality, high transaction costs." By keeping enforcement out of the bureaucracy, it also makes the system far less accountable.[6] In a European parliamentary system, a new rule or regulation promulgated by a bureaucracy is subject to scrutiny and debate, and can be changed through political action at the next election. In the United States, policy is made piecemeal in a highly specialized and therefore nontransparent process by judges who are often unelected and serve with lifetime tenure.

The explosion of opportunities for litigation gave access and therefore power to many formerly excluded groups, beginning with African Americans. For this reason, litigation and the right to sue has been jealously guarded by many on the progressive left. But it also entailed large costs in terms of the quality of public policy. Kagan illustrates this with the case of the dredging of Oakland Harbor. During the 1970s, the Port of Oakland initiated plans to dredge the harbor in anticipation of the new, larger classes of container ships that were then coming into service. The plan had to be approved by a host of governmental agencies including the Army Corps of Engineers, the Fish and Wildlife Service, the National Marine Fisheries Service, the EPA, and their counterparts in the state of California. A series of alternative plans for disposing of toxic materials dredged from the harbor were challenged in the courts, and each successive plan entailed prolonged delays and higher costs. The reaction of the EPA to these lawsuits was to retreat into a defensive crouch and not take action. The final plan to proceed with the dredging was not forthcoming until 1994, at an ultimate cost many times the original estimates.[7]

Examples like this can be found across the entire range of activities undertaken by the U.S. government. Many of the travails of the Forest Service described earlier can be attributed to the ways its judgments could be second-guessed through the court system. This had the effect of effectively bringing to a halt all logging on lands it and the Bureau of Land Management operated in the Pacific Northwest during the early 1990s, as a result of threats to the spotted owl under the Endangered Species Act.[8]

When used as an instrument of enforcement, the courts have morphed from constraints on government to mechanisms by which the scope of government has enormously expanded. For example, special education programs for handicapped and disabled children have mushroomed in size and cost since the mid-1970s due to an expansive mandate legislated by Congress in 1974. This mandate was built on earlier findings by federal district courts that special needs children had "rights," which are much harder than mere interests to trade off against other goods or to subject to cost-benefit criteria. Congress, moreover, threw the interpretation of the mandate and its enforcement back into the lap of the courts, which are singularly poor institutions for operating within budget constraints or making complex political trade-offs. The result has been an increasing flow of limited education dollars going to special education in school districts around the country.[9]

The solution to this problem is not necessarily the one advocated by many American conservatives and libertarians, which is to simply eliminate regulation and close down bureaucracies. The ends that government is serving, like regulation of toxic wastes or environmental protection, are important ones that private markets will not pursue if left to their own devices. Conservatives often fail to see that it is the very distrust of government that leads the American system into a far less efficient court-based approach to regulation than that of democracies with stronger executive branches.

But American progressives and liberals are complicit in creating this system as well. They were equally distrustful of bureaucracies that had produced segregated school systems in the South, or that had been influenced by big business interests, and were happy to inject unelected judges into social policy making when legislators proved insufficiently supportive.

This decentralized, legalistic approach to administration then dove-tails with the other notable feature of the American political system, its openness to the influence of interest groups. Interest groups get their way through their ability to use the court system to sue the government di-rectly. But they have another, even more powerful channel that controls significantly more power and resources: the U.S. Congress.

33

CONGRESS AND THE REPATRIMONIALIZATION OF AMERICAN POLITICS

How nineteenth-century clientelism has been replaced by interest group reciprocity; how interest groups affect the quality of public policies; whether interest groups are good or bad for democracy; repatrimonialization of the American state

American politics during most of the nineteenth century was, as we have seen, thoroughly clientelistic. Politicians mobilized voters to go to the polls by making promises of individualized benefits, sometimes in the form of small favors or outright cash payments, but most often through offers of jobs in government bureaucracies on a federal, state, and municipal level. This easy ability to distribute patronage had big spillover effects in terms of official corruption, in which political bosses and members of Congress would skim off benefits for themselves out of the resources they controlled.

These historical forms of clientelism and corruption were largely ended as a result of the civil service reform movement described in chapters 10 and 11, and it is safe to say that neither is the chief threat facing the American political system today. While each incoming administration makes more than four thousand political appointments in the federal government—far more than in any other advanced democracy—political parties are no longer in the business of the wholesale distribution of petty government offices to loyal supporters. There have of course been egregious cases of outright individual corruption, such as those leading to the convictions of California congressman Randy "Duke" Cunningham in 2006, and Illinois governor Rod Blagojevich in 2011. But rules against this type of corruption are extensive and strict, to the point where compliance with the government's voluminous disclosure and conflict of interest rules has become a deterrent to the willingness of many qualified people to serve.

RECIPROCAL ALTRUISM

Unfortunately, the trading of political influence for money has come back in a big way in American politics, this time in a form that is perfectly legal and much harder to eradicate. Criminalized bribery is narrowly defined in American law as a transaction in which a politician and a private party explicitly agree upon a specific quid pro quo exchange. What is not covered by the law is what biologists call reciprocal altruism, or what an anthropologist might label a gift exchange. In a relationship of reciprocal altruism, one person confers a benefit on another with no explicit expectation that it will immediately buy a return favor, unlike an impersonal market transaction. Indeed, if one gives someone a gift and then demands a gift in return, the recipient is likely to feel offended and refuse what is offered. In a gift exchange, the receiver incurs a moral obligation to the other party, and is then inclined at another time or place to return the favor. The law bans only the market transaction but not the exchange of favors, and that is what the American lobbying industry is built around.[1]

I argued earlier that kin selection and reciprocal altruism are the two natural modes of human sociability. They are not learned behaviors but are genetically encoded in our brains and emotions. A human being in any culture who receives a gift from another member of the community will feel a moral obligation to reciprocate. Early states were called patrimonial because they were regarded as the personal property of the ruler, who used his family or household, and friends—oftentimes the warriors who helped him conquer the territory in the first place—to staff his administration. Such states were built around these natural modes of sociability.

Modern states create strict rules and incentives to overcome the tendency to favor family and friends. These include civil service examinations, merit qualifications, conflict-of-interest rules, and antibribery and corruption laws. But the force of natural sociability is so strong that it keeps coming back, like the proverbial thief who, being blocked by a locked front door, tries the back door, windows, and basement crawl space.

It seems to me fair to say that the American state has been repatrimonialized in the second half of the twentieth century, much in the same way as the Chinese state in the Later Han Dynasty, or the Mamluk regime in the century prior to its defeat by the Ottomans, or the French state under the Old Regime. The rules today blocking overt nepotism are still strong enough to prevent this from being a common political transaction in American politics, though it is interesting to note how powerful the urge to form political dynasties is, with all of the Kennedys, Bushes, Clintons, and the like.

Reciprocal altruism, on the other hand, is rampant in Washington, D.C., and is the primary channel through which interest groups have succeeded in corrupting government. As legal scholar Lawrence Lessig points out, interest groups are able to influence members of Congress in perfectly legal ways simply by making donations and waiting for unspecified return favors. At other times it is the member of Congress who is initiating the gift exchange, favoring an interest group in the expectation that he or she will be rewarded down the line with campaign contributions. Often the exchange does not involve money. A congressperson attending a conference in a fancy resort on, say, derivatives regulation, will hear presentations on why the banking industry does not need to be regulated without hearing credible alternative arguments. The politician will be captured in this case not by money (though there is plenty of that to go around), but intellectually, since he or she will have only positive associations with the interest group's point of view.[2]

The explosion of interest groups and lobbying in Washington has been astonishing, with 175 registered lobbying firms in 1971 rising to 2,500 ten years later, and then to more than 12,000 registered lobbyists spending more than $3.2 billion by 2013.[3] The distortive effects of this activity on American public policies can be seen in a host of areas, beginning with the tax code. Economists agree that all taxes potentially detract from the ability of markets to allocate resources efficiently, and the least inefficient types of taxation are those that are simple, uniform, and predictable, which allow businesses to plan and invest around them. The U.S. tax code is exactly the opposite. While nominal corporate tax rates in the United States are much higher than in other developed countries, very few American corporations actually pay taxes at that rate, because they have negotiated special exemptions and benefits for themselves.[4]

Of the old elites in France prior to the revolution, Alexis de Tocqueville said that they mistook privilege for liberty, that is, protection from state power that applied to themselves alone and not generally to all citizens. In the contemporary United States, elites speak the language of liberty but are perfectly happy to settle for privilege.

Some political scientists have argued that all of this money and activity have not resulted in measurable changes in policy along the lines desired by the lobbyists, implausible as this may seem given the sums readily invested in the process.[5] Often, however, the goal of interest groups and lobbyists is not to stimulate new policies but to prevent outcomes unfavorable to themselves but in the public interest from ever seeing the light of day. In other cases, they make existing legislation much worse than it would otherwise be. The American legislative process has always been much more fragmented than in countries with parliamentary systems and disciplined parties. The welter of congressional committees with overlapping jurisdiction often produces multiple and conflicting mandates for action, like the "three separate proposals embodying radically different theories about the nature of the problem" that were embodied in the 1990 National Affordable Housing Act, or the multiplicity of mandated ways of enforcing the Clean Air Act. This decentralized legislative process produces incoherent laws and virtually invites involvement by interest groups which, if not powerful enough to shape overall legislation, can at least protect their specific interests.[6]

For example, Barack Obama's Affordable Care Act in 2010 turned into something of a monstrosity during the legislative process as a result of all the concessions and side payments that had to be made to interest groups, including doctors, insurance companies, and the pharmaceutical industry. The bill itself ran to nine hundred pages, which very few members of Congress were able to review in any detail. In other cases, interest groups have been able to block legislation harmful to their interests. The simplest and most effective response to the financial crisis of 2008–2009 and the hugely unpopular taxpayer bailouts of large banks would have been a law that put a hard cap on the size of financial institutions, or else dramatically raised capital requirements that would have had much the same effect.[7] If such constraints existed, banks taking foolish risks could go bankrupt without triggering a systemic crisis and government bailout. Like the Depression-era Glass-Steagall Act, such a law could have been written on a few of sheets of paper. But this possibility was not seriously considered during the congressional deliberations on financial regulation. What emerged instead was the Wall Street Reform and Consumer Protection, or Dodd-Frank, Act, which, while better than no regulation at all, extended to hundreds of pages of legislation and mandated reams of further detailed rules that will impose huge costs on banks and consumers down the road. Rather than simply capping bank size, it creates a Financial Stability Oversight Council tasked with the enormous job of assessing and managing institutions deemed to pose systemic risks, which in the end will still not solve the problem of banks being too big to fail. Though no one will ever find a smoking gun linking bank campaign contributions to the votes of specific congressmen, it defies belief that the banking industry's legions of lobbyists did not have a major impact in preventing the simpler solution of simply breaking up the big banks or subjecting them to stringent capital requirements.[8]

PASSIONS AND INTERESTS

Ordinary Americans express widespread disdain for interest groups and their sway over Congress. The perception that the democratic process has been corrupted or hijacked is not an exclusive concern of either end of the political spectrum; both Tea Party Republicans on the right and liberal Democrats on the left believe that interest groups are exercising undue political influence and feathering their own nests. As a result, trust in Congress has fallen to historically low levels barely above double digits.[9]

The economist Mancur Olson made one of the most famous arguments about the malign effects of interest group politics on economic growth and ultimately democracy in *The Rise and Decline of Nations*. Looking particularly at the long-term economic decline of Britain throughout the twentieth century, Olson argued that democracies in times of peace and stability tended to accumulate ever-increasing numbers of interest groups. These groups, instead of pursuing wealth-creating economic activities, made use of the political system to extract benefits or rents for themselves. These rents were unproductive in the aggregate and costly to the public as a whole. But the general public had a collective action problem or could not organize as effectively as, for example, the banking industry and corn producers to protect their interests. The result was the steady diversion of energy into rent-seeking activities over time, a process that could be halted only by a large shock like war or revolution.[10]

This highly negative narrative about interest groups stands in sharp contrast, however, to a much more positive one about the benefits of civil society, or voluntary associations, to the health of democracy. Alexis de

Tocqueville in *Democracy in America* noted that Americans had a strong propensity for organizing private associations, which he argued were "schools for democracy" because they taught private individuals the skills of coming together for public purposes. Individuals by themselves were weak; only by joining with others for common purposes could they, among other things, resist tyrannical government. This line of argument has been carried forward by scholars like Robert Putnam, who argues that this very propensity to organize—"social capital"—is both good for democracy and became endangered in the second half of the twentieth century.[11]

Founding Father James Madison also had a relatively benign view of interest groups. Even if one did not approve of the ends that a particular group was seeking, their diversity over a large country, he argued, would be sufficient to prevent domination by any one group. As political scientist Theodore Lowi noted, "pluralist" political theory in the mid-twentieth century concurred with Madison: the cacophony of interest groups would collectively interact to produce a public interest, just as competition in a free market would provide public benefit through individuals following their narrow self-interests. There were no grounds for the government to regulate this process, since there was no higher ground that could define a "public interest" standing above the narrow concerns of interest groups. The Supreme Court in its *Buckley v. Valeo* and *Citizens United* decisions was in effect affirming the benign interpretation of what Lowi labeled "interest group liberalism."[12]

How, then, do we reconcile these diametrically opposed narratives— that interest groups are corrupting democracy and harming economic growth, and that they are necessary conditions for a healthy democracy?

The most obvious way is to try to distinguish a "good" civil society organization from a "bad" interest group. The former could be said to be driven by what Albert Hirschman called the passions, the latter by the interests.[13] The former might be a nonprofit organization like a church group seeking to build houses for the poor, or a lobbying organization promoting a policy it believes to be in the public interest, like protection of coastal habitats. An interest group might be a lobbyist for the tobacco industry or large banks, whose only objective is to maximize the profits of the companies supporting it. Robert Putnam tried to make a distinction between small associations that invited active participation by their members and "membership organizations" that simply involved paying a membership fee.[14]

Unfortunately, this distinction does not hold up to theoretical scrutiny. Just because a group proclaims that it is acting in the public interest does not mean that it is actually doing so. For example, a medical advocacy group that wants more dollars allocated to combating a particular disease may actually distort public priorities by diverting funds from more widespread and damaging diseases, simply because it is better at public relations. Just because an interest group is self-interested doesn't mean that its claims are illegitimate or that it does not have a right to be represented within the political system. If a poorly thought-out regulation will seriously damage the interests of an industry and its workers, they have a right to make that known to Congress. Indeed, lobbyists are often some of the most important sources of information about the consequences of government action. In the long-running battles between environmental groups and corporations, environmentalists purporting to represent the public interest are not always right with respect to the trade-offs between sustainability, profits, and jobs, as the Oakland Harbor dredging case illustrates.[15]

The most salient argument against interest group pluralism has to do with distorted representation. E. E. Schattschneider, in *The Semisovereign People*, argued that the actual practice of democracy in America had nothing to do with its popular image as government "of the people, by the people, and for the people." He noted that political outcomes seldom correspond with popular preferences, that there is a very low level of participation and political awareness, and that real decisions are taken by much smaller groups of organized interests.[16] A similar argument is buried in Mancur Olson's framework: he notes that not all groups are equally capable of organizing for collective action. His earlier work, *The Logic of Collective Action*, in fact explained that it is much more difficult to organize large as opposed to small groups, since large groups that provide benefits to all their members invite free riding. In a democratic context, the whole body of citizens (or at least large majorities within them) may share a long-term interest in, for example, a fiscally responsible budget, but any one American feels this much less powerfully than an interest group that would get its subsidy or tax break cut as the result of a budget consolidation. The interest groups that contend for the attention of Congress are therefore not collectively representative of the whole American people. They are representative of the best-organized and (what often amounts to the same thing) richly endowed parts of American society. This bias is not a random one but tends to work against the interests of the unorganized, who are often poor, poorly educated, or otherwise marginalized.[17]

Morris Fiorina has provided substantial evidence that what he labels the American "political class" is far more polarized than the American people themselves. He presents a wide variety of data showing that on many supposedly contentious issues, from abortion to deficits to school prayer to gay marriage, poll data show that majorities of the American public support compromise positions—for example, use of federal funding to support stem cell research on excess embryos in fertility clinics. Party activists are invariably more ideological and take more extreme positions, whether on the left or right, than the rank-and-file party voters. But the majorities supporting middle-of-the-road positions do not feel very passionately about them, and they are largely unorganized. This means that politics is defined by well-organized activists, whether in the parties and Congress, the media, or lobbying and interest groups. The sum of these activist groups does not yield a compromise position; it leads to polarization and deadlocked politics.[18]

Unrepresentative interest groups are not simply creatures of corporate America and the Right. Some of the most powerful organizations in democratic countries have been trade unions, followed by environmental groups, women's organizations, advocates of gay rights, the aged, the disabled, indigenous peoples, and virtually every other sector of society. In contemporary America, it seems that every disease or medical condition has spawned its own advocacy organization lobbying for increased attention and resources. Pluralist theory holds that the aggregation of all these groups contending with one another constitutes a democratic public interest. But one could argue instead that due to their intrinsic overrepresentation of narrow interests, they undermine the possibility of representative democracy expressing a true public interest.

INTEREST GROUPS AND THE QUALITY OF GOVERNMENT

Interest groups undermine bureaucratic autonomy when they persuade their agents in Congress to issue complex and often self-contradictory mandates to agencies, which are then highly constrained in their ability to exercise independent judgment or make commonsense decisions.

Examples of this abound. Congress wants the federal government to procure goods and services cheaply and efficiently, and yet it mandates a cumbersome set of rules known as the Federal Acquisition Regulation (FAR) on all government procurement agencies. In contrast to private-sector procurement, government purchasing is minutely procedural and subject to endless right of appeal. In many cases, individual members of Congress intervene directly to make sure procurement is done in ways that benefit their own constituents. This is particularly true for the big-ticket items procured by the Pentagon, which become virtual jobs programs to be distributed by lucky members of Congress. While Congress and the public decry "waste, fraud, and abuse" in procurement, fixing the problem by mandating even more detailed and constraining rules only serves to drive up the costs of procurement and to reduce its quality.

There is a further problem with interest groups and the pluralist view that sees public interest as nothing more than the aggregation of individual private interests: they undermine the possibility of deliberation and the way that individual preferences are shaped by dialogue and communication. In both classical Athenian democracy and the New England town hall meetings celebrated by Tocqueville, citizens spoke directly to each other about the common interests of their community. It is easy to idealize these instances of small-scale democracy, or minimize the real differences that exist in large societies. But as any organizer of focus groups will tell you, people's views on highly emotional subjects from immigration to abortion to drugs will change just thirty minutes into a face-to-face discussion with people of differing views, provided that they are given common information and ground rules that enforce civility. Few single-issue advocates will ever maintain that their cause will trump all other good things if forced to directly confront those alternative needs. One of the problems of pluralist theory, then, is the assumption that interests are fixed, and that the goal of the legislator is simply to act as a transmission belt for them, rather than having his or her own views that can be shaped by deliberation.

It is commonly observed that no one in Congress deliberates anymore. Congressional "debate" amounts to a sequential series of talking points aimed not at colleagues but at activist audiences, who are perfectly happy to punish a legislator who deviates from their agenda as a result of deliberation or greater knowledge.

In well-functioning governance systems, a great deal of deliberation occurs not just in legislatures but also in bureaucracies. This is not a matter of bureaucrats simply talking with one another but rather a complex series of consultations among government officials and businesses, outside implementers and service providers, civil society groups, the media, and other sources of information about societal interests and opinions.[19] Congress mandated consultation in the landmark 1946 Administrative Procedure Act, which required regulatory agencies to publicly post proposed rule changes and to solicit notice and comment. But these consultative procedures often become highly routinized and pro forma, with actual decisions resulting not from internal deliberation but from political confrontations between well-organized interest groups.[20]

POLITICAL DECAY

The rule of law constitutes a basic protection of individuals against tyrannical government. But in the second half of the twentieth century, law lost its focus as a constraint on government and became instead an instrument for widening the scope of government. In the process, functions that could have been efficiently and accountably carried out in a bureaucracy were given over to a mixture of courts, executive agencies, and private individuals. For fear of empowering "big government," the United States has ended up with a government that is equally large but actually less accountable because it is in the hands of the courts.

Similarly, legislators as representatives of the people's will are supposed to act to ensure that policies reflect public purposes. But political parties have become hostage to powerful interest groups that collectively do not represent the American electorate. The hold of these groups is strong enough to block sensible public policies on issues from farm subsidies to bank regulation. They have turned the tax code into a confusing welter of privileges and made difficult any kind of impersonal public administration.

The United States tried to establish a modern, Weberian state during the Progressive Era and New Deal. It succeeded in many respects: the Food and Drug Administration, the Centers for Disease Control, the armed services, and the Federal Reserve are among the most technically competent, well-run, and autonomous government bodies anywhere in the world. But the overall quality of American public administration remains very problematic, precisely because of the country's continuing reliance on courts and parties at the expense of state administration.

Part of the phenomenon of decay has to do with intellectual rigidity. The idea that lawyers and litigation should be such an integral part of public administration is not a view widely shared in other democracies, and yet it has become such an entrenched way of doing business in the United States that no one sees any alternatives. Strictly speaking, this is less an ideological matter than a political tradition shared by both Left and Right. Similarly, despite a widespread populist outcry against the influence of interest groups in Congress, many people (beginning with members of the Supreme Court) fail to see that a problem even exists, and no one sees a realistic way of curbing their influence.

The underlying sources of political decay—intellectual rigidity and the influence of elite groups—are generic to democracies as a whole. Indeed, they are problems faced by all governments whether democratic or not. The problems identified here of excessive judicialization and interest groups exist in other developed democracies. But the impact of interest groups depends heavily on the specific nature of institutions. There is a wide variation in the way that democracies structure the incentives facing political actors, which make governments more or less susceptible to these forces. In the following chapter, I will argue that the United States, as the world's first and most advanced liberal democracy, suffers from the problem of political decay in a more acute form than other democratic political systems. The long-standing distrust of the state that has always characterized American politics has led to an unbalanced form of government that undermines the prospects of necessary collective action. The result is what I label "vetocracy."

34

AMERICA THE VETOCRACY

How the American system of checks and balances has become a vetocracy; how other democracies have stronger mechanisms to force collective decisions; how strong authority is nonetheless delegated to the executive in certain areas; how the European Union is becoming more like the United States

The American Constitution protects individual liberties through a complex system of checks and balances that was deliberately designed by the Founders to constrain the power of the state. American government arose in the context of a revolution against British monarchical authority and drew on even older wellsprings of resistance to the king in the English Civil War. Intense distrust of government and reliance on the spontaneous activities of dispersed individuals has been a hallmark of American politics ever since.

The American constitutional system checks power in any number of ways. In contrast to a parliamentary system, in which a unified executive (that is, an executive centralized under a single authority) carries out the wishes of legislative majorities, the American presidential system splits authority between an elected president and a Congress that have equal democratic legitimacy and whose survival is independent of one another. The Constitution also establishes a judicial branch that over time acquired the power to invalidate legislation coming from Congress. It further distributes powers to the states—or rather, the states, which were the original holders of power, gave up authority to a federal government only slowly and grudgingly in the course of the two hundred years following ratification of the Constitution. Congress itself is divided into two houses, the upper one originally designed to be a bastion of state power. In many democratic systems like that of Britain, the upper house has largely ceremonial powers; in the United States, it is very strong and exercises specific powers such as confirmation of executive appointments and authority over war and peace. The American executive branch itself does not always answer to the president; many regulatory commissions are under the control of commissioners appointed by the parties in Congress.

As Huntington pointed out, powers in America are not so much functionally divided as replicated across the branches, leading to periodic usurpations of one branch by another and conflicts over which branch should predominate. Congressional authority over national security policy and the influence of the courts over social policies like abortion are recent examples of this. American federalism oftentimes does not cleanly delegate powers to the appropriate level of government; instead it duplicates them at multiple levels, giving federal, state, and local authorities jurisdiction over, for example, toxic waste disposal. Under such a system of redundant and nonhierarchical authority, different parts of the government are easily able to block one another.

POLARIZATION

Of the most important challenges facing developed democracies is the unsustainability of their welfare-state commitments. The existing social contracts underlying contemporary welfare states were negotiated generations ago, when birth rates were higher, people didn't live as long, and economic growth was more robust. The availability of finance has allowed all modern democracies to keep pushing this problem into the future, but at some point the underlying demographic reality will set in.

These problems are not insuperable. The debt-to-GDP ratios of both Britain and the United States coming out of World War II were higher than they are today.[1] Sweden, Finland, and other Scandinavian countries found their large welfare states in crisis during the 1990s and were able to make adjustments to their tax and spending levels. Australia succeeded in eliminating almost all of its external debt, even prior to the huge resource boom of the 2000s.

The American political system early in the twenty-first century has failed to deal with this issue. The fundamental reason for this failure has to do with the two dominant political parties, which have become more ideologically polarized than they have been since the late nineteenth century. There has been a large geographical sorting of the parties that began in the 1960s, with virtually the entire South moving from the Democratic to the Republican Party, and Republicans becoming almost extinct in the Northeast. Since the breakdown of the New Deal coalition and the end of the Democrats' hegemony in Congress in the 1980s, the two parties have become more evenly balanced and have repeatedly exchanged control over the presidency and the two houses of Congress. This higher degree of partisan competition has fueled an arms race between the parties for funding and has undermined personal comity between them.[2]

As noted in the previous chapter, there is disagreement among social scientists as to how deeply rooted this polarization is in American society. But there is no question that the parties and the activist groups driving their behavior have sorted themselves into far more rigid and ideologically cohesive groups. They have increased their homogeneity through their control, in most states, over redistricting, which allows them to gerrymander voting districts to increase their chances of reelection. The spread of primaries has put the choice of party candidates into the hands of the relatively small numbers of activists who turn out for these elections.[3]

Polarization is not the end of the story, however. Democratic political systems are not supposed to end conflict; they are supposed to peacefully resolve and lessen conflicts through agreed-upon rules. Americans have always been divided on issues from slavery to abortion to gun control. A good political system mitigates underlying polarizations and encourages the emergence of political outcomes representing the interests of as large a part of the population as possible. But when polarization confronts America's Madisonian check-and-balance political system, the result is particularly devastating.[4]

VETO PLAYERS

Ideally, a democracy provides equal opportunity for participation on the part of every member of the political community. Democratic decisions should be taken by consensus, where every single member of the community agrees on a particular decision. This is what typically happens in families, and in band- and tribal-level societies.

However, the efficiency of consensual decision making deteriorates rapidly as groups become more diverse and as their size increases. This means that for most groups, decisions are made not on the basis of consensus but on the basis of assent on the part of some portion of the whole group. The smaller the percentage of the group necessary to take a decision, the easier and more efficiently it can be made. The trade-off between the percentage of votes required and the costs of decision making, in terms of both time and effort, is illustrated by Figure 22. As anyone who has chaired a meeting of a club or committee knows, decision costs rise exponentially if one needs consensus in large groups.

Decisions taken under a majority voting rule (50 percent plus one) often used in democratic countries thus deviate very far from an ideal democratic procedure, since they can disenfranchise nearly half the population. Indeed, under plurality (or what is sometimes known as first-past-the-post) voting, decisions can be taken on behalf of the whole community by a minority of voters. (The United States and the United Kingdom, both of which have such voting systems, elected Bill Clinton in 1992 with 43 percent of the vote, and Tony Blair with 42 percent in 2001.)[5]

FIGURE 22. Political Participation vs. Cost of Decision Making

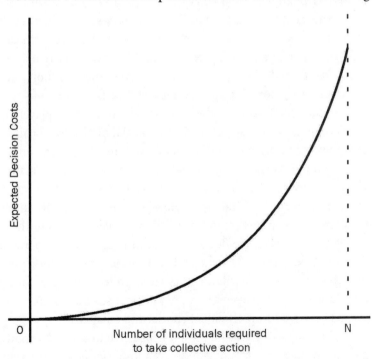

SOURCE: James M. Buchanan and Gordon Tullock, *The Calculus of Consent*

It is evident that rules like majority voting are not adopted on the basis of any deep principle of justice but rather as an expedient that reduces decision costs and allows large communities to make a decision of some sort. Democracies impose other mechanisms to force decisions and decrease the number of potential veto players. These include cloture rules that allow for cutoff of debate, rules restricting the ability of legislators to offer amendments, and what are called "reversionary" rules in the event that the legislature can't agree on important matters like budgets. Under the Meiji Constitution, if the Diet couldn't agree on a new budget, the previous year's budget was automatically adopted. Under the reversionary rules adopted in Chile and other Latin American countries, failure to pass a budget meant that budgetary authority went back to the president and the executive.[6]

Other types of rules are meant to promote stability, which they do at the expense of minority prerogatives. The postwar German Federal Republic, learning from the weaknesses of Weimar democracy, has provisions for what is called a "positive" vote of no confidence: a party cannot topple a government coalition (that is, exercise a veto) unless it can put together an alternative government. Parliamentary systems have evolved one of the best mechanisms for forcing legislative decisions ever invented: if there is deadlock or a high degree of contention over a particular issue, the government can dissolve parliament and call for new elections, allowing a democratic electorate to speak directly to the issue at hand.

Political scientist George Tsebelis coined the term "veto players" as a means of comparing diverse political systems. All institutional rules that delegate powers to different political actors within the system constitute potential veto points where individual veto players can block action by the whole body. Virtually all features of a constitution—presidentialism, bicameralism, federalism, judicial review—while functionally different from one another can be thought of as potential veto points in the process of reaching a collective decision. In addition, there are many nonconstitutional rules that affect the ability of minorities to block the will of majorities, such as the parliamentary rules under which amendments can be offered. A veto player is simply political science lingo for what Americans have traditionally called checks and balances.[7]

Using the concept of veto players, it is possible to array different political systems on a linear scale going from an absolute dictatorship, in which there is only one veto player (the dictator), to a consensus system in which every citizen wields a potential veto over action by the whole. Democratic political systems grant many more vetoes to players within the system than do authoritarian states; that's why they are democracies. But within the universe of democracies, there are substantial differences in the number of veto players permitted. Figure 23 reproduces the Buchanan-Tullock curve, but with the horizontal axis representing the number of veto players able to block decisions rather than percentages of the electorate needed to make them.

FIGURE 23. Veto Players and the Difficulty of Decision Making

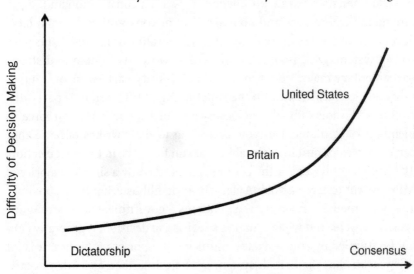

In terms of the sheer number of veto players, the American political system is an outlier among contemporary democracies. It has become unbalanced and in certain areas has acquired too many checks and balances, which raise the costs of collective action, sometimes making it impossible altogether. It is a system that might be labeled a vetocracy. In earlier periods of American history, when one or the other party dominated, this system served to moderate the will of the majority and force it to pay greater attention to minorities than it otherwise might. But in the more evenly balanced, highly competitive party system that has arisen since the 1980s, it has become a formula for gridlock.

America's large number of veto players becomes evident when the U.S. system is compared to that of another long-standing democracy, Britain. The Westminster system, which evolved in the years following the Glorious Revolution, is one of the most decisive in the democratic world because, in its pure form, it creates a much smaller number of veto players. In Britain, citizens have one large, formal check on government— their ability to periodically elect Parliament. (There is another important check, a free media, which is not part of the formal political system.) In all other respects, however, the system concentrates rather than diffuses power. A pure Westminster system has only a single all-powerful legislative chamber, no separate presidency, no written constitution and therefore no judicial review, and no federalism or constitutionally mandated devolution of powers to localities. It has a plurality, or first-past-the-post, voting system, which tends to produce a two-party system and strong parliamentary majorities even when the majority party wins only a plurality of the vote.[8] Critical to the functioning of this system is party discipline; the leadership of the Conservative or Labour Party can force its members of Parliament to vote according to their wishes because they can deny recalcitrant MPs the ability to run for office in the next election. The British equivalent of the cloture rule needs only a simple majority of MPs present to force a vote; American-style filibustering is not possible. The parliamentary majority then chooses a government with strong executive powers, and when it makes a legislative decision, it generally cannot be stymied by courts, states, municipalities, or other bodies. It is for this reason that the British system is often described as a "democratic dictatorship."[9]

The Westminster system understandably produces governments with more formal powers than in the United States. This greater degree of decisiveness can be seen clearly with respect to the budget process. In Britain, national budgets are not drawn up in Parliament, but in Whitehall, the seat of the bureaucracy, where professional civil servants act under instructions from the cabinet and prime minister. The budget is then presented by the chancellor of the exchequer (equivalent of the U.S. treasury secretary) to the House of Commons, which votes to approve it in a single up-or-down vote. This usually takes place within a week or two of its promulgation by the government.

The process in the United States is totally different. The Constitution grants Congress primary authority over the budget. While presidents formulate budgets through the executive branch Office of Management and Budget, this office often becomes more like another lobbying organization supporting the president's preferences. The budget, put before Congress in February, works its way through a complex set of committees over a period of months, and what finally emerges for ratification (we hope) by the two houses toward the end of the summer is the product of innumerable deals struck with individual members to secure their support. The nonpartisan Congressional Budget Office was established in 1974 to provide Congress with greater technocratic support in drawing up budgets, but in the end the making of an American budget is a highly decentralized and nonstrategic process in comparison to what happens in Britain.

The openness and never-ending character of the American budget process in turn gives lobbyists and interest groups multiple opportunities to exercise influence. In most European parliamentary systems, it makes no sense for an interest group to lobby an individual MP, since the rules of party discipline give him or her little or no influence over the party leadership's position. In the United States, by contrast, committee chairs and party leaders have enormous powers to modify legislation and therefore become the target of lobbying activity.

The Westminster system for all of its concentrated powers nonetheless remains fundamentally democratic. It is democratic because if voters don't like the kinds of policies and state performance it produces, they are free to vote the current government out and replace it with another. Indeed, with a vote of no confidence, they do not have to wait until the end of a presidential term or congressional cycle; they can immediately dethrone a prime minister. Governments are judged much more on their overall performance than on their ability to provide specific pork barrel benefits to particular interest groups or lobbies.

The classic Westminster system no longer exists anywhere in the world, including Britain itself, which has gradually adopted more checks and balances. Nonetheless, in terms of its position on the horizontal axis of Figure 23, Britain still remains far to the left of the United States in terms of numbers of veto players. While the Westminster system may represent something of an extreme among contemporary democracies, most other parliamentary systems in Europe and Asia provide their governments with stronger mechanisms for forcing decisions than does the United States. The United States tends to share the space at the right end of Figure 23's horizontal axis with those Latin American countries which, having copied the U.S. presidential system in the nineteenth century, have faced similar problems with gridlock and politicized administration.

Budgeting is not the only aspect of American government that differs systematically from its democratic counterparts in terms of proliferating veto players. In a parliamentary system, a great deal of legislation is formulated in the executive branch with heavy technocratic input from the permanent civil service. Ministries are accountable to parliament and hence ultimately to voters through the ministers who head them, but this type of hierarchical system can take a longer-term strategic view and produce much more coherent legislation. In Sweden, for example, there is a small civil service separate from the implementing agencies that actually deliver services; the former's main function is to help parliament prepare legislation.[10]

Such a system is utterly foreign to American political culture, where Congress jealously guards its right to legislate. Bill Clinton's health care plan was formulated in the executive branch by a group of experts operating under the leadership of First Lady Hillary Clinton away from the glare of immediate public scrutiny. This was one important reason that it failed ignominiously to get through Congress in 1993. Barack Obama was able to get the Affordable Care Act passed in 2010 only because he abdicated virtually any role in shaping the legislation, leaving the final bill in the hands of multiple congressional committees.

The lack of legislative coherence in turn produces a large, sprawling, and often unaccountable government. Congress's multiple committees frequently produce duplicative and overlapping programs, or create multiple agencies with similar mandates. Moreover, a system that is fragmented at the center gets further fragmented as a result of American federalism. In the words of legal scholar Gerhard Casper,

> In our system of public administration and adjudication of public law issues, we suffer from too many layers of government with concurrent jurisdiction . . . Where just a single level of government would busily produce a regulatory maze, complex and internally inconsistent enough to employ legions of handholding lawyers, we allow two, three, or four to have their say. Not only do multiple government agencies have a say, but so do innumerable citizens acting as private attorney generals, empow-

ered to bring private suits. Government decisionmaking is further distorted when enforcement rights, over matters concerning the public interest, are granted to private parties.[11]

The Pentagon in this system is mandated to produce close to five hundred reports to Congress on various issues annually, more than one for every day of the year. These mandates are often duplicative and never expire, consuming huge amounts of bureaucratic time and energy.[12] Congress created fifty-one separate programs for worker retraining, and eighty-two projects to improve teacher quality.[13] Financial sector regulation is shared by the Federal Reserve Board, the Treasury Department, the Securities and Exchange Commission, the Federal Deposit Insurance Corporation, the National Credit Union Administration, the Commodity Futures Trading Commission, the Office of Thrift Supervision, the Federal Housing Finance Agency, and the New York Federal Reserve Bank, as well as a host of state attorneys general who have broadened their mandates to take on the banking sector. The federal agencies are overseen by different congressional committees who are loath to give up their turf to a more coherent and unified regulator. It was easy for the banking sector to game this system to bring about deregulation of the financial sector in the late 1990s; reregulating it after the crisis proved much more difficult.[14]

THE PERILS OF PRESIDENTIALISM

Vetocracy is only half the story of the American political system. In other respects, Congress delegates huge powers to the executive branch, allowing it to operate rapidly and sometimes with a very low degree of accountability. Our overall evaluation of the system therefore needs to be tempered by an appreciation of areas in which it can act with strength and decisiveness.

There are several areas of delegation to highly autonomous bureaucracies. These include the Federal Reserve Board, the intelligence agencies, the military, and specialized agencies like NASA and the Centers for Disease Control.[15] On the state and local levels, attorneys general or prosecutors are given a great deal of discretion over whether to bring charges against individuals accused of crimes, and they are free to enter into plea bargains—much more so than, say, their German counterparts.

The military is typically allowed substantial autonomy with regard to operational matters. And, as the world has come to know through the revelations of Edward Snowden, the National Security Agency has been given broad leave to collect data not just on foreign activities but also on American citizens since September 11, 2001.[16]

While many American libertarians and conservatives would like to abolish these agencies altogether, it is hard to see how it would be possible to govern properly without them under modern circumstances. America today has a vast, diverse, complex national economy, connected to a globalized world economy that moves with extraordinary speed and that takes a great deal of expertise to master. It faces serious external security threats. During the acute phase of the financial crisis that unfolded after the collapse of Lehman Brothers in September 2008, the Federal Reserve and Treasury Department had to make massive decisions literally overnight, decisions that involved flooding the market with trillions of dollars of liquidity, propping up individual banks, and imposing new regulations. The severity of the crisis led Congress to an emergency appropriation of $700 billion for the Troubled Asset Relief Program, largely on the say-so of the Treasury Department and the Bush administration. There has been a large amount of after-the-fact second-guessing of specific decisions made during this period. But the idea that such a crisis could be managed by any other branch of government—and in particular by Congress, exercising detailed oversight—is ludicrous. The same applies to national security issues, where the president is in effect delegated to decide how to respond to nuclear and terrorist threats that potentially affect the lives of millions of Americans. It is for this reason that Alexander Hamilton in Federalist No. 70 spoke of the need for "energy in the executive."

There is intense populist distrust of elite institutions and demand either to abolish them (as in the case of the Federal Reserve) or to open up their internal deliberations to television and public scrutiny. Ironically, however, Americans when polled show the highest degree of approval precisely for those institutions—the military, NASA, the CDC—that are the least subject to immediate democratic oversight. Part of the reason they are admired is that they actually get things done. By contrast, the institution most directly accountable to the people, the U.S. Congress, receives disastrously low levels of approval (see Figure 24). Congress is typically regarded as a talking shop where only lobbyist influence produces results and partisanship prevents commonsense solutions.

FIGURE 24. Americans' View of Their Institutions (percent)

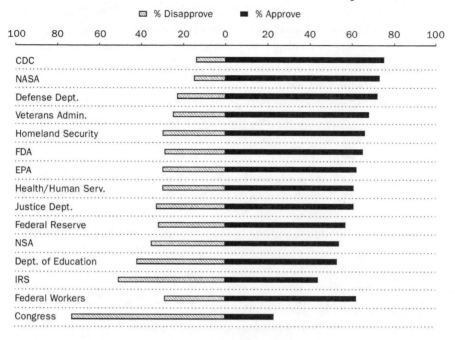

SOURCE: Pew Research Center

The American political system thus presents a complex picture in which checks and balances excessively constrain decision making on the part of majorities, as well as instances of excessive or potentially dangerous delegations of authority to poorly accountable institutions. So simple a delegated power as prosecutorial discretion is easily abused, particularly by high-profile prosecutors responding to political pressures to get tough on crime. The same goes, it would seem, for the NSA.

The problem in the American system is that these delegations are seldom made cleanly. Congress frequently fails in its duty to provide clear legislative guidance on how a particular agency is to perform its task, leaving it up to the agency itself to write its own mandate. In doing so, Congress hopes that if things don't work out, the courts will step in to correct abuses. We saw this process unfold in the case of the first national regulator in the United States, the ICC, which was given a very unclear mandate about its powers over railroads and was then wrapped up in litigation for the first twenty years of its existence as a variety of private parties challenged its authority to make decisions. The same process is unfolding in the early twenty-first century with passage of the Dodd-Frank bill regulating the financial sector: Congress delegated to the regulators the responsibility of writing many of the detailed provisions, which will inevitably be challenged in the courts. Ironically, excessive delegation and vetocracy are intertwined.

Many of these problems stem from America's presidential system itself. In a parliamentary system, the majority party or coalition controls the government directly; members of parliament become ministers who have the hierarchical authority to direct the bureaucracies they control. Parliamentary systems can be blocked if parties are excessively fragmented and coalitions unstable, as has been the case frequently in Italy. But once a parliamentary majority has been established, there is a relatively clean delegation of authority to an executive agency. Such straightforward delegations are harder to achieve in a presidential system, where the two branches often find themselves competing with each other. Simply strengthening one branch at the expense of the others does not overcome the problem posed by the original separation of powers.

The United States has needed presidential power at many junctures in its history, but it has always been leery of potential abuses of executive authority. This is particularly true under conditions of divided government, when the party controlling one or both houses of Congress is different from the one controlling the presidency. Congress needs to delegate authority, but it does not want to give up control. Thus, although the Constitution clearly delegates to the executive branch authority over national defense and foreign relations, this does not prevent Congress from constantly dragging secretaries of defense and state before it, mandating detailed rules regarding, for example, embassy security, and requiring them to produce hundreds of annual reports on subjects from environmental damage to human rights. Distrust of presidential authority has led to the peculiar independent commission structure that characterized the Interstate Commerce Commission and other regulators. Instead of straightforwardly delegating power to a single agency head who is then accountable to the president, early regulatory agencies reported instead to a group of commissioners balanced between the two parties. Congress was in effect delegating control to the executive while at the same time strictly controlling that delegation. An election that in a European parliamentary system would lead to a swift change in policy slows down in the United States as commissioners cycle through their fixed terms. The independent commission structure preserved party dominance, but in the end ironically made regulators less democratically accountable.

HOW DIFFERENT IS THE UNITED STATES?

In many respects, the American system of checks and balances compares unfavorably with parliamentary systems in its ability to balance the need for strong state action with law and accountability. These systems tend not to judicialize administration to nearly the same extent; they have fewer government agencies; they write more coherent legislation; and they are less subject to interest group influence. Germany, Scandinavia, the Netherlands, and Switzerland have been able to sustain higher levels of trust in government, which makes public administration less adversarial, more consensus based and, in the early twenty-first century, better able to adapt to changing conditions of globalization. For example, the privatization of many welfare services and the concessions by trade unions on job security were facilitated by high-trust institutions like the corporatist framework within which wages and benefits are set across the whole economy. These assertions are true, however, only at the level of individual countries. When we consider the European Union as a whole, the comparisons are not nearly as favorable.

Take interest groups and their impact on public policy. It is clear from the academic literature that there has been a large increase in the number and sophistication of lobbying groups in Europe as well as in America. Numbers are difficult to compare, since Europe does not have the same strict requirements for the registration of lobbyists that the United States does. But it is still the case that corporations, trade associations, and environmental, consumer, and labor rights groups all operate both at national and EU-wide levels much as they do in the United States.[17] With the growth of the European Union and the shift of policy making away from national capitals to Brussels, the European system as a whole is beginning to resemble that of the United States to an increasing degree. Europe's individual parliamentary systems may allow for fewer veto players than the American system of checks and balances, but with the addition of a large European layer, many more veto points have been added. This means that European interest groups can jurisdiction-shop to an increasing extent: if they cannot get favorable treatment at a national level they can go to Brussels, or vice versa. Although, as political scientist Christine Mahoney has noted, "outside" groups representing social movements have significantly less access to European institutions than they do in the United States, interest groups still have many more opportunities to lay their case before policy makers and regulators than they did when they were confined to their own national systems.[18]

Indeed, the consensual nature of the EU itself has meant that EU-level institutions are far weaker than certain federal institutions in the United States. These weaknesses were made painfully evident in the European debt crisis of 2010–2013. The United States Federal Reserve, Treasury, and Congress responded quite forcefully to its financial crisis, with a massive expansion of the Federal Reserve's balance sheet, the $700 billion TARP, a second $700 billion stimulus package in 2009, and continuing asset purchases by the Fed under successive versions of quantitative easing. Under emergency circumstances, the executive branch was able to browbeat the Congress into supporting its initiatives. The European Union, by contrast, has taken a much more hesitant and piecemeal approach to the euro crisis. Lacking a monetary authority with the same powers as the Federal Reserve, and with fiscal policy remaining the preserve of national-level governments, European policy makers have had fewer tools than their American counterparts to deal with economic shocks.

Growth of the EU has also Americanized Europe with respect to the role of the judiciary. Many European governments began adding bills of fundamental rights to their constitutional systems after World War II and empowered constitutional courts to act as the defenders of these rights against state authority. A higher layer of judicial review was introduced with the creation of the European Court of Justice, which is tasked with interpreting European law, and the European Court of Human Rights, which emerged out of the European Convention on Human Rights. In addition, courts in individual European countries have made novel assertions of universal jurisdiction, as when a Spanish court indicted Chilean dictator Augusto Pinochet for crimes committed on Chilean soil. While European judges remain more reticent overall than their American counterparts to insert themselves into political matters, the formal structure of jurisprudence has tended toward the multiplication of judicial vetoes rather than the reverse.

THE MADISONIAN REPUBLIC

The American political system has decayed over time because its traditional system of checks and balances has deepened and become increasingly rigid. With sharp political polarization, this decentralized system is less and less able to represent majority interests but gives excessive representation to the views of interest groups and activist organizations that collectively do not add up to a sovereign American people.

This is not the first time that the American political system has been polarized and indecisive. The Madisonian system of checks and balances and the clientelistic, party-driven political system that emerged in the early nineteenth century were adequate for governing a largely agrarian country where most citizens lived on isolated family farms. It could not, however, resolve the acute political crisis produced by the institution of slavery and its extension to the territories. Nor was this decentralized system sufficient to deal with a continental-scale national economy increasingly knit together by new transportation and communications technologies of the sort that emerged after the Civil War. Political coalitions were assembled to create a modern, merit-based civil service, but these changes were resisted by the entrenched political actors at every step of the way. In light of these obstacles, the state building that occurred during the Progressive Era and New Deal was remarkable; the United States could have evolved like Greece or Italy with entrenched clientelism and individual corruption stretching into the modern era. The American state grew enormously in the subsequent period into the bloated and inefficient monstrosity it is today. But this outcome was in large measure a consequence of the fact that law and democracy, so deeply rooted in American political culture, continued to trump the state even as the state expanded.

The United States is trapped in a bad equilibrium. Because Americans historically distrust the government, they typically aren't willing to delegate to the government authority to make decisions in the manner of other democratic societies. Instead, Congress mandates complex rules that reduce the government's autonomy and make decisions slow and expensive. The government then doesn't perform well, which confirms people's original distrust. Under these circumstances, they are reluctant to pay higher taxes, which they feel the government will waste. But while resources are not the only, or even the main, source of government inefficiency, without them the government won't function properly. Hence distrust of government becomes a self-fulfilling prophecy.

Is it possible to reverse these tendencies toward decay and reform the system? There are two obstacles that stand in the way, both related to the phenomenon of decay itself. The first is a simple matter of politics. A lot of political actors in the United States recognize that the system isn't working very well but nonetheless have very deep interests in keeping things the way they are. Neither political party has an incentive to cut itself off from access to interest group money, and the interest groups don't want a system where money no longer buys influence. As in the 1880s, a reform coalition has to emerge that unites groups that don't have a stake in the current system. But achieving collective action among these out-groups is very difficult; they need leadership and a clear-cut agenda, which is not automatically forthcoming. External shocks were critical in crystallizing reform, events like the Garfield assassination, the requirements of America's rise as a global power, entry into the world wars, and the crisis of the Great Depression.

The second problem is a cognitive one that has to do with ideas. The typical American solution to perceived government dysfunction has been to try to expand democratic participation and transparency. This happened at a national level after the turbulent Vietnam and Watergate years as reformers pushed for more open primaries, greater citizen access to the courts, and round-the-clock media coverage of Congress. California and other states expanded use of ballot initiatives to get around unresponsive government. Almost all of these reforms failed in their objectives of creating higher levels of accountable government. The reason, as Bruce Cain has suggested, is that democratic publics are not in fact able by background or temperament to make large numbers of complex public policy choices; what has filled the void are well-organized groups of activists who are unrepresentative of the public as a whole. The obvious solution to this problem would be to roll back some of the would-be democratizing reforms, but no one dares suggest that what the country needs is a bit less participation and transparency.

I promised in the first chapter that this book would not suggest concrete policies or a short-term solution to the problems outlined here. A realistic reform agenda would have to balance long-term objectives against political realities. A system of checks and balances that gives undue weight to interest groups and fails to aggregate majority interests cannot be fixed with a few simple changes. For example, the temptation in presidential systems to prevent legislative gridlock by piling on new executive powers often creates as many problems as it solves. Getting rid of earmarks and increasing party discipline may actually make it harder to achieve broad legislative compromises. Using the courts to implement administrative decisions may be highly inefficient, but in the absence of a stronger and more unified bureaucracy, there may be no alternative. It makes little sense to delegate more autonomy to the executive branch until the capacity of that branch has been upgraded and the bureaucracy reformed.

Many of these problems could be solved if the United States moved to a more unified parliamentary system of government, but so radical a change in the country's institutional structure is inconceivable. Americans regard their Constitution as a quasi-religious document, so getting them to rethink its most basic tenets would be an uphill struggle. I think that any realistic reform program would try to trim veto points or insert parliamentary-style mechanisms to promote stronger hierarchical authority within the existing system of separated powers.

The Madisonian system of checks and balances that makes decision making so hard delayed the onset of the American welfare state and ensured that it never grew to the extent of its European counterparts.[19] Many Americans would count this as a blessing; it has liberated the U.S. economy from many of the damaging regulations and disincentives imposed by European social policy. But it also means that reform of the system— cutting it down in size and making it work more effectively—is also much more difficult. The many veto points that throw sand in the gears prevent the shaft from turning forward, but mean it can't turn backward either.

35

AUTONOMY AND SUBORDINATION

How private and public sector governance differ; state capacity and bureaucratic autonomy as measures of the quality of government; how good government requires finding the proper balance between expertise and democratic control

An effective modern government finds the appropriate balance between a strong and capable state, and institutions of law and accountability that restrain the state and force it to act in the broad interests of citizens. This is the "getting to Denmark" problem described earlier. Since the beginning of the Third Wave of democratization, however, democratic institutions have spread farther and faster than strong, effective modern states. Many countries therefore face a dual task of state building even as they consolidate their democratic institutions. In the long run, these two processes are complementary and should be mutually supportive. But in the short run, as we have seen, they can run afoul of one another.

How, then, do we get to a productive, administratively capable state? Many international development agencies, recognizing the importance of having such states, have promoted efforts to reform broken public sectors. The expectation is that the best way to strengthen states is to increase transparency and democratic accountability. This theory assumes that if voters have good information about public officials who are corrupt or incompetent, they will use the power of the ballot to throw them out of office. In addition, many reform efforts have sought to decrease the scope of government, in order to reduce opportunities for corruption. They have also tried to increase the number of rules—for example, regarding conflicts of interest—that officials have to follow. By reducing official discretion, it is believed that corruption will be correspondingly reduced.[1]

These practical measures for improving performance of the public sector are tied to a larger body of theoretical work formulated largely by economists, who understand the effectiveness of bureaucracies in terms of so-called principal-agent theory. (I've alluded to this theory at numerous points in discussions of specific cases earlier in the two volumes.) The principal is the chief decision maker who gives instructions to the agent, or to a hierarchy of agents, whose function is to carry out the principal's wishes. This framework can be applied to both private- and public-sector organizations: in a private-sector firm, the principal is the owner of the business (or the shareholders in a publicly traded firm), who delegates authority to a board of directors, then to a CEO, and then to the company's administrative hierarchy. In a democracy, the principal is the whole people, who through elections delegate authority to a legislature, president, or other officials, who in turn establish bureaucratic hierarchies to carry out their wishes.

Organizational dysfunction is said to occur because the agents often act self-interestedly, for example, diverting money to their own bank accounts or promoting their careers at the expense of the organization. This is the source of corruption in both private and public organizations. The cure is said to be an alignment of incentives that motivate the agents to properly implement the principal's commands. Principal-agent theory ends up endorsing a version of the transparency and accountability path to good government: principals need to increase the transparency of agent behavior in order to be able to monitor them better, and then to create incentives that allow them to be held strictly accountable to their wishes.[2]

In the political sphere, this theory implies that more democracy should lead to less corruption and better government. It certainly seems logical that corrupt or incompetent officials should not be able to hide their actions, and they will have few incentives to change their behavior without some mechanism of accountability. However, there are a number of reasons for thinking that this theory is a very incomplete one.

In the first place, it assumes that ordinary voters, if told about the corrupt or clientelistic distribution of public resources, will inevitably demand programmatic public policies that will distribute goods on an impersonal basis, as democratic theory says they should. This ignores the fact that voters in many societies, particularly poor ones, want the clientelistic distribution of resources because they hope to personally benefit from it. Indeed, citizen demand for payoffs may be what creates the clientelism in the first place.

Moreover, the idea that greater transparency and accountability is a necessary path to better bureaucracy flies in the face of a great deal of history, in which relatively clean, modern bureaucracies have been built under nondemocratic circumstances. We saw this most clearly in the stories of bureaucratic development in Part I of this book. A number of the most successful modern states were created under authoritarian conditions, often by countries facing severe national security threats. This is true of ancient China, Prussia/Germany, modern Japan, and a handful of other countries. By contrast, when democracy is introduced prior to the consolidation of a modern state, it often has the effect of weakening the quality of government. The prime example of this is the United States, which invented clientelistic party government after the opening up of the democratic franchise in the 1820s and was thereafter saddled with a patronage-riddled bureaucracy for much of the next century. This is also the story of Greece and Italy, both of which developed sophisticated clientelistic systems that impeded the growth of modern state administrations. Clientelism remains pervasive among democratic countries in the developing world and undermines the quality of governments from India and Mexico to Kenya and the Philippines.

And finally, the idea that public officials should be constrained by strict rules and stripped of administrative discretion runs contrary to the most common complaint about government, namely, that it is too rule bound, rigid, and lacking in common sense. The modern nightmare is the bureaucrat demanding mountains of paperwork before the smallest decision can be made. Many attempted reforms of the American public sector have involved dismantling rules and granting greater discretion in government decision making. How, then, do we square this with the notion that good government is the product of strict rules?

All of this suggests that state building and democracy building are not the same thing, and in the short run they often exist in a great deal of tension with one another. There may be other routes to good government, and indeed democracy may under certain circumstances be an obstacle rather than an advantage. We need a more sophisticated theory of public administration, one that pays particular attention to the interface among state administration, law, and democratic accountability.

STATE CAPACITY

One of the big problems with the principal-agent framework is that it takes for granted the existence of state capacity. That is, it formulates the problem of managing an organization primarily as one of incentives and will: the principal commands that the agents do certain things, and the agents fail to do so because they are opportunistic or self-interested. But agents can be completely loyal and motivated to do the right thing and yet fail because they simply do not have the knowledge, competence, or technical ability to carry out the principal's wishes.

Modern government, in addition to being very large, is a provider of a wide variety of complex services. The government forecasts the weather, operates aircraft carriers, regulates derivatives, oversees pharmaceutical safety, provides agricultural extension services, manages public health emergencies, judges complex criminal and civil cases, and controls monetary policy. Many of these activities require high levels of professionalism and education: the staff of the U.S. Federal Reserve Board, for example, consists mostly of PhD economists, while the Centers for Disease Control is run by doctors and biomedical researchers.

This need for technocratic competence is the first thing that puts good government on a collision course with democracy. As we saw, one of Andrew Jackson's assertions as president was that there wasn't a single job in the U.S. government that couldn't be performed by an ordinary American, and he went on to staff the bureaucracy with plenty of ordinary Americans who happened to be his political supporters. The populist Jackson was elected in part out of distrust of the Harvard-educated elites represented by his opponent, John Quincy Adams, and that distrust continues down to the present day. Establishment of a merit-based civil service under the Pendleton Act represented an effort to remove bureaucratic recruitment from democratic political contestation and to create expanding islands of autonomous technocratic competence within the government.

Building technocratic capacity in government is not just a matter of sending bureaucrats to a few weekend executive training sessions. It requires huge investments in higher educational systems. The Stein-Hardenberg reforms in Prussia could not have had the positive effect they did without the simultaneous creation of new universities by reformers like Wilhelm von Humboldt, who established the new University of Berlin, while the Northcote-Trevelyan reforms in Britain were accompanied by Benjamin Jowett's shake-up of Oxford and Cambridge. One of the most impressive accomplishments of the Meiji oligarchs in the late nineteenth century was their creation of a network of modern universities in Japan, whose graduates went on to staff the new bureaucracies in Tokyo.

While bureaucratic capacity is built on the human capital of individual bureaucrats, the performance of actual government agencies is critically dependent on the kind of organizational culture, or social capital, they possess. Two organizations with identical staffing and resources will perform at vastly different levels depending on the degree of internal cohesion they enjoy. Part of the reason that the German Wehrmacht proved to be such a formidable fighting machine in World War II was that it was able to foster enormous unit cohesion through the leadership of its noncommissioned officers. As military historian Martin van Creveld has shown, German regiments were recruited from the same region, trained, fought, and died together, and when exhausted were withdrawn in groups. This produced strong unit identification and substantially higher fighting power than the American system that continually formed and re-formed units, and replaced casualties on an individual basis.[3]

Civilian organizations do not have the same ability to shape their staff, but they can still benefit from strong cohesion based on shared norms. The modern Forest Service was built around a shared commitment to scientific forestry. The contemporary Japanese and South Korean bureaucracies, like the British one before them, were staffed with graduates from the same elite schools who knew each other from their days as students. They entered public service in classes that were subsequently promoted as a group, and since their ministries did not permit lateral entry of political appointees into the bureaucracy, they developed a strong esprit de corps. But even in the United States with its weak traditions of bureaucratic solidarity, there are pockets of excellence that show astonishing levels of commitment to public service, like the federal prison system described by political scientist John DiIulio.[4] Bureaucratic capacity is therefore something much more than the sum of the capacities of the officials who make up a bureaucracy; it also is a function of the social capital they possess.[5]

Finally, state capacity is a function of resources. The best-trained and most enthusiastic officials will not remain committed if they are not paid adequately, or if they find themselves lacking the tools for doing their jobs. This is one of the reasons that poor countries have poorly functioning governments. Melissa Thomas notes that while a rich country like the United States spends approximately $17,000 per year per capita on government services of all sorts, the government of Afghanistan spends only $17 when foreign donor contributions are excluded. Much of the money it does collect is wasted through corruption and fraud. It is therefore not surprising that the central Afghan government is barely sovereign throughout much of its own territory.[6]

BUREAUCRATIC AUTONOMY

State capacity is by itself an inadequate measure of the quality of government. One of the constant themes throughout this book has been the importance of bureaucratic autonomy for the proper functioning of government. Agents who are not given sufficient leeway to exercise judgment in the crafting and implementation of policies will not perform their jobs well, no matter how capable they are as individuals or as organizations.

In ancient China, the Legalists and Confucians engaged in a long-running debate over what contemporary administrative lawyers would call the issue of "rules versus discretion."[7] The Legalists thought that society needed clear legal rules to govern behavior, to help stabilize expectations, and to leave no uncertainties about the intentions of the state. The Confucians, by contrast, criticized law (or *fa*) on the grounds that no written law could ever be correct in all circumstances. Proper judgment would require knowledge of the circumstances of the specific case: who committed the crime, what his or her motives were, how a given decision would affect the interests of the broader community. The Confucians argued that only a learned sage taking full account of context could arrive at a correct judgment. This view is similar to Aristotle's description of the "great-souled man" in the *Nicomachean Ethics* who is capable of exercising proper moral choice.

Actual Chinese law, as we saw in chapter 24 above, evolved as a mixture of Legalist and Confucian doctrines. Chinese practice has always tended to favor discretion over strict rules, reflecting the weak rule of law in the Chinese tradition. But the Confucians had a point: too many strict rules oftentimes impede good decision making.

Bureaucratic autonomy lies in the precise way that principals impose mandates or rules on their agents. An organization's degree of autonomy will depend on the number and types of mandates handed down from the principal or, to put it in slightly different terms, the degree of authority granted to the agent. A completely subordinated organization will have no independent authority whatsoever and will be required to robotically carry out the principal's detailed mandates. An autonomous organization, by contrast, will be able to make decisions on its own without detailed second-guessing from the principal.

There are a wide variety of responsibilities that can be delegated by principals. One of the most important concerns staffing. As we saw in Volume 1, one of the most important developments in the establishment of the rule of law in Europe was the investiture conflict, which revolved around the Catholic church's ability to appoint its own priests and bishops. Up until the eleventh century, the church was necessarily subordinate to the political authority of the Holy Roman Emperor since he could influence personnel decisions, including the choice of popes. The church's independence as a lawmaking institution was therefore tightly bound to its control over its own cadres. The civil service reform struggles in nineteenth-century America were similarly about the bureaucracy's ability to set its own standards for hiring and promotion, rather than being subordinated to patronage politicians.

Political principals often issue overlapping and sometimes downright contradictory mandates. Indeed, there are often multiple principals—that is, political authorities with equal legitimacy issuing potentially contradictory mandates. State-owned utilities, for example, often have mandates to simultaneously do cost recovery, universal service to the poor, and efficient pricing to business clients, each promoted by a different part of the political system. These mandates obviously cannot be simultaneously achieved and generate bureaucratic dysfunction. The quasi-public railroad Amtrak could become a profitable and effective railway if it were not under congressional mandates to serve various low-volume rural communities. In China there are often duplicate functional agencies, one reporting to a chain of command that goes through national ministries, the other reporting to municipal or provincial governments; the result is inconsistent and ineffective policy.

A high degree of autonomy is what permits innovation, experimentation, and risk taking in a bureaucracy. In a well-functioning organization, the boss gives general orders to get something done, and the subordinates figure out how best to do it. High-quality military organizations understand that junior officers have to be given the "freedom to fail": if the slightest mistake can end a career, then no one will ever take risks. This insight was embedded in the evolution of the U.S. army's field manual for combined arms operations, FM 100-5. In rethinking combined arms doctrine in light of the Vietnam War, the drafters of the manual shifted emphasis from centralized command and control to more flexible mission orders under which the commander is supposed to only set broad goals and devolve implementation to the lowest possible echelon of the command structure. In other words, junior officers were permitted a high degree of autonomy, which included toleration of failure if they sought to innovate or experiment.[8]

Lack of autonomy is a major cause of poor government. People around the world hate the rule-bound, rigid, paperwork-driven nature of bureaucracy. Bureaucrats themselves derive power and authority from their ability to manipulate rules and therefore have an interest in expanding their reach. But their political masters are complicit in this process, in the number and types of mandates that they issue. The solution to this problem is to change the mandate to permit greater bureaucratic autonomy.

On the other hand, bureaucracies can have too much autonomy. I described what were perhaps the two most notorious cases of this in modern history, the German and Japanese military bureaucracies prior to the first and second world wars. In both cases a strong tradition of autonomy led to high-quality military organizations, but it also led to their usurping of the goal-setting authority of the political leaders that were nominally their principals. The German navy and General Staff in the early years of the twentieth century co-opted the emperor and set a course of foreign policy that brought the country as a whole into conflict with Britain and France. The Japanese Kwantung Army in Manchuria was even more directly involved in launching an aggression against China, and it eventually took over political authority for Japan as a whole in all but name. Even short of these extreme cases, tightly bonded, highly autonomous bureaucratic organizations can be highly resistant to political direction; they can become inbred, resistant to change, and unresponsive to societal needs.

Ironically, sometimes an excessive number of rules actually increases rather than decreases bureaucratic autonomy, but in a very unhealthy direction. Bureaucratic red tape is often so mind-numbingly complex that no one is able to actually monitor whether or not the rules are being followed. This allows the bureaucrats themselves to decide which ones to enforce since only they can navigate the system. This is frequently said about the bureaucracy in India, which is famous for being simultaneously rule bound and arbitrary.

The appropriate degree of autonomy needed to produce high-quality government would thus look like the curve shown in Figure 25. At one extreme, that of complete subordination, the bureaucracy has no room for discretion or independent judgment and is completely bound by detailed rules set by the political principal. At the other end of the horizontal axis, that of complete autonomy, governance outcomes would also be very bad, because the bureaucracy has escaped all political control and sets not just internal procedures but its goals as well. The inflection point of the curve is shifted to the right, however, due to a general recognition that the dangers of excessive micromanagement are often greater than those posed by excessive autonomy.

FIGURE 25. Bureaucratic Autonomy and the Quality of Government

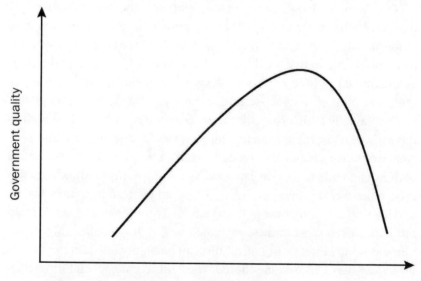

Capacity and autonomy interact with one another. One can control the behavior of an agent through either explicit formal rules and incentives or informal norms and habits. Of the two, the latter involves substantially lower transaction costs. Many highly skilled professionals are basically self-regulating, due to the fact that it is hard for people outside their profession to judge the quality of their work. The higher the capacity of a bureaucracy, then, the more autonomy one would want to grant it. In judging the quality of government, therefore, we want to know about both the capacity and the autonomy of the bureaucrats.

The effort to grant workers greater autonomy based on rising levels of capacity has already occurred in many private-sector workplaces. The classic automobile factory of the early twentieth century, like Henry Ford's Highland Park facility, was staffed with an extremely low-skilled blue-collar workforce. In 1915, most auto workers in Detroit were recent immigrants; half could not speak English, and the average level of education was not much beyond elementary school. It was under these conditions that "Taylorism" developed. Scientific management segregated the organization's intelligence at the top of a hierarchy, where white-collar managers directed a blue-collar workforce by issuing detailed rules about where to stand, how to operate the machines, and how many bathroom breaks a worker could take. This kind of low-trust workplace did not permit the lower levels of the organization to exercise any autonomous judgment whatsoever.

This type of work environment has been replaced with a much flatter form of organization. The lean manufacturing plant, pioneered by Toyota, delegates substantially higher degrees of discretion to assembly-line workers, who are encouraged to discuss among themselves how better to organize their joint production. Autonomy is even higher in firms that rely on highly educated professionals. Law firms, architectural firms, research labs, software companies, universities, and similar organizations cannot possibly be organized along Taylorite lines. In such organizations, the managers who exercise nominal authority over their highly educated "workers" actually know less about the work being done than do those at the bottom of the hierarchy. In such flat organizations, authority does not flow only from principals to agents; the agents themselves are often involved in goal setting and use their expertise to control the principals. These organizations, needless to say, require substantially higher levels of trust than the old Taylorite ones.

The optimal level of autonomy thus depends on the organization's capacity. Figure 26 illustrates the optimal autonomy curves for four hypothetical organizations of differing levels of capacity. For each, the curve slopes downward at the extremes, since every bureaucracy can have too much or too little autonomy. But in the lower-capacity organizations, the inflection points shift to the left, while in higher-capacity organizations, they shift to the right. The early twentieth-century Ford factory would be at level 1, while a high-tech company like Google would be at level 4.

What applies to private-sector organizations is also valid for the public-sector organizations that make up a state. As societies become wealthier and develop governments with higher capacity, they can afford to grant them much greater autonomy. The assertion embedded in Figure 25 that the optimal amount of autonomy is shifted to the right is true only in high-capacity countries. In very low-capacity countries, the opposite is the case: one would want to circumscribe the behavior of government officials with more rather than fewer rules because one could not trust them to exercise good judgment or refrain from corrupt behavior.

FIGURE 26. Optimal Levels of Autonomy for Differing
Levels of Capacity

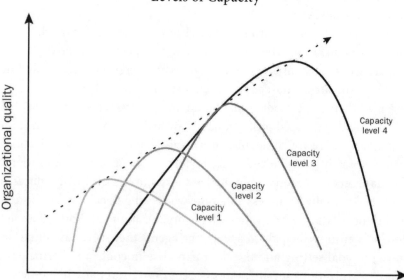

On the other hand, if the same developing country agency were full of professionals with graduate degrees from internationally recognized schools rather than political cronies, one would not only feel safer granting them considerable autonomy, but would actually want to reduce rule-boundedness in hopes of encouraging the exercise of judgment and innovative behavior.

If we locate countries on a matrix that arrays state capacity against bureaucratic autonomy (see Figure 27), we can compare the overall quality of state institutions. Each country is actually a collection of different government institutions of varying capacities and degrees of autonomy, which is why each is portrayed as an oval rather than a single point. The diagonal line is derived from Figure 26 and consists of the inflection points representing the optimal degree of autonomy for a given degree of capacity. All organizations should want to increase capacity (move up the vertical axis), but this involves costly long-term investments. In the short run, their strategy should be to move as close to the line as possible.

As is evident from Figure 28, there is not one single formula for making all governments work better. The route to better performance depends on where a country is on the matrix. Indeed, paths may differ within the same country, since the many bureaucracies that make up a government will have different capacities and degrees of autonomy.

This framework explains the conundrum of why some countries need

FIGURE 27. Autonomy and Capacity

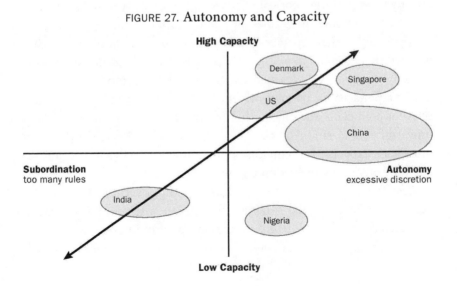

FIGURE 28. Pathways to Reform

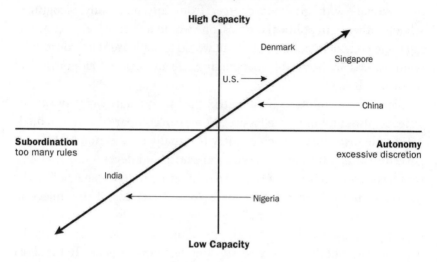

to reduce discretion and impose more rules while others should seek to do the reverse. In *Controlling Corruption*, Robert Klitgaard coined the formula

$$\text{Corruption} = \text{Discretion} - \text{Accountability}.$$

International development agencies like the World Bank have consequently been pushing poor countries with low capacity to reduce discretion (that is, impose more rules on public officials) while improving the transparency of their operations and setting up mechanisms to increase democratic accountability. This advice is largely correct for poor, low-capacity countries. Greater media scrutiny and democratic elections may not be a panacea for corruption, but they at least provide some incentives for politicians and officials to improve their behavior. But it is not a universally valid rule that necessarily applies to richer countries with more state capacity. In many cases, government effectiveness is best secured by increasing discretion and relaxing rules.

The path, then, to improved performance by governments varies depending on the particular situation they find themselves in. Even within a single government, different parts may require different approaches: military procurement may need to be subject to less red tape, while the banks and special prosecutors may be dangerously unaccountable. Analyzing these problems requires knowledge of context; fixing them, even more so.

DEMOCRATIC ACCOUNTABILITY

How do democratic electorates grant their governments an appropriate degree of discretion and yet remain in firm control of the policies and goals that bureaucracies are meant to serve? Whatever else it may imply, bureaucratic autonomy does not mean turning over the process of decision making to "experts" who somehow know better than the public at large what's best for them. The autonomous platoon leader, to return to the military example, does not weigh in on grand strategy; that's the appropriate function of generals. In a democracy, the people are ultimately the generals.

Democratic accountability is critical to the proper functioning of political systems because it is ultimately the basis for authority, that is, the legitimate exercise of power. Compliance with the state's wishes can be achieved coercively, and there have of course been many examples of this in history. But governments work much better when power is converted into authority, when citizens comply with laws and policies voluntarily because they believe in the system's basic legitimacy.

The importance of legitimacy was illustrated in Volume 1 by the contrast between England and France following the Glorious Revolution of 1688–1689. England established the principle of "no taxation without representation," meaning that the state had access only to revenues approved by Parliament, which at that moment consisted of the nation's wealthiest taxpayers. In the decades after 1689, both the percentage of taxes taken by the government, and the perceived security of English public debt, soared. France, by contrast, had a much more coercive tax system, where the wealthy could exempt themselves and the army was frequently called upon to extract taxes from unwilling peasants. French taxes as a percentage of GDP were a fraction of England's. As a consequence, French public finances crumbled in the eighteenth century. Britain, working off of a smaller resource base, was able to defeat France in a series of wars that stretched to the eve of the French Revolution.

Perceived legitimacy is important to government effectiveness because governments have always relied on nonstate actors to help execute public purposes. Many people believe that outsourcing, public-private partnerships, and state reliance on faith-based groups to deliver social services are innovations of the late twentieth century. But public-private collaborations have a long history. In Europe, social services from population registration to poor relief were traditionally delivered by churches; those functions were absorbed into the state only in the twentieth century. English and Dutch colonialism was carried out by semiprivate organizations like their East India Companies, which worked in parallel with the government. Stein Ringen points out that the military governments ruling South Korea after 1961 nonetheless relied heavily on a variety of private organizations to carry out their policies, not just giant corporations like Samsung and Hyundai, but a welter of private voluntary associations as well.[9]

As populations become wealthier and better educated, and as technology provides them with more access to information, the difficulty of exercising authority increases. When people discover they can think for themselves, or know things that the government doesn't, they are much less willing to obey an edict simply because it was issued by an official. It is the broad social mobilization reflecting the rise of middle classes that has led to the spread of formal democracy around the world over the past four decades. But it constitutes a challenge for democratic systems as well, which are perceived as being out of touch and unresponsive to their citizens.

Formal procedures like regular free and fair elections were designed to achieve democratic accountability. But elections by themselves do not guarantee a substantive outcome of government truly responsive to popular wishes. Elections and electorates can be manipulated; entrenched parties may offer inadequate choices to voters; participation may be low. There is a large information problem: my casting a vote every few years may signal my general approval or disapproval of the policies of a party or administration, but what I am really concerned about is a particular regulation affecting my business, or the fact that my child doesn't have good teachers in her public school. There is theoretically a route of accountability that stretches from voter to government and back down to the citizen via a bureaucracy. But that route is extremely long, and in the process of communicating choices, the signal is often lost in a lot of noise.

There are a number of formal, procedural approaches designed to address these issues and make governments more responsive. The most obvious is to shorten the route of accountability by devolving power to the lowest possible level where it can be more directly responsive to popular will. Since the time of the American Founding Fathers, this has gone under the heading of federalism (it is called subsidiarity in Europe). Another approach is to balance the branches of government against one another, using the judiciary to force the executive to respond to public demands. In Europe's civil law systems, there has long been a hierarchy of administrative courts that allow citizens to sue the government. I have already discussed the way the American system gives legal standing to private citizens, allowing them to sue agencies to require them to enforce or to prevent them from enforcing laws. Finally, there are mechanisms like the landmark Administrative Procedure Act, passed in 1946, that forces federal agencies to publicly post rule changes and to solicit comment on them. Similar processes to increase democratic participation at a state and local level have proliferated across the world, such as participatory budgeting pioneered in Brazil.

Many of these approaches work as advertised and force governments to be more responsive. But all formal procedures have a tendency to multiply, and then to be gamed over time by powerful actors within the system. Federalism often duplicates levels of government rather than truly devolving powers; decentralization, especially in poor countries, simply hands over power to local elites. I have already noted the impact of adversarial legalism on the quality of public administration in the United States. The notice-and-comment provisions of the Administrative Procedure Act over the years have evolved into an often meaningless ritual, where well-paid lobbyists for powerful interest groups post predictable comments.

All of these formal procedures are designed to increase accountability and therefore the democratic legitimacy of decision making. But they also multiply rules, impose large transaction costs, and slow government action. The cumulative impact of these procedures is often to rob administrative agencies of the autonomy they need to do their jobs effectively. Too much transparency can and has undercut the possibility of deliberation, as in the U.S. Congress. If demands for accountability become just another weapon in partisan political combat, they will not achieve their purpose. Formal systems that minutely measure performance and punish poor performance often produce what the political scientist Jane

Mansbridge labels "sanction-based accountability," a modern version of Taylorism that is based more on fear than loyalty. Such systems are premised on the idea that workers cannot be trusted to do their jobs in the absence of careful external monitoring; they are surefire ways of killing risk taking and innovation on the part of those being evaluated. Because these procedures, designed to increase accountability and therefore legitimacy, have the ultimate impact of making the government less effective, they paradoxically undercut its legitimacy.

THE BALANCE

The solution to the problem of improving democratic accountability therefore does not necessarily lie in the proliferation of formal accountability mechanisms or in absolute government transparency. The Confucians were right in arguing that no set of rules can ever be adequate to produce good results in all cases. There is an intangible factor that needs to be present to make the political system work, which is trust. Citizens must trust the government to make good decisions reflecting their interests most of the time, while governments for their part must earn that trust by being responsive and delivering on their promises. A properly autonomous bureaucracy is not one that is walled off from citizens, but rather one that Peter Evans describes as "embedded" in society and responsive to its demands. This constitutes a high-level equilibrium in which trust in government begets effective government, which in turn increases trust on all sides.

The opposite, low-level equilibrium, is one in which low-quality government breeds distrust on the part of citizens, who then withhold from the state both the compliance and resources necessary for government to function effectively. Lacking proper authority, such governments turn to coercion to achieve compliance. It is far easier to see how a political system falls out of a high-level equilibrium than rises out of a low-level one, which is perhaps why the latter are so much more prevalent around the world. It is also possible that as citizens' expectations and demands multiply, all governments are headed toward the low-level trap.

If there is a path out of this situation, it is tied to the two characteristics of effective governments described above: capacity and autonomy. Governments need the human and fiscal resources to do their jobs adequately, along with organizational capital. And the handoff of authority from the democratic principals to the bureaucratic agents needs to grant the latter a degree of autonomy matched to the existing level of capacity. No existing government ever achieved this kind of transition overnight; it usually occurs piecemeal, and in political struggle. Getting to Denmark is therefore a very long-term goal.

36

POLITICAL ORDER AND POLITICAL DECAY

Political development and biological evolution; political development and its relation to the other dimensions of development; the importance of international influences; getting to a modern state; the role of violence in political development; is liberal democracy a developmental universal?

The two volumes of this book have traced the origin, evolution, and decay of political institutions over time.

Political development is similar to biological evolution in a number of respects. The latter is based on the interaction of two principles, variation and selection. So too in politics: there is variation in the nature of political institutions; as a result of competition and interaction with the physical environment, certain institutions survive over time while others prove inadequate. And just as certain species turn out to be maladapted when their environments change, so too political decay occurs when institutions prove unable to adapt.

But while variation in biological evolution is random, human beings exercise some degree of agency over the design of their institutions. It is true, as authors like Friedrich A. Hayek have argued, that human beings are never knowledgeable or wise enough to be able to predict the outcomes of their efforts to design institutions or plan policies with full *ex ante* knowledge of the results.[1] But the exercise of human agency is not a one-shot affair: human beings learn from their mistakes and take actions to correct them in an iterative process. The constitution adopted by the Federal Republic of Germany in 1949 differed in significant ways from the constitution of the Weimar Republic, precisely because Germans had learned from the failure of democracy during the 1930s.

In biological evolution, there are separate specific and general processes. Under specific evolution, organisms adapt to particular environments and diverge in their characteristics. This produces speciation; Charles Darwin's famous finches were the result of the birds' adaptation to a host of microenvironments. In the process of general evolution, disparate species evolve similar characteristics because they have to solve similar problems: thus sensory organs like eyes evolved independently across different species.

So too with human beings. When the first small group of behaviorally modern humans walked out of Africa into the Middle East about fifty thousand years ago, they began to diverge, to some extent genetically but more dramatically in terms of culture. There was a real precedent for the story of the Tower of Babel in the Bible: as humans spread to Europe, Asia, South Asia, Oceana, and eventually to the Americas, their languages and cultural practices began to differentiate as they settled into a wide variety of ecological niches. But there was at the same time a process of general political evolution at work: culturally diverse peoples had to solve similar problems, and they therefore came up with parallel solutions even though they had limited or no physical contact with one another.

I have described a number of major transitions in political institutions that have taken place across diverse societies around the world:

- from band-level to tribal-level societies
- from tribal-level societies to states
- from patrimonial to modern states
- the development of independent legal systems
- the emergence of formal institutions of accountability

These political transitions occurred independently in societies with very different cultural norms. Segmentary lineages—tribalism—appeared in virtually all parts of the world at a certain moment in human development. All are based on a principle of descent from a common ancestor, and all are sustained by religious belief in the power of dead ancestors and unborn descendants over the living. Despite the minute variations in kinship organization that are the bread and butter of anthropology, the basic structure of tribal societies is remarkably similar across geographically separated societies.

Similarly, states began to appear at roughly the same point in history in Mesopotamia, China, Egypt, and Mexico, with generally similar political structures. They constituted larger-scale and wealthier societies that could generate sufficient military power to maintain their autonomy against less organized competitors. To do this, however, they all faced the problem of overcoming kinship as the primary principle of political organization and replacing it with a more impersonal form of rule. Different societies solved this problem in different ways, from the Chinese invention of the bureaucratic state to the Arab-Ottoman institution of military slavery, to the undermining of kinship itself and its replacement with feudal contract in the lands of Western Christianity. Finally, independent legal systems evolved in ancient Israel, the Christian West, India, and the Muslim world in the form of religious law administered by a hierarchy of priests, who had at least nominal authority over secular rulers. The content of these laws varied considerably from culture to culture, as did the degree and nature of institutionalization. But the basic structure of law as a set of community rules limiting the sovereignty of those holding the means of coercion was the same for all of these societies. Laws regulated family life, inheritance, and property, and provided for dispute resolution in a sphere somewhat protected from the state. The only major world civilization that did not develop rule of law in this sense was China, largely because it never developed a transcendental religion on which law could be based.

Not one of these transitions was universally achieved across all human societies. There are still a small number of surviving band-level societies in remote niches like the Kalahari Desert and the Arctic, and a significantly larger number of tribal societies in mountainous, desert, and jungle regions. One level of political organization is never fully superseded by another: thus in China, India, and the Middle East, segmentary lineages continued to exist long after the invention of the state. Only in Western Europe were segmentary lineages largely eliminated at a social level prior to the emergence of modern states. In other societies, the political power of the state was simply layered over existing lineage structures, and when it waned, the power of lineages revived. In the Middle East, tribalism remains a powerful force and competes with states for authority.

Under natural selection, individuals compete with one another and those that are best adapted to their environments survive. But Charles Darwin described a second evolutionary process, that of sexual selection, which at times operated at cross-purposes with the first. Males compete for access to females and oftentimes develop characteristics (like the antlers on bucks) that are markers for overall reproductive fitness within the species. But these same characteristics are not necessarily adaptive vis-à-vis other species and constitute a liability when a new type of predator is introduced into the environment. Specific evolution within a protected niche is often driven by sexual rather than natural selection, as local "arms races" between males of the same species play themselves out.

As the economist Robert Frank has pointed out, there is a political counterpart to sexual selection. Not every political or social institution that arises is the product of a remorseless struggle for group survival. Existing institutions can channel competitive behavior into alternative venues. Thus wealthy hedge fund managers do not compete through displays of physical prowess or combat with knives and clubs. They compete on the basis of the size of their funds or their art collections. As Frank points out, many of these competitions are over relative status and are zero-sum in character. That is, consumption has value only by virtue of being conspicuous, which leads to unwinnable races for ostentatious display. Thus the petty princes of Renaissance Italy competed to be patrons of the arts. While these investments had great value for subsequent generations, they did not help much in their military struggles against larger and better-organized external enemies like the Spanish and French kings.[2]

DIMENSIONS OF DEVELOPMENT

This volume covers a period marked by the onset of the Industrial Revolution in Europe and America, and the remarkably high sustained levels of economic growth it made possible. By contrast, the agrarian societies in Europe, China, India, and the Middle East described in the first volume existed in a Malthusian economic world that made predation an economically rational mode of activity. Technological change occurred, but so slowly that per capita increases in output were quickly dissipated by population increase. With few opportunities for productive investment, political activity centered around one group organizing itself to extract agricultural surpluses from another group. This system produced magnificent cultural works and lavish lifestyles for elites, but condemned the vast majority of the population to hard lives as subsistence farmers.

The main benefit it returned to the nonelites was a degree of security and political peace.

This was not a trivial advantage. In an age in which populations could drop by half or three-quarters as a result of hunger, disease, and outright butchery brought on by war and invasion, the sovereign's guarantee of peace was a critical public good. This system could be stable over many centuries because the differential in organizational ability between the elites and everyone else was self-reinforcing. While peasant revolts periodically broke out in agrarian societies from China and Turkey to France and Germany, they could always be contained and were usually savagely suppressed by the landowning elites. The reigning ideologies underpinning these systems all legitimated the stratification of human beings into different status groups or castes, and actively discouraged social mobility.

This low-growth, zero-sum economic world actually describes the situation of many extremely poor developing countries today. While it may in some theoretical sense be possible for a country like Sierra Leone or Afghanistan to turn itself into an industrial powerhouse like South Korea through appropriate investment, these countries' lack of strong institutions forecloses this option for all practical purposes. Rather than starting a business, a young entrepreneur is much more likely to enrich himself by entering politics, organizing a militia, or otherwise scheming to grab a share of the country's resource wealth.

As we have seen, this agrarian equilibrium was dramatically upset with the onset of industrialization in the nineteenth century. Continuous high levels of economic growth driven by technologically induced increases in productivity reordered societies in dramatic ways. Peasants who had been politically inert over the preceding centuries moved to cities or other centers of manufacturing employment, where they were transformed into an industrial working class. Residents of cities acquired higher levels of education and emerged as a new middle class. As Adam Smith explained, improved transportation and communications technology centered around waterways began to expand the size of markets dramatically in the seventeenth and eighteenth centuries. This facilitated a massive change in the division of labor, which was the main driver of social change in Britain, Belgium, Germany, and France, a process that began to unfold in East Asia in the late twentieth century and is still ongoing in China in the early twenty-first.

The model of development described in chapter 2 shows that the three central political institutions—the state, rule of law, and accountability—come under pressure as rapid social mobilization fosters demands for political participation. This is the critical juncture at which the political institutions of the agrarian order either adapt to accommodate demands for participation, or else they decay (see Figure 29). The old social groups like large landowners or the parts of the state that allied to them (for example, the military) will try to block demands for participation. The ability of the newer social groups to force their way into the political system depends in turn on their degree of organization. In Europe and America, this proceeded in two stages, through the development of trade unions and then the organization of new political parties representing their interests. If those parties are accommodated within an expanded political system, the system will remain stable; if those demands are repressed, the stage is set for substantial political instability.

The outcome of these struggles is highly context dependent and never fully determined by structural factors alone. In Britain, the old agrarian elites either imperceptibly melded through intermarriage with the new bourgeoisie or else found new ways of maintaining their political status even as their economic position was eroded. In Prussia, Argentina, and other Latin American countries, they allied themselves with the state and used authoritarian power to suppress these new actors. In contemporary China, the state has sought to forestall this process by blocking the formation of independent trade unions that would facilitate collective action by workers, and by maintaining a high level of employment growth to keep workers satisfied.

In Italy, Greece, and nineteenth-century America, and in contemporary developing countries like India, Brazil, and Mexico, class issues could be partially diffused by traditional political parties recruiting new social actors into clientelistic political machines. These machines were extremely effective in accommodating rising demands for political participation and therefore contributed to the system's overall stability. On the other hand, clientelism encouraged outright corruption on the part of the political class and blocked the emergence of programmatic demands for policies that in the end would much better serve the interests of the new social groups being brought into the system.

The sequence illustrated in Figure 29 represents the classic path toward modernization taken by a number of countries in Western Europe, North America, and East Asia. It is not, however, the only possible route

FIGURE 29. Dimensions of Development

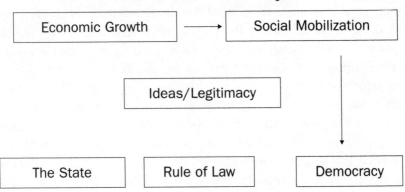

to modernization. Oftentimes, social mobilization has occurred in the absence of sustained economic growth, a phenomenon referred to earlier as "modernization without development" (see Figure 30). Under this scenario, social change occurs not under the pull of new industrial employment but under the push of rural poverty. Peasants flock to cities because they seemingly offer more choices and opportunities, but they are not subject to the rigors of an expanding division of labor as in the classic industrialization scenario. Instead of Gemeinschaft being transformed into Gesellschaft, Gemeinschaft simply implants itself in cities—kin groups and rural villages move intact to urban slums but retain much of their rural social organization and values under extremely marginal economic conditions. This is the type of modernization that occurred in Greece and southern Italy; it has taken place in countless developing countries from the Indian subcontinent to Latin America to the Middle East and sub-Saharan Africa, where enormous cities have emerged in the absence of a vibrant industrial economy.

Modernization without development has been widespread among many developing countries outside of East Asia. It has important political consequences when compared to the classic path of modernization via industrialization. It can destabilize existing traditional political systems that do not provide routes to political participation—the classic Huntington scenario of political decay. But it can also lead to a stable system of clientelism and elite coalitions built around the distribution of rents. Since the division of labor is much less extensive when there is no vigorous development of a capitalist industrial sector, different types of social

FIGURE 30. Modernization Without Development

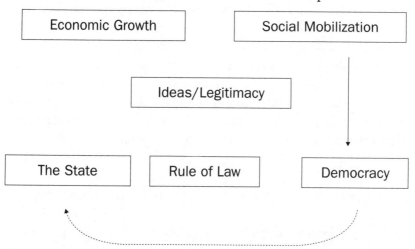

groups emerge compared to nineteenth-century Europe. There is neither a large emerging group of middle-class individuals, professionals with higher levels of education, nor a strong industrial proletariat. Rather, such societies have a large, amorphous group of urbanized poor who eke out livings in the informal sector. Many of these people can be highly entrepreneurial when given access to capital and markets. The contemporary microfinance industry and property rights movements are built around providing the poor with such tools.[3] But there is no clear path from informal employment to true growth- and job-generating industrialization. Clientelism thrives under these conditions, since the individualized benefits offered by politicians, and the ability to generate rents in the public sector, are often a much more effective path to economic security than the private sector. Politics then centers around zero-sum struggles over rent distribution rather than over programmatic policies. This kind of clientelism poses a big obstacle to reform of the public sector and the upgrading of state capacity, as indicated by the dotted lines in Figure 30.

Ideas concerning legitimacy are an independent dimension of development and have a large effect on the way political institutions evolve. Their primary impact is on the nature of social mobilization. Identity politics—based on nationalism, ethnicity, or religion—has frequently trumped class, or acted as a substitute for class, as the rallying point for social mobilization. This happened in nineteenth-century Europe, when workers were more easily mobilized by appeals to nationalism than to their status as workers. It is also true in the contemporary Middle East, where religion is a powerful mobilizational tool. This has diverted political agendas from questions of economic policy into issues like the establishment of sharia and fights over the status of women. In Kenya and Nigeria, politics has descended into interethnic struggles over rents. As the cases of Indonesia and Tanzania indicated, this was not a natural or inevitable outcome: political leaders in these countries formulated alternative concepts of national identity that reduced the salience of ethnicity.

ALL GOOD THINGS DO NOT NECESSARILY GO TOGETHER

The three components of political order that constitute modern liberal democracy—the state, rule of law, and accountability—are in many ways complementary. In order to be effective and impersonal, states need to operate through law. The most successful absolutist regimes were those that possessed rule by rather than of law, such as the Chinese Empire that could rule vast territories and populations through a bureaucracy, and the Prussian Rechtsstaat that established clear property rights and laid the basis for Germany's economic development. Accountability, whether formal through democratic elections, or informal through a government that serves the substantive needs of its population, is also critical to the good functioning of a state. States accumulate and use power, but they are much more effective and stable if they exercise legitimate authority instead and achieve voluntary compliance on the part of citizens. When governments cease being accountable, they invite passive noncompliance, protest, violence, and in extreme cases, revolution. When liberal democracies work well, state, law, and accountability all reinforce one another (see Figure 31).

There is, nonetheless, a permanent tension among the three components of political order. We have seen many examples of the collision of the imperatives of state building and democracy. Effective modern states are built around technical expertise, competence, and autonomy. This is why they could be established under authoritarian conditions, from Prussia and Meiji Japan to Singapore and China today. Democracy, on the other hand, demands political control over the state that in turn reflects popular wishes, and indeed ever-higher levels of participation. This control is nec-

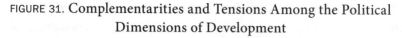

FIGURE 31. Complementarities and Tensions Among the Political Dimensions of Development

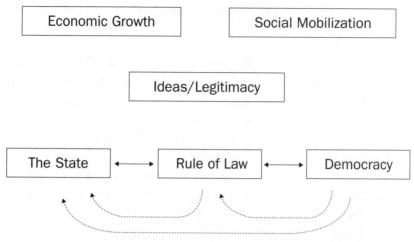

essary and legitimate with regard to the political ends that states pursue. But political control can take the form of contradictory and/or overly detailed mandates, and often seeks to use the state itself as a source of rents and employment. Clientelism emerges in young democracies precisely because the state and its resources constitute useful piggy banks for democratic politicians seeking to mobilize supporters. The nascent American state was captured and controlled by democratic politicians and has been repatrimonialized through interest group influence over Congress. This same process has taken place in countless developing world democracies.

There is also a tension between a high-quality state and rule of law. Effective states operate through law, but formal law can itself become an obstacle to the exercise of an appropriate level of administrative discretion. This tension was well understood in ancient China and was reflected in the debate between Legalists and Confucians. So too in modern debates over rules versus discretion in administrative law. Rules need to be clear and impersonal, but every legal system adjusts the application of rules to fit particular circumstances. Prosecutors are allowed to exercise discretion over when and how to charge defendants; judges exercise discretion in sentencing. The best bureaucracies have the autonomy to use judgment in decision making, to take risks, and to innovate. The worst mechanically carry out detailed rules written by other people. Ordinary citizens are driven crazy by bureaucrats who can't use common sense and insist on mindless rule following. Policy makers occasionally need to take risks and try things that haven't been done before. Excessive deference to rules often makes this impossible and reinforces government's status quo bent.

There is also a long-standing tension between rule of law and democratic accountability. For rule of law to exist, it must be binding on all citizens, including democratic majorities. In many democracies, majorities are content to violate the rights of individuals and minorities, and find legal rules to be inconvenient obstacles to their goals. On the other hand, the ultimate legitimacy of law itself arises out of the degree to which it reflects the norms of justice of the larger community. Moreover, laws are administered by the human beings who operate the judicial branches of government. These individuals have their own beliefs and opinions that may not correspond to the desires of the broader public. Judicial activism can be as much of a danger as weak or politically compliant judiciaries.

Finally, democracy can be in tension with itself: efforts to increase levels of democratic participation and transparency can actually decrease the democratic representativeness of the system as a whole. The great mass of individuals living in democracy are not able by background or temperament to make complex public policy decisions, and when they are asked to do so repeatedly the process is often taken over by well-organized interest groups that can manipulate the process to serve their narrow purposes. Excessive transparency can undermine deliberation.

The tensions that exist between the different components of political order mean that all good things do not necessarily go together. A good liberal democracy is one that holds all three components in some kind of balance. But state, law, and accountability can impede one another's development as well. This is why the sequence in which different institutions were introduced becomes important.

THE INTERNATIONAL DIMENSION

I have portrayed the six dimensions of development as interacting in the context of single societies in a closed system. But the truth of the matter is that every single one of these dimensions is heavily influenced by what goes on at an international level. This is most evident with respect to ideas concerning legitimacy. Well before the Industrial Revolution, ideas could pass from one society to another—indeed, from one civilization to another—and were in fact often the main agents of social change. Islam as an ideology transformed a marginal and backward tribal people on the Arabian peninsula into a major world power, and spread as far as Southeast Asia. Chinese Confucianism migrated to neighboring Japan, Korea, and Vietnam, where it induced the formation of Chinese-style institutions even in the absence of invasion and occupation. Buddhism crossed from India into Southeast and East Asia, where it often became, unlike in its home country, something akin to a state religion. Ideological diffusion has of course become much more intense with the development of modern communications technology. Books and newspapers were critical to the rise and spread of nationalism as an organizing principle. Liberalism, Marxism, fascism, Islamism, and democracy all readily crossed borders in the twentieth century due to electronic technologies from radio and television to the Internet and social media. It is hard to envision the democratic transitions that occurred in sub-Saharan Africa in the early 1990s absent the power of the images of the crumbling Berlin Wall that echoed around the world. Similarly, the timing of protests against autocratic regimes during the Arab Spring was driven by television stations like Al Jazeera and by Twitter and Facebook as much as by domestic causes. By the early twenty-first century, democracy has become truly globalized.

Unfortunately, many of the mechanisms for the transmission of institutions across borders were much less gentle: through conquest, occupation, and often the physical enslavement or elimination of indigenous populations. But even the most coercive colonial powers found that they could not re-create their own institutions in different places at will: geography, climate, local populations, and indigenous institutions all interacted to create new forms that diverged from those in the home country.

The most successful instances of institutional transfer were those in which colonial powers settled lightly populated territories with their own people. In North America, Australia, Argentina, Chile, and parts of South Africa, the colonial powers encountered hunter-gatherer and pastoral peoples who were not, with some exceptions, organized into state-level societies. Conquest was often prolonged, bitter, and bloody, but in the end relatively little survived of indigenous political institutions. In Peru and Mexico, the Spanish encountered densely populated state-level societies. But the Inca and Aztec state institutions were neither old nor highly sophisticated, and under the pressure of conquest and disease dis-integrated even more rapidly than the tribal societies of North and South America. The Spanish conquests became settler colonies, albeit ones whose Creole populations were smaller relative to the indigenous peoples over whom they ruled and with whom they intermarried. The institutions implanted in Latin America were therefore similar to those of Spain and Portugal at the time of settlement, whether mercantilist in Peru and Mexico, or liberal as in Argentina.

Settler regimes never simply replicated the institutions of their home countries, however, since transplanted populations confronted local conditions that were often substantially different from the ones they left behind. Specific evolution created great variation in outcomes. Thus cli-mate and geography played important roles in shaping the slave societies that emerged in different parts of Latin America, the Caribbean, and the American South. These reinforced imported European traditions of hi-erarchy and authoritarian government, and in the American South re-versed the trend toward increasing social equality that characterized the rest of the country.

In those parts of the world that were not extensively settled by Euro-peans, the nature of preexisting institutions was critical in shaping the kinds of political order that eventually emerged. Sub-Saharan Africa and East Asia in this respect stand at opposite ends of the spectrum. Much of the former region did not possess strong state-level institutions at the time of colonization, and the state-level societies that did exist were not highly developed in terms of either state scope or strength. Dis-eases and lack of attractive economic opportunities prevented Europe-ans from settling Africa in large numbers (with the exception of South Africa), and the colonial powers consequently did not find it worth their while to invest heavily in re-creating their own institutions there. The short period of European colonialism in Africa thus succeeded in under-mining the region's traditional institutions while failing to implant more modern ones in their place.

By contrast, China, Japan, and Korea had traditions of stateness that were in some cases longer and deeper than those of the Europeans them-selves. This allowed them to be much more successful in resisting con-quest and colonization in the first place. Attempts to settle or annex their territories in the nineteenth century were all defeated or reversed, up to the reversion of Hong Kong to Chinese sovereignty in 1997. While traditional East Asian regimes all collapsed after confronting the West, they were eventually able to rebuild strong new state institutions based on a mixing of indigenous political traditions with modern practices. The states that emerged were greatly influenced by Western ideas: China is ruled by a regime that claims to be based on Marxism-Leninism, and Japan and South Korea have Western-style liberal democracies. East Asian borrowings from Western practice are substantial: for all of China's trumpeting of its own governance model, its legal system and micro-level institutions are all heavily shaped by Western and international practices. But the major states of East Asia were constructed around bureaucratic cores that owe more to their own historical experience than to anything imported from the West.

VIOLENCE AND POLITICAL DEVELOPMENT

One of the tragic aspects of the human situation is that violence has been integral to the process of political development in a host of ways, particularly with respect to the creation of modern states. Human beings compete to cooperate, and cooperate to compete; cooperation and competition are not alternatives but two sides of the same coin. And competition frequently takes a violent form.

We do not, unfortunately, have historical records of the early transitions from band to tribe, or from tribe to pristine state, and can only speculate about the factors motivating them. The shift to larger-scale societies depended, of course, on technological changes and the economic surpluses they permitted, and were facilitated by the physical environment. But economic incentives by themselves do not seem to have been sufficient to bring these transitions about. Just as peasants today in developing countries frequently refuse to adopt productivity-enhancing technologies, so too these early societies were often subject to institutional rigidities in production methods and social organization that blocked change.

The archaeological record suggests instead that the dynamic force that induced the major transitions from band to tribe to state to modern state was military competition. It was only the threat of violence that created strong demand for new forms of political organization to ensure the community's physical survival. The Tilly hypothesis that "the state made war and war made the state" was meant to apply to state formation in early modern Europe. But military competition drove the formation of modern states in ancient China as well. When historical records begin to appear in ancient China's Zhou Dynasty, violence figures front and center as the source of state building and state modernization. As we saw, military competition was critical in compelling France, Prussia, and Japan to build modern bureaucracies under absolutist conditions. The military fiascoes of the Crimean War played a role in motivating passage of the Northcote-Trevelyan reform in Britain; many of the major expansions of the state in the United States were made for reasons of national security during the two world wars, the cold war, and the so-called war on terrorism. Conversely, it was the infrequency of interstate war in Latin America that explains in part the relative weakness of states there.

The role of violence in producing political order may seem contradictory, since political order exists in the first place to overcome the problem of violence. But no political orders have ever permanently eliminated violence; they simply pushed the organization of violence to higher levels. In the contemporary world, state power can provide basic peace and security for individuals in societies that encompass more than a billion people. But those states are still capable of organizing highly destructive violence between themselves, and they are never fully capable of maintaining domestic order.

External competition is not the only way that violence or the threat of violence has driven political institution building. Violence has frequently been necessary to overcome institutional rigidity and political decay. Decay occurs when incumbent political actors entrench themselves within a political system and block possibilities for institutional change. Oftentimes these actors are so powerful that they can be eliminated only through violent means. This was true of the venal officeholders of the ancien régime in France, who as a class had to be physically dispossessed during the revolution. Other powerful agrarian oligarchies—the Prussian Junkers and the landowning classes in Russia and China—lost their holdings only as a result of war and revolution. The landowning classes in Japan, South Korea, and Taiwan were forced to divest their holdings against the backdrop of American military power. At other times, it was nonelites who were the obstacles to modernizing change. Barrington Moore noted that the commercialization of agriculture in England under the parliamentary enclosure movement, necessary to create a modern capitalist land tenure system, required a slow-motion revolution under which peasants were forcibly driven off the lands their families had inhabited for generations.

A final respect in which violence or the threat of violence is important to political development is in the formation of national identities, which are an often critical adjunct to successful state building and political order more generally. The idea that territorial boundaries should correspond to cultural units required the redrawing of borders or the physical removal of populations, neither of which could be accomplished without substantial violence. Even where national identity was deliberately designed to be inclusive and nonethnic, as in Tanzania and Indonesia, lingua francas and coherent stories of nationhood had to be imposed through authoritarian political methods. In Europe, nations that became successful liberal democracies in the second half of the twentieth century were all the products of violent nation building in the preceding centuries.

Fortunately, military struggle is not the only route to a modern state. Although Britain and the United States constructed state bureaucracies in response to national security imperatives, they both undertook reforms of their state administrations in peacetime through the building of reform coalitions. These coalitions consisted chiefly, though not exclusively, of new social groups that did not have a stake in the old systems of political patronage. In Britain it was middle classes wanting to break into the circle of privilege held by the old aristocracy. Once the country's relatively small elite decided that the old system was not efficient and was failing to meet the needs of empire, it shifted course relatively rapidly. The country's Westminster system concentrated power in such a way that the reform could be put in place in less than two decades. In the United States, the reform coalition was more complex. The new middle and professional classes were themselves divided on the issue of patronage, with some business interests having found a way to work within the old system. Conversely, some of the older agrarian interests being left behind by industrialization also joined the reform coalition out of hostility to those same interests. Culture played an important but hard to quantify role as well. The moralism of a Protestant elite resentful of the corruption being fostered by urban party machines with their immigrant clients joined in mobilizing support for reform.

These cases suggest that economic development in itself can be the starting point for the shift from a patrimonial or clientelistic state to a modern one. But growth alone provides no guarantee that modern states will emerge. The cases of Greece and Italy show how clientelism can survive into the present, despite high levels of per capita wealth. Newly mobilized social groups like middle-class professionals may or may not support reform of the state; they could just as easily get sucked into the web of clientelistic politics. This is particularly true when economic growth is not based on market-centered entrepreneurship, and when an unreformed state takes the lead in promoting economic development.

There are thus a number of ways of getting to a modern state. Violence was important in incentivizing political innovation as a historical matter, but it does not remain a necessary condition for reform in cases that come later. Those societies have the option of learning from earlier experiences and adapting other models to their own societies.

POLITICAL UNIVERSALS

In the course of the two volumes of this book, I have emphasized general over specific evolution in political development. That is, societies have diverged in their forms of political organization as they adapted to the specific environmental niches they occupied. But they have also, as noted, generated remarkably similar solutions to problems of organization across different environments.

I have argued that a well-functioning political order must consist of the three sets of political institutions—state, law, and accountability—in some kind of balance. Implicit in this argument is a normative preference. In my view, liberal democracies that combine effective and powerful states with institutions of constraint based on law and democratic accountability are more just and serve their citizens better than ones in which the state is dominant. This is because the kind of political agency implied by democratic politics serves an important end of human life in its own right, independently of the quality of government that such a system produces. I agree with Aristotle's assertion in the *Politics* that human beings are political by nature and can achieve their highest level of flourishing only to the extent that they participate in a shared life. There is a similar argument to be made for the intrinsic value of market-based economic systems. Amartya Sen notes that the latter are not simply more efficient; even if a planned economy grew at an equal rate, a citizen "may still have very good reason to prefer the scenario of free choice over that of submission to order."[4] The exercise of political and economic agency is an important end of human life itself, apart from the effects of that exercise.

The rule of law that grants rights to citizens also has an intrinsic value independent of whether those rights are useful in promoting economic growth. Individual rights—to speak freely, to assemble, to criticize, and to participate in politics—constitute recognition by the state of the dignity of its citizens. An authoritarian state at best treats its citizens as if they were ignorant or immature children who need adult supervision for their own good; at worst it treats them as resources to be exploited or trash to be disposed of. A rule of law that protects individual rights in effect recognizes that citizens are adults who are capable of independent moral choice. This is why so many tyrants, from Qin Shi Huangdi, the unifier of ancient China, to Mubarak and Qaddafi during the Arab Spring, have ultimately faced revolts of outraged dignity on the part of their own citizens.[5]

A broader question raised by this study is whether a regime that is balanced among state, law, and accountability—that is, liberal democracy—itself constitutes some kind of political universal, or whether it simply reflects the cultural preferences of people who live in Western liberal democracies.

This kind of regime clearly does not represent a human universal, since it came into being only a few centuries ago, a mere speck of time in the history of human political order. To the extent that liberal democracy does constitute a more generally applicable form of government, we would have to argue that it does so as a matter of general political evolution, much as band-, tribe-, and state-level institutions came to be dominant forms of political organization across different cultures and regions at different historical moments. That is, this kind of regime becomes necessary in conjunction with the other dimensions of development—economic growth, social mobilization, and changes in ideas. Band- and tribal-level societies had no state or law enforced by third parties, though they arguably had a strong form of accountability. State-level societies presiding over agrarian economies could persist for centuries, sometimes with law but never with democratic accountability. The functional need for a balanced regime incorporating all three components becomes necessary only as high levels of economic growth kick in and countries modernize along their economic and social dimensions.

It is very difficult to run large-scale societies with highly mobilized populations in the absence of legal rules and formal mechanisms of accountability. The large markets that underpin economic growth and efficiency require consistent, predictable, and well-enforced rules. Highly mobilized and ever-changing populations make constant demands of rulers; free press and elections can be seen as crucial information channels by which governments can keep abreast of this kaleidoscopic process. Moreover, as Tocqueville observed, the idea of human equality has been growing inexorably over the past several centuries, even if it is not respected by many regimes in practice. People believe they have rights and will take whatever opportunities exist to assert them. Under these conditions, the need to balance state power with rule of law and democratic accountability becomes not just a normative preference but the necessary condition for the stable organization of politics if a society hopes to be modern in other respects. Huntington believed authoritarian parties could satisfy popular demands for participation, but we see in retrospect that this was not true.

But while a regime that is balanced among state, law, and accountability is in fact a general condition of successful modern politics, we need to acknowledge that there is considerable variation in the specific institutional forms that law and accountability can take; the institutional forms adopted by particular countries like the United States do not constitute universal models. Different societies can implement these institutions differently.

In particular, we need to pay attention to the substantive ends that law and accountability are meant to serve, rather than their strict procedural forms. The purpose of law is to codify and make transparent the community's rules of justice and to enforce them evenhandedly. The vast procedural apparatus that is the specialty of the legal profession in the contemporary world is a means to the end of evenhanded justice, not an end in itself. Yet procedure often takes precedence and stymies the substantive ends of justice. Countless rule-of-law societies have legal systems that are excessively slow and costly, in ways that benefit those who are in a position to take advantage of their knowledge of procedure at the expense of justice.

Similarly, democratic procedures regarding free and fair elections do not guarantee the substantive end of accountability. Electoral procedures themselves can be gamed, from outright fraud and vote rigging to more subtle efforts to redraw electoral districts to suit one party, or to disqualify voters of the other. Even under the best electoral procedures, politicians can recruit supporters through clientelistic methods and use markers like ethnicity and religion for their own purposes. In other cases, powerful interest groups can take advantage of existing procedures to protect narrow interests and block broader public goals. Public interest under these circumstances often faces a collective action problem and fails to receive adequate representation.

The worship of procedure over substance is a critical source of political decay in contemporary liberal democracies. Political decay can occur in any regime simply because of the nature of institutions themselves. Institutions are rules that persist beyond the lifetimes of the individuals who created them. They persist partly because they are useful and partly because they are believed to have intrinsic value. The human propensity to invest rules with emotional meaning is what makes them stable over long periods of time, but their rigidity becomes a liability when circumstances change. The problem is often more acute when change occurs after a prolonged period of peace and stability. Moreover, there is a natural tendency to backslide into the default form of sociability, one based on favoring family and engaging in reciprocal exchange of benefits with friends, particularly among elites that have privileged access to the political system. The result is that both law and procedural accountability are used to defeat the substantive ends that they were originally designed to serve.

FUTURE MODELS

There are a number of governments in the early twenty-first century world that see themselves as principled alternatives to liberal democracy. These include Iran and the monarchies of the Persian Gulf, Russia, and the People's Republic of China. Iran, however, is seriously divided, with a large middle class that contests many of the regime's claims to legitimacy. The Gulf monarchies have always been exceptional cases, viable in their present forms only because of their huge energy resources. Putin's Russia, likewise, has emerged as a rentier state, regionally powerful largely because it sits on reserves of gas and oil; outside of the world of Russian speakers, it is no one's idea of a political system worth emulating.

Of the nondemocratic alternatives, China poses the most serious challenge to the idea that liberal democracy constitutes a universal evolutionary model. China, as noted many times in these volumes, builds on a two-millennia-long tradition of strong centralized government and is one of the few state-level societies never to have developed an indigenous tradition of rule of law. China's rich and complex tradition has substituted Confucian morality for formal procedural rules as a constraint on rulers. It was this tradition that was bequeathed to other countries in East Asia and is one important source of the success of post–World War II Japan, South Korea, and Taiwan. Authoritarian governments can sometimes be more capable than democratic ones of breaking decisively with the past. One of the great advantages that post-Mao China enjoyed was that it was led by a highly autonomous Communist Party.

The central issue facing China today is whether, a mere thirty-five years since the initiation of Deng's reforms, the Chinese regime is itself now suffering from political decay and losing the autonomy that was the source of its earlier success. China's policy agenda in the coming decade will be very different from what it was over the past generation. It is now a middle-income country striving to become a high-income one. The old export-driven model has run its course and needs to rely much more heavily on domestic demand. China can no longer exploit extensive economic growth and the mass mobilization of people into an industrial economy. In its quest for high growth, China has built up huge environmental liabilities that become manifest in unbreathable air, "cancer villages" dotting the country, a failing food safety system, and other daunting problems. It is not clear whether China's educational system is capable of supplying the kinds of skills necessary to sustain broad-based improvements in productivity. A deeper question is whether true innovation can be sustained in the absence of greater individual freedom. With the complexity of the Chinese economy, informational requirements for managing it have also grown. As in dynastic China, the ability of a top-down command-and-control system to stay abreast of what is actually happening in the society is questionable.[6]

Most important, China has experienced an enormous mobilization of its own population, far more massive and rapid than the shift that occurred in nineteenth- and early-twentieth-century Europe. China's rapidly expanding population of educated and increasingly wealthy citizens has different demands and aspirations than the peasants that made up the bulk of Chinese society in the past.

In light of these challenges, the central question is whether the Chinese regime has the autonomy to shift course toward a more liberal system that will encourage greater economic competition and permit a freer flow of information throughout the society. China's rapid growth has created new vested interests that are powerful and have influence over the party's decision making, even in the absence of a legislature and lobbyists. The state-owned enterprises are larger and wealthier than ever. The party leadership itself has fallen into patterns of corruption that make reform personally dangerous for many of them. The party continues to cling to Marxism-Leninism as an ideology, despite the fact that most Chinese ceased to believe in it many years ago.

How the new Chinese middle class behaves in the coming years will be the most important test of the universality of liberal democracy. If it continues to grow in absolute and relative size, and yet remains content to live under the benevolent tutelage of a single-party dictatorship, one would have to say that China is culturally different from other societies around the world in its support for authoritarian government. If, however, it generates demands for participation that cannot be accommodated within the existing political system, then it is simply behaving in a manner similar to middle classes in other parts of the world. The real test of the legitimacy of the Chinese system will come not when the economy is expanding and jobs are abundant but when growth slows and the system faces crisis, as it inevitably will.

Perhaps the greater developmental challenge lies not in the existence of an alternative, more attractive form of political organization, but rather in the fact that many countries will aspire to be rich, liberal democracies, but will never be able to get there. Some observers have suggested that poor countries may be "trapped" in poverty because of the intertwined dimensions of political and economic development.[7] Economic growth requires certain minimal political institutions to occur; on the other hand, institutions are very hard to create in conditions of extreme poverty and political fractionalization. How to break out of this trap? Throughout the two volumes of this book, we have seen the role played by accident and contingency—how fortuitous leadership, the unplanned sequencing of the introduction of institutions, or unintended consequences of activities undertaken for other purposes like fighting wars—led certain countries to evolve in unexpected ways. Could it be the case that societies escaping this trap historically were simply lucky, and that others ones not similarly blessed may never develop?

This view is too pessimistic. It is true that luck and accidents have played a role in kick-starting political and economic change historically. But luck and accidents may have been more important for the first societies building new institutions than for ones that come later. Today, there is a large body of accumulated experience about institutions, and a growing international community that shares information, knowledge, and resources. There are, moreover, multiple paths and entry points toward development. If progress fails to materialize along one dimension, it may happen along another over time, and then the interconnected chains of causality will start to kick in. All of this is suggested by the general framework for understanding development presented here, with its economic, political, social, and ideological dimensions.

Does the existence of political decay in modern democracies mean that the overall model of a regime balanced among state, law, and accountability is somehow fatally flawed? This is definitely not my conclusion: all societies, authoritarian and democratic, are subject to decay over time. The real issue is their ability to adapt and eventually fix themselves. I do not believe that there is a systemic "crisis of governability" among established democracies. Democratic political systems have faced such crises in the past, notably during the 1930s when they fell into economic depression and were challenged by alternative fascist and communist competitors, or again in the 1960s and '70s, when they were destabilized by popular protests, economic stagnation, and high inflation. It is very difficult to judge a political system's long-term prospects by its performance in any given decade; problems that seem insuperable in one time period vanish in another. Democratic political systems are often slower to respond to mounting problems than authoritarian ones, but when they do, they are often more decisive because the decision to act is based on broader buy-in.

If there has been a single problem facing contemporary democracies, either aspiring or well established, it has been centered in their failure to provide the substance of what people want from government: personal security, shared economic growth, and quality basic public services like education, health, and infrastructure that are needed to achieve individual opportunity. Proponents of democracy focus, for understandable reasons, on limiting the powers of tyrannical or predatory states. But they do not spend as much time thinking about how to govern effectively—they are, in Woodrow Wilson's phrase, more interested in "controlling than in energizing government."

This was the failure of the 2004 Orange Revolution in Ukraine, which toppled Viktor Yanukovich for the first time. Had an effective democratic administration come to power that cleaned up corruption and improved the trustworthiness of state institutions, it would have cemented its legitimacy across not just western but Russian-speaking eastern Ukraine as well, long before Vladimir Putin was strong enough to undermine its actions. Instead, the Orange Coalition wasted its energy on internal squabbling and shady deals, paving the way for Yanukovich's return in 2010 and the crisis following on his departure in 2014.

India has been held back by a similar gap in performance when compared to authoritarian China. It is very impressive that India has held together, with one brief exception, as an electoral democracy since its founding in 1947. But Indian democracy, like sausage-making, does not look very appealing on closer inspection. The system is rife with corruption and patronage; 34 percent of the winners of India's 2014 elections have *criminal* indictments pending against them, including serious charges like murder, kidnapping, and sexual assault. A rule of law exists, but it is so slow and ineffective that many plaintiffs die before their cases come to trial. Compared to China, the country has been completely hamstrung in its ability to provide modern infrastructure or services like clean water, electricity, or basic education to its population. It was for this reason that Narendra Modi, a Hindu nationalist with a troubled past, was elected prime minister in 2014 by an impressive majority in the hope that he will somehow be able to cut through all the blather of routine Indian politics and actually get something done.

The inability to govern effectively extends, unfortunately, to the United States itself. The country's Madisonian Constitution, deliberately designed to prevent tyranny by multiplying checks and balances at all levels of government, has become a vetocracy. When combined with political polarization, it has proven unable to move either forward or backward effectively. The United States faces a very serious long-term fiscal problem that is nonetheless solvable through appropriate political compromises. But Congress has not passed a budget, according to its own rules, in several years, and in fall 2013 shut down the entire government because it couldn't agree on paying for past debts. While the American economy remains a source of miraculous innovation, American government is hardly a source of inspiration around the world at the present moment.

No one living in an established liberal democracy should therefore be complacent about the inevitability of its survival. There is no automatic historical mechanism that makes progress inevitable, or that prevents decay and backsliding. Democracies exist and survive only because people want and are willing to fight for them; leadership, organizational ability, and oftentimes sheer good luck are needed for them to prevail. As we have seen, there is a trade-off between the level of popular participation and the effectiveness of government; how to strike that balance is not something that can be theoretically determined with any ease. So while general evolution may dictate the emergence of certain broad institutional forms over time, specific evolution means that no particular political system will be in equilibrium with its environment forever.

But if the supply of high-quality democratic government is sometimes lacking, the demand for it is large and growing day by day. New social groups have been mobilized all over the world. We continue to see evidence of this in the mass protests that continue to erupt unexpectedly in places from Tunis to Kiev to Istanbul to São Paulo, where people want governments that recognize their equal dignity as human beings and perform as promised. It is evident also in the millions of poor people desperate to move from places like Guatemala City or Karachi to Los Angeles or London each year. These facts alone suggest that there is a clear directionality to the process of political development, and that accountable governments recognizing the equal dignity of their citizens have a universal appeal.

NOTES

INTRODUCTION

1. See for example Peter J. Wallison, *Bad History, Worse Policy: How a False Narrative About the Financial Crisis Led to the Dodd-Frank Act* (Washington, D.C.: American Enterprise Institute, 2013).
2. Anat Admati and Martin Hellwig, *The Banker's New Clothes: What's Wrong with Banking and What to Do About It* (Princeton: Princeton University Press, 2013).
3. For a broader account of how politics affected banking regulation after the financial crisis, see Simon Johnson and James Kwak, *13 Bankers: The Wall Street Takeover and the Next Financial Meltdown* (New York: Pantheon, 2010).
4. This definition is taken from Samuel P. Huntington, *Political Order in Changing Societies* (New Haven: Yale University Press, 2006), p. 12.
5. In Britain, a similar long-term battle was fought out during the nineteenth and early twentieth centuries, where class rather than race was the fundamental issue. Perhaps because the principle of equality was less clearly articulated (Britain has no equivalent of the Bill of Rights and remains a constitutional monarchy), it took far longer to achieve universal white male suffrage there than in the United States.
6. Edmund Burke, *Reflections on the Revolution in France* (Stanford, CA: Stanford University Press, 2001); Alexis de Tocqueville, *The Old Regime and the Revolution,* Vol. 1 (Chicago: University of Chicago Press, 1998); François Furet, *Interpreting the French Revolution* (New York: Cambridge University Press, 1981).
7. For an overview of these events, see Georges Lefebvre, *The Coming of the French Revolution, 1789* (Princeton: Princeton University Press, 1947).
8. Napoleon himself had pushed for a new code in 1800 shortly after his takeover of the revolutionary government on 18 Brumaire, and he personally attended

many sessions of the Conseil d'État, which oversaw its drafting. The code was finally promulgated in 1804. Carl J. Friedrich, "The Ideological and Philosophical Background," in Bernard Schwartz, ed., *The Code Napoléon and the Common Law World* (New York: New York University Press, 1956).

9. Martyn Lyons, *Napoleon Bonaparte and the Legacy of the French Revolution* (London: Macmillan, 1994), pp. 94–96.

10. Jean Limpens, "Territorial Expansion of the Code," in Schwartz, *Code Napoléon.*

11. See Tocqueville, *The Old Regime*, pp. 118–24.

1: WHAT IS POLITICAL DEVELOPMENT?

1. For a survey of existing definitions, see Rachel Kleinfeld, "Competing Definitions of the Rule of Law," in Thomas Carothers, ed., *Promoting the Rule of Law Abroad: In Search of Knowledge* (Washington, D.C.: Carnegie Endowment, 2006).

2. S. N. Eisenstadt, *Traditional Patrimonialism and Modern Neopatrimonialism* (Beverly Hills, CA: Sage, 1973).

3. Douglass C. North, John Wallis, and Barry R. Weingast, *Violence and Social Orders: A Conceptual Framework for Interpreting Recorded Human History* (New York: Cambridge University Press, 2009).

4. Daron Acemoglu and James A. Robinson, *Why Nations Fail: The Origins of Power, Prosperity, and Poverty* (New York: Crown, 2012).

5. For definitions of these terms, see Huntington, *Political Order in Changing Societies*, pp. 12–24; also the discussion in Francis Fukuyama, *The Origins of Political Order: From Prehuman Times to the French Revolution* (New York: Farrar, Straus and Giroux, 2011), pp. 450–51.

6. The argument that democracies will self-correct when faced by elite challenges is made in Mancur Olson, "Dictatorship, Democracy, and Development," *American Political Science Review* 87, no. 9 (1993): 567–76; North, Wallis, and Weingast, *Violence and Social Orders*; and Acemoglu and Robinson, *Why Nations Fail*.

7. See for example Larry Diamond, Juan J. Linz, and Seymour Martin Lipset, eds., *Democracy in Developing Countries* (Boulder, CO: Lynne Rienner, 1988); Guillermo O'Donnell, Philippe C. Schmitter, and Laurence Whitehead, eds., *Transitions from Authoritarian Rule: Comparative Perspectives* (Baltimore: Johns Hopkins University Press, 1986); Samuel P. Huntington, *The Third Wave: Democratization in the Late Twentieth Century* (Oklahoma City: University of Oklahoma Press, 1991); Juan J. Linz and Alfred C. Stepan, eds., *The Breakdown of Democratic Regimes: Crisis, Breakdown and Reequilibration. An Introduction* (Baltimore: Johns Hopkins University Press, 1978); Larry Diamond, *The Spirit of Democracy: The Struggle to Build Free Societies Throughout the World* (New York: Times Books, 2008).

8. For a critique of contemporary definitions of "governance," see Claus Offe, "Governance: An 'Empty Signifier'?" *Constellations* 16, no. 4 (2009): 550–62;

and Marc F. Plattner, "Reflections on 'Governance,'" *Journal of Democracy* 24, no. 4 (2013): 17–28.

9. I express some views on a desirable structure of international institutions in *America at the Crossroads: Democracy, Power, and the Neoconservative Legacy* (New Haven: Yale University Press, 2006), chap. 6.

10. Michael Mann, *The Sources of Social Power*, Vol. 1: *A History of Power from the Beginning to AD 1760* (Cambridge: Cambridge University Press, 1986).

2: THE DIMENSIONS OF DEVELOPMENT

1. For an overview, see Eric Hobsbawm, *The Age of Capital, 1848–1875* (New York: Vintage Books, 1996), chap. 1.

2. Ferdinand Tönnies, *Community and Association (Gemeinschaft und Gesellschaft)* (London: Routledge, 1955).

3. Max Weber, *Economy and Society* (Berkeley: University of California Press, 1978); Émile Durkheim, *The Division of Labor in Society* (New York: Macmillan, 1933); Henry Maine, *Ancient Law: Its Connection with the Early History of Society and Its Relation to Modern Ideas* (Boston: Beacon Press, 1963).

4. See for example Joel Mokyr, ed., *The Economics of the Industrial Revolution* (Totowa, NJ: Rowman & Allanheld, 1985); Mokyr, *The British Industrial Revolution: An Economic Perspective* (Boulder, CO: Westview Press, 1999); Douglass C. North and Robert P. Thomas, *The Rise of the Western World* (New York: Cambridge University Press, 1973); Nathan Rosenberg and L. E. Birdzell, *How the West Grew Rich* (New York: Basic Books, 1986); David S. Landes, *The Wealth and Poverty of Nations: Why Some Are So Rich and Some So Poor* (New York: Norton, 1998).

5. For an overview, see Nils Gilman, *Mandarins of the Future: Modernization Theory in Cold War America* (Baltimore: Johns Hopkins University Press, 2003).

6. Huntington, *Political Order in Changing Societies*, pp. 32–92.

7. See for example James D. Fearon and David Laitin, "Ethnicity, Insurgency, and Civil War," *American Political Science Review* 97 (2003): 75–90; Paul Collier, *The Bottom Billion: Why the Poorest Countries Are Failing and What Can Be Done About It* (New York: Oxford University Press, 2007); Collier, *Economic Causes of Civil Conflict and Their Implications for Policy* (Oxford: Oxford Economic Papers, 2006); Collier, Anke Hoeffler, and Dominic Rohner, *Beyond Greed and Grievance: Feasibility and Civil War* (Oxford: Oxford Economic Papers, 2007).

8. World Bank, *World Development Report 2011: Conflict, Security, and Development* (Washington, D.C.: World Bank, 2011).

9. William R. Easterly, "Can Institutions Resolve Ethnic Conflict?" *Economic Development and Cultural Change* 49, no. 4 (2001); Fearon and Laitin, "Ethnicity, Insurgency and Civil War."

10. World Bank Development Indicators and Global Development Finance; U.S. Bureau of Labor Statistics.

11. Figures are taken from Larry Diamond, "The Financial Crisis and the Democratic Recession," in Nancy Birdsall and Francis Fukuyama, eds., *New Ideas in Development after the Financial Crisis* (Baltimore: Johns Hopkins University Press, 2011). See also Huntington, *The Third Wave*.
12. See Alfred C. Stepan and Graeme B. Robertson, "An 'Arab' More Than a 'Muslim' Electoral Gap," *Journal of Democracy* 14, (no. 3) (2003): 30–44.
13. United Nations Development Program, Arab Human Development Reports, www.arab-hdr.org/.
14. UNDP, Arab Human Development Reports, www.arab-hdr.org/data/indicators /2012-31.aspx.
15. On the impact of social media on the Arab Spring, see Eric Schmidt and Jared Cohen, *The New Digital Age: Reshaping the Future of People, Nations and Business* (New York: Knopf, 2013).

3: BUREAUCRACY

1. This is described in Lant Pritchett, Michael Woolcock, and Matt Andrews, *Capability Traps? The Mechanisms of Persistent Implementation Failure* (Washington, D.C.: Center for Global Development Working Paper No. 234, 2010).
2. See World Bank DataBank, http://databank.worldbank.org/data/home.aspx.
3. Karl Polanyi and C. W. Arensberg, *Trade and Market in the Early Empires* (New York: Free Press, 1957).
4. Weber's criteria:
    1. Bureaucrats are personally free and subject to authority only within a defined area.
    2. They are organized into a clearly defined hierarchy of offices.
    3. Each office has a defined sphere of competence.
    4. Offices are filled by free contractual relationship.
    5. Candidates are selected on the basis of technical qualifications.
    6. Bureaucrats receive fixed salaries.
    7. The office is treated as the sole occupation of the incumbent.
    8. The office constitutes a career.
    9. There is a separation between ownership and management.
    10. Officials are subject to strict discipline and control.
    Economy and Society (Berkeley: University of California Press, 1978), 1: 220–21.
5. Two of the few studies to try to quantify the Weberian characteristics of governments and to correlate them against outcomes are James E. Rauch and Peter B. Evans, "Bureaucratic Structure and Bureaucratic Performance in Less Developed Countries," *Journal of Public Economics* 75 (2000): 45–71; and Rauch and Evans, "Bureaucracy and Growth: A Cross-National Analysis of the Effects of 'Weberian' State Structures on Economic Growth," *American Sociological Review* 64 (1999): 748–65.

6. Bo Rothstein, *The Quality of Government: Corruption, Social Trust, and Inequality in International Perspective* (Chicago: University of Chicago Press, 2011).

7. This index is based on surveys of people doing business in different countries, at http://transparency.org/policy_research/surveys_indices/cpi.

8. Max Weber, *The Protestant Ethic and the Spirit of Capitalism* (New York: Scribner, 1930), p. 181.

9. Joel Migdal, *Strong Societies and Weak States: State-Society Relations and State Capabilities in the Third World* (Princeton: Princeton University Press, 1988), p. 4.

10. Pritchett, Woolcock, and Andrews, *Capability Traps?*

11. James S. Coleman et al., *Equality of Educational Opportunity* (Washington, D.C.: Department of Health, Education and Welfare, 1966).

12. China's position well to the left of Russia is a bit misleading. China retains a large state-owned enterprise sector whose revenues are at the disposal of the state sector but don't necessarily show up as taxes.

4: PRUSSIA BUILDS A STATE

1. Hajo Holborn, *A History of Modern Germany 1648–1840* (Princeton: Princeton University Press, 1982), pp. 22–23.

2. Hans Rosenberg, *Bureaucracy, Aristocracy, and Autocracy: The Prussian Experience, 1660–1815* (Cambridge, MA: Harvard University Press, 1958), pp. 8–10.

3. For a discussion of early Hohenzollern efforts to subdue the warlord aristocracy, see Otto Hintze, *The Historical Essays of Otto Hintze* (New York: Oxford University Press, 1975), pp. 38–39. On roving and stationary bandits, see Olson, "Dictatorship, Democracy, and Development." For a discussion of this concept, see Fukuyama, *Origins of Political Order*, pp. 303–304.

4. Rosenberg, *Bureaucracy, Aristocracy, and Autocracy*, pp. 36–37.

5. Holborn, *History of Modern Germany*, pp. 190–91.

6. Rosenberg, *Bureaucracy, Aristocracy, and Autocracy*, p. 40.

7. Philip S. Gorski, *The Disciplinary Revolution: Calvinism and the Rise of the State in Early Modern Europe* (Chicago: University of Chicago Press, 2003), pp. 79–113.

8. See Hintze, *Historical Essays*, p. 45. Philip Gorski points out, however, that some of the most important institutional changes came during Frederick William's reign, when Prussia was not under intense military pressure. This suggests that Prussian state building had religious rather than simply national security roots. *Disciplinary Revolution*, pp. 12–15.

9. On this period, see Holborn, *History of Modern Germany*, pp. 246–48.

10. Hans-Eberhard Mueller, *Bureaucracy, Education, and Monopoly: Civil Service*

Reforms in Prussia and England (Berkeley: University of California Press, 1984), pp. 43–45.

11. See Rosenberg, *Bureaucracy, Aristocracy, and Autocracy*, pp. 73–87; Mueller, *Bureaucracy, Education, and Monopoly*, pp. 58–61.
12. Alexandre Kojève, *Introduction à la Lecture de Hegel* (Paris: Gallimard, 1947).
13. Holborn, *History of Modern Germany*, pp. 396–97.
14. Ibid., p. 413.
15. Mueller, *Bureaucracy, Education, and Monopoly*, pp. 136–37, 162–63.
16. Rosenberg, *Bureaucracy, Aristocracy, and Autocracy*, p. 211.
17. Ibid., p. 182.
18. On the theoretical origins of the impersonal state and the importance of Hobbes, see Harvey C. Mansfield, Jr., *Machiavelli's Virtue* (Chicago: University of Chicago Press, 1996), pp. 281–94.
19. Rosenberg, *Bureaucracy, Aristocracy, and Autocracy*, pp. 46–56.
20. See Fukuyama, *Origins of Political Order*, p. 276.
21. René David, *French Law: Its Structure, Sources, and Methodology* (Baton Rouge: Louisiana State University Press, 1972), p. 36.
22. Holborn, *History of Modern Germany*, pp. 272–74; Rosenberg, *Bureaucracy, Aristocracy, and Autocracy*, pp. 190–91.
23. James J. Sheehan, *German History, 1770–1866* (New York: Oxford University Press, 1989), p. 428.
24. Huntington, *Political Order in Changing Societies*, p. 20.
25. Fukuyama, *Origins of Political Order*, pp. 264–67.
26. The degree to which Chinese emperors in the late Ming Dynasty were prisoners of their own bureaucracies is illustrated in Ray Huang, *1587, a Year of No Significance: The Ming Dynasty in Decline* (New Haven: Yale University Press, 1981). See also Fukuyama, *Origins of Political Order*, pp. 307–308.
27. Rosenberg, *Bureaucracy, Aristocracy, and Autocracy*, p. 191. Even under Frederick, the Prussian bureaucracy was so large that he could not control it particularly well beyond Berlin, and outside of areas of particular interest to him such as the army and foreign policy.
28. Quoted in Rosenberg, *Bureaucracy, Aristocracy, and Autocracy*, p. 201.
29. Martin Shefter, *Political Parties and the State: The American Historical Experience* (Princeton: Princeton University Press, 1994).
30. Ibid., p. 41.
31. Gordon A. Craig, *The Politics of the Prussian Army, 1640–1945* (New York: Oxford University Press, 1964), pp. 76–81.
32. Ibid., pp. 217–19, 255–95.
33. David Schoenbaum, *Hitler's Social Revolution* (Garden City, NY: Doubleday, 1966), pp. 202–207.
34. Ibid., p. 205.
35. Shefter, *Political Parties and the State*, p. 42.

5: CORRUPTION

1. On this speech and Wolfenson's role in promoting a good governance agenda, see Sebastian Mallaby, *The World's Banker: A Story of Failed States, Financial Crises, and the Wealth and Poverty of Nations* (New York: Penguin Press, 2004), pp. 176–77.
2. Anne O. Krueger, "The Political Economy of the Rent-Seeking Society," *American Economic Review* 64, no. 3 (1974): 291–303.
3. Basic works on the general phenomenon of corruption include Robert Brooks, "The Nature of Political Corruption," *Political Science Quarterly* 24, no. 1 (1909): 1–22; Joseph S. Nye, Jr., "Corruption and Political Development: A Cost-Benefit Analysis," *American Political Science Review* 61, no. 2 (1967): 417–27; James C. Scott, *Comparative Political Corruption* (Englewood Cliffs, NJ: Prentice-Hall, 1972); Susan Rose-Ackerman, *Corruption: A Study in Political Economy* (New York: Academic Press, 1978), and *Corruption and Government: Causes, Consequences, and Reform* (New York: Cambridge University Press, 1999); Daniel Kaufmann, "Corruption: The Facts," *Foreign Policy* 107 (1997): 114–31; A. W. Goudie and David Stasavage, "A Framework for an Analysis of Corruption," *Crime, Law and Social Change* 29, no. 2–3 (1998): 113–59; Arnold J. Heidenheimer and Michael Johnston, eds., *Political Corruption*, 3rd ed. (New Brunswick, NJ: Transaction, 2001); Robert Leiken, "Controlling the Global Corruption Epidemic," *Foreign Policy* 105 (1997): 55–73; Robert Klitgaard, *Controlling Corruption* (Berkeley: University of California Press, 1988), and *Tropical Gangsters: One Man's Experience with Development and Decadence in Deepest Africa* (New York: Basic Books, 1990); Andrei Shleifer and Robert W. Vishny, "Corruption," *Quarterly Journal of Economics* 108, no. 3 (1993): 599–617; Johnston, *Syndromes of Corruption: Wealth, Power, and Democracy* (New York: Cambridge University Press, 2005.
4. See for example the definition in Johnston, *Syndromes of Corruption*, p. 11.
5. On the Wanli emperor, see Fukuyama, *Origins of Political Order*, p. 312.
6. See José Anson, Oliver Cadot, and Marcelo Olarreaga, *Import-Tariff Evasion and Customs Corruption: Does Pre-Shipment Inspection Help?* (Washington, D.C.: World Bank, 2003).
7. North, Wallis, and Weingast, *Violence and Social Orders*.
8. Mushtaq H. Khan and Jomo Kwame Sundaram, eds., *Rents, Rent-Seeking and Economic Development: Theory and Evidence in Asia* (New York: Cambridge University Press, 2000).
9. There is a large literature on clientelism. See Herbert Kitschelt and Steven I. Wilkinson, eds., *Patrons, Clients, and Policies: Patterns of Democratic Accountability and Political Competition* (New York: Cambridge University Press, 2007); Frederic Charles Schaffer, ed., *Elections for Sale: The Causes and Consequences of Vote Buying* (Boulder, CO: Lynne Rienner, 2007); Paul D. Hutchcroft, "The Politics of Privilege: Assessing the Impact of Rents, Corruption, and Clientelism on Third World Development," *Political Studies* 45, no. 3 (1997): 649–58; Luigi Manzetti and Carole J. Wilson, "Why Do Corrupt Governments Maintain

Public Support?" *Comparative Political Studies* 40, no. 8 (2007): 949–70; Philip Keefer and Razvan Vlaicu, "Democracy, Credibility, and Clientelism," *Journal of Law, Economics, and Organization* 24, no. 2 (2008): 371–406.

10. S. N. Eisenstadt and L. Roniger, *Patrons, Clients, and Friends: Interpersonal Relations and the Structure of Trust in Society* (New York: Cambridge University Press, 1984), p. 43.

11. Thus James Scott, *Comparative Political Corruption*, describes a patronage system in predemocratic Thailand and a clientelistic system in Ghana and India.

12. See the definition in Simona Piattoni, ed., *Clientelism, Interests, and Democratic Representation: The European Experience in Historical and Comparative Perspective* (New York: Cambridge University Press, 2001), pp. 6–7.

13. For a broad analysis of this phenomenon, see Susan Stokes et al., *Brokers, Voters, and Clientelism: The Puzzle of Distributive Politics* (New York: Cambridge University Press, 2013).

14. For an overview of the ways clientelism undermines democracy, see Susan C. Stokes, "Is Vote Buying Undemocratic?" in Schaffer, *Elections for Sale*.

15. For further discussion of this issue, see Merilee S. Grindle, *Jobs for the Boys: Patronage and the State in Comparative Perspective* (Cambridge, MA: Harvard University Press, 2012), chap. 1.

16. See Fukuyama, *Origins of Political Order*, chap. 2.

17. On this problem, see Susan C. Stokes, "Perverse Accountability: A Formal Model of Machine Politics with Evidence from Argentina," *American Political Science Review* 99, no. 3 (2005): 315–25; and Simeon Nichter, "Vote Buying or Turnout Buying? Machine Politics and the Secret Ballot," *American Political Science Review* 102, no. 1 (2008): 19–31.

18. On this point, see Elizabeth Carlson, *Great Expectations: Explaining Ugandan Voters' Ethnic Preferences* (forthcoming); Kanchan Chandra, *Why Ethnic Parties Succeed: Patronage and Ethnic Head Counts in India* (New York: Cambridge University Press, 2004).

19. Eric Kramon's study of vote buying in Kenya shows that the areas most subject to clientelistic campaigning during elections receive higher levels of patronage goods, including targeted public goods. "Vote Buying and Accountability in Democratic Africa" (PhD diss., University of California, Los Angeles, 2013).

20. This term was used in relationship to contemporary Africa in Richard A. Joseph, *Democracy and Prebendal Politics in Nigeria: The Rise and Fall of the Second Republic* (New York: Cambridge University Press, 1987). Joseph's use of "prebendal" is broader than mine, however, because it encompasses clientelism.

21. Nicolas van de Walle, "Meet the New Boss, Same as the Old Boss? The Evolution of Political Clientelism in Africa," in Kitschelt and Wilkinson, *Patrons, Clients, and Policies*.

22. On this point, see Philip Keefer, "Clientelism, Credibility, and the Policy Choices of Young Democracies," *American Journal of Political Science* 51, no. 4 (2007): 804–21.

23. Chin-Shou Wang and Charles Kurzman, "The Logistics: How to Buy Votes," in Schaffer, *Elections for Sale.*

24. Kanchan Chandra, "Ethnicity and the Distribution of Public Goods in India" (draft paper, 2010).

25. This argument is made in Mushtaq H. Khan, "Markets, States, and Democracy: Patron-Client Networks and the Case for Democracy in Developing Countries," *Democratization* 12, no. 5 (2005): 704–24.

26. Shefter, *Political Parties and the State.* For a broad comparative overview of patronage systems, see Grindle, *Jobs for the Boys.*

6: THE BIRTHPLACE OF DEMOCRACY

1. Friedrich Schneider and Dominik H. Enste, *The Shadow Economy: An International Survey* (New York: Cambridge University Press, 2002), pp. 34–36.

2. See Jane Schneider, *Italy's "Southern Question": Orientalism in One Country* (New York: Berg, 1998); Judith Chubb, *Patronage, Power, and Poverty in Southern Italy: A Tale of Two Cities* (New York: Cambridge University Press, 1982); P. A. Allum, *Politics and Society in Post-War Naples* (Cambridge: Cambridge University Press, 1973); Sidney G. Tarrow, *Peasant Communism in Southern Italy* (New Haven: Yale University Press, 1967).

3. Diego Gambetta, *The Sicilian Mafia: The Business of Private Protection* (Cambridge, MA: Harvard University Press, 1993), pp. 75–78.

4. Edward C. Banfield, *The Moral Basis of a Backward Society* (Glencoe, IL: Free Press, 1958), pp. 85, 115–16.

5. Joseph LaPalombara, *Interest Groups in Italian Politics* (Princeton: Princeton University Press, 1964), p. 38.

6. Tarrow, *Peasant Communism,* pp. 54–55.

7. Robert D. Putnam, *Making Democracy Work: Civic Traditions in Modern Italy* (Princeton: Princeton University Press, 1993).

8. Apostolis Papakostas, "Why Is There No Clientelism in Scandinavia?" in Piattoni, *Clientelism, Interests, and Democratic Representation,* p. 46.

9. Keith R. Legg, *Politics in Modern Greece* (Stanford, CA: Stanford University Press, 1969), pp. 36–37.

10. Francis Fukuyama, *Trust: The Social Virtues and the Creation of Prosperity* (New York: Free Press, 1995), pp. 97–101.

11. Papakostas, "Why Is There No Clientelism in Scandinavia?" p. 48.

12. I am grateful to Elena Panaritis for this observation.

13. Legg, *Politics in Modern Greece,* pp. 52–56.

14. Nicos P. Mouzelis, *Politics in the Semi-Periphery: Early Parliamentarism and Late Industrialization in the Balkans and Latin America* (New York: St. Martin's Press, 1986), pp. 40–41.

15. Nicos P. Mouzelis, "Capitalism and the Development of the Greek State," in

Richard Scase, ed., *The State in Western Europe* (New York: St. Martin's Press, 1980), pp. 245–46.

16. Constantine Tsoucalas, "On the Problem of Political Clientelism in Greece in the Nineteenth Century," *Journal of the Hellenic Diaspora* 5, no. 1 (1978): 1–17.

17. Mouzelis, "Capitalism and the Development of the Greek State," p. 242.

18. Ibid., p. 244; George Th. Mavrogordatos, "From Traditional Clientelism to Machine Politics: the Impact of PASOK Populism in Greece," *South European Society and Politics* 2, no. 3 (1997): 1–26.

19. Legg, *Politics in Modern Greece*, pp. 128–29; Christos Lyrintzis, "Political Parties in Post-Junta Greece: A Case of 'Bureaucratic Clientelism'?" *West European Politics* 7, no. 2 (1984): 99–118.

20. On the interwar period, see George Th. Mavrogordatos, *Stillborn Republic: Social Coalitions and Party Strategies in Greece, 1922–1936* (Berkeley: University of California Press, 1983).

21. Lyrintzis, "Political Parties in Post-Junta Greece," p. 103; Takis S. Pappas, *Making Party Democracy in Greece* (New York: St. Martin's Press, 1999).

22. These cases and two others are discussed in Mavrogordatos, "From Traditional Clientelism to Machine Politics."

23. John Sfakianakis, "The Cost of Protecting Greece's Public Sector," *International Herald Tribune*, October 10, 2012. A report on the Greek public sector by the OECD estimates that government employment in 2008 amounted to a million employees, or 22.3 percent of the workforce. See Organization for Economic Cooperation and Development, *Greece: Review of the Central Administration* (Paris: OECD Public Governance Reviews, 2011), pp. 71–72.

24. Susan Daley, "Greek Wealth Is Everywhere but Tax Forms," *New York Times*, May 1, 2010; see also Daley, "Greece's Efforts to Limit Tax Evasion Have Little Success," *New York Times*, May 29, 2010; Schneider and Enste, *Shadow Economy*, p. 36; Friedrich Schneider and Robert Klinglmair, "Shadow Economies Around the World: What Do We Really Know?" *European Journal of Political Economy* 21 (2005): 598–642.

25. See Fukuyama, *Trust*, chap. 1.

7: ITALY AND THE LOW-TRUST EQUILIBRIUM

1. Judith Chubb, *Patronage, Power, and Property in Southern Italy: A Tale of Two Cities* (New York: Cambridge University Press, 1983), p. 1.

2. See "Naples Blasts Berlusconi as Garbage Piles Up," *Newsweek*, October 27, 2010.

3. Rachel Donadio, "Corruption Seen as Steady Drain on Italy's South," *New York Times*, October 8, 2012, p. A1.

4. Putnam, *Making Democracy Work*, pp. 67–82.

5. Putnam looked at other possible explanatory factors such as level of education, ideological polarization, voter consensus on policy issues, strike rates, and rule

by Communist parties. None of these correlated strongly with observed differences in government performance. Ibid., pp. 116–17.

6. Ibid., pp. 121–36.

7. In Poland and Hungary, the power of the monarchy was limited by constitutions and checks on the power of the king. The inability of kings to check the power of the aristocracy in return is one of the reasons why the landowning elites progressively eliminated the rights of the peasantry from the end of the fifteenth century on. The situation of southern Italy on the eve of unification thus seems more similar to these countries than to a country like Prussia with a strong centralized monarchy. See Fukuyama, *Origins of Political Order*, pp. 373–85.

8. This was argued by Paolo Mattia Doria and criticized by Benedetto Croce. See Gambetta, *Sicilian Mafia*, p. 77.

9. P. A. Allum, *Italy—Republic Without Government?* (New York: Norton, 1973), p. 9.

10. Ibid., pp. 3–4.

11. Chubb, *Patronage, Power, and Poverty*, p. 20.

12. For a history of this term, see Richard P. Saller, *Personal Patronage Under the Early Empire* (Cambridge: Cambridge University Press, 1982), pp. 8–11.

13. Luigi Graziano, "Patron-Client Relationships in Southern Italy," *European Journal of Political Research* 1, no. 1 (1973): 3–34.

14. Chubb, *Patronage, Power, and Poverty*, pp. 19–21; James Walston, *The Mafia and Clientelism: Roads to Rome in Post-War Calabria* (New York: Routledge, 1988), pp. 48–49.

15. Graziano, "Patron-Client Relationships," p. 13; Chubb, *Patronage, Power, and Poverty*, pp. 16–17. The southern landowning elite, like that in Latin America but different from the landed classes in England, tended to be rentier landlords who lived in cities (Chubb, p. 17). This meant there was no entrepreneurial landowning class of the sort that powered the revolution in commercial agriculture in England, and also that the norms of city life were set by this traditional elite rather than by an industrial bourgeoisie.

16. Graziano, "Patron-Client Relationships," pp. 8–9.

17. Gambetta, *Sicilian Mafia*, pp. 15–33, 83.

18. On the origins of the Mafia, see also Alexander Stille, *Excellent Cadavers: The Mafia and the Death of the First Italian Republic* (New York: Pantheon, 1995), pp. 14–17. The Mafia was neither the first nor the last criminal organization to fill a vacuum left by a weak state. Contemporary examples are the paramilitaries that plague Colombia, a mountainous country with dense jungles where the state has historically had tremendous difficulty exerting its authority. Wealthy Colombian landowners threatened by guerrillas from leftist groups including the Fuerzas Armadas Revolucionarios de Colombia (FARC) and the Ejército de Liberación National (ELN) began hiring paramilitaries to protect their farms and ranches. These groups evolved into autonomous organizations

with substantial firepower that began branching out into drug trafficking, extortion, and a host of other criminal activities. The drug cartels operating in twenty-first-century Mexico as well take advantage of a state that historically has been (and remains) weak in police enforcement of citizens' basic rights.

19. The classic definition is given in Carl J. Friedrich and Zbigniew K. Brzezinski, *Totalitarian Dictatorship and Autocracy*, 2nd ed. (Cambridge, MA: Harvard University Press, 1965). See also Juan J. Linz, *Totalitarian and Authoritarian Regimes* (Boulder, CO: Lynne Rienner, 2000).

20. Chubb, *Patronage, Power, and Poverty*, pp. 24–27.

21. Tarrow, *Peasant Communism in Southern Italy*, pp. 101–102.

22. Walston, *The Mafia and Clientelism*, pp. 52–56; Robert Leonardi and Douglas A. Wertman, *Italian Christian Democracy: The Politics of Dominance* (New York: St. Martin's Press, 1989); Chubb, *Patronage, Power, and Poverty*, pp. 56–64; Allum, *Politics and Society in Post-War Naples*, pp. 62–68; Graziano, "Patron-Client Relationships," pp. 24–27.

23. On Italy's White and Red subcultures, see Paul Ginsborg, *Italy and Its Discontents: Family, Civil Society, State 1980–2001* (New York: Palgrave Macmillan, 2003), pp. 102–104.

24. Tarrow, *Peasant Communism in Southern Italy*, pp. 25–26.

25. Chubb, *Patronage, Power, and Poverty*, p. 30.

26. Quoted ibid., p. 75.

27. Ginsborg, *Italy and Its Discontents*, p. 203.

28. Quoted ibid., p. 181.

29. Alexander Stille, *The Sack of Rome: How a Beautiful European Country with a Fabled History and a Storied Culture Was Taken Over by a Man Named Silvio Berlusconi* (New York: Penguin Press, 2006), pp. 120–26.

30. Ginsborg, *Italy and Its Discontents*, pp. 204–205.

31. Ibid., pp. 205–208.

32. On the histories of Falcone and Borsellino, see Stille, *Excellent Cadavers*.

33. Stille, *Sack of Rome*, pp. 189–96.

34. See Rachel Donadio, "Sicily's Fiscal Problems Threaten to Swamp Italy," *New York Times*, July 23, 2012, p. A4.

35. This point is made in Gianfranco Pasquino, "Leaders, Institutions, and Populism: Italy in a Comparative Perspective," in Gianfranco Pasquino, James L. Newell, and Paolo Mancini, eds., *The Future of the Liberal Western Order: The Case of Italy* (Washington, D.C.: Transatlantic Academy, 2013).

36. Chubb, *Patronage, Power, and Poverty*, pp. 219–32; Simona Piattoni, "'Virtuous Clientelism': The Southern Question Resolved?" in Schneider, *Italy's "Southern Question"*; Mario Caciagli, "The Long Life of Clientelism in Southern Italy," in Junichi Kawata, ed., *Comparing Political Corruption and Clientelism* (Hampshire, UK: Ashgate, 2006).

37. On the general subject of the relationship of trust and good government, see Rothstein, *The Quality of Government*, pp. 164–92.

8: PATRONAGE AND REFORM

1. For a discussion of the nature of government service in eighteenth-century England, see Henry Parris, *Constitutional Bureaucracy: The Development of British Central Administration Since the Eighteenth Century* (New York: Augustus M. Kelley, 1969), pp. 22–28.

2. Quoted ibid., pp. 53–54.

3. J. M. Bourne, *Patronage and Society in Nineteenth-Century England* (Baltimore: Edward Arnold, 1986), pp. 18–19.

4. E. N. Gladden, *Civil Services of the United Kingdom, 1855–1970* (London: Frank Cass, 1967), p. 2.

5. Bourne, *Patronage and Society*, p. 59.

6. Richard A. Chapman, *The Higher Civil Service in Britain* (London: Constable, 1970), pp. 12–13.

7. Ibid., p. 15.

8. Bourne, *Patronage and Society*, p. 32.

9. Edward Hughes, "Sir Charles Trevelyan and Civil Service Reform, 1853–5," *English Historical Review* 64, no. 250 (1949): 53–88.

10. John Greenaway, "Celebrating Northcote/Trevelyan: Dispelling the Myths," *Public Policy and Administration* 19, no. 1 (2004): 1–14.

11. Chapman, *Higher Civil Service*, p. 20; Gladden, *Civil Services of the United Kingdom*, pp. 19–21.

12. See S. E. Finer, "The Transmission of Benthamite Ideas 1820–50," and Alan Ryan, "Utilitarianism and Bureaucracy: The Views of J. S. Mill," in Gillian Sutherland, ed., *Studies in the Growth of Nineteenth-Century Government* (Totowa, NJ: Rowman and Littlefield, 1972).

13. Shefter, *Political Parties and the State*, p. 47.

14. Albert O. Hirschman, *The Passions and the Interests: Political Arguments for Capitalism Before Its Triumph* (Princeton: Princeton University Press, 1977).

15. Chapman, *Higher Civil Service*, pp. 18–19.

16. Richard A. Chapman, *The Civil Service Commission 1855–1991: A Bureau Biography* (New York: Routledge, 2004), p. 12.

17. Jennifer Hart, "The Genesis of the Northcote-Trevelyan Report," in Sutherland, *Studies in the Growth of Nineteenth-Century Government*.

18. Chapman, *Civil Service Commission*, pp. 17–24.

19. Chapman, *Higher Civil Service*, pp. 29–30.

20. Leon Epstein, *Political Parties in Western Democracies* (New York: Praeger, 1969), p. 24.

21. Morton Keller, *America's Three Regimes: A New Political History* (New York: Oxford University Press, 2007), pp. 136–37.

22. Shefter, *Political Parties and the State*, pp. 50–51.

23. Henry Pelling, *The Origins of the Labour Party, 1880–1900* (Oxford: Clarendon Press, 1965), chap. 8.

24. Gladden, *Civil Services of the United Kingdom*, pp. 18–40.

25. For an account of reform in the 1990s, see Michael Barber, *Instruction to De-liver: Fighting to Transform Britain's Public Services* (London: Methuen, 2008).

9: THE UNITED STATES INVENTS CLIENTELISM

1. Huntington, *Political Order in Changing Societies*, pp. 93–139.
2. Before Huntington, this argument was made in Louis Hartz, *The Founding of New Societies* (New York: Harcourt, 1964).
3. Huntington, *Political Order in Changing Societies*, p. 98; see also Huntington, "Political Modernization: America vs. Europe," *World Politics* 18 (1966): 378–414.
4. Louis Hartz, *The Liberal Tradition in America* (New York: Harcourt, 1955).
5. See Seymour Martin Lipset, *The First New Nation* (New York: Basic Books, 1963), and Lipset, *American Exceptionalism: A Double-Edged Sword* (New York: Norton, 1996).
6. Lipset, *American Exceptionalism*, pp. 113–16.
7. The other four components were individualism, equality (understood as equal-ity of opportunity and not result), populism, and laissez-faire.
8. Frederick C. Mosher, *Democracy and the Public Service*, 2nd ed. (New York: Oxford University Press, 1982), pp. 58–64.
9. Patricia W. Ingraham, *The Foundation of Merit: Public Service in American Democracy* (Baltimore: Johns Hopkins University Press, 1995), pp. 17–18.
10. Mosher, *Democracy and the Public Service*, p. 63.
11. Ibid., p. 62.
12. Stephen Skowronek, *Building a New American State: The Expansion of National Administrative Capacities, 1877–1920* (New York: Cambridge University Press, 1982), pp. 31–32.
13. Paul P. Van Riper, *History of the United States Civil Service* (Evanston, IL: Row, Peterson, 1958), p. 24.
14. Michael C. LeMay, ed., *Transforming America: Perspectives on U.S. Immigration* (Santa Barbara, CA: Praeger, 2013), chap. 3, table 3.11.
15. Mosher, *Democracy and the Public Service*, p. 61.
16. See Susan E. Scarrow, "The Nineteenth-Century Origins of Modern Political Parties: The Unwanted Emergence of Party-Based Politics," in Richard S. Katz and William J. Crotty, eds., *Handbook of Party Politics* (Thousand Oaks, CA: Sage, 2006).
17. William J. Crotty, "Party Origins and Evolution in the United States," ibid., p. 27; Epstein, *Political Parties in Western Democracies*, pp. 20–21.
18. For overviews of the functions of political parties, see Gabriel A. Almond et al., *Comparative Politics: A Theoretical Framework*, 5th ed. (New York: Pearson Longman, 2004), chap. 5; and Richard Gunther and Larry Diamond, "Types and Functions of Political Parties," in Larry Diamond and Richard Gunther,

eds., *Political Parties and Democracy* (Baltimore: Johns Hopkins University Press, 2001).

19. For this reason, the development of political parties is central to Huntington's theory of political development. See *Political Order in Changing Societies*, pp. 397–461.

20. On Jackson's background, see Harry L. Watson, "Old Hickory's Democracy," *Wilson Quarterly* 9, no. 4 (1985): 100–33.

21. Walter Russell Mead, "The Jacksonian Tradition and American Foreign Policy," *National Interest* 58 (1999): 5–29; Mead, *Special Providence: American Foreign Policy and How It Changed the World* (New York: Knopf, 2001); Mead, "The Tea Party and American Foreign Policy," *Foreign Affairs* 90, no. 2 (2011).

22. For an overview, see David Hackett Fischer, *Albion's Seed: Four British Folkways in America* (New York: Oxford University Press, 1991), pp. 605–782.

23. Ibid., p. 615.

24. Ibid., pp. 621–32.

25. Jack H. Knott and Gary J. Miller, *Reforming Bureaucracy: The Politics of Institutional Choice* (Englewood Cliffs, NJ: Prentice-Hall, 1987), p. 16.

26. Quoted in Ingraham, *Foundation of Merit*, p. 20.

27. Kenneth J. Meier, "Ode to Patronage: A Critical Analysis of Two Recent Supreme Court Decisions," *Public Administration Review* 41, no. 5 (1981): 558–63.

28. David A. Schultz and Robert Maranto, *The Politics of Civil Service Reform* (New York: Peter Lang, 1998), p. 38. Jackson actually did not engage in a wholesale purge of earlier officeholders; the system of rotation would evolve gradually over the coming decades. Matthew A. Crenson, *The Federal Machine: Beginning of Bureaucracy in Jacksonian America* (Baltimore: Johns Hopkins University Press, 1975), p. 55.

29. The politicization of the executive branch did not occur at once; Jackson himself made only a limited number of appointments, and the number of elite officeholders fell only 7 percent from Jefferson's presidency. Mosher, *Democracy and the Public Service*, p. 63; Erik M. Eriksson, "The Federal Civil Service Under President Jackson," *Mississippi Valley Historical Review* 13, no. 4 (1927): 517–40.

30. Skowronek, *Building a New American State*, p. 24.

31. Ibid., p. 25.

32. Skowronek points to the 1857 Dred Scott case as an example of the courts making substantive policy when Congress failed to do so (ibid., p. 29). One could point to *Roe v. Wade* or the AT&T divestiture decisions in the twentieth century as instances of courts taking on legislative and administrative functions, respectively.

33. See Michael Mann, "The Autonomous Power of the State: Its Origins, Mechanisms, and Results," *European Journal of Sociology* 25, no. 2 (1984): 185–213.

34. Schultz and Maranto, *Politics of Civil Service Reform*, p. 43; Ingraham, *Foundation of Merit*, p. 21.

35. Harry J. Carman and Reinhard H. Luthin, *Lincoln and the Patronage* (New York: Columbia University Press, 1943), p. 300.

36. T. Harry Williams, *Lincoln and His Generals* (New York: Vintage Books, 2011), pp. 10–11.

37. Margaret Susan Thompson, *The "Spider Web": Congress and Lobbying in the Age of Grant* (Ithaca, NY: Cornell University Press, 1985), p. 215.

38. Clayton R. Newell and Charles R. Shrader, *Of Duty Well and Faithfully Done: A History of the Regular Army in the Civil War* (Lincoln: University of Nebraska Press, 2011), p. 3.

39. Keller, *America's Three Regimes*, p. 137.

40. Scott C. James, "Patronage Regimes and American Party Development from 'The Age of Jackson' to the Progressive Era," *British Journal of Political Science* 36, no. 1 (2006): 39–60.

41. Quoted in Keller, *America's Three Regimes*, p. 136.

42. On why political machines were so durable in the East and Midwest but never got established in the West, see Martin Shefter, "Regional Receptivity to Reform: The Legacy of the Progressive Era," *Political Science Quarterly* 98, no. 3 (1983): 459–83.

43. Edward C. Banfield and James Q. Wilson, *City Politics* (Cambridge, MA: Harvard University Press, 1963), chap. 9.

44. For an overview of the literature on municipal machine politics in the United States, see David R. Colburn and George E. Pozzetta, "Bosses and Machines: Changing Interpretations in American History," *The History Teacher* 9, no. 3 (1976): 445–63.

45. James Duane Bolin, *Bossism and Reform in a Southern City: Lexington, Kentucky, 1880–1940* (Lexington: University Press of Kentucky, 2000), pp. 35–47.

46. See for example Roger Biles, *Big City Boss in Depression and War: Mayor Edward J. Kelly of Chicago* (DeKalb: Northern Illinois University Press, 1984); Richard J. Connors, *A Cycle of Power: The Career of Jersey City Mayor Frank Hague* (Metuchen, NJ: Scarecrow Press, 1971); Rudolph H. Hartmann, *The Kansas City Investigation: Pendergast's Downfall, 1938–1939* (Columbia: University of Missouri Press, 1999); John R. Schmidt, *"The Mayor Who Cleaned Up Chicago": A Political Biography of William E. Dever* (DeKalb: Northern Illinois University Press, 1989); Frederick Shaw, *The History of the New York State Legislature* (New York: Columbia University Press, 1954); Joel A. Tarr, *A Study in Boss Politics: William Lorimer of Chicago* (Urbana: University of Illinois Press, 1971).

47. Knott and Miller, *Reforming Bureaucracy*, p. 18.

48. See Richard Oestreicher, "Urban Working-Class Political Behavior and Theories of American Electoral Politics, 1870–1940," *Journal of American History* 74, no. 4 (1988): 1257–86.

49. Thompson, *The "Spider Web,"* p. 35.

50. Ibid., pp. 215–18.

10: THE END OF THE SPOILS SYSTEM

1. For an overview, see Thompson, *The "Spider Web,"* chap. 1.
2. Ingraham, *Foundation of Merit*, pp. 23–24; Schultz and Maranto, *Politics of Civil Service Reform*, pp. 60–61.
3. For an account of Garfield's shooting and the poor medical attention he received, see Candice Millard, *Destiny of the Republic: A Tale of Madness, Medicine and the Murder of a President* (New York: Doubleday, 2011).
4. Sean M. Theriault, "Patronage, the Pendleton Act, and the Power of the People," *Journal of Politics* 65, no. 1 (2003): 50–68; Ingraham, *Foundation of Merit*, pp. 26–27.
5. Paul P. Van Riper, "The American Administrative State: Wilson and the Founders—An Unorthodox View," *Public Administration Review* 43, no. 6 (1983): 477–90; Skowronek, *Building a New American State*, pp. 47–48.
6. Woodrow Wilson, "The Study of Administration," *Political Science Quarterly* 2, no. 2 (1887): 197–222. Van Riper, "American Administrative State," argues that Eaton had much more influence than Wilson on the climate of opinion in this period, and that this article's fame arose only ex post. This article was preceded in 1885 by "Notes on Administration," which made the case for a division of responsibilities between politics and administration.
7. The politics-administration distinction is made in Max Weber's 1919 essay "Politics as a Vocation," in *From Max Weber: Essays in Sociology* (New York: Oxford University Press, 1946).
8. Wilson, "Study of Administration," p. 206.
9. Van Riper, "American Administrative State"; H. Eliot Kaplan, "Accomplishments of the Civil Service Reform Movement," *Annals of the American Academy of Political and Social Science* 189 (1937): 142–47; Skowronek, *Building a New American State*, p. 64.
10. Ingraham, *Foundation of Merit*, pp. 27–28.
11. Ibid., pp. 32–33; Van Riper, "American Administrative State," p. 483.
12. Ari Hoogenboom, "The Pendleton Act and the Civil Service," *American Historical Review* 64, no. 2 (1959): 301–18; Knott and Miller, *Reforming Bureaucracy*, p. 44.
13. Hoogenboom, "Pendleton Act," pp. 305–306; Ingraham, *Foundation of Merit*, pp. 33–34; Skowronek, *Building a New American State*, pp. 68, 72.
14. Tarr, *A Study in Boss Politics*, pp. 72–73.
15. Knott and Miller, *Reforming Bureaucracy*, pp. 44–47.
16. Skowronek, *Building a New American State*, p. 51.
17. Ibid., pp. 61–62; Knott and Miller, *Reforming Bureaucracy*, pp. 36–37.
18. Knott and Miller, *Reforming Bureaucracy*, pp. 35–36.
19. Ibid., pp. 37–38; Jean Bethke Elshtain, *Jane Addams and the Dream of American Democracy: A Life* (New York: Basic Books, 2002).
20. Among Goodnow's books are *Comparative Administrative Law: An Analysis of*

the Administrative Systems, National and Local, of the United States, England, France and Germany, 2 vols. (New York: G. P. Putnam's Sons, 1893); and *Politics and Administration: A Study in Government* (New York: Macmillan, 1900).

21. Skowronek, *Building a New American State*, p. 53; Knott and Miller, *Reforming Bureaucracy*, pp. 39–40.

22. Frederick Winslow Taylor, *The Principles of Scientific Management* (New York: Harper, 1911). See the discussion of Taylorism in Fukuyama, *Trust*, pp. 225–27.

23. Edmund Morris, *The Rise of Theodore Roosevelt* (New York: Modern Library, 2001), pp. 404–405.

24. Skowronek, *Building a New American State*, p. 53.

25. Robert H. Wiebe, *The Search for Order: 1877–1920* (New York: Hill and Wang, 1967), p. 165.

26. For an overview of the social backgrounds of the reformers, see Blaine A. Brownell, "Interpretations of Twentieth-Century Urban Progressive Reform," in David R. Colburn and George E. Pozzetta, eds., *Reform and Reformers in the Progressive Era* (Westport, CT: Greenwood Press, 1983); and Michael McGerr, *A Fierce Discontent: The Rise and Fall of the Progressive Movement in America, 1870–1920* (New York: Free Press, 2003).

27. Skowronek, *Building a New American State*, p. 167.

28. E. E. Schattschneider, *The Semisovereign People: A Realist's View of Democracy in America* (New York: Holt, 1960), pp. 78–85.

29. Skowronek, *Building a New American State*, pp. 179–80; Keller, *America's Three Regimes*, pp. 182–83; Van Riper, *History of the United States Civil Service*, pp. 205–207.

30. Skowronek, *Building a New American State*, pp. 197–200.

31. Ingraham, *Foundation of Merit*, pp. 42–47.

32. For example, efforts to reduce the head count in overstaffed African agencies simply led to the same individuals finding employment in other parts of the government. Teacher absenteeism in India is often the result of the fact that teaching jobs are given out as political favors; the politician doesn't care that much whether the teacher shows up for work, unless somehow the political incentives facing him or her are changed. See Nicolas van de Walle, *African Economies and the Politics of Permanent Crisis, 1979–1999* (New York: Cambridge University Press, 2001), pp. 101–109.

33. Skowronek, *Building a New American State*, pp. 180–82, 191–94.

11: RAILROADS, FORESTS, AND AMERICAN STATE BUILDING

1. Richard D. Stone, *The Interstate Commerce Commission and the Railroad Industry: A History of Regulatory Policy* (New York: Praeger, 1991), p. 2.

2. Skowronek, *Building a New American State*, p. 123.

3. Gabriel Kolko, *Railroads and Regulation, 1877–1916* (Princeton: Princeton University Press, 1965), p. 7.

4. Skowronek, *Building a New American State*, pp. 124–25; Kolko, *Railroads and Regulation*, pp. 7–20; Ari Hoogenboom and Olive Hoogenboom, *A History of the ICC: From Panacea to Palliative* (New York: Norton, 1976), pp. 1–6.

5. Robin A. Prager, "Using Stock Price Data to Measure the Effects of Regulation: The Interstate Commerce Act and the Railroad Industry," *RAND Journal of Economics* 20, no. 2 (1989).

6. Kaiser Family Foundation, *Health Care Costs: A Primer. Key Information on Health Care Costs and Their Impact* (Menlo Park, CA: Kaiser Family Foundation, 2012).

7. *Munn* concerned the regulation of grain elevators but was soon extended to include railroads.

8. Alfred Marshall's *Principles of Economics*, on which much of modern neoclassical economics is based, was only published in 1890.

9. Skowronek, *Building a New American State*, pp. 135–37.

10. For example, pooling traffic and earnings was made illegal, but collective rate making was neither legalized nor outlawed. See Hoogenboom and Hoogenboom, *History of the ICC*, p. 18.

11. Keller, *America's Three Regimes*, pp. 158–62.

12. Skowronek, *Building a New American State*, p. 151.

13. Stone, *Interstate Commerce Commission*, pp. 10–15.

14. Kolko, *Railroads and Regulation*, pp. 1–6.

15. Stone, *Interstate Commerce Commission*, pp. 17–22; Skowronek, *Building a New American State*, pp. 248–83.

16. Skowronek, *Building a New American State*, p. 283.

17. This rate-setting decision was eventually overturned by the Supreme Court. Stone, *Interstate Commerce Commission*, p. 51.

18. Ibid., p. 113.

19. Daniel P. Carpenter, *The Forging of Bureaucratic Autonomy: Reputations, Networks, and Policy Innovation in Executive Agencies, 1862–1928* (Princeton: Princeton University Press, 2001), pp. 191–98.

20. Herbert Kaufman, *The Forest Ranger: A Study in Administrative Behavior* (Baltimore: Johns Hopkins University Press, 1960), pp. 26–29; www.foresthistory.org/ASPNET/Places/National%20Forests%20of%20the%20U.S.pdf.

21. On Pinchot's family background and early life, see Char Miller, *Gifford Pinchot and the Making of Modern Environmentalism* (Washington, D.C.: Island Press/Shearwater Books, 2001), pp. 15–54.

22. Harold K. Steen, *The U.S. Forest Service: A History* (Seattle: University of Washington Press, 1976), p. 49.

23. Brian Balogh, "Scientific Forestry and the Roots of the Modern American State: Gifford Pinchot's Path to Progressive Reform," *Environmental History* 7, no. 2 (2002): 198–225.

24. Carpenter, *Forging of Bureaucratic Autonomy*, pp. 205–207; Kaufman, *Forest Ranger*, pp. 26–27; Steen, *U. S. Forest Service*, pp. 47–48.

25. Balogh, "Scientific Forestry," p. 199; Carpenter, *Forging a Bureaucratic Autonomy*, p. 280; Steen, *U.S. Forest Service*, p. 71.
26. Carpenter, *Forging a Bureaucratic Autonomy*, pp. 212–16.
27. See Miller, *Gifford Pinchot*, pp. 149–50.
28. Steen, *U.S. Forest Service*, pp. 71–78.
29. Carpenter, *Forging a Bureaucratic Autonomy*, pp. 1, 280–82.
30. Ibid., p. 282.
31. Gifford Pinchot, *Breaking New Ground* (Washington, D.C.: Island Press, 1947), p. 392.
32. Ibid., pp. 395–403; Carpenter, *Forging a Bureaucratic Autonomy*, pp. 285–86; Skowronek, *Building a New American State*, pp. 190–91.
33. Kaufman, *Forest Ranger*, pp. 28–29.

12: NATION BUILDING

1. On the idea of social cooperation arising out of competitive pressures, see Fukuyama, *Origins of Political Order*, chap. 2.
2. This is the definition given in Ernest Gellner, *Nations and Nationalism*, 2nd ed. (Malden, MA: Blackwell, 2006), p. 1.
3. See Charles Taylor, ed., *Multiculturalism: Examining the Politics of Recognition* (Princeton: Princeton University Press, 1994).
4. Benedict Anderson, *Imagined Communities: Reflections on the Origins and Spread of Nationalism*, rev. ed. (New York: Verso, 1991), pp. 37–46. Similar points are made in Elizabeth L. Eisenstein, *The Printing Revolution in Early Modern Europe*, 2nd ed. (New York: Cambridge University Press, 2005).
5. Ernest Gellner, "Nationalism and the Two Forms of Cohesion in Complex Societies," in *Culture, Identity, and Politics* (New York: Cambridge University Press, 1987), pp. 15–16.
6. See Gellner, *Nations and Nationalism*, pp. 38–42.
7. Eugen Weber, *Peasants into Frenchmen: The Modernization of Rural France, 1870–1914* (Stanford, CA: Stanford University Press, 1976), pp. 67, 84, 86.
8. See Émile Durkheim, *Suicide* (Glencoe, IL: Free Press, 1951).
9. Liah Greenfeld, *Nationalism: Five Roads to Modernity* (Cambridge, MA: Harvard University Press, 1992), p. 14.
10. The general point about the current constructivist consensus is made by Keith Darden, *Resisting Occupation: Mass Schooling and the Creation of Durable National Loyalties* (New York: Cambridge University Press, 2013). For different types of constructivist arguments, see Rogers Brubaker, *Nationalism Reframed: Nationhood and the National Question in the New Europe* (New York: Cambridge University Press, 1996), and *Ethnicity without Groups* (Cambridge, MA: Harvard University Press, 2004); David D. Laitin, *Nations, States, and Violence* (New York: Oxford University Press, 2007).

11. Ernest Renan, *Qu'est-ce qu'une nation? What Is a Nation?* (Toronto: Tapir Press, 1996), p. 19.
12. On this point, see Mansfield, *Machiavelli's Virtue*, pp. 64–66, 262.

13: GOOD GOVERNMENT, BAD GOVERNMENT

1. The term "limited access" comes from North, Wallis, and Weingast, *Violence and Social Orders*. This book's distinction between limited-access and open-access orders is a very useful way of thinking about the transition between patrimonial and modern states. It does not, however, provide a dynamic theory of how the transition from one order to the other comes about. The "doorstep conditions" it lists for making the transition like rule of law for elites or civilian control over the military simply beg the question of how those conditions are themselves met, or why those and not other seemingly important conditions are critical to the transition.
2. In his study of the growth of state sectors in Eastern Europe after the fall of communism, Conor O'Dwyer adds another factor to the Shefter framework: the nature of party competition. When competition is robust, parties monitor one another and prevent the expansion of patronage appointments; when parties are fragmented and weak, patronage tends to expand. This explains why the Polish and Slovak states expanded so quickly, whereas the Czech one did not. See Conor O'Dwyer, *Runaway State-Building: Patronage Politics and Democratic Development* (Baltimore: Johns Hopkins University Press, 2006).
3. Alexander Gerschenkron, *Economic Backwardness in Historical Perspective* (Cambridge, MA: Harvard University Press, 1962).
4. This point is made in Khan, "Markets, States, and Democracy."
5. Gorski, *The Disciplinary Revolution*, pp. 39–77.
6. For an account of state building in this region, see Dan Slater, *Ordering Power: Contentious Politics and Authoritarian Leviathans in Southeast Asia* (New York: Cambridge University Press, 2010), pp. 135–63.
7. Edward N. Luttwak, "Give War a Chance," *Foreign Affairs* 78, no. 4 (1999): 36–44.
8. Huntington, *Political Order in Changing Societies*, pp. 315–24.
9. Fareed Zakaria, *The Future of Freedom: Illiberal Democracy at Home and Abroad* (New York: Norton, 2003).
10. See Thomas Carothers, "The 'Sequencing' Fallacy," *Journal of Democracy* 18, no. 1 (2007): 13–27; Robert Kagan, "The Ungreat Washed: Why Democracy Must Remain America's Goal Abroad," *New Republic*, July 7 and 14, 2003, 27–37; Francis Fukuyama, "Is There a Proper Sequence in Democratic Transitions?" *Current History* 110, no. 739 (2011): 308–10.

14: NIGERIA

1. Peter Cunliffe-Jones, *My Nigeria: Five Decades of Independence* (New York: Palgrave Macmillan, 2010), pp. 148–49.
2. Peter Lewis, *Growing Apart: Oil, Politics, and Economic Change in Indonesia and Nigeria* (Ann Arbor: University of Michigan Press, 2007).
3. Tom Forrest, *Politics and Economic Development in Nigeria* (Boulder, CO: Westview Press, 1993), pp. 133–36.
4. Lewis, *Growing Apart*, pp. 184–88.
5. Cunliffe-Jones, *My Nigeria*, p. 129. It is very hard to get accurate statistics on oil exports, given the overall nontransparency of this sector in Nigeria.
6. www.forbes.com/billionaires/#tab:overall_page:3.
7. Cunliffe-Jones, *My Nigeria*, pp. 131–32.
8. World Bank Worldwide Governance Indicators 2010; Transparency International Corruption Perceptions Index 2011.
9. Toyin Falola and Matthew M. Heaton, *A History of Nigeria* (New York: Cambridge University Press, 2008), p. 187.
10. Daniel Jordan Smith, *A Culture of Corruption: Everyday Deception and Popular Discontent in Nigeria* (Princeton: Princeton University Press, 2007), pp. 19–24, 33–39.
11. John Campbell, *Nigeria: Dancing on the Brink* (Lanham, MD: Rowman and Littlefield, 2011), pp. 63–78.
12. See Eghosa E. Osaghae, *Crippled Giant: Nigeria Since Independence* (Bloomington: Indiana University Press, 1998), pp. 54–69.
13. Campbell, *Nigeria*, pp. 97–113. The 2011 election that continued the term of Goodluck Jonathan was evidently conducted in a fairer manner. Peter Lewis, "Nigeria Votes: More Openness, More Conflict," *Journal of Democracy* 22, no. 4 (2011): 59–74.
14. Cunliffe-Jones, *My Nigeria*, pp. 179–94, poses the perfectly reasonable question of why there isn't more popular anger and mobilization in Nigeria.
15. Joseph, *Democracy and Prebendal Politics in Nigeria*.
16. See Daniel N. Posner, *Institutions and Ethnic Politics in Africa* (New York: Cambridge University Press, 2005).

15: GEOGRAPHY

1. For an overview of social Darwinism and the role of biology in understandings of human behavior, see Fukuyama, *Origins of Political Order*, chap. 2.
2. For an overview of recent research linking geography to economic growth, see World Bank, *World Development Report 2009: Reshaping Economic Geography* (Washington, D.C.: World Bank, 2008).
3. Jeffrey Sachs, "Tropical Underdevelopment" (Cambridge, MA: National Bu-

reau of Economic Research Working Paper No. 8119, 2001); John L. Gallup and Jeffrey D. Sachs, "The Economic Burden of Malaria," *American Journal of Tropical Medicine and Hygiene* 64, no. 1–2 (2001): 85–96.

4. Jared Diamond, *Guns, Germs, and Steel: The Fates of Human Societies* (New York: Norton, 1997).

5. See for example North and Thomas, *The Rise of the Western World*.

6. Stanley L. Engerman and Kenneth L. Sokoloff, "Factor Endowments, Institutions, and Differential Paths of Growth Among New World Economies: A View from Economic Historians of the United States," in Stephen Haber, ed., *How Latin America Fell Behind: Essays on the Economic Histories of Brazil and Mexico, 1800–1914* (Stanford, CA: Stanford University Press, 1997); Stanley L. Engerman and Kenneth L. Sokoloff, "Factor Endowments, Inequality, and Paths of Development Among New World Economies," *Economia* 3, no. 1 (2002): 41–101. Stephen Haber makes a similar case based on average rainfall. He argues that regions receiving moderate amounts of rainfall are more likely to produce democratic governments because such climates tend to encourage smallholder agriculture and a more equitable distribution of land, and hence more distributed political power. Neither desert areas with limited rainfall nor tropical regions with heavy rainfall are as likely to support this type of agriculture. Stephen Haber, "Rainfall and Democracy: Climate, Technology, and the Evolution of Economic and Political Institutions" (unpublished paper, August 24, 2012).

7. Daron Acemoglu, Simon Johnson, and James A. Robinson, "The Colonial Origins of Comparative Development: An Empirical Investigation," *American Economic Review* 91, no. 5 (2001): 1369–1401. These findings have been incorporated into Acemoglu and Robinson, *Why Nations Fail*.

8. Daron Acemoglu, Simon Johnson, and James A. Robinson, "Reversal of Fortune: Geography and Institutions in the Making of the Modern World Income Distribution," *Quarterly Journal of Economics* 107 (2002): 1231–94; David Eltis, Frank D. Lewis, and Kenneth L. Sokoloff, eds., *Slavery in the Development of the Americas* (New York: Cambridge University Press, 2004), pp. 1–27; Eric E. Williams, *Capitalism and Slavery* (Chapel Hill: University of North Carolina Press, 1994), pp. 51–84.

9. This and other theories are discussed in Fukuyama, *Origins of Political Order*, chap. 5; Robert L. Carneiro, "A Theory of the Origin of the State," *Science* 159 (1970): 733–38; Ian Morris, *Why the West Rules—For Now* (New York: Farrar, Straus and Giroux, 2010).

10. On the inability of states in Southeast Asia to subdue their hinterlands, see James C. Scott, *The Art of Not Being Governed: An Anarchist History of Upland Southeast Asia* (New Haven: Yale University Press, 2009).

11. Jack Goody, *Technology, Tradition, and the State in Africa* (Oxford: Oxford University Press, 1971); Jeffrey Herbst, *States and Power in Africa* (Princeton: Princeton University Press, 2000), pp. 39–41.

16: SILVER, GOLD, AND SUGAR

1. J. H. Elliott, *Empires of the Atlantic World: Britain and Spain in America, 1492–1830* (New Haven: Yale University Press, 2006), p. 23; James Mahoney, *Colonialism and Postcolonial Development* (New York: Cambridge University Press, 2000), pp. 69–70; D. K. Fieldhouse, *The Colonial Empires: A Comparative Survey from the Eighteenth Century,* 2nd ed. (London: Macmillan, 1982), pp. 22–23.

2. Elliott, *Empires of the Atlantic World,* pp. 41–42; Mahoney, *Colonialism and Postcolonial Development,* p. 63.

3. Fieldhouse, *Colonial Empires,* p. 14.

4. Philip D. Curtin, *The Rise and Fall of the Plantation Complex: Essays in Atlantic History,* 2nd ed. (New York: Cambridge University Press, 1998), pp. 16–25.

5. Ibid., pp. 42–45; Thomas E. Skidmore and Peter H. Smith, *Modern Latin America,* 6th ed. (New York: Oxford University Press, 2004), pp. 22–26.

6. Gavin Wright, *Slavery and American Economic Development* (Baton Rouge: Louisiana State University Press, 2006), p. 14. Philip Curtin notes that the sugar island of Barbados had a larger population than Massachusetts or Virginia in the 1680s, and was four times more densely settled than England (*Rise and Fall of the Plantation Complex,* p. 83).

7. Wright, *Slavery and American Economic Development,* p. 16.

8. The view that slavery was inefficient is made by Ulrich B. Phillips, *American Negro Slavery* (Baton Rouge: Louisiana State University Press, 1966). The arguments for the economic viability of slavery are in Alfred H. Conrad and John R. Meyer, "The Economics of Slavery in the Ante Bellum South: Comment," *American Economic Review* 66, no. 2 (1979): 95–130; Robert W. Fogel and Stanley Engerman, *Time on the Cross: The Economics of American Negro Slavery* (Boston: Little, Brown, 1974); Robert W. Fogel and Stanley L. Engerman, "Explaining the Relative Efficiency of Slave Agriculture in the Antebellum South," *American Economic Review* 67, no. 3 (1977): 275–96.

9. William H. Prescott, *History of the Conquest of Peru* (Philadelphia: J. B. Lippincott, 1902), and Prescott, *History of the Conquest of Mexico* (Philadelphia: J. B. Lippincott, 1904); Hugh Thomas, *The Conquest of Mexico* (London: Hutchinson, 1993); Diamond, *Guns, Germs, and Steel.*

10. Diamond, *Guns, Germs, and Steel,* pp. 67–81.

11. Ferrel Heady, *Public Administration: A Comparative Perspective,* 6th ed. (New York: Marcel Dekker, 2001), pp. 163–64; Jean-Claude Garcia-Zamor, "Administrative Practices of the Aztecs, Incas, and Mayas: Lessons for Modern Development Administration," *International Journal of Public Administration* 21, no. 1 (1998): 145–71. One archaeologist suggests that early Spanish observers interpreted the impressive network of roads linking Inca land as signs of a large military-bureaucratic establishment, but that their use was much more religious and ceremonial. It is not clear what degree of bureaucracy existed in this empire. See Craig Morris, "The Infrastructure of Inka Control in the Peruvian Central High-

lands," in George A. Collier, Renato I. Rosaldo, and John D. Wirth, eds., *The Inca and Aztec States, 1400–1800: Anthropology and History* (New York: Academic Press, 1982).

12. On the Mauryas and the Indian-Chinese comparison, see Fukuyama, *Origins of Political Order*, pp. 163–88.

13. Mahoney, *Colonialism and Postcolonial Development*, pp. 60, 68; Diamond, *Guns, Germs, and Steel*, pp. 210–14.

14. For an account of these developments, see Fukuyama, *Origins of Political Order*, chap. 8.

15. Fieldhouse, *Colonial Empires*, p. 16; Curtin, *Rise and Fall of the Plantation Complex*, pp. 62–63.

16. Elliott, *Empires of the Atlantic World*, pp. 59–60.

17. Mahoney, *Colonialism and Postcolonial Development*, pp. 44–47; Skidmore and Smith, *Modern Latin America*, pp. 26–27.

18. Mahoney, *Colonialism and Postcolonial Development*, pp. 46–49; Skidmore and Smith, *Modern Latin America*, pp. 27–28.

19. For an overview of this process, see Francis Fukuyama, ed., *Falling Behind: Explaining the Development Gap Between Latin America and the United States* (New York: Oxford University Press, 2008), chap. 10.

20. Mahoney, *Colonialism and Postcolonial Development*, pp. 143–46.

21. Enrique Cárdenas, "A Macroeconomic Interpretation of Nineteenth-Century Mexico," in Haber, *How Latin America Fell Behind*, pp. 66–74; John H. Coatsworth, "Obstacles to Economic Growth in Nineteenth-Century Mexico," *American Historical Review* 83 (1978): 80–100.

22. Jeffrey Bortz and Stephen Haber, "The New Institutional Economics and Latin American Economic History," and Noel Maurer and Stephen Haber, "Institutional Change and Economic Growth: Banks, Financial Markets, and Mexican Industrialization, 1878–1913," in Jeffrey Bortz and Stephen Haber, eds. *The Mexican Economy, 1870–1930: Essays on the Economic History of Institutions, Revolution, and Growth* (Stanford, CA: Stanford University Press, 2002).

17: DOGS THAT DIDN'T BARK

1. Miguel Angel Centeno, *Blood and Debt: War and the Nation-State in Latin America* (University Park: Pennsylvania State University Press, 2002), pp. 35–47. A similar point on the relative absence of war and state building in Latin America is made by Georg Sørensen, "War and State-Making: Why Doesn't It Work in the Third World?" *Security Dialogue* 32, no. 3 (2001): 341–54; and Cameron G. Thies, "War, Rivalry, and State Building in Latin America," *American Journal of Political Science* 49, no. 3 (2005): 451–65.

2. Skidmore and Smith, *Modern Latin America*, pp, 28–34; David Bushnell and Neill Macaulay, *The Emergence of Latin America in the Nineteenth Century*, 2nd ed. (New York: Oxford University Press, 1994), pp. 14–20.

3. Bushnell and Macaulay, *Emergence of Latin America*, pp. 22–26; Skidmore and Smith, *Modern Latin America*, pp. 36–40.

4. Centeno, *Blood and Debt*, p. 56.

5. Ibid., pp. 52–81.

6. On how this process played out in China and Europe, see Fukuyama, *Origins of Political Order*, pp. 110–27, 321–35.

7. Ibid., p. 361.

8. Marcus Kurtz documents this using three measures of state effectiveness: tax extraction rates, percentage of children enrolled in secondary education, and miles of railways built relative to land area. Kurtz, *Latin American State Building in Comparative Perspective* (New York: Cambridge University Press, 2013), pp. 10–17.

9. Kurtz shows the limits of existing state-building theories that focus on war and resource extraction. Chile, Bolivia, and Peru are resource-dependent countries that fought wars with one another in the nineteenth century, yet only Chile ended up with a relatively strong state (ibid., pp. 48–54).

10. Barbara Geddes, *Politician's Dilemma: Building State Capacity in Latin America* (Berkeley: University of California Press, 1994), pp. 24–42.

11. See the Organization for Economic Cooperation and Development, *OECD Integrity Review of Brazil: Managing Risks for a Cleaner Public Sector* (Paris: OECD, 2012).

18: THE CLEAN SLATE

1. Figures are in constant 2005 parity purchasing power terms. World Bank Data-Bank, http://databank.worldbank.org/ddp/home.do?Step=3&id=4.

2. For an overview of the Costa Rican economy since 1948, see Helen L. Jacobstein, *The Process of Economic Development in Costa Rica, 1948–1970: Some Political Factors* (New York: Garland Publishing, 1987).

3. Lawrence E. Harrison, *Underdevelopment Is a State of Mind: The Latin American Case* (Lanham, MD: Center for International Affairs, 1985), p. 49.

4. See Jeffery M. Paige, *Coffee and Power: Revolution and the Rise of Democracy in Central America* (Cambridge, MA: Harvard University Press, 1997), pp. 16–19, 24–25.

5. John A. Booth, *Costa Rica: Quest for Democracy* (Boulder, CO: Westview Press, 1998), pp. 32–35.

6. Skidmore and Smith, *Modern Latin America*, pp. 371–72; Booth, *Costa Rica*, pp. 42–50.

7. Paige, *Coffee and Power*, pp. 141–52.

8. Ibid., pp. 127–40.

9. Mahoney, *Colonialism and Postcolonial Development*, pp. 130–31; Bushnell and Macaulay, *Emergence of Latin America*, p. 224.

10. Skidmore and Smith, *Modern Latin America*, pp. 72–73; Carlos Newland, "Eco-

nomic Development and Population Change: Argentina, 1810–1870," in Coatsworth and Taylor, *Latin America and the World Economy*, pp. 210–13.

11. Carlos Waisman, *Reversal of Development in Argentina: Postwar Counterrevolutionary Policies and their Structural Consequences* (Princeton: Princeton University Press, 1987), p. 5.
12. Mahoney, *Colonialism and Postcolonial Development*, pp. 129, 211.
13. Quoted ibid., p. 131.
14. Waisman, *Reversal of Development*, p. 9.
15. See V. S. Naipaul, *The Return of Eva Perón, with The Killings in Trinidad* (New York: Knopf, 1980).
16. Paul W. Gates, "The Homestead Act: Free Land Policy in Operation, 1862–1935," in Gates, ed., *The Jeffersonian Dream: Studies in the History of American Land Policy and Development* (Albuquerque: University of New Mexico Press, 1996); Harold M. Hyman, *American Singularity: The 1787 Northwest Ordinance, the 1862 Homestead and Morrill Acts, and the 1944 G.I. Bill* (Athens: University of Geogia Press, 1986).
17. Mouzelis, *Politics in the Semi-Periphery*, pp. 16–17.
18. Bushnell and Macaulay, *Emergence of Latin America*, pp. 128–29.
19. Ibid., pp. 227–32.
20. The comparison to Greece is made in Mouzelis, *Politics in the Semi-Periphery*, pp. 21–22. See also Skidmore and Smith, *Modern Latin America*, pp. 80–81.
21. Skidmore and Smith, *Modern Latin America*, pp. 82–86.
22. Mouzelis, *Politics in the Semi-Periphery*, pp. 2–27.
23. Roberto Cortés Condé, *The Political Economy of Argentina in the Twentieth Century* (New York: Cambridge University Press, 2009), pp. 125–44.
24. The problem got much worse under Perón, who impeached four of five sitting justices of the Supreme Court. Matías Iaryczower, Pablo T. Spiller, and Mariano Tommasi, "Judicial Independence in Unstable Environments, Argentina 1935–1998," *American Journal of Political Science* 46, no. 4 (2002): 699–716.

19: STORMS IN AFRICA

1. See the World Bank DataBank, http://databank.worldbank.org/ddp/home.do?Step=12&id=4&CNO=2.
2. Steven Radelet, *Emerging Africa: How 17 Countries Are Leading the Way* (Baltimore: Center for Global Development, 2010). Since the publication of this book, one of the seventeen countries, Mali, suffered a coup and needs to be stricken from the list.
3. On this period, see William Reno, *Warlord Politics and African States* (Boulder, CO: Lynne Rienner, 1998).
4. Collier, *The Bottom Billion*; Collier and Hoeffler, *Economic Causes of Civil Conflict*; Collier, "Implications of Ethnic Diversity," *Economic Policy* 32 (2001): 129–66.

5. Michael Bratton and Nicolas van de Walle, *Democratic Experiments in Africa: Regime Transitions in Comparative Perspective* (New York: Cambridge University Press, 1997), pp. 61–63.

6. van de Walle, *African Economies*, p. 117.

7. At the time his regime fell, Mobutu's army was staffed with fifty generals and six hundred colonels. Michela Wrong, *In the Footsteps of Mr. Kurtz: Living on the Brink of Disaster in Mobutu's Congo* (New York: Harper, 2001), pp. 90, 95, 229.

8. van de Walle, *African Economics*, p. 65.

9. Herbst, *States and Power in Africa*.

10. van de Walle, *African Economics*, pp. 73–74.

11. Nicolas van de Walle, *Overcoming Stagnation in Aid-Dependent Countries* (Washington, D.C.: Center for Global Development, 2004), p. 33.

12. Bratton and van de Walle, *Democratic Experiments*; Robert Bates, *Markets and States in Tropical Africa: The Political Basis of Agricultural Policies* (Berkeley: University of California Press, 2005).

13. Wrong, *In the Footsteps of Mr. Kurtz*, pp. 104–108.

14. David B. Abernethy, *The Dynamics of Global Dominance: European Overseas Empires, 1415–1980* (New Haven: Yale University Press, 2000), pp. 81–82; Fieldhouse, *Colonial Empires*, pp. 177–78.

15. Abernethy, *Dynamics of Global Dominance*, p. 92.

16. Fieldhouse, *Colonial Empires*, pp. 178, 207–10.

17. Abernethy, *Dynamics of Global Dominance*, pp. 94–95; Mahmood Mamdani, *Citizen and Subject: Contemporary Africa and the Legacy of Late Colonialism* (Princeton: Princeton University Press, 1996).

18. Herbst, *States and Power in Africa*, p. 15.

19. Crawford Young, *The African Colonial State in Comparative Perspective* (New Haven: Yale University Press, 1994), pp. 74–75.

20. Carneiro, "A Theory of the Origin of the State."

21. Herbst, *States and Power in Africa*, pp. 40–57.

22. Young, *African Colonial State*, pp. 80–90; Fieldhouse, *Colonial Empires*, pp. 211–16.

20: INDIRECT RULE

1. See for example Human Rights Watch, www.hrw.org/en/news/2000/05/31/sierra-leone-rebels-forcefully-recruit-child-soldiers.

2. Robert D. Kaplan, *The Coming Anarchy: Shattering the Dreams of the Post Cold War* (New York: Random House, 2000), pp. 4–19.

3. Economist Nathan Nunn in a careful study shows that there is a strong correlation between high levels of distrust in West Africa today and places where the slave trade was practiced several centuries ago. The taking of slaves involved a great deal of violence, and in the South particularly the polities involved in the

slave trade were constantly fighting over routes and access to foreign markets. Nunn, "Historical Legacies: A Model Linking Africa's Past to Its Current Underdevelopment," *Journal of Development Economics* 83, no. 1 (2007): 157–75; and Nunn, "The Long-Term Effects of Africa's Slave Trades," *Quarterly Journal of Economics* 123, no. 1 (2008): 139–76.

4. Wrong, *In the Footsteps of Mr. Kurtz*, p. 47.

5. Lansana Gberie, *A Dirty War in West Africa: The RUF and the Destruction of Sierra Leone* (Bloomington: Indiana University Press, 2005), p. 40.

6. Quoted in Jean Suret-Canale, *French Colonialism in Tropical Africa, 1900–1945* (New York: Pica Press, 1971), p. 90.

7. Mann, *Sources of Social Power*, pp. 169–70.

8. There were of course some important exceptions of countries that could rule with a minimum of despotism, like Botswana and Mauritius.

9. Karen E. Fields, *Revival and Rebellion in Colonial Central Africa* (Princeton: Princeton University Press, 1985), p. 32.

10. Sara Berry, *No Condition Is Permanent: The Social Dynamics of Agrarian Change in Sub-Saharan Africa* (Madison: University of Wisconsin Press, 1993), pp. 22, 24; Fields, *Revival and Rebellion*, p. 39.

11. See for example Charles K. Meek, *Land Law and Custom in the Colonies*, 2nd ed. (London: Frank Cass, 1968); E. E. Evans-Pritchard, *Kinship and Marriage Among the Nuer* (Oxford: Clarendon Press, 1951), and Evans-Pritchard, *The Political System of the Anuak of the Anglo-Egyptian Sudan* (New York: AMS Press, 1977); Julius Lewin, *Studies in African Native Law* (Philadelphia: University of Pennsylvania Press, 1947); Abernethy, *Dynamics of Global Dominance*, p. 115; Berry, *No Condition Is Permanent*, p. 30.

12. Berry, *No Condition Is Permanent*, p. 27.

13. Mamdani, *Citizen and Subject*, pp. 79–81; William B. Cohen, "The French Colonial Service in French West Africa," in Gifford Prosser and William R. Louis, eds., *France and Britain in Africa: Imperial Rivalry and Colonial Rule* (New Haven: Yale University Press, 1971), p. 498.

14. Terence Ranger, "The Invention of Tradition in Colonial Africa," in E. J. Hobsbawm and Terence Ranger, eds., *The Invention of Tradition* (New York: Cambridge University Press, 1983), p. 248.

15. Land in tribal societies is usually controlled by both individual families and lineage segments as a whole. Individuals do not possess free ownership, however; rights to land alienation are usually severely entailed by obligations to kin. The chief is more like a custodian acting on behalf of the group. See Francis Fukuyama, *Origins of Political Order*, chap. 4; T. Olawale Elias, *The Nature of African Customary Law* (Manchester, UK: Manchester University Press, 1956), pp. 162–66.

16. Mamdani, *Citizen and Subject*, pp. 138–45.

17. Ibid., p. 44.

18. On the dual land law system in Kenya, see Ann P. Munro, "Land Law in Kenya," in Thomas W. Hutchison et al., eds., *Africa and Law: Developing Legal Systems in*

African Commonwealth Nations (Madison: University of Wisconsin Press, 1968).

19. Thomas Spear, "Neo-Traditionalism and the Limits of Invention in British Colonial Africa," *Journal of African History* 44, no. 1 (2003): 3–27; Emily Lynn Osborn, " 'Circle of Iron': African Colonial Employees and the Interpretation of Colonial Rule in French West Africa," *Journal of African History* 44 (2003): 29–50; Fields, *Revival and Rebellion*, pp. 31, 38; Berry, *No Condition Is Permanent*, p. 32.

20. See Martin Chanock, "Paradigms, Policies and Property: A Review of the Customary Law of Land Tenure," in Kristin Mann and Richard Roberts, eds., *Law in Colonial Africa* (Portsmouth, NH: Heinemann, 1991).

21. Cohen, "French Colonial Service," p. 500; Michael Crowder, "The White Chiefs of Tropical Africa," in Lewis H. Gann and Peter Duignan, eds., *Colonialism in Africa, 1870–1960.* Vol. 2: *The History and Politics of Colonialism 1914–1960* (London: Cambridge University Press, 1970), p. 320.

22. Crowder, "White Chiefs of Tropical Africa," p. 344.

23. Suret-Canale, *French Colonialism*, pp. 71–83. A number of communities in Senegal did in fact win French citizenship.

24. James C. Scott, *Seeing Like a State: How Certain Schemes to Improve the Human Condition Have Failed* (New Haven: Yale University Press, 1998), chap. 9.

25. Suret-Canale, *French Colonialism*, pp. 313–14.

26. Ibid., p. 371; Cohen, "French Colonial Service," pp. 492, 497.

27. See Fukuyama, *Origins of Political Order*, chap. 3.

28. Quoted in Abernethy, *Dynamics of Global Dominance*, p. 120.

29. Melissa Thomas, "Hard Choices: Why U.S. Policies Towards Poor Governments Fail" (unpublished manuscript), chap. 6.

30. Collier and Rohner, "Beyond Greed and Grievance."

31. Matthew Lange, *Lineages of Despotism and Development: British Colonialism and State Power* (Chicago: University of Chicago Press, 2009), pp. 96–100; Gberie, *A Dirty War in West Africa*, pp. 17–38. It was Sierra Leone's misfortune that its diamonds were, unlike those of Botswana, alluvial, which made them relatively easy for individuals to mine. Siaka Stevens's early political career was built around his championing of poor miners against the state-controlled mining industry, which weakened the state's overall ability to control trade in diamonds.

32. Gberie, *A Dirty War in West Africa*, p. 196.

21: INSTITUTIONS, DOMESTIC OR IMPORTED

1. There is a huge literature on the subject of peacekeeping and postconflict interventions. See James Dobbins et al., *America's Role in Nation-Building: From Germany to Iraq* (Santa Monica, CA: RAND Corp., 2003); Simon Chesterman, *You, the People: The United Nations, Transitional Administration, and State-*

Building (New York: Oxford University Press, 2004); World Bank, *World Development Report 2011*.

2. See Fukuyama, *America at the Crossroads*; and Fukuyama, ed., *Nation-Building: Beyond Afghanistan and Iraq* (Baltimore: Johns Hopkins University Press, 2006).

3. James Dobbins et al., *The UN's Role in Nation-Building: From the Congo to Iraq* (Santa Monica, CA: RAND Corp., 2005). See Michael Maren, *The Road to Hell: The Ravaging Effects of Foreign Aid and International Charity* (New York: Free Press, 1997), for how humanitarian assistance to Somalia benefited the Siad Barre government. In the case of eastern Congo, the charge is made that UN refugee camps were sheltering Rwandan Hutu *génocidaires* until they were broken up by invading Rwandan forces.

4. See Fukuyama, *Origins of Political Order*, p. 14.

5. Pritchett, Woolcock, and Andrews, *Capability Traps?*

6. Thomas, "Hard Choices"; Merilee S. Grindle, "Good Enough Governance: Poverty Reduction and Reform in Developing Countries," *Governance* 17, no. 4 (2004): 525–48.

7. On the origins of community-driven development, see Mallaby, *The World's Banker*, pp. 202–206.

8. Jean Ensminger, "Inside Corruption Networks: Community Driven Development in the Village" (unpublished paper, May 2012).

9. Reo Matsuzaki, "Why Accountable Agents Are More Likely to Fail: Explaining Variation in State-Building Outcomes across Colonial Taiwan and the Philippines" (unpublished paper); Paul D. Hutchcroft, "Colonial Masters, National Politicos, and Provincial Lords: Central Authority and Local Autonomy in the American Philippines, 1900–1913," *Journal of Asian Studies* 59, no. 2 (2000): 277–306.

22: LINGUA FRANCAS

1. Some historians talk about the existence of states and kingdoms in the western and eastern halves of southern Nigeria, but few of these polities rose past the level of chiefdoms to become true states. The dominant form of social organization remained tribal. There had been some unification of Yoruba-speaking peoples under the kingdoms of Oyo, centered on the city of Ife, and Benin near the Niger River delta (not to be confused with the present-day country of Benin). But these had begun to break down in internecine warfare by the time the British arrived in force late in the nineteenth century. Northern Nigeria had larger political structures, primarily due to the influence of Islam as an organizing ideology. The North had long been linked to the Middle East through trans-Saharan trade routes, leading to the conversion of the Hausa polities and Borno to Islam late in the eleventh century. The Caliphate of Sokoto was formed early in the nineteenth century when the Fulani people under a charismatic leader

named Usman dan Fodio launched a jihad and conquered the Hausa dynasties. As Atul Kohli has pointed out, even though the Sokoto Caliphate was one of the largest political units in West Africa, it remained far less developed than states in other parts of the world. It had no centralized army or bureaucracy and could not enforce its writ over a clearly defined territory. It was more properly a chiefdom or center of a large tribal confederation than a state. See Falola and Heaton, *A History of Nigeria*, pp. 23, 29–34, 62–73; Atul Kohli, *State-Directed Development: Political Power and Industrialization in the Global Periphery* (New York: Cambridge University Press, 2004), p. 297.

2. Osaghae, *Crippled Giant*, pp. 1–4.
3. Sunil Khilnani, *The Idea of India* (New York: Farrar, Straus and Giroux, 1998).
4. Kohli, *State-Directed Development*, pp. 313, 318.
5. For an overview, see Osaghae, *Crippled Giant*, pp. 54–69.
6. Robert E. Elson, *The Idea of Indonesia* (New York: Cambridge University Press, 2008), pp. 1–4.
7. Jean Gelman Taylor, *Indonesia: Peoples and Histories* (New Haven: Yale University Press, 2003), pp. 238–39.
8. Elson, *Idea of Indonesia*, pp. 64–65.
9. Soekarno, *Nationalism, Islam, and Marxism* (Ithaca, NY: Cornell University Southeast Asia Program, 1969); Bernhard Dahm, *Sukarno and the Struggle for Indonesian Independence* (Ithaca, NY: Cornell University Press, 1969), pp. 340–41.
10. Dahm, *Sukarno*, pp. 336–43; Eka Darmaputera, *Pancasila and the Search for Identity and Modernity in Indonesian Society* (New York: E. J. Brill, 1988), pp. 147–64.
11. Dahm, *Sukarno*, pp. 331–35.
12. Taylor, *Indonesia*, pp. 356–60; John Hughes, *Indonesian Upheaval* (New York: David McKay, 1967).
13. Benjamin Fleming Intan, *"Public Religion" and the Pancasila-Based State of Indonesia* (New York: Peter Lang, 2006), pp. 50–68.
14. Taufik Abdullah, *Indonesia: Towards Democracy* (Singapore: ISEAS, 2009), pp. 215, 434; Elson, *Idea of Indonesia*, p. 65.
15. On the struggles to integrate places like Ambon, Aceh, and Sulawesi in the 1950s, see Abdullah, *Indonesia*, pp. 221–40.
16. Taylor, *Indonesia*, pp. 350–52; Elson, *Idea of Indonesia*, p. 69; see Dahm, *Sukarno*, p. 179, who describes Sukarno's desolation when exiled to the eastern island of Flores in 1934.
17. On postauthoritarian Indonesia, see Donald K. Emmerson, "Indonesia's Approaching Elections: A Year of Voting Dangerously?" *Journal of Democracy* 15, no. 1 (2004): 94–108, and "Southeast Asia: Minding the Gap Between Democracy and Governance," *Journal of Democracy* 23, no. 2 (2012): 62–73.
18. Joel D. Barkan, ed., *Beyond Capitalism vs. Socialism in Kenya and Tanzania* (Boulder, CO: Lynne Rienner, 1994), p. xiii.
19. Joel D. Barkan, "Divergence and Convergence in Kenya and Tanzania: Pressures for Reform," ibid., p. 10. See also Barkan, "To Fault or Not to Fault? Ethnic

Fractionalisation, Uneven Development and the Propensity for Conflict in Tanzania, Uganda and Kenya," in Jeffrey Herbst, Terence McNamee, and Greg Mills, eds., *On the Fault Line: Managing Tensions and Divisions Within Societies* (London: Profile Books, 2012).

20. Julius Nyerere argued that heavy German repression fostered Tanzanian unity by bringing the country's tribes together in nationalist resistance. Henry S. Bienen, *Tanzania: Party Transformation and Economic Development* (Princeton: Princeton University Press, 1970), p. 36.

21. Goran Hyden, *Beyond Ujamaa in Tanzania: Underdevelopment and an Uncaptured Peasantry* (Berkeley: University of California Press, 1980), pp. 98–105.

22. Cranford Pratt, *The Critical Phase in Tanzania, 1945–1968: Nyerere and the Emergence of a Socialist Strategy* (New York: Cambridge University Press, 1976), pp. 64–77; Bismarck U. Mwansasu and Cranford Pratt, eds., *Towards Socialism in Tanzania* (Toronto: University of Toronto Press, 1979), pp. 3–15.

23. Bienen, *Tanzania*, p. 43.

24. Michela Wrong, *It's Our Turn to Eat: The Story of a Kenyan Whistle-Blower* (New York: Harper, 2010), p. 52; see also Barkan, "Divergence and Convergence," pp. 23–28; Goran Hyden, "Party, State and Civil Society: Control versus Openness," in Barkan, *Beyond Capitalism and Socialism*, pp. 81–82.

25. Maina Kiai, "The Crisis in Kenya," *Journal of Democracy* 19, no. 3 (2008): 162–68; Michael Chege, "Kenya: Back from the Brink?" *Journal of Democracy* 19, no. 4 (2008): 125–39.

26. Edward Miguel, "Tribe or Nation? Nation Building and Public Goods in Kenya versus Tanzania," *World Politics* 56, no. 3 (2004): 327–62. See also Goran Hyden, *Political Development in Rural Tanzania* (Lund: Bokforlaget Universitet och Skola, 1968), pp. 150–53.

27. Barkan, "Divergence and Convergence," pp. 5, 20; Scott, *Seeing Like a State*, pp. 223–61; Hyden, *Beyond Ujamaa*, pp. 129–53.

23: THE STRONG ASIAN STATE

1. For a study emphasizing the promarket nature of policy in East Asia, see World Bank, *The East Asian Miracle: Economic Growth and Public Policy* (New York: Oxford University Press, 1993). The classic studies of industrial policy in East Asia include Chalmers Johnson, *MITI and the Japanese Miracle* (Stanford, CA: Stanford University Press, 1982); Robert Wade, *Governing the Market: Economic Theory and the Role of Government in East Asian Industrialization* (Princeton: Princeton University Press, 1990); and Alice H. Amsden, *Asia's Next Giant: South Korea and Late Industrialization* (New York: Oxford University Press, 1989). For a more contemporary account of industrial policy in China, see Justin Yifu Lin, "Lessons from the Great Recession," in Birdsall and Fukuyama, eds., *New Ideas in Development After the Financial Crisis*. For cultural interpretations, see Lee Kuan Yew's interview with Fareed Zakaria, "A

Conversation with Lee Kuan Yew," *Foreign Affairs* 73, no. 2 (1994): 109–27; and Lawrence E. Harrison, *Jews, Confucians, and Protestants: Cultural Capital and the End of Multiculturalism* (Lanham, MD: Rowman and Littlefield, 2013).

2. One of the most successful instances of industrial policy occurred in the United States with the development of the Internet. The Internet was originally developed by the Pentagon's Defense Advanced Research Projects Agency, with the TCP/IP protocol underlying it mandated by the government for use in its own networks. This early investment was based on security concerns rather than economic considerations, but it nonetheless succeeded in seeding one of the most important technologies of the twentieth century. Government investment was also critical in the development of semiconductors, radar, jet aircraft, and a host of other technologies.

3. Peter B. Evans, *Embedded Autonomy: States and Industrial Transformation* (Princeton: Princeton University Press, 1995).

4. Peter Duus, *The Rise of Modern Japan* (Boston: Houghton Mifflin, 1976), pp. 21–31.

5. For an overview of the origins of Japanese technonationalism, see Richard J. Samuels, *"Rich Nation, Strong Army": National Security and the Technological Transformation of Japan* (Ithaca, NY: Cornell University Press, 1994), pp. 33–78.

6. Duus, *Rise of Modern Japan*, pp. 94–95.

7. James L. McClain, *Japan, A Modern History* (New York: Norton, 2002), pp. 267–71.

8. B. C. Koh, *Japan's Administrative Elite* (Berkeley: University of California Press, 1989), p. 20.

9. Bernard S. Silberman, "Bureaucratic Development and the Structure of Decision-making in Japan: 1868–1925," *Journal of Asian Studies* 29, no. 2 (1970): 347–62.

10. Bernard S. Silberman, "The Bureaucratic Role in Japan, 1900–1945: The Bureaucrat as Politician," in Bernard S. Silberman and H. D. Harootunian, eds., *Japan in Crisis: Essays on Taishō Democracy* (Princeton: Princeton University Press, 1974).

11. Silberman, "Bureaucratic Development," p. 349.

12. Yasukuni was one of twenty-seven new Shinto shrines that were built in this period. McClain, *Japan*, p. 268.

13. John O. Haley and Veronica Taylor, "Rule of Law in Japan," in Randall Peerenboom, ed., *Asian Discourses of Rule of Law: Theories and Implementation of Rule of Law in Twelve Asian Countries, France, and the U. S.* (New York: Routledge, 2004), pp. 449–50.

14. Carl F. Goodman, *The Rule of Law in Japan: A Comparative Analysis*, 3rd ed. (The Hague: Kluwer Law International, 2003), pp. 17–18; Shigenori Matsui, *The Constitution of Japan: A Contextual Analysis* (Portland, OR: Hart Publishing, 2011), p. 9.

15. Haley and Taylor, "Rule of Law in Japan," pp. 452–53; Goodman, *Rule of Law in Japan*, pp. 18–19.

16. George Akita, *Foundations of Constitutional Government in Modern Japan, 1868–1900* (Cambridge, MA: Harvard University Press, 1967), pp. 59–64.

17. Duus, *Rise of Modern Japan*, pp. 114–15; Lawrence W. Beer and John M. Maki, *From Imperial Myth to Democracy: Japan's Two Constitutions, 1889–2002* (Boulder: University Press of Colorado, 2002), pp. 17–18, 24–29; Matsui, *The Constitution of Japan*, pp. 9–11.

18. Tetsuo Najita, *Hara Kei in the Politics of Compromise 1905–1915* (Cambridge, MA: Harvard University Press, 1967); Akita, *Foundations of Constitutional Government*, pp. 159–61; Duus, *Rise of Modern Japan*, pp. 114–15; Matsui, *Constitution of Japan*, pp. 9–11; McClain, *Japan*, pp. 184–87.

19. Stephen Vlastos, "Opposition Movements in Early Meji, 1868–1885," in Marius B. Jansen, ed., *The Emergence of Meiji Japan* (New York: Cambridge University Press, 1995).

20. Akita, *Foundations of Constitutional Government*, pp. 2–3.

21. The signing of an Anglo-Japanese Commercial Treaty in 1894 provided for the abolition of extraterritoriality in five years; the other Western powers followed suit by 1897. Goodman, *Rule of Law in Japan*, p. 19.

22. Barrington Moore, Jr., *Social Origins of Dictatorship and Democracy* (Boston: Beacon Press, 1966), pp. 433–52.

23. See Fukuyama, *Trust*, pp. 83–95.

24. Moore, *Social Origins of Dictatorship*, pp. 254–75.

25. This point is made in Theda Skocpol, "A Critical Review of Barrington Moore's *Social Origins of Dictatorship and Democracy*," *Politics & Society* 4 (1973): 1–34. Rural tenancy actually declined and the number of small and medium-sized farms steadily increased during the 1920s. See Duus, *Rise of Modern Japan*, pp. 182–85.

26. McClain, *Japan*, pp. 345–56; Andrew Gordon, *Labor and Imperial Democracy in Prewar Japan* (Berkeley: University of California Press, 1991), pp. 1–10.

27. Duus, *Rise of Modern Japan*, pp. 206–19; on the role of the Washington Naval Treaty, see James B. Crowley, *Japan's Quest for Autonomy: National Security and Foreign Policy, 1930–1938* (Princeton: Princeton University Press, 1966).

28. McClain, *Japan*, p. 410.

29. Beer and Maki, *Imperial Myth*, pp. 58–59, 68–69.

30. Ibid., pp. 81–87; Theodore McNelly, *The Origins of Japan's Democratic Constitution* (Lanham, MD: University Press of America, 2000), pp. 1–14.

31. Sirota had grown up in Japan and had the presence of mind to demand inclusion of provisions on women's rights that were taken up by Japanese feminists like Sato Shizue. Beer and Maki, *Imperial Myth*, p. 87.

32. For an account of this effort by a participant, see Eleanor M. Hadley, *Memoir of a Trustbuster: A Lifelong Adventure with Japan* (Honolulu: University of Hawai'i Press, 2003). See also Fukuyama, *Trust*, pp. 195–207.

33. Frank Upham, "Mythmaking in the Rule-of-Law Orthodoxy," in Carothers, *Promoting the Rule of Law Abroad*; see also Upham's *Law and Social Change in Postwar Japan* (Cambridge, MA: Harvard University Press, 1987).

34. Janis Mimura, *Planning for Empire: Reform Bureaucrats and the Japanese Wartime State* (Ithaca, NY: Cornell University Press, 2011).

35. Akita, *Foundations of Constitutional Government*, pp. 162–63.

24: THE STRUGGLE FOR LAW IN CHINA

1. This story is told in Fukuyama, *Origins of Political Order*, chaps. 7–8.

2. See Frederic Wakeman, Jr., *The Great Enterprise: The Manchu Reconstruction of Imperial Order in Seventeenth-Century China*. 2 vols. (Berkeley: University of California Press, 1985), 1:414–24, 2:1006–16; Evelyn S. Rawski, *The Last Emperors: A Social History of Qing Imperial Institutions* (Berkeley: University of California Press, 1998).

3. Jack A. Goldstone, *Revolution and Rebellion in the Early Modern World* (Berkeley: University of California Press, 1991), pp. 355–62.

4. Kenneth Pomeranz, *The Great Divergence: Europe, China, and the Making of the Modern World Economy* (Princeton: Princeton University Press, 2000), pp. 16–25. See also Jean-Laurent Rosenthal and R. Bin Wong, *Before and Beyond Divergence: The Politics of Economic Change in China and Europe* (Cambridge, MA: Harvard University Press, 2011).

5. There is an older literature on the causes of China's intellectual and social stagnation in the period 1500–1800 that still has considerable validity. See Joseph Needham, *Science and Civilisation in China*. Vol. 1: *Introductory Orientations* (New York: Cambridge University Press, 1954); see also the discussion of early modern China versus the West in Morris, *Why the West Rules—For Now*, pp. 481–507.

6. For a general description of late Qing China and the revolution, see John King Fairbank, *The Great Chinese Revolution, 1800–1985* (New York: Harper, 1986).

7. Derk Bodde and Clarence Morris, *Law in Imperial China, Exemplified by 190 Ch'ing Dynasty Cases* (Cambridge, MA: Harvard University Press, 1967), pp. 4, 8.

8. Bodde and Morris, *Law in Imperial China*, pp. 19–23; Stanley B. Lubman, *Bird in a Cage: Legal Reform in China after Mao* (Stanford, CA: Stanford University Press, 1999), pp. 13–14.

9. Bodde and Morris, *Law in Imperial China*, pp. 23–27.

10. The Confucian view is not unknown in the Western tradition. Plato in designing a just city in the *Republic* does not argue for formal laws or procedures but for the education of a guardian class and philosopher king that would be able to rule justly.

11. For a list of premodern Chinese legal codes, see Bodde and Morris, *Law in Imperial China*, pp. 55–57.

12. Ibid., pp. 3–6; Lubman, *Bird in a Cage*, pp. 23–29.

13. Philip C. C. Huang, ed., *Code, Custom, and Legal Practice in China: The Qing*

and the Republic Compared (Stanford, CA: Stanford University Press, 2001), p. 33; Jianfu Chen, *Chinese Law: Context and Transformation* (Boston: Martinus Nijhoff, 2008), p. 29.

14. Chen, *Chinese Law: Context*, pp. 23–28; Huang, *Code, Custom, and Legal Practice*, pp. 15–18.

15. On the factionalism and the failure of constitutionalism during this period of Chinese history, see Andrew J. Nathan, *Peking Politics, 1918–1923: Factionalism and the Failure of Constitutionalism* (Ann Arbor, MI: Center for Chinese Studies, 1998), pp. 4–26.

16. Chen, *Chinese Law: Context*, pp. 80–85. On the continuities of the Chinese civil law tradition, see Kathryn Bernhardt and Philip C. C. Huang, eds., *Civil Law in Qing and Republican China* (Stanford, CA: Stanford University Press, 1994).

17. Huang, *Code, Custom, and Legal Practice*, pp. 50–62. In Europe, the Catholic church's decision to grant women inheritance rights at the expense of the patrilineal family had taken place early in the Middle Ages and was responsible for the breakdown of extended kinship groups there. Thus in China, where segmentary lineages survive in some areas to the present day, this milestone was achieved only in the third decade of the twentieth century. See Fukuyama, *Origins of Political Order*, chap. 17.

18. See the account of the Confucian-Legalist debate given in the Maoist-era book Li Yu-ning, *Shang Yang's Reforms and State Control in China* (White Plains, NY: M. E. Sharpe, 1977).

19. Quoted in Chen, *Chinese Law: Context*, p. 49. See also Lubman, *Bird in a Cage*, pp. 72–74.

20. Yang Jisheng, *Tombstone: The Great Chinese Famine, 1958–1962* (New York: Farrar, Straus and Giroux, 2012).

21. Chen, *Chinese Law: Context*, p. 41.

22. Quoted in Lubman, *Bird in a Cage*, p. 124.

23. Kenneth Lieberthal, *Governing China: From Revolution to Reform*, 2nd ed. (New York: Norton, 2004), pp. 176–77.

24. Chen, *Chinese Law: Context*, pp. 70–83.

25. Jianfu Chen, *Chinese Law: Towards an Understanding of Chinese Law, Its Nature and Development* (Boston: Kluwer Law International, 1999), p. 220; Lubman, *Bird in a Cage*, p. 178.

26. Minxin Pei, "Citizens v. Mandarins: Administrative Litigation in China," *China Quarterly* 152 (1997): 832–62; Kevin J. O'Brien and Lianjiang Li, "Suing the State: Administrative Litigation in Rural China," *China Journal* 51 (2004): 75–96; Lubman, *Bird in a Cage*, pp. 212–14.

27. Chen, *Chinese Law: Towards an Understanding*, pp. 237–42, 337–38; Lubman, *Bird in a Cage*, pp. 178–80; Chen, *Chinese Law: Context*, pp. 374–78. These laws were further extended and modified in a major revision that was passed by the NPC in 2007.

28. The first statutes applied to contracts between foreigners and the state, implemented early in China's reform to promote foreign direct investment. This was

superseded in 1999 by a more general Contract Law of the People's Republic of China that covers contractual relationships entered into by the state and by private individuals, with provisions for things like liquidated damages and arbitration procedures.

29. Chen, *Chinese Law: Towards an Understanding*, pp. 224–27.

30. See Franz Schurmann, "Traditional Property Concepts in China," *Far Eastern Quarterly* 15, no. 4 (1956): 507–16.

31. Kevin J. O'Brien, "Villagers, Elections, and Citizenship in Contemporary China," *Modern China* 27, no. 4 (2001): 407–35; Mary E. Gallagher, "Mobilizing the Law in China: 'Informed Disenchantment' and the Development of Legal Consciousness," *Law & Society Review* 40, no. 4 (2006): 783–816.

32. Chen, *Chinese Law: Towards an Understanding*, pp. 341–53.

33. The issue of weak property rights comes up most prominently in land use cases. As geographer You-tien Hsing points out, control over land is *the* central power that the different arms of the Chinese government possess, particularly local governments that have a direct economic stake in pushing outward the urban-rural boundaries of their jurisdictions. Conflicts over land are often settled not through a neutral court system but politically by administrative agencies that seek to balance their interest in economic growth with a desire for social stability. During the Hu Jintao years of the 2000s and into the present, the party has placed heavy emphasis on stability, which often meant making concessions to existing property holders. See Hsing, *The Great Urban Transformation: Politics of Land and Property in China* (New York: Oxford University Press, 2010); and Jean C. Oi and Andrew Walder, eds., *Property Rights and Economic Reform in China* (Stanford, CA: Stanford University Press, 1999).

34. The inability of Communist states to institutionalize succession rules was noted many years ago in Myron Rush, *How Communist States Change Their Rulers* (Ithaca, NY: Cornell University Press, 1974).

35. Lieberthal, *Governing China*, p. 211; Melanie Manion, *Retirement of Revolutionaries in China: Public Policies, Social Norms, Private Interests* (Princeton: Princeton University Press, 1993), pp. 3–15.

36. This point is made in Andrew J. Nathan, "China's Constitutionalist Option," *Journal of Democracy* 7, no. 4 (1996): 43–57.

25: THE REINVENTION OF THE CHINESE STATE

1. See Fukuyama, *Origins of Political Order*, chaps. 7–8.

2. Frederick C. Teiwes, "The Chinese State During the Maoist Era," in David L. Shambaugh, ed., *The Modern Chinese State* (New York: Cambridge University Press, 2000), pp. 112–20.

3. Ibid., pp. 120–24. The prestige of the Soviet military increased after World War II and its role in defeating Nazi Germany, but it still remained highly subordinate to the Communist Party of the Soviet Union.

4. Ibid., pp. 136–48.
5. Dali Yang, *Remaking the Chinese Leviathan: Market Transition and the Politics of Governance in China* (Stanford, CA: Stanford University Press, 2004), pp. 175–83.
6. Xinhua, http://news.xinhuanet.com/english/china/2012-11/25/c_131997757.htm.
7. One recent effort to measure meritocracy in China is Victor Shih, Christopher Adolph, and Mingxing Liu, "Getting Ahead in the Communist Party: Explaining the Advancement of Central Committee Members in China," *American Political Science Review* 106, no. 1 (2012): 166–87.
8. Selina Ho, "Decentralization and Local Variations in China's Development: Case Studies from the Urban Water Sector" (PhD diss., Johns Hopkins School of Advanced International Studies, 2013), chap. 8.
9. Minxin Pei, *China's Trapped Transition: The Limits of Developmental Autocracy* (Cambridge, MA: Harvard University Press, 2006), p. 136; Lieberthal, *Governing China*, pp. 173–79; Ho, "Decentralization and Local Variations."
10. Jean C. Oi, *Rural China Takes Off: Institutional Foundations of Economic Reform* (Berkeley: University of California Press, 1999).
11. James Q. Wilson, *Bureaucracy: What Government Agencies Do and Why They Do It* (New York: Basic Books, 1989), p. 115.
12. Oi, *Rural China Takes Off*, pp. 61–64.
13. On this shift, see Yasheng Huang, "China: Getting Rural Issues Right," in Birdsall and Fukuyama, *New Ideas in Development*.
14. Dingxin Zhao and Hongxing Yang, "Performance Legitimacy, State Autonomy and China's Economic Miracle," working paper (Center on Democracy, Development, and the Rule of Law, Stanford University, 2013).
15. Yang, *Remaking the Chinese Leviathan*, pp. 110–49.
16. Pei, *China's Trapped Transition*, pp. 102–18.
17. Edward Wong, "China's Railway Minister Loses Post in Corruption Inquiry," *New York Times*, February 12, 2011.
18. Keith Zhai, "Railway Ministry a Bloated Outfit Few Will Mourn," *South China Morning Post*, March 12, 2013.
19. Pei, *China's Trapped Transition*, pp. 132–66.
20. Melanie Manion, "Authoritarian Parochialism: Congressional Representation in China" (unpublished paper, 2012).
21. Lily L. Tsai, *Accountability Without Democracy: Solidary Groups and Public Goods Provision in Rural China* (New York: Cambridge University Press, 2007); Lily Tsai, "The Political Payoffs of Governance Reforms: How Citizens See and Judge the State in Authoritarian China" (unpublished paper, 2012).
22. Christian Göbel and Lynette Ong, *Social Unrest in China* (London: Europe China Research and Advice Network, 2012).
23. Zhao Shukai, "Rural China: Poor Governance in Story Development," working paper (Center on Democracy, Development, and the Rule of Law, Stanford University, 2013).
24. See for example Anthony Saich, "The Quality of Governance in China: The

Citizen's View," working paper (Center on Democracy, Development, and the Rule of Law, Stanford University, 2013).

25. The argument that political reform ought to start with expanding constitutionalism is made in Nathan, "China's Constitutionalist Option."

26: THREE REGIONS

1. Data are for different years, based on availability: Japan, 1993; Ethiopia, 2005; South Korea, 1998; Indonesia, 2005; Tanzania, 2007; China, 2005; Philippines, 2009; Argentina, 2010; Kenya, 2005; Mexico, 2008; Nigeria, 2010; Brazil, 2009; Angola, 2000.

2. See Luis F. López-Calva and Nora Lustig, eds., *Declining Inequality in Latin America: A Decade of Progress?* (Washington, D.C.: Brookings Institution Press, 2010).

3. The only country typically put in this category in Latin America is Chile under the dictator Augusto Pinochet, which achieved relatively high rates of economic growth as a result of market-friendly policies he put in place. In addition, Ethiopia under Meles Zenawi and Rwanda under Paul Kagame have been seen as incipient developmental states.

4. On the premodern state in Southeast Asia, see Tony Day, *Fluid Iron: State Formation in Southeast Asia* (Honolulu: University of Hawai'i Press, 2002). For one account of state building in postcolonial Singapore and Malaysia, see Slater, *Ordering Power.*

27: WHY DID DEMOCRACY SPREAD?

1. Diamond, *The Spirit of Democracy.*

2. Tocqueville, *Democracy in America*, introduction; Francis Fukuyama, "The March of Equality," *Journal of Democracy* 11, no. 1 (2000): 11–17.

3. On this correlation, see Seymour Martin Lipset, "Some Social Requisites of Democracy: Economic Development and Political Legitimacy," *American Political Science Review* 53 (1959): 69–105; Larry Diamond, "Economic Development and Democracy Reconsidered," *American Behavioral Scientist* 15, nos. 4–5 (1992): 450–99; Adam Przeworski et al., *Democracy and Development: Political Institutions and Material Well-Being in the World, 1950–1990* (Cambridge: Cambridge University Press, 2000). See also Acemoglu and Robinson, *Why Nations Fail*, which links development and democracy but shifts the causal direction.

4. For an overview of this whole literature, see James Mahoney, "Knowledge Accumulation in Comparative Historical Research: The Case of Democracy and Authoritarianism," in James Mahoney and Dietrich Rueschemeyer, eds., *Comparative Historical Analysis in the Social Sciences* (New York: Cambridge University Press, 2003). Dietrich Rueschemeyer and coauthors Evelyne and John Stephens, for example, went over Moore's cases as well as additional ones from

Latin America, and argue that the working class rather than the bourgeoisie were the main supporters of democracy, and that the middle classes as often as not were willing to ally themselves with reactionary landowners in supporting authoritarian governments. See Dietrich Rueschemeyer, Evelyne Huber Stephens, and John D. Stephens, *Capitalist Development and Democracy* (Chicago: University of Chicago Press, 1992); Guillermo A. O'Donnell, *Modernization and Bureaucratic-Authoritarianism: Studies in South American Politics* (Berkeley: University of California Press, 1973). A later study by Ruth Collier argues by contrast that the working classes were not the primary drivers of democracy in many of the nineteenth-century transitions, though they played a larger role in the Third Wave transitions than commonly acknowledged. Her analysis of the European cases in some ways restores the validity of Moore's original linkage of the middle classes to democracy. Ruth Berins Collier, *Paths Toward Democracy: The Working Class and Elites in Western Europe and South America* (New York: Cambridge University Press, 1999).

5. Guillermo O'Donnell (*Modernization and Bureaucratic-Authoritarianism*), writing primarily about Latin America, put forward a theory about bureaucratic authoritarianism, which maintained that the bourgeoisie in countries at the periphery of the global system tended to support authoritarian governments as a means of coping with the problems created by deepening industrialization.

6. Collier, *Paths Toward Democracy*, p. 35.

7. Ibid., p. 80.

8. On the role of large Prussian landowners blocking expansion of the franchise, see Daniel Ziblatt, "Does Landholding Inequality Block Democratization? A Test of the 'Bread and Democracy' Thesis and the Case of Prussia," *World Politics* 60 (2008): 610–41.

28: THE LONG ROAD TO DEMOCRACY

1. S. N. Eisenstadt and Stein Rokkan, eds., *Building States and Nations* (Beverly Hills, CA: Sage, 1973), pp. 84–85; Charles Tilly, *Democracy* (New York: Cambridge University Press, 2007), pp. 97–98.

2. Jonathan Sperber, *The European Revolutions, 1848–1851*, 2nd ed. (New York: Cambridge University Press, 2005), pp. 56–58.

3. Hobsbawm, *The Age of Capital*, p. 15.

4. See Kurt Weyland, "The Diffusion of Revolution: '1848' in Europe and Latin America," *International Organization* 63, no. 3 (2009): 391–423.

5. On the level of development in Europe in the early nineteenth century, see Eric Hobsbawm, *The Age of Revolution, 1789–1848* (New York: Vintage Books, 1996), pp. 11–18; Sperber, *European Revolutions*, pp. 5, 59–62.

6. John Stuart Mill, *Essays on Politics and Society*, vol. 19 (Buffalo, NY: University of Toronto Press, 1977), p. 471.

7. Ibid., pp. 322–23.

8. Ibid., p. 327.

9. Edmund Burke, *On Empire, Liberty, and Reform: Speeches and Letters* (New Haven: Yale University Press, 2000), p. 277.

10. From *Reflections on the Revolution in France*, quoted in Albert O. Hirschman, *The Rhetoric of Reaction: Perversity, Futility, Jeopardy* (Cambridge, MA: Belknap Press, 1991), p. 20.

11. Walter Bagehot, *The English Constitution* (New York: Oxford University Press, 2001), p. 186.

12. Ibid., pp. 4–5, 32.

13. Gaetano Mosca, *The Ruling Class* (New York: McGraw-Hill, 1939); Vilfredo Pareto, *Sociological Writings* (New York: Praeger, 1966). See the discussion of Mosca and Pareto in Hirschman, *Rhetoric of Reaction*, pp. 50–57.

14. On scientific racism, see Stephen Jay Gould, *The Mismeasure of Man* (New York: Norton, 1981).

15. Bruce E. Cain, *Regulating Politics? The Democratic Imperative and American Political Reform* (New York: Cambridge University Press, 2014).

16. The contemporary rational choice version of this Marxist tale can be found in Carles Boix, *Democracy and Redistribution* (New York: Cambridge University Press, 2003), and Daron Acemoglu and James A. Robinson, *Economic Origins of Dictatorship and Democracy* (New York: Cambridge University Press, 2005). Both theories point to the degree of inequality as the key determinant of the demand for democracy on the part of the poor and the willingness to concede democracy on the part of the rich, but differ as to the specific ways inequality triggers democratic change. For an overview of the contemporary literature, see Daniel Ziblatt, "How Did Europe Democratize?" *World Politics* 58 (2006): 311–38.

17. Adam Przeworski, "Conquered or Granted? A History of Suffrage Extensions," *British Journal of Political Science* 39, no. 2 (2009): 291–321.

18. The 1832 Reform eliminated many of the rotten boroughs, which returned Conservative MPs despite the fact that they had no inhabitants. The 1867 Reform extended the franchise to most urban male householders, which included about 40 percent of the total population. The 1884 Reform Act extended the same voting rights to rural areas and increased participation to about 60 percent of the male population. Further reforms in 1918 and 1929 finally gave the vote to all adult males, and then to women as well. Under these conditions, a truly popular politics could emerge, permitting the rise of the British Labour Party and its displacement of the Liberals as the alternative to the Tories. Each of these Reform Bills engendered huge public controversy, in which the pros and cons of democracy were actively debated. For a general account of these reforms, see Asa Briggs, *The Age of Improvement, 1783–1867* (New York: Longman, 1959), chaps. 5 and 10.

19. Gladstone introduced his own limited reform bill in 1866 that would have marginally increased the franchise to households with an annual income of £7 (the average annual income was £42), but he, like John Stuart Mill, was eager to "ex-

clude those who are, presumably, in themselves unfitted to exercise it with intelligence and integrity." His bill was defeated by the Tories acting together with a conservative wing of his own party known as the Adullamites. William Ewart Gladstone, "Speech on the Bill of Mr. Baines," in Sarah Richardson, ed. *History of Suffrage, 1760–1867,* 6 vols. (Brookfield, VT: Pickering and Chatto, 2000), 5:107; Briggs, *Age of Improvement,* p. 494.

20. Gertrude Himmelfarb, *Victorian Minds* (New York: Knopf, 1968), p. 357.
21. James Cornford, "The Transformation of Conservatism in the Late Nineteenth Century," *Victorian Studies* 7 (1963): 41–66.
22. Collier, *Paths Toward Democracy,* pp. 54–76.
23. See for example "Speech of Edward Baines," in Richardson, *History of Suffrage,* 5:95; and Martin J. Wiener, *English Culture and the Decline of the Industrial Spirit, 1850–1980,* 2nd ed. (New York: Cambridge University Press, 2004).

29: FROM 1848 TO THE ARAB SPRING

1. On cultural arguments about the failure of democracy in the Middle East, see Elie Kedourie, *Politics in the Middle East* (New York: Oxford University Press, 1992). For a more insightful view of the obstacles to democratization in the region, see Stepan and Robertson, "An 'Arab' More Than a 'Muslim' Electoral Gap."
2. See for example Seth Jones, "The Mirage of the Arab Spring: Deal with the Region You Have, Not the Region You Want," *Foreign Affairs* 92, no. 1 (2013): 47–54. For a more general argument about the potentially malign effects of democratization, see Edward D. Mansfield and Jack Snyder, *Electing to Fight: Why Emerging Democracies Go to War* (Cambridge, MA: MIT Press, 2005).
3. See Barry Mirkin, "Population Levels, Trends and Policies in the Arab Region: Challenges and Opportunities" (New York: UNDP Research Paper, 2010), p. 16.
4. This argument is made in Huntington, *The Third Wave.*
5. Gellner makes the comparison of European nationalism and Middle Eastern Islamism in *Nations and Nationalism,* pp. 75–89. A variant of this argument is also made in Olivier Roy, *Globalized Islam: The Search for a New Ummah* (New York: Columbia University Press, 2004). See also Francis Fukuyama, "Identity, Immigration, and Liberal Democracy," *Journal of Democracy* 17, no. 2 (2006): 5–20.

30: THE MIDDLE CLASS AND DEMOCRACY'S FUTURE

1. This chapter expands on Francis Fukuyama, "The Future of History," *Foreign Affairs* 91, no. 1 (2012): 53–61.
2. Gellner, *Nations and Nationalism,* p. 124. Gellner also makes this argument in *Culture, Identity, and Politics.* See also Fukuyama, "Identity, Immigration, and Liberal Democracy."

3. See *The Global Middle Class* (Washington, D.C.: Pew Research Global Attitudes Project, 2009); Ronald Inglehart, *Modernization and Postmodernization: Cultural, Economic, and Political Change in 43 Societies* (Princeton: Princeton University Press, 1997); and Inglehart and Christian Welzel, *Modernization, Cultural Change, and Democracy: The Human Development Sequence* (New York: Cambridge University Press, 2005); William Easterly, *The Middle Class Consensus and Economic Development* (Washington, D.C.: World Bank Policy Research Paper No. 2346, 2000); Luis F. López-Calva et al., *Is There Such a Thing as Middle-Class Values? Class Differences, Values, and Political Orientations in Latin America* (Washington, D.C.: Center for Global Development Working Paper No. 286, 2012).

4. See Thitinan Pongsudhirak, "Thailand's Uneasy Passage," *Journal of Democracy* 23, no. 2 (2012): 47–61.

5. Dominic Wilson and Raluca Dragusanu, *The Expanding Middle: The Exploding World Middle Class and Falling Global Inequality* (New York: Goldman Sachs Global Economics Paper No. 170, 2008), p. 4.

6. European Union Institute for Security Studies, *Global Trends 2030—Citizens in an Interconnected and Polycentric World* (Paris: EUISS, 2012), p. 28.

7. China's Gini index was 42.5 in 2005 (World Bank).

8. López-Calva and Lustig, *Declining Inequality in Latin America.*

9. This figure quoted in Francesca Castellani and Gwenn Parent, *Being "Middle Class" in Latin America* (Paris: OECD Development Centre Working Paper No. 305, 2011), p. 9.

10. Thomas Piketty and Emmanuel Saez, "Income Inequality in the United States, 1913–1998," *Quarterly Journal of Economics* 118, no. 1 (2003): 1–39; see also Jacob S. Hacker and Paul Pierson, "Winner-Take-All Politics: Public Policy, Political Organization, and the Precipitous Rise of Top Incomes in the United States," *Politics and Society* 38, no. 2 (2010): 152–204; Hacker and Pierson, *Winner-Take-All Politics: How Washington Made the Rich Richer—and Turned Its Back on the Middle Class* (New York: Simon & Schuster, 2010).

11. See Raghuram G. Rajan, *Fault Lines: How Hidden Fractures Still Threaten the World Economy* (Princeton: Princeton University Press, 2010).

12. See Erik Brynjolfsson and Andrew McAfee, *The Second Machine Age: Work, Progress, and Prosperity in a Time of Brilliant Technologies* (New York: Norton, 2014).

13. Robert H. Frank and Philip J. Cook, *The Winner-Take-All Society* (New York: Free Press, 1995).

14. See Fukuyama, *Origins of Political Order*, pp. 460–68.

15. I discuss the social and political consequences of life extension in *Our Posthuman Future: Consequences of the Biotechnology Revolution* (New York: Farrar, Straus and Giroux, 2002), pp. 57–71.

16. Karl Polanyi, *The Great Transformation* (New York: Rinehart, 1944).

31: POLITICAL DECAY

1. Robert H. Nelson, *A Burning Issue: A Case for Abolishing the U.S. Forest Service* (Lanham, MD: Rowman and Littlefield, 2000).
2. Eliza Wing Yee Lee, "Political Science, Public Administration, and the Rise of the American Administrative State," *Public Administration Review* 55, no. 6 (1995): 538–46; Knott and Miller, *Reforming Bureaucracy*, pp. 38–39.
3. Dean Lueck, "Economics and the Organization of Wildfire Suppression," in Karen M. Bradshaw and Dean Lueck, eds., *Wildfire Policy: Law and Economics Perspectives* (New York: RFF Press, 2012); Nelson, *A Burning Issue*, p. 4; Stephen J. Pyne, "Fire Policy and Fire Research in the U.S. Forest Service," *Journal of Forest History* 25, no. 2 (1981): 64–77.
4. Nelson, *A Burning Issue*, p. 38.
5. Sarah E. Anderson and Terry L. Anderson, "The Political Economy of Wildfire Management," in Bradshaw and Lueck, *Wildfire Policy*, p. 110.
6. Nelson, *A Burning Issue*, p. xiii.
7. Dennis Roth, "The National Forests and the Campaign for Wilderness Legislation," *Journal of Forest History* 28, no. 3 (1984): 112–25.
8. See Randal O'Toole, *Reforming the Forest Service* (Washington, D.C.: Island Press, 1988), pp. 98–111.
9. Paul C. Light, *A Government Ill Executed: The Decline of the Federal Service and How to Reverse It* (Cambridge, MA: Harvard University Press, 2008), p. 126; Patricia W. Ingraham and David H. Rosenbloom, "Political Foundations of the American Federal Service: Rebuilding a Crumbling Base," *Public Administration Review* 50 (1990): 212.
10. National Commission on the Public Service, *Rebuilding the Public Service* (Washington, D.C., 1989); and *Revitalizing the Federal Government for the 21st Century* (Washington, D.C., 2003).
11. Public authorities (like the Port Authority of New York and New Jersey) are more common at state and municipal levels than at the federal level, and have a cumulative public debt significantly larger than direct state and municipal debt. See Gail Radford, *The Rise of the Public Authority: Statebuilding and Economic Development in Twentieth-Century America* (Chicago: University of Chicago Press, 2013). On contractors, see Light, *A Government Ill Executed*, pp. 192ff. The 2.25 million threshold was breached only once, in 1968.
12. Light, *A Government Ill Executed*, p. 106; supporting data given on pp. 108–20.
13. *Revitalizing the Federal Government for the 21st Century*, p. 1.
14. Light, *A Government Ill Executed*, p. 115; Ingraham and Rosenbloom, "Political Foundations of the American Federal Service."
15. Oswald Spengler, *The Decline of the West* (New York: Knopf, 1926); Arnold Toynbee, *A Study of History* (London: Oxford University Press, 1972); Paul Kennedy, *The Rise and Fall of the Great Powers: Economic Change and Military Conflict from 1500 to 2000* (New York: Random House, 1987); Diamond, *Collapse*.

16. Samuel P. Huntington, "Political Development and Political Decay," *World Politics* 17, (no. 3) (1965).
17. See Fukuyama, *Origins of Political Order*, chap. 2.
18. Diamond, *Collapse*, pp. 136–56.
19. See for example Fareed Zakaria, *The Post-American World* (New York: Norton, 2003); Thomas L. Friedman and Michael Mandelbaum, *That Used to Be Us: How America Fell Behind in the World It Invented and How We Can Come Back* (New York: Farrar, Straus and Giroux, 2011); Edward Luce, *Time to Start Thinking: America in the Age of Descent* (New York: Atlantic Monthly Press, 2012); Josef Joffe, *The Myth of America's Decline: Politics, Economics, and a Half Century of False Prophecies* (New York: Liveright, 2014).

32: A STATE OF COURTS AND PARTIES

1. Skowronek, *Building a New American State*.
2. Robert A. Kagan, *Adversarial Legalism: The American Way of Law* (Cambridge, MA: Harvard University Press, 2001). See also Mary Ann Glendon, *A Nation Under Lawyers: How the Crisis in the Legal Profession Is Transforming American Society* (New York: Farrar, Straus and Giroux, 1994).
3. For an example of these differences with regard to occupational safety and health, see Steven Kelman, *Regulating America, Regulating Sweden: A Comparative Study of Occupational Safety and Health Policy* (Cambridge, MA: MIT Press, 1981).
4. R. Shep Melnick, "Adversarial Legalism, Civil Rights, and the Exceptional American State" (unpublished paper, 2012). Quotation is from Sean Farhang, *The Litigation State: Public Regulation and Private Lawsuits in the U.S.* (Princeton: Princeton University Press, 2010), cited in Melnick.
5. Kagan, *Adversarial Legalism*, p. 50.
6. Quoted in Melnick, "Adversarial Legalism," p. 18.
7. Kagan, *Adversarial Legalism*, pp. 36–42.
8. Ibid., p. 236.
9. See R. Shep Melnick, "Separation of Powers and the Strategy of Rights: The Expansion of Special Education," in Marc K. Landy and Martin A. Levin, eds., *The New Politics of Public Policy* (Baltimore: Johns Hopkins University Press, 1995).

33: CONGRESS AND THE REPATRIMONIALIZATION OF AMERICAN POLITICS

1. See the discussion of reciprocal altruism in Fukuyama, *Origins of Political Order*, pp. 30–31; see also the discussion of moral reciprocity in Francis Fukuyama,

The Great Disruption: Human Nature and the Reconstitution of Social Order (New York: Free Press, 1999), pp. 259–62.

2. Lawrence Lessig, *Republic, Lost: How Money Corrupts Congress—and a Plan to Stop It* (New York: Twelve, 2011), pp. 24–38. For an earlier study of interest groups, see Kay Lehmen Schlozman and John T. Tierney, *Organized Interests and American Democracy* (New York: Harper, 1986).

3. Hacker and Pierson, *Winner-Take-All Politics*, p. 118.

4. Oftentimes these benefits take the form of loopholes permitting the offshoring of profits or tax arbitrage. Hence it was revealed that General Electric paid no taxes in 2010, a fact that became a campaign issue in the 2012 election. See David Kocieniewski, "G.E.'s Strategies Let It Avoid Taxes Altogether," *New York Times*, March 24, 2011.

5. See for example Frank R. Baumgartner et al., *Lobbying and Policy Change: Who Wins, Who Loses, and Why* (Chicago: University of Chicago Press, 2009); Derek Bok, *The Trouble With Government* (Cambridge, MA: Harvard University Press, 2001), pp. 85–94.

6. Bok, *Trouble with Government*, p. 100.

7. See Admati and Hellwig, *The Banker's New Clothes*, pp. 169–91.

8. On the impact of lobbyists on financial sector reform, see Johnson and Kwak, *13 Bankers*. For a discussion of solutions to the too-big-to-fail problem, see Admati and Hellwig, *The Banker's New Clothes*. I'm grateful to Paul Ockelmann, who did useful research on this topic.

9. Average approval ratings of Congress in the 2000s were 13 percent according to Gallup. See www.realclearpolitics.com/epolls/other/congressional_job_approval-903.html for aggregated polling data; also www.gallup.com/poll/152528/congress-job-approval-new-low.aspx.

10. Mancur Olson, *The Rise and Decline of Nations* (New Haven: Yale University Press, 1982).

11. Tocqueville's discussion of voluntary associations can be found in *Democracy in America*, vol. 2, part 2, chaps. 5–7. Robert D. Putnam, *Bowling Alone: The Collapse and Revival of American Community* (New York: Simon & Schuster, 2000).

12. Theodore J. Lowi, *The End of Liberalism: Ideology, Policy, and the Crisis of Public Authority* (New York: Norton, 1969), pp. 51–61; Robert A. Dahl, *Pluralist Democracy in the United States: Conflict and Consent* (Chicago: Rand McNally, 1967); and Dahl, *Dilemmas of Pluralist Democracy: Autonomy vs. Control* (New Haven: Yale University Press, 1982).

13. Hirschman, *The Passions and the Interests*.

14. Robert D. Putnam, "Bowling Alone: America's Declining Social Capital," *Journal of Democracy* 6, no. 1 (1995): 65–78.

15. Another possible way of distinguishing between a good civil society and bad interest-group advocacy is that good organizations do not seek rents or favors from the government but rather exist to provide services directly to their

members. Again, this kind of categorical distinction is not tenable: it is perfectly legitimate, if not always wise, for private parties to seek government help on specific issues.

16. Schattschneider, *The Semisovereign People*, pp. 129–41.

17. Mancur Olson, *The Logic of Collective Action: Public Goods and the Theory of Groups* (Cambridge, MA: Harvard University Press, 1965). For further discussion of representation in democracies, see Bernard Manin, Adam Przeworski, and Susan C. Stokes, "Elections and Representation," in Adam Przeworski, Susan C. Stokes, and Bernard Manin, eds., *Democracy, Accountability, and Representation* (New York: Cambridge University Press, 1999).

18. Morris P. Fiorina, *Disconnect: The Breakdown of Representation in American Politics* (Norman: University of Oklahoma Press, 2009); and Morris P. Fiorina, Samuel J. Abrams, and Jeremy C. Pope, eds., *Culture War? The Myth of a Polarized America*, 3rd ed. (Boston: Longman, 2010).

19. Stein Ringen makes the point that such consultation occurred even in authoritarian South Korea under Park Chung Hee. See *Nation of Devils: Democratic Leadership and the Problem of Obedience* (New Haven: Yale University Press, 2013), pp. 24–28. This is also the meaning of Peter Evans's concept of "embedded autonomy."

20. For an account of how information consultation operates within the European Union, see Charles Sabel and Jonathan Zeitlin, "Learning from Difference: The New Architecture of Experimentalist Governance in the European Union," *European Law Journal* 14, no. 3 (2008): 271–317.

34: AMERICA THE VETOCRACY

1. U.S. debt in 1945 was 112.7 percent of GDP (www.cbo.gov/publication/21728), that of Britain 225 percent (www.res.org.uk/view/article5jan12Correspondence.html).

2. William A. Galston, *Can a Polarized American Party System Be "Healthy"?* (Washington, D.C.: Brookings Institution, 2010).

3. Morris Fiorina points out that the strongly conservative candidate Rick Santorum was briefly declared the Republican front-runner in the 2012 primaries based on the votes of 1.2, 1.8, and 7.4 percent of the electorates of just three states. Fiorina, "America's Missing Moderates: Hiding in Plain Site," *American Interest* 8(4): 58–67.

4. Thomas E. Mann and Norman J. Ornstein, *It's Even Worse Than It Looks: How the American Constitutional System Collided with the New Politics of Extremism* (New York: Basic Books, 2012), p. 154.

5. This has been characterized as a trade-off between decisiveness and resoluteness (Gary Cox and Mathew McCubbins, "The Institutional Determinants of Economic Policy Outcomes," in Stephan Haggard and Mathew D. McCubbins, eds., *Presidents, Parliaments, and Policy* [New York: Cambridge University Press, 2001], pp. 21–64), or between decisiveness and credibility (Andrew MacIntyre, *The*

Power of Institutions: Political Architecture and Governance [Ithaca, NY: Cornell University Press, 2003], pp. 17–36).

6. Gary Cox, "The Power of the Purse and the Reversionary Budget" (unpublished paper, Stanford University, Department of Political Science, 2013).

7. George Tsebelis, *Veto Players: How Political Institutions Work* (Princeton: Princeton University Press, 2002).

8. The coalition government combining the Conservative and Liberal Democratic Parties that took power in 2010 was highly unusual in British practice. It is more often the case that strong parliamentary majorities are elected by pluralities of actual voters.

9. Herbert Döring, *Parliaments and Majority Rule in Western Europe* (New York: St. Martin's Press, 1995), pp. 223–46.

10. See Jacqueline Yates, "Sweden," in J. A. Chandler, ed., *Comparative Public Administration* (New York: Routledge, 2000).

11. Gerhard Casper, "The United States at the End of the 'American Century': The Rule of Law or Enlightened Absolutism?" *Washington University Journal of Law and Policy* 4 (2000): 149–73.

12. "Statement by George Little on Length of Congressional Reports," U.S. Department of Defense, press release, July 11, 2007, www.defense.gov/releases/release .aspx?releaseid=15437.

13. Luce, *Time to Start Thinking*, chap. 4.

14. On the general issue of the lack of legislative coherence, see Bok, *Trouble With Government*, pp. 98–103.

15. Eric A. Posner and Adrian Vermeule, *The Executive Unbound: After the Madisonian Republic* (New York: Oxford University Press, 2010).

16. See Joachim Herrmann, "The German Prosecutor," in Kenneth Culp Davis et al., eds., *Discretionary Justice in Europe and America* (Urbana: University of Illinois Press, 1976).

17. Christine Mahoney, "The Power of Institutions: State and Interest-Group Activity and the European Union," *European Union Politics* 5, no. 4 (2004): 441–66; Mahoney, *Brussels versus the Beltway: Advocacy in the United States and the European Union* (Washington, D.C.: Georgetown University Press, 2008); Darren Halpin and Grant Jordan, eds., *The Scale of Interest Organization in Democratic Politics: Data and Research Methods* (New York: Palgrave Macmillan, 2012); Robin Pedler, ed., *European Union Lobbying: Changes in the Arena* (New York: Palgrave, 2002); Jan Beyers, Rainer Eising, and William Maloney, eds., *Interest Group Politics in Europe: Lessons from EU Studies and Comparative Politics* (New York: Routledge, 2010); Sonia Mazey and Jeremy Richardson, eds., *Lobbying in the European Community* (New York: Oxford University Press, 1993).

18. See Mahoney, *Brussels versus the Beltway*, pp. 147–65. The reason for this difference is not simply the nature of EU institutions; civil society groups find it harder to organize across national media and language boundaries in Europe than in the United States.

19. Theda Skocpol, *Protecting Soldiers and Mothers: The Political Origins of Social Policy in the United States* (Cambridge, MA: Harvard University Press, 1992); Desmond King et al., eds., *Democratization in America: A Comparative-Historical Analysis* (Baltimore: Johns Hopkins University Press, 2009). For a general comparison of welfare states in Europe and the United States, see Arnold J. Heidenheimer and Peter Flora, eds., *The Development of the Welfare States in Europe and America* (New Brunswick, NJ: Transaction, 1987).

35: AUTONOMY AND SUBORDINATION

1. World Bank, *World Development Report 2004: Making Services Work for Poor People* (Washington, D.C.: World Bank, 2003).
2. For a longer discussion of principal-agent theory and its limitations, see Francis Fukuyama, *State-Building: Governance and World Order in the 21st Century* (Ithaca, NY: Cornell University Press, 2004), chap. 2.
3. Martin van Creveld, *Fighting Power: German and U.S. Army Performance, 1939–1945* (Westport, CT: Greenwood Press, 1982). See also Wilson, *Bureaucracy*, pp. 3–6, on the contrasts between the German and French armies on the eve of World War II.
4. DiIulio describes a situation in 1987 in which serious prison riots broke out simultaneously in Louisiana and Georgia. A group of retired prison officials, all members of the Federal Prison Retirees Association, put on their old uniforms and paid their own way to the riot scenes to assist in the crisis. As the author points out, the principal-agent framework, seeing human beings as motivated primarily by material rewards, can't account for this kind of public-spirited behavior. John J. DiIulio, Jr., "Principled Agents: The Cultural Bases of Behavior in a Federal Government Bureaucracy," *Journal of Public Administration Research and Theory* 4, no. 3 (1994): 277–318.
5. On the role of the Huguenots in creating the Swiss watch industry, see David S. Landes, *Revolution in Time: Clocks and the Making of the Modern World*, rev. ed. (Cambridge, MA: Harvard University Press, 2000), pp. 248–57: On the role of Orthodox Jews in the diamond trade, see James S. Coleman, "Social Capital in the Creation of Human Capital," *American Journal of Sociology* 94 (1988): S95–S120.
6. Melissa Thomas, "Great Expectations: Rich Donors and Poor Country Governments," http://papers.ssrn.com/sol3/papers.cfm?abstract_id=1333618.
7. See Davis, *Discretionary Justice in Europe and America*.
8. This field manual was based on the operational doctrine that had been developed by the German army from the end of World War I through the beginning of World War II; mission orders are an American version of *Aufstragstaktik*. See Francis Fukuyama and Abram N. Shulsky, *The "Virtual Corporation" and Army Organization* (Santa Monica, CA: RAND Corp., 1997).
9. Ringen, *Nation of Devils*, pp. 24–29.

36: POLITICAL ORDER AND POLITICAL DECAY

1. For Friedrich Hayek's arguments against rationalist planning and in favor of spontaneous order, see *Law, Legislation and Liberty* (Chicago: University of Chicago Press, 1976), and *The Constitution of Liberty* (Chicago: University of Chicago Press, 2011).
2. See Robert H. Frank, *The Darwin Economy: Liberty, Competition, and the Common Good* (Princeton: Princeton University Press, 2011).
3. On the limitations of the contemporary microfinance movement, see David Roodman, *Due Diligence: An Impertinent Inquiry into Microfinance* (Washington, D.C.: Center for Global Development, 2012). On extending property rights to the poor, see Hernando de Soto, *The Mystery of Capital: Why Capitalism Triumphs in the West and Fails Everywhere Else* (London: Bantam Press, 2000).
4. Amartya Sen, *Development as Freedom* (New York: Knopf, 1999), p. 27.
5. For a much longer discussion of the role of recognition and dignity in politics, see Fukuyama, *The End of History and the Last Man*, pp. 162–208.
6. On China's challenges in moving from middle- to high-income status, see the World Bank, *China 2030: Building a Modern, Harmonious, and Creative Society* (Washington, D.C.: World Bank, 2013).
7. See, for example, Gary Cox, Douglass North, and Barry Weingast, "The Violence Trap: A Political-Economic Approach to the Problems of Development" (unpublished paper, September 2013).

BIBLIOGRAPHY

Abdullah, Taufik. 2009. *Indonesia: Towards Democracy*. Singapore: ISEAS.

Abernethy, David B. 2000. *The Dynamics of Global Dominance: European Overseas Empires, 1415–1980*. New Haven: Yale University Press.

Acemoglu, Daron, Simon Johnson, and James A. Robinson. 2001. "The Colonial Origins of Comparative Development: An Empirical Investigation." *American Economic Review* 91(5):1369–1401.

———. 2002. "Reversal of Fortune: Geography and Institutions in the Making of the Modern World Income Distribution." *Quarterly Journal of Economics* 107:1231–94.

Acemoglu, Daron, and James A. Robinson. 2005. *Economic Origins of Dictatorship and Democracy*. New York: Cambridge University Press.

———. 2012. *Why Nations Fail: The Origins of Power, Prosperity and Poverty*. New York: Crown.

Admati, Anat, and Martin Hellwig. 2013. *The Banker's New Clothes: What's Wrong with Banking and What to Do About It*. Princeton: Princeton University Press.

Akita, George. 1967. *Foundations of Constitutional Government in Modern Japan, 1868–1900*. Cambridge, MA: Harvard University Press.

Allum, P. A. 1973. *Italy—Republic Without Government?* New York: Norton.

———. 1973. *Politics and Society in Post-War Naples*. Cambridge: Cambridge University Press.

Almond, Gabriel A., et al. 2004. *Comparative Politics: A Theoretical Framework*. 5th ed. New York: Pearson/Longman.

Amsden, Alice H. 1989. *Asia's Next Giant: South Korea and Late Industrialization*. New York: Oxford University Press.

Anderson, Benedict. 1991. *Imagined Communities: Reflections on the Origins and Spread of Nationalism*. New York: Verso.

Ang, Yuen Yuen. 2012. "Bureaucratic Incentives, Local Development, and Petty Rents." Paper presented at the Conference on the Quality of Governance. Stanford University.

Anson, José, Oliver Cadot, and Marcelo Olarreaga. 2003. *Import Tariff Evasion and Customs Corruption: Does Pre-Shipment Inspection Help?* Washington, D.C.: World Bank.

Auyero, Javier. 2000. "The Logic of Clientelism in Argentina: An Ethnographic Account." *Latin American Research Review* 35(3):55–81.

Ayittey, George B. N. 2006. *Indigenous African Institutions.* 2nd ed. Ardsley-on-Hudson, NY: Transactional Publishers.

Bagehot, Walter. 2001. *The English Constitution.* New York: Oxford University Press.

Balogh, Brian. 2002. "Scientific Forestry and the Roots of the Modern American State: Gifford Pinchot's Path to Progressive Reform." *Environmental History* 7(2):198–225.

Banerjee, Abhijit, and Lakshmi Iyer. 2005. "History, Institutions, and Economic Performance: The Legacy of Colonial Land Tenure Systems in India." *American Economic Review* 95(4):1190–1213.

Banfield, Edward C. 1958. *The Moral Basis of a Backward Society.* Glencoe, IL: Free Press.

———, and James Q. Wilson. 1963. *City Politics.* Cambridge, MA: Harvard University Press.

Barber, Michael. 2008. *Instruction to Deliver: Fighting to Transform Britain's Public Services.* London: Methuen.

Barkan, Joel D., ed. 1994. *Beyond Capitalism vs. Socialism in Kenya and Tanzania.* Boulder, CO: Lynne Rienner.

Barro, Robert J. 1997. *Determinants of Economic Growth: A Cross-Country Survey.* Cambridge, MA: MIT Press.

———. 1999. "Determinants of Democracy." *Journal of Political Economy* 107: 158–83.

Bates, Robert. 2005. *Markets and States in Tropical Africa: The Political Basis of Agricultural Policies.* Berkeley: University of California Press.

Baumgartner, Frank R., and Beth L. Leech. 1998. *Basic Interests: The Importance of Groups in Politics and in Political Science.* Princeton: Princeton University Press.

Baumgartner, Frank R., et al. 2009. *Lobbying and Policy Change: Who Wins, Who Loses, and Why.* Chicago: University of Chicago Press.

Beer, Lawrence W., and John M. Maki. 2002. *From Imperial Myth to Democracy: Japan's Two Constitutions, 1889–2002.* Boulder: University Press of Colorado.

Bell, Daniel. 1973. *The Coming of Post-Industrial Society: A Venture in Social Forecasting.* New York: Basic Books.

Berman, Sheri. 2013. "The Promise of the Arab Spring: In Political Development, No Gain Without Pain." *Foreign Affairs* 92(1):64–74.

Bernhardt, Kathryn, and Philip C. C. Huang, eds. 1994. *Civil Law in Qing and Republican China*. Stanford, CA: Stanford University Press.

Berry, Sara. 1993. *No Condition Is Permanent: The Social Dynamics of Agrarian Change in Sub-Saharan Africa*. Madison: University of Wisconsin Press.

Beyers, Jan, Rainer Eising, and William Maloney, eds. 2010. *Interest Group Politics in Europe: Lessons from EU Studies and Comparative Politics*. New York: Routledge.

Bienen, Henry S. 1970. *Tanzania: Party Transformation and Economic Development*. Princeton: Princeton University Press.

Biles, Roger. 1984. *Big City Boss in Depression and War: Mayor Edward J. Kelly of Chicago*. DeKalb: Northern Illinois University Press.

Birdsall, Nancy, and Francis Fukuyama, eds. 2001. *New Ideas in Development After the Financial Crisis*. Baltimore: Johns Hopkins University Press.

Bodde, Derk, and Clarence Morris. 1967. *Law in Imperial China, Exemplified by 190 Ch'ing Dynasty Cases*. Cambridge, MA: Harvard University Press.

Boix, Carles. 2003. *Democracy and Redistribution*. New York: Cambridge University Press.

Bok, Derek. 2001. *The Trouble With Government*. Cambridge, MA: Harvard University Press.

Bolin, James Duane. 2000. *Bossism and Reform in a Southern City: Lexington, Kentucky, 1880–1940*. Lexington: University Press of Kentucky.

Booth, John A. 1998. *Costa Rica: Quest for Democracy*. Boulder, CO: Westview Press.

Bortz, Jeffrey, and Stephen Haber, eds. 2002. *The Mexican Economy, 1870–1930: Essays on the Economic History of Institutions, Revolution, and Growth*. Stanford, CA: Stanford University Press.

Böss, Michael, ed. 2011. *Narrating Peoplehood Amidst Diversity: Historical and Theoretical Perspectives*. Aarhus, Denmark: Aarhus University Press.

Bourne, J. M. 1986. *Patronage and Society in Nineteenth-Century England*. Baltimore: Edward Arnold.

Bradshaw, Karen M., and Dean Lueck. 2012. *Wildfire Policy: Law and Economics Perspectives*. New York: RFF Press.

Bratton, Michael, and Nicolas van de Walle. 1997. *Democratic Experiments in Africa: Regime Transitions in Comparative Perspective*. New York: Cambridge University Press.

Briggs, Asa. 1959. *The Age of Improvement, 1783–1867*. New York: Longman.

Brooks, Robert. 1909. "The Nature of Political Corruption." *Political Science Quarterly* 24(1):1–22.

Brubaker, Rogers. 1996. *Nationalism Reframed: Nationhood and the National Question in the New Europe*. New York: Cambridge University Press.

———. 2004. *Ethnicity without Groups*. Cambridge, MA: Harvard University Press.

Brusco, Valeria, Marcelo Nazareno, and Susan Carol Stokes. 2004. "Vote Buying in Argentina." *Latin American Research Review* 39(2):66–88.

Brynjolfsson, Erik, and Andrew McAfee. 2014. *The Second Machine Age: Work, Progress, and Prosperity in a Time of Brilliant Technologies*. New York: Norton.

Buchanan, James M., and Gordon Tullock. 1962. *The Calculus of Consent: Logical Foundations of Constitutional Democracy*. Ann Arbor: University of Michigan Press.

Burke, Edmund. 2000. *On Empire, Liberty, and Reform: Speeches and Letters*. New Haven: Yale University Press.

———. 2001. *Reflections on the Revolution in France*. Stanford, CA: Stanford University Press.

Bushnell, David, and Neill Macaulay. 1994. *The Emergence of Latin America in the Nineteenth Century*. 2nd ed. New York: Oxford University Press.

Cain, Bruce E. 2014. *Regulating Politics? The Democratic Imperative and American Political Reform*. New York: Cambridge University Press.

Calvo, Ernesto, and Maria Victoria Murillo. 2004. "Who Delivers? Partisan Clients in the Argentine Electoral Market." *American Journal of Political Science* 48(4):742–57.

Campbell, John. 2011. *Nigeria: Dancing on the Brink*. Lanham, MD: Rowman and Littlefield.

Carman, Harry J., and Reinhard H. Luthin. 1943. *Lincoln and the Patronage*. New York: Columbia University Press.

Carneiro, Robert L. 1970. "A Theory of the Origin of the State," *Science* 169: 733–38.

Carothers, Thomas. 2007. "The 'Sequencing' Fallacy." *Journal of Democracy* 18(1):12–27.

———, ed. 2006. *Promoting the Rule of Law Abroad: In Search of Knowledge*. Washington, D.C.: Carnegie Endowment.

Carpenter, Daniel P. 2001. *The Forging of Bureaucratic Autonomy: Reputations, Networks, and Policy Innovation in Executive Agencies, 1862–1928*. Princeton: Princeton University Press.

Casper, Gerhard. 1985. "The Constitutional Organization of the Government." *William and Mary Law Review* 26(2):177–98.

———. 2000. "The United States at the End of the 'American Century': The Rule of Law or Enlightened Absolutism?" *Washington University Journal of Law and Policy* 4:149–73.

Castellani, Francesca, and Gwenn Parent. 2011. *Being "Middle Class" in Latin America*. Paris: OECD Development Centre Working Paper, No. 305.

Centeno, Miguel Angel. 1997. "Blood and Debt: War and Taxation in Nineteenth-Century Latin America." *American Journal of Sociology* 102(6):1565–1605.

———. 2002. *Blood and Debt: War and the Nation-State in Latin America*. University Park: Pennsylvania State University Press.

Chadwick, Mary E. J. 1976. "The Role of Redistribution in the Making of the Third Reform Act." *The Historical Journal* 19(3):665–83.

Chandler, J. A., ed. 2000. *Comparative Public Administration*. New York: Routledge.

Chandra, Kanchan. 2004. *Why Ethnic Parties Succeed: Patronage and Ethnic Head Counts in India*. New York: Cambridge University Press.

Chapman, Richard. 1970. *The Higher Civil Service in Britain*. London: Constable.

———. 2004. *The Civil Service Commission 1855–1991: A Bureau Biography*. New York: Routledge.

Chege, Michael. 2008. "Kenya: Back from the Brink?" *Journal of Democracy* 19(4):125–39.

Chen, Jianfu. 1999. *Chinese Law: Towards an Understanding of Chinese Law, Its Nature and Development*. Boston: Kluwer Law International.

———. 2008. *Chinese Law: Context and Transformation*. Leiden: Martinus Nijhoff.

Chesterman, Simon. 2004. *You, the People: The United Nations, Transitional Administration, and State-Building*. New York: Oxford University Press.

Chubb, Judith. 1982. *Patronage, Power, and Poverty in Southern Italy: A Tale of Two Cities*. New York: Cambridge University Press.

Clark, Gregory. 2007. *A Farewell to Alms: A Brief Economic History of the World*. Princeton: Princeton University Press.

Cleary, Matthew R., and Susan C. Stokes. 2006. *Democracy and the Culture of Skepticism: Political Trust in Argentina and Mexico*. New York: Russell Sage Foundation.

Coatsworth, John H. 1978. "Obstacles to Economic Growth in Nineteenth-Century Mexico." *American Historical Review* 83:80–100.

Coatsworth, John H., and Alan M. Taylor, eds. 1999. *Latin America and the World Economy Since 1800*. Cambridge, MA: Harvard University Press.

Colburn, David R., and George E. Pozzetta. 1976. "Bosses and Machines: Changing Interpretations in American History." *The History Teacher* 9(3):445–63.

———, eds. 1983. *Reform and Reformers in the Progressive Era*. Westport, CT: Greenwood Press.

Coleman, James S. 1988. "Social Capital in the Creation of Human Capital." *American Journal of Sociology* 94:S95–S120.

Coleman, James S., et al. 1966. *Equality of Educational Opportunity*. Washington, D.C.: Department of Health, Education and Welfare.

Collier, George A., Renato I. Rosaldo, and John D. Wirth, eds. 1982. *The Inca and Aztec States, 1400–1800: Anthropology and History*. New York: Academic Press.

Collier, Paul. 2001. "Implications of Ethnic Diversity." *Economic Policy* 32:129–66.

———. 2007. *The Bottom Billion: Why the Poorest Countries Are Failing and What Can Be Done About It*. New York: Oxford University Press.

Collier, Paul, and Anke Hoeffler. 2006. *Economic Causes of Civil Conflict and Their Implications for Policy*. Oxford: Oxford Economic Papers.

Collier, Paul, and Dominic Rohner. 2007. "Beyond Greed and Grievance: Feasibility and Civil War." *Oxford Economic Papers* 61:1–27.

Collier, Ruth Berins. 1999. *Paths Toward Democracy: The Working Class and Elites in Western Europe and South America*. New York: Cambridge University Press.

Connors, Richard J. 1971. *A Cycle of Power: The Career of Jersey City Mayor Frank Hague*. Metuchen, NJ: Scarecrow Press.

Conrad, Alfred H., and John R. Meyer. 1979. "The Economics of Slavery in the Ante Bellum South: Comment." *American Economic Review* 66(2):95–130.

Cornford, James. 1963. "The Transformation of Conservatism in the Late Nineteenth Century." *Victorian Studies* 7:35–66.

Cortés Condé, Roberto. 2009. *The Political Economy of Argentina in the Twentieth Century*. New York: Cambridge University Press.

Cowen, Tyler. 2011. *The Great Stagnation: How America Ate All the Low-Hanging Fruit of Modern History, Got Sick, and Will (Eventually) Feel Better*. New York: Dutton.

Cox, Gary. 2013. "The Power of the Purse and the Reversionary Budget." Unpublished paper.

Cox, Gary, Douglass North, and Barry Weingast. 2013. "The Violence Trap: A Political-Economic Approach to the Problem of Development." Unpublished paper.

Craig, Gordon A. 1964. *The Politics of the Prussian Army, 1640–1945*. New York: Oxford University Press.

Crenson, Matthew A. 1975. *The Federal Machine: Beginning of Bureaucracy in Jacksonian America*. Baltimore: Johns Hopkins University Press.

Crowley, James B. 1966. *Japan's Quest for Autonomy: National Security and Foreign Policy, 1930–1938*. Princeton: Princeton University Press.

Cunliffe-Jones, Peter. 2010. *My Nigeria: Five Decades of Independence*. New York: Palgrave Macmillan.

Curtin, Philip D. 1998. *The Rise and Fall of the Plantation Complex: Essays in Atlantic History*. 2nd ed. New York: Cambridge University Press.

Dahl, Robert A. 1956. *A Preface to Democratic Theory*. Chicago: University of Chicago Press.

———. 1967. *Pluralist Democracy in the United States: Conflict and Consent*. Chicago: Rand McNally.

———. 1982. *Dilemmas of Pluralist Democracy: Autonomy vs. Control*. New Haven: Yale University Press.

Dahm, Bernhard. 1969. *Sukarno and the Struggle for Indonesian Independence*. Ithaca, NY: Cornell University Press.

Darden, Keith. 2013. *Resisting Occupation: Mass Schooling and the Creation of Durable National Loyalties*. New York: Cambridge University Press.

Darmaputera, Eka. 1988. *Pancasila and the Search for Identity and Modernity in Indonesian Society*. New York: E. J. Brill.

David, René. 1972. *French Law: Its Structure, Sources, and Methodology*. Baton Rouge: Louisiana State University Press.

Davis, Kenneth Culp, et al. 1976. *Discretionary Justice in Europe and America*. Urbana: University of Illinois Press.

Day, Tony. 2002. *Fluid Iron: State Formation in Southeast Asia.* Honolulu: University of Hawai'i Press.

Debusmann, Robert, and Stefan Arnold, eds. 1996. *Land Law and Land Ownership in Africa: Case Studies from Colonial and Contemporary Cameroon and Tanzania.* Bayreuth, Germany: Eckhard Breitinger.

Diamond, Jared. 1997. *Guns, Germs, and Steel: The Fates of Human Societies.* New York: Norton.

———. 2005. *Collapse: How Societies Choose to Fail or Succeed.* New York: Viking.

Diamond, Larry, 1992. "Economic Development and Democracy Reconsidered." *American Behavioral Scientist* 15(4–5):450–99.

———. 2008. *The Spirit of Democracy: The Struggle to Build Free Societies Throughout the World.* New York: Times Books.

Diamond, Larry, and Richard Gunther, eds. 2001. *Political Parties and Democracy.* Baltimore: Johns Hopkins University Press.

Diamond, Larry, Juan J. Linz, and Seymour Martin Lipset, eds., 1988. *Democracy in Developing Countries.* Boulder, CO: Lynne Rienner.

DiIulio, John J., Jr. 1994. "Principled Agents: The Cultural Bases of Behavior in a Federal Government Bureaucracy." *Journal of Public Administration Research and Theory* 4(3): 277–320.

Dobbins, James, et al. 2003. *America's Role in Nation-Building: From Germany to Iraq.* Santa Monica, CA: RAND Corp.

———. 2005. *The UN's Role in Nation-Building: From the Congo to Iraq.* Santa Monica, CA: RAND.

Döring, Herbert. 1995. *Parliaments and Majority Rule in Western Europe.* New York: St. Martin's Press.

Durkheim, Émile. 1933. *The Division of Labor in Society.* New York: Macmillan.

———. 1951. *Suicide.* Glencoe, IL: Free Press.

Duus, Peter. 1976. *The Rise of Modern Japan.* Boston: Houghton Mifflin.

Easterly, William R. 2000. *The Middle Class Consensus and Economic Development.* Washington, D.C.: World Bank Policy Research Paper No. 2346.

———. 2001. "Can Institutions Resolve Ethnic Conflict?" *Economic Development and Cultural Change* 49(4):687–706.

Eisenstadt, S. N. 1973. *Traditional Patrimonialism and Modern Neopatrimonialism.* Beverly Hills, CA: Sage.

Eisenstadt, S. N., and Stein Rokken, eds. 1973. *Building States and Nations.* Beverly Hills, CA: Sage.

Eisenstadt, S. N., and L. Roniger. 1984. *Patrons, Clients, and Friends: Interpersonal Relations and the Structure of Trust in Society.* New York: Cambridge University Press.

Eisenstein, Elizabeth L. 2005. *The Printing Revolution in Early Modern Europe.* 2nd ed. New York: Cambridge University Press.

Elias, T. Olawale. 1956. *The Nature of African Customary Law.* Manchester, UK: Manchester University Press.

Elliott, J. H. 2006. *Empires of the Atlantic World: Britain and Spain in America, 1492–1830*. New Haven: Yale University Press.

Elshtain, Jean Bethke. 2002. *Jane Addams and the Dream of American Democracy: A Life*. New York: Basic Books.

Elson, R. E. 2008. *The Idea of Indonesia*. New York: Cambridge University Press.

Eltis, David, Frank D. Lewis, and Kenneth L. Sokoloff, eds. 2004. *Slavery in the Development of the Americas*. New York: Cambridge University Press.

Emmerson, Donald K. 2004. "Indonesia's Approaching Elections: A Year of Voting Dangerously?" *Journal of Democracy* 15(1):94–108.

———. 2012. "Southeast Asia: Minding the Gap Between Democracy and Governance." *Journal of Democracy* 23(2):62–73.

Engerman, Stanley L., and Kenneth L. Sokoloff. 2002. "Factor Endowments, Inequality, and Paths of Development Among New World Economies." *Economia* 3(1):41–101.

Epstein, Leon D. 1967. *Political Parties in Western Democracies*. New York: Praeger.

Eriksson, Erik McKinley. 1927. "The Federal Civil Service Under President Jackson." *Mississippi Valley Historical Review* 13(4):517–40.

European Union Institute for Security Studies. 2012. *Global Trends 2030—Citizens in an Interconnected and Polycentric World*. Paris: EUISS.

Evans, Peter B. 1989. "Predatory, Developmental, and Other Apparatuses: A Comparative Analysis of the Third World State." *Sociological Forum* 4(4):561–82.

———. 1995. *Embedded Autonomy: States and Industrial Transformation*. Princeton: Princeton University Press.

Evans, Peter B., and James E. Rauch. 1999. "Bureaucracy and Growth: A Cross-National Analysis of the Effects of 'Weberian' State Structures on Economic Growth. *American Sociological Review* 64:748–65.

Evans-Pritchard, E. E. 1951. *Kinship and Marriage Among the Nuer*. Oxford: Oxford University Press.

———. 1977. *The Political System of the Anuak of the Anglo-Egyptian Sudan*. New York: AMS Press.

Fairbank, John King. 1986. *The Great Chinese Revolution, 1800–1985*. New York: Harper.

Falola, Toyin. 2009. *Colonialism and Violence in Nigeria*. Bloomington: Indiana University Press.

Falola, Toyin, and Matthew M. Heaton. 2008. *A History of Nigeria*. New York: Cambridge University Press.

Fearon, James D., and David Laitin. 2003. "Ethnicity, Insurgency, and Civil War." *American Political Science Review* 97:75–90.

Felice, Emanuele. 2010. "Regional Inequalities in Italy in the Long Run (1891–2001): The Pattern and Some Ideas to Explain It." University of Siena, Department of Economics.

Ferguson, Niall. 2003. *Empire: The Rise and Demise of the British World Order and Its Lessons for Global Power*. New York: Basic Books.

Fieldhouse, D. K. 1982. *The Colonial Empires: A Comparative Survey from the Eighteenth Century.* 2nd ed. London: Macmillan.

Fields, Karen E. 1985. *Revival and Rebellion in Colonial Central Africa.* Princeton: Princeton University Press.

Fiorina, Morris P. 2009. *Disconnect: The Breakdown of Representation in American Politics.* Norman: University of Oklahoma Press.

———. 2013. "America's Missing Moderates: Hiding in Plain Sight." *American Interest* 8(4):58–67.

Fiorina, Morris P., Samuel J. Abrams, and Jeremy C. Pope, eds. 2010. *Culture War? The Myth of a Polarized America.* 3rd ed. Boston: Longman.

Fischer, David Hackett. 1991. *Albion's Seed: Four British Folkways in America.* New York: Oxford University Press.

Fogel, Robert W., and Stanley L. Engerman. 1974. *Time on the Cross: The Economics of American Negro Slavery.* Boston: Little, Brown.

———. 1977. "Explaining the Relative Efficiency of Slave Agriculture in the Antebellum South." *American Economic Review* 67(3):275–96.

Forrest, Tom. 1993. *Politics and Economic Development in Nigeria.* Boulder, CO: Westview Press.

Frank, Robert H. 2011. *The Darwin Economy: Liberty, Competition, and the Common Good.* Princeton: Princeton University Press.

———, and Philip J. Cook. 1995. *The Winner-Take-All Society.* New York: Free Press.

Friedman, Thomas L., and Michael Mandelbaum. 2011. *That Used to Be Us: How America Fell Behind in the World It Invented and How We Can Come Back.* New York: Farrar, Straus and Giroux.

Friedrich, Carl J., and Zbigniew K. Brzezinski. 1965. *Totalitarian Dictatorship and Autocracy.* 2nd ed. Cambridge, MA: Harvard University Press.

Fukuyama, Francis. 1992. *The End of History and the Last Man.* New York: Free Press.

———. 1995. *Trust: The Social Virtues and the Creation of Prosperity.* New York: Free Press.

———. 1999. *The Great Disruption: Human Nature and the Reconstitution of Social Order.* New York: Free Press.

———. 2000. "The March of Equality." *Journal of Democracy* 11(1):11–17.

———. 2004. *State-Building: Governance and World Order in the 21st Century.* Ithaca, NY: Cornell University Press.

———. 2006. *America at the Crossroads: Democracy, Power, and the Neoconservative Legacy.* New Haven: Yale University Press.

———. 2006. "Identity, Immigration, and Liberal Democracy." *Journal of Democracy* 17(2):5–20.

———. 2011. "Is There a Proper Sequence in Democratic Transitions?" *Current History* 110(739):308–10.

———. 2011. *The Origins of Political Order: From Prehuman Times to the French Revolution.* New York: Farrar, Straus and Giroux.

———. 2012. "The Future of History." *Foreign Affairs* 91(1):53–61.

———. 2013. "What Is Governance?" *Governance* 26(3):347–68.

———. 2014. *Our Posthuman Future: Consequences of the Biotechnology Revolution.* New York: Farrar, Straus and Giroux.

———, ed. 2006. *Nation-Building: Beyond Afghanistan and Iraq.* Baltimore: Johns Hopkins University Press.

———, ed. 2008. *Falling Behind: Explaining the Development Gap Between Latin America and the United States.* New York: Oxford University Press.

Fukuyama, Francis, and Abram N. Shulsky. 1997. *The "Virtual Corporation" and Army Organization.* Santa Monica, CA: RAND Corp.

Furet, François. 1981. *Interpreting the French Revolution.* New York: Cambridge University Press.

———. 2006. "Democracy Without Nations?" *Journal of Democracy* 8:92–102.

Gallagher, Mary E. 2006. "Mobilizing the Law in China: 'Informed Disenchantment' and the Development of Legal Consciousness." *Law & Society Review* 40(4):783–816.

Gallup, John L., and Jeffrey D. Sachs. 2001. "The Economic Burden of Malaria." *American Journal of Tropical Medicine & Hygiene* 64(1–2):85–96.

Galston, William A. 2010. *Can a Polarized American Party System Be "Healthy"?* Washington, D.C.: Brookings Institution.

Gambetta, Diego. 1993. *The Sicilian Mafia: The Business of Private Protection.* Cambridge, MA: Harvard University Press.

Gann, L. H., and Peter Duignan, eds. 1970. *Colonialism in Africa, 1870–1960.* Vol. 2: *The History and Politics of Colonialism 1914–1960.* London: Cambridge University Press.

Garcia-Zamor, Jean-Claude. 1998. "Administrative Practices of the Aztecs, Incas, and Mayas: Lessons for Modern Development Administration." *International Journal of Public Administration* 21(1):145–71.

Gates, Paul W. 1996. *The Jeffersonian Dream: Studies in the History of American Land Policy and Development.* Albuquerque: University of New Mexico Press.

Gberie, Lansana. 2005. *A Dirty War in West Africa: The RUF and the Destruction of Sierra Leone.* Bloomington: Indiana University Press.

Geddes, Barbara. 1994. *Politician's Dilemma: Building State Capacity in Latin America.* Berkeley: University of California Press.

Gellner, Ernest. 1987. *Culture, Identity, and Politics.* New York: Cambridge University Press.

———. 1997. *Nationalism.* New York: NYU Press.

———. 2006. *Nations and Nationalism.* 2nd ed. Malden, MA: Blackwell.

Gerschenkron, Alexander. 1962. *Economic Backwardness in Historical Perspective.* Cambridge, MA: Harvard University Press.

Gilman, Nils. 2003. *Mandarins of the Future: Modernization Theory in Cold War America.* Baltimore: Johns Hopkins University Press.

Ginsborg, Paul. 2003. *Italy and Its Discontents: Family, Civil Society, State, 1980–2001.* New York: Palgrave Macmillan.

Gladden, E. N. 1967. *Civil Services of the United Kingdom, 1855–1970*. London: Frank Cass.

Gladstone, David. 1999. *The Twentieth-Century Welfare State*. New York: St. Martin's Press.

Gleditsch, Nils Petter, et al. 2002. "Armed Conflict 1946–2001: A New Dataset." *Journal of Peace Research* 39(5):615–37.

Glendon, Mary Ann. 1994. *A Nation Under Lawyers: How the Crisis in the Legal Profession Is Transforming American Society*. New York: Farrar, Straus and Giroux.

Göbel, Christian, and Lynette Ong. 2012. *Social Unrest in China*. London: Europe China Research and Advice Network.

Goldstone, Jack A. 1991. *Revolution and Rebellion in the Early Modern World*. Berkeley: University of California Press.

Goodman, Carl F. 2012. *The Rule of Law in Japan: A Comparative Analysis*. 3rd ed. The Hague: Kluwer Law International.

Goodnow, Frank J. 1893. *Comparative Administrative Law: An Analysis of the Administrative Systems, National and Local, of the United States, England, France and Germany*. 2 vols. New York: G. P. Putnam's Sons.

———. 1900. *Politics and Administration: A Study in Government*. New York: Macmillan.

Goody, Jack. 1971. *Technology, Tradition, and the State in Africa*. Oxford: Oxford University Press.

Gordon, Andrew. 1991. *Labor and Imperial Democracy in Prewar Japan*. Berkeley: University of California Press.

Gorski, Philip S. 2003. *The Disciplinary Revolution: Calvinism and the Rise of the State in Early Modern Europe*. Chicago: University of Chicago Press.

Goudie, A. W., and David Stasavage. 1998. "A Framework for an Analysis of Corruption." *Crime, Law & Social Change* 29(2–3):113–59.

Gould, Stephen Jay. 1981. *The Mismeasure of Man*. New York: Norton.

Graziano, Luigi. 1973. "Patron-Client Relationships in Southern Italy." *European Journal of Political Research* 1(1):3–34.

Greenaway, John. 2004. "Celebrating Northcote/Trevelyan: Dispelling the Myths." *Public Policy and Administration* 19(1):1–14.

Greenfeld, Liah. 1992. *Nationalism: Five Roads to Modernity*. Cambridge, MA: Harvard University Press.

Grindle, Merilee S. 2004. "Good Enough Governance: Poverty Reduction and Reform in Developing Countries." *Governance* 17(4):525–48.

———. 2012. *Jobs for the Boys: Patronage and the State in Comparative Perspective*. Cambridge, MA: Harvard University Press.

Haber, Stephen, ed. 1997. *How Latin America Fell Behind: Essays on the Economic Histories of Brazil and Mexico, 1800–1914*. Stanford, CA: Stanford University Press.

Hacker, Jacob S., and Paul Pierson. 2010. *Winner-Take-All Politics: How Washington Made the Rich Richer—and Turned Its Back on the Middle Class*. New York: Simon & Schuster.

———. 2010. "Winner-Take-All Politics: Public Policy, Political Organization, and the Precipitous Rise of Top Incomes in the United States." *Politics and Society* 38(2):152–204.

Hadley, Eleanor M. 2003. *Memoir of a Trustbuster: A Lifelong Adventure with Japan.* Honolulu: University of Hawai'i Press.

Haggard, Stephan, and Mathew D. McCubbins, eds. 2001. *Presidents, Parliaments, and Policy.* New York: Cambridge University Press.

Halpin, Darren, and Grant Jordan, eds. 2012. *The Scale of Interest Organization in Democratic Politics: Data and Research Methods.* New York: Palgrave Macmillan.

Hariri, Jacob Gerner. 2012. "The Autocratic Legacy of Early Statehood." *American Political Science Review* 106(3):471–94.

Harrison, Lawrence E. 1985. *Underdevelopment Is a State of Mind: The Latin American Case.* Lanham, MD: Center for International Affairs.

———. 2013. *Jews, Confucians, and Protestants: Cultural Capital and the End of Multiculturalism.* Lanham, MD: Rowman and Littlefield.

Harriss, John, Janet Hunter, and Colin M. Lewis, eds. 1997. *The New Institutional Economics and Third World Development.* New York: Routledge.

Hartmann, Rudolph H. 1999. *The Kansas City Investigation: Pendergast's Downfall, 1938–1939.* Columbia: University of Missouri Press.

Hartz, Louis. 1955. *The Liberal Tradition in America.* New York: Harcourt.

———. 1964. *The Founding of New Societies.* New York: Harcourt.

Hausmann, Ricardo, Lant Pritchett, and Dani Rodrik. 2005. "Growth Accelerations." *Journal of Economic Growth* 10(4):303–29.

Hayek, Friedrich A. 1944. *The Road to Serfdom.* Chicago: University of Chicago Press.

———. 1976. *Law, Legislation and Liberty.* Chicago: University of Chicago Press.

———. 2011. *The Constitution of Liberty.* Definitive edition. Chicago: University of Chicago Press.

Heady, Ferrel. 2001. *Public Administration: A Comparative Perspective.* 6th ed. New York: Marcel Dekker.

Heidenheimer, Arnold J., and Peter Flora, eds. 1981. *The Development of the Welfare States in Europe and America.* New Brunswick, NJ: Transaction.

Heidenheimer, Arnold J., and Michael Johnston, eds. 2002. *Political Corruption.* 3rd ed. New Brunswick, NJ: Transaction.

Herbst, Jeffrey. 2000. *States and Power in Africa.* Princeton: Princeton University Press.

Herbst, Jeffrey, Terence McNamee, and Greg Mills, eds. 2012. *On the Fault Line: Managing Tensions and Divisions Within Societies.* London: Profile Books.

Himmelfarb, Gertrude. 1968. *Victorian Minds.* New York: Knopf.

Hintze, Otto. 1975. *The Historical Essays of Otto Hintze.* New York: Oxford University Press.

Hirschman, Albert O. 1977. *The Passions and the Interests: Political Arguments for Capitalism Before Its Triumph.* Princeton: Princeton University Press.

———. 1991. *The Rhetoric of Reaction: Perversity, Futility, Jeopardy.* Cambridge, MA: Belknap Press.

Hobsbawm, Eric. 1996. *The Age of Capital, 1848–1875*. New York: Vintage Books.

———. 1996. *The Age of Revolution, 1789–1848*. New York: Vintage Books.

Hobsbawm, Eric, and Terence Ranger, eds. 1983. *The Invention of Tradition*. New York: Cambridge University Press.

Hofler, Richard A., and Sherman T. Folland. 1991. "The Relative Efficiency of Slave Agriculture: A Comment." *Applied Economics* 23(5):861–68.

Holborn, Hajo. 1982. *A History of Modern Germany 1648–1840*. Princeton: Princeton University Press.

Hoogenboom, Ari. 1959. "The Pendleton Act and the Civil Service." *American Historical Review* 64(2): 301–18.

Hoogenboom, Ari, and Olive Hoogenboom. 1976. *A History of the ICC: From Panacea to Palliative*. New York: Norton.

Hsing, You-tien. 2010. *The Great Urban Transformation: Politics of Land and Property in China*. New York: Oxford University Press.

Huang, Philip C. C., ed. 2001. *Code, Custom, and Legal Practice in China: The Qing and the Republic Compared*. Stanford, CA: Stanford University Press.

Huang, Ray. 1981. *1587, a Year of No Significance: The Ming Dynasty in Decline*. New Haven: Yale University Press.

Hughes, Edward. 1949. "Sir Charles Trevelyan and Civil Service Reform, 1853–5." *English Historical Review* 64(250):53–88.

Hughes, John. 1967. *Indonesian Upheaval*. New York: David McKay.

Huntington, Samuel P. 1965. "Political Development and Political Decay." *World Politics* 17(3).

———. 1966. "Political Modernization: America vs. Europe." *World Politics* 18:378–414.

———. 1991. *The Third Wave: Democratization in the Late Twentieth Century*. Oklahoma City: University of Oklahoma Press.

———. 2004. *Who Are We? The Challenges to America's National Identity*. New York: Simon & Schuster.

———. 2006. *Political Order in Changing Societies*. With a New Foreword by Francis Fukuyama. New Haven: Yale University Press.

Hutchcroft, Paul D. 1997. "The Politics of Privilege: Assessing the Impact of Rents, Corruption, and Clientelism on Third World Development." *Political Studies* 45(3):639–58.

———. 2000. "Colonial Masters, National Politicos, and Provincial Lords: Central Authority and Local Autonomy in the American Philippines, 1900–1913." *Journal of Asian Studies* 59(2):277–306.

Hutchison, Thomas W., et al., eds. 1968. *Africa and Law: Developing Legal Systems in African Commonwealth Nations*. Madison: University of Wisconsin Press.

Hyden, Goran. 1968. *Political Development in Rural Tanzania*. Lund: Bokforlaget Universitet och Skola.

———. 1980. *Beyond Ujamaa in Tanzania: Underdevelopment and an Uncaptured Peasantry*. Berkeley: University of California Press.

Hyden, Goran, and Colin Leys. 1972. "Elections and Politics in Single-Party Systems: The Case of Kenya and Tanzania." *British Journal of Political Science* 2(4):389–420.

Hyman, Harold M. 1986. *American Singularity: The 1787 Northwest Ordinance, the 1862 Homestead and Morrill Acts, and the 1944 G.I. Bill*. Athens: University of Georgia Press.

Iaryczower, Matías, Pablo T. Spiller, and Mariano Tommasi. 2002. "Judicial Independence in Unstable Environments, Argentina 1935–1998." *American Journal of Political Science* 46(4):699–716.

Inglehart, Ronald. 1997. *Modernization and Postmodernization: Cultural, Economic, and Political Change in 43 Societies*. Princeton: Princeton University Press.

Inglehart, Ronald, and Christian Welzel. 2005. *Modernization, Cultural Change, and Democracy: The Human Development Sequence*. New York: Cambridge University Press.

Ingraham, Patricia W. 1995. *The Foundation of Merit: Public Service in American Democracy*. Baltimore: Johns Hopkins University Press.

Ingraham, Patricia W., and David H. Rosenbloom. 1990. "Political Foundations of the American Federal Service: Rebuilding a Crumbling Base." *Public Administration Review* 50(2):210–19.

Intan, Benjamin Fleming. 2006. *"Public Religion" and the Pancasila-Based State of Indonesia*. New York: Peter Lang.

Iyer, Lakshmi. 2010. "Direct v. Indirect Colonial Rule in India: Long-Term Consequences." *Review of Economics and Statistics* 92(4):693–713.

Jacobstein, Helen L. 1987. *The Process of Economic Development in Costa Rica, 1948–1970: Some Political Factors*. New York: Garland Publishing.

James, Scott C. 2006. "Patronage Regimes and American Party Development from 'The Age of Jackson' to the Progressive Era." *British Journal of Political Science* 36(1):39–60.

Jamison, Kay Redfield. 2004. *Exuberance: The Passion for Life*. New York: Knopf.

Jansen, Marius B. 1995. *The Emergence of Meiji Japan*. New York: Cambridge University Press.

Jensen, Erik G., and Thomas C. Heller. 2003. *Beyond Common Knowledge: Empirical Approaches to the Rule of Law*. Stanford, CA: Stanford University Press.

Joffe, Josef. 2014. *The Myth of America's Decline: Politics, Economics, and a Half Century of False Prophecies*. New York: Liveright.

Johnson, Chalmers. 1982. *MITI and the Japanese Miracle*. Stanford, CA: Stanford University Press.

Johnson, Simon. 2010. *13 Bankers: The Wall Street Takeover and the Next Financial Meltdown*. New York: Pantheon.

Johnston, Michael. 2005. *Syndromes of Corruption*. New York: Cambridge University Press.

Jones, Seth. 2013. "The Mirage of the Arab Spring: Deal with the Region You Have, Not the Region You Want." *Foreign Affairs* 92(1):47–54.

Joseph, Richard A. 1987. *Democracy and Prebendal Politics in Nigeria: The Rise and Fall of the Second Republic.* New York: Cambridge University Press.

Kagan, Robert. 2003. "The Ungreat Washed: Why Democracy Must Remain America's Goal Abroad." *New Republic* (July 7 and 14):27–37.

Kagan, Robert A. 1997. "Should Europe Worry About Adversarial Legalism?" *Oxford Journal of Legal Studies* 17(2):165–83.

———. 2001. *Adversarial Legalism: The American Way of Law.* Cambridge, MA: Harvard University Press.

Kaiser Family Foundation. 2012. *Health Care Costs: A Primer. Key Information on Health Care Costs and Their Impact.* Menlo Park, CA: Kaiser Family Foundation.

Kaplan, H. Eliot. 1937. "Accomplishments of the Civil Service Reform Movement." *Annals of the American Academy of Political and Social Science* 189:142–47.

Kaplan, Robert D. 2000. *The Coming Anarchy: Shattering the Dreams of the Post Cold War.* New York: Random House.

Katz, Richard S., and William J. Crotty, eds. 2006. *Handbook of Party Politics.* Thousand Oaks, CA: Sage.

Kaufman, Herbert. 1960. *The Forest Ranger: A Study in Administrative Behavior.* Baltimore: Johns Hopkins University Press.

Kaufmann, Daniel. 1997. "Corruption: The Facts." *Foreign Policy* 107:114–31.

Kawata, Junichi, ed. 2006. *Comparing Political Corruption and Clientelism.* Hampshire, UK: Ashgate.

Kedourie, Elie. 1992. *Politics in the Middle East.* New York: Oxford University Press.

Keefer, Philip. 2007. "Clientelism, Credibility, and the Policy Choices of Young Democracies." *American Journal of Political Science* 51(4):804–21.

Keefer, Philip, and Razvan Vlaicu. 2008. "Democracy, Credibility, and Clientelism." *Journal of Law, Economics, and Organization* 24(2):371–406.

Keller, Morton. 2007. *America's Three Regimes: A New Political History.* New York: Oxford University Press.

Kelman, Steven. 1981. *Regulating America, Regulating Sweden: A Comparative Study of Occupational Safety and Health Policy.* Cambridge, MA: MIT Press.

Kennedy, Paul. 1987. *The Rise and Fall of the Great Powers: Economic Change and Military Conflict from 1500 to 2000.* New York: Random House.

Khan, Mushtaq H. 2005. "Markets, States, and Democracy: Patron-Client Networks and the Case for Democracy in Developing Countries." *Democratization* 12(5):704–24.

Khan, Mushtaq H., and Jomo Kwame Sundaram, eds. 2000. *Rents, Rent-Seeking and Economic Development: Theory and Evidence in Asia.* New York: Cambridge University Press.

Khilnani, Sunil. 1998. *The Idea of India.* New York: Farrar, Straus and Giroux.

Kiai, Maina. 2008. "The Crisis in Kenya." *Journal of Democracy* 19(3):162–68.

King, Desmond, et al., eds. 2009. *Democratization in America: A Comparative-Historical Analysis.* Baltimore: Johns Hopkins University Press.

Kitschelt, Herbert, and Steven I. Wilkinson, eds. 2007. *Patrons, Clients, and Policies: Patterns of Democratic Accountability and Political Competition.* New York: Cambridge University Press.

Klitgaard, Robert. 1988. *Controlling Corruption.* Berkeley: University of California Press.

———. 1990. *Tropical Gangsters: One Man's Experience with Development and Decadence in Deepest Africa.* New York: Basic Books.

Knack, Stephen, and Philip Keefer. 1995. "Institutions and Economic Performance: Cross-Country Tests Using Alternative Measures." *Economics and Politics* 7:207–27.

Knott, Jack H., and Gary J. Miller. 1987. *Reforming Bureaucracy: The Politics of Institutional Choice.* Englewood Cliffs, NJ: Prentice-Hall.

Koh, B. C. 1989. *Japan's Administrative Elite.* Berkeley: University of California Press.

Kohli, Atul. 2004. *State-Directed Development: Political Power and Industrialization in the Global Periphery.* New York: Cambridge University Press.

Kolko, Gabriel. 1965. *Railroads and Regulation, 1877–1916.* Princeton: Princeton University Press.

Kojève, Alexandre. 1947. *Introduction à la Lecture de Hegel.* Paris: Gallimard.

Krastev, Ivan. 2013. "The Rise and Fall of Democracy? Meritocracy?" *Russia in Global Affairs* 11(2):8–22.

Krueger, Anne O. 1974. "The Political Economy of the Rent-Seeking Society." *American Economic Review* 64(3):291–303.

Kuper, Hilda, and Leo Kuper, eds. 1965. *African Law: Adaptation and Development.* Berkeley: University of California Press.

Kurtz, Marcus J. 2013. *Latin American State Building in Comparative Perspective.* New York: Cambridge University Press.

Laitin, David D. 2007. *Nations, States, and Violence.* New York: Oxford University Press.

Landes, David S. 1998. *The Wealth and Poverty of Nations: Why Some Are So Rich and Some So Poor.* New York: Norton.

———. 2000. *Revolution in Time: Clocks and the Making of the Modern World.* Rev. ed. Cambridge, MA: Harvard University Press.

Landis, James M. 1938. *The Administrative Process.* New Haven: Yale University Press.

Landy, Marc K., and Martin A. Levin, eds. 1995. *The New Politics of Public Policy.* Baltimore: Johns Hopkins University Press.

Lange, Matthew. 2009. *Lineages of Despotism and Development: British Colonialism and State Power.* Chicago: University of Chicago Press.

Lange, Matthew, and Dietrich Rueschemeyer, eds. 2005. *States and Development: Historical Antecedents of Stagnation and Advance.* New York: Palgrave Macmillan.

LaPalombara, Joseph. 1964. *Interest Groups in Italian Politics.* Princeton: Princeton University Press.

Lee, Eliza Wing-yee. 1995. "Political Science, Public Administration, and the Rise of the American Administrative State." *Public Administration Review* 55(6):538–46.

Lefevbre, Georges. 1947. *The Coming of the French Revolution, 1789*. Princeton: Princeton University Press.

Legg, Keith R. 1969. *Politics in Modern Greece*. Stanford, CA: Stanford University Press.

Leiken, Robert. 1997. "Controlling the Global Corruption Epidemic." *Foreign Policy* 105:55–73.

LeMay, Michael C., ed. 2013. *Transforming America: Perspectives on U.S. Immigration*. Santa Barbara, CA: Praeger.

Leonardi, Robert, and Douglas A. Wertman. 1989. *Italian Christian Democracy: The Politics of Dominance*. New York: St. Martin's Press.

Lessig, Lawrence. 2011. *Republic, Lost: How Money Corrupts Congress—and a Plan to Stop It*. New York: Twelve.

Levinson, Sanford. 2006. *Our Undemocratic Constitution: Where the Constitution Goes Wrong (And How We the People Can Correct It)*. New York: Oxford University Press.

———. 2013. *Framed: America's 51 Constitutions and the Crisis of Governance*. New York: Oxford University Press.

Levitsky, Steven, and Lucan A. Way. 2002. "The Rise of Competitive Authoritarianism." *Journal of Democracy* 13(2):51–65.

Lewin, Julius. 1947. *Studies in African Native Law*. Philadelphia: University of Pennsylvania Press.

Lewis, Peter. 2007. *Growing Apart: Oil, Politics, and Economic Change in Indonesia and Nigeria*. Ann Arbor: University of Michigan Press.

———. 2011. "Nigeria Votes: More Openness, More Conflict." *Journal of Democracy* 22(4):59–74.

Li, Lianjiang. 2010. "Rights Consciousness and Rules Consciousness in Contemporary China." *China Journal* (64):47–68.

Li, Yu-ning. 1977. *Shang Yang's Reforms and State Control in China*. White Plains, NY: M. E. Sharpe.

Lieberthal, Kenneth. 2004. *Governing China: From Revolution to Reform*. 2nd ed. New York: Norton.

Light, Paul C. 2008. *A Government Ill Executed: The Decline of the Federal Service and How to Reverse It*. Cambridge, MA: Harvard University Press.

Linz, Juan J. 2000. *Totalitarian and Authoritarian Regimes*. Boulder, CO: Lynne Rienner.

Linz, Juan J., and Alfred Stephan, eds. 1978. *The Breakdown of Democratic Regimes: Crisis, Breakdown, and Reequilibration*. Baltimore: Johns Hopkins University Press.

Lipset, Seymour Martin. 1959. "Some Social Requisites of Democracy: Economic Development and Political Legitimacy." *American Political Science Review* 53:69–105.

———. 1963. *The First New Nation*. New York: Basic Books.

———. 1995. *American Exceptionalism: A Double-Edged Sword*. New York: Norton.

López-Calva, Luis F., and Nora Lustig, eds. 2010. *Declining Inequality in Latin America: A Decade of Progress?* Washington, D.C.: Brookings Institution Press.

López-Calva, Luis F., et al. 2012. *Is There Such a Thing as Middle-Class Values? Class Differences, Values, and Political Orientations.* Washington, D.C.: Center for Global Development Working Paper.

Lowi, Theodore J. 1969. *The End of Liberalism: Ideology, Policy, and the Crisis of Public Authority.* New York: Norton.

Lubman, Stanley B. 1999. *Bird in a Cage: Legal Reform in China after Mao.* Stanford, CA: Stanford University Press.

Lubove, Roy. 1986. *The Struggle for Social Security, 1900–1935.* 2nd ed. Pittsburgh, PA: University of Pittsburgh Press.

Luce, Edward. 2012. *Time to Start Thinking: America in the Age of Descent.* New York: Atlantic Monthly Press.

Lust, Ellen. 2009. "Competitive Clientelism in the Middle East." *Journal of Democracy* 20(3):122–35.

Luttwak, Edward N. 1999. "Give War a Chance." *Foreign Affairs* 78(4):36–44.

Lyons, Martyn. 1994. *Napoleon Bonaparte and the Legacy of the French Revolution.* New York: St. Martin's Press.

Lyrintzis, Christos. 1984. "Political Parties in Post-Junta Greece: A Case of 'Bureaucratic Clientelism'?" *West European Politics* 7(2):99–118.

MacIntyre, Andrew. 2003. *The Power of Institutions: Political Architecture and Governance.* Ithaca, NY: Cornell University Press.

Maddox, Gregory H., and James L. Giblin. 2005. *In Search of a Nation: Histories of Authority and Dissidence in Tanzania.* Oxford: James Currey.

Mahoney, Christine. 2004. "The Power of Institutions: State and Interest-Group Activity and the European Union." *European Union Politics* 5(4):441–66.

———. 2008. *Brussels versus the Beltway: Advocacy in the United States and the European Union.* Washington, D.C.: Georgetown University Press.

Mahoney, Christine, and Frank R. Baumgartner. 2008. "Converging Perspectives on Interest Group Research in Europe and America." *West European Politics* 31(6):1251–71.

Mahoney, James. 2010. *Colonialism and Postcolonial Development: Spanish America in Comparative Perspective.* New York: Cambridge University Press.

Mahoney, James, and Dietrich Rueschemeyer, eds. 2003. *Comparative Historical Analysis in the Social Sciences.* New York: Cambridge University Press.

Maine, Henry. 1963. *Ancient Law: Its Connection with the Early History of Society and Its Relation to Modern Ideas.* Boston: Beacon Press.

Mallaby, Sebastian. 2004. *The World's Banker: A Story of Failed States, Financial Crises, and the Wealth and Poverty of Nations.* New York: Penguin Press.

Mallat, Chibli, and Jane Connors. 1990. *Islamic Family Law.* Boston: Graham and Trotman.

Mamdani, Mahmood. 1996. *Citizen and Subject: Contemporary Africa and the Legacy of Late Colonialism.* Princeton: Princeton University Press.

Manent, Pierre. 1997. "Democracy Without Nations?" *Journal of Democracy* 8:92–102.

———. 2006. *A World Beyond Politics? A Defense of the Nation-State*. Princeton: Princeton University Press.

Manion, Melanie. 1993. *Retirement of Revolutionaries in China: Public Policies, Social Norms, Private Interests*. Princeton: Princeton University Press.

Mann, Kristin, and Richard Roberts, eds. 1991. *Law in Colonial Africa*. Portsmouth, NH: Heinemann.

Mann, Michael. 1984. "The Autonomous Power of the State: Its Origins, Mechanisms, and Results." *European Journal of Sociology* 25(2):185–213.

———. 1986. *The Sources of Social Power*. Vol. I: *A History of Power from the Beginning to AD 1760*. New York: Cambridge University Press.

Mann, Thomas E., and Norman J. Ornstein. 2012. *It's Even Worse Than It Looks: How the American Constitutional System Collided with the New Politics of Extremism*. New York: Basic Books.

Mansfield, Edward D., and Jack Snyder. 2005. *Electing to Fight: Why Emerging Democracies Go to War*. Cambridge, MA: MIT Press.

Mansfield, Harvey C., Jr. 1996. *Machiavelli's Virtue*. Chicago: University of Chicago Press.

Manzetti, Luigi, and Carole J. Wilson. 2007. "Why Do Corrupt Governments Maintain Public Support?" *Comparative Political Studies* 40(8):949–70.

Maren, Michael. 1997. *The Road to Hell: The Ravaging Effects of Foreign Aid and International Charity*. New York: Free Press.

Matsui, Shigenori. 2011. *The Constitution of Japan: A Contextual Analysis*. Portland, OR: Hart Publishing.

Mavrogordatos, George Th. 1983. *Stillborn Republic: Social Coalitions and Party Strategies in Greece, 1922–1936*. Berkeley: University of California Press.

———. 1997. "From Traditional Clientelism to Machine Politics: The Impact of PASOK Populism in Greece." *South European Society and Politics* 2(3):1–26.

Mayhew, David R. 2011. *Partisan Balance: Why Political Parties Don't Kill the U.S. Constitutional System*. Princeton: Princeton University Press.

Mazey, Sonia, and Jeremy Richardson, eds. 1993. *Lobbying in the European Community*. New York: Oxford University Press.

McClain, James L. 2002. *Japan: A Modern History*. New York: Norton.

McGerr, Michael. 2003. *A Fierce Discontent: The Rise and Fall of the Progressive Movement in America, 1870–1920*. New York: Free Press.

McNelly, Theodore. 2000. *The Origins of Japan's Democratic Constitution*. Lanham, MD: University Press of America.

Mead, Walter Russell. 1999. "The Jacksonian Tradition and American Foreign Policy." *National Interest* 58:5–29.

———. 2001. *Special Providence: American Foreign Policy and How It Changed the World*. New York: Knopf.

———. 2011. "The Tea Party and American Foreign Policy." *Foreign Affairs* 90(2).

Meek, Charles K. 1968. *Land Law and Custom in the Colonies*. 2nd ed. London: Frank Cass.

Meier, Kenneth J. 1981. "Ode to Patronage: A Critical Analysis of Two Recent Supreme Court Decisions." *Public Administration Review* 41(5):558–63.

Melnick, R. Shep. 2012. "Adversarial Legalism, Civil Rights, and the Exceptional American State." Unpublished paper.

Migdal, Joel. 1988. *Strong Societies and Weak States: State-Society Relations and State Capabilities in the Third World.* Princeton: Princeton University Press.

Miguel, Edward. 2004. "Tribe or Nation? Nation Building and Public Goods in Kenya versus Tanzania." *World Politics* 56(3):327–62.

Mill, John Stuart. 1977. *Essays on Politics and Society.* Buffalo, NY: University of Toronto Press.

Millard, Candice. 2011. *Destiny of the Republic: A Tale of Madness, Medicine and the Murder of a President.* New York: Doubleday.

Miller, Char. 2001. *Gifford Pinchot and the Making of Modern Environmentalism.* Washington, D.C.: Island Press/Shearwater Books.

Mimura, Janis. 2011. *Planning for Empire: Reform Bureaucrats and the Japanese Wartime State.* Ithaca, NY: Cornell University Press.

Mirkin, Barry. 2010. "Population Levels, Trends and Policies in the Arab Region: Challenges and Opportunities." Research paper. New York: UNDP.

Mokyr, Joel. 1999. *The British Industrial Revolution: An Economic Perspective.* 2nd ed. Boulder, CO: Westview Press.

——, ed. 1985. *The Economics of the Industrial Revolution.* Totowa, NJ: Roman and Allanheld.

Moore, Barrington, Jr. 1966. *Social Origins of Dictatorship and Democracy.* Boston: Beacon Press.

Morris, Edmund. 2001. *The Rise of Theodore Roosevelt.* New York: Modern Library.

Morris, Ian. 2010. *Why the West Rules—For Now: The Patterns of History, and What They Reveal About the Future.* New York: Farrar, Straus and Giroux.

Mosca, Gaetano. 1939. *The Ruling Class.* New York: McGraw-Hill.

Mosher, Frederick C. 1982. *Democracy and the Public Service.* 2nd ed. New York: Oxford University Press.

Mouzelis, Nicos P. 1986. *Politics in the Semi-Periphery: Early Parliamentarism and Late Industrialization in the Balkans and Latin America.* New York: St. Martin's Press.

Mueller, Hans-Eberhard. 1984. *Bureaucracy, Education, and Monopoly: Civil Service Reforms in Prussia and England.* Berkeley: University of California Press.

Mwansasu, Bismarck U., and Cranford Pratt, eds. 1979. *Towards Socialism in Tanzania.* Buffalo, NY: University of Toronto Press.

Myers, Ramon H., and Mark R. Peattie, eds. 1984. *The Japanese Colonial Empire, 1895–1945.* Princeton: Princeton University Press.

Naipaul, V. S. 1980. *The Return of Eva Perón, with the Killings in Trinidad.* New York: A. Knopf.

Najita, Tetsuo. 1967. *Hara Kei in the Politics of Compromise, 1905–1915.* Cambridge, MA: Harvard University Press.

Nathan, Andrew J. 1996. "China's Constitutionalist Option." *Journal of Democracy* 7(4):43–57.

———. 1998. *Peking Politics, 1918–1923: Factionalism and the Failure of Constitutionalism.* Ann Arbor, MI: Center for Chinese Studies.

National Commission on the Public Service. 1989. *Rebuilding the Public Service.* Washington, D.C.

———. 2003. *Revitalizing the Federal Government for the 21st Century.* Washington, D.C.

Needham, Joseph. 1954. *Science and Civilization in China.* Vol. 1: *Introductory Orientations.* New York: Cambridge University Press.

Nelson, Robert H. 2000. *A Burning Issue: A Case for Abolishing the U.S. Forest Service.* Lanham, MD: Rowman and Littlefield.

Newell, Clayton R., and Charles R. Shrader. 2011. *Of Duty Well and Faithfully Done: A History of the Regular Army in the Civil War.* Lincoln: University of Nebraska Press.

Nichter, Simeon. 2008. "Vote Buying or Turnout Buying? Machine Politics and the Secret Ballot." *American Political Science Review* 102(1):19–31.

Niskanen, William A. 1973. *Bureaucracy—Servant or Master? Lessons from America.* London: Institute of Economic Affairs.

North, Douglass C., and Robert Paul Thomas. 1973. *The Rise of the Western World: A New Economic History.* New York: Cambridge University Press.

North, Douglass C., John Wallis, and Barry R. Weingast. 2009. *Violence and Social Orders: A Conceptual Framework for Interpreting Recorded Human History.* New York: Cambridge University Press.

Nunn, Nathan. 2007. "Historical Legacies: A Model Linking Africa's Past to Its Current Underdevelopment." *Journal of Development Economics* 83(1): 157–75.

———. 2008. "The Long-Term Effects of Africa's Slave Trades." *Quarterly Journal of Economics* 123(1):139–76.

Nye, Joseph S., Jr. 1967. "Corruption and Political Development: A Cost-Benefit Analysis." *American Political Science Review* 61(2):417–27.

O'Brien, Kevin J. 2001. "Villagers, Elections, and Citizenship in Contemporary China." *Modern China* 27(4):407–35.

O'Brien, Kevin J., and Lianjiang Li. 2004. "Suing the State: Administrative Litigation in Rural China." *China Journal* (51):75–96.

O'Donnell, Guillermo A. 1973. *Modernization and Bureaucratic-Authoritarianism: Studies in South American Politics.* Berkeley: University of California Press.

O'Donnell, Guillermo, Philippe C. Schmitter, and Laurence Whitehead, eds. 1986. *Transitions from Authoritarian Rule: Comparative Perspectives.* Baltimore: Johns Hopkins University Press.

O'Dwyer, Conor. 2006. *Runaway State-Building: Patronage Politics and Democratic Development.* Baltimore: Johns Hopkins University Press.

Oestreicher, Richard. 1988. "Urban Working-Class Political Behavior and Theories of American Electoral Politics, 1870–1940." *Journal of American History* 74(4):1257–86.

Offe, Claus. 2009. "Governance: An 'Empty Signifier'?" *Constellations* 16(4):550–62.

Oi, Jean C. 1999. *Rural China Takes Off: Institutional Foundations of Economic Reform*. Berkeley: University of California Press.

Oi, Jean C., and Andrew Walder, eds. 1999. *Property Rights and Economic Reform in China*. Stanford, CA: Stanford University Press.

Olson, Mancur. 1965. *The Logic of Collective Action. Public Goods and the Theory of Groups*. Cambridge, MA: Harvard University Press.

———. 1982. *The Rise and Decline of Nations*. New Haven: Yale University Press.

———. 1993. "Dictatorship, Democracy, and Development." *American Political Science Review* 87(9):567–76.

Organization for Economic Cooperation and Development. 2011. *Greece: Review of the Central Administration*. Public Governance Reviews. Paris: OECD.

———. 2012. *OECD Integrity Review of Brazil: Managing Risks for a Cleaner Public Sector*. Paris: OECD.

———. 2013. *Revenue Statistics*. Paris: OECD.

Osaghae, Eghosa E. 1998. *Crippled Giant: Nigeria Since Independence*. Bloomington: Indiana University Press.

Osborn, Emily Lynn. 2003. " 'Circle of Iron': African Colonial Employees and the Interpretation of Colonial Rule in French West Africa." *Journal of African History* 44:29–50.

O'Toole, Randal. 1988. *Reforming the Forest Service*. Washington, D.C.: Island Press.

Paige, Jeffery M. 1997. *Coffee and Power: Revolution and the Rise of Democracy in Central America*. Cambridge, MA: Harvard University Press.

Pappas, Takis S. 1999. *Making Party Democracy in Greece*. New York: St. Martin's Press.

Pareto, Vilfredo. 1966. *Sociological Writings*. New York: Praeger.

Parris, Henry. 1969. *Constitutional Bureaucracy: The Development of British Central Administration Since the Eighteenth Century*. New York: Augustus M. Kelley.

Pasquino, Gianfranco, James L. Newell, and Paolo Mancini, eds. 2013. *The Future of the Liberal Western Order: The Case of Italy*. Washington, D.C.: Transatlantic Academy.

Pedler, Robin, ed. 2002. *European Union Lobbying: Changes in the Arena*. New York: Palgrave.

Peerenboom, Randall, ed. 2004. *Asian Discourses of Rule of Law: Theories and Implementation of Rule of Law in Twelve Asian Countries, France, and the U.S.* New York: Routledge.

Pei, Minxin. 1997. "Citizens v. Mandarins: Administrative Litigation in China." *China Quarterly* (152):832–62.

———. 2006. *China's Trapped Transition: The Limits of Developmental Autocracy*. Cambridge, MA: Harvard University Press.

Pelling, Henry. 1965. *The Origins of the Labour Party, 1880–1900*. Oxford: Clarendon Press.

Pew Research Center. 2013. "Trust in Government Nears Record Low, But Most Federal Agencies Are Viewed Favorably." Washington, D.C.: Pew Research Center.

Pfiffner, James P., ed. 1999. *The Managerial Presidency*. 2nd ed. College Station: Texas A&M University Press.

Phillips, Ulrich B. 1966. *American Negro Slavery*. Baton Rouge: Louisiana State University Press.

Piattoni, Simona, ed. 2001. *Clientelism, Interests, and Democratic Representation: The European Experience in Historical and Comparative Perspective*. New York: Cambridge University Press.

Piketty, Thomas, and Emmanuel Saez. 2003. "Income Inequality in the United States, 1913–1998." *Quarterly Journal of Economics* 118(1):1–39.

Pinchot, Gifford. 1947. *Breaking New Ground*. Washington, D.C.: Island Press.

Plattner, Marc F. 2013. "Reflections on 'Governance.'" *Journal of Democracy* 24(4):17–28.

Polanyi, Karl. 1944. *The Great Transformation*. New York: Rinehart.

Polanyi, Karl, and C. W. Arensberg, eds. 1957. *Trade and Market in the Early Empires*. New York: Free Press.

Pomeranz, Kenneth. 2000. *The Great Divergence: Europe, China, and the Making of the Modern World Economy*. Princeton: Princeton University Press.

Pongsudhirak, Thitinan. 2012. "Thailand's Uneasy Passage." *Journal of Democracy* 23(2):47–61.

Posner, Daniel N. 2005. *Institutions and Ethnic Politics in Africa*. New York: Cambridge University Press.

Posner, Eric A., and Adrian Vermeule. 2010. *The Executive Unbound: After the Madisonian Republic*. New York: Oxford University Press.

Prager, Robin A. 1989. "Using Stock Price Data to Measure the Effects of Regulation: the Interstate Commerce Act and the Railroad Industry." *RAND Journal of Economics* 20(2):280–90.

Pratt, Cranford. 1976. *The Critical Phase in Tanzania 1945–1968: Nyerere and the Emergence of a Socialist Strategy*. New York: Cambridge University Press.

Prescott, William H. 1902. *History of the Conquest of Peru*. Philadelphia: J. B. Lippincott.

———. 1904. *History of the Conquest of Mexico*. Philadelphia: J. B. Lippincott.

Pritchett, Lant, Michael Woolcock, and Matt Andrews. 2010. *Capability Traps? The Mechanisms of Persistent Implementation Failure*. Washington, D.C.: Center for Global Development.

Prosser, Gifford, and William R. Louis, eds. 1971. *France and Britain in Africa: Imperial Rivalry and Colonial Rule*. New Haven: Yale University Press.

Przeworski, Adam. 2009. "Conquered or Granted? A History of Suffrage Extensions." *British Journal of Political Science* 39(2):291–321.

Przeworski, Adam, et al. 2000. *Democracy and Development: Political Institutions and Material Well-Being in the World, 1950–1990*. Cambridge: Cambridge University Press.

Przeworski, Adam, Susan C. Stokes, and Bernard Manin, eds. 1999. *Democracy, Accountability, and Representation*. New York: Cambridge University Press.

Putnam, Robert D. 1993. *Making Democracy Work: Civic Traditions in Modern Italy*. Princeton: Princeton University Press.

———. 1995. "Bowling Alone: America's Declining Social Capital." *Journal of Democracy* 6(1):65–78.

———. 2000. *Bowling Alone: The Collapse and Revival of American Community*. New York: Simon & Schuster.

Pyne, Stephen J. 1981. "Fire Policy and Fire Research in the U.S. Forest Service." *Journal of Forest History* 25(2):64–77.

Radelet, Steven. 2010. *Emerging Africa: How 17 Countries Are Leading the Way*. Baltimore: Center for Global Development.

Radford, Gail. 2013. *The Rise of the Public Authority: Statebuilding and Economic Development in Twentieth-Century America*. Chicago: University of Chicago Press.

Rajan, Raghuram G. 2010. *Fault Lines: How Hidden Fractures Still Threaten the World Economy*. Princeton: Princeton University Press.

Rauch, James E., and Peter B. Evans. 2000. "Bureaucratic Structure and Bureaucratic Performance in Less Developed Countries." *Journal of Public Economics* 75:49–71.

Rawski, Evelyn S. 1998. *The Last Emperors: A Social History of Qing Imperial Institutions*. Berkeley: University of California Press.

Renan, Ernest. 1996. *Qu'est-ce qu'une nation? (What Is a Nation?)* Toronto: Tapir Press.

Reno, William. 1998. *Warlord Politics and African States*. Boulder, CO: Lynne Rienner.

Richardson, Sarah, ed. 2000. *History of Suffrage, 1760–1867*. Brookfield, VT: Pickering and Chatto.

Ringen, Stein. 2013. *Nation of Devils: Democratic Leadership and the Problem of Obedience*. New Haven: Yale University Press.

Roodman, David. 2012. *Due Diligence: An Impertinent Inquiry into Microfinance*. Washington, D.C.: Center for Global Development.

Rose-Ackerman, Susan. 1978. *Corruption: A Study in Political Economy*. New York: Academic Press.

———. 1999. *Corruption and Government: Causes, Consequences, and Reform*. New York: Cambridge University Press.

Rosenberg, Hans. 1958. *Bureaucracy, Aristocracy, and Autocracy: The Prussian Experience, 1660–1815*. Cambridge, MA: Harvard University Press.

Rosenberg, Nathan, and L. E. Birdzell. 1986. *How the West Grew Rich*. New York: Basic Books.

Rosenthal, Jean-Laurent, and R. Bin Wong. 2011. *Before and Beyond Divergence: The Politics of Economic Change in China and Europe.* Cambridge, MA: Harvard University Press.

Roth, Dennis. 1984. "The National Forests and the Campaign for Wilderness Legislation." *Journal of Forest History* 28(3):112–25.

Rothstein, Bo. 2011. *The Quality of Government: Corruption, Social Trust, and Inequality in International Perspective.* Chicago: University of Chicago Press.

Roy, Olivier. 2004. *Globalized Islam: The Search for a New Ummah.* New York: Columbia University Press.

Rueschemeyer, Dietrich, Evelyn Huber Stephens, and John D. Stephens. 1992. *Capitalist Development and Democracy.* Chicago: University of Chicago Press.

Ruhil, Anirudh V. S. 2003. "Urban Armageddon or Politics as Usual? The Case of Municipal Civil Service Reform." *American Journal of Political Science* 47(1):159–70.

Rush, Myron. 1974. *How Communist States Change Their Rulers.* Ithaca, NY: Cornell University Press.

Rweyémamu, Anthony H., ed. 1970. *Nation-Building in Tanzania: Problems and Issues.* Nairobi: East African Publishing House.

Sabel, Charles F., and Jonathan Zeitlin. 2008. "Learning from Difference: The New Architecture of Experimentalist Governance in the European Union." *European Law Journal* 14(3):271–327.

Sachs, Jeffrey D. 2001. "Tropical Underdevelopment." Cambridge, MA: National Bureau of Economic Research Working Paper No. 8119.

Saller, Richard P. 1982. *Personal Patronage Under the Early Empire.* New York: Cambridge University Press.

Samuels, Richard J. 1994. *"Rich Nation, Strong Army": National Security and the Technological Transformation of Japan.* Ithaca, NY: Cornell University Press.

Scase, Richard, ed. 1980. *The State in Western Europe.* New York: St. Martin's Press.

Schaffer, Frederic Charles, ed. 2007. *Elections for Sale: The Causes and Consequences of Vote Buying.* Boulder, CO: Lynne Rienner.

Schattschneider, E. E. 1960. *The Semisovereign People: A Realist's View of Democracy in America.* New York: Holt.

Schedler, Andreas. 2002. "The Menu of Manipulation." *Journal of Democracy* 13(2):36–50.

Schlozman, Kay Lehman, and John T. Tierney. 1986. *Organized Interests and American Democracy.* New York: Harper.

Schmidt, Eric, and Jared Cohen. *The New Digital Age: Reshaping the Future of People, Nations and Business.* New York: Knopf.

Schmidt, John R. 1989. *"The Mayor Who Cleaned Up Chicago": A Political Biography of William E. Dever.* DeKalb: Northern Illinois University Press.

Schneider, Friedrich, and Dominik H. Enste. 2002. *The Shadow Economy: An International Survey.* New York: Cambridge University Press.

Schneider, Friedrich, and Robert Klinglmair. 2005. "Shadow Economies Around the World: What Do We Really Know?" *European Journal of Political Economy* 21:598–642.

Schneider, Jane. 1998. *Italy's "Southern Question": Orientalism in One Country.* New York: Berg.

Schoenbaum, David. 1966. *Hitler's Social Revolution.* Garden City, NY: Doubleday.

Schultz, David A., and Robert Maranto. 1998. *The Politics of Civil Service Reform.* New York: Peter Lang.

Schurmann, Franz. 1956. "Traditional Property Concepts in China." *Far Eastern Quarterly* 15(4):507–16.

Schwartz, Bernard, ed. 1956. *The Code Napoléon and the Common-Law World.* New York: New York University Press.

Scott, James C. 1972. *Comparative Political Corruption.* Englewood Cliffs, NJ: Prentice-Hall.

———. 1998. *Seeing Like a State: How Certain Schemes to Improve the Human Condition Have Failed.* New Haven: Yale University Press.

———. 2009. *The Art of Not Being Governed: An Anarchist History of Upland Southeast Asia.* New Haven: Yale University Press.

Sen, Amartya. 1999. *Development as Freedom.* New York: Knopf.

Shambaugh, David L., ed. 2000. *The Modern Chinese State.* New York: Cambridge University Press.

Shaw, Frederick. 1954. *The History of the New York State Legislature.* New York: Columbia University Press.

Sheehan, James J. 1989. *German History, 1770–1866.* New York: Oxford University Press.

Shefter, Martin. 1983. "Regional Receptivity to Reform: The Legacy of the Progressive Era." *Political Science Quarterly* 98(3):459–83.

———. 1994. *Political Parties and the State: The American Historical Experience.* Princeton: Princeton University Press.

Shih, Victor, Christopher Adolph, and Mingxing Liu. 2012. "Getting Ahead in the Communist Party: Explaining the Advancement of Central Committee Members in China." *American Political Science Review* 106(1):166–87.

Shleifer, Andrei, and Robert W. Vishny. 1993. "Corruption." *Quarterly Journal of Economics* 108(3):599–617.

Silberman, Bernard S. 1970. "Bureaucratic Development and the Structure of Decision-making in Japan: 1868–1925." *Journal of Asian Studies* 29(2):347–62.

Silberman, Bernard S., and H. D. Harootunian. 1974. *Japan in Crisis: Essays on Taishō Democracy.* Princeton: Princeton University Press.

Skidmore, Thomas E., and Peter H. Smith. 2004. *Modern Latin America.* 6th ed. New York: Oxford University Press.

Skocpol, Theda. 1973. "A Critical Review of Barrington Moore's *Social Origins of Dictatorship and Democracy.*" *Politics & Society* 4:1–34.

———. 1992. *Protecting Soldiers and Mothers: The Political Origins of Social Policy in the United States.* Cambridge, MA: Harvard University Press.

Skowronek, Stephen. 1982. *Building a New American State: The Expansion of National Administrative Capacities, 1877–1920*. New York: Cambridge University Press.

Slater, Dan. 2010. *Ordering Power: Contentious Politics and Authoritarian Leviathans in Southeast Asia*. New York: Cambridge University Press.

Small, Melvin, and J. David Singer. 1982. *Resort to Arms: International and Civil Wars, 1816–1980*. Thousand Oaks, CA: Sage.

Smith, Daniel Jordan. 2007. *A Culture of Corruption: Everyday Deception and Popular Discontent in Nigeria*. Princeton: Princeton University Press.

Soekarno. 1969. *Nationalism, Islam, and Marxism*. Ithaca, NY: Cornell University, Southeast Asia Program.

Soifer, Hillel. 2008. "State Infrastructural Power: Approaches to Conceptualization and Measurement." *Studies in Comparative International Development* 43:231–51.

Soifer, Hillel, and Matthias vom Hau. 2008. "Unpacking the Strength of the State: The Utility of State Infrastructural Power." *Studies in Comparative International Development* 43:219–30.

Soto, Hernando de. 2000. *The Mystery of Capital: Why Capitalism Triumphs in the West and Fails Everywhere Else*. New York: Basic Books.

Sørensen, Georg. 2001. "War and State-Making: Why Doesn't It Work in the Third World?" *Security Dialogue* 32(3): 341–54.

Spear, Thomas. 2003. "Neo-Traditionalism and the Limits of Invention in British Colonial Africa." *Journal of African History* 44(1):3–27.

Spengler, Oswald. 1926. *The Decline of the West*. New York: Knopf.

Sperber, Jonathan. 2005. *The European Revolutions, 1848–1851*. 2nd ed. New York: Cambridge University Press.

Steen, Harold K. 1976. *The U.S. Forest Service: A History*. Seattle: University of Washington Press.

Stepan, Alfred C., and Juan J. Linz. 2011. "Comparative Perspectives on Inequality and the Quality of Democracy in the United States." *Perspectives on Politics* 9(4):841–56.

Stepan, Alfred C., and Graeme B. Robertson. 2003. "An 'Arab' More Than a 'Muslim' Electoral Gap." *Journal of Democracy* 14(3):30–44.

Stepan, Alfred C., Juan J. Linz, and Yogendra Yadav. 2010. "The Rise of 'State-Nations.'" *Journal of Democracy* 21(3):50–68.

Stille, Alexander. 1995. *Excellent Cadavers: The Mafia and the Death of the First Italian Republic*. New York: Pantheon.

———. 2006. *The Sack of Rome: How a Beautiful European Country with a Fabled History and a Storied Culture Was Taken Over by a Man Named Silvio Berlusconi*. New York: Penguin Press.

Stokes, Susan C. 2005. "Perverse Accountability: A Formal Model of Machine Politics with Evidence from Argentina." *American Political Science Review* 99(3): 315–25.

Stokes, Susan, et al. 2013. *Brokers, Voters, and Clientelism: The Puzzle of Distributive Politics*. New York: Cambridge University Press.

Stone, Richard D. 1991. *The Interstate Commerce Commission and the Railroad Industry: A History of Regulatory Policy.* New York: Praeger.

Suret-Canale, Jean. 1971. *French Colonialism in Tropical Africa, 1900–1945.* New York: Pica Press.

Sutherland, Gillian, ed. 1972. *Studies in the Growth of Nineteenth-Century Government.* Totowa, NJ: Rowman and Littlefield.

Tanzi, Vito. 2011. *Government versus Markets: The Changing Economic Role of the State.* New York: Cambridge University Press.

Tarr, Joel A. 1971. *A Study in Boss Politics: William Lorimer of Chicago.* Urbana: University of Illinois Press.

Tarrow, Sidney G. 1967. *Peasant Communism in Southern Italy.* New Haven: Yale University Press.

Taylor, Charles. 1989. *Sources of the Self: The Making of the Modern Identity.* Cambridge, MA: Harvard University Press.

———, ed. 1994. *Multiculturalism: Examining the Politics of Recognition.* Princeton: Princeton University Press.

Taylor, Frederick Winslow. 1911. *The Principles of Scientific Management.* New York: Harper.

Taylor, Jean Gelman. 2003. *Indonesia: Peoples and Histories.* New Haven: Yale University Press.

Theriault, Sean M. 2003. "Patronage, the Pendleton Act, and the Power of the People." *Journal of Politics* 65(1):50–68.

Thies, Cameron G. 2005. "War, Rivalry, and State Building in Latin America." *American Journal of Political Science* 49(3):451–65.

Thomas, Hugh. 1993. *The Conquest of Mexico.* London: Hutchinson.

Thomas, Melissa. 2009. "Great Expectations: Rich Donors and Poor Country Governments." Paper. Washington, D.C.: Johns Hopkins University, School of Advanced International Studies. http://papers.ssrn.com/sol3/papers.cfm?abstract-id=1333618.

Thompson, Margaret Susan. 1985. *The "Spider Web": Congress and Lobbying in the Age of Grant.* Ithaca, NY: Cornell University Press.

Tilly, Charles. 1990. *Coercion, Capital, and European States AD 990–1990.* Cambridge, MA: Blackwell.

———. 2007. *Democracy.* New York: Cambridge University Press.

Titmuss, Richard M. 1971. *The Gift Relationship: From Human Blood to Social Policy.* New York: Vintage Books.

Tocqueville, Alexis de. 1998. *The Old Regime and the Revolution.* Vol. 1. Chicago: University of Chicago Press.

———. 2000. *Democracy in America.* Chicago: University of Chicago Press.

Tönnies, Ferdinand. 1955. *Community and Association (Gemeinschaft und Gesellschaft).* London: Routledge.

Torsvik, Per. 1981. *Mobilization, Center-Periphery Structures and Nation-Building.* Bergen: Universitetsforlaget.

Toynbee, Arnold. 1972. *A Study of History*. London: Oxford University Press.

Trebilcock, Michael J., and Robert J. Daniels. 2008. *Rule of Law Reform and Development: Charting the Fragile Path of Progress*. Northampton, MA: Edward Elgar.

Tsai, Lily L. 2007. *Accountability Without Democracy: Solidary Groups and Public Goods Provision in Rural China*. New York: Cambridge University Press.

——. 2012. "The Political Payoffs of Governance Reforms: How Citizens See and Judge the State in Authoritarian China." Unpublished paper.

Tsebelis, George. 2002. *Veto Players: How Political Institutions Work*. Princeton: Princeton University Press.

Tsoucalas, Constantine. 1978. "On the Problem of Political Clientelism in Greece in the Nineteenth Century." *Journal of the Hellenic Diaspora* 5(2):5–17.

Upham, Frank K. 1987. *Law and Social Change in Postwar Japan*. Cambridge, MA: Harvard University Press.

van Creveld, Martin. 1982. *Fighting Power: German and U.S. Army Performance, 1939–1945*. Westport, CT: Greenwood Press.

van de Walle, Nicolas. 2001. *African Economies and the Politics of Permanent Crisis, 1979–1999*. New York: Cambridge University Press.

——. 2004. *Overcoming Stagnation in Aid-Dependent Countries*. Washington, D.C.: Center for Global Development.

Van Riper, Paul P. 1958. *History of the United States Civil Service*. Evanston, IL: Row, Peterson.

——. 1983. "The American Administrative State: Wilson and the Founders—An Unorthodox View." *Public Administration Review* 43(6):477–90.

Wade, Robert. 1990. *Governing the Market: Economic Theory and the Role of Government in East Asian Industrialization*. Princeton: Princeton University Press.

Waisman, Carlos. 1987. *Reversal of Development in Argentina: Postwar Counterrevolutionary Policies and Their Structural Consequences*. Princeton: Princeton University Press.

Wakeman, Frederic, Jr. 1985. *The Great Enterprise: The Manchu Reconstruction of Imperial Order in Seventeenth-Century China*. 2 vols. Berkeley: University of California Press.

Wallace, Elisabeth. 1977. *The British Caribbean from the Decline of Colonialism to the End of Federation*. Buffalo, NY: University of Toronto Press.

Wallison, Peter J. 2013. *Bad History, Worse Policy: How a False Narrative About the Financial Crisis Led to the Dodd-Frank Act*. Washington, D.C.: American Enterprise Institute.

Walston, James. 1988. *The Mafia and Clientelism: Roads to Rome in Post-War Calabria*. New York: Routledge.

Watson, Harry L. 1985. "Old Hickory's Democracy." *Wilson Quarterly* 9(4):100–33.

Weber, Eugen. 1976. *Peasants into Frenchmen: The Modernization of Rural France, 1870–1914*. Stanford, CA: Stanford University Press.

Weber, Max. 1930. *The Protestant Ethic and the Spirit of Capitalism*. New York: Scribner.

———. 1946. *From Max Weber: Essays in Sociology*. New York: Oxford University Press.

———. 1978. *Economy and Society*. 2 vols. Berkeley: University of California Press.

Weyland, Kurt. 2009. "The Diffusion of Revolution: '1848' in Europe and Latin America." *International Organization* 63(3):391–423.

Wiebe, Robert H. 1967. *The Search for Order: 1877–1920*. New York: Hill and Wang.

Wiener, Martin J. 2004. *English Culture and the Decline of the Industrial Spirit, 1850–1980*. 2nd ed. New York: Cambridge University Press.

Wilensky, Harold L. 1975. *The Welfare State and Equality*. Berkeley: University of California Press.

Williams, Eric E. 1994. *Capitalism and Slavery*. Chapel Hill: University of North Carolina Press.

Williams, T. Harry. 2011. *Lincoln and His Generals*. New York: Vintage Books.

Wilson, Dominic, and Raluca Dragusanu. 2008. *The Expanding Middle: The Exploding World Middle Class and Falling Global Inequality*. New York: Goldman Sachs Global Economics Paper No. 170.

Wilson, James Q. 1989. *Bureaucracy: What Government Agencies Do and Why They Do It*. New York: Basic Books.

Wilson, Woodrow. 1887. "The Study of Administration." *Political Science Quarterly* 2(2):197–222.

Woo, Jung-En. 1991. *Race to the Swift: State and Finance in Korean Industrialization*. New York: Columbia University Press.

World Bank. 1993. *World Development Report 1993: The East Asian Miracle: Economic Growth and Public Policy*. New York: Oxford University Press.

———. 1997. *World Development Report 1997: The State in a Changing World*. Oxford: Oxford University Press.

———. 2003. *World Development Report 2004: Making Services Work for Poor People*. Washington, D.C.: World Bank.

———. 2008. *World Development Report 2009: Reshaping Economic Geography*. Washington, D.C.: World Bank.

———. 2011. *World Development Report 2011: Conflict, Security, and Development*. Washington, D.C.: World Bank.

———. 2013. *China 2030: Building a Modern, Harmonious, and Creative Society*. Washington, D.C.: World Bank.

Wright, Gavin. 2006. *Slavery and American Economic Development*. Baton Rouge: Louisiana State University Press.

Wrong, Michela. 2001. *In the Footsteps of Mr. Kurtz: Living on the Brink of Disaster in Mobutu's Congo*. New York: Harper.

———. 2010. *It's Our Turn to Eat: The Story of a Kenyan Whistle-Blower*. New York: Harper Perennial.

Yang Jisheng. 2012. *Tombstone: The Great Chinese Famine, 1958–1962*. New York: Farrar, Straus and Giroux.

Yang, Dali L. 2004. *Remaking the Chinese Leviathan: Market Transition and the Politics of Governance in China*. Stanford, CA: Stanford University Press.

Young, Crawford. 1994. *The African Colonial State in Comparative Perspective*. New Haven: Yale University Press.

Zakaria, Fareed. 2003. *The Future of Freedom: Illiberal Democracy at Home and Abroad*. New York: Norton.

———. 2008. *The Post-American World*. New York: Norton.

Zhao, Dingxin, and John A. Hall. 1994. "State Power and Patterns of Late Development: Resolving the Crisis of the Sociology of Development." *Sociology* 28(1):211–30.

Ziblatt, Daniel. 2006. "How Did Europe Democratize?" *World Politics* 58:311–38.

———. 2008. "Does Landholding Inequality Block Democratization? A Test of the 'Bread and Democracy' Thesis and the Case of Prussia." *World Politics* 60:610–41.

ACKNOWLEDGMENTS

I'm very grateful to a number of people and institutions that have helped me in the preparation of this volume, as well as its predecessor. I have found a wonderful institutional home at the Center for Democracy, Development, and the Rule of Law (CDDRL) at Stanford's Freeman Spogli Institute for International Studies, under the leadership of CDDRL's director, Larry Diamond. There are many people who read parts or all of the manuscript and provided comments as well as valuable insights into the many issues covered. My wife, Laura Holmgren, read the manuscript early on and has been completely supportive over the years it has taken to write this book, as well as in all of the ones preceding.

I would like to pay special thanks to David Abernethy, the late Joel Barkan, Margaret Boittin, Bruce Cain, Gerhard Casper, Roberto D'Alimonte, Tino Cuéllar, Larry Diamond, Giovanna Dore, Peter Duns, Karl Eikenberry, Don Emmerson, Morris Fiorina, Adam Garfinkle, Elira Karaja, Eric Kramon, Steven Krasner, Melissa Lee, Peter Lewis, Reo Matsuzaki, Ian Morris, Paul Ockelmann, Dan Okimoto, Elena Panaritis, Minxin Pei, Marc Plattner, Alastair Roberts, Richard Roberts, Eric E. Schmidt, Jim Sheehan, Landry Signé, Peter Skerry, Melissa Thomas, Lucan Way, Daniel Ziblatt, and research assistants Jason Wu, Purun Cheong, Priscilla Choi, Kamil Dada, Nicholas Dugdale, Alana Kirkland, and Devanshi Patel. Samantha Maskey and Lauren Weitzman both helped on research and on the production of the book as a whole. Parts of this book were presented at the Berkeley Global History Seminar, the University of Puget Sound, the Belfer Center at Harvard's Kennedy School, the Center for Global Development, and the Europe Center and CDDRL at Stanford; I'm appreciative of the comments received.

I am extremely grateful to my editor at Farrar, Straus and Giroux, Eric Chinski, who (as in the case of Volume 1) provided invaluable guidance and judgment on how to refine and present my arguments. I would also like to extend special thanks to Andrew Franklin of Profile Books, Paulo Rocco at Editora Rocco, and Mizzi van der Pluijm at Contact, who over the years have published every single book I've written. In addition, Cynthia Merman did a heroic job copyediting and fact-checking the manuscript. This book would not be possible without my terrific literary agents, Esther Newberg, Sophie Baker, and Betsy Robbins.

INDEX

Abe, Shinzō, 352
Abernethy, David, 292
accountability, 12–15, 23–25, 28, 33, 37,
    52, 64, 211, 337, 376, 395, 405, 412–13,
    422, 506–508, 518–22, 529, 532,
    540–43; of Chinese state, 380–85,
    399; clientelism and, 90; procedural,
    24; rule of law and, 534; sanction-
    based, 522; substantive, 24
Acemoglu, Daron, 26, 234, 235
Adams, Henry Carter, 168
Adams, John, 137, 139, 140
Adams, John Quincy, 141, 142, 175,
    182, 509
Addams, Jane, 157
Admati, Anat, 5
Administrative Procedure Act,
    486, 521
adversarial legalism, 473–76, 521
Affordable Care Act, 56, 480, 496
Afghanistan, 25, 52–53, 91, 237, 298,
    312, 313–15, 317, 511, 528
Africa, 4, 30–33, 39, 41, 48, 49, 53, 91,
    99, 209–10, 219, 225, 227, 234, 238,
    240–41, 285–98, 299–312, 318, 335,
    336, 367, 386–89, 392–95, 400, 443,
    530, 535, 536; agriculture in, 290–91;

Britain and, 222, 297–98, 300–301,
    303, 305, 308–10, 312, 315–17, 323–24;
    clientelism in, 288–89; colonialism
    in, 283–84, 291–94, 296–98, 300–312,
    315–17, 322, 392, 393, 536; democracy
    in, 291; East Asia compared with,
    286, 290, 291; economic growth in,
    285–86, 386–87; French and, 297,
    308–12, 315–17; geography in,
    294–95, 390; native law and custom
    in, 303–308, 317; neopatrimonial
    rule in, 287–89, 392; population
    densities in, 294; states in, 287–96,
    322, 392; taxes in, 289–90, 305–306,
    392; tribalism and ethnic groups in,
    296, 300, 304, 306, 393
African Americans, 14, 136, 170, 474;
    Brown v. Board of Education and,
    471–72; franchise and, 140, 414,
    419–20, 422
agrarian societies, 187, 188, 259, 410,
    416, 447, 527–29; shift to industrial
    societies from, 47, 101, 131, 150,
    188–89, 436–37
Aitken, James, 175
Akita, George, 343–44, 352
Alamieyeseigha, Diepreye, 220

A Note About the Author

.

Francis Fukuyama is the Olivier Nomellini Senior Fellow at Stanford University's Freeman Spogli Institute for International Studies. He has previously taught at the Paul H. Nitze School of Advanced International Studies of the Johns Hopkins University and at the George Mason University School of Public Policy. Fukuyama was a researcher at the RAND Corporation and served on the State Department's Policy Planning Staff. He is the author of *The Origins of Political Order*, *The End of History and the Last Man*, *Trust*, and *America at the Crossroads*. He lives with his wife in California.